CANADA

THE NORTHEAST
26–53

THE MIDWEST
84–113

THE WEST
128–155

THE SOUTHEAST
54–83

THE SOUTHWEST
114–127

MEXICO

BAHAMAS

CUBA

It's a BIG country. Learn it. Love it. Explore it.

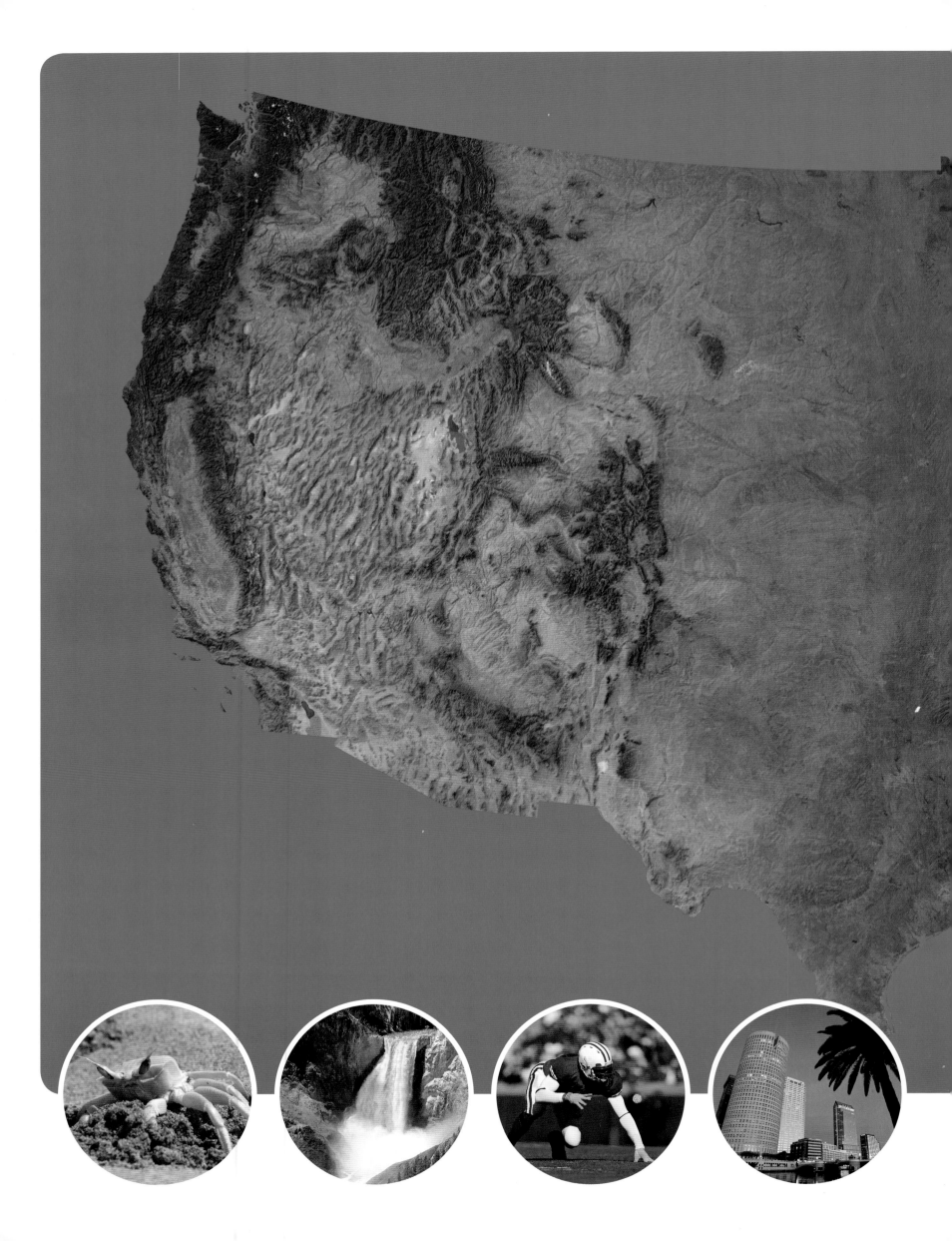

NATIONAL GEOGRAPHIC

UNITED STATES
ATLAS

FOR YOUNG EXPLORERS

THIRD EDITION

NATIONAL GEOGRAPHIC
WASHINGTON, DC

TABLE OF CONTENTS

FRONT OF THE BOOK

GETTING STARTED
How to Use This Atlas   6
How to Use the
   Atlas Web Site   8

THE PHYSICAL UNITED STATES   10
Natural Environment   12
Natural Hazards   14

THE POLITICAL UNITED STATES   16
Population   18
People on the Move   20
Getting Green   22
The Nation's Capital   24

THE NORTHEAST 26

PHYSICAL & POLITICAL MAPS   28
About the Northeast   30
Connecticut   32
Delaware   34
Maine   36
Maryland   38
Massachusetts   40
New Hampshire   42
New Jersey   44
New York   46
Pennsylvania   48
Rhode Island   50
Vermont   52

THE SOUTHEAST 54

PHYSICAL & POLITICAL MAPS   56
About the Southeast   58
Alabama   60
Arkansas   62
Florida   64
Georgia   66
Kentucky   68
Louisiana   70
Mississippi   72
North Carolina   74
South Carolina   76
Tennessee   78
Virginia   80
West Virginia   82

THE MIDWEST 84

PHYSICAL & POLITICAL MAPS   86
About the Midwest   88
Illinois   90
Indiana   92
Iowa   94
Kansas   96
Michigan   98
Minnesota   100
Missouri   102
Nebraska   104
North Dakota   106
Ohio   108
South Dakota   110
Wisconsin   112

Northeast: Maine lighthouse, pp. 36–37

Southeast:
Florida manatee, p. 64

Midwest: Illinois hay field with tractor, pp. 90–91

Title page: Atlantic sand crab; Lower Falls of the Yellowstone, MT; football player; Tampa, FL;
sage grouse; skyline, Seattle, WA; Organ Pipe Cactus National Monument, AZ.

THE SOUTHWEST 114

PHYSICAL & POLITICAL MAPS 116
About the Southwest 118
Arizona 120
New Mexico 122
Oklahoma 124
Texas 126

THE WEST 128

PHYSICAL & POLITICAL MAPS 130
About the West 132
Alaska 134
California 136
Colorado 138
Hawai'i 140
Idaho 142
Montana 144
Nevada 146
Oregon 148
Utah 150
Washington 152
Wyoming 154

THE TERRITORIES 156

POLITICAL MAP & FACT BOXES 156
U.S. Caribbean Territories
    Puerto Rico,
    Virgin Islands
U.S. Pacific Territories
    American Samoa,
    Guam, Northern
    Mariana Islands
Other U.S. Territories
    Baker Is., Howland Is.,
    Jarvis Is., Johnston Atoll,
    Kingman Reef, Midway
    Islands, Navassa Is.,
    Palmyra Atoll, Wake Is.
About the Territories 158

BACK OF THE BOOK

U.S. FACTS & FIGURES 160
GLOSSARY 161
OUTSIDE WEB SITES 161
PLACE-NAME INDEX 162
CREDITS 176

Southwest: Albuquerque balloon festival, p. 122

Territories: Festival dancers, American Samoa, pp. 158–159

West: Wyoming ranch, p. 154

HOW TO USE THIS ATLAS

This atlas is much more than just another book of maps about the United States. Of course you'll find all the things you'd expect to find—country, regional, and state maps, essays, photos, flags, graphs, and fact boxes—for the country as a whole as well as for each region and state (even the territories). But there's much more. This atlas, through a specially designed Web site (see pages 8–9), not only leads you to places where you can find more information and keep up-to-date about all kinds of things, it also allows you to go beyond the flat page and experience the sights and sounds of the country through the multimedia archives of National Geographic.

STATE FACT BOX
The fact box has all the key information you need at a glance about a state, its flag and nickname, statistics about area, cities, population, ethnic and racial makeup,* statehood, industry, and agriculture, plus some fun Geo Whiz facts and the state bird and flower.

*The ethnic/racial percentages total more than 100 percent because Hispanics can be included with any race or ethnic group.

WEB LINKS
Throughout the atlas you will find black-and-yellow Web link icons for photos, videos, sounds, games, and more information. You can get to all of these links through one URL: www.nationalgeographic.com/kids-usa-atlas. This link will take you to the Web site specially designed to go with this atlas (see pages 8–9). Bookmark it so you can use it often.

COLOR BARS
Each section of the atlas has its own color to make it easy to move from one to another. Look for the color on the Table of Contents and across the top of the pages in the atlas. The name of the section and the title for each topic or map is in the color bar.

The Northeast
The Southeast
The Midwest
The Southwest
The West
The Territories

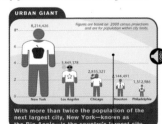

WHERE ARE THE PICTURES?
If you want to know where a picture in any of the regional sections in the atlas was taken, check the map in the regional photo essay. Find the label that describes the photograph you are curious about, and follow the line to its location.

CHARTS AND GRAPHS
The photo essay for each state includes a chart or graph that highlights economic, physical, cultural, or some other type of information related to the state.

BAR SCALE
Each map has a bar scale in miles and kilometers to help you find out how far it is from one place to another on the map.

"YOU ARE HERE"
Locator maps show you where each region and state within the region is in relation to the rest of the United States. Regions are shown in the regional color; featured states are in yellow.

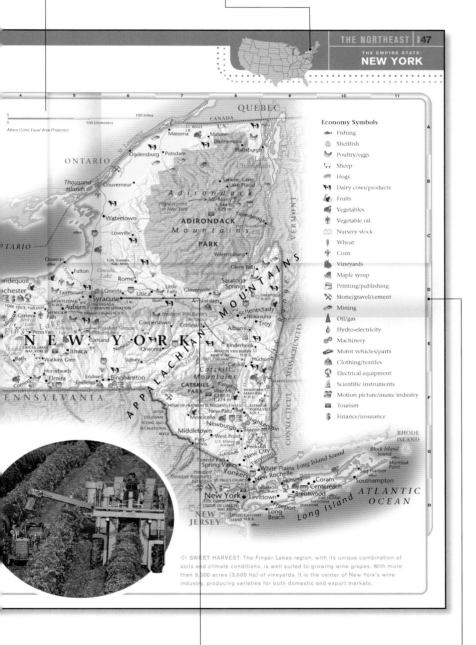

THE NORTHEAST | 47

THE EMPIRE STATE:
NEW YORK

Economy Symbols
- Fishing
- Shellfish
- Poultry/eggs
- Sheep
- Hogs
- Dairy cows/products
- Fruits
- Vegetables
- Vegetable oil
- Nursery stock
- Wheat
- Corn
- Vineyards
- Maple syrup
- Printing/publishing
- Stone/gravel/cement
- Mining
- Oil/gas
- Hydro-electricity
- Machinery
- Motor vehicles/parts
- Clothing/textiles
- Electrical equipment
- Scientific instruments
- Motion picture/music industry
- Tourism
- Finance/insurance

SWEET HARVEST. The Finger Lakes region, with its unique combination of soils and climate conditions, is well suited to growing wine grapes. With more than 9,000 acres (3,600 ha) of vineyards, it is the center of New York's wine industry, producing varieties for both domestic and export markets.

Sycamore, IL **91** B4
Sycan (river), OR **149** F4
Sycan N.W.&S.R., OR **149** F4
Sylacauga, AL **61** D4
Sylvania, OH **109** A3
Syracuse, NY **47** D5
Sysladobsis Lake, ME

INDEX AND GRID
A grid system makes it easy to find places listed in the index. For example, the listing for Syracuse, New York, is followed by **47** D5. The bold type is the page number; D5 tells you the city is near the point where imaginary lines drawn from D and 5 on the grid bars meet.

MAP ICONS

Maps use symbols to stand for many physical, political, and economic features. Below is a complete list of the map symbols used in this atlas. In addition, each state map has its own key featuring symbols for major economic activities. Additional abbreviations used in this atlas as well as metric conversion tables are listed on the endsheets at the back of the book.

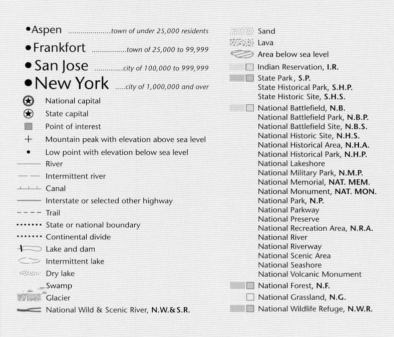

- •Aspen ....town of under 25,000 residents
- •Frankfort ....town of 25,000 to 99,999
- •San Jose ....city of 100,000 to 999,999
- •New York .....city of 1,000,000 and over
- ★ National capital
- ★ State capital
- ■ Point of interest
- + Mountain peak with elevation above sea level
- Low point with elevation below sea level
- River
- Intermittent river
- Canal
- Interstate or selected other highway
- Trail
- State or national boundary
- Continental divide
- Lake and dam
- Intermittent lake
- Dry lake
- Swamp
- Glacier
- National Wild & Scenic River, N.W.&S.R.

- Sand
- Lava
- Area below sea level
- Indian Reservation, I.R.
- State Park, S.P.
- State Historical Park, S.H.P.
- State Historic Site, S.H.S.
- National Battlefield, N.B.
- National Battlefield Park, N.B.P.
- National Battlefield Site, N.B.S.
- National Historic Site, N.H.S.
- National Historical Area, N.H.A.
- National Historical Park, N.H.P.
- National Lakeshore
- National Military Park, N.M.P.
- National Memorial, NAT. MEM.
- National Monument, NAT. MON.
- National Park, N.P.
- National Parkway
- National Preserve
- National Recreation Area, N.R.A.
- National River
- National Riverway
- National Scenic Area
- National Seashore
- National Volcanic Monument
- National Forest, N.F.
- National Grassland, N.G.
- National Wildlife Refuge, N.W.R.

Economy Symbols

Fishing	Stone/gravel/cement
Lobster fishing	Mining
Shellfish	Coal
Poultry/eggs	Oil/gas
Sheep	Hydro-electricity
Hogs	Machinery
Dairy cows/products	Metal manufacturing
Beef cattle	Metal products
Fruits	Shipbuilding
Vegetables	Railroad equipment
Vegetable oil	Motor vehicles/parts
Peanuts	Rubber/plastics
Nursery stock	Chemistry
Wheat	Food processing
Corn	Clothing/textiles
Rice	Leather products
Soybeans	Glass/clay products
Sugarcane	Jewelry
Cotton	Electrical equipment
Tobacco	Computers/electronics
Coffee	Scientific instruments
Vineyards	Aircraft/parts
Maple syrup	Aerospace
Timber/forest products	Motion picture/music industry
Furniture	Tourism
Printing/publishing	Finance/insurance

HOW TO USE THE ATLAS WEB SITE

As you can see by flipping through the pages, this atlas is chock full. There are photographs, statistics, quick facts, and—most of all—lots of charts and detailed maps. Plus there is a companion Web site that adds even more. You can watch videos of animals in their natural surrounds or of a volcano erupting, listen to the sounds of people, places, and animals, find lots of state information, download pictures and maps for school reports, and play games that allow you to explore the United States. You can even send e-postcards to your friends. The Web site provides added value to specific subjects in the atlas and also helps you explore on your own, taking you deep into the resources of National Geographic and beyond. Throughout the atlas you will find these icons.

PHOTOS   VIDEO   AUDIO   GAMES   INFO

The icons are placed near pictures, on maps, or next to text. Each icon tells you that you can find more on that subject on the Web site. To follow any icon link, go to www.nationalgeographic.com/kids-usa-atlas.

⇨ START HERE.

There are three ways to find what you are looking for from the Home Page:

1. BY ATLAS PAGE NUMBER
2. BY TOPIC
3. BY ICON

www.nationalgeographic.com/kids-usa-atlas

1. SEARCH BY ATLAS PAGE NUMBER

⇐ **PAGE NUMBER PULL-DOWN MENU.** If you find an icon in the atlas and want to go directly to that link, use the page number pull-down menu. Just drag and click.

2. SEARCH BY TOPIC

⇨ **LIST OF TOPICS.** If you want to explore a specific topic, click on the entry in the topic list. This list is your portal to vast quantities of National Geographic information, photos, videos, games, and more, all arranged by subject. Say you're interested in Animals. One click takes you to the Animals choice page (below).

⇩ **CREATURE FEATURES.** Click to go to the National Geographic Kids' animal site. Click on an animal, and you will find a full feature about it, including photos, video, a range map, and other fun info.

⇩ **CRITTERCAM.** Scientists put video cameras on animals to learn about the animal from its point of view. Click to see those videos, learn about the project, play games such as exploring the virtual world of a seal, and more.

⇐ **ANIMALS A–Z.** This choice takes you to the animal site for adults and older kids. Use the list of animals in the upper right-hand corner of the page. Clicking on an animal name takes you to the profile of that animal.

3. SEARCH BY ICON

⇐ **SELECT ONE OF FIVE ICONS.** If you want to find all the videos referenced in the atlas, or all of the audios, photos, or games, click on one of the icons. A list will drop down. Choose from the list, and you're there! Clicking on Blackbeard takes you to a trailer for a National Geographic Channel film.

THE PHYSICAL UNITED STATES

Stretching from the Atlantic in the east to the Pacific in the west, the United States is the third largest country in area in the world. Its physical diversity ranges from mountains to fertile plains and dry deserts. Shading on the map indicates changes in elevation, while colors suggest different vegetation patterns.

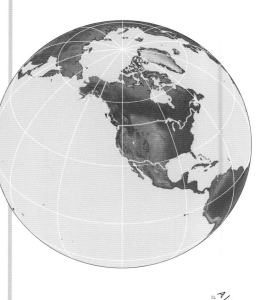

⇨ ALASKA AND HAWAI'I. In addition to the states located on the main landmass, the U.S. has two states—Alaska and Hawai'i—that are not directly connected to the other 48 states. If Alaska and Hawai'i were shown in their correct relative sizes and locations, the map would not fit on the page. The locator globe shows the correct relative size and location of each.

San Francisco

Coast Ranges   Sierra Nevada   Great Basin   Rocky Mountains

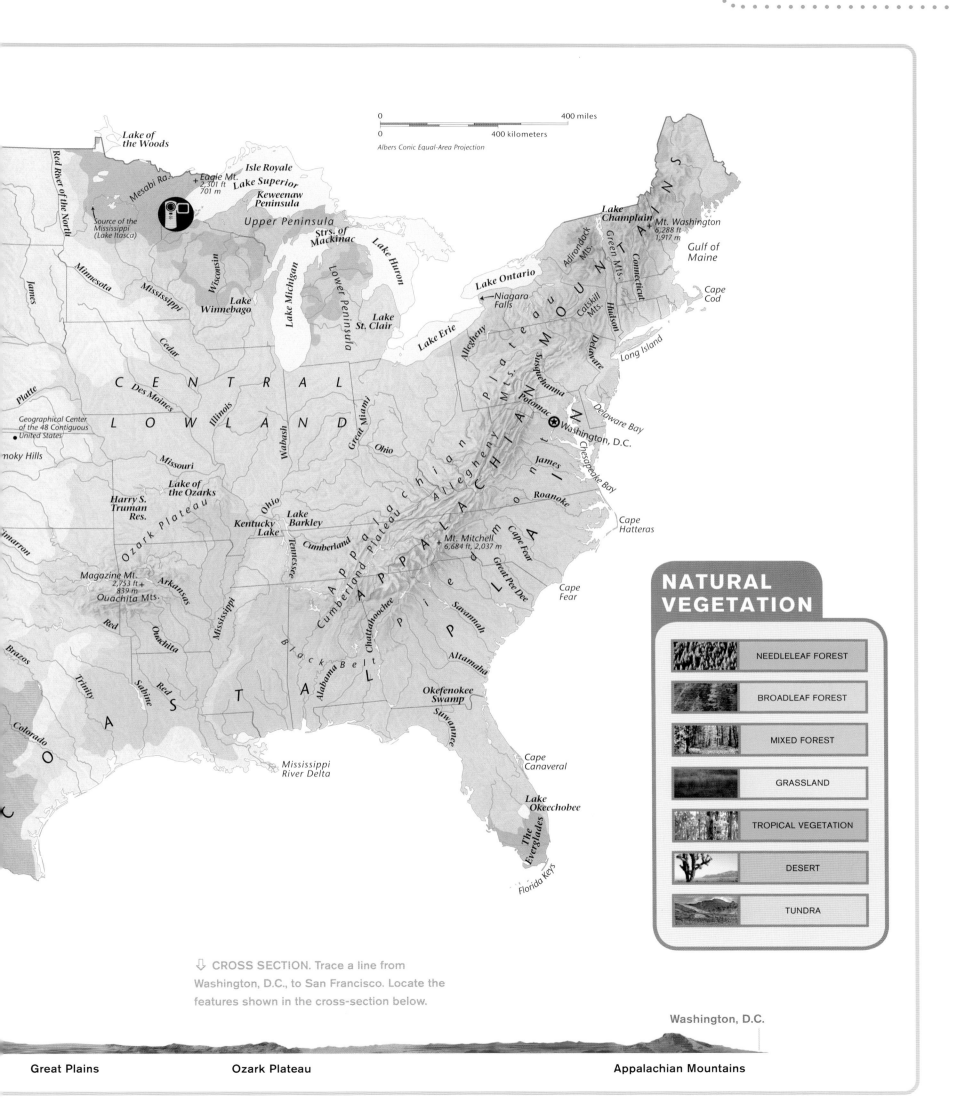

0 _____ 400 miles
0 _____ 400 kilometers
Albers Conic Equal-Area Projection

Lake of
the Woods

Red River of the North

Mesabi Ra.

Eagle Mt.
2,301 ft
701 m

Isle Royale

Lake Superior

Keweenaw
Peninsula

Source of the
Mississippi
(Lake Itasca)

Upper Peninsula

Strs. of
Mackinac

Minnesota

Mississippi

Wisconsin

Lake Huron

Lower Peninsula

Lake
Michigan

Lake
Winnebago

Lake
St. Clair

Lake Erie

James

Cedar

Platte

Des Moines

C E N T R A L

Illinois

Great Miami

Lake Ontario

Niagara
Falls

Allegheny

Geographical Center
of the 48 Contiguous
United States

L O W L A N D

Wabash

Ohio

Ohio

Lake
Champlain

Adirondack
Mts.

Green Mts.

Mt. Washington
6,288 ft
1,917 m

Connecticut

Hudson

Catskill
Mts.

Delaware

Gulf of
Maine

Cape
Cod

Long Island

Smoky Hills

Missouri

Lake of
the Ozarks

Harry S.
Truman
Res.

Ozark Plateau

Kentucky
Lake

Ohio

Lake
Barkley

Cumberland

Tennessee

Cumberland Plateau

Appalachian Plateau

Allegheny

Susquehanna

Potomac

Delaware Bay

Washington, D.C.

Chesapeake Bay

James

Roanoke

M O U N T A I N S

A P P A L A C H I A N

Cape
Hatteras

Cinnarron

Magazine Mt.
2,753 ft
839 m
Ouachita Mts.

Arkansas

Mississippi

Mt. Mitchell
6,684 ft, 2,037 m

Cape Fear

Great Pee Dee

Piedmont

Cape
Fear

Red

Ouachita

Black

Savannah

Brazos

Sabine

Red

Alabama Belt

Chattahoochee

Altamaha

Trinity

C O A S T A L   P L A I N

Okefenokee
Swamp

Colorado

Suwannee

Cape
Canaveral

Mississippi
River Delta

Lake
Okeechobee

The
Everglades

Florida Keys

⇩ CROSS SECTION. Trace a line from
Washington, D.C., to San Francisco. Locate the
features shown in the cross-section below.

Washington, D.C.

Great Plains   Ozark Plateau   Appalachian Mountains

NATURAL ENVIRONMENT

NATURAL ENVIRONMENT

A big part of the natural environment of the United States is the climate. With humid areas near the coasts, dry interior regions far from any major water body, and land areas that extend from northern Alaska to southern Florida and Hawai'i, the country experiences great variation in climate. Location is the key. Distance from the Equator, nearness to water, wind patterns, temperature of nearby water bodies, and elevation are things that influence temperature and precipitation. Climate affects the types of vegetation that grow in a particular place and plays a part in soil formation.

CHANGING CLIMATE

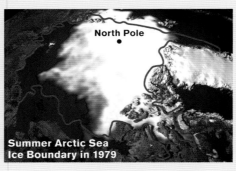

Summer Arctic Sea Ice Boundary in 1979

Scientists are concerned that a recent warming trend may be more than a natural cycle and that human activity may be a contributing factor. An increase in average temperatures could result in more severe storms, changes in precipitation patterns, and the spread of deserts. Rising temperatures may also play a part in the melting of glaciers, which could lead to a rise in ocean levels and the shrinking of the Arctic ice cover. NASA satellite images indicate that Arctic ice is shrinking as much as 9 percent each decade. Many believe that this puts polar bears at risk, since they normally hunt and raise their young on ice floes.

0 — 400 miles
0 — 400 kilometers

ALASKA

HAWAI'I

0 — 150 miles
0 — 150 kilometers

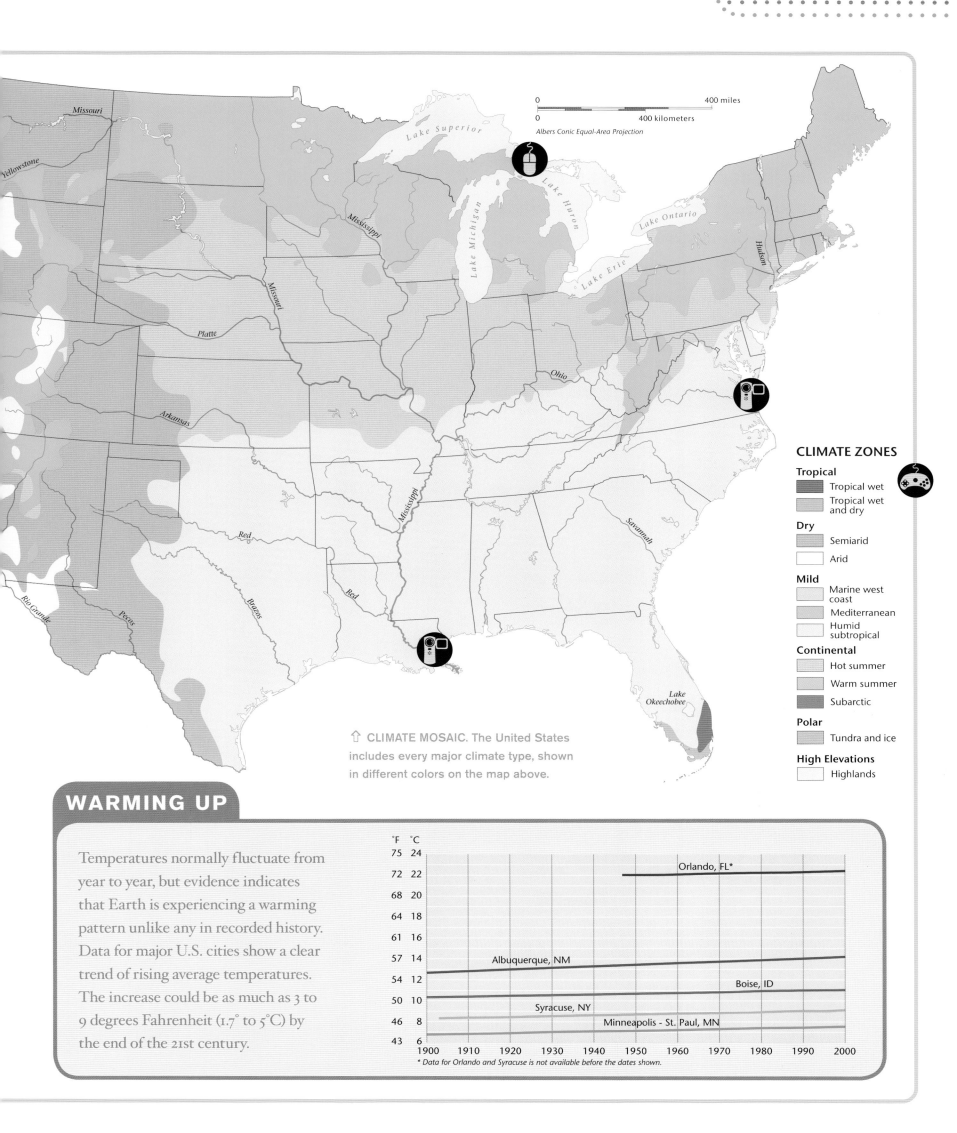

0
400 miles
0
400 kilometers
Albers Conic Equal-Area Projection

CLIMATE ZONES

Tropical
- Tropical wet
- Tropical wet and dry

Dry
- Semiarid
- Arid

Mild
- Marine west coast
- Mediterranean
- Humid subtropical

Continental
- Hot summer
- Warm summer
- Subarctic

Polar
- Tundra and ice

High Elevations
- Highlands

⇧ CLIMATE MOSAIC. The United States includes every major climate type, shown in different colors on the map above.

WARMING UP

Temperatures normally fluctuate from year to year, but evidence indicates that Earth is experiencing a warming pattern unlike any in recorded history. Data for major U.S. cities show a clear trend of rising average temperatures. The increase could be as much as 3 to 9 degrees Fahrenheit (1.7° to 5°C) by the end of the 21st century.

°F	°C
75	24
72	22
68	20
64	18
61	16
57	14
54	12
50	10
46	8
43	6

Orlando, FL*

Albuquerque, NM

Boise, ID

Syracuse, NY

Minneapolis - St. Paul, MN

1900 1910 1920 1930 1940 1950 1960 1970 1980 1990 2000

* Data for Orlando and Syracuse is not available before the dates shown.

NATURAL HAZARDS

The natural environment of the United States provides much diversity, but it also poses many dangers, especially when people locate homes and businesses in places at risk of natural disasters. Tornados bring destructive winds, and hurricanes bring strong winds, rain, and more; shifting of Earth's crust along fault lines rattles buildings; flood waters and wildfires threaten lives and property. More than one-third of the U.S. population lives in hazard-prone areas. Compare this natural disasters map to the population map on pages 18–19.

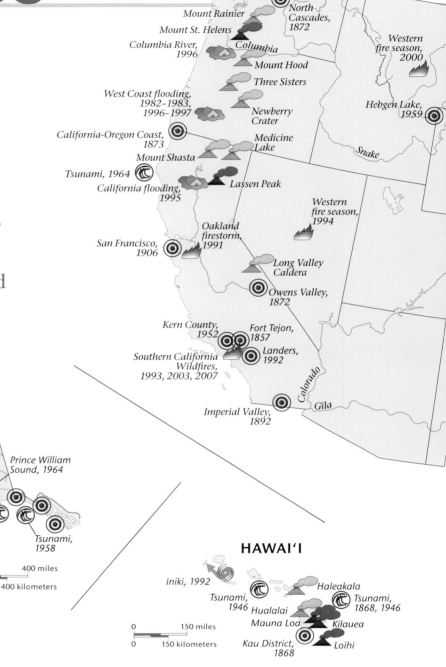

Mount Baker
Glacier Peak
Mount Rainier
Mount St. Helens
Columbia River, 1996
Columbia
Mount Hood
Three Sisters
North Cascades, 1872
Western fire season, 2000
West Coast flooding, 1982–1983, 1996–1997
Newberry Crater
Hebgen Lake, 1959
California-Oregon Coast, 1873
Medicine Lake
Mount Shasta
Tsunami, 1964
California flooding, 1995
Lassen Peak
Snake
Western fire season, 1994
Oakland firestorm, 1991
Long Valley Caldera
San Francisco, 1906
Owens Valley, 1872
Kern County, 1952
Fort Tejon, 1857
Landers, 1992
Southern California Wildfires, 1993, 2003, 2007
Colorado
Imperial Valley, 1892
Gila

ALASKA

Alaska has about 80 major volcanic centers.
More earthquakes occur in Alaska than in the other 49 states combined.

Prince William Sound, 1964
Novarupta, 1912
Tsunami, 1964
Tsunami, 1958
Tsunami, 1946, 1957

0   400 miles
0   400 kilometers

HAWAI'I

Iniki, 1992
Tsunami, 1946
Hualalai
Haleakala
Tsunami, 1868, 1946
Mauna Loa
Kilauea
Kau District, 1868
Loihi

0   150 miles
0   150 kilometers

NATURAL HAZARDS

BLIZZARD. Severe storm with bitter cold temperatures and wind-whipped snow and ice particles that reduce visibility to less than 650 feet (198 m), paralyzing transportation systems

FLOOD. Inundation of buildings or roadways caused by overflow of a river or stream swollen by heavy rainfall or rapid snowmelt; may involve displacement of people

DROUGHT. Long and continuous period of abnormally low precipitation, resulting in water shortages that negatively impact people, animals, and plant life; may result in crop loss

HURRICANE. Tropical storm in the Atlantic, Caribbean, Gulf of Mexico, or eastern Pacific with a minimum sustained wind speed of 74 miles per hour (119 kmph)

ICE STORM. Damaging accumulations of ice associated with freezing rain; may pull down trees or utility lines, causing extensive damage and creating dangerous travel conditions

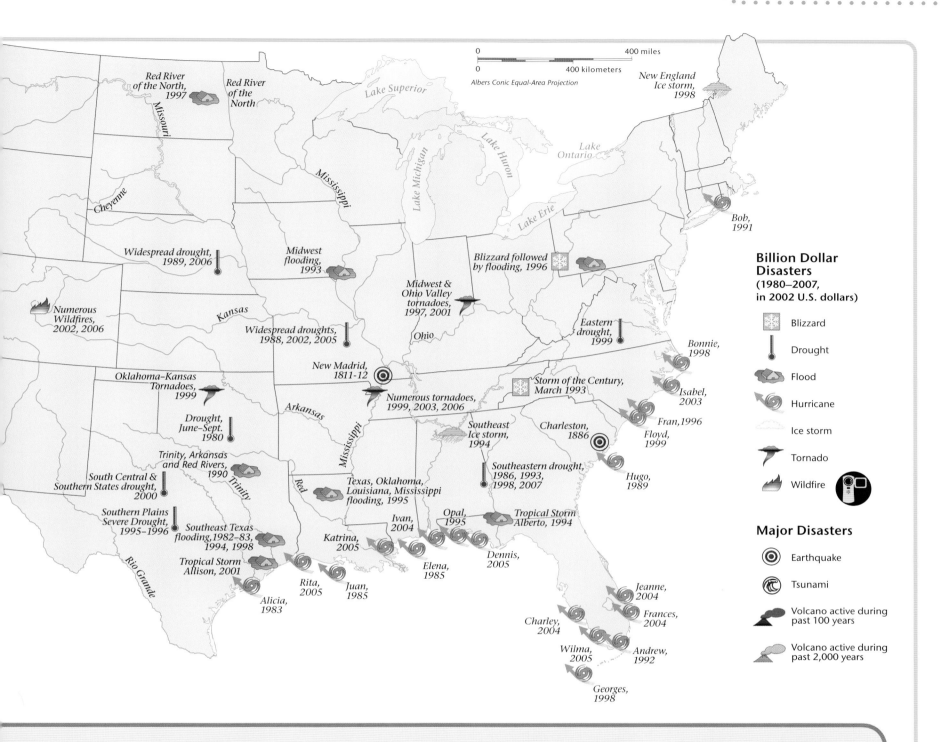

0 400 miles
0 400 kilometers
Albers Conic Equal-Area Projection

Red River of the North, 1997

Red River of the North

Missouri

New England Ice storm, 1998

Lake Superior

Lake Michigan

Lake Huron

Lake Ontario

Lake Erie

Cheyenne

Bob, 1991

Widespread drought, 1989, 2006

Midwest flooding, 1993

Blizzard followed by flooding, 1996

Numerous Wildfires, 2002, 2006

Kansas

Midwest & Ohio Valley tornadoes, 1997, 2001

Eastern drought, 1999

Bonnie, 1998

Widespread droughts, 1988, 2002, 2005

Ohio

Isabel, 2003

Oklahoma-Kansas Tornadoes, 1999

New Madrid, 1811-12

Numerous tornadoes, 1999, 2003, 2006

Storm of the Century, March 1993

Fran, 1996

Drought, June–Sept. 1980

Arkansas

Southeast Ice storm, 1994

Charleston, 1886

Floyd, 1999

South Central & Southern States drought, 2000

Trinity, Arkansas and Red Rivers, 1990

Trinity

Mississippi

Texas, Oklahoma, Louisiana, Mississippi flooding, 1995

Southeastern drought, 1986, 1993, 1998, 2007

Hugo, 1989

Southern Plains Severe Drought, 1995–1996

Red

Ivan, 2004

Opal, 1995

Tropical Storm Alberto, 1994

Southeast Texas flooding, 1982–83, 1994, 1998

Katrina, 2005

Dennis, 2005

Tropical Storm Allison, 2001

Rita, 2005

Juan, 1985

Elena, 1985

Jeanne, 2004

Alicia, 1983

Frances, 2004

Rio Grande

Charley, 2004

Wilma, 2005

Andrew, 1992

Georges, 1998

Billion Dollar Disasters
(1980–2007, in 2002 U.S. dollars)

Blizzard

Drought

Flood

Hurricane

Ice storm

Tornado

Wildfire

Major Disasters

Earthquake

Tsunami

Volcano active during past 100 years

Volcano active during past 2,000 years

TORNADO. Violently rotating column of air that, when it reaches the ground, is the most damaging of all atmospheric phenomena; most common in the central U.S.

WILDFIRE. Free-burning, uncontained fire in a forest or grassland; may result from lightning strikes or accidental or deliberate human activity in areas where conditions are dry

EARTHQUAKE. Shaking or vibration created by the energy released by movement of Earth's crust along plate boundaries; can cause structural damage and loss of life

TSUNAMI. Series of unusually large ocean waves caused by an underwater earthquake, landslide, or volcanic eruption; very destructive in coastal areas

VOLCANO. Vent or opening in Earth's surface through which molten rock called lava, ash, and gases are released; often associated with tectonic plate boundaries

THE POLITICAL UNITED STATES

Like a giant patchwork quilt, the United States is made up of 50 states, each uniquely different but together making a national fabric held together by a Constitution and a federal government. State boundaries, outlined in various colors on the map, set apart internal political units within the country. The national capital—Washington, D.C.—is marked by a star in a double circle on the map. The capital of each state is marked by a star in a single circle.

9:00 AM
PACIFIC TIME

10:00 AM
MOUNTAIN TIME

Cape Flattery

Seattle
Olympia • Tacoma
WASHINGTON
Spokane
Yakima

Portland
Salem
Eugene
OREGON
Columbia

Great Falls
Missouri
MONTANA
Butte • Helena
Billings

Medford
Klamath Falls

Boise
IDAHO
Idaho Falls
Snake

Cody
Yellowstone L.

Eureka
Redding

Pocatello

WYOMING
Casper
Cheyenne
Laramie
N. Platte

Sacramento
San Francisco • Oakland
San Jose
Salinas
Fresno

Reno
Carson City
Lake Tahoe

Great Salt Lake
Ogden
Salt Lake City
Provo

Great Basin
NEVADA

UTAH
Grand Junction
Lake Powell
Colorado

Fort Collins
Denver
Boulder
COLORADO
Colorado Springs
Pueblo

Bakersfield
Point Conception

Mojave Desert

Las Vegas
Lake Mead

Grand Canyon

St. George

Flagstaff

Santa Fe

Los Angeles
Long Beach • Riverside
San Diego
Salton Sea
Colorado

Phoenix • Mesa
Yuma
ARIZONA

Tucson

Albuquerque
NEW MEXICO

Roswell
Rio Grande
Las Cruces
El Paso

7:00 AM
HAWAI'I-ALEUTIAN TIME

0 ──── 400 miles
0 ──── 400 kilometers

North Slope
Brooks Range
ALASKA
Yukon
Alaska Range
Juneau
Anchorage

ALEUTIAN ISLANDS
Alaska Peninsula

8:00 AM
ALASKA TIME

7:00 AM
HAWAI'I-ALEUTIAN TIME

Kaua'i
Ni'ihau • O'ahu
Honolulu
HAWAI'I
Moloka'i
Lana'i • Maui
Kaho'olawe
Hilo
Hawai'i

0 ──── 150 mi
0 ──── 150 km

⇧ TIME ZONES. Earth is divided into 24 time zones, each about 15 degrees of longitude wide, reflecting the distance Earth turns from west to east each hour. The U.S. is divided into six time zones, indicated by red dotted lines on the maps. When it is noon in Boston, what is the time in Seattle?

11:00 AM

CENTRAL TIME

12:00 noon

EASTERN TIME

0   300 miles
0   300 kilometers
Albers Conic Equal-Area Projection

Lake of the Woods

Isle Royale

Lake Superior

MAINE

Bangor

Minot

International Falls

Grand Forks

NORTH DAKOTA

Bismarck   Fargo

Duluth   Marquette

MINNESOTA   Superior

MICHIGAN

Burlington

VT.

Montpelier

Augusta

N.H.

Portland

Concord

Aberdeen

SOUTH DAKOTA

Pierre

Minneapolis

St. Paul

WISCONSIN

Green Bay

Lake Michigan

Lake Huron

Lake Champlain

Boston

MASS.

Cape Cod

Rapid City

Sioux Falls

Madison

Milwaukee

Grand Rapids

Lansing

Lake Ontario

Rochester

Syracuse Albany

NEW YORK

Buffalo

Hartford

CONN. RHODE ISLAND

Providence

NEBRASKA

Cedar Rapids

IOWA

Rockford

Chicago

Detroit

Lake Erie

Erie

Cleveland

Newark

New York

Long Island

Grand Island

Omaha

Des Moines

Davenport

Gary

Toledo

PENNSYLVANIA

Harrisburg

Pittsburgh

Trenton

NEW JERSEY

Philadelphia

Platte

Lincoln

Peoria

Fort Wayne

OHIO

Columbus

Baltimore

Dover

DELAWARE

Springfield

ILLINOIS

INDIANA

Indianapolis

Dayton

Cincinnati

WEST VIRGINIA

Washington D.C.

Annapolis

MARYLAND

Chesapeake Bay

Kansas City

Jefferson City

St. Louis

Louisville

Frankfort

Lexington

Evansville

Charleston

Richmond

VIRGINIA

Virginia Beach

Roanoke

Norfolk

Topeka

KANSAS

MISSOURI

KENTUCKY

Paducah

Greensboro

Raleigh

Cape Hatteras

Dodge City

Wichita

Springfield

Knoxville

NORTH CAROLINA

Charlotte

Tulsa

Nashville

TENNESSEE

Chattanooga

Greenville

OKLAHOMA

Amarillo

Oklahoma City

Fort Smith

Memphis

Huntsville

Columbia

SOUTH CAROLINA

Lawton

ARKANSAS

Little Rock

Birmingham

Atlanta

GEORGIA

Charleston

Lubbock

Wichita Falls

Red

Jackson

ALABAMA

Macon

Columbus

Savannah

Fort Worth

Dallas

Shreveport

MISSISSIPPI

Montgomery

Savannah

Midland

Abilene

Waco

Brazos

LOUISIANA

Red

Natchez

Biloxi

Mobile

Tallahassee

Jacksonville

Odessa

TEXAS

Austin

Beaumont

Lafayette

Baton Rouge

New Orleans

Mobile Bay

Gainesville

Houston

Mississippi River Delta

Apalachee Bay

FLORIDA

Orlando

Cape Canaveral

San Antonio

Tampa

St. Petersburg

Lake Okeechobee

Corpus Christi

Rio Grande

Laredo

Fort Lauderdale

Miami

The Everglades

Brownsville

Florida Keys

Red River basin ceded by Great Britain, 1818

Ceded by Great Britain, 1842

Ceded by Great Britain, 1842

Oregon Country ceded by Great Britain, 1846

Louisiana Purchase from France, 1803

United States, 1783

Ceded by Mexico, 1848

Texas annexed by U.S., 1845

Western boundary of original 13 colonies, 1775

Alaska purchased from Russia, 1867

Gadsden Purchase from Mexico, 1853

Florida ceded by Spain, 1819

Hawai'i annexed in 1898

⇐ WESTWARD EXPANSION. The United States had its origins in 13 British colonies established along the Atlantic coast. After gaining independence in 1783, the young country began adding new territories—some by treaty, others by purchase or by war. The map traces the country's expansion and shows the date each territory was acquired.

POPULATION

Three hundred million and growing! The population of the United States topped the 300 million mark in 2006, and it continues to grow by more than 2 million people each year. Before the arrival of European settlers, the population consisted of Native Americans living in tribal groups scattered across the country. In the 16th and 17th centuries, Europeans, some with slaves from Africa, settled first along the eastern seaboard and later moved westward. In 1790 the U.S. population was not quite 4 million people. Today, New York City alone has a population more than double that number. The country's population is unevenly distributed. The map shows the number of people per square mile for each county in every state. Greatest densities are in the East and along the West Coast, especially around major cities. The most rapid growth is occurring in the South and the West—an area referred to as the Sunbelt—as well as in suburban areas around cities.

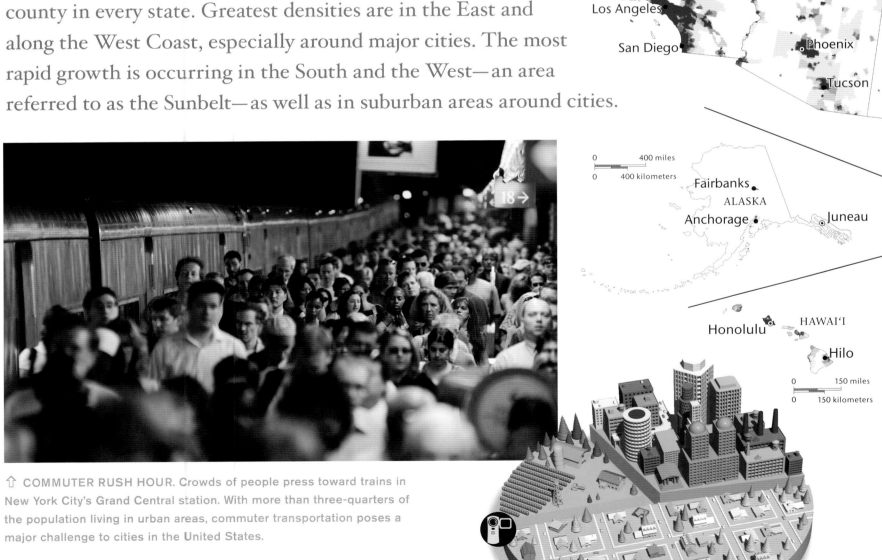

⇧ COMMUTER RUSH HOUR. Crowds of people press toward trains in New York City's Grand Central station. With more than three-quarters of the population living in urban areas, commuter transportation poses a major challenge to cities in the United States.

⇨ WHERE WE LIVE. The first U.S. census in 1790 revealed that only 5 percent of people lived in towns. As industry has grown and agriculture has become increasingly mechanized, people have left farms (green), moving to urban places (blue) and their surrounding suburbs (orange).

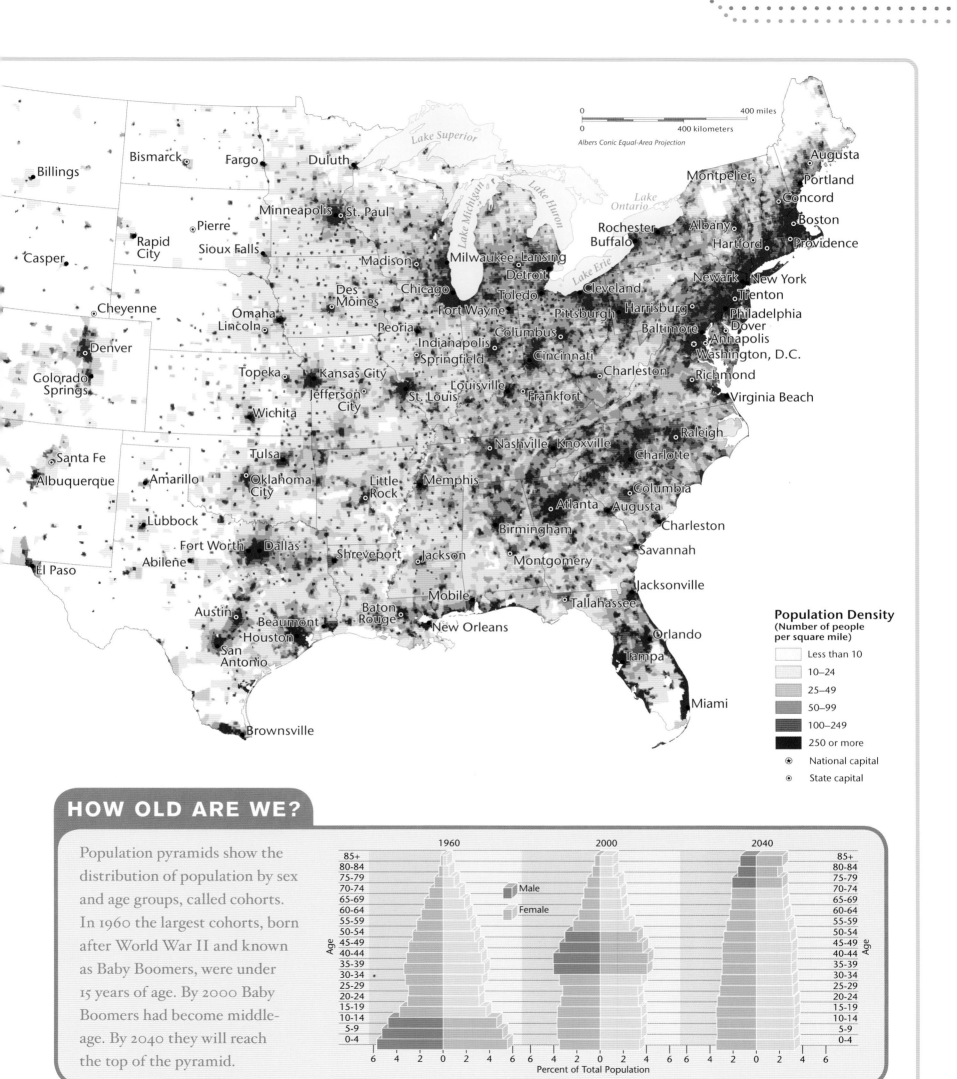

0   400 miles
0   400 kilometers
Albers Conic Equal-Area Projection

Population Density
(Number of people
per square mile)

Less than 10
10–24
25–49
50–99
100–249
250 or more

⊛   National capital
⊙   State capital

HOW OLD ARE WE?

Population pyramids show the distribution of population by sex and age groups, called cohorts. In 1960 the largest cohorts, born after World War II and known as Baby Boomers, were under 15 years of age. By 2000 Baby Boomers had become middle-age. By 2040 they will reach the top of the pyramid.

1960   2000   2040

85+
80-84
75-79
70-74   ■ Male
65-69
60-64   ■ Female
55-59
50-54
45-49
40-44
35-39
30-34
25-29
20-24
15-19
10-14
5-9
0-4

6 4 2 0 2 4 6   6 4 2 0 2 4 6   6 4 2 0 2 4 6
Percent of Total Population

Age

PEOPLE ON THE MOVE

From earliest human history, the land of the United States has been a focus of migration. Native peoples arrived thousands of years ago. The first European settlers came in the 16th and 17th centuries, and slave ships brought people from Africa. Today, people are still on the move. Since the mid-20th century, most international migrants have come from Latin America—especially Mexico and countries of Central America and the Caribbean—and Asia, particularly China, the Philippines, and India. While most of the population is still of European descent, certain regions have large minority concentrations, as shown on the map, that influence local cultural landscapes.

⇧ BRIDGE OF HOPE. Many Mexicans enter the U.S. (foreground) by bridges across the Rio Grande, such as this one between Nuevo Laredo, Mexico, and Laredo, Texas.

⇧ IMMIGRANT INFLUENCE. With Hispanics making up almost 15 percent of the population, signs in Spanish are popping up everywhere—even at voting areas.

⇧ SUNBELT SPRAWL. Spreading suburbs are becoming a common feature of the desert Southwest as people flock to the Sunbelt.

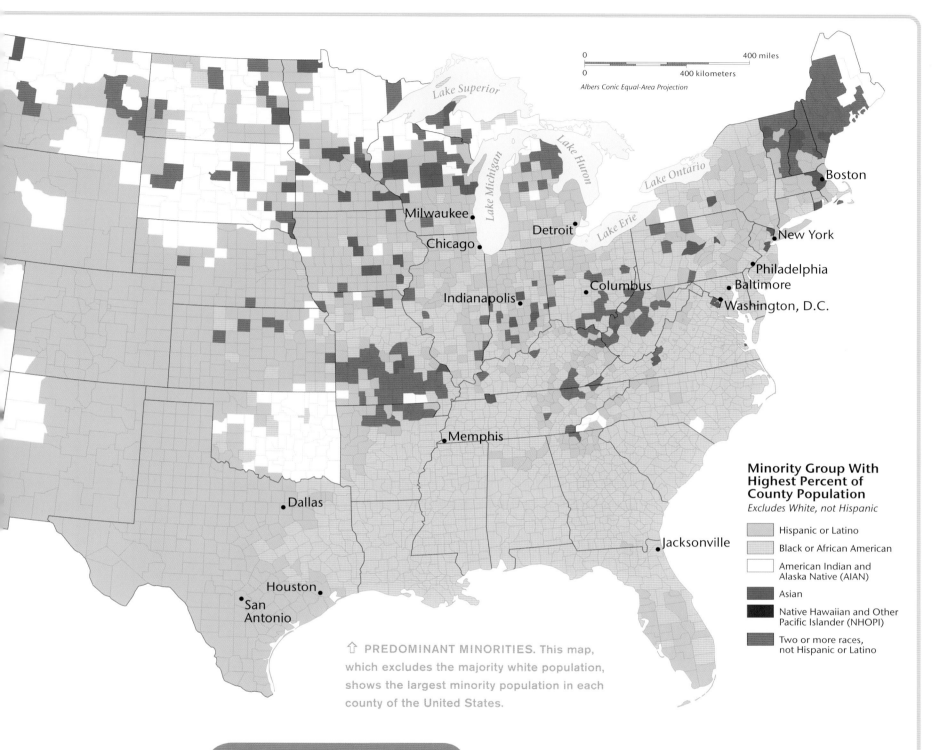

Milwaukee
Detroit
Chicago
New York
Philadelphia
Columbus
Baltimore
Indianapolis
Washington, D.C.
Boston

Memphis

Dallas

Jacksonville

Houston
San
Antonio

Lake Superior
Lake Michigan
Lake Huron
Lake Erie
Lake Ontario

0   400 miles
0   400 kilometers
Albers Conic Equal-Area Projection

Minority Group With Highest Percent of County Population
Excludes White, not Hispanic

- Hispanic or Latino
- Black or African American
- American Indian and Alaska Native (AIAN)
- Asian
- Native Hawaiian and Other Pacific Islander (NHOPI)
- Two or more races, not Hispanic or Latino

⇧ PREDOMINANT MINORITIES. This map, which excludes the majority white population, shows the largest minority population in each county of the United States.

POPULATION SHIFT

In the last half century, people have begun moving from the historical industrial and agricultural regions of the Northeast and Midwest toward the South and West, attracted by the promise of jobs, generally lower living costs, and a more relaxed way of life. This trend can be seen in the population growth patterns, shown in the map at right.

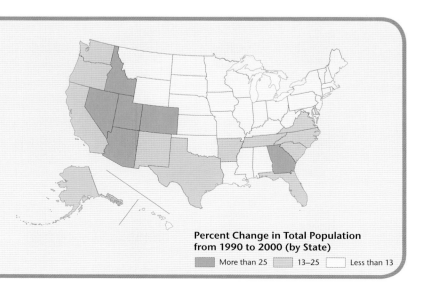

Percent Change in Total Population from 1990 to 2000 (by State)

- More than 25
- 13–25
- Less than 13

GETTING GREEN

Every day the media is filled with stories about global warming, pollution, and dwindling resources. Headlines warn of environmental risks that may threaten our way of life. The United States is the source of a quarter of the world's greenhouse gas emissions, and Americans generate more than 250 million tons of trash each year. The average American also uses 32 times more resources than a person in the African country of Kenya. But there's a bright side to these grim statistics. We can make a positive difference to the environment by making simple lifestyle changes. Scientists and engineers have developed energy efficient appliances, cars that run on alternative fuels, and products made from recycled paper and plastics. But it is up to each of us to make changes that take advantage of these environment-friendly developments.

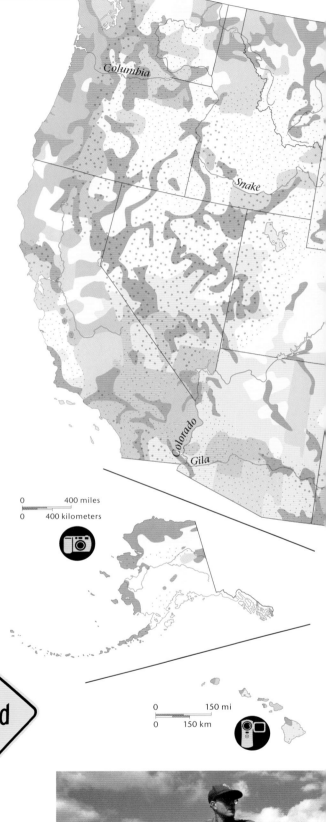

THINGS YOU CAN DO

Each year the average American household generates more than 80 tons of carbon dioxide gases, uses 102,000 gallons (386,111 l) of water, and creates 3.3 tons of landfill waste. Improving the health of our environment begins with you. You can make a difference if you practice the 3 R's of "getting green."

• REDUCE resource consumption by turning off lights, the TV, computers, and other electronic devices when you leave the room. Close the faucet when you are not using the water. Avoid buying things you do not need.

• REUSE items whenever possible, rather than throwing things away. Consider whether a container can be used again or a pair of shoes repaired.

• RECYCLE paper, plastic, glass, and aluminum cans. Recycling makes for less landfill trash, plus it preserves resources by reusing old products to make new ones.

Visit the library or go online to learn what your community is doing to protect the environment.

⇧ GREEN STREETS. Biking to work or school reduces use of gasoline, a source of greenhouse gases, and it is healthy, too.

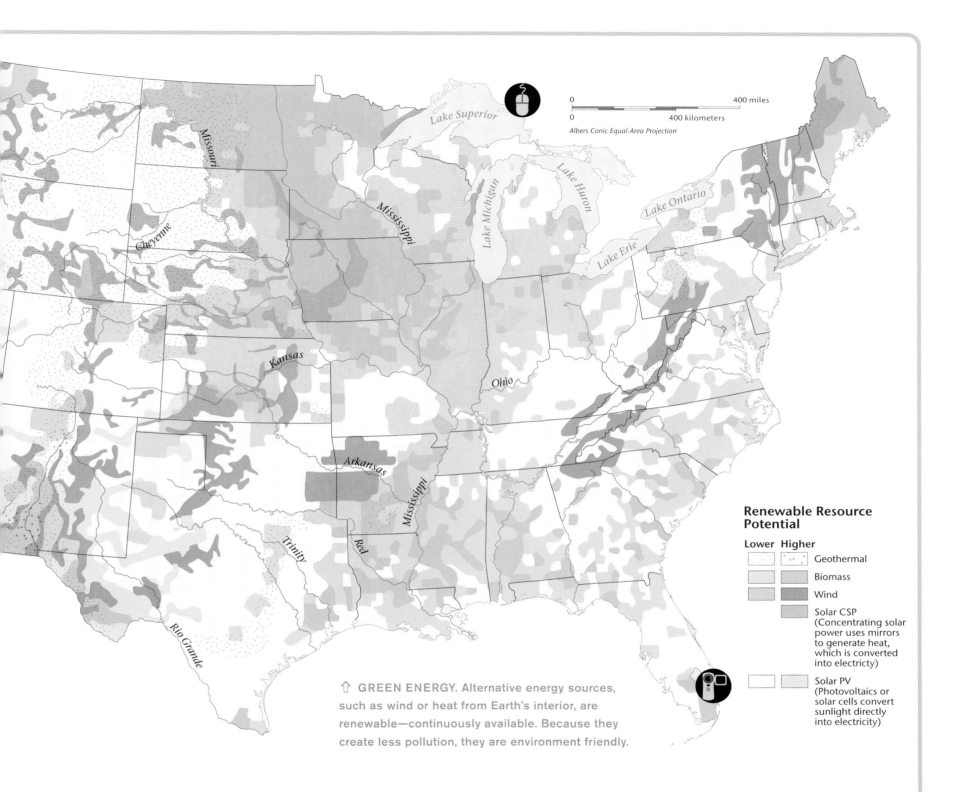

0   400 miles

0   400 kilometers

Albers Conic Equal-Area Projection

Renewable Resource Potential

Lower Higher

- Geothermal
- Biomass
- Wind
- Solar CSP (Concentrating solar power uses mirrors to generate heat, which is converted into electricty)
- Solar PV (Photovoltaics or solar cells convert sunlight directly into electricity)

⇑ GREEN ENERGY. Alternative energy sources, such as wind or heat from Earth's interior, are renewable—continuously available. Because they create less pollution, they are environment friendly.

⇐ GREEN GARDENING. An organic farmer turns a compost pile with a pitchfork. Compost is a natural fertilizer made from decayed plant material. It is good for the environment because it reuses natural materials and avoids the use of chemicals that can pollute soil and water.

⇐ RECYCLE. Bright blue trash collectors overflow with plastic containers waiting to go to a recycling center. Citizen participation is an important step toward reducing landfill waste and restoring the health of the environment.

THE NATION'S CAPITAL

THE NATION'S CAPITAL

Chosen as a compromise location between Northern and Southern interests and built on land ceded by Virginia and Maryland in the late 1700s, Washington, D.C., sits on a bank of the Potomac River. It is the seat of U.S. government and symbol of the country's history. Pierre L'Enfant, a French architect, was appointed by President George Washington to design the city, which is distinguished by a grid pattern cut by diagonal avenues. At the city's core is the National Mall, a broad park lined by monuments, museums, and stately government buildings.

← DISTRICT OF COLUMBIA. Originally on both sides of the Potomac River, the city returned land to Virginia in 1846.

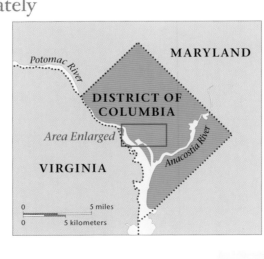

← GREAT LEADER. Abraham Lincoln, who was president during the Civil War and a strong opponent of slavery, is remembered in a monument that houses this seated statue at the west end of the National Mall.

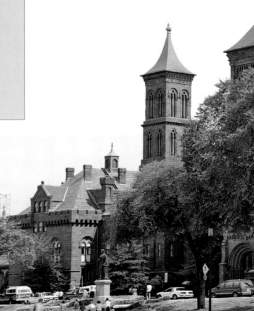

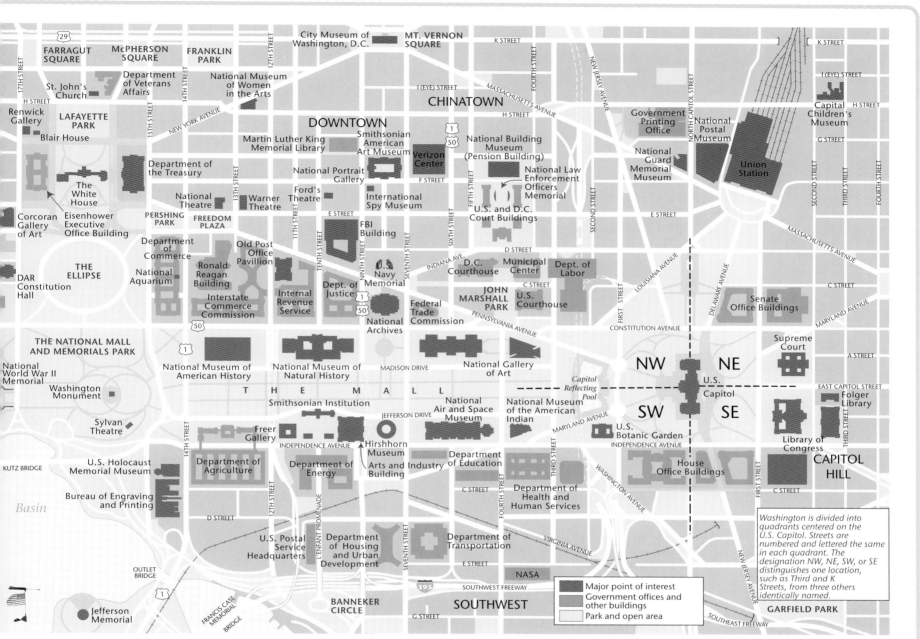

FARRAGUT SQUARE
McPHERSON SQUARE
FRANKLIN PARK
City Museum of Washington, D.C.
MT. VERNON SQUARE
K STREET
I (EYE) STREET
Capital Children's Museum
H STREET

17TH STREET
St. John's Church
Department of Veterans Affairs
14TH STREET
12TH STREET
National Museum of Women in the Arts
FOURTH STREET
NEW JERSEY AVENUE
Government Printing Office
National Postal Museum
G STREET

Renwick Gallery
LAFAYETTE PARK
H STREET
NEW YORK AVENUE
CHINATOWN
MASSACHUSETTS AVENUE
H STREET
NORTH CAPITOL STREET
National Guard Memorial Museum
Union Station

Blair House
15TH STREET
DOWNTOWN
Martin Luther King Memorial Library
Smithsonian American Art Museum
Verizon Center
U.S. 50
National Building Museum (Pension Building)

The White House
Department of the Treasury
National Portrait Gallery
F STREET
FIFTH STREET
National Law Enforcement Officers Memorial
SECOND STREET
E STREET
SECOND STREET
THIRD STREET
FOURTH STREET

Corcoran Gallery of Art
Eisenhower Executive Office Building
PERSHING PARK
FREEDOM PLAZA
National Theatre
13TH STREET
Warner Theatre
11TH STREET
Ford's Theatre
E STREET
International Spy Museum
U.S. and D.C. Court Buildings

DAR Constitution Hall
THE ELLIPSE
Department of Commerce
TENTH STREET
FBI Building
NINTH STREET
SEVENTH STREET
D STREET
LOUISIANA AVENUE
FIRST STREET

National Aquarium
Ronald Reagan Building
Old Post Office Pavillion
INDIANA AVE.
U.S. Navy Memorial
D.C. Courthouse
Municipal Center
Dept. of Labor
C STREET
DELAWARE AVENUE
Senate Office Buildings
MASSACHUSETTS AVENUE

Interstate Commerce Commission
Internal Revenue Service
Dept. of Justice
U.S. 1 50
JOHN MARSHALL PARK
U.S. Courthouse
CONSTITUTION AVENUE
C STREET
MARYLAND AVENUE

THE NATIONAL MALL AND MEMORIALS PARK
National Archives
Federal Trade Commission
PENNSYLVANIA AVENUE
Supreme Court
A STREET

National World War II Memorial
U.S. 1
National Museum of American History
National Museum of Natural History
MADISON DRIVE
National Gallery of Art
NW   NE
Folger Library
EAST CAPITOL STREET

Washington Monument
14TH STREET
Smithsonian Institution
Capitol Reflecting Pool
U.S. Capitol
THIRD STREET

T H E   M A L L
National Air and Space Museum
JEFFERSON DRIVE
National Museum of the American Indian
SW   SE
Library of Congress
CAPITOL HILL

Sylvan Theatre
Freer Gallery
INDEPENDENCE AVENUE
Hirshhorn Museum
MARYLAND AVENUE
U.S. Botanic Garden
INDEPENDENCE AVENUE

KUTZ BRIDGE
U.S. Holocaust Memorial Museum
Department of Agriculture
Department of Energy
Arts and Industry Building
Department of Education
Department of Industry
WASHINGTON AVENUE
House Office Buildings
FIRST STREET

Basin
Bureau of Engraving and Printing
D STREET
Department of Health and Human Services
THIRD STREET
C STREET

OUTLET BRIDGE
U.S. Postal Service Headquarters
L'ENFANT PROMENADE
Department of Housing and Urban Development
12TH STREET
SEVENTH STREET
Department of Transportation
E STREET
VIRGINIA AVENUE
NEW JERSEY AVENUE

Jefferson Memorial
U.S. 1
FRANCIS CASE MEMORIAL BRIDGE
BANNEKER CIRCLE
G STREET
I-395
SOUTHWEST FREEWAY
NASA
SOUTHWEST
GARFIELD PARK
SOUTHEAST FREEWAY

Washington is divided into quadrants centered on the U.S. Capitol. Streets are numbered and lettered the same in each quadrant. The designation NW, NE, SW, or SE distinguishes one location, such as Third and K Streets, from three others identically named.

■ Major point of interest
■ Government offices and other buildings
□ Park and open area

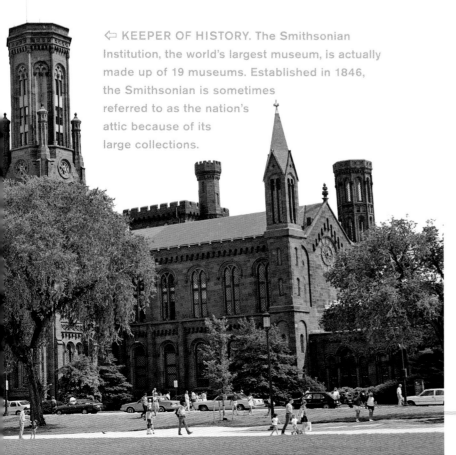

⇐ KEEPER OF HISTORY. The Smithsonian Institution, the world's largest museum, is actually made up of 19 museums. Established in 1846, the Smithsonian is sometimes referred to as the nation's attic because of its large collections.

⇑ NATIONAL ICON. The gleaming dome of the U.S. Capitol, home to the Senate and House of Representatives, rises above a group of protesters on the eastern end of the National Mall.

THE REGION

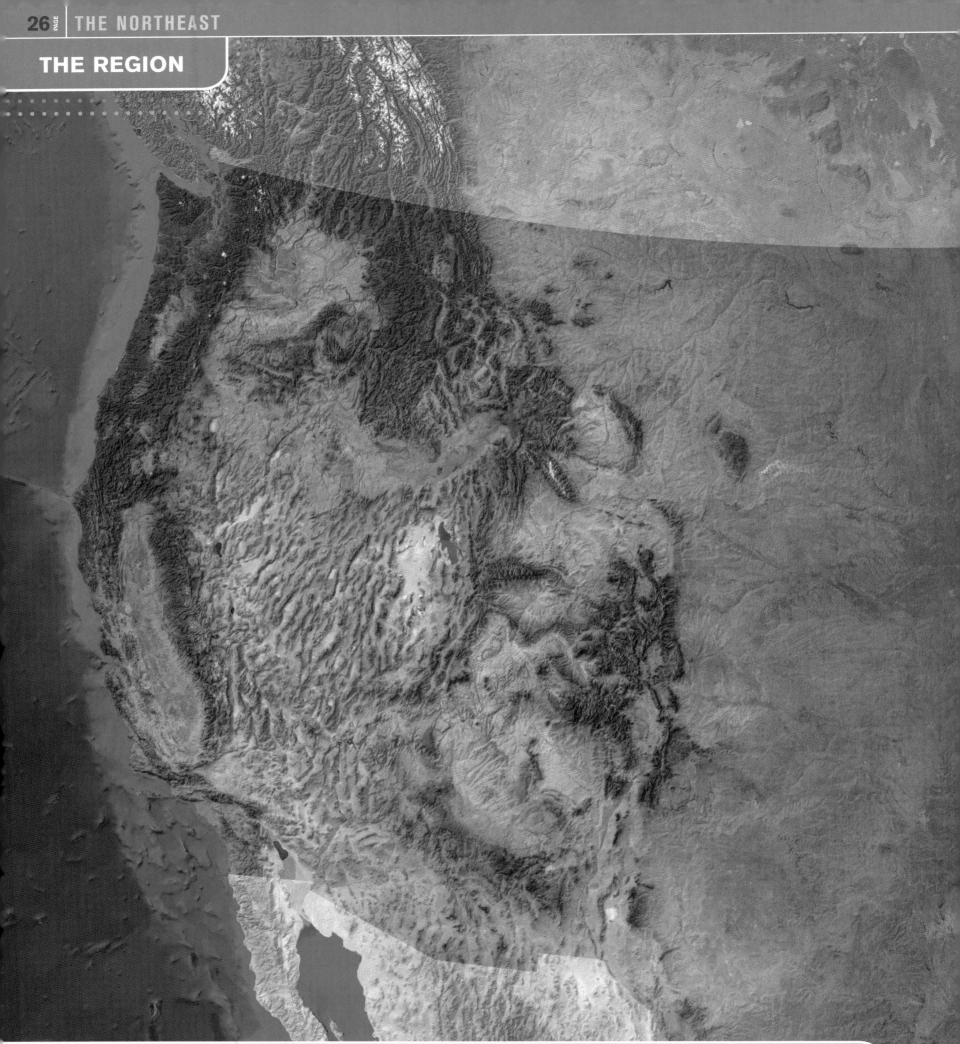

PHYSICAL			POLITICAL	
Total area 196,220 sq mi (508,209 sq km)	**Lowest point** Sea level, shores of the Atlantic Ocean	**Vegetation** Needleleaf, broadleaf, and mixed forest	**Total population** 61,163,734	**Smallest state** Rhode Island: 1,545 sq mi (4,002 sq km)
Highest point Mount Washington, NH 6,288 ft (1,917 m)	**Longest rivers** St. Lawrence, Susquehanna, Connecticut, Hudson	**Climate** Continental to mild, with cool to warm summers, cold winters, and moderate precipitation throughout the year	**States (11):** Connecticut, Delaware, Maine, Maryland, Massachusetts, New Hampshire, New Jersey, New York, Pennsylvania, Rhode Island, Vermont	**Most populous state** New York: 19,297,729
	Largest lakes Erie, Ontario, Champlain			**Least populous state** Vermont: 621,254
			Largest state New York: 54,556 sq mi (141,300 sq km)	**Largest city proper** New York, NY: 8,214,426

The Northeast

ATLANTIC OCEAN

100 miles
100 kilometers
Albers Conic Equal-Area Projection

NOVA SCOTIA

NEW BRUNSWICK

Bay of Fundy

St. John

St. Croix

CANADA
U.S.

Mt. Katahdin
+5,268 ft
1,605 m

Allagash

St. John

MAINE

Penobscot

Mt. Desert Island

Gulf of Maine

Kennebec

Saco

Cape Ann

Massachusetts Bay

Cape Cod

Nantucket Island

Martha's Vineyard

Mt. Washington
6,288 ft
1,917 m

White Mts.

N.H.

Merrimack

MOUNTAINS

Mt. Mansfield
+4,393 ft
1,339 m

Green Mts.

VT.

Connecticut

Mt. Greylock
3,491 ft
1,064 m

MASSACHUSETTS

Jerimoth Hill
+812 ft
247 m

R.I.

Mt. Frissell
2,380 ft
725 m

CONN.

Long Island Sound

Long Island

QUEBEC

CANADA
U.S.

Lake Champlain

Mt. Marcy
+5,344 ft
1,629 m

Adirondack Mts.

Hudson

Raquette

Black

Mohawk

NEW YORK

APPALACHIAN

Catskill Mts.

High Point
1,803 ft
550 m

NEW JERSEY

Fall Line

COASTAL

Pine Barrens

Cape May

Delaware Bay

CANADA

Oneida Lake

Finger Lakes

Genesee

Erie Canal

St. Lawrence

Niagara Falls

ONTARIO

Lake Ontario

Plateau

PENNSYLVANIA

Allegheny

Susquehanna

Delaware

448 ft
137 m

PLAIN

DEL.

MARYLAND

Delmarva Peninsula

Chesapeake Bay

D.C.

Blue Ridge

PIEDMONT

Allegheny Mountains

Appalachian Mountains

Potomac

VIRGINIA

Lake Erie

Monongahela

Ohio

Mt. Davis
3,213 ft
979 m

Backbone Mt.
3,360 ft
1,024 m

WEST VIRGINIA

OHIO

Lake Huron

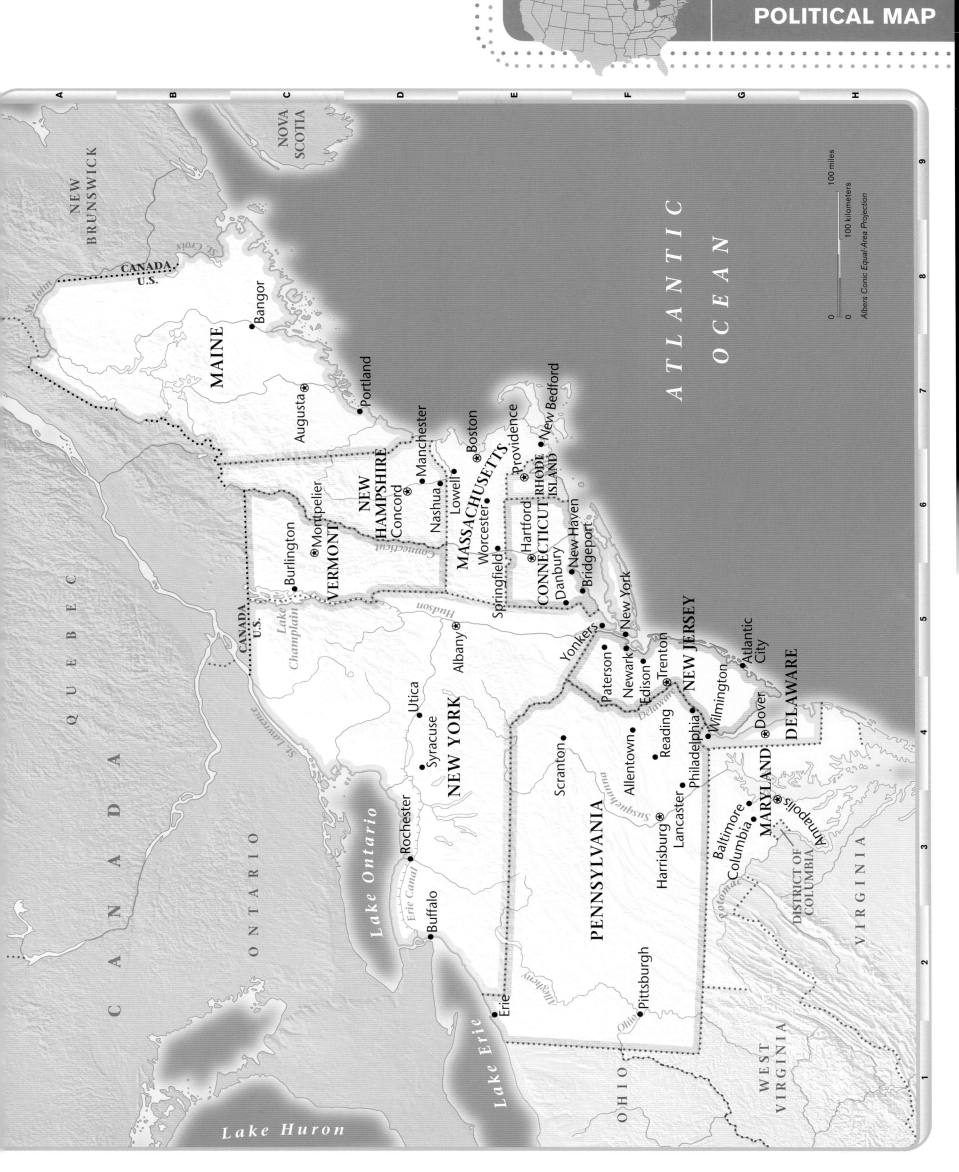

ATLANTIC OCEAN

100 miles
100 kilometers
Albers Conic Equal-Area Projection

NEW BRUNSWICK

NOVA SCOTIA

St. Croix

St. John

CANADA
U.S.

MAINE

Bangor

Augusta

Portland

QUEBEC

CANADA

ONTARIO

St. Lawrence

NEW HAMPSHIRE

VERMONT

Montpelier

Burlington

Lake Champlain

Concord

Manchester

Nashua

Lowell

Worcester

Boston

Providence

New Bedford

MASSACHUSETTS

RHODE ISLAND

CONNECTICUT

Springfield

Hartford

New Haven

Danbury

Bridgeport

Connecticut

Lake Ontario

Rochester

Buffalo

Erie Canal

Erie

NEW YORK

Utica

Syracuse

Albany

Hudson

Yonkers

New York

Paterson

Newark

Edison

Trenton

NEW JERSEY

Atlantic City

Delaware

Lake Erie

Lake Huron

OHIO

Pittsburgh

Ohio

Allegheny

PENNSYLVANIA

Scranton

Allentown

Reading

Susquehanna

Harrisburg

Lancaster

Philadelphia

Wilmington

DELAWARE

Dover

Baltimore

Columbia

MARYLAND

Annapolis

Potomac

DISTRICT OF COLUMBIA

VIRGINIA

WEST VIRGINIA

⇨ DINNER DELICACY. Lobsters, a favorite food for many people, turn bright red when cooked. These crustaceans live in the cold waters of the Atlantic Ocean and are caught using baited traps.

The Northeast
BIRTHPLACE OF A NATION

The United States had its beginnings in the Northeast region. Early European traders and settlers were quickly followed by immigrants from around the globe, making the region's population the most diverse in the country. The region includes the country's financial center, New York City, and its political capital, Washington, D.C. While the region boasts tranquil mountains, lakes, and rivers, its teeming cities have always been the heart of the Northeast. First there were water-powered textile mills, followed by manufacturing and shipbuilding industries. Today, service industries dominate the scene, but the economic pulse continues to beat strongly.

⇩ MELTING POT. From colonial times, the Northeast has been a gateway for immigration. These young girls, dressed in traditional saris and performing in an India Cultural Festival in New Jersey, reflect the rich diversity of the region.

⇨ DEFENDER OF FREEDOM. Rising 548 feet (167 m) above Penn Square, Philadelphia's City Hall, with its statue of William Penn, is the country's largest municipal building. Penn was founder of the Pennsylvania colony and defender of equal rights for men and women.

⇧ DAWN'S EARLY LIGHT. The lights of New York City's skyline sparkle against the early morning sky. The tall buildings of Lower Manhattan, reflected in the dark waters of the East River, are home to companies whose influence reaches around the world.

⇧ STILL WATERS. A father and son enjoy a quiet day of fishing on the smooth-as-glass waters of Lake Chocurua in New Hampshire's White Mountains. Deciduous trees turning red and gold will soon shed their leaves, and the hillsides will turn white with winter's snow, attracting skiers to the valley.

WHERE THE PICTURES ARE

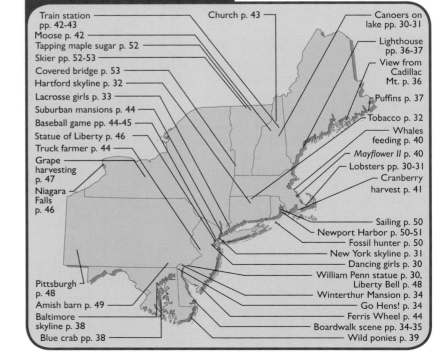

Train station pp. 42-43
Moose p. 42
Tapping maple sugar p. 52
Skier pp. 52-53
Covered bridge p. 53
Hartford skyline p. 32
Lacrosse girls p. 33
Suburban mansions p. 44
Baseball game pp. 44-45
Statue of Liberty p. 46
Truck farmer p. 44
Grape harvesting p. 47
Niagara Falls p. 46

Church p. 43

Canoers on lake pp. 30-31
Lighthouse pp. 36-37
View from Cadillac Mt. p. 36
Puffins p. 37
Tobacco p. 32
Whales feeding p. 40
Mayflower II p. 40
Lobsters pp. 30-31
Cranberry harvest p. 41
Sailing p. 50
Newport Harbor p. 50-51
Fossil hunter p. 50
New York skyline p. 31
Dancing girls p. 30
William Penn statue p. 30, Liberty Bell p. 48
Winterthur Mansion p. 34
Go Hens! p. 34
Ferris Wheel p. 44
Boardwalk scene pp. 34-35
Wild ponies p. 39

Pittsburgh p. 48
Amish barn p. 49
Baltimore skyline p. 38
Blue crab pp. 38

THE BASICS

STATS

Area
5,543 sq mi (14,357 sq km)

Population
3,502,309

Capital
Hartford
Population 124,512

Largest city
Bridgeport
Population 137,912

Ethnic/racial groups
84.6% white; 10.2% African American;
3.4% Asian; .4% Native American.
Hispanic (any race) 11.2%.

Industry
Transportation equipment, metal
products, machinery, electrical
equipment, printing and publishing,
scientific instruments, insurance

Agriculture
Nursery stock, dairy products, poultry,
eggs, shellfish

Statehood
January 9, 1788; 5th state

GEO WHIZ

The sperm whale, Connecticut's
state animal, is known for its massive head. Its brain is larger than
that of any other creature known to
have lived on Earth.

The first hamburgers in U.S. history
were served by Louis Lassen at his New
Haven lunch wagon in 1895. He didn't
like to waste the excess beef left after
the daily noon rush, so he ground
it up, grilled it, and served it
between two slices of bread.

The nuclear-powered U.S.S.
Virginia, the world's most tech-
nologically advanced submarine,
was built at Groton, home of
the U.S. Naval Submarine Base.

ROBIN
MOUNTAIN LAUREL

CONNECTICUT

As early as 1614, Dutch explorers founded trading posts along the coast of Connecticut, but the first permanent European settlements were established in 1635 by English Puritans from nearby Massachusetts. The Connecticut Fundamental Orders, which in 1639 estab-lished a democratic system of government in the colony, were an important model for the writing of the U.S. Constitution in 1787. This earned the state its nickname—Constitution State. Even in colonial times, Connecticut was an important industrial center, producing goods that competed with factories in England. During the Revolutionary War, Connecticut produced military goods for the colonial army. Today, Connecticut industries produce jet aircraft engines, helicopters, and nuclear submarines. Connecticut is home to many international corporations, but it is best known as the "insurance state." Following independence, businessmen offered to insure ship cargoes in exchange for a share of the profits. Soon after, other types of insurance were offered. Today, Connecticut is home to more than 100 insurance companies.

⇧ LEAFY HARVEST. The Connecticut
River Valley is a major source of
world-class premium cigar tobacco
in the United States. Most of the
harvest is used for cigar wrappers.

⇦ BRIGHT CITY LIGHTS. Established as
a fort in the early 1600s, Hartford was one
of the earliest cities of colonial America.
Today, this modern state capital is a center
of economic growth and cultural diversity.

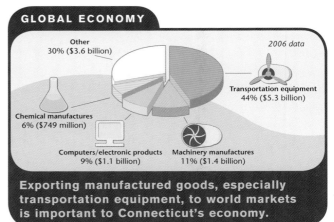

GLOBAL ECONOMY

2006 data

Other
30% ($3.6 billion)

Transportation equipment
44% ($5.3 billion)

Chemical manufactures
6% ($749 million)

Computers/electronic products
9% ($1.1 billion)

Machinery manufactures
11% ($1.4 billion)

**Exporting manufactured goods, especially
transportation equipment, to world markets
is important to Connecticut's economy.**

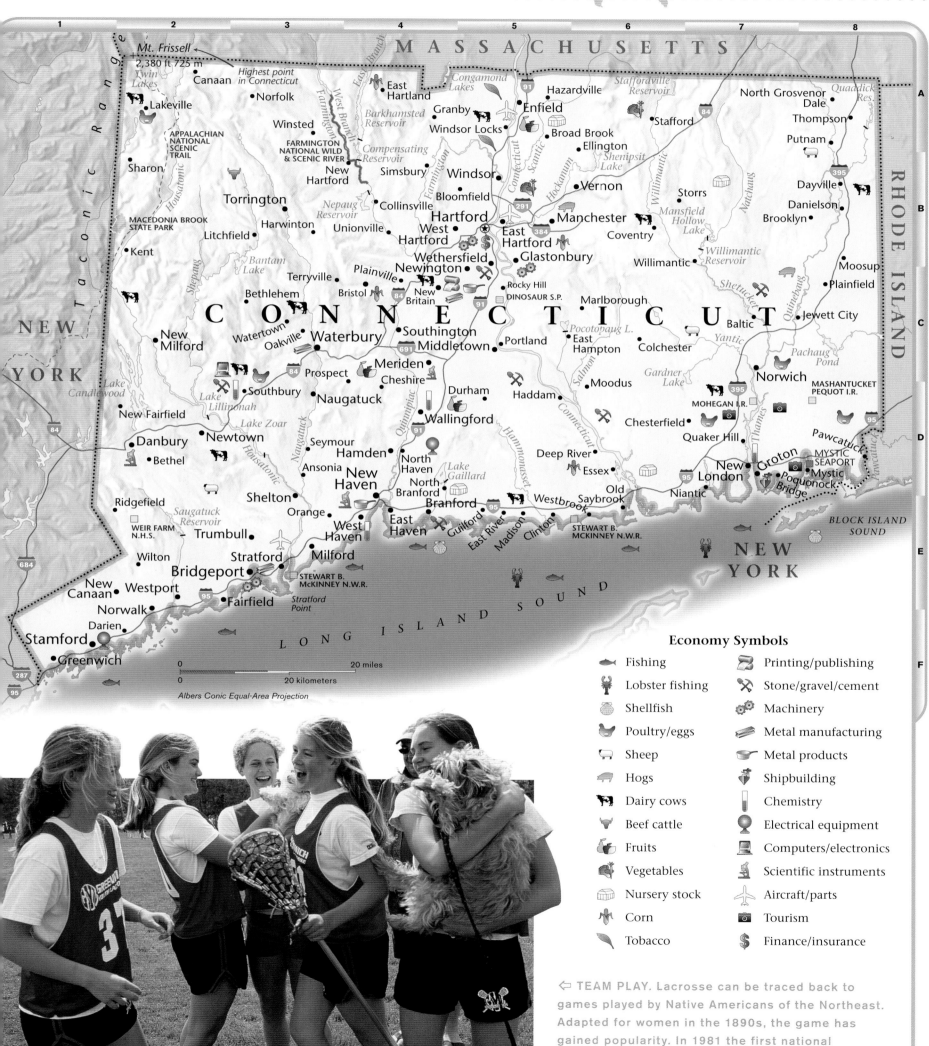

Map labels

MASSACHUSETTS

RHODE ISLAND

NEW YORK

NEW YORK

CONNECTICUT

Mt. Frissell
2,380 ft 725 m
Highest point in Connecticut

Taconic Range

Twin Lakes
Canaan
Lakeville
Norfolk
East Hartland
Congamond Lakes
Hazardville
Staffordville Reservoir
North Grosvenor Dale
Quaddick Res.
Thompson
Winsted
Granby
Enfield
Stafford
Putnam
Windsor Locks
Broad Brook
Appalachian National Scenic Trail
Barkhamsted Reservoir
Ellington
Shenipsit Lake
Dayville
Sharon
Farmington National Wild & Scenic River
New Hartford
Simsbury
Windsor
Vernon
Storrs
Danielson
Compensating Reservoir
West Branch Farmington
Bloomfield
Mansfield Hollow Lake
Brooklyn
Torrington
Nepaug Reservoir
Collinsville
Hartford
Manchester
Macedonia Brook State Park
Harwinton
Unionville
West Hartford
East Hartford
Coventry
Willimantic Reservoir
Moosup
Litchfield
Wethersfield
Glastonbury
Willimantic
Plainfield
Kent
Bantam Lake
Plainville
Newington
Terryville
Bethlehem
Bristol
New Britain
Rocky Hill
DINOSAUR S.P.
Marlborough
Shetucket
Baltic
Jewett City
New Milford
Watertown
Waterbury
Southington
Middletown
Portland
East Hampton
Colchester
Yantic
Pocotopaug L.
Pachaug Pond
Oakville
Prospect
Meriden
Gardner Lake
Norwich
Shepaug
Lake Candlewood
Southbury
Cheshire
Durham
Moodus
Salmon
MASHANTUCKET PEQUOT I.R.
Lake Lillinonah
Naugatuck
Wallingford
Haddam
Chesterfield
MOHEGAN I.R.
Lake Zoar
Quinnipiac
Connecticut
Quaker Hill
Pawcatuck
New Fairfield
Newtown
Seymour
Hamden
North Haven
Deep River
New London
Groton
MYSTIC SEAPORT
Danbury
Bethel
Ansonia
New Haven
North Branford
Lake Gaillard
Essex
Niantic
Mystic
Poquonock Bridge
Housatonic
Shelton
Orange
Branford
Saybrook
Hammonasset
Ridgefield
Saugatuck Reservoir
East Haven
Guilford
Westbrook
Old Saybrook
BLOCK ISLAND SOUND
Weir Farm N.H.S.
Trumbull
West Haven
East River
Madison
Clinton
STEWART B. McKINNEY N.W.R.
Wilton
Stratford
Milford
Stratford Point
Bridgeport
STEWART B. McKINNEY N.W.R.
New Canaan
Westport
Fairfield
NEW YORK
Norwalk
Darien
Stamford
Greenwich

LONG ISLAND SOUND

0 ——— 20 miles
0 ——— 20 kilometers
Albers Conic Equal-Area Projection

Economy Symbols

Fishing	Printing/publishing
Lobster fishing	Stone/gravel/cement
Shellfish	Machinery
Poultry/eggs	Metal manufacturing
Sheep	Metal products
Hogs	Shipbuilding
Dairy cows	Chemistry
Beef cattle	Electrical equipment
Fruits	Computers/electronics
Vegetables	Scientific instruments
Nursery stock	Aircraft/parts
Corn	Tourism
Tobacco	Finance/insurance

← TEAM PLAY. Lacrosse can be traced back to games played by Native Americans of the Northeast. Adapted for women in the 1890s, the game has gained popularity. In 1981 the first national women's lacrosse championship was held.

DECEMBER 7, 1787

THE BASICS

STATS

Area
2,489 sq mi (6,447 sq km)

Population
864,764

Capital
Dover
Population 32,808

Largest city
Wilmington
Population 72,051

Ethnic/racial groups
74.5% white; 20.9% African American; 2.8% Asian; .4% Native American. Hispanic (any race) 6.3%.

Industry
Food processing, chemicals, rubber and plastic products, scientific instruments, printing and publishing, financial services

Agriculture
Poultry, soybeans, nursery stock, corn, vegetables, dairy products

Statehood
December 7, 1787; 1st state

GEO WHIZ

Each year contestants bring their pumpkins and launching machines to the Punkin Chunkin World Championship in Bridgeville to see who can catapult their big, orange squash the farthest.

The Delaware Estuary is one of the four most important shorebird migration sites in the world and has the second-highest concentration of shorebirds in North America. The estuary also provides wintering and migratory habitat to many species of songbirds and raptors.

The first steam railroad to provide regular service began operations in New Castle in 1831.

BLUE HEN CHICKEN
PEACH BLOSSOM

DELAWARE

Second smallest among the states in area, Delaware has played a big role in the history of the U.S. Explored at various times by the Spanish, Portuguese, and Dutch, it was Swedes who established the first permanent European settlement in 1638 in the Delaware River Valley. In 1655 the colony fell under Dutch authority, but in 1682 the land was annexed by William Penn and the Pennsylvania colony. In 1787, Delaware was the first state to ratify the new U.S. Constitution. Delaware's Atlantic coast beaches are popular with tourists. Its fertile farmland, mainly in the south, produces soybeans, corn, dairy products, and poultry. But the state's real economic power is located in the north, around Wilmington, where factories employ thousands of workers to process food products and produce machinery and chemicals. Industry has been a source of wealth, but it also poses a danger to the environment. Protecting the environment is a high priority for Delaware.

⇩ TEAM SPIRIT. Enthusiastic fans and the University of Delaware band support the "Fightin' Blue Hens." Located in Newark, the university was founded in 1743.

⇧ PAST GRANDEUR. Built in 1837 in the fashion of a British country house, Winterthur was expanded from 12 to 196 rooms by the du Ponts, chemical industry tycoons. In 1951 the house was opened to the public as a museum for the family's extensive collection of antiques and Americana.

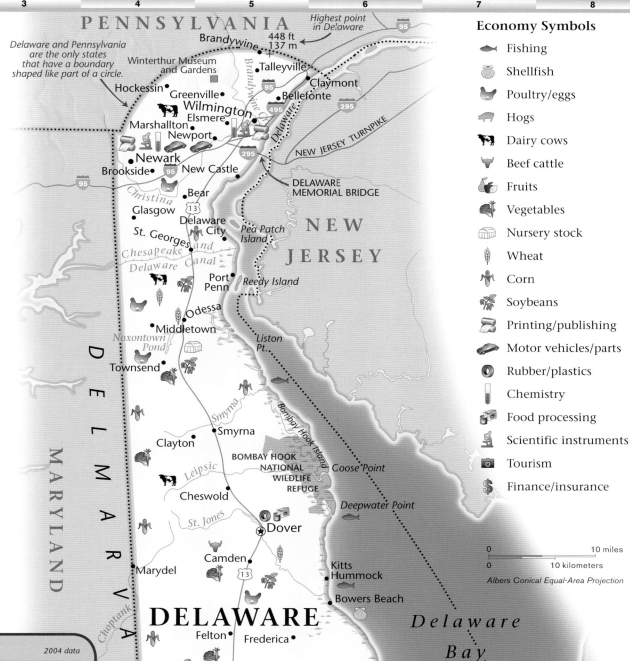

PENNSYLVANIA

Delaware and Pennsylvania are the only states that have a boundary shaped like part of a circle.

Highest point in Delaware

Brandywine
448 ft
137 m

Winterthur Museum and Gardens

Talleyville

Hockessin

Greenville

Claymont

Bellefonte

Wilmington
Elsmere

Marshallton
Newport

Newark
Brookside New Castle

Bear

Glasgow

Delaware City

St. Georges

Pea Patch Island

NEW JERSEY

DELAWARE MEMORIAL BRIDGE

NEW JERSEY TURNPIKE

Christina

Chesapeake and Delaware Canal

Port Penn

Reedy Island

Odessa

Noxontown Pond

Middletown

Townsend

Liston Pt.

Smyrna

Bombay Hook Island

Goose Point

Clayton

Leipsic

BOMBAY HOOK NATIONAL WILDLIFE REFUGE

Cheswold

Deepwater Point

St. Jones

Dover

Camden

Kitts Hummock

Marydel

Bowers Beach

DELAWARE

Felton Frederica

Delaware Bay

Choptank

Houston

Harrington

Milford
Lincoln

Slaughter Beach

Greenwood

PRIME HOOK NATIONAL WILDLIFE REFUGE

Ellendale

Broadkill Beach

Marshyhope Creek

Bridgeville

Milton

Cape Henlopen

Lewes

Lewes & Rehoboth Canal

Harbeson

Midway

ATLANTIC

Rehoboth Beach

Georgetown

Dewey Beach

Rehoboth Bay

Seaford
Blades

Nanticoke

OCEAN

Oak Orchard

Indian River Bay

Indian River Inlet

Laurel

Millsboro

Dagsboro

Ocean View

Assawoman Canal

Bethany Beach

Frankford

Cypress Swamp

Delmar

Selbyville

Fenwick Island

PENINSULA

DELMARVA

MARYLAND

Economy Symbols

- Fishing
- Shellfish
- Poultry/eggs
- Hogs
- Dairy cows
- Beef cattle
- Fruits
- Vegetables
- Nursery stock
- Wheat
- Corn
- Soybeans
- Printing/publishing
- Motor vehicles/parts
- Rubber/plastics
- Chemistry
- Food processing
- Scientific instruments
- Tourism
- Finance/insurance

0   10 miles
0   10 kilometers
Albers Conical Equal-Area Projection

⇧ **SEASIDE RETREAT.** Originally established in 1873 as a church campground, Rehoboth Beach is still a popular getaway destination on Delaware's Atlantic coastline. A concrete dolphin overlooks the town's boardwalk, a popular promenade that separates shops and restaurants from the beach. The boardwalk has been destroyed on several occasions by storms.

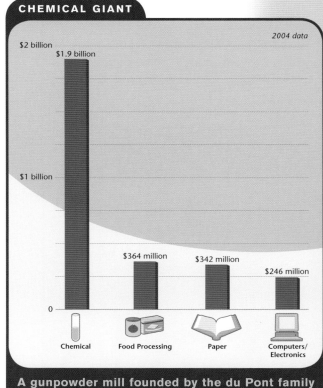

CHEMICAL GIANT

2004 data

$2 billion
$1.9 billion

$1 billion

$364 million
$342 million
$246 million

Chemical | Food Processing | Paper | Computers/Electronics

A gunpowder mill founded by the du Pont family in 1802 gave rise to a chemical industry that is now the state's leading industry and employer.

THE BASICS

STATS

Area
35,385 sq mi (91,646 sq km)

Population
1,317,207

Capital
Augusta
Population 18,560

Largest city
Portland
Population 63,635

Ethnic/racial groups
96.7% white; .9% Asian; .8% African American; .6% Native American. Hispanic (any race) 1.0%.

Industry
Health services, tourism, forest products, leather products, electrical equipment, food processing, textiles

Agriculture
Seafood, potatoes, dairy products, poultry and eggs, livestock, apples, blueberries, vegetables

Statehood
March 15, 1820; 23rd state

GEO WHIZ

With world shark populations declining, some conservation-minded deep-sea fishermen in Maine have turned the idea of a shark tournament upside-down. They still compete to see who can catch the biggest fish, but then they tag and release the sharks.

Eartha, a scale model of our planet, holds the Guinness World Record as the World's Largest Revolving/Rotating Globe. It is on display in a three-story glass building in Yarmouth.

Forests cover nearly 90 percent of Maine. No wonder it is called the Pine Tree State.

Until the last ice age, Maine's coast was relatively straight. Glaciers carved hundreds of bays and inlets out of its shoreline and created some 2,000 islands off the coast.

CHICKADEE
WHITE PINE CONE AND TASSEL

MAINE

Maine's story begins long before the arrival of European settlers in the 1600s. Evidence of native people dates back to at least 3000 B.C., and Leif Erikson and his Viking sailors may have explored Maine's coastline 500 years before Columbus crossed the Atlantic. English settlements were established along the southern coast in the 1620s, and in 1677 the territory of Maine came under control of Massachusetts. Following the Revolutionary War, the people of Maine pressed for separation from Massachusetts, and in 1820 Maine entered the Union as a non-slave state under the terms of the Missouri Compromise. Most of Maine's population is concentrated in towns along the coast. Famous for its rugged beauty, it is the focus of the tourist industry. Cold offshore waters contribute to a lively fishing industry, while timber from the state's mountainous interior supports wood product and paper businesses. Maine, a leader in environmental awareness, seeks a balance between economic growth and environmental protection.

⇩ ACADIA NATIONAL PARK, established in 1929, attracts thousands of tourists each year. The park includes Cadillac Mountain, the highest point along the North Atlantic coast and the site from which the earliest sunrises in the United States can be viewed from October 7 through March 6.

BLUEBERRY LEADER

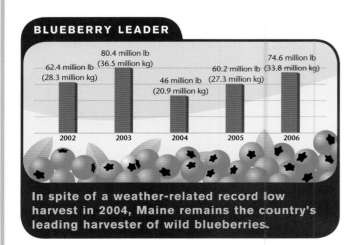

	80.4 million lb (36.5 million kg)		74.6 million lb (33.8 million kg)
62.4 million lb (28.3 million kg)		60.2 million lb (27.3 million kg)	
	46 million lb (20.9 million kg)		
2002	2003	2004	2005	2006

In spite of a weather-related record low harvest in 2004, Maine remains the country's leading harvester of wild blueberries.

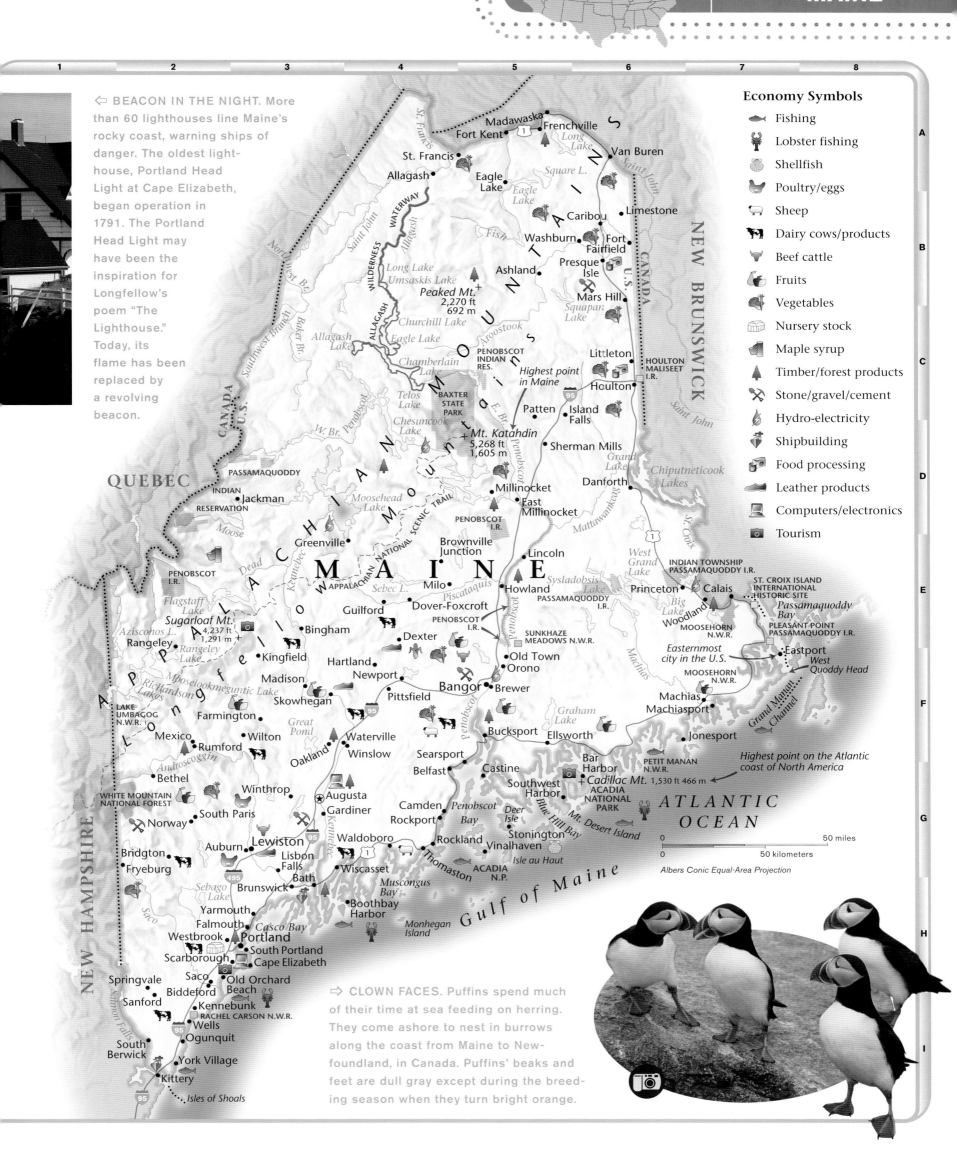

⇐ BEACON IN THE NIGHT. More than 60 lighthouses line Maine's rocky coast, warning ships of danger. The oldest lighthouse, Portland Head Light at Cape Elizabeth, began operation in 1791. The Portland Head Light may have been the inspiration for Longfellow's poem "The Lighthouse." Today, its flame has been replaced by a revolving beacon.

Economy Symbols

- Fishing
- Lobster fishing
- Shellfish
- Poultry/eggs
- Sheep
- Dairy cows/products
- Beef cattle
- Fruits
- Vegetables
- Nursery stock
- Maple syrup
- Timber/forest products
- Stone/gravel/cement
- Hydro-electricity
- Shipbuilding
- Food processing
- Leather products
- Computers/electronics
- Tourism

NEW BRUNSWICK

QUEBEC

CANADA
U.S.

PASSAMAQUODDY INDIAN RESERVATION

PENOBSCOT I.R.

MAINE

APPALACHIAN MOUNTAINS

Longfellow

NEW HAMPSHIRE

Madawaska
Fort Kent
Frenchville
St. Francis
Van Buren
Allagash
Eagle Lake
Square L.
Long Lake
Caribou
Limestone
Washburn
Fort Fairfield
Ashland
Presque Isle
Mars Hill
Squapan Lake
Peaked Mt. 2,270 ft 692 m
Churchill Lake
Eagle Lake
Allagash Lake
Chamberlain Lake
PENOBSCOT INDIAN RES.
Littleton
HOULTON MALISEET I.R.
Highest point in Maine
Houlton
Telos Lake
BAXTER STATE PARK
Patten
Island Falls
Chesuncook Lake
Mt. Katahdin 5,268 ft 1,605 m
Sherman Mills
Danforth
Grand Lake
Chiputneticook Lakes
Millinocket
East Millinocket
Moosehead Lake
PENOBSCOT I.R.
Jackman
Moose
Greenville
Brownville Junction
Lincoln
West Grand Lake
INDIAN TOWNSHIP PASSAMAQUODDY I.R.
ST. CROIX ISLAND INTERNATIONAL HISTORIC SITE
Milo
Howland
Sysladobsis Lake
Princeton
Calais
Flagstaff Lake
Sugarloaf Mt. 4,237 ft 1,291 m
Guilford
Dover-Foxcroft
PENOBSCOT I.R.
PASSAMAQUODDY I.R.
Big Lake
Woodland
Passamaquoddy Bay
Rangeley
Bingham
Dexter
SUNKHAZE MEADOWS N.W.R.
MOOSEHORN N.W.R.
PLEASANT POINT PASSAMAQUODDY I.R.
Sebec L.
Piscataquis
Kingfield
Old Town
Orono
Easternmost city in the U.S.
Eastport
West Quoddy Head
Madison
Hartland
Newport
MOOSEHORN N.W.R.
Machias
Machiasport
Mexico
Rumford
Skowhegan
Pittsfield
Bangor
Brewer
Graham Lake
Jonesport
Farmington
Wilton
Great Pond
Waterville
Bucksport
Ellsworth
PETIT MANAN N.W.R.
Highest point on the Atlantic coast of North America
Bethel
Oakland
Winslow
Searsport
Castine
Bar Harbor
Cadillac Mt. 1,530 ft 466 m
Winthrop
Belfast
Southwest Harbor
ACADIA NATIONAL PARK
WHITE MOUNTAIN NATIONAL FOREST
South Paris
Augusta
Gardiner
Camden
Rockport
Penobscot Bay
Deer Isle
Mt. Desert Island
ATLANTIC OCEAN
Norway
Bridgton
Auburn
Lewiston
Waldoboro
Rockland
Stonington
Vinalhaven
Blue Hill Bay
Fryeburg
Lisbon Falls
Bath
Wiscasset
Thomaston
ACADIA N.P.
Isle au Haut
Sebago Lake
Brunswick
Muscongus Bay
Yarmouth
Boothbay Harbor
Monhegan Island
Gulf of Maine
Falmouth
Casco Bay
Westbrook
Portland
Scarborough
South Portland
Cape Elizabeth
Springvale
Saco
Old Orchard Beach
Biddeford
Sanford
Kennebunk
RACHEL CARSON N.W.R.
Wells
South Berwick
Ogunquit
York Village
Kittery
Isles of Shoals

50 miles
50 kilometers
Albers Conic Equal-Area Projection

⇒ CLOWN FACES. Puffins spend much of their time at sea feeding on herring. They come ashore to nest in burrows along the coast from Maine to Newfoundland, in Canada. Puffins' beaks and feet are dull gray except during the breeding season when they turn bright orange.

THE BASICS

STATS

Area
12,407 sq mi (32,133 sq km)

Population
5,618,344

Capital
Annapolis
Population 36,178

Largest city
Baltimore
Population 631,366

Ethnic/racial groups
63.6% white; 29.5% African American; 4.9% Asian; .3% Native American. Hispanic (any race) 6.0%.

Industry
Real estate, federal government, health services, business services, engineering services, electrical and gas services, communications, banking, insurance

Agriculture
Poultry and eggs, dairy products, nursery stock, soybeans, corn, seafood, cattle, vegetables

Statehood
April 28, 1788; 7th state

GEO WHIZ

The Captain John Smith Chesapeake National Historic Water Trail, which traces some 3,000 miles (4,800 km) of Smith's 1607–1608 explorations of the bay, is the first national water trail in the United States.

The Naval Support Facility Thurmont, better known as Camp David, the mountain retreat of American presidents, is part of Catoctin Mountain Park in north-central Maryland.

Residents on Smith Island, in the lower Chesapeake Bay, are being robbed of their land by rising sea levels and of their traditional livelihood by dwindling blue crab harvests. They fear a major Atlantic hurricane could wipe out their island home.

The name of Baltimore's professional football team—the Ravens—may have been inspired by the title of a poem written by noted American author Edgar Allan Poe, who lived in Baltimore in the mid-1800s and whose grave is in that city.

NORTHERN
(BALTIMORE)
ORIOLE

BLACK-EYED
SUSAN

MARYLAND

Native Americans, who raised crops and harvested oysters from the nearby waters of Chesapeake Bay, lived on the land that would become Maryland long before early European settlers arrived. In 1608 Captain John Smith explored the waters of the bay, and in 1634 English settlers established the colony of Maryland. In 1788 Maryland became the 7th state to ratify the new U.S. Constitution. Chesapeake Bay, the largest estuary in the U.S., almost splits Maryland into two parts. East of the bay lies the flat coastal plain, while to the west the land rises through the hilly piedmont and mountainous panhandle. Chesapeake Bay, the state's economic and environmental focal point, supports a busy seafood industry. It is also a major transportation artery, linking Baltimore and other Maryland ports to the Atlantic Ocean. Most of the people of Maryland live in an urban corridor between Baltimore and Washington, D.C., where jobs in government, research, and high-tech businesses provide employment.

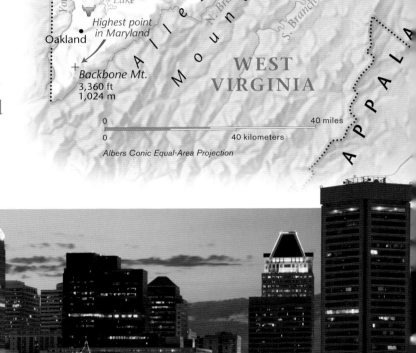

⇑ GATEWAY CITY. Since the early 1700s, Baltimore, near the upper Chesapeake Bay, has been a major seaport and focus of trade, industry, and immigration. Today, the Inner Harbor is not only a modern working port, but also the city's vibrant cultural center.

⇐ COLORFUL CRUSTACEAN. Blue crabs, found in Maryland's Chesapeake Bay waters, were a staple in the diet of Native Americans. They have been harvested commercially since the mid-1800s, and the tasty meat is a popular menu item—especially crab cakes—in seafood restaurants throughout the area.

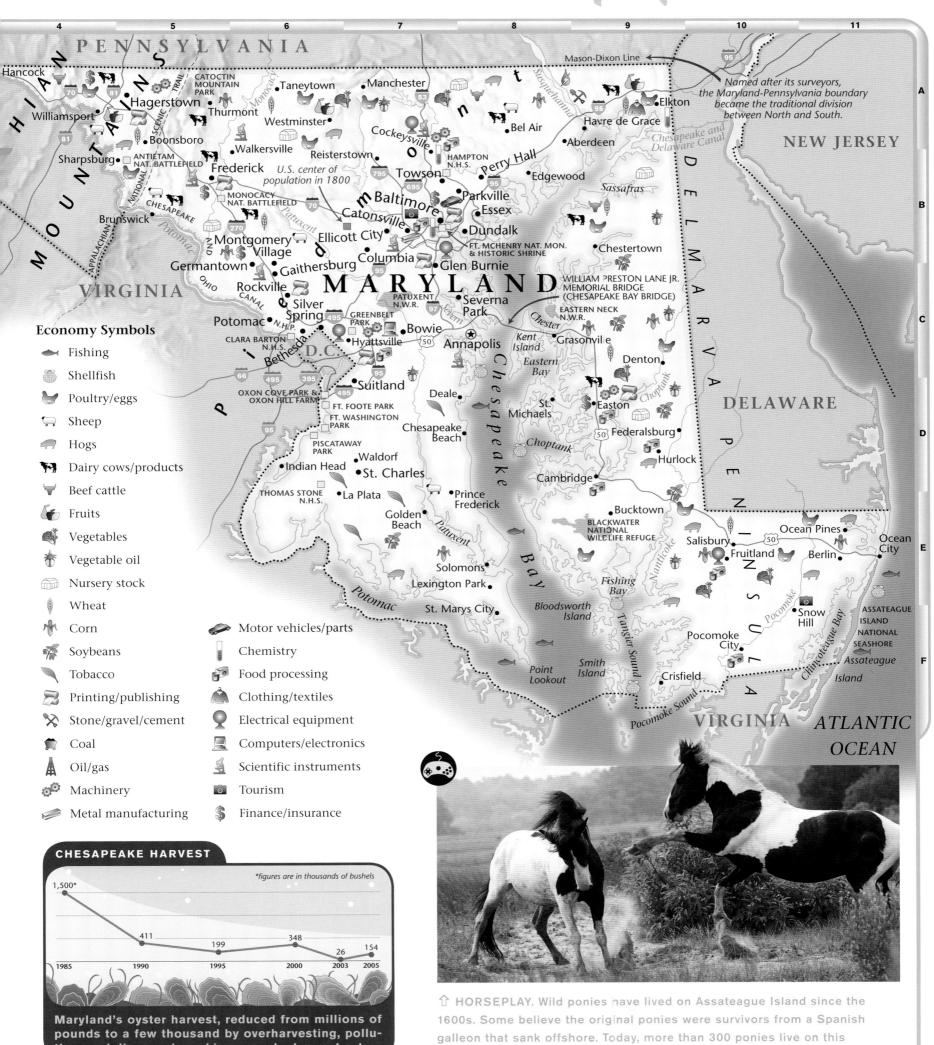

PENNSYLVANIA

Mason-Dixon Line

Named after its surveyors, the Maryland-Pennsylvania boundary became the traditional division between North and South.

NEW JERSEY

Hancock

Williamsport

Hagerstown

Thurmont

Taneytown

Manchester

Elkton

Havre de Grace

Boonsboro

Westminster

Cockeysville

Bel Air

Aberdeen

CATOCTIN MOUNTAIN PARK

Sharpsburg

ANTIETAM NAT. BATTLEFIELD

Walkersville

Reisterstown

HAMPTON N.H.S.

Edgewood

Frederick

U.S. center of population in 1800

Towson

Parkville

Brunswick

CHESAPEAKE

MONOCACY NAT. BATTLEFIELD

Baltimore

Catonsville

Essex

Chestertown

Montgomery Village

Ellicott City

Dundalk

FT. MCHENRY NAT. MON. & HISTORIC SHRINE

Germantown

Gaithersburg

Columbia

Glen Burnie

VIRGINIA

Rockville

MARYLAND

WILLIAM PRESTON LANE JR. MEMORIAL BRIDGE (CHESAPEAKE BAY BRIDGE)

EASTERN NECK N.W.R.

DELAWARE

Silver Spring

PATUXENT N.W.R.

Severna Park

Potomac

N.H.P.

GREENBELT PARK

Bowie

Chester

Grasonville

Denton

CLARA BARTON N.H.S.

Bethesda

Hyattsville

Annapolis

Kent Island

Eastern Bay

D.C.

Suitland

Deale

St. Michaels

Easton

OXON COVE PARK & OXON HILL FARM

FT. FOOTE PARK

Chesapeake Beach

Federalsburg

FT. WASHINGTON PARK

PISCATAWAY PARK

Waldorf

Choptank

Hurlock

Indian Head

St. Charles

Cambridge

THOMAS STONE N.H.S.

La Plata

Prince Frederick

Bucktown

BLACKWATER NATIONAL WILDLIFE REFUGE

Ocean Pines

Golden Beach

Salisbury

Ocean City

Solomons

Fruitland

Berlin

Lexington Park

St. Marys City

Bloodsworth Island

Fishing Bay

ASSATEAGUE ISLAND NATIONAL SEASHORE

Snow Hill

Pocomoke City

Assateague Island

Point Lookout

Smith Island

Crisfield

VIRGINIA

ATLANTIC OCEAN

Chesapeake Bay

Potomac

Patuxent

Choptank

Nanticoke

Pocomoke

Tangier Sound

Pocomoke Sound

Chincoteague Bay

Sassafras

DELMARVA PENINSULA

Economy Symbols

- Fishing
- Shellfish
- Poultry/eggs
- Sheep
- Hogs
- Dairy cows/products
- Beef cattle
- Fruits
- Vegetables
- Vegetable oil
- Nursery stock
- Wheat
- Corn
- Soybeans
- Tobacco
- Printing/publishing
- Stone/gravel/cement
- Coal
- Oil/gas
- Machinery
- Metal manufacturing

- Motor vehicles/parts
- Chemistry
- Food processing
- Clothing/textiles
- Electrical equipment
- Computers/electronics
- Scientific instruments
- Tourism
- Finance/insurance

CHESAPEAKE HARVEST

figures are in thousands of bushels

1,500*

411

199

348

26

154

1985 | 1990 | 1995 | 2000 | 2003 | 2005

Maryland's oyster harvest, reduced from millions of pounds to a few thousand by overharvesting, pollution, and disease, is making a gradual comeback.

⇧ HORSEPLAY. Wild ponies have lived on Assateague Island since the 1600s. Some believe the original ponies were survivors from a Spanish galleon that sank offshore. Today, more than 300 ponies live on this Atlantic barrier island shared by Maryland and Virginia.

THE BASICS

STATS

Area
10,555 sq mi (27,336 sq km)

Population
6,449,755

Capital
Boston
Population 590,763

Largest city
Boston
Population 590,763

Major ethnic/racial groups
86.5% white; 6.9% African American; 4.9% Asian; .3% Native American. Hispanic (any race) 7.9%.

Industry
Electrical equipment, machinery, metal products, scientific instruments, printing and publishing, tourism

Agriculture
Fruits, nuts and berries, nursery stock, dairy products

Statehood
February 6, 1788; 6th state

GEO WHIZ

In 1717 the pirate ship *Whydah*, under the command of Captain Samuel Bellamy (also known as Black Sam), went down in a storm off Cape Cod. Treasure and artifacts recovered from the ship are on display at the Whydah Museum, in Provincetown, and are also part of a National Geographic traveling exhibit.

Massachusetts is the birthplace of several famous inventors, including Eli Whitney, Samuel Morse, and Benjamin Franklin.

The country's first lighthouse was built on Little Brewster Island in Boston Harbor in 1716. It is the last manned lighthouse in the United States. Use the online link to see what it's like to be a lighthouse keeper for Boston Light.

Cape Cod is considered one of the world's best spots for whale watching, thanks to Stellwagen Bank, a protected area at the mouth of Massachusetts Bay.

CHICKADEE
MAYFLOWER

MASSACHUSETTS

Earliest human inhabitants of Massachusetts were Native Americans who arrived more than 10,000 years ago. The first Europeans to visit Massachusetts may have been Norsemen around A.D. 1000, and later fishermen from France and Spain. But the first permanent European settlement was established in 1620 when people aboard the sailing ship *Mayflower* landed near Plymouth on the coast of Massachusetts. The Puritans arrived soon after, and by 1630 they had established settlements at Salem and Boston. By 1640 more than 16,000 people, most seeking religious freedom, had settled in Massachusetts. In the early days, the economy of Massachusetts was based on shipping, fishing, and whaling. By the 19th century, industry, taking advantage of abundant water power, had a firm foothold. Factory jobs attracted thousands of immigrants, mainly from Europe. In the late 20th century, Massachusetts experienced a boom in high-tech jobs, drawing on the state's skilled labor force and its more than 80 colleges and universities.

⇧ REMINDER OF TIMES PAST. Shrouded in morning mist, this replica of the *Mayflower* docked in Plymouth Harbor is a reminder of Massachusetts's early history.

⇨ LEVIATHANS OF THE DEEP. In the 19th century, Massachusetts was an important center for the whaling industry, with more than 300 registered whaling ships. Today, humpback whales swim in the protected waters of a marine sanctuary in Massachusetts Bay.

NEW HAMPSHIRE

ATLANTIC OCEAN

Amesbury
Haverhill
Newburyport
Methuen
Lawrence
PARKER RIVER N.W.R.
Ipswich
Winchenden
Lowell N.H.P.
Dracut
Turners Falls
Orange
Athol
Lowell
Gloucester
Cape Ann
Greenfield
Fitchburg
Gardner
Chelmsford
Wilmington
Danvers
Beverly
Salem Maritime N.H.S.
One of the ten most populous cities in the U.S. in 1790
Deerfield
Leominster
OXBOW N.W.R.
SUDBURY, ASSABET & CONCORD NATIONAL WILD & SCENIC RIVER
Peabody
Salem
Marblehead
MASSACHUSETTS
Concord
MINUTE MAN N.H.P.
SAUGUS IRON WORKS N.H.S.
Lynn
Massachusetts
STELLWAGEN BANK NATIONAL MARINE SANCTUARY
Amherst
GREAT MEADOWS N.W.R.
Woburn
Boston N.H.P.
Medford
Malden
Bay
Northampton
Marlborough
Cambridge
Wachusett Res.
Shrewsbury
Wellesley
Brookline
Boston
BOSTON HARBOR ISLANDS N.R.A.
South Hadley
Worcester
Sudbury Res.
Framingham
Milton
Quincy
Weymouth
Birthplace of Presidents John Adams and John Quincy Adams
Holyoke
Ware
Lake Quinsigamond
President Kennedy's birthplace
Spencer
Auburn
President Bush's birthplace
Norwood
Randolph
Rockland
Ludlow
Chicopee
Springfield
Sturbridge
Oxford
Milford
Stoughton
Brockton
Whitman
Agawam
Springfield Armory N.H.S.
Southbridge
Webster
Bellingham
Franklin
Bridgewater
Silver Lake
Plymouth
Plimoth Plantation
CAPE COD NATIONAL SEASHORE
Provincetown
Truro
CONNECTICUT
RHODE ISLAND
North Attleboro
Attleboro
Taunton
Middleboro
Assawompset Pond
Cape Cod Canal
Cape Cod Bay
Wellfleet
Seekonk
Long Pond
Great Quittacus Pond
Buzzards Bay
Sandwich
Orleans
Somerset
Dennis
Barnstable
Chatham
Fall River
New Bedford Whaling N.H.P.
Hyannis
S. Yarmouth
New Bedford
Fairhaven
East Falmouth
Monomoy Island
MONOMOY N.W.R.
CAPE
COD
Falmouth
Nantucket Sound
Woods Hole
Vineyard Haven
Oak Bluffs
NANTUCKET N.W.R.
Rhode Island Sound
Elizabeth Islands
Vineyard Sound
Buzzards Bay
Edgartown
Chappaquiddick Island
Gay Head WAMPANOAG I.R.
Martha's Vineyard
Nantucket
Nomans Land
Nantucket Island

0 ____ 30 miles
0 ____ 30 kilometers
Albers Conic Equal-Area Projection

Economy Symbols

- Fishing
- Lobster fishing
- Shellfish
- Poultry/eggs
- Sheep
- Hogs
- Dairy cows/products
- Beef cattle
- Fruits
- Vegetables
- Nursery stock
- Wheat

- Tobacco
- Maple syrup
- Printing/publishing
- Stone/gravel/cement
- Hydro-electricity
- Machinery
- Metal products
- Computers/electronics
- Scientific instruments
- Aerospace
- Tourism

⇧ BIG BUSINESS. Cranberries, grown in fields called bogs, are the state's largest agricultural crop. These tiny berries, one of only three fruits native to North America, are consumed mainly in the form of juice or as a tasty accompaniment to holiday dishes. Workers flood fields to make harvesting the floating berries easier.

TRACING OUR ROOTS

Massachusetts, 2000 census data

Not Specified 12%
Multi-ancestry 33%
Single Ancestry 55%

Polish	Portuguese	French	Italian	English	Irish	Other
5.1%	6%	9.9%	13.6%	14.5%	21%	29.9%

Most new immigrants to the U.S. are from Latin America and Asia, but many people in Massachusetts trace their ancestry to Europe.

THE GRANITE STATE:
NEW HAMPSHIRE

NEW HAMPSHIRE

The territory that would become the state of New Hampshire, the 9th state to approve the U.S. Constitution in 1788, began as a fishing colony established along the short 18-mile- (29-km-) long coastline in 1623. New Hampshire was named a royal colony in 1679, but as the Revolutionary War approached, it was the first colony to declare its independence from English rule.

In the early 19th century, life in New Hampshire followed two very different paths. Near the coast, villages and towns grew up around sawmills, shipyards, and warehouses. But in the forested, mountainous interior, people lived on small isolated farms, and towns provided only basic services. Today, New Hampshire is one of the fastest growing states in the Northeast. Modern industries, such as computers and electronics, and high-tech companies have brought prosperity to the state. Its natural beauty attracts tourists year-round to hike on forest trails, swim in pristine lakes, and ski on snow-covered mountain slopes.

THE BASICS

STATS

Area
9,350 sq mi (24,216 sq km)

Population
1,315,828

Capital
Concord
Population 41,823

Largest city
Manchester
Population 109,497

Ethnic/racial groups
95.8% white; 1.9% Asian; 1.1% African American; .3% Native American. Hispanic (any race) 2.3%.

Industry
Machinery, electronics, metal products

Agriculture
Nursery stock, poultry and eggs, fruits and nuts, vegetables

Statehood
June 21, 1788; 9th state

GEO WHIZ

About ten million tourists visit New Hampshire each year, nearly ten times the number of people who live in the state.

The Granite State boasts more than 200 different kinds of rocks and minerals. Use the icon to play Rock Stars and test your knowledge.

The first potato grown in the United States was planted in 1719 in Londonderry on the Common Field, now known simply as the Commons.

Ben Kilham's unique ways of rehabilitating abandoned black bear cubs he finds in the New Hampshire woods has earned him the nickname Bear Man by residents of Lyme. He has been working with orphaned, sick, and injured cubs for more than nine years.

PURPLE FINCH
PURPLE LILAC

⇧ LUMBERING GIANT. Averaging 6 feet (2 m) tall at the shoulders, moose are the largest of North America's deer. Moose are found throughout New Hampshire.

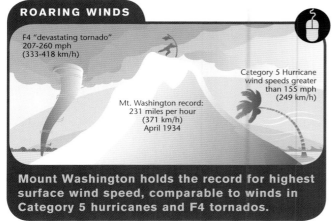

ROARING WINDS

F4 "devastating tornado"
207-260 mph
(333-418 km/h)

Category 5 Hurricane wind speeds greater than 155 mph
(249 km/h)

Mt. Washington record:
231 miles per hour
(371 km/h)
April 1934

Mount Washington holds the record for highest surface wind speed, comparable to winds in Category 5 hurricanes and F4 tornados.

⇨ ALL ABOARD. Tourists traveling by train through the White Mountains enjoy the cool autumn weather and the colorful fall foliage of deciduous trees that cover the mountains.

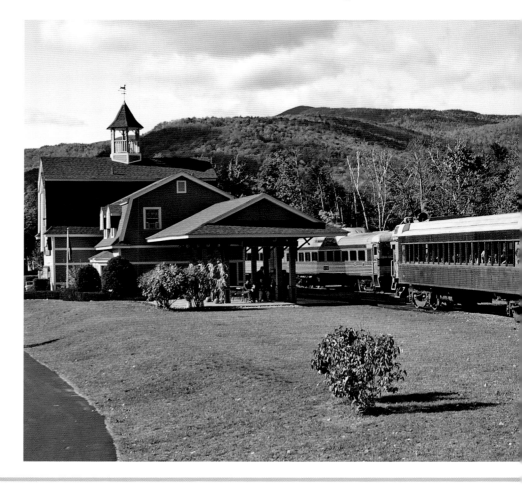

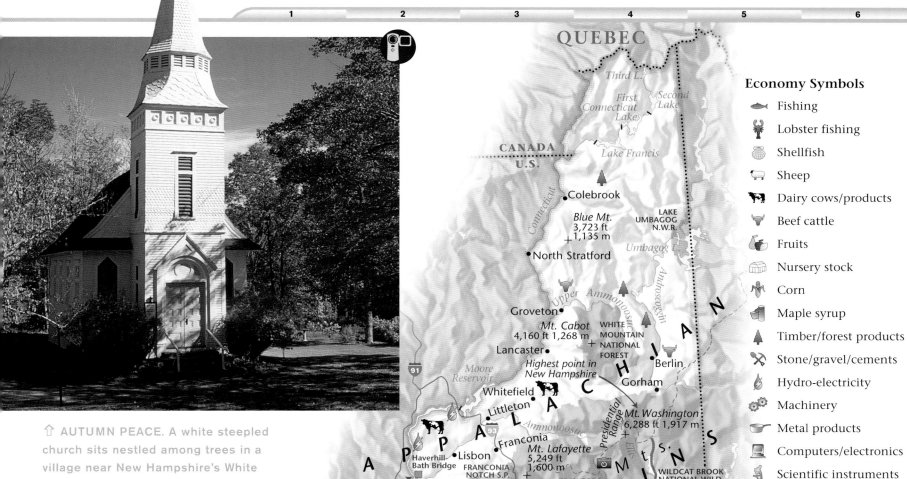

QUEBEC

Third L.

First
Connecticut
Lake

Second
Lake

Lake Francis

CANADA
U.S.

Lake
Umbagog
N.W.R.

Colebrook

Blue Mt.
3,723 ft
1,135 m

Umbagog L.

North Stratford

Groveton

Mt. Cabot
4,160 ft 1,268 m

Lancaster

WHITE
MOUNTAIN
NATIONAL
FOREST

Berlin

Gorham

Whitefield

Highest point in
New Hampshire

Littleton

Mt. Washington
6,288 ft 1,917 m

Franconia

Mt. Lafayette
5,249 ft
1,600 m

Presidential Range

Lisbon

Haverhill
Bath Bridge

FRANCONIA
NOTCH S.P.

CRAWFORD
NOTCH
S.P.

WILDCAT BROOK
NATIONAL WILD
& SCENIC RIVER

Woodsville

Oldest covered bridge
in the U.S. (1827)

Lincoln

WHITE MOUNTAIN
NATIONAL FOREST

North
Conway

Haverhill

Conway

VERMONT

Orford

Warren

Conway
Lake

MAINE

NEW
HAMPSHIRE

Squam
Lake

Bearcamp

Ossipee

Center
Sandwich

Ossipee
Lake

Center
Ossipee

Hanover

Newfound
Lake

Meredith

Ashland

Lake
Wentworth

APPALACHIAN

Enfield

Canaan

Lebanon

Mascoma
Lake

Bristol

Wolfeboro

Sanbornville

SAINT-GAUDENS
N.H.S.

Winnisquam
Lake

Laconia

Merrymeeting
Lake

Franklin

Tilton

Crystal
Lake

Alton Bay

Milton

New
London

Northfield

Suncook
Lakes

Farmington

Claremont

Sunapee
Lake

Newport

MT. SUNAPEE
S.P.

JOHN HAY
N.W.R.

Mt. Sunapee
2,743 ft
836 m

Canterbury

Rochester

Pittsfield

Somersworth

Charlestown

President Pierce's
birthplace

Contoocook

Concord

Bow
Lake

Dover

Durham

Henniker

Suncook

LAMPREY NATIONAL
WILD & SCENIC RIVER

North
Walpole

Hillsboro

Highland
Lake

Newmarket

Great
Bay

Portsmouth

Walpole

Antrim

Raymond

Rye

Nubanusit
Lake

Massabesic
Lake

Exeter

Kingston

Isles of
Shoals

Keene

Monadnock Mt.
3,165 ft
965 m

Manchester

Peterborough

WAPACK
N.W.R.

East Derry

Hampton

PISGAH
S.P.

Troy

Jaffrey

Wilton

Milford

Londonderry

Merrimack

Derry

Atkinson

Plaistow

ATLANTIC
OCEAN

Hinsdale

Winchester

New Ipswich

Greenville

Nashua

Salem

MASSACHUSETTS

Economy Symbols

- Fishing
- Lobster fishing
- Shellfish
- Sheep
- Dairy cows/products
- Beef cattle
- Fruits
- Nursery stock
- Corn
- Maple syrup
- Timber/forest products
- Stone/gravel/cements
- Hydro-electricity
- Machinery
- Metal products
- Computers/electronics
- Scientific instruments
- Tourism

0   20 miles
0   20 kilometers

Albers Conic Equal-Area Projection

⇧ AUTUMN PEACE. A white steepled church sits nestled among trees in a village near New Hampshire's White Mountains. Such traditional churches, common in the New England landscape, are a reminder of early settlers' search for religious freedom.

THE BASICS

STATS

Area
8,721 sq mi (22,588 sq km)

Population
8,685,920

Capital
Trenton
Population 85,314

Largest city
Newark
Population 281,402

Ethnic/racial groups
76.4% white; 14.5% African American; 7.4% Asian; .3% Native American. Hispanic (any race) 15.6%.

Industry
Machinery, electronics, metal products, chemicals

Agriculture
Nursery stock, poultry and eggs, fruits and nuts, vegetables

Statehood
December 18, 1787; 3rd state

GEO WHIZ

Site of a one-time trash heap, the Meadowlands, a swampy lowland on either side of the Hackensack River, is now home to a major sports complex, bustling suburban neighborhoods, and congested roadways. Parts of it are isolated enough to allow days of quiet canoeing.

In 1930 New Jerseyite Charles Darrow developed the game Monopoly. He named Boardwalk and other streets in the game after those in Atlantic City.

The first dinosaur skeleton found in North America was excavated at Haddonfield in 1858. It was named *Hadrosaurus* in honor of its discovery site.

AMERICAN GOLDFINCH
VIOLET

NEW JERSEY

Long before Europeans settled in New Jersey, the region was home to hunting and farming communities of Delaware Indians. The Dutch set up a trading post in northern New Jersey in 1618, calling it New Netherland, but yielded the land in 1664 to the English, who named it New Jersey after the English Channel Isle of Jersey. New Jersey saw more than 90 battles during the Revolutionary War. It became the 3rd U.S. state in 1787 and the first to sign the Bill of Rights. In the 19th century southern New Jersey remained largely agricultural, while the northern part of the state rapidly industrialized. Today highways and railroads link the state to urban centers along the Atlantic seaboard. Nearly 10,000 farms grow fruits and vegetables for nearby urban markets. Industries as well as services and trade are thriving. Beaches along the Atlantic coast attract thousands of tourists each year.

⇧ HOLD ON! New Jersey's Atlantic coast is lined with sandy beaches that attract vacationers from near and far. Amusement parks, such as this one in Wildwood, add to the fun.

⇨ HEADED TO MARKET. New Jersey is a leading producer of fresh fruits and vegetables. These organic vegetables are headed for urban markets in the Northeast.

⇦ SUBURBAN SPRAWL. With more than 90 percent of the state's population living in urban areas, housing developments, with close-set, look-alike houses, are a common characteristic of the suburban landscape. Residents commute to jobs in the city.

⇧ PLAY BALL! Fans pack the seats at Newark's Bear and Eagles Riverfront Stadium to watch a minor league baseball game. Built in 1999, the stadium is a part of Newark's plan to revitalize the downtown area, drawing people into the city.

Economy Symbols

- 🐟 Fishing
- 🐚 Shellfish
- 🐔 Poultry/eggs
- 🐑 Sheep
- 🐖 Hogs
- 🐄 Dairy cows/products
- 🐃 Beef cattle
- 🍓 Fruits
- 🌱 Vegetables
- 🏠 Nursery stock
- 🌾 Wheat

- 🌽 Corn
- 🌿 Soybeans
- 🖨 Printing/publishing
- ⚒ Stone/gravel/cement
- ⚙ Machinery
- 🧪 Chemistry
- 📷 Food processing
- 💻 Computers/electronics
- 🚀 Aerospace
- 📷 Tourism

CROWDED

Average number of people per square mile of land, 2006 data

1171.1 New Jersey
822.7 Massachusetts
408.7 New York
67.2 Vermont
42.7 Maine
85.8 U.S. Average

Although it ranks 47th among the states in area, New Jersey has the highest population density—people per square mile—in the country.

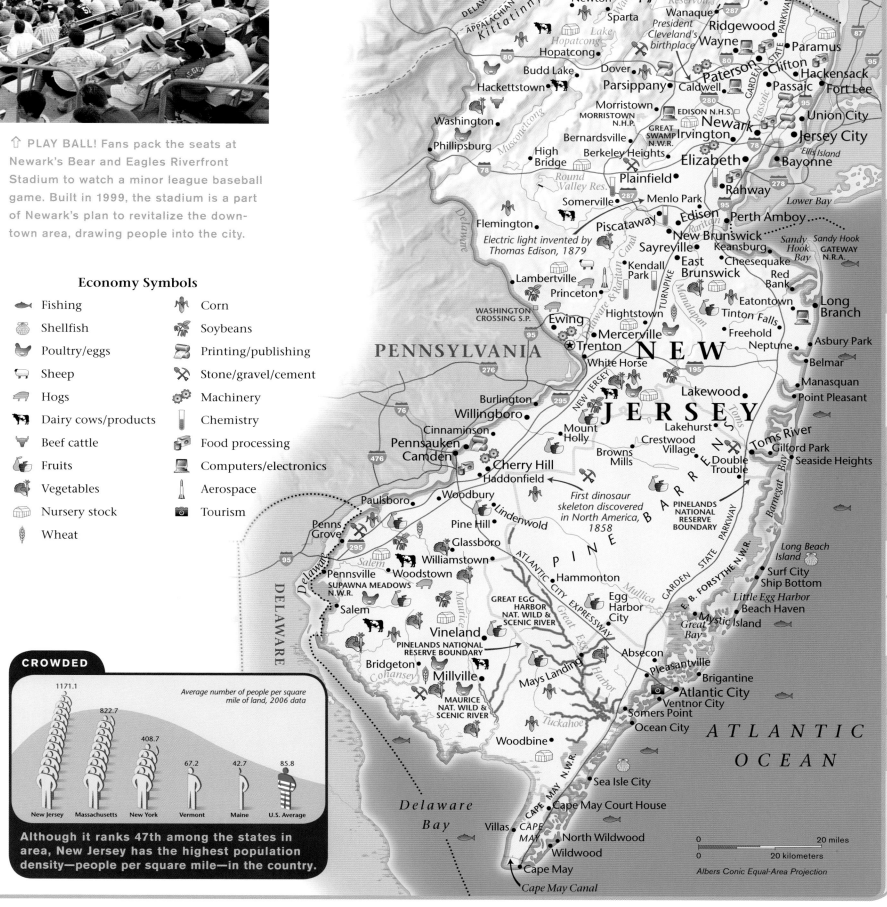

NEW YORK

High Point 1,803 ft 550 m
Highest point in New Jersey

DELAWARE WATER GAP N.R.A.
WALLKILL RIVER N.W.R.
APPALACHIAN TRAIL
Kittatinny Mountains
SCENIC
Highland Lakes
Ringwood
West Milford
Franklin
Newton
Sparta
Wanaque
Wanaque Reservoir
Ramsey
Ridgewood
Paramus
Lake Hopatcong
Hopatcong
President Cleveland's birthplace
Wayne
Budd Lake
Dover
Paterson
Clifton
Hackensack
Hackettstown
Parsippany
Caldwell
Passaic
Fort Lee
Morristown
MORRISTOWN N.H.P.
EDISON N.H.S.
Newark
Union City
Washington
Bernardsville
GREAT SWAMP N.W.R.
Irvington
Jersey City
Phillipsburg
High Bridge
Berkeley Heights
Elizabeth
Ellis Island
Bayonne
Round Valley Res.
Plainfield
Rahway
Somerville
Menlo Park
Edison
Perth Amboy
Lower Bay
Flemington
Piscataway
New Brunswick
Electric light invented by Thomas Edison, 1879
Sayreville
Keansburg
Sandy Hook Bay
Sandy Hook GATEWAY N.R.A.
Lambertville
Kendall Park
East Brunswick
Cheesequake
Red Bank
Princeton
WASHINGTON CROSSING S.P.
Hightstown
Matawan
Eatontown
Tinton Falls
Long Branch
Ewing
Mercerville
Freehold
Neptune
Asbury Park
Trenton
White Horse
NEW JERSEY
Belmar
PENNSYLVANIA
Manasquan
Point Pleasant
Burlington
Willingboro
Lakewood
Mount Holly
Lakehurst
Toms River
Cinnaminson
Crestwood Village
Gilford Park
Pennsauken
Camden
Browns Mills
Double Trouble
Seaside Heights
Cherry Hill
Haddonfield
First dinosaur skeleton discovered in North America, 1858
PINELANDS NATIONAL RESERVE BOUNDARY
Woodbury
Lindenwold
PINE BARRENS
Paulsboro
Pine Hill
Penns Grove
Glassboro
Long Beach Island
Williamstown
Surf City
Ship Bottom
Pennsville
Woodstown
Hammonton
Little Egg Harbor
Beach Haven
SUPAWNA MEADOWS N.W.R.
Salem
GREAT EGG HARBOR NAT. WILD & SCENIC RIVER
Egg Harbor City
Mystic Island
Vineland
Great Bay
PINELANDS NATIONAL RESERVE BOUNDARY
Absecon
Bridgeton
Pleasantville
Brigantine
Millville
Mays Landing
Atlantic City
Ventnor City
MAURICE NAT. WILD & SCENIC RIVER
Somers Point
Ocean City
Woodbine
ATLANTIC OCEAN
Sea Isle City
Delaware Bay
Cape May Court House
Villas
CAPE MAY
North Wildwood
Wildwood
Cape May
Cape May Canal

Albers Conic Equal-Area Projection

0 ___ 20 miles
0 ___ 20 kilometers

THE BASICS

STATS

Area
54,556 sq mi (141,300 sq km)

Population
19,297,729

Capital
Albany
Population 93,919

Largest city
New York City
Population 8,214,426

Ethnic/racial groups
73.7% white; 17.4% African American;
6.9% Asian; .5% Native American.
Hispanic (any race) 16.3%.

Industry
Printing and publishing, machinery,
computer products, finance, tourism

Agriculture
Dairy products, cattle and other livestock, vegetables, nursery stock, apples

Statehood
July 26, 1788; 11th state

GEO WHIZ

Each year at Halloween the
Headless Horseman rides again
through the countryside of Sleepy
Hollow as residents reenact
Washington Irving's *The Legend
of Sleepy Hollow.*

The Erie Canal, built in the 1820s
between Albany and Buffalo, helped
New York City become a worldwide
trading center and opened the Midwest
to development by linking the Hudson
River and the Great Lakes.

Cooperstown, New York,
home of the National
Baseball Hall of Fame,
takes its name from
a town established in
the late 1700s by the father
of James Fenimore Cooper,
author of such American
classics as *The Last of the
Mohicans* and *The Deerslayer.*

EASTERN
BLUEBIRD

ROSE

NEW YORK

When Englishman Henry Hudson explored New York's Hudson River Valley in 1609, the territory was already inhabited by large tribes of Native Americans, including the powerful Iroquois. In 1624 a Dutch trading company established the New Netherland colony, but after just 40 years the colony was taken over by the English and renamed for England's Duke of York. In 1788 New York became the 11th state. The state can be divided into two parts. The powerful port city of New York, center of trade and commerce and gateway to immigrants, is the largest city in the U.S. Its metropolitan area has more than 18 million people. Everything north of the city is simply referred to as "Upstate." Cities such as Buffalo and Rochester are industrial centers, while Ithaca and Syracuse boast major universities. Agriculture is also important in New York. With almost 5 million acres in cropland, the state is a major producer of dairy products, fruits, and vegetables.

⇧ LADY LIBERTY.
Standing in New York
Harbor, the Statue of
Liberty, a gift from the
people of France, is
a symbol of freedom
and democracy.

⇦ NATURAL WONDER.
As many as 12 million
tourists annually visit
Niagara Falls on the
U.S.-Canada border.
Visitors in rain slickers
trek through the mists
below Bridal Veil Falls
on the American side.

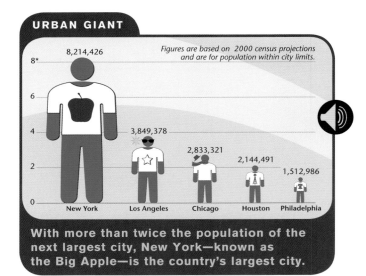

URBAN GIANT

Figures are based on 2000 census projections
and are for population within city limits.

8* — 8,214,426

3,849,378

2,833,321

2,144,491

1,512,986

New York | Los Angeles | Chicago | Houston | Philadelphia

With more than twice the population of the
next largest city, New York—known as
the Big Apple—is the country's largest city.

4 5 6 7 8 9 10 11

0 _____ 100 miles
0 _____ 100 kilometers

Albers Conic Equal-Area Projection

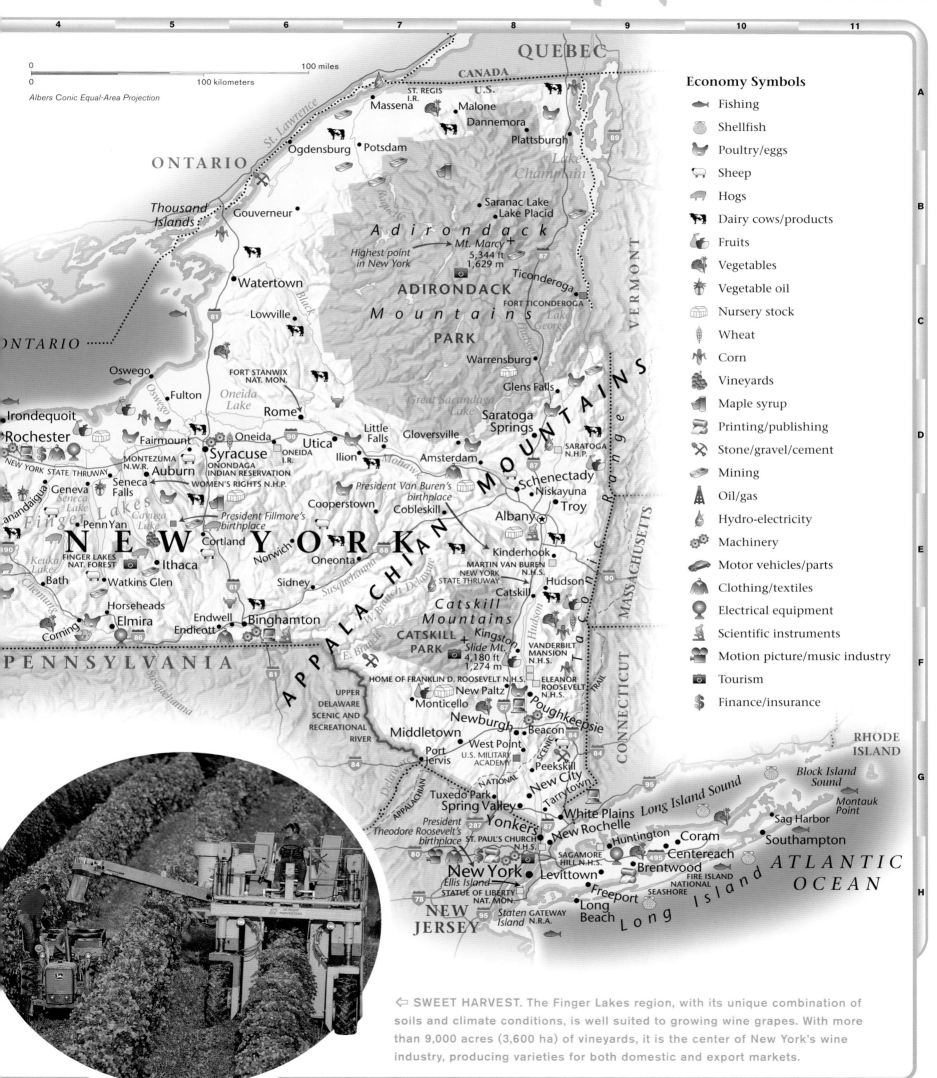

Economy Symbols

- Fishing
- Shellfish
- Poultry/eggs
- Sheep
- Hogs
- Dairy cows/products
- Fruits
- Vegetables
- Vegetable oil
- Nursery stock
- Wheat
- Corn
- Vineyards
- Maple syrup
- Printing/publishing
- Stone/gravel/cement
- Mining
- Oil/gas
- Hydro-electricity
- Machinery
- Motor vehicles/parts
- Clothing/textiles
- Electrical equipment
- Scientific instruments
- Motion picture/music industry
- Tourism
- Finance/insurance

QUEBEC
CANADA
U.S.
ONTARIO
ONTARIO
VERMONT
MASSACHUSETTS
CONNECTICUT
RHODE ISLAND
PENNSYLVANIA
NEW JERSEY

St. Lawrence
Thousand Islands
Lake Champlain

ST. REGIS I.R.
Massena
Malone
Dannemora
Plattsburgh
Ogdensburg
Potsdam
Gouverneur
Saranac Lake
Lake Placid

Adirondack
Mt. Marcy 5,344 ft 1,629 m
Highest point in New York
Ticonderoga
FORT TICONDEROGA
Lake George

Watertown
Lowville
Black
Raquette

ADIRONDACK
Mountains
PARK

Warrensburg
Glens Falls
Great Sacandaga Lake
Saratoga Springs
SARATOGA N.H.P.
Gloversville
Amsterdam
Schenectady
Niskayuna
Troy
Albany ★
Hudson

Oswego
Fulton
Oneida Lake
Rome
FORT STANWIX NAT. MON.
Little Falls
Utica
Ilion
Oneida
ONEIDA I.R.
Mohawk
President Van Buren's birthplace
Cobleskill
Kinderhook
MARTIN VAN BUREN N.H.S.

Irondequoit
Rochester
NEW YORK STATE THRUWAY
Fairmount
Syracuse
MONTEZUMA N.W.R.
Auburn
ONONDAGA INDIAN RESERVATION
WOMEN'S RIGHTS N.H.P.
Seneca Falls
Geneva
Cooperstown
President Fillmore's birthplace
Cortland
Norwich
Oneonta
Susquehanna
MARTIN VAN BUREN NEW YORK STATE THRUWAY
Catskill

Canandaigua
Penn Yan
Finger Lakes
Cayuga Lake
Seneca Lake
Keuka Lake

N E W   Y O R K

FINGER LAKES NAT. FOREST
Ithaca
Watkins Glen
Bath
Horseheads
Elmira
Corning
Chemung
Endwell
Endicott
Binghamton
Sidney
Delaware
W. Branch Delaware
E. Branch

APPALACHIAN MOUNTAINS
Taconic Range
Taconic Range

Catskill Mountains
CATSKILL PARK
Slide Mt. 4,180 ft 1,274 m
Kingston
VANDERBILT MANSION N.H.S.
HOME OF FRANKLIN D. ROOSEVELT N.H.S.
ELEANOR ROOSEVELT N.H.S.
New Paltz
Monticello
Poughkeepsie
Newburgh
Beacon
Middletown
Port Jervis
West Point
U.S. MILITARY ACADEMY
Peekskill
New City
UPPER DELAWARE SCENIC AND RECREATIONAL RIVER

Tuxedo Park
Spring Valley
President Theodore Roosevelt's birthplace
ST. PAUL'S CHURCH N.H.S.
Yonkers
White Plains
New Rochelle
Tarrytown

APPALACHIAN NATIONAL SCENIC TRAIL

Long Island Sound
Block Island Sound
Montauk Point
Huntington
Coram
Sag Harbor
Southampton
Centereach
Brentwood
SAGAMORE HILL N.H.S.
New York
Levittown
Freeport
Long Beach
FIRE ISLAND NATIONAL SEASHORE

Long Island
ATLANTIC OCEAN

Ellis Island
STATUE OF LIBERTY NAT. MON.
Staten Island
GATEWAY N.R.A.
Hudson

← SWEET HARVEST. The Finger Lakes region, with its unique combination of soils and climate conditions, is well suited to growing wine grapes. With more than 9,000 acres (3,600 ha) of vineyards, it is the center of New York's wine industry, producing varieties for both domestic and export markets.

THE KEYSTONE STATE:
PENNSYLVANIA

PENNSYLVANIA

Pennsylvania, the 12th of England's 13 American colonies, was established in 1682 by Quaker William Penn and 360 settlers seeking religious freedom and fair government. The colony enjoyed abundant natural resources—dense woodlands, fertile soils, industrial minerals, and water power—which soon attracted Germans, Scotch-Irish, and other immigrants. Pennsylvania played a central role in the move for independence from Britain, and Philadelphia served as the new country's capital from 1790 to 1800. In the 19th century Philadelphia, in the east, and Pittsburgh, in the west, became booming centers of industrial growth. Philadelphia produced ships, locomotives, and textiles, while the iron and steel industry fueled Pittsburgh's growth. Jobs in industry as well as agriculture attracted immigrants from around the world. Today, Pennsylvania's economy has shifted toward information technology, health care, financial services, and tourism, but the state remains a leader in coal and steel production.

⇧ **LET FREEDOM RING.** The Liberty Bell, cast in 1753 by Pennsylvania craftsmen, hangs silent in Philadelphia. Because of a crack, it is no longer rung.

THE BASICS

STATS

Area
46,055 sq mi (119,283 sq km)

Population
12,432,792

Capital
Harrisburg
Population 48,322

Largest city
Philadelphia
Population 1,448,394

Ethnic/racial groups
85.7% white; 10.7% African American; 2.4% Asian; .2% Native American. Hispanic (any race) 4.2%.

Industry
Machinery, printing and publishing, forest products, metal products

Agriculture
Dairy products, poultry and eggs, mushrooms, cattle, hogs, grains

Statehood
December 12, 1787; 2nd state

GEO WHIZ

If you are into guitars or other acoustical instruments, you will want to put the Martin Guitar Company, in Nazareth, on your list of places to visit. It has been handcrafting these instruments for musicians all over the world for more than 150 years.

For more than a century, the streets of Philadelphia have been transformed on New Year's Day as some 15,000 revelers dressed in sequined and feathered costumes "strut their stuff" to the sound of string-band music in the Mummers Parade past millions of onlookers.

RUFFED GROUSE
MOUNTAIN LAUREL

LAKE ERIE

Erie
Millcreek
Corry
Meadville
ERIE NATIONAL WILDLIFE REFUGE
Pymatuning Reservoir
Titusville
Greenville
Oil City
Sharon
Grove City
New Castle
Butler
Beaver Falls
McCandless
Aliquippa
Plum
Pittsburgh
Penn Hills
McKeesport
Jeannette
Washington
Monessen
Connellsville
Waynesburg
Uniontown
FRIENDSHIP HILL N.H.S.
FT. NECESSITY NATIONAL BATTLEFIELD
OHIO
WEST VIRGINIA

⇨ **RIVER TOWN.** Pittsburgh, one of the largest inland ports in the U.S., was established in 1758 where the Monongahela and Allegheny Rivers meet to form the Ohio River. Once a booming steel town, Pittsburgh is now a center of finance, medicine, and education.

MAKING COINS

4.3 billion

Annual output, 2006 data

693 million

1.4 billion

1.4 billion

PENNIES

DIMES

The 1792 Coinage Act established the first U.S. mint in Philadelphia. It is still one of the country's main coin-producing facilities.

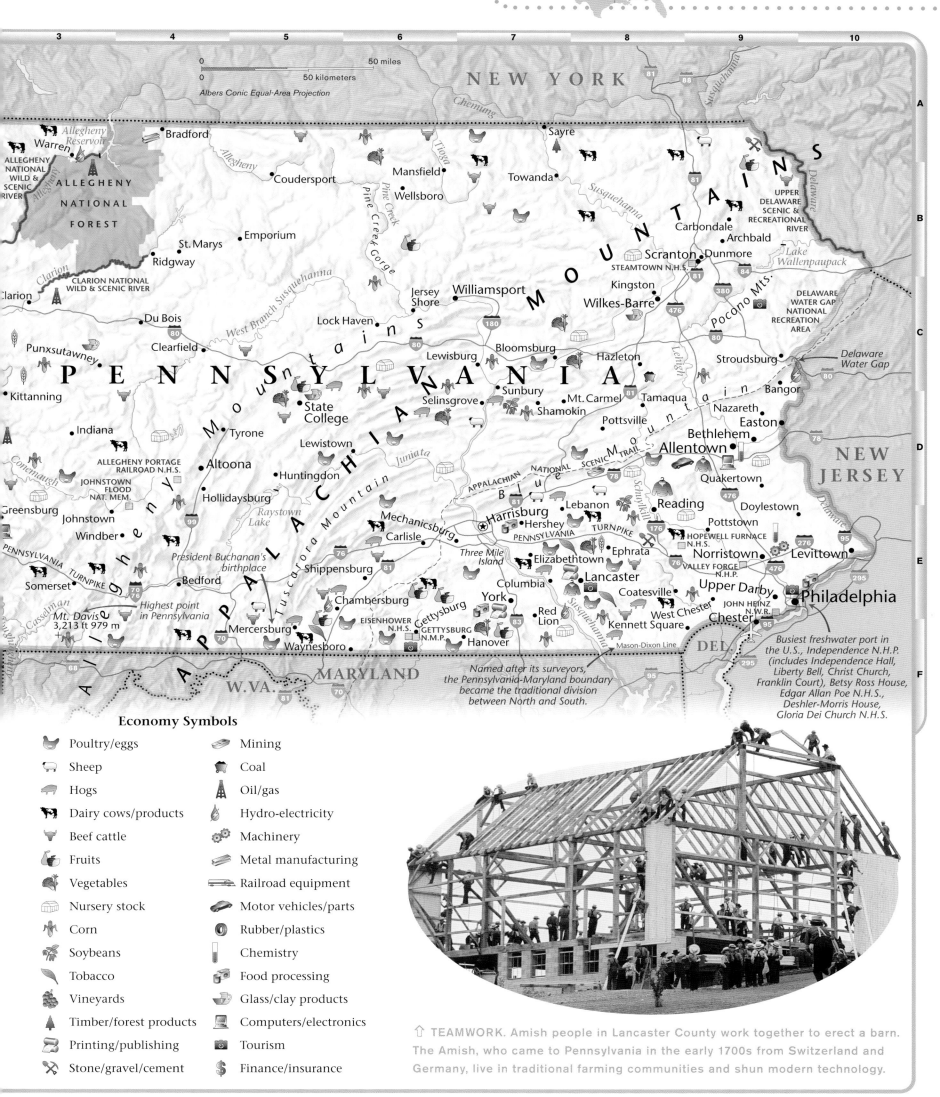

NEW YORK

50 miles

50 kilometers

Albers Conic Equal-Area Projection

Allegheny Reservoir

Warren

ALLEGHENY NATIONAL WILD & SCENIC RIVER

Bradford

ALLEGHENY NATIONAL FOREST

St. Marys

Emporium

Ridgway

Coudersport

Mansfield

Wellsboro

Sayre

Towanda

Carbondale

Archbald

UPPER DELAWARE SCENIC & RECREATIONAL RIVER

Lake Wallenpaupack

Clarion

CLARION NATIONAL WILD & SCENIC RIVER

Pine Creek Gorge

Williamsport

Scranton Dunmore

STEAMTOWN N.H.S.

Kingston

Wilkes-Barre

Pocono Mts.

DELAWARE WATER GAP NATIONAL RECREATION AREA

Du Bois

West Branch Susquehanna

Jersey Shore

Lock Haven

Clearfield

Lewisburg

Bloomsburg

Hazleton

Stroudsburg

Delaware Water Gap

Punxsutawney

PENNSYLVANIA

Kittanning

State College

Selinsgrove

Sunbury

Mt. Carmel

Shamokin

Tamaqua

Pottsville

Nazareth

Bangor

Easton

Indiana

Tyrone

Lewistown

Bethlehem

Allentown

Quakertown

NEW JERSEY

ALLEGHENY PORTAGE RAILROAD N.H.S.

JOHNSTOWN FLOOD NAT. MEM.

Altoona

Huntingdon

Juniata

APPALACHIAN NATIONAL SCENIC TRAIL

Reading

Doylestown

Greensburg

Johnstown

Windber

Hollidaysburg

Raystown Lake

Mechanicsburg

Harrisburg

Hershey

Lebanon

Ephrata

Pottstown

HOPEWELL FURNACE N.H.S.

Norristown

Levittown

Conemaugh

Carlisle

PENNSYLVANIA TURNPIKE

Elizabethtown

PENNSYLVANIA TURNPIKE

VALLEY FORGE N.H.P.

Somerset

President Buchanan's birthplace

Bedford

Shippensburg

Three Mile Island

Columbia

Lancaster

Coatesville

Upper Darby

JOHN HEINZ N.W.R.

Philadelphia

Highest point in Pennsylvania

Chambersburg

York

West Chester

Kennett Square

Chester

Casselman

Mt. Davis 3,213 ft 979 m

Mercersburg

Waynesboro

EISENHOWER N.H.S.

GETTYSBURG N.M.P.

Hanover

Red Lion

Mason-Dixon Line

DEL.

Busiest freshwater port in the U.S., Independence N.H.P. (includes Independence Hall, Liberty Bell, Christ Church, Franklin Court), Betsy Ross House, Edgar Allan Poe N.H.S., Deshler-Morris House, Gloria Dei Church N.H.S.

W.VA.

MARYLAND

Named after its surveyors, the Pennsylvania-Maryland boundary became the traditional division between North and South.

Economy Symbols

- Poultry/eggs
- Sheep
- Hogs
- Dairy cows/products
- Beef cattle
- Fruits
- Vegetables
- Nursery stock
- Corn
- Soybeans
- Tobacco
- Vineyards
- Timber/forest products
- Printing/publishing
- Stone/gravel/cement

- Mining
- Coal
- Oil/gas
- Hydro-electricity
- Machinery
- Metal manufacturing
- Railroad equipment
- Motor vehicles/parts
- Rubber/plastics
- Chemistry
- Food processing
- Glass/clay products
- Computers/electronics
- Tourism
- Finance/insurance

⇧ TEAMWORK. Amish people in Lancaster County work together to erect a barn. The Amish, who came to Pennsylvania in the early 1700s from Switzerland and Germany, live in traditional farming communities and shun modern technology.

RHODE ISLAND

STATS

Area
1,545 sq mi (4,002 sq km)

Population
1,057,832

Capital
Providence
Population 175,255

Largest city
Providence
Population 175,255

Ethnic/racial groups
88.7% white; 6.3% African American; 2.7% Asian; .6% Native American. Hispanic (any race) 11.0%.

Industry
Health services, business services, silver and jewelry products, metal products

Agriculture
Nursery stock, vegetables, dairy products, eggs

Statehood
May 29, 1790; 13th state

GEO WHIZ

Pawtucket is one of several communities in Rhode Island that have become home to a growing number of people from Cape Verde. Drought has forced people from this African country to find a new place to live. Massachusetts and North Dakota are the only other states with measurable Cape Verdean populations.

Wild coyotes are living and thriving on islands in Narragansett Bay. Researchers have outfitted some of the animals with radio collars so that their numbers and whereabouts can be tracked online—even by schoolkids.

RHODE ISLAND RED
VIOLET

In 1524 Italian navigator Giovanni Verrazzano was the first European explorer to visit Rhode Island, but place names such as Quonochontaug and Narragansett tell of an earlier Native American population. In 1636 Roger Williams, seeking greater religious freedom, left Massachusetts and established the first European settlement in what was to become the colony of Rhode Island. In the years following the Revolutionary War, Rhode Island pressed for fairness in trade, taxes, and representation in Congress, as well as greater freedom of worship, before becoming the 13th state. By the 19th century, Rhode Island had become an important center of trade and textile factories, attracting many immigrants from Europe. In addition to commercial activities, Rhode Island's coastline became a popular vacation retreat for the wealthy. Today, Rhode Island, like many other states, has seen its economy shift toward high-tech jobs and service industries. It is also promoting its coastline and bays, as well as its rich history, to attract tourists.

⇧ CLUES TO THE PAST. Fossils embedded in rocks left behind 10,000 years ago by retreating glaciers tell of Block Island's past.

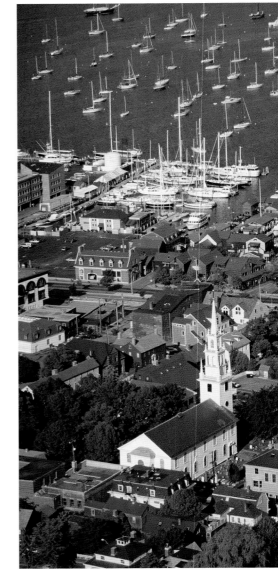

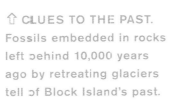

⇐ SETTING SAIL. Newport Harbor invites sailors of all ages. From 1930 to 1983, the prestigious America's Cup Yacht Race took place in the waters off Newport. Today, the town provides 900 moorings for boats of all types.

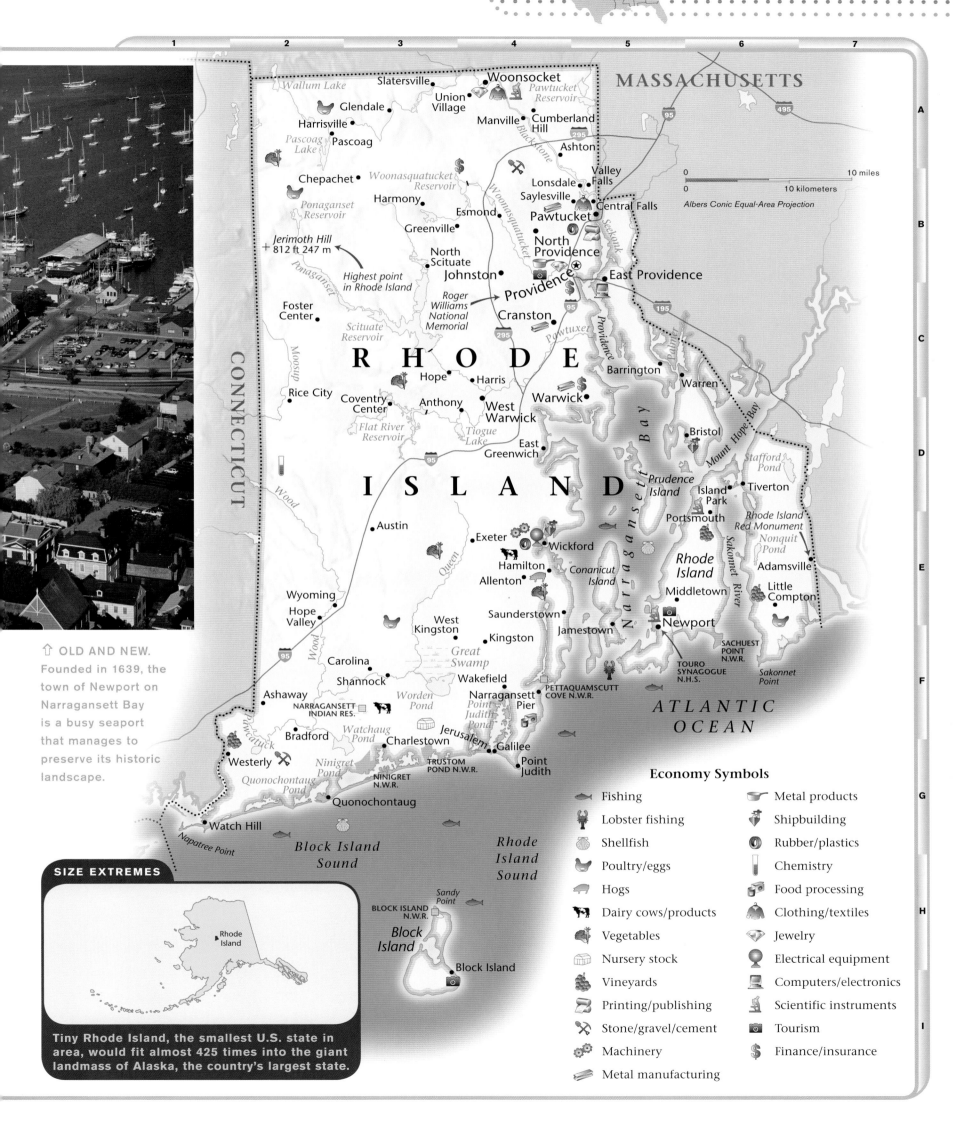

1 2 3 4 5 6 7

MASSACHUSETTS

Wallum Lake Slatersville **Woonsocket** *Pawtucket Reservoir*

Glendale Union Village Manville **Cumberland Hill**

Harrisville Ashton

Pascoag Lake Pascoag Lonsdale Valley Falls

Chepachet *Woonasquatucket Reservoir* Saylesville Central Falls

Harmony Esmond **Pawtucket**

Ponaganset Reservoir Greenville **North Providence**

Jerimoth Hill North Scituate Johnston

+812 ft 247 m *Highest point in Rhode Island* **Providence** **East Providence**

Foster Center *Roger Williams National Memorial* **Cranston**

Scituate Reservoir Barrington

R H O D E Warren

Rice City Hope Harris Bristol

Coventry Center Anthony **Warwick** *Stafford Pond*

Flat River Reservoir **West Warwick** *Prudence Island* Tiverton

Tiogue Lake East Greenwich Island Park *Rhode Island Red Monument*

I S L A N D Portsmouth *Nonquit Pond*

Austin Exeter Wickford *Rhode Island* Adamsville

Hamilton *Conanicut Island* Little Compton

Allenton Middletown

Wyoming Saunderstown **Newport** SACHUEST POINT N.W.R.

Hope Valley West Kingston Jamestown TOURO SYNAGOGUE N.H.S. *Sakonnet Point*

Kingston *Great Swamp*

Carolina Wakefield PETTAQUAMSCUTT COVE N.W.R. *A T L A N T I C*

Shannock Narragansett Pier *O C E A N*

Ashaway NARRAGANSETT INDIAN RES. *Worden Pond* *Point Judith Pond*

Bradford *Watchaug Pond* Jerusalem Galilee

Westerly *Ninigret Pond* Charlestown Point Judith

Quonochontaug Pond NINIGRET N.W.R. TRUSTOM POND N.W.R.

Watch Hill Quonochontaug

Napatree Point *Block Island Sound* *Rhode Island Sound*

CONNECTICUT

Moosup *Ponaganset* *Wood* *Queen* *Wood* *Pawcatuck*

Blackstone *Woonasquatucket* *Seekonk* *Providence* *Pawtuxet* *Narragansett Bay* *Mount Hope Bay* *Sakonnet River*

0 _____ 10 miles
0 _____ 10 kilometers
Albers Conic Equal-Area Projection

⇧ **OLD AND NEW.**
Founded in 1639, the town of Newport on Narragansett Bay is a busy seaport that manages to preserve its historic landscape.

SIZE EXTREMES

Rhode Island

Tiny Rhode Island, the smallest U.S. state in area, would fit almost 425 times into the giant landmass of Alaska, the country's largest state.

BLOCK ISLAND N.W.R. *Sandy Point*

Block Island Block Island

Economy Symbols

- Fishing
- Lobster fishing
- Shellfish
- Poultry/eggs
- Hogs
- Dairy cows/products
- Vegetables
- Nursery stock
- Vineyards
- Printing/publishing
- Stone/gravel/cement
- Machinery
- Metal manufacturing
- Metal products
- Shipbuilding
- Rubber/plastics
- Chemistry
- Food processing
- Clothing/textiles
- Jewelry
- Electrical equipment
- Computers/electronics
- Scientific instruments
- Tourism
- Finance/insurance

VERMONT

THE BASICS

STATS

Area
9,614 sq mi (24,901 sq km)

Population
621,254

Capital
Montpelier
Population 7,954

Largest city
Burlington
Population 39,148

Ethnic/racial groups
96.7% white; 1.1% Asian; .7% African American; .4% Native American. Hispanic (any race) 1.1%.

Industry
Health services, tourism, finance, real estate, computer components, electrical parts, printing and publishing, machine tools

Agriculture
Dairy products, maple products, apples

Statehood
March 4, 1791; 14th state

GEO WHIZ

Barre is famous for producing granite gravestones. The tombstones of President Harry Truman, industrialist John D. Rockefeller, Sr., songwriter Stephen Foster, and fast-food-chain founder Col. Harland Sanders are all made of Barre Gray granite, as are the steps of the U.S. Capitol in Washington, D.C.

Burlington is the home of Ben & Jerry's ice cream. The company gives its leftovers to local farmers, who feed it to their hogs. The hogs seem to like every flavor except Mint Oreo.

From 1777 until it became a state in 1791, Vermont was an independent country. It had its own postal and monetary systems.

Vermont, the third-largest state in New England, is the only state in the region that does not border the Atlantic Ocean.

HERMIT THRUSH
RED CLOVER

When French explorer Jacques Cartier arrived in Vermont in 1535, Native Americans living in woodland villages had been there for hundreds of years. Settled first by the French in 1666 and then by the English in 1724, the territory of Vermont became an area of conflict between these colonial powers. The French finally withdrew, but conflict continued between New York and New Hampshire, both of which wanted to take over Vermont. The people of Vermont declared their independence in 1777 and became the 14th U.S. state in 1791. Vermont's name, which means "Green Mountain," comes from the extensive forests that cover much of the state and that provide the basis for furniture and pulp industries. Vermont also boasts the world's largest granite quarry and the largest underground marble quarry, both of which produce valuable building materials. Tourism and recreation are also important in Vermont. Lakes, rivers, and mountain trails are popular summer attractions, while snow-covered mountains attract skiers throughout the winter.

⇧ LIQUID GOLD. In spring, sap from maple trees is collected in buckets by drilling a hole in the tree trunk—called "tapping." The sap is boiled to remove water, then filtered, and finally bottled.

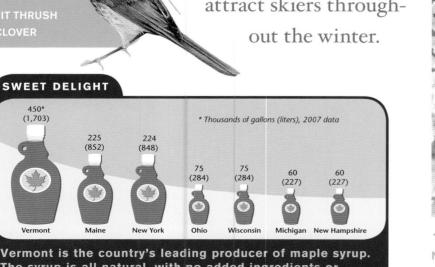

SWEET DELIGHT

* Thousands of gallons (liters), 2007 data

450* (1,703)	225 (852)	224 (848)	75 (284)	75 (284)	60 (227)	60 (227)
Vermont	Maine	New York	Ohio	Wisconsin	Michigan	New Hampshire

Vermont is the country's leading producer of maple syrup. The syrup is all natural, with no added ingredients or preservatives, just boiled sap collected from maple trees.

⇧ WINTER WONDERLAND. One of the snowiest places in the Northeast, Jay Peak averages 355 inches (900 cm) of snow each year. With 76 trails, the mountain, near Vermont's border with Canada, attracts beginner and expert skiers from near and far.

Economy Symbols

- Poultry/eggs
- Sheep
- Dairy cows/products
- Beef cattle
- Fruits
- Vegetables
- Nursery stock
- Corn
- Maple syrup
- Timber/forest products
- Printing/publishing
- Stone/gravel/cement
- Hydro-electricity
- Metal products
- Food processing
- Computers/electronics
- Tourism

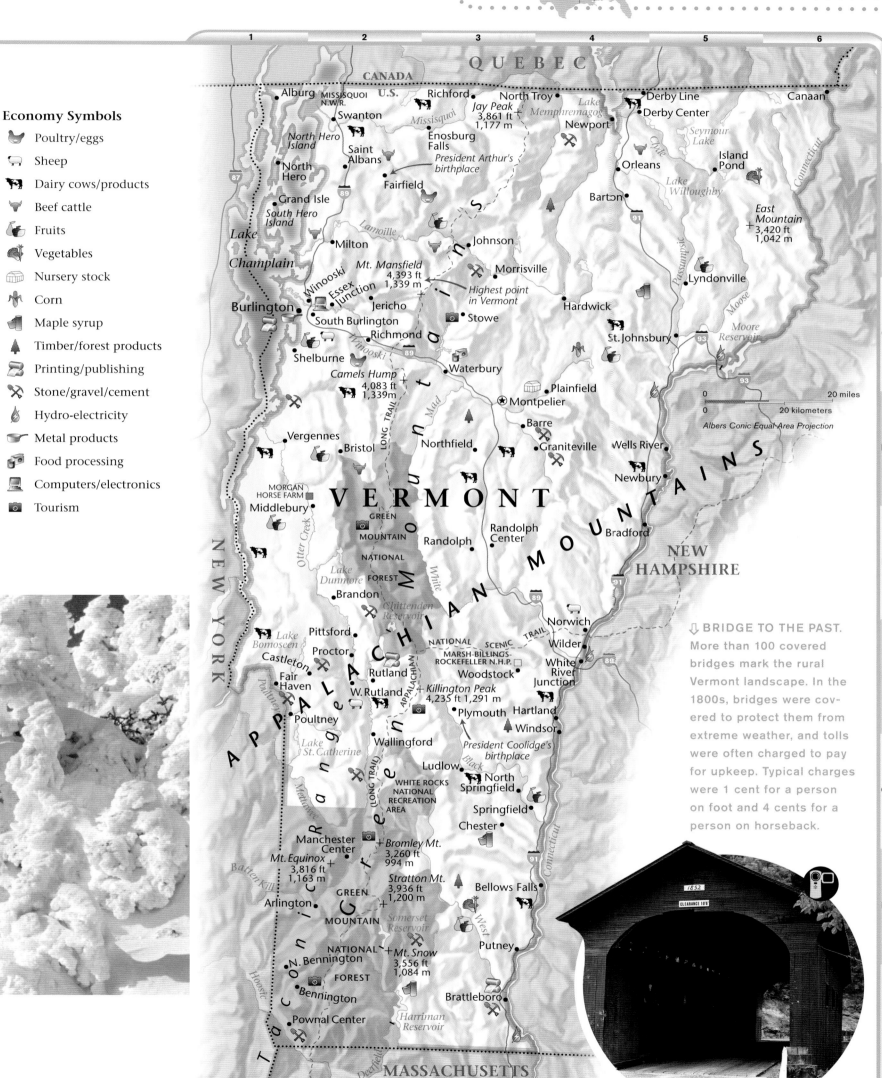

QUEBEC

CANADA
U.S.

Alburg
MISSISQUOI N.W.R.
Swanton
Richford
North Troy
Jay Peak 3,861 ft 1,177 m
Derby Line
Derby Center
Canaan

Lake Memphremagog
Newport

North Hero Island
Missisquoi
Enosburg Falls
President Arthur's birthplace
Seymour Lake

Saint Albans
Fairfield
Orleans
Island Pond

North Hero
Barton
Lake Willoughby

Grand Isle
South Hero Island
East Mountain 3,420 ft 1,042 m

Lake Champlain
Lamoille
Milton
Johnson

Mt. Mansfield 4,393 ft 1,339 m
Morrisville

Winooski
Essex Junction
Highest point in Vermont
Hardwick
Lyndonville

Burlington
Jericho
Stowe
St. Johnsbury

South Burlington
Richmond
Moore Reservoir

Winooski
Waterbury

Shelburne
Camels Hump 4,083 ft 1,339 m
Plainfield

★ Montpelier

Vergennes
Northfield
Barre
Wells River

Bristol
Graniteville
Newbury

VERMONT

MORGAN HORSE FARM
GREEN MOUNTAIN
Randolph
Randolph Center
Bradford

NEW HAMPSHIRE

Middlebury
NATIONAL FOREST

Lake Dunmore
White

Brandon

Chittenden Reservoir

Lake Bomoseen
Pittsford
Norwich

Castleton
Proctor
Wilder

Fair Haven
Rutland
White River Junction

W. Rutland
Killington Peak 4,235 ft 1,291 m
Hartland

Poultney
Wallingford
Plymouth
Windsor

Lake St. Catherine

NATIONAL SCENIC TRAIL
MARSH-BILLINGS-ROCKEFELLER N.H.P.
Woodstock

President Coolidge's birthplace

Ludlow
North Springfield

WHITE ROCKS NATIONAL RECREATION AREA
Springfield

Chester

Manchester Center
Bromley Mt. 3,260 ft 994 m

Mt. Equinox 3,816 ft 1,163 m

Stratton Mt. 3,936 ft 1,200 m
Bellows Falls

GREEN MOUNTAIN

Arlington
Somerset Reservoir
Putney

NATIONAL
Mt. Snow 3,556 ft 1,084 m

N. Bennington
FOREST

Bennington
Brattleboro

Pownal Center
Harriman Reservoir

NEW YORK

APPALACHIAN MOUNTAINS

LONG TRAIL

Taconic Range
Green Mountains

MASSACHUSETTS

Deerfield

Otter Creek
Mad
White
Black
West
Connecticut
Clyde
Passumpsic
Moose
Batten Kill
Hoosic
Poultney
Metawee

0   20 miles
0   20 kilometers
Albers Conic Equal-Area Projection

⇩ BRIDGE TO THE PAST.
More than 100 covered bridges mark the rural Vermont landscape. In the 1800s, bridges were covered to protect them from extreme weather, and tolls were often charged to pay for upkeep. Typical charges were 1 cent for a person on foot and 4 cents for a person on horseback.

1852
CLEARANCE 10'6"

THE REGION

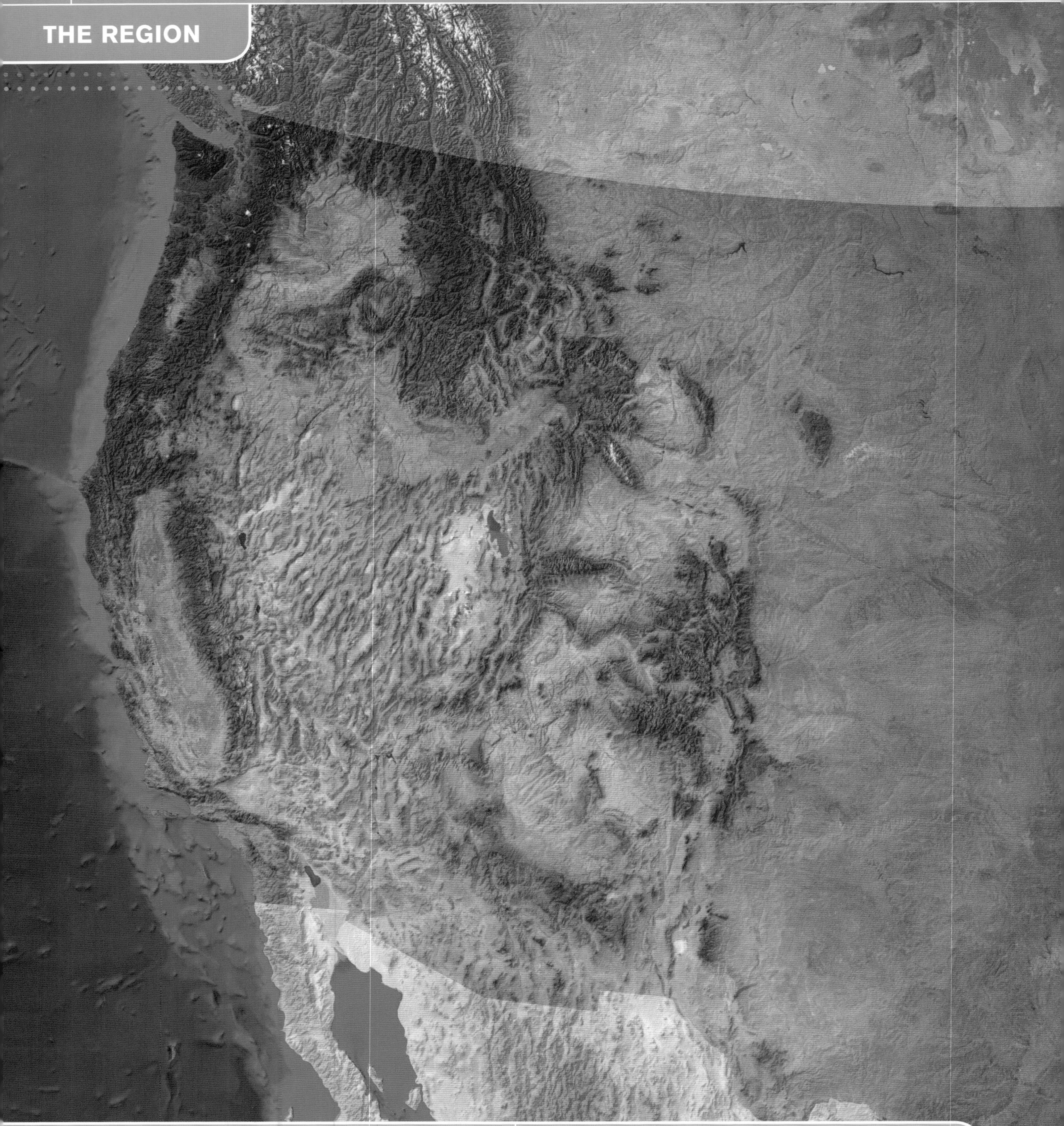

PHYSICAL

Total area
566,443 sq mi
(1,467,082 sq km)

Highest point
Mount Mitchell, NC
6,684 ft (2,037 m)

Lowest point
New Orleans, LA
8 ft (2 m) below sea level

Longest rivers
Mississippi, Arkansas,
Red, Ohio

Largest lakes
Okeechobee, Pontchartrain,
Kentucky (reservoir)

Vegetation
Needleleaf, broadleaf, and
mixed forest

Climate
Continental to mild, ranging
from cool summers in the
north to humid, subtropical
conditions in the south

POLITICAL

Total population
75,861,690

States (12):
Alabama, Arkansas, Florida, Georgia,
Kentucky, Louisiana, Mississippi, North
Carolina, South Carolina, Tennessee,
Virginia, West Virginia

Largest state
Florida: 65,755 sq mi (170,304 sq km)

Smallest state
West Virginia: 24,230 sq mi (62,755 sq km)

Most populous state
Florida: 18,251,243

Least populous state
West Virginia: 1,812,035

Largest city proper
Jacksonville, FL: 794,555

The Southeast

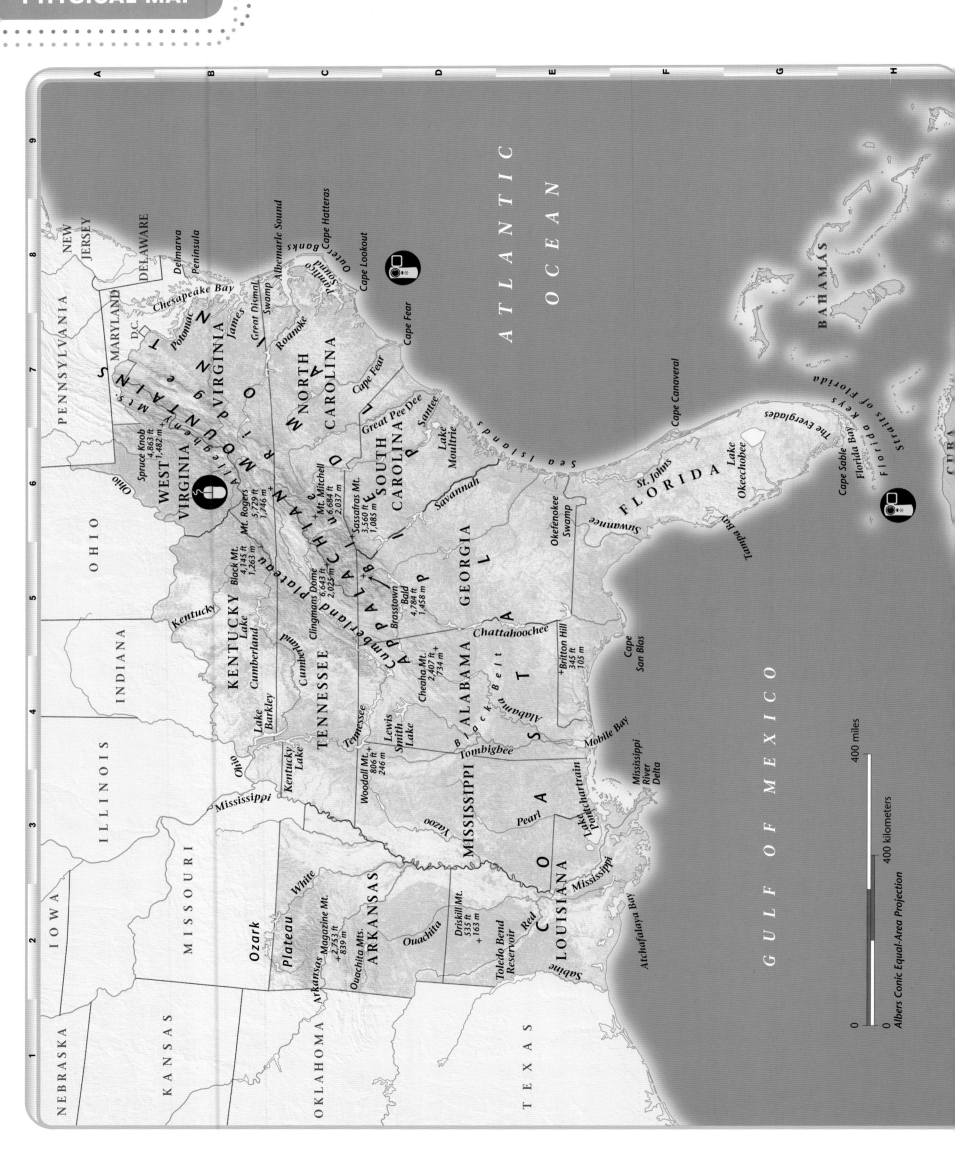

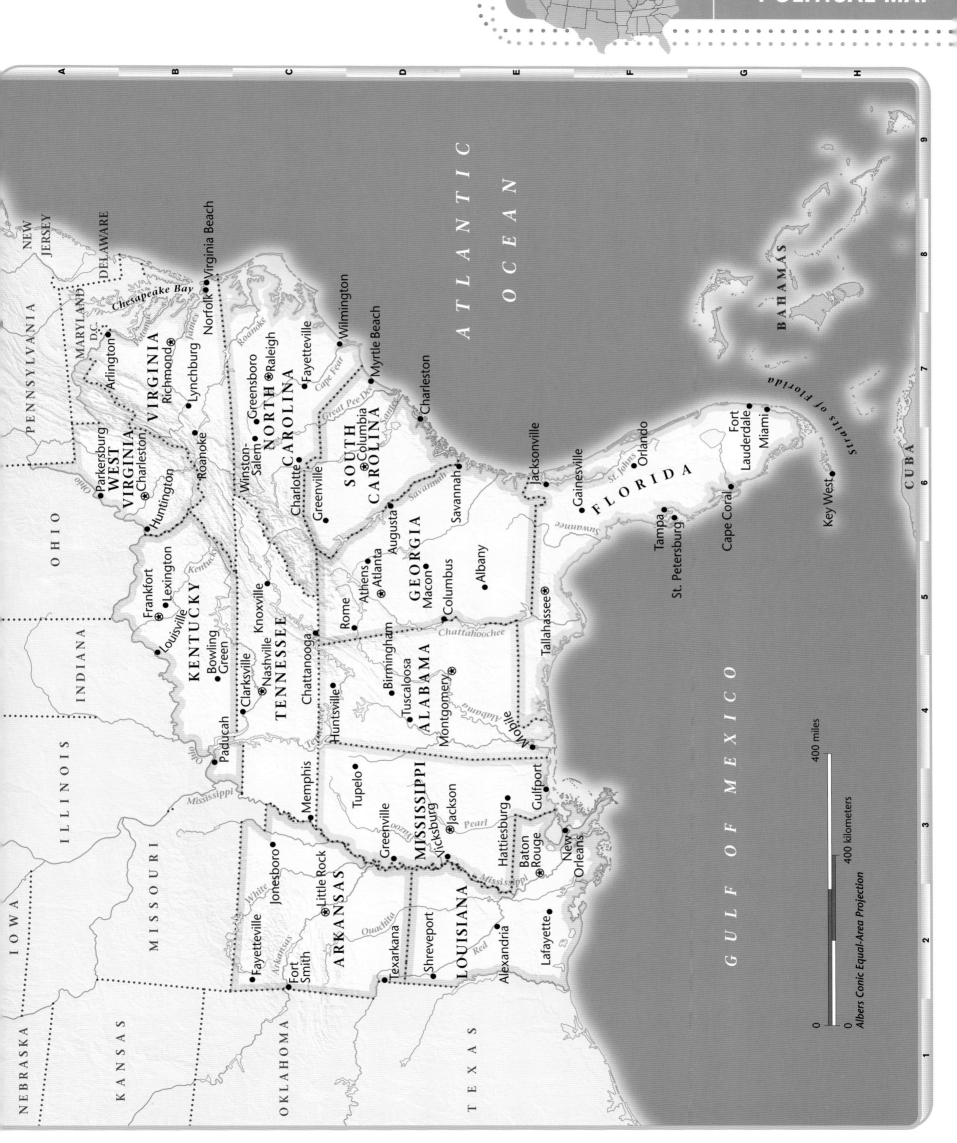

400 miles

400 kilometers

Albers Conic Equal-Area Projection

⇨ OPEN WIDE. An American alligator in Florida's Big Cypress Swamp shows off sharp teeth. These large reptiles live mainly in fresh-water swamps and marshes in coastal areas of the Southeast. Adult males average 14 feet (4 m) in length.

The Southeast
TRADITION MEETS TECHNOLOGY

From deeply weathered mountains in West Virginia to warm, humid wetlands in south Florida and the Mississippi River's sprawling delta in southern Louisiana, the Southeast is marked by great physical diversity. The region's historical roots are in agriculture—especially cotton and tobacco. The Civil War brought economic and political upheaval in the mid-19th century, but today the Southeast is part of the Sunbelt, where 3 of the top 20 metropolitan areas of the U.S. are found and where high-tech industries are redefining the way people earn a living and the way the region is connected to the global economy.

⇨ ENCHANTED KINGDOM. Fireworks light up the night sky above Cinderella's Castle at Walt Disney World near Orlando, Florida. The park, which accounts for more than 12 percent of all jobs in the Orlando area, attracts millions of tourists from around the world each year.

⇧ SOCIAL CONSCIENCE. Members of the Big Nine Social Aid and Pleasure Club of New Orleans's Lower Ninth Ward march in a parade through a neighborhood devastated by Hurricane Katrina. Such clubs, which date back to late 19th-century benevolent societies, bring support and hope to communities in need.

WHERE THE PICTURES ARE

Banjo playing p. 69
River rafting p. 83
Coal miner p. 82
Horse race p. 68
Cyclists on outcrop pp. 58-59
Black bear family p. 78
Harpers Ferry p. 82
Motorboats p. 79
Luray Caverns p. 80
Grand Ole Opry p. 79
Indian Woman p. 75
Cyclists pp. 80-81
Space camp p. 60
Dice p. 80
Race car p. 59
Rockclimber p. 62
Bird-watchers p. 62
Wright Brothers Memorial p. 74
Blackbeard's cannon p. 59
Boys playing basketball p. 74
Diamond hunter p. 63
Beach scene p. 76
Paddleboat p. 72
Wild turkey p. 77
Blues guitarist p. 72
Atlanta p. 66
Historic Charleston pp. 76-77
Oil rig p. 60
Catfish p. 73
Peanuts p. 66
Aerial of Sea Islands p. 66
Oak Alley Plantation p. 70
Manatee p. 64
Shuttle launch pp. 64-65
Katrina parade p. 58
Cinderella's Castle p. 58, Girl in parade p. 64
Shrimp fisherman p. 70
Alligator p. 58

⇧ VIEW FROM ABOVE. Cyclists look out from a rocky ledge across West Virginia's Germany Valley. The area took its name from German immigrants who moved there in the mid-1700s from North Carolina and Pennsylvania and established farming villages.

⇨ CAR STARS. For more than 50 years, auto racing has been a leading sport in the U.S., especially in the Southeast. The International Motorsports Hall of Fame, located adjacent to the Talledega Superspeedway in Alabama, features racing cars, motorcycles, and vintage cars.

⇦ PIRATE'S DEFENSE. This 4.5-foot (1.4-m) cast-iron cannon was recovered from the wreck of the *Queen Anne's Revenge* off North Carolina's coast. The vessel, which probably belonged to the notorious pirate Blackbeard, grounded on a sandbar and sank in 1718 near Cape Lookout.

THE BASICS

STATS

Area
52,419 sq mi (135,765 sq km)

Population
4,627,851

Capital
Montgomery
Population 201,998

Largest city
Birmingham
Population 229,424

Ethnic/racial groups
71.2% white; 26.3% African American; .9% Asian; .5% Native American. Hispanic (any race) 2.5%.

Industry
Retail and wholesale trade, services, government, finance, insurance, real estate, transportation, construction, communication

Agriculture
Fruits and vegetables, dairy products, cattle, forest products, commercial fishing

Statehood
December 14, 1819; 22nd state

GEO WHIZ

Condoleezza Rice, the first African-American woman to serve as U.S. Secretary of State, and Rosa Parks, whose refusal to give up her seat on a Montgomery bus earned her the title "mother of the modern-day civil rights movement," were both born in Alabama: Rice in Birmingham and Parks in Tuskegee.

Russell Cave, near Bridgeport, was home to prehistoric peoples for more than 10,000 years. In 1961 a national monument was established on land donated by the National Geographic Society. Today, visitors can take guided tours of the cave and see the kinds of tools and weapons its early inhabitants used.

In 2004 Hurricane Ivan, one of the worst storms to batter Alabama's Gulf coast since 1900, struck Orange Beach.

NORTHERN FLICKER

CAMELLIA

ALABAMA

Alabama has a colorful story. The French established the first permanent European settlement at Mobile Bay in 1702, but different groups—British, Native Americans, and U.S. settlers—struggled over control of the land for more than 100 years. In 1819 Alabama became the 22nd state, but in 1861 it joined the Confederacy. During the Civil War, Montgomery was the capital of the secessionist South for a time. After the war Alabama struggled to rebuild its agriculture-based economy. By 1900 the state was producing more than one million bales of cotton annually. In the mid-20th century, Alabama was at the center of the civil rights movement, which pressed for equal rights for all people regardless of race or social status. Key players included Martin Luther King, Jr., and Rosa Parks. Modern industries, including the NASA space program, have given the state's economy a big boost. In 2002 assembly plants built by automakers from Asia created thousands of new jobs.

⇧ UNDERWATER RESOURCE. A massive drill descends from an offshore oil rig to tap petroleum deposits beneath the water of the Gulf of Mexico off Alabama's shore.

⇧ ROCKET POWER. Students inspect giant booster rockets during Space Camp at Marshall Space Flight Center, in Huntsville, Alabama. The center is one of NASA's largest installations, providing support to space shuttle missions and the International Space Station.

ON THE ROAD

Alabama car and light-truck production

2002	2003	2004	2005	2006	2007
196,291	252,025	253,200	479,465	698,086	800,000 (estimated)

Since the first vehicles rolled off the assembly line in 1993, Alabama has risen to #5 in national automotive production.

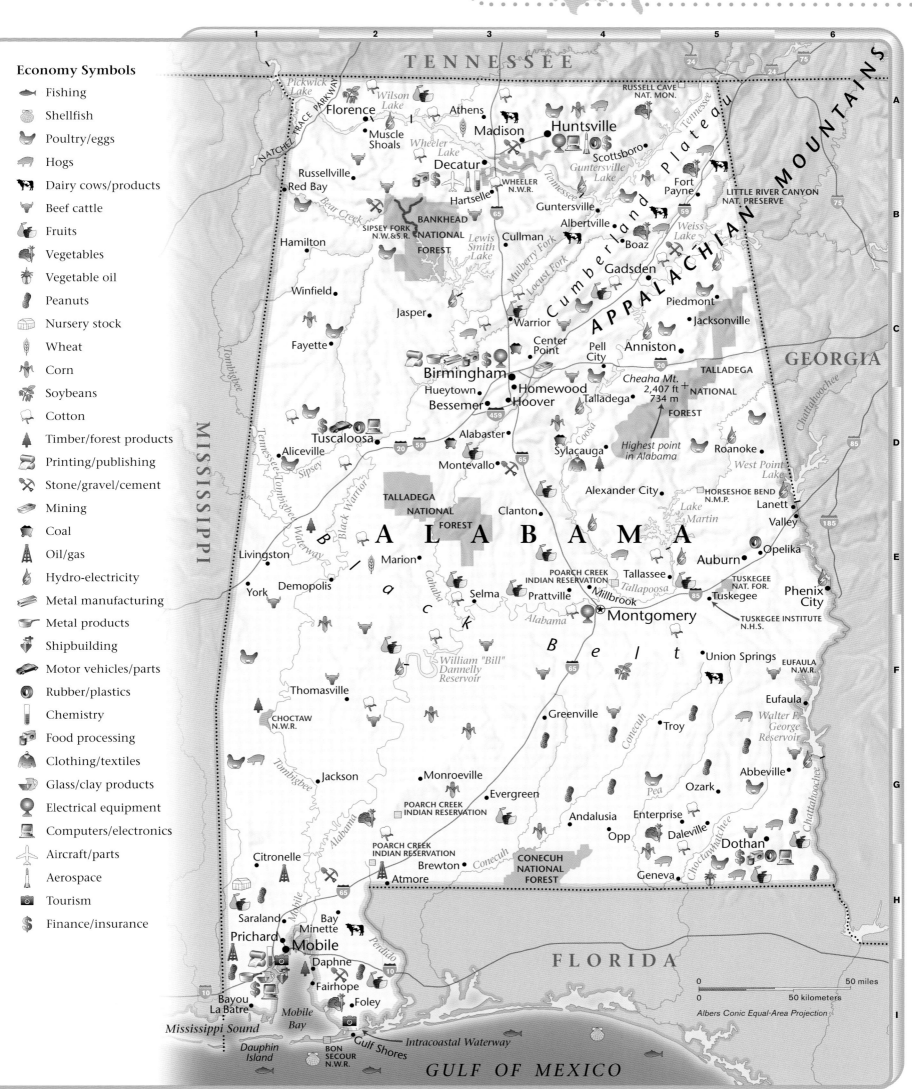

Economy Symbols

- Fishing
- Shellfish
- Poultry/eggs
- Hogs
- Dairy cows/products
- Beef cattle
- Fruits
- Vegetables
- Vegetable oil
- Peanuts
- Nursery stock
- Wheat
- Corn
- Soybeans
- Cotton
- Timber/forest products
- Printing/publishing
- Stone/gravel/cement
- Mining
- Coal
- Oil/gas
- Hydro-electricity
- Metal manufacturing
- Metal products
- Shipbuilding
- Motor vehicles/parts
- Rubber/plastics
- Chemistry
- Food processing
- Clothing/textiles
- Glass/clay products
- Electrical equipment
- Computers/electronics
- Aircraft/parts
- Aerospace
- Tourism
- Finance/insurance

TENNESSEE

MISSISSIPPI

GEORGIA

FLORIDA

GULF OF MEXICO

APPALACHIAN MOUNTAINS

Cumberland Plateau

A L A B A M A

Black Warrior

Black Belt

Places labeled on map

Pickwick Lake, Natchez Trace Parkway, Florence, Wilson Lake, Muscle Shoals, Athens, Madison, Huntsville, Russell Cave Nat. Mon., Wheeler Lake, Decatur, Scottsboro, Russellville, Red Bay, Hartselle, Wheeler N.W.R., Guntersville Lake, Fort Payne, Little River Canyon Nat. Preserve, Guntersville, Bankhead National Forest, Sipsey Fork N.W.&S.R., Lewis Smith Lake, Cullman, Albertville, Boaz, Weiss Lake, Hamilton, Mulberry Fork, Locust Fork, Gadsden, Winfield, Piedmont, Jasper, Warrior, Jacksonville, Fayette, Center Point, Pell City, Anniston, Birmingham, Hueytown, Homewood, Bessemer, Hoover, Talladega, Cheaha Mt. 2,407 ft + 734 m, Talladega National Forest, Tuscaloosa, Aliceville, Alabaster, Sylacauga, Highest point in Alabama, Roanoke, West Point Lake, Montevallo, Lanett, Clanton, Lake Martin, Valley, Alexander City, Horseshoe Bend N.M.P., Livingston, Demopolis, Marion, Opelika, Auburn, Tallassee, Poarch Creek Indian Reservation, Tuskegee Nat. For., Phenix City, York, Selma, Prattville, Millbrook, Tuskegee, Tuskegee Institute N.H.S., William "Bill" Dannelly Reservoir, Montgomery, Union Springs, Eufaula N.W.R., Thomasville, Greenville, Troy, Eufaula, Walter F. George Reservoir, Jackson, Monroeville, Evergreen, Abbeville, Choctaw N.W.R., Ozark, Andalusia, Enterprise, Daleville, Dothan, Poarch Creek Indian Reservation, Opp, Geneva, Citronelle, Brewton, Conecuh National Forest, Atmore, Saraland, Bay Minette, Prichard, Mobile, Daphne, Fairhope, Bayou La Batre, Foley, Mississippi Sound, Mobile Bay, Dauphin Island, Bon Secour N.W.R., Gulf Shores, Intracoastal Waterway

Cheaha Mt.
2,407 ft +
734 m

Highest point
in Alabama

0   50 miles
0   50 kilometers
Albers Conic Equal-Area Projection

THE NATURAL STATE:
ARKANSAS

ARKANSAS

THE BASICS

STATS

Area
53,179 sq mi (137,732 sq km)

Population
2,834,797

Capital
Little Rock
Population 184,422

Largest city
Little Rock
Population 184,422

Ethnic/racial groups
81.1% white; 15.7% African American;
1.0% Asian; .8% Native American.
Hispanic (any race) 5.0%.

Industry
Services, food processing, paper products, transportation, metal products, machinery, electronics

Agriculture
Poultry and eggs, rice, soybeans, cotton, wheat

Statehood
June 15, 1836; 25th state

GEO WHIZ

In 1924 Arkansas's Crater of Diamonds State Park yielded the largest natural diamond ever found in the United States—a 40.23-carat whopper named "Uncle Sam." A 13-year-old girl from Missouri found a 2.93 carat diamond there in 2007.

Since 1936 Stuttgart has been the site of the annual World Championship Duck Calling Contest. The first winner took home a grand total of $6.60. Today, the prize package is worth more than $15,000.

The city of Texarkana is divided by the Arkansas-Texas border. It has two governments, one for each state.

MOCKINGBIRD
APPLE BLOSSOM

ARKANSAS

The land that is Arkansas was explored by the Spanish in 1541 and later by the French, but it came under U.S. control with the Louisiana Purchase in 1803. As settlers arrived, Native Americans were pushed out, and cotton fields spread across the fertile valleys of the Arkansas and Mississippi Rivers. Arkansas became the 25th state in 1836, but joined the Confederacy in 1861. Following the war, Arkansas faced hard times, and many people moved away in search of jobs. Today, agriculture remains an important part of the economy. Rice has replaced cotton as the state's main crop, and poultry and grain production are also important. Natural gas, in the northwestern part of the state, and petroleum, along the southern border with Louisiana, are key mining products in Arkansas. The state is headquarters for Wal-Mart, the world's largest retail chain, and tourism is growing as visitors are attracted to the natural beauty of the Ozark and Ouachita Mountains.

⇧ HOLD ON! A rock climber clings to a sandstone cliff in northwest Arkansas, where the Ozark and Ouachita Mountains make up the Interior Highlands of the United States. The Ouachita are folded mountains, but the Ozarks are really a deeply eroded plateau.

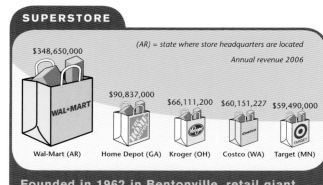

SUPERSTORE

(AR) = state where store headquarters are located

Annual revenue 2006

$348,650,000

$90,837,000 $66,111,200 $60,151,227 $59,490,000

Wal-Mart (AR)   Home Depot (GA)   Kroger (OH)   Costco (WA)   Target (MN)

Founded in 1962 in Bentonville, retail giant Wal-Mart, with more than 4,000 stores nationwide, leads the country in annual revenues.

⇦ BIRDWATCHERS. Biologists and volunteers scan the treetops for a rare ivory-billed woodpecker in the White River National Wildlife Refuge. Established in 1935 along the White River near where it joins the Mississippi, the refuge provides a protected habitat for migratory birds.

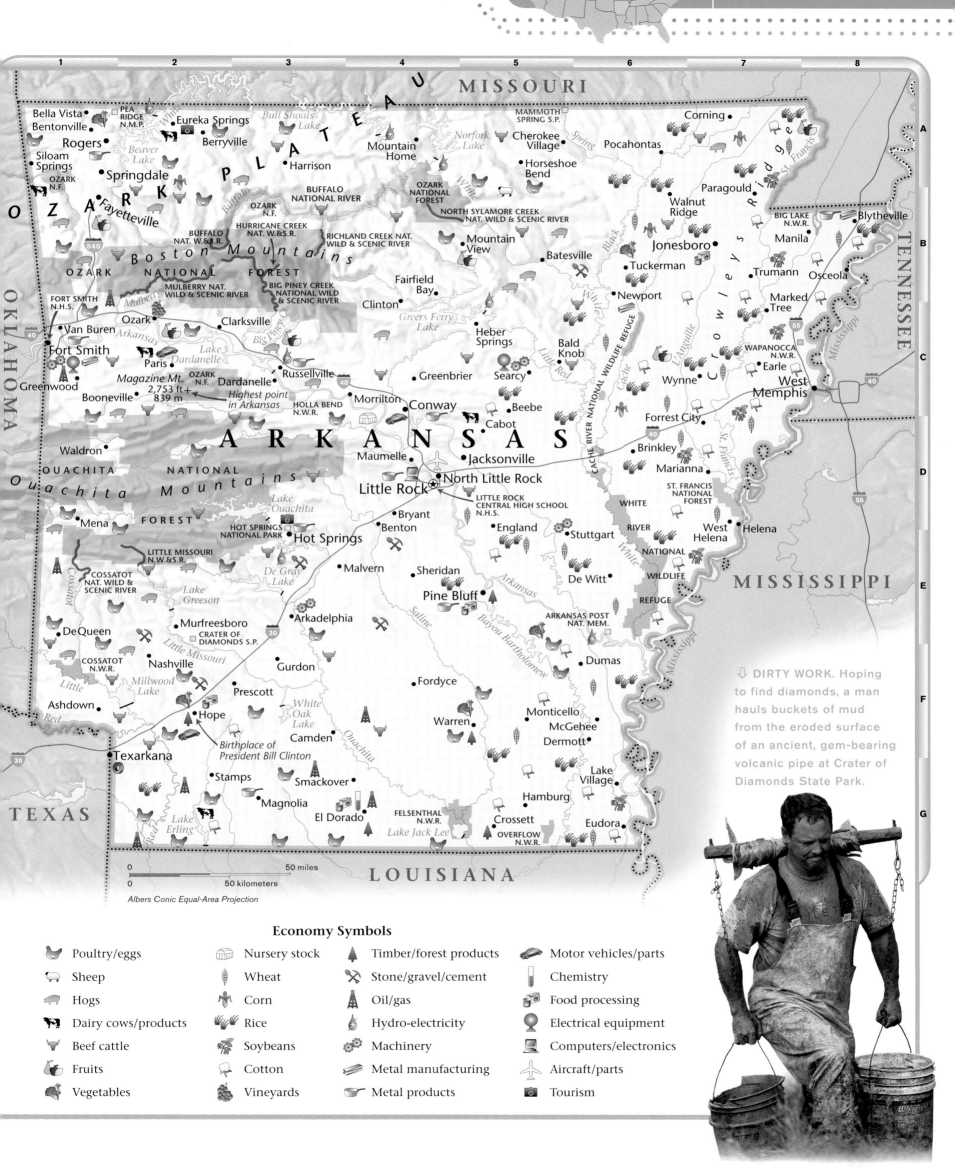

MISSOURI

Bella Vista
Bentonville
PEA RIDGE N.M.P.
Rogers
Eureka Springs
Berryville
Siloam Springs
Springdale
OZARK N.F.
Beaver Lake
White
Bull Shoals Lake
Norfork Lake
Spring
Corning
MAMMOTH SPRING S.P.
Cherokee Village
Pocahontas
Horseshoe Bend
Mountain Home
Harrison
Fayetteville
O Z A R K   P L A T E A U
Buffalo
OZARK N.F.
BUFFALO NATIONAL RIVER
OZARK NATIONAL FOREST
NORTH SYLAMORE CREEK NAT. WILD & SCENIC RIVER
Walnut Ridge
Paragould
Jonesboro
Manila
Blytheville
BIG LAKE N.W.R.
Boston Mountains
HURRICANE CREEK NAT. W.&S.R.
RICHLAND CREEK NAT. WILD & SCENIC RIVER
Mountain View
Batesville
Tuckerman
Trumann
Osceola
OZARK   NATIONAL   FOREST
BUFFALO NAT. W.&S.R.
MULBERRY NAT. WILD & SCENIC RIVER
BIG PINEY CREEK NATIONAL WILD & SCENIC RIVER
Fairfield Bay
Newport
Marked Tree
540
FORT SMITH N.H.S.
Mulberry
Clinton
Greers Ferry Lake
Heber Springs
White
WAPANOCCA N.W.R.
Earle
Crowleys Ridge
St. Francis
Black
Ozark
Clarksville
Arkansas
Van Buren
Fort Smith
40
Paris
Lake Dardanelle
Big Piney
OZARK N.F.
Dardanelle
Russellville
40
Morrilton
Bald Knob
Greenbrier
Searcy
Little Red
L'Anguille
Cache
Wynne
West Memphis
40
Greenwood
Magazine Mt. 2,753 ft+ 839 m
Highest point in Arkansas
HOLLA BEND N.W.R.
Conway
Beebe
Cabot
Forrest City
55
TENNESSEE
Booneville
A R K A N S A S
Maumelle
Jacksonville
Brinkley
Marianna
St. Francis
ST. FRANCIS NATIONAL FOREST
Waldron
O U A C H I T A   N A T I O N A L
North Little Rock
Little Rock
LITTLE ROCK CENTRAL HIGH SCHOOL N.H.S.
CACHE RIVER NATIONAL WILDLIFE REFUGE
WHITE
55
Mena
M o u n t a i n s
Bryant
Benton
England
RIVER
West Helena
Helena
F O R E S T
Lake Ouachita
HOT SPRINGS NATIONAL PARK
Hot Springs
Stuttgart
NATIONAL
LITTLE MISSOURI N.W.&S.R.
De Gray Lake
Malvern
Sheridan
De Witt
WILDLIFE
Ouachita
COSSATOT NAT. WILD & SCENIC RIVER
Lake Greeson
Pine Bluff
Arkansas
REFUGE
DeQueen
Murfreesboro
CRATER OF DIAMONDS S.P.
Arkadelphia
30
ARKANSAS POST NAT. MEM.
Mississippi
MISSISSIPPI
Cossatot
COSSATOT N.W.R.
Nashville
Gurdon
Fordyce
Bayou Bartholomew
Dumas
Little Missouri
Little
Millwood Lake
Prescott
White Oak Lake
Monticello
McGehee
Dermott
Ashdown
Hope
Birthplace of President Bill Clinton
Camden
Warren
Lake Village
30
Red
Texarkana
Stamps
Smackover
Hamburg
TEXAS
Magnolia
El Dorado
FELSENTHAL N.W.R.
Crossett
Eudora
Lake Erling
Lake Jack Lee
OVERFLOW N.W.R.

⬇ DIRTY WORK. Hoping to find diamonds, a man hauls buckets of mud from the eroded surface of an ancient, gem-bearing volcanic pipe at Crater of Diamonds State Park.

LOUISIANA

0   50 miles
0   50 kilometers
Albers Conic Equal-Area Projection

Economy Symbols

Poultry/eggs	Nursery stock	Timber/forest products	Motor vehicles/parts
Sheep	Wheat	Stone/gravel/cement	Chemistry
Hogs	Corn	Oil/gas	Food processing
Dairy cows/products	Rice	Hydro-electricity	Electrical equipment
Beef cattle	Soybeans	Machinery	Computers/electronics
Fruits	Cotton	Metal manufacturing	Aircraft/parts
Vegetables	Vineyards	Metal products	Tourism

THE BASICS

STATS

Area
65,755 sq mi (170,304 sq km)

Population
18,251,243

Capital
Tallahassee
Population 159,012

Largest city
Jacksonville
Population 794,555

Ethnic/racial groups
80.2% white; 15.8% African American; 2.2% Asian; .4% Native American. Hispanic (any race) 20.2%.

Industry
Tourism, health services, business services, communications, banking, electronic equipment, insurance

Agriculture
Citrus fruits, vegetables, field crops, nursery stock, cattle, dairy products

Statehood
March 3, 1845; 27th state

GEO WHIZ

Key West, the southernmost point in the continental U.S., is just 90 miles (145 km) from Cuba.

In 1937 Amelia Earhart and her navigator took off from Miami with the goal of making an around-the-world flight, but disappeared over the Pacific Ocean and were never seen again. You can read all about this famous flying ace in our children's book *Sky Pioneer*, by Corine Szabo.

Everglades National Park, the largest subtropical wilderness in the United States, is home to rare and endangered species such as the American crocodile, Florida panther, and West Indian manatee.

Britton Hill, Florida's highest point, is only 345 feet (105 m) above sea level.

Lightning strikes occur more often in Florida than in any other U.S. state.

MOCKINGBIRD
ORANGE BLOSSOM

FLORIDA

Florida is home to St. Augustine, the country's oldest permanent European settlement, established by the Spanish in 1565. But native peoples had called Florida home long before then. Florida became a U.S. territory in 1821 and a state in 1845. The state's turbulent early history included the Civil War and three wars with Native Americans over control of the land. Railroads opened Florida to migration from the northern states as early as the 1890s. The mild climate and sandy beaches attracted people seeking to escape cold winters in the north. This trend continues today and includes both tourists and retirees. South Florida has a large Hispanic population that has migrated from all over Latin America—especially from nearby Cuba. Florida is working to solve many challenges: competition between city-dwellers and farmers for limited water resources; the annual risk of tropical storms; and the need to preserve its natural environment, including the vast Everglades wetland.

⇧ CULTURAL PRIDE. A young girl marches in Orlando's Puerto Rican Parade, a celebration of the music, dance, and culture of this U.S. island territory.

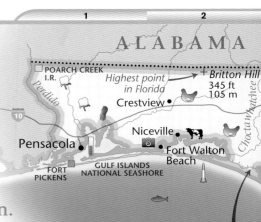

ALABAMA

POARCH CREEK I.R.
Perdido
Highest point in Florida
Crestview
+ Britton Hill 345 ft 105 m
Niceville
Pensacola
Fort Walton Beach
FORT PICKENS
GULF ISLANDS NATIONAL SEASHORE
Choctawhatchee

Intracoasta Waterway

⇨ LIFTOFF! Crowds watch as a space shuttle rises amid clouds of steam at NASA's Kennedy Space Center on Florida's Atlantic coast. The center has been the launch site for all U.S. human space flight missions.

1   2

JUICY HARVEST

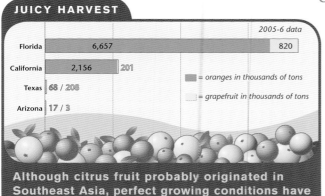

		2005-6 data
Florida	6,657	820
California	2,156	201
Texas	68 / 208	
Arizona	17 / 3	

■ = oranges in thousands of tons
□ = grapefruit in thousands of tons

Although citrus fruit probably originated in Southeast Asia, perfect growing conditions have made Florida the leading producer in the U.S.

⇨ GENTLE GIANT. The manatee, which is closely related to the elephant, is Florida's state marine mammal. Averaging 10 feet (3 m) in length and 1,000 pounds (453 kg), these endangered animals live on a diet of sea grasses.

GEORGIA

Marianna
Lake Seminole
Panama City
Tallahassee
St. Marks N.W.R.
Perry
Live Oak
Lake City
Apalachicola National Forest
St. Vincent N.W.R.
Ochlockonee
Apalachicola

OKEFENOKEE NATIONAL WILDLIFE REFUGE

FLORIDA

Fernandina Beach
TIMUCUAN ECOLOGICAL AND HISTORIC PRESERVE
FORT CAROLINE NAT. MEM.
Jacksonville
Jacksonville Beach

ATLANTIC OCEAN

Suwannee
Gainesville
Palatka
St. Johns

CASTILLO DE SAN MARCOS NAT. MON.
St. Augustine
FORT MATANZAS NAT. MON.
Palm Coast

Oldest permanent European settlement on the continent, est. 1565

LOWER SUWANNEE NATIONAL WILDLIFE REFUGE
Ocala
CEDAR KEYS N.W.R.
Homosassa Springs
CHASSAHOWITZKA N.W.R.
CRYSTAL RIVER N.W.R.
Leesburg

OCALA NATIONAL FOREST
Lake George
Sanford
De Land
Deltona

Daytona Beach
LAKE WOODRUFF N.W.R.
New Smyrna Beach

CANAVERAL NATIONAL SEASHORE

Spring Hill
Bayonet Point
Tarpon Springs
Clearwater
TAMPA I.R.
Lakeland
St. Petersburg
PINELLAS N.W.R.
Tampa
EGMONT KEY N.W.R.
DE SOTO NAT. MEM.
Bradenton
Sarasota
Venice
Port Charlotte

Walt Disney World & EPCOT Center
Orlando
Kissimmee
Haines City
Winter Haven
Tampa Bay
Sebring
Arcadia
BRIGHTON SEMINOLE I.R.
Punta Gorda

Titusville
MERRITT ISLAND N.W.R.
John F. Kennedy Space Center
Cape Canaveral
Merritt Island
Melbourne
Palm Bay
PELICAN ISLAND N.W.R.
Vero Beach
Fort Pierce
FORT PIERCE I.R.
Port St. Lucie

FLORIDA'S TURNPIKE
Indian
Kissimmee
Peace
St. Lucie Canal
Lake Okeechobee
Caloosahatchee

HOBE SOUND N.W.R.
LOXAHATCHEE NAT. WILD & SCENIC RIVER
Jupiter
West Palm Beach

Charlotte Harbor
Cape Coral
Fort Myers
J. N. "DING" DARLING N.W.R.
Immokalee
Sanibel Island

Belle Glade
ARTHUR R. MARSHALL LOXAHATCHEE N.W.R.
IMMOKALEE I.R.
BIG CYPRESS SEMINOLE I.R.
COCONUT CREEK I.R.

Delray Beach
Boca Raton
Coral Springs
Fort Lauderdale

Naples
Big Cypress Swamp
BIG CYPRESS NATIONAL PRESERVE
MICCOSUKEE INDIAN RES.
SEMINOLE I.R.
HOLLYWOOD I.R.
Hollywood
Hialeah
Kendall
Miami
Miami Beach

GULF OF MEXICO
Ten Thousand Islands
The Everglades
EVERGLADES NATIONAL PARK
BISCAYNE N.P.
Biscayne Bay

Largest subtropical wilderness in the 48 contiguous states

Cape Sable
Florida Bay
Homestead
Key Largo

FLORIDA KEYS NATIONAL MARINE SANCTUARY
DRY TORTUGAS NATIONAL PARK
GREAT WHITE HERON N.W.R.
KEY WEST N.W.R.
NAT. KEY DEER REFUGE
Marathon
FLORIDA KEYS
Key West

Southernmost point in the continental United States

STRAITS OF FLORIDA

0 100 miles
0 100 kilometers
Albers Conic Equal-Area Projection

Economy Symbols

- Fishing
- Lobster fishing
- Shellfish
- Poultry/eggs
- Hogs
- Dairy cows
- Beef cattle
- Fruits
- Vegetables
- Peanuts
- Nursery stock
- Corn
- Rice
- Sugarcane
- Cotton

- Tobacco
- Timber/forest products
- Printing/publishing
- Hydro-electricity
- Metal products
- Shipbuilding
- Chemistry
- Food processing
- Electrical equipment
- Computers/electronics
- Scientific instruments
- Aerospace
- Tourism
- Finance/insurance

25
HOUR MINUTE SECOND
00 06

THE BASICS

STATS

Area
59,425 sq mi (153,910 sq km)

Population
9,544,750

Capital
Atlanta
Population 486,411

Largest city
Atlanta
Population 486,411

Ethnic/racial groups
65.8% white; 29.9% African American; 2.8% Asian; .3% Native American. Hispanic (any race) 7.5%.

Industry
Textiles and clothing, transportation equipment, food processing, paper products, chemicals, electrical equipment, tourism

Agriculture
Poultry and eggs, cotton, peanuts, vegetables, sweet corn, melons, cattle

Statehood
January 2, 1788; 4th state

GEO WHIZ

The Okefenokee Swamp, the largest swamp in North America, is home to many meat-eating plants, which capture animals for food. The swamp was also the setting for the adventures of Pogo the Possum, Albert the Alligator, and other characters created by cartoonist Walt Kelly.

The Georgia Aquarium in Atlanta, the world's largest, features more than 100,000 animals in more than 8 million gallons (30.3 million liters) of water.

Stone Mountain near Atlanta is famous for its enormous carving of three historic figures from the Confederate States of America: Stonewall Jackson, Robert E. Lee, and Jefferson Davis. It is one of the largest single masses of exposed granite in the world.

BROWN THRASHER
CHEROKEE ROSE

GEORGIA

When Spanish explorers arrived in the mid-1500s in what would become Georgia, they found the land already occupied by Cherokees, Creeks, and other native peoples. Georgia was the frontier separating Spanish Florida and English South Carolina, but in 1733 James Oglethorpe founded a new colony on the site of present-day Savannah. Georgia became the 4th state in 1788 and built an economy based on agriculture and slave labor. The state suffered widespread destruction during the Civil War and endured a long period of poverty in the years that followed. Modern-day Georgia is part of the fast-changing Sunbelt region. Agriculture—especially poultry, cotton, and forest products—remains important. Atlanta has emerged as a regional center of banking, telecommunications, and transportation, and Savannah is a major container port near the Atlantic coast, linking the state to the global economy. Historic sites, sports, and beaches draw thousands of tourists to the state every year.

⇧ CASH CROP. Peanuts are a big moneymaker in Georgia, where almost half the U.S. crop is grown—about half of which is used to make peanut butter.

⇧ LIGHT SHOW. Busy Interstate traffic appears as ribbons of light below Atlanta's nighttime skyline. Atlanta is a center of economic growth, leading all cities in the region with 12 Fortune 500 companies. Its metropolitan area leads the country in population growth, adding almost one million people since 2000.

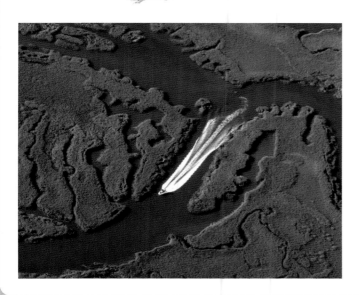

⇦ PAST MEETS PRESENT. Georgia's 100-mile (160-km) coastline is laced with barrier islands, wetlands, and winding streams. In the 19th century plantations grew Sea Island cotton here. Today, tourists are attracted to the area's natural beauty and beaches.

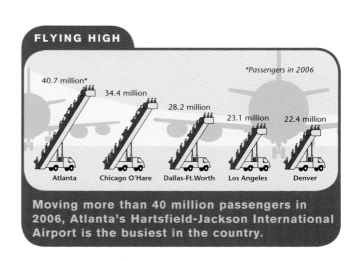

FLYING HIGH

*Passengers in 2006

40.7 million* — Atlanta
34.4 million — Chicago O'Hare
28.2 million — Dallas-Ft.Worth
23.1 million — Los Angeles
22.4 million — Denver

Moving more than 40 million passengers in 2006, Atlanta's Hartsfield-Jackson International Airport is the busiest in the country.

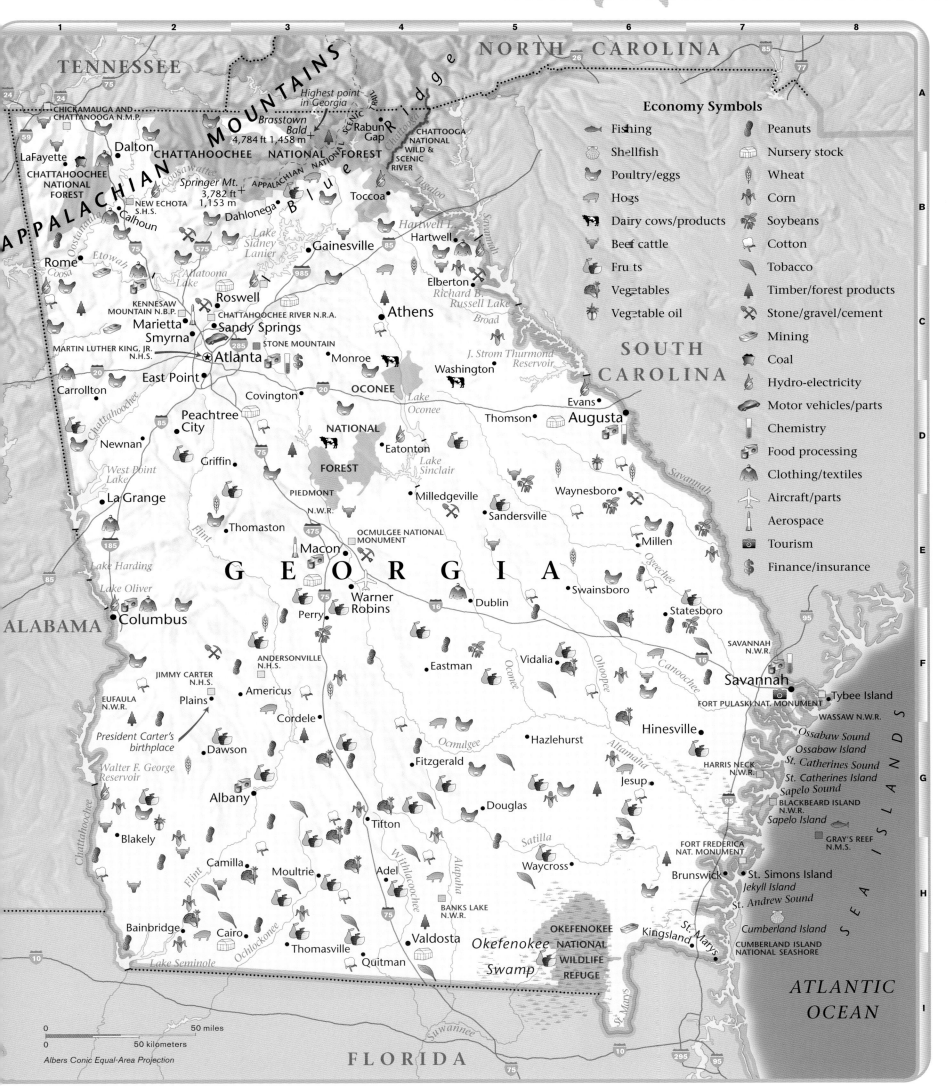

TENNESSEE

NORTH CAROLINA

APPALACHIAN MOUNTAINS

Blue Ridge

Highest point in Georgia
Brasstown Bald
4,784 ft 1,458 m

Rabun Gap

CHICKAMAUGA AND CHATTANOOGA N.M.P.

LaFayette
Dalton

CHATTAHOOCHEE NATIONAL FOREST

CHATTAHOOCHEE NATIONAL FOREST

APPALACHIAN NATIONAL FOREST

CHATTOOGA NATIONAL WILD & SCENIC RIVER

Springer Mt.
3,782 ft
1,153 m

NEW ECHOTA S.H.S.

Calhoun

Dahlonega

Toccoa

Rome

Etowah

Lake Sidney Lanier

Gainesville

Hartwell L.
Hartwell

Allatoona Lake

Elberton

Richard B. Russell Lake

Roswell

KENNESAW MOUNTAIN N.B.P.

CHATTAHOOCHEE RIVER N.R.A.

Athens

Broad

Marietta
Smyrna

Sandy Springs

STONE MOUNTAIN

SOUTH CAROLINA

MARTIN LUTHER KING, JR. N.H.S.

Atlanta

Monroe

Washington

J. Strom Thurmond Reservoir

East Point

Carrollton

Covington

OCONEE

Lake Oconee

Evans

Thomson
Augusta

Peachtree City

NATIONAL

Eatonton

Newnan

West Point Lake

Griffin

FOREST

Lake Sinclair

Savannah

La Grange

PIEDMONT N.W.R.

Milledgeville

Waynesboro

Thomaston

Sandersville

Lake Harding

Flint

OCMULGEE NATIONAL MONUMENT

Macon

Millen

Lake Oliver

GEORGIA

Warner Robins

Dublin

Swainsboro

Ogeechee

ALABAMA

Columbus

Perry

Statesboro

SAVANNAH N.W.R.

ANDERSONVILLE N.H.S.

Eastman

Vidalia

Ocmulgee

Ohoopee

Canoochee

Savannah

JIMMY CARTER N.H.S.

Americus

Plains

EUFAULA N.W.R.

Cordele

Hazlehurst

Altamaha

Hinesville

FORT PULASKI NAT. MONUMENT

WASSAW N.W.R.

President Carter's birthplace

Dawson

Fitzgerald

Ocmulgee

Jesup

HARRIS NECK N.W.R.

Ossabaw Sound
Ossabaw Island

Walter F. George Reservoir

Albany

Tifton

Satilla

Douglas

St. Catherines Sound
St. Catherines Island

Sapelo Sound

BLACKBEARD ISLAND N.W.R.

Sapelo Island

GRAY'S REEF N.M.S.

Blakely

Chattahoochee

Camilla

Moultrie

Adel

Withlacoochee

Alapaha

Waycross

FORT FREDERICA NAT. MONUMENT

Brunswick

St. Simons Island
Jekyll Island

St. Andrew Sound

Bainbridge

Cairo

BANKS LAKE N.W.R.

OKEFENOKEE NATIONAL WILDLIFE REFUGE

Kingsland

Cumberland Island

CUMBERLAND ISLAND NATIONAL SEASHORE

Thomasville

Valdosta

Okefenokee Swamp

St. Marys

SEA ISLANDS

Lake Seminole

Ochlockonee

Quitman

Suwannee

ATLANTIC OCEAN

FLORIDA

Economy Symbols

- Fishing
- Shellfish
- Poultry/eggs
- Hogs
- Dairy cows/products
- Beef cattle
- Fruits
- Vegetables
- Vegetable oil
- Peanuts
- Nursery stock
- Wheat
- Corn
- Soybeans
- Cotton
- Tobacco
- Timber/forest products
- Stone/gravel/cement
- Mining
- Coal
- Hydro-electricity
- Motor vehicles/parts
- Chemistry
- Food processing
- Clothing/textiles
- Aircraft/parts
- Aerospace
- Tourism
- Finance/insurance

0   50 miles
0   50 kilometers
Albers Conic Equal-Area Projection

THE BASICS

STATS

Area
40,409 sq mi (104,659 sq km)

Population
4,241,474

Capital
Frankfort
Population 27,408

Largest city
Louisville Metro
Population 701,500

Ethnic/racial groups
90.2% white; 7.5% African American;
1.0% Asian; .2% Native American.
Hispanic (any race) 2.0%.

Industry
Manufacturing, services, government,
finance, insurance, real estate, retail
trade, transportation, wholesale trade,
construction, mining

Agriculture
Horses, tobacco, cattle, corn, dairy
products

Statehood
June 1, 1792; 15th state

GEO WHIZ

A favorite Kentucky dessert is Derby
Pie, a rich chocolate-and-walnut
pastry that was first created by George
Kern, manager of the Melrose Inn, in
Prospect, in the 1950s. It became so
popular that the name was registered
with the U.S. Patent Office and the
Commonwealth of Kentucky.

 Pleasant Hill, near Lexington, was
the site of a Shaker religious
community. It is now a National
Historic Site where visitors can
tour the living history museum.

The song "Happy Birthday to You,"
one of the most popular songs in the
English language, was the creation of
two Louisville sisters in 1893.

Post-it notes are manufactured
exclusively in Cynthiana. Millions
of self-stick notes in 27 sizes
and 57 colors are produced
each year.

CARDINAL

GOLDENROD

KENTUCKY

1   2   3

The original inhabitants of the area known today as Kentucky were Native Americans, but a treaty with the Cherokees, signed in 1775, opened the territory to settlers—including the legendary Daniel Boone—from the soon-to-be independent eastern colonies. In 1776 Kentucky became a western county of the state of Virginia. In 1792 it became the 15th state of the young U.S. Eastern Kentucky is a part of Appalachia, a region rich in soft bituminous coal but burdened with environmental problems that often accompany the mining industry. The region is known for crafts and music that can be traced back to Scotch-Irish immigrants who settled there. In central Kentucky, the Bluegrass region produces some of the finest Thoroughbred horses in the world, and the Kentucky Derby, held in Louisville, is a part of racing's coveted Triple Crown. In western Kentucky, coal found near the surface is strip mined, leaving scars on the landscape, but federal laws now require that the land be restored.

BENEATH THE SURFACE

Mammoth Cave System, KY	367 miles/591 km
Jewel Cave, SD	140 miles/225 km
Wind Cave, SD	125 miles/201 km
Lechuguilla Cave, NM	121 miles/195 km
Fisher Ridge Cave System, KY	110 miles/177 km

Caves, natural openings in Earth's surface extending beyond the reach of sunlight, are often created by water dissolving limestone.

⇧ THEY'RE OFF! Riders and horses press for the finish line at Churchill Downs, in Louisville. Kentucky is a major breeder of Thoroughbred race horses, and horses are the leading source of farm income in the state.

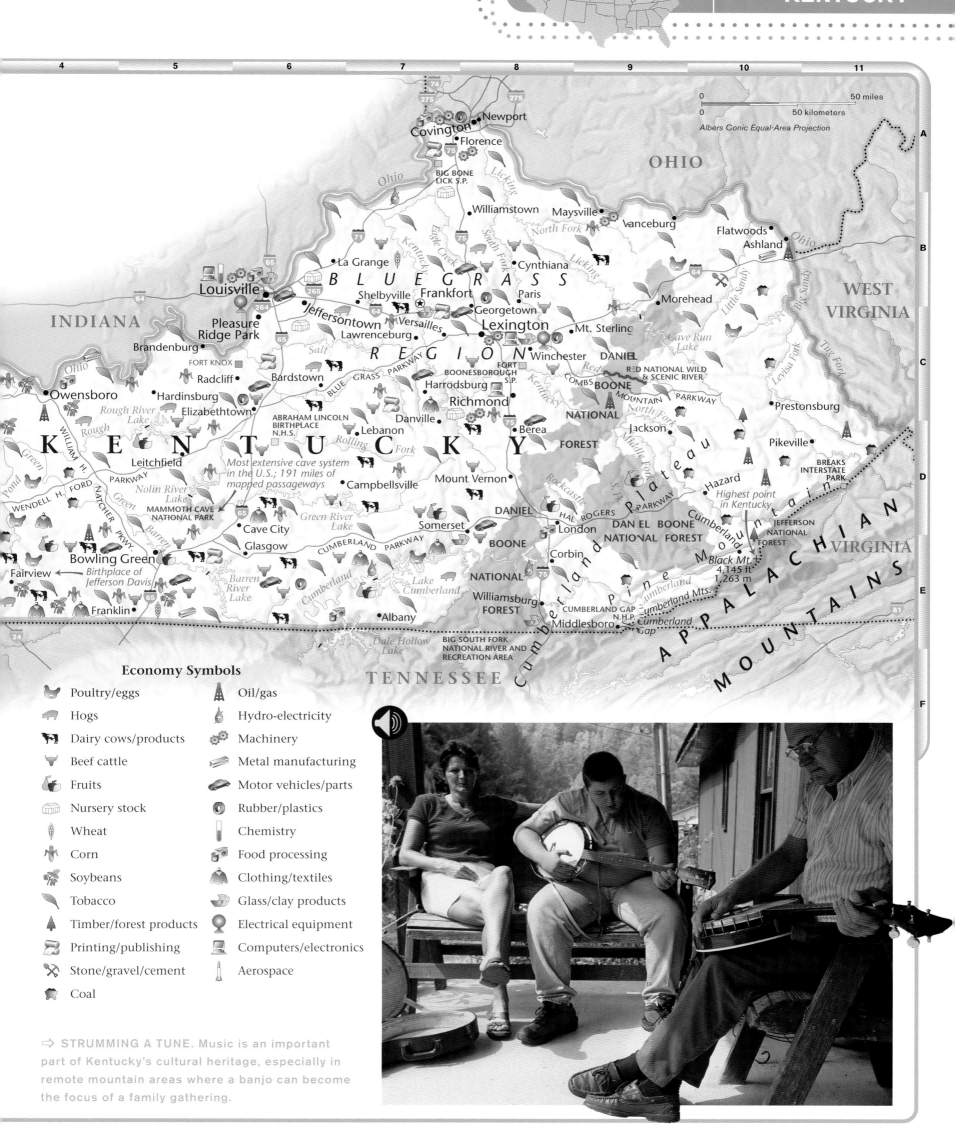

OHIO

WEST
VIRGINIA

INDIANA

K E N T U C K Y

B L U E G R A S S

R E G I O N

VIRGINIA

APPALACHIAN MOUNTAINS

TENNESSEE

Newport
Covington
Florence
BIG BONE LICK S.P.
Williamstown
Maysville
Vanceburg
Flatwoods
Ashland
La Grange
Cynthiana
Louisville
Shelbyville
Frankfort
Paris
Georgetown
Morehead
Jeffersontown
Versailles
Lexington
Mt. Sterling
Pleasure Ridge Park
Lawrenceburg
Winchester
DANIEL
Cave Run Lake
Brandenburg
Salt
FORT KNOX
BLUE GRASS PARKWAY
FORT BOONESBOROUGH S.P.
RED NATIONAL WILD & SCENIC RIVER
Radcliff
Bardstown
Harrodsburg
COMBS
BOONE
Prestonsburg
Owensboro
Hardinsburg
Richmond
MOUNTAIN PARKWAY
Rough River Lake
Elizabethtown
Danville
Berea
NATIONAL
Jackson
Pikeville
Rough
ABRAHAM LINCOLN BIRTHPLACE N.H.S.
Lebanon
FOREST
BREAKS INTERSTATE PARK
Leitchfield
Most extensive cave system in the U.S.; 191 miles of mapped passageways
Campbellsville
Mount Vernon
Highest point in Kentucky
WENDELL H. FORD PARKWAY
Nolin River Lake
DANIEL
HAL ROGERS PARKWAY
Hazard
JEFFERSON NATIONAL FOREST
MAMMOTH CAVE NATIONAL PARK
Green River Lake
BOONE
DANIEL BOONE
Cave City
Somerset
London
NATIONAL FOREST
Glasgow
CUMBERLAND PARKWAY
Corbin
Black Mt. 4,145 ft 1,263 m
Bowling Green
Lake Cumberland
Pine Mountain
Fairview
Birthplace of Jefferson Davis
Barren River Lake
NATIONAL
Williamsburg
FOREST
CUMBERLAND GAP N.H.P.
Cumberland Mts.
Franklin
Albany
Middlesboro
Cumberland Gap
BIG SOUTH FORK NATIONAL RIVER AND RECREATION AREA
Dale Hollow Lake

50 miles
50 kilometers
Albers Conic Equal-Area Projection

Economy Symbols

Poultry/eggs		Oil/gas	
Hogs		Hydro-electricity	
Dairy cows/products		Machinery	
Beef cattle		Metal manufacturing	
Fruits		Motor vehicles/parts	
Nursery stock		Rubber/plastics	
Wheat		Chemistry	
Corn		Food processing	
Soybeans		Clothing/textiles	
Tobacco		Glass/clay products	
Timber/forest products		Electrical equipment	
Printing/publishing		Computers/electronics	
Stone/gravel/cement		Aerospace	
Coal			

⇨ STRUMMING A TUNE. Music is an important part of Kentucky's cultural heritage, especially in remote mountain areas where a banjo can become the focus of a family gathering.

THE PELICAN STATE:
LOUISIANA

LOUISIANA

THE BASICS

STATS

Area
51,840 sq mi (134,265 sq km)

Population
4,293,204

Capital
Baton Rouge
Population 229,553

Largest city
Baton Rouge
Population 229,553

Ethnic/racial groups
65.4% white; 31.7% African
American; 1.4% Asian; .6% Native
American. Hispanic (any race) 2.9%.

Industry
Chemicals, petroleum products,
food processing, health services,
tourism, oil and natural gas extraction,
paper products

Agriculture
Forest products, poultry, marine
fisheries, sugarcane, rice, dairy
products, cotton, cattle, aquaculture

Statehood
April 30, 1812; 18th state

GEO WHIZ

The brown pelican, the state bird
of Louisiana, was placed on the
endangered species list in 1970.
The species has made a remarkable
recovery in the Atlantic coastal states,
but it is still considered endangered in
the Gulf Coast area.

The magnolia, Louisiana's state flower,
is the oldest flowering plant in the
world. Some species are believed to
be 100 million years old.

Cajuns, people whose French-
speaking ancestors were exiled
by the British from Acadia,
in what is now Canada,
live primarily in the bayou
region of Louisiana. Their
distinctive music and spicy
food have become popular
throughout the country.

BROWN PELICAN
MAGNOLIA

Louisiana's Native American heritage is evident in place-names such as Natchitoches and Opelousas. Spanish sailors explored the area in 1528, but the French, traveling down the Mississippi River, established permanent settlements in the mid-17th century and named the region for King Louis XIV. The U.S. gained possession of the territory as part of the Louisiana Purchase in 1803, and Louisiana became the 18th state in 1812. New Orleans and the Port of South Louisiana, located near the delta of the Mississippi River, are Louisiana's main ports. Trade from the interior of the U.S. moves through these ports and out to world markets. Oil and gas are drilled in the Mississippi Delta area, and coastal waters are an important source of seafood. Louisiana is vulnerable to tropical storms. In late August 2005 Hurricane Katrina roared in off the Gulf of Mexico, flooding towns, breaking through levees, and changing forever the lives of everyone in southern Louisiana.

⇧ TASTY HARVEST.
Louisiana produces
almost half of all shrimp
caught in the U.S. Most
of this harvest comes
from the Barataria-
Terrebonne region, an
estuary at the mouth of
the Mississippi River
that supports shrimp,
oysters, crabs, and fish.

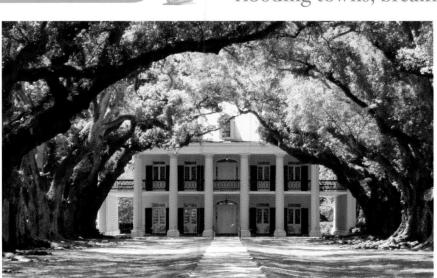

⇦ AVENUE TO THE PAST. Stately
live oaks, believed to be 300 years
old, frame Oak Alley Plantation on
the banks of the Mississippi River
west of New Orleans. Built in 1839,
the house has been restored to its
former grandeur and is open to the
public for tours and private events.

1 2

Springhill
Vivian
Caddo
Lake
KISATCHI
NATIONAL
FOREST
Red
Minder
220
Shreveport Bossier
City
20
Lake
Bistineau
49
Mansfield
Red
Natchitoches
CANE RIVER CREOLE N.H.P.
AND HERITAGE AREA
Many
Toledo
Bend
Reservoir
Leesville
TEXAS
Rosepine
De Ridder
Sabine
De Quincy
Sulphur
10
Lake
Charle
Intracoastal
CAMERON
PRAIRIE
N.W.R.
Calcasieu
Lake
Sabine
Lake SABINE NAT. WILDLIFE REFUGE

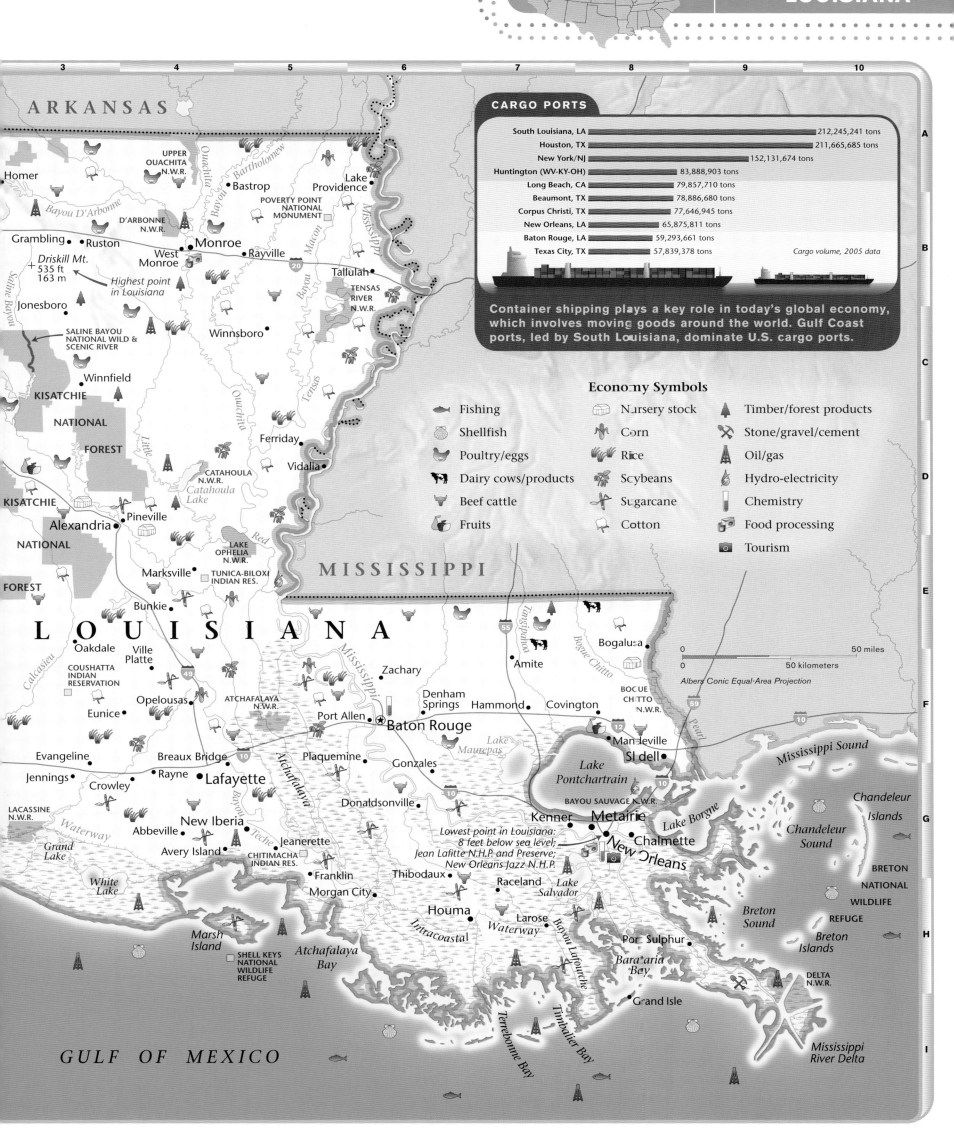

3 4 5 6 7 8 9 10

ARKANSAS

Homer

Bayou D'Arbonne

UPPER
OUACHITA
N.W.R.

Bastrop

Lake
Providence

POVERTY POINT
NATIONAL
MONUMENT

D'ARBONNE
N.W.R.

Grambling Ruston West
Monroe Monroe Rayville

Driskill Mt.
+ 535 ft
163 m

Tallulah

Highest point
in Louisiana

TENSAS
RIVER
N.W.R.

Jonesboro

SALINE BAYOU
NATIONAL WILD &
SCENIC RIVER

Winnsboro

Winnfield

KISATCHIE

Ferriday

NATIONAL

Vidalia

FOREST

CATAHOULA
N.W.R.
Catahoula
Lake

KISATCHIE

Alexandria Pineville

NATIONAL

LAKE
OPHELIA
N.W.R.

FOREST

Marksville

TUNICA-BILOXI
INDIAN RES.

MISSISSIPPI

Bunkie

L O U I S I A N A

Oakdale Ville
Platte

COUSHATTA
INDIAN
RESERVATION

Zachary

Opelousas

ATCHAFALAYA
N.W.R.

Denham
Springs Hammond Covington

Amite

Bogalusa

BOC UE
CHITTO
N.W.R.

Eunice

Port Allen Baton Rouge

Mandeville

Evangeline Breaux Bridge

Plaquemine

Gonzales

Lake
Maurepas

Slidell

Jennings Rayne Lafayette

Crowley

Lake
Pontchartrain

Donaldsonville

Abbeville New Iberia

BAYOU SAUVAGE N.W.R.

Chandeleur
Islands

LACASSINE
N.W.R.

Waterway

Avery Island

Jeanerette

CHITIMACHA
INDIAN RES.

Lowest point in Louisiana:
8 feet below sea level;
Jean Lafitte N.H.P. and Preserve;
New Orleans Jazz N.H.P.

Kenner Metairie

Lake Borgne

Chandeleur
Sound

Grand
Lake

White
Lake

Franklin

Morgan City

Thibodaux

Raceland

Chalmette

New Orleans

BRETON

NATIONAL

Marsh
Island

SHELL KEYS
NATIONAL
WILDLIFE
REFUGE

Atchafalaya
Bay

Houma

Larose

Lake
Salvador

Intracoastal
Waterway

Breton
Sound

WILDLIFE

REFUGE

Por Sulphur

Barataria
Bay

Breton
Islands

DELTA
N.W.R.

Grand Isle

GULF OF MEXICO

Mississippi
River Delta

CARGO PORTS

South Louisiana, LA	212,245,241 tons
Houston, TX	211,665,685 tons
New York/NJ	152,131,674 tons
Huntington (WV-KY-OH)	83,888,903 tons
Long Beach, CA	79,857,710 tons
Beaumont, TX	78,886,680 tons
Corpus Christi, TX	77,646,945 tons
New Orleans, LA	65,875,811 tons
Baton Rouge, LA	59,293,661 tons
Texas City, TX	57,839,378 tons

Cargo volume, 2005 data

Container shipping plays a key role in today's global economy,
which involves moving goods around the world. Gulf Coast
ports, led by South Louisiana, dominate U.S. cargo ports.

Economy Symbols

- Fishing
- Shellfish
- Poultry/eggs
- Dairy cows/products
- Beef cattle
- Fruits
- Nursery stock
- Corn
- Rice
- Soybeans
- Sugarcane
- Cotton
- Timber/forest products
- Stone/gravel/cement
- Oil/gas
- Hydro-electricity
- Chemistry
- Food processing
- Tourism

0   50 miles
0   50 kilometers

Albers Conic Equal-Area Projection

THE BASICS

STATS

Area
48,430 sq mi (125,434 sq km)

Population
2,918,785

Capital
Jackson
Population 176,614

Largest city
Jackson
Population 176,614

Ethnic/racial groups
60.9% white; 37.1% African American;
.8% Asian; .5% Native American.
Hispanic (any race) 1.8%.

Industry
Petroleum products, health services,
electronic equipment, transportation, banking, forest products,
communications

Agriculture
Poultry and eggs, cotton, catfish,
soybeans, cattle, rice, dairy products

Statehood
December 10, 1817; 20th state

GEO WHIZ

The Windsor Ruins, located near Port
Gibson, are 23 monolithic columns that
once made up the largest antebellum
mansion in the state. The mansion
survived the Civil War but was destroyed
by a fire in 1890.

The Marine Life Oceanarium in Gulfport
was almost completely destroyed
by Hurricane Katrina in 2005. Eight
of its 14 bottlenose dolphins were
swept into the Gulf of Mexico by a
40-foot (12-m) wave. These animals
and two sea lions named Splash and
Elliot were eventually rescued.
Others were not so lucky.

Greenville is the birthplace of
Jim Henson, creator of Kermit
the Frog, Miss Piggy, Big Bird,
and other famous Muppets.

MOCKINGBIRD

MAGNOLIA

MISSISSIPPI

Mississippi is named for the river that forms its western boundary. The name comes from the Chippewa words *mici zibi,* meaning "great river." Indeed it is a great river, draining much of the interior U.S. and providing a trade artery to the world. Explored by the Spanish in 1540 and claimed by the French in 1699, the territory of Mississippi passed to the U.S. in 1783 and became the 20th state in 1817. For more than a hundred years following statehood, Mississippi was the center of U.S. cotton production and trade. The fertile soils and mild climate of the delta region in northwestern Mississippi provided a perfect environment for cotton, a crop that depended on slave labor. When the Civil War broke out, it took a heavy toll on the state. Today, poverty, especially in rural areas, is a major challenge for the state where agriculture—poultry, cotton, soybeans, and rice—is still the base of the economy.

⇧ SINGING THE BLUES. B.B. King
sings the soulful sounds of the blues,
a music form that traces its roots to
Mississippi's cotton fields and the
sorrows of West Africans traveling
on slave ships to the Americas.

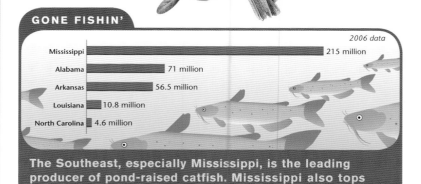

GONE FISHIN'

2006 data

Mississippi	215 million
Alabama	71 million
Arkansas	56.5 million
Louisiana	10.8 million
North Carolina	4.6 million

The Southeast, especially Mississippi, is the leading
producer of pond-raised catfish. Mississippi also tops
all other states in revenue for catfish sales.

⇨ BIG WHEEL TURNING. Now popular with tourists,
paddlewheel boats made the Mississippi River a
major artery for trade and travel in the 19th century.

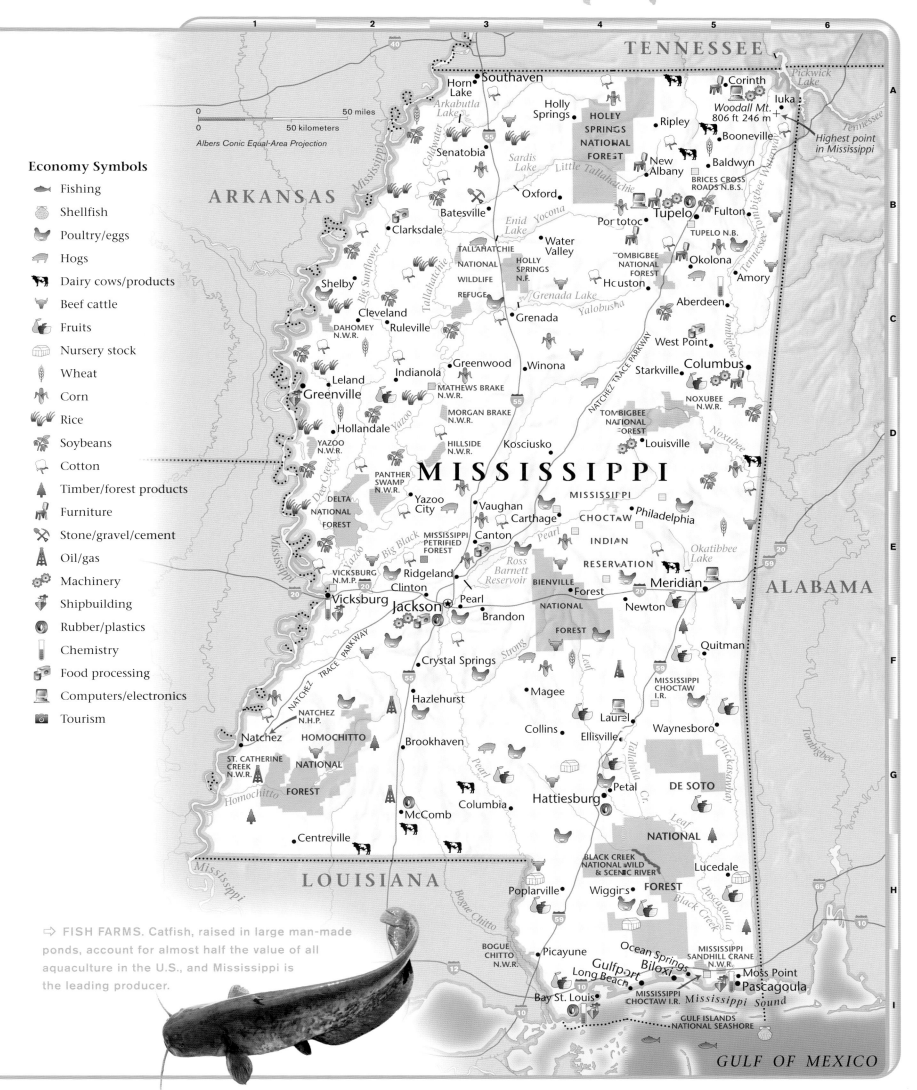

Economy Symbols

- Fishing
- Shellfish
- Poultry/eggs
- Hogs
- Dairy cows/products
- Beef cattle
- Fruits
- Nursery stock
- Wheat
- Corn
- Rice
- Soybeans
- Cotton
- Timber/forest products
- Furniture
- Stone/gravel/cement
- Oil/gas
- Machinery
- Shipbuilding
- Rubber/plastics
- Chemistry
- Food processing
- Computers/electronics
- Tourism

0   50 miles
0   50 kilometers
Albers Conic Equal-Area Projection

TENNESSEE

ARKANSAS

ALABAMA

LOUISIANA

MISSISSIPPI

Pickwick Lake

Southaven
Horn Lake
Arkabutla Lake
Holly Springs
HOLLY SPRINGS NATIONAL FOREST
Corinth
Iuka
Woodall Mt. 806 ft 246 m
Highest point in Mississippi
Ripley
Booneville
Baldwyn
New Albany
BRICES CROSS ROADS N.B.S.
Senatobia
Sardis Lake
Oxford
Little Tallahatchie
Coldwater
Tupelo
Fulton
Batesville
Enid Lake
Yocona
Por totoc
TUPELO N.B.
Clarksdale
Water Valley
OMBIGBEE NATIONAL FOREST
Okolona
Amory
TALLAHATCHIE NATIONAL WILDLIFE REFUGE
HOLLY SPRINGS N.F.
Hcuston
Aberdeen
Shelby
Big Sunflower
Grenada Lake
Grenada
Tallahatchie
Yalobusha
Cleveland
Ruleville
West Point
DAHOMEY N.W.R.
Greenwood
Winona
Starkville
Columbus
Leland
Indianola
Natchez Trace Parkway
NOXUBEE N.W.R.
Greenville
MATHEWS BRAKE N.W.R.
TOMBIGBEE NATIONAL FOREST
Louisville
Noxubee
Hollandale
Yazoo
MORGAN BRAKE N.W.R.
YAZOO N.W.R.
HILLSIDE N.W.R.
Kosciusko
Deer Creek
PANTHER SWAMP N.W.R.
MISSISSIPPI
DELTA NATIONAL FOREST
Yazoo City
Vaughan
Carthage
CHOCTAW
Philadelphia
INDIAN
Okatibbee Lake
MISSISSIPPI PETRIFIED FOREST
Canton
Pearl
RESERVATION
Ross Barnett Reservoir
VICKSBURG N.M.P.
Ridgeland
Clinton
BIENVILLE NATIONAL FOREST
Meridian
ALABAMA
Vicksburg
Jackson
Pearl
Brandon
Forest
Newton
Big Black
Quitman
Crystal Springs
Strong
Leaf
MISSISSIPPI CHOCTAW I.R.
Natchez Trace Parkway
Hazlehurst
Magee
Laurel
Waynesboro
Natchez
NATCHEZ N.H.P.
Collins
Ellisville
Chickasawhay
HOMOCHITTO
Brookhaven
ST. CATHERINE CREEK N.W.R.
NATIONAL
Petal
DE SOTO
Columbia
Hattiesburg
Tallahala Cr.
FOREST
McComb
Leaf
Centreville
Homochitto
NATIONAL
Lucedale
Mississippi
BLACK CREEK NATIONAL WILD & SCENIC RIVER
FOREST
Pascagoula
LOUISIANA
Bogue Chitto
Poplarville
Wiggins
Black Creek
Tombigbee
BOGUE CHITTO N.W.R.
Picayune
Ocean Springs
MISSISSIPPI SANDHILL CRANE N.W.R.
Moss Point
Gulfport
Biloxi
Pascagoula
Long Beach
Bay St. Louis
MISSISSIPPI CHOCTAW I.R.
Mississippi Sound
GULF ISLANDS NATIONAL SEASHORE
GULF OF MEXICO

⇨ **FISH FARMS.** Catfish, raised in large man-made ponds, account for almost half the value of all aquaculture in the U.S., and Mississippi is the leading producer.

THE BASICS

STATS

Area
53,819 sq mi (139,390 sq km)

Population
9,061,032

Capital
Raleigh
Population 356,321

Largest city
Charlotte
Population 630,478

Ethnic/racial groups
74.0% white; 21.7% African American;
1.9% Asian; 1.3% Native American.
Hispanic (any race) 6.7%.

Industry
Real estate, health services, chemicals,
tobacco products, finance, textiles

Agriculture
Poultry, hogs, tobacco, nursery stock,
cotton, soybeans

Statehood
November 21, 1789; 12th state

GEO WHIZ

The University of North Carolina at
Chapel Hill, which opened its doors
in 1795, is the oldest state university in
the United States.

The Biltmore estate in Asheville is
the largest private residence in the
United States. Built to resemble a
French chateau, the mansion is still
owned by descendants of Cornelius
Vanderbilt, who made the family's
original fortune in the late 1800s.

Standing 208 feet (63 m) high, Cape
Hatteras Light is the tallest lighthouse
in the U.S. Its beacon can be seen
some 20 miles (32 km) out to sea
and has warned sailors for more
than a century about the
shallow waters around a
group of treacherous sandbars
called Diamond Shoals.

CARDINAL

**FLOWERING
DOGWOOD**

NORTH CAROLINA

Before European contact, the land that became North Carolina was inhabited by numerous Native American groups. Early attempts to settle the area met with strong resistance, and one early colony established in 1587 on Roanoke Island disappeared without a trace. More attempts at settlement came in 1650, and in 1663 King Charles granted a charter for the Carolina colony, which included present-day North Carolina, South Carolina, and part of Georgia. In 1789 North Carolina became the 12th state, but in 1861 it joined the Confederacy, supplying more men and equipment to the Southern cause than any other state. In 1903 the Wright brothers piloted the first successful airplane near Kitty Hawk, foreshadowing the change and growth coming to the Tar Heel State. Traditional industries included agriculture, textiles, and furniture making. Today, these, plus high-tech industries and education in the Raleigh-Durham Research Triangle area, as well as banking and finance in Charlotte, are important to the economy.

⇨ FAVORITE PASTIME.
With four of the state's
major schools represented
in the powerful Atlantic
Coast Conference, it is not
surprising that basketball is
a popular sport among all
ages, whether on the court
or in the backyard.

⇦ TAKING FLIGHT.
The Wright Brothers
Memorial on Kill Devil
Hill, near Kitty Hawk on
North Carolina's Outer
Banks, marks the site
of the first successful
airplane flight in 1903.

VIRGINIA

NEW NATIONAL WILD & SCENIC RIVER
Mt. Airy
Eden
Reidsville
Roxboro
Oxford
Henderson
John H. Kerr Reservoir
Lake Gaston
Roanoke Rapids
GREAT DISMAL SWAMP N.W.R.
Great Dismal Swamp
MACKAY ISLAND N.W.R.
CURRITUCK N.W.R.
Ahoskie
Elizabeth City
Kitty Hawk
Kernersville
GUILFORD COURTHOUSE N.M.P.
Burlington
Durham
Rocky Mount
Tarboro
Edenton
WRIGHT BROTHERS NAT. MEM.
FORT RALEIGH N.H.S.
Winston-Salem
Greensboro
Chapel Hill
Cary
Raleigh
Williamston
Albemarle Sound
ROANOKE RIVER N.W.R.
Roanoke Island
High Point
Thomasville
Lexington
Lenoir
Wilson
PEA ISLAND N.W.R.
POCOSIN LAKES N.W.R.
Hickory
Statesville
Salisbury
Asheboro
Garner
Greenville
Washington
Hatteras Island
NORTH CAROLINA
Newton
Kannapolis
UWHARRIE NATIONAL FOREST
Sanford
Smithfield
Goldsboro
MATTAMUSKEET N.W.R.
Pamlico R.
CAPE HATTERAS NATIONAL SEASHORE
Concord
Albemarle
Dunn
SWANQUARTER N.W.R.
Lincolnton
Shelby
Gastonia
Charlotte
L. Tillery
Pinehurst
Southern Pines
Spring Lake
Kinston
New Bern
Cape Hatteras
Kings Mountain
Matthews
PEE DEE N.W.R.
Fayetteville
Clinton
CROATAN NAT. FOREST
Havelock
CEDAR ISLAND N.W.R.
Ocracoke Island
President Polk's birthplace
Monroe
Rockingham
LUMBER NATIONAL WILD & SCENIC RIVER
Hope Mills
Jacksonville
Morehead City
CAPE LOOKOUT NATIONAL SEASHORE
CAROLINA
Laurinburg
Lumberton
MOORES CREEK NATIONAL BATTLEFIELD
Whiteville
Lake Waccamaw
Wilmington
Wrightsville Beach
Cape Lookout
ATLANTIC OCEAN
Green Swamp
Intracoastal Waterway
Southport
Long Bay
Cape Fear
Onslow Bay

50 miles
50 kilometers
Albers Conic Equal-Area Projection

Economy Symbols

Fishing	Peanuts	Stone/gravel/cement
Shellfish	Nursery stock	Hydro-electricity
Poultry/eggs	Wheat	Chemistry
Sheep	Corn	Food processing
Hogs	Soybeans	Clothing/textiles
Dairy cows/products	Cotton	Computers/electronics
Fruits	Tobacco	Tourism
Vegetables	Furniture	Finance/insurance

⇧ SKILLED ARTISAN. A Cherokee woman sews a beaded belt in Oconaluftee Indian Village in western North Carolina. Cherokees in this mountainous region are descendants of Indians who hid in the hills to avoid the forced migration known as the Trail of Tears. The village preserves traditional 18th-century crafts, customs, and lifestyles.

REGIONAL GIANTS

West:
Mt. McKinley (Denali), AK
20,320 feet (6,194 m)

Southwest:
Wheeler Peak, NM
13,161 feet (4,011 m)

Midwest:
Harney Peak, SD
7,242 feet (2,207 m)

Southeast:
Mt. Mitchell, NC
6,684 feet (2,037 m)

Northeast:
Mt. Washington, NH
6,288 feet (1,917 m)

Mt. Mitchell in the Southeast is the tallest peak east of the Mississippi, but young mountains in the West and Southwest tower above older eastern peaks.

SOUTH CAROLINA

A ttempts in the 16th century by the Spanish and the French to colonize the area that would become South Carolina met fierce resistance from local Native American groups, but in 1670 the English were the first to establish a permanent European settlement at present-day Charleston. The colony prospered by relying on slave labor to produce first cotton, then rice and indigo. South Carolina became the 8th state in 1788 and the first to leave the Union just months before the first shots of the Civil War were fired on Fort Sumter in 1861. After the war, South Carolina struggled to rebuild its economy.

Early in the 20th century, textile mills introduced new jobs. Today, agriculture remains important, manufacturing and high-tech industries are expanding along interstate highway corridors, and tourists and retirees are drawn to the state's Atlantic coastline. But these coastal areas are not without risk. In 1989 Hurricane Hugo's 135-mile-per-hour (217-kmph) winds left a trail of destruction.

THE BASICS

STATS

Area
32,020 sq mi (82,932 sq km)

Population
4,407,709

Capital
Columbia
Population 119,961

Largest city
Columbia
Population 119,961

Ethnic/racial groups
68.5% white; 29.0% African American; 1.1% Asian; .4% Native American. Hispanic (any race) 3.5%.

Industry
Service industries, tourism, chemicals, textiles, machinery, forest products

Agriculture
Chickens, tobacco, nursery stock, beef cattle, dairy products, cotton

Statehood
May 23, 1788; 8th state

GEO WHIZ

The loggerhead sea turtle, South Carolina's state reptile, is threatened throughout its range. These turtles weigh between 200–450 pounds (90–204 kg).

North America's largest remnant of old-growth bottomland hardwood forest towers above the Congaree River and is protected as a 22,000-acre (8,903-ha) refuge called Congaree National Park.

Sweetgrass basketmaking, a traditional art form of African origin, has been a part of the Mount Pleasant community for more than 300 years. The baskets were originally used by slaves in the planting and processing of rice in coastal lowland regions.

Bobcats are thriving on Kiawah Island, a resort community southeast of Charleston. The elusive, nocturnal cats, which are about twice the size of an average house cat, play an important role in controlling the island's deer population.

CAROLINA WREN
YELLOW JESSAMINE

⇧ GLOW OF DAWN. The rising sun reflects off the water along the Atlantic coast. Beaches attract visitors year-round, contributing to tourism, the state's largest industry.

Highest point in South Carolina

CHATTOOGA NATIONAL WILD & SCENIC RIVER

SUMTER

NATIONAL FOREST

Sassafras Mt.
3,560 ft
1,085 m

Lake Keowee

Greenville
Easley • Gantt

Seneca

Clemson

Belton

Anderson

Hartwell Lake

Richard B. Russell Lake

Abbeville

J. Strom Thurmond Reservoir

⇩ SOUTHERN CHARM. Twilight settles over antebellum homes in the historic district of Charleston. The city, established in 1670, is an important port located where the Ashley and Cooper Rivers merge before flowing to the Atlantic Ocean.

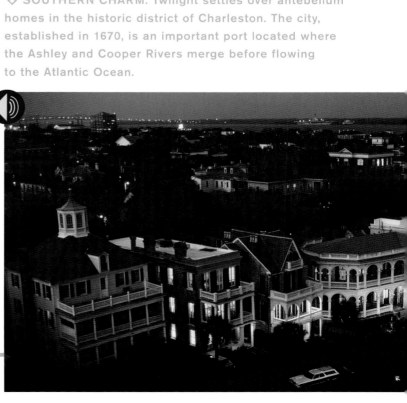

TRADE PARTNERS

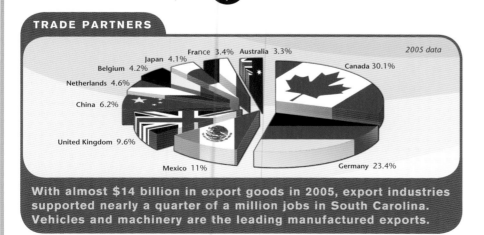

2005 data

Japan 4.1%
France 3.4%   Australia 3.3%
Belgium 4.2%
Netherlands 4.6%
China 6.2%
Canada 30.1%
United Kingdom 9.6%
Mexico 11%
Germany 23.4%

With almost $14 billion in export goods in 2005, export industries supported nearly a quarter of a million jobs in South Carolina. Vehicles and machinery are the leading manufactured exports.

3   4   5   6   7   8   9   10

0 ————— 50 miles
0 ————— 50 kilometers
Albers Conic Equal-Area Projection

➔ SHOWING OFF. Feathers extended, a male wild turkey struts through Francis Beicler Forest, a wildlife sanctuary and the world's largest virgin cypress-tupelo swamp forest.

COWPENS N.B.
Gaffney
Greer
Taylors
Spartanburg
Mauldin
Simpsonville
Union
Laurens
Clinton
Greenwood
NINETY SIX N.H.S.
Newberry
Batesburg-Leesville
KINGS MOUNTAIN N.M.P.
York
Rock Hill
Fort Mill
CATAWBA I.R.
Chester
Lancaster
Cheraw
Bennettsville
CAROLINA SANDHILLS N.W.R.
Hartsville
Darlington
Florence
Dillon
Mullins
Marion
Loris
Conway
North Myrtle Beach
Myrtle Beach
Socastee
Surfside Beach
Garden City
SUMTER NATIONAL FOREST
Winnsboro
Camden
Wateree Lake
Lake Murray
Saluda
Irmo
West Columbia
Cayce
Columbia
Forest Acres
SOUTH CAROLINA
Sumter
Lake City
Manning
Kingstree
Georgetown
North Island
Intracoastal Waterway
Long Bay
ATLANTIC OCEAN
NORTH CAROLINA
Wylie Lake
Broad
Catawba
Congaree
Wateree
Lynches
Great Pee Dee
Little Pee Dee
Black
Waccamaw
Santee
Edgefield
Aiken
Clearwater
North Augusta
Williston
Bamberg
Barnwell
Orangeburg
S. Fork Edisto
N. Fork Edisto
CONGAREE NATIONAL PARK
SANTEE N.W.R.
Lake Marion
Santee Dam
Lake Moultrie
Moncks Corner
FRANCIS MARION NATIONAL FOREST
Cape Island
CAPE ROMAIN N.W.R.
GEORGIA
Savannah
Coosawhatchie
Combahee
Edisto
Cooper
Allendale
Hampton
Walterboro
Summerville
Ladson
Goose Creek
Hanahan
North Charleston
Charleston
Mt. Pleasant
FT. SUMTER NAT. MON.
CHARLES PINCKNEY N.H.S.
ACE BASIN N.W.R.
Edisto Island
Burton
Beaufort
Port Royal
St. Helena Sound
St. Helena Island
Parris Island
Port Royal Sound
SEA ISLANDS
SAVANNAH NATIONAL WILDLIFE REFUGE
PINCKNEY ISLAND N.W.R.
Hilton Head Island
Daufuskie Island

Economy Symbols

Fishing		Soybeans	
Shellfish		Cotton	
Poultry/eggs		Tobacco	
Hogs		Timber/forest products	
Dairy cows/products		Stone/gravel/cement	
Fruits		Hydro-electricity	
Vegetables		Machinery	
Peanuts		Rubber/plastics	
Nursery stock		Chemistry	
Wheat		Clothing/textiles	
Corn		Tourism	

THE VOLUNTEER STATE:
TENNESSEE

STATS

Area
42,143 sq mi (109,151 sq km)

Population
6,156,719

Capital
Nashville
Population 552,120

Largest city
Memphis
Population 670,902

Ethnic/racial groups
80.4% white; 16.9% African American; 1.3% Asian; .3% Native American. Hispanic (any race) 3.2%.

Industry
Service industries, chemicals, transportation equipment, processed foods, machinery

Agriculture
Cattle, cotton, dairy products, hogs, poultry, nursery stock

Statehood
June 1, 1796; 16th state

GEO WHIZ

Twenty-seven species of salamanders live in Great Smoky Mountains National Park, earning it the nickname Salamander Capital of the World. Among the species are the spotted, the Jordans, which is found nowhere else, and the five-foot- (1.5-m-) long hellbender.

The New Madrid Earthquakes of 1811–1812, some of the largest earthquakes in the history of the U.S., created Reelfoot Lake in northwestern Tennessee. It is the state's only large, natural lake; others were created by damming waterways.

The Tennessee-Tombigbee Waterway is a 234-mile (376-km) artificial waterway that connects the Tennessee and Tombigbee Rivers. This water transportation route provides inland ports with an outlet to the Gulf of Mexico.

MOCKINGBIRD

IRIS

TENNESSEE

Following the last ice age, Native Americans moved onto the fertile lands of Tennessee. The earliest Europeans in Tennessee were Spanish explorers who passed through in 1541. In 1673 both the English and French made claims on the land, hoping to develop trade with the powerful Cherokees, whose town, called *Tanasi,* gave the state its name. Originally part of North Carolina, Tennessee was ceded to the federal government and became the 16th state in 1796. Tennessee was the last state to join the Confederacy and endured years of hardship after the war. Beginning in the 1930s, the federally funded Tennessee Valley Authority (TVA) set a high standard in water management in the state, and the hydropower it generated supported major industrial development. Tennessee played a key role in the civil rights movement of the 1960s. Today, visitors to Tennessee are drawn to national parks, Nashville's country music, and the mournful sound of the blues in Memphis.

Map of western Tennessee showing cities including Memphis, Jackson, Dyersburg, Union City, Martin, Paris, McKenzie, Trenton, Milan, Humboldt, Ripley, Brownsville, Lexington, Henderson, Millington, Bartlett, Bolivar, Savannah, Germantown, Collierville. Bordered by Missouri, Arkansas, Mississippi, Kentucky Lake, Reelfoot Lake, and features such as Land Between the Lakes National Recreation Area, Fort Donelson N.B., Shiloh N.M.P., Pickwick Lake.

⇐ OUT FOR A STROLL. Black bear cubs are usually born in January and remain with their mother for about 18 months. The Great Smoky Mountains National Park is one of the few remaining natural habitats for black bears in the eastern U.S.

NATURE'S PLAYGROUND

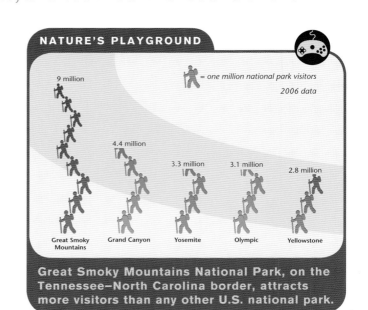

= one million national park visitors
2006 data

9 million — Great Smoky Mountains
4.4 million — Grand Canyon
3.3 million — Yosemite
3.1 million — Olympic
2.8 million — Yellowstone

Great Smoky Mountains National Park, on the Tennessee–North Carolina border, attracts more visitors than any other U.S. national park.

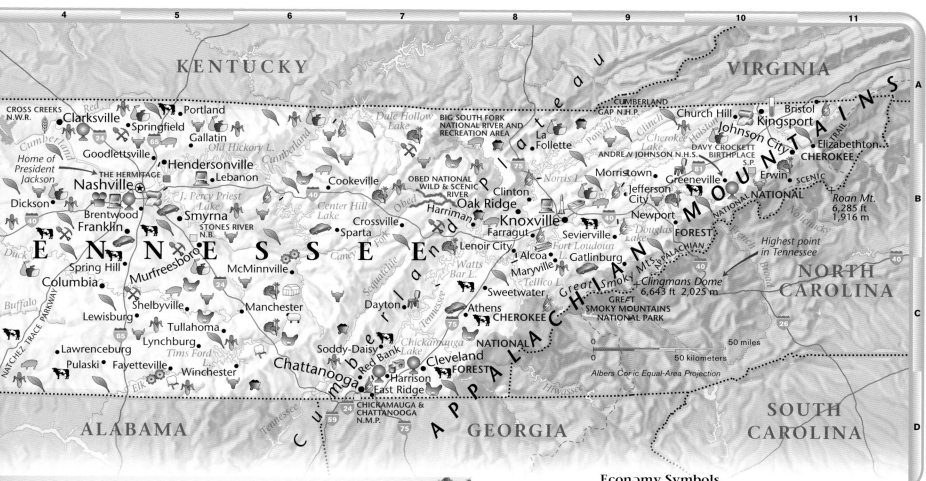

KENTUCKY

VIRGINIA

CROSS CREEKS N.W.R.
Clarksville
Portland
Springfield
Gallatin
Goodlettsville
Hendersonville
Home of President Jackson
THE HERMITAGE
Nashville
Lebanon
Old Hickory L.
Cookeville
CUMBERLAND GAP N.H.P.
Church Hill
Bristol
Kingsport
La Follette
Johnson City
Elizabethton
ANDREW JOHNSON N.H.S.
DAVY CROCKETT BIRTHPLACE
CHEROKEE
Morristown
Greeneville
Erwin
SCENIC
Jefferson City
OBED NATIONAL WILD & SCENIC RIVER
Clinton
Oak Ridge
Newport
NATIONAL
Roan Mt. 6,285 ft 1,916 m
Dickson
Brentwood
Smyrna
STONES RIVER N.B.
Crossville
Sparta
Harriman
Knoxville
Farragut
Sevierville
FOREST
Highest point in Tennessee
Franklin
Center Hill Lake
Lenoir City
Fort Loudoun
Alcoa
Gatlinburg
NORTH CAROLINA
Spring Hill
Murfreesboro
McMinnville
Maryville
Clingmans Dome 6,643 ft 2,025 m
Columbia
Shelbyville
Manchester
Dayton
Sweetwater
GREAT SMOKY MOUNTAINS NATIONAL PARK
Lewisburg
Tullahoma
Athens
CHEROKEE
Pulaski
Lynchburg
Tims Ford L.
Soddy-Daisy
Red Bank
Cleveland
NATIONAL FOREST
Lawrenceburg
Fayetteville
Winchester
Chattanooga
Harrison
East Ridge
CHICKAMAUGA & CHATTANOOGA N.M.P.
ALABAMA
GEORGIA
SOUTH CAROLINA

50 miles
50 kilometers
Albers Conic Equal-Area Projection

Economy Symbols

Poultry/eggs		Printing/publishing	
Sheep		Stone/gravel/cement	
Hogs		Mining	
Dairy cows/products		Coal	
Beef cattle		Hydro-electricity	
Fruits		Machinery	
Vegetables		Metal manufacturing	
Nursery stock		Motor vehicles/parts	
Wheat		Chemistry	
Corn		Food processing	
Soybeans		Electrical equipment	
Cotton		Computers/electronics	
Tobacco		Aerospace	
Furniture		Motion picture/music industry	

⇧ WATTS BAR DAM is one of nine TVA dams built on the Tennessee River to aid navigation and flood control and to supply power. The large reservoir behind the dam provides a recreation area that attracts millions of vacationers each year. Without the dam, cities such as Chattanooga would face devastating floods.

⇨ SOUTHERN TRADITION. Nashville's Grand Ole Opry is the home of country music. Originally a 1925 radio show called "Barn Dance," the Opry now occupies a theater with a seating capacity of 4,400 and the largest broadcasting studio in the world. Country music, using mainly stringed instruments, evolved from traditional folk tunes of the Appalachians.

THE OLD DOMINION STATE:
VIRGINIA

VIRGINIA

1   2   3   4

Long before Europeans arrived in present-day Virginia, Native Americans populated the area. Early Spanish attempts to establish a colony failed, but in 1607 merchants established the first permanent English settlement in North America at Jamestown. Virginia became a prosperous colony, growing tobacco using slave labor. Virginia played a key role in the drive for independence, and the final battle of the Revolutionary War was at Yorktown, near Jamestown. In 1861 Virginia joined the Confederacy and became a major battleground of the Civil War, which left the state in financial ruin. Today, Virginia has a diversified economy. Farmers still grow tobacco, along with other crops. The Hampton Roads area, near the mouth of Chesapeake Bay, is a center for shipbuilding and home to major naval bases. Northern Virginia, across the Potomac River from Washington, D.C., boasts federal government offices and high-tech businesses. And the state's natural beauty and many historic sites attract tourists from around the world.

⇧ EARLY ENTER-
TAINMENT. Dating
back to ancient
Greece and Rome,
dice made of bone,
ivory, or lead were
popular during
colonial times.

THE BASICS

STATS

Area
42,774 sq mi (110,785 sq km)

Population
7,712,091

Capital
Richmond
Population 192,913

Largest city
Virginia Beach
Population 435,619

Ethnic/racial groups
73.3% white; 19.9% African American; 4.8% Asian; .3% Native American. Hispanic (any race) 6.3%.

Industry
Food processing, communication and electronic equipment, transportation equipment, printing, shipbuilding, textiles

Agriculture
Tobacco, poultry, dairy products, beef cattle, soybeans, hogs

Statehood
June 25, 1788; 10th state

GEO WHIZ

In the early 1700s the bustling port of Hampton was a major target for pirates, including the notorious Blackbeard. Today, each spring the city hosts the Blackbeard Festival, complete with pirate re-enactors, live music, games, and fireworks.

Virginia is the birthplace of eight U.S. presidents—more than any other state. They are: George Washington, Thomas Jefferson, James Madison, James Monroe, William Harrison, John Tyler, Zachary Taylor, and Woodrow Wilson. Learn about them and more in our book *Our Country's Presidents.*

During the Battle of Hampton Roads in 1862, the USS *Monitor* and the CSS *Virginia* (a rebuilt version of the USS *Merrimac*) met in one of the most famous naval engagements in U.S. history. It marked the dawn of a new era of naval warfare.

More than 200,000 telephone calls are made each day at the Pentagon, the headquarters for the U.S. Department of Defense, through phones connected by 100,000 miles (160,000 km) of telephone cable. It is one of the largest office buildings in the world.

CARDINAL
FLOWERING
DOGWOOD

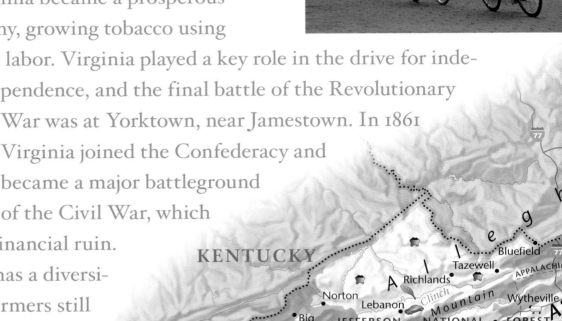

KENTUCKY

Bluefield
Tazewell   APPALACHIA
Richlands
Norton
Lebanon   Clinch   Wytheville
Big
Stone   JEFFERSON   Mountain
CUMBERLAND   Gap
GAP   Clinch   NATIONAL   FOREST
N.H.P.   Powell   Marion   MT. ROGER RECREATIO
North Fork   Mt. Rogers
Bristol   Abingdon   +5,729 ft
Holston   1,746 m
S. Fork   Highest point
in Virginia
TENNESSEE

⇨ NATURAL WONDER.
Winding under the Appalachian Mountains, Luray Caverns formed as water dissolved limestone rocks and precipitated calcium deposits to form stalactites and stalagmites.

⇩ PAST AND PRESENT. Cyclists speed past a statue of Confederate General Robert E. Lee on Richmond's Monument Avenue. The street has drawn criticism for recognizing leaders of the Confederacy.

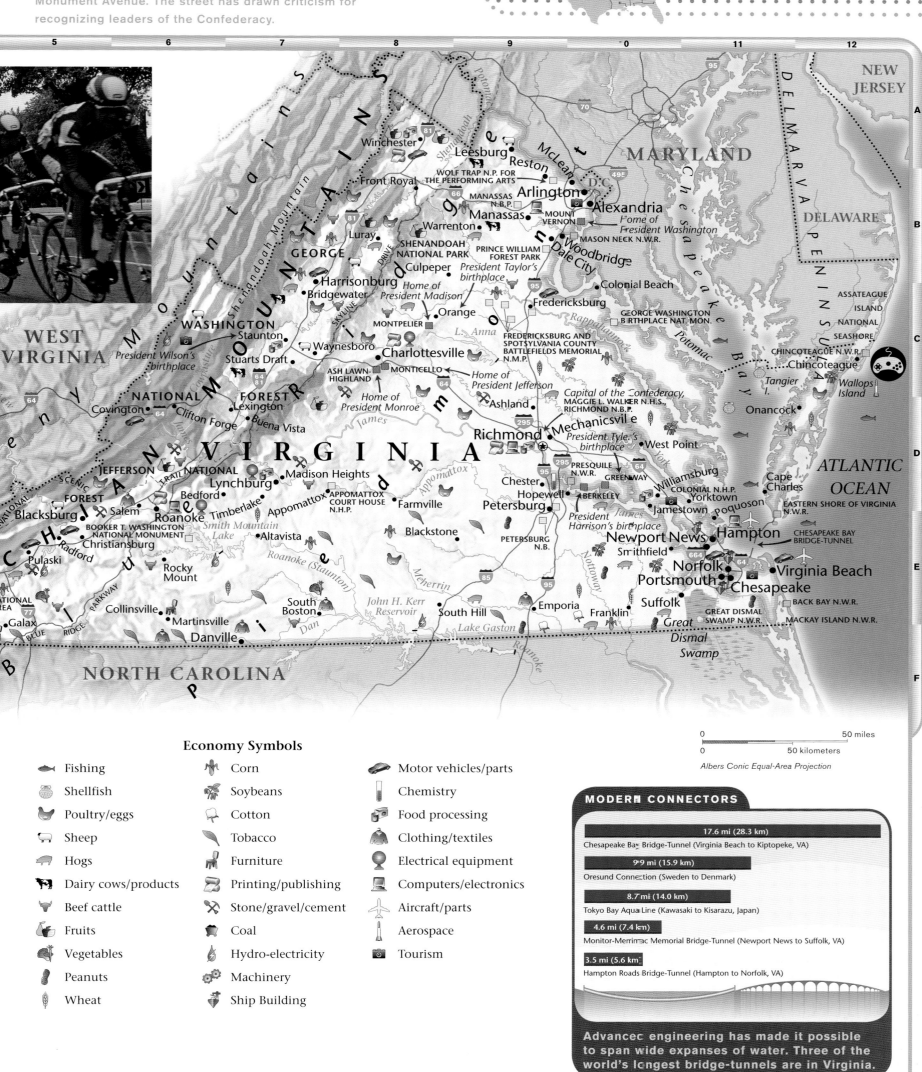

Economy Symbols

- Fishing
- Shellfish
- Poultry/eggs
- Sheep
- Hogs
- Dairy cows/products
- Beef cattle
- Fruits
- Vegetables
- Peanuts
- Wheat

- Corn
- Soybeans
- Cotton
- Tobacco
- Furniture
- Printing/publishing
- Stone/gravel/cement
- Coal
- Hydro-electricity
- Machinery
- Ship Building

- Motor vehicles/parts
- Chemistry
- Food processing
- Clothing/textiles
- Electrical equipment
- Computers/electronics
- Aircraft/parts
- Aerospace
- Tourism

0   50 miles
0   50 kilometers
Albers Conic Equal-Area Projection

MODERN CONNECTORS

17.6 mi (28.3 km)
Chesapeake Bay Bridge-Tunnel (Virginia Beach to Kiptopeke, VA)

9.9 mi (15.9 km)
Oresund Connection (Sweden to Denmark)

8.7 mi (14.0 km)
Tokyo Bay Aqua-Line (Kawasaki to Kisarazu, Japan)

4.6 mi (7.4 km)
Monitor-Merrimac Memorial Bridge-Tunnel (Newport News to Suffolk, VA)

3.5 mi (5.6 km)
Hampton Roads Bridge-Tunnel (Hampton to Norfolk, VA)

Advanced engineering has made it possible to span wide expanses of water. Three of the world's longest bridge-tunnels are in Virginia.

THE MOUNTAIN STATE:
WEST VIRGINIA

WEST VIRGINIA

1   2

THE BASICS

STATS

Area
24,230 sq mi (62,755 sq km)

Population
1,812,035

Capital
Charleston
Population 51,394

Largest city
Charleston
Population 51,394

Ethnic/racial groups
94.9% white; 3.3% African American;
.6% Asian; .2% Native American.
Hispanic (any race) .9%.

Industry
Tourism, coal mining, chemicals,
metal manufacturing, forest products,
stone, clay, oil, glass products

Agriculture
Poultry and eggs, cattle, dairy
products, apples

Statehood
June 20, 1863; 35th state

GEO WHIZ

The FBI crime data center in
Clarksburg has the largest collection of fingerprints in the world.
The center processes some 50,000
fingerprints each day.

The city of Weirton is nestled in the panhandle between Ohio and Pennsylvania.
It is the only city in the U.S. that sits in
one state and borders two others.

Bridge Day, held each October, is
the only day of the year when it
is legal to jump off the
876-foot- (267-m-) high
New River Gorge Bridge using
bungee cords, parachutes,
or other equipment.

The first rural free mail delivery
in the United States started in
Charles Town on October 1, 1896.

CARDINAL
RHODODENDRON

⬆ HARD LABOR.
Coal miners work
under difficult
conditions. In 2006
West Virginia mined
more than 152
million tons of coal,
or 13 percent of
U.S. production.

Mountainous West Virginia was first settled by Native Americans who favored the wooded region for hunting. The first Europeans to settle in what originally was an extension of Virginia were Germans and Scotch-Irish, who came through mountain valleys of Pennsylvania in the early 1700s. Because farms in West Virginia did not depend upon slaves, residents opposed secession during the Civil War and broke away from Virginia, becoming the 35th state in 1863. In the early 1800s West Virginia harvested forest products and mined salt, but it was the exploitation of vast coal deposits that brought industrialization to the state. Coal fueled steel mills, steamboats, and trains, and jobs in the mines attracted immigrants from far and near. However, poor work conditions resulted in a legacy of poverty, illness, and environmental degradation— problems the state continues to face. Today, the state is working to build a tourist industry based on its natural beauty and mountain crafts and culture.

OHIO

Point
Pleasant

Hurricane
Huntington Nitro
Kenova   St. Alban

Madison

Logan

Williamson

KENTUCKY

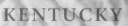

⬅ STRATEGIC
LOCATION.
Founded in 1751
by Robert Harper,
who built a ferry to
cross the Shenandoah
River, Harpers Ferry was
a departure point for pioneers
heading West as well as the site
of many battles during the Civil War.

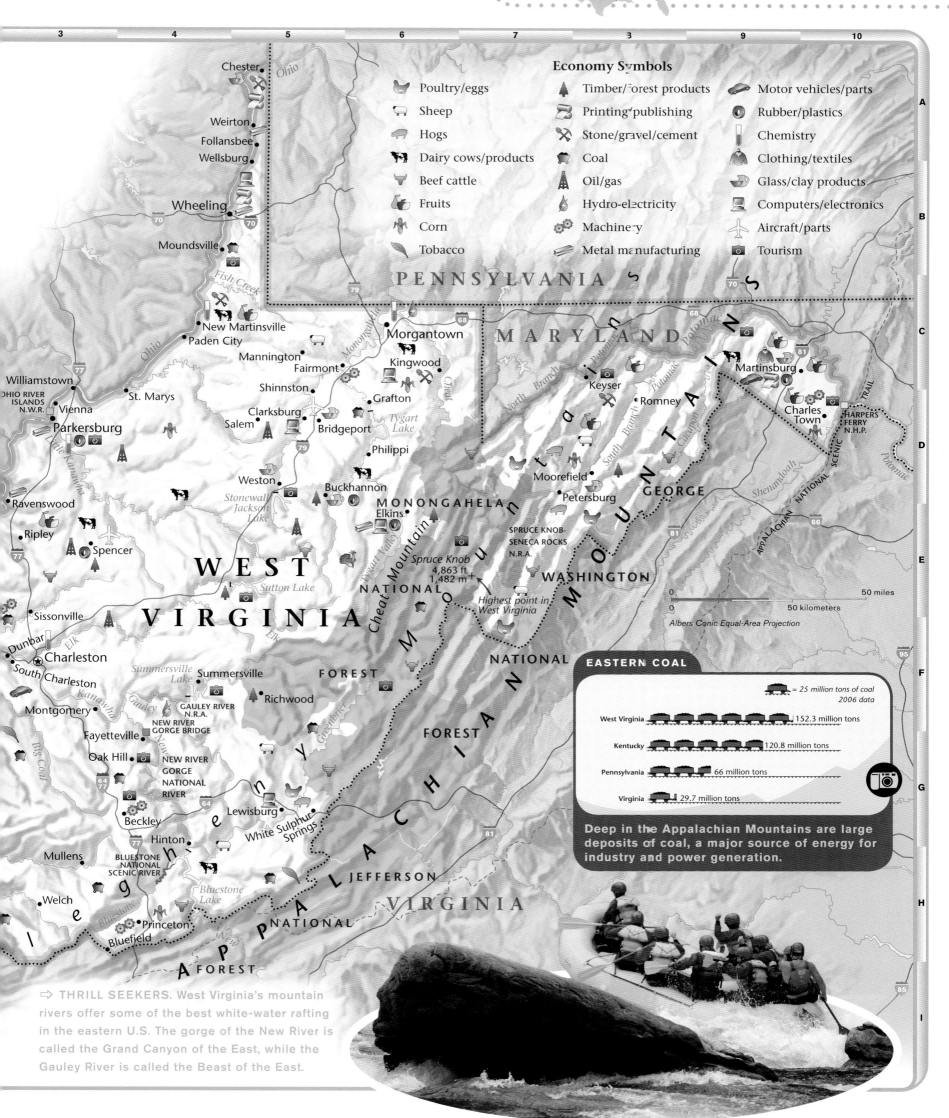

Economy Symbols

Poultry/eggs	Timber/forest products	Motor vehicles/parts
Sheep	Printing/publishing	Rubber/plastics
Hogs	Stone/gravel/cement	Chemistry
Dairy cows/products	Coal	Clothing/textiles
Beef cattle	Oil/gas	Glass/clay products
Fruits	Hydro-electricity	Computers/electronics
Corn	Machinery	Aircraft/parts
Tobacco	Metal manufacturing	Tourism

PENNSYLVANIA

MARYLAND

Chester
Weirton
Follansbee
Wellsburg
Wheeling
Moundsville

New Martinsville
Paden City
Mannington
Fairmont
Morgantown
Kingwood
Williamstown
OHIO RIVER ISLANDS N.W.R.
St. Marys
Shinnston
Grafton
Vienna
Clarksburg
Salem
Bridgeport
Parkersburg
Philippi
Tygart Lake
Ravenswood
Weston
Buckhannon
Stonewall Jackson Lake
MONONGAHELA
Ripley
Spencer
Elkins
SPRUCE KNOB-SENECA ROCKS N.R.A.
Keyser
Romney
Martinsburg
Charles Town
HARPERS FERRY N.H.P.
Moorefield
Petersburg
GEORGE

WEST VIRGINIA

Sissonville
NATIONAL
Spruce Knob
4,863 ft
1,482 m
Highest point in West Virginia
WASHINGTON
Sutton Lake
Dunbar
Charleston
South Charleston
Summersville Lake
Summersville
FOREST
NATIONAL

Montgomery
GAULEY RIVER N.R.A.
Richwood
Fayetteville
NEW RIVER GORGE BRIDGE
Oak Hill
NEW RIVER GORGE NATIONAL RIVER
FOREST
Beckley
Lewisburg
White Sulphur Springs
Hinton
Mullens
BLUESTONE NATIONAL SCENIC RIVER
Welch
Bluestone Lake
Princeton
Bluefield
JEFFERSON
VIRGINIA
NATIONAL
APPALACHIAN
FOREST

APPALACHIAN MOUNTAINS

0   50 miles
0   50 kilometers
Albers Conic Equal-Area Projection

EASTERN COAL

= 25 million tons of coal
2006 data

West Virginia	152.3 million tons
Kentucky	120.8 million tons
Pennsylvania	66 million tons
Virginia	29.7 million tons

Deep in the Appalachian Mountains are large deposits of coal, a major source of energy for industry and power generation.

⇨ THRILL SEEKERS. West Virginia's mountain rivers offer some of the best white-water rafting in the eastern U.S. The gorge of the New River is called the Grand Canyon of the East, while the Gauley River is called the Beast of the East.

THE REGION

PHYSICAL			POLITICAL	
Total area 821,739 sq mi (2,128,287 sq km)	**Lowest point** St. Francis River, MO 230 ft (70 m)	**Vegetation** Grassland; broadleaf, needleleaf, and mixed forest	**Total population** 66,388,795	**Smallest state** Indiana: 36,418 sq mi (94,322 sq km)
Highest point Harney Peak, SD 7,242 ft (2,207 m)	**Longest rivers** Mississippi, Missouri, Arkansas, Ohio	**Climate** Continental to mild, ranging from cold winters and cool summers in the north to mild winters and humid summers in the south	**States (12):** Illinois, Indiana, Iowa, Kansas, Michigan, Minnesota, Missouri, Nebraska, North Dakota, Ohio, South Dakota, Wisconsin	**Most populous state** Illinois: 12,852,548
	Largest lakes Superior, Michigan, Huron, Erie		**Largest state** Michigan: 96,716 sq mi (250,495 sq km)	**Least populous state** North Dakota: 639,715
				Largest city proper Chicago, IL: 2,833,321

The Midwest

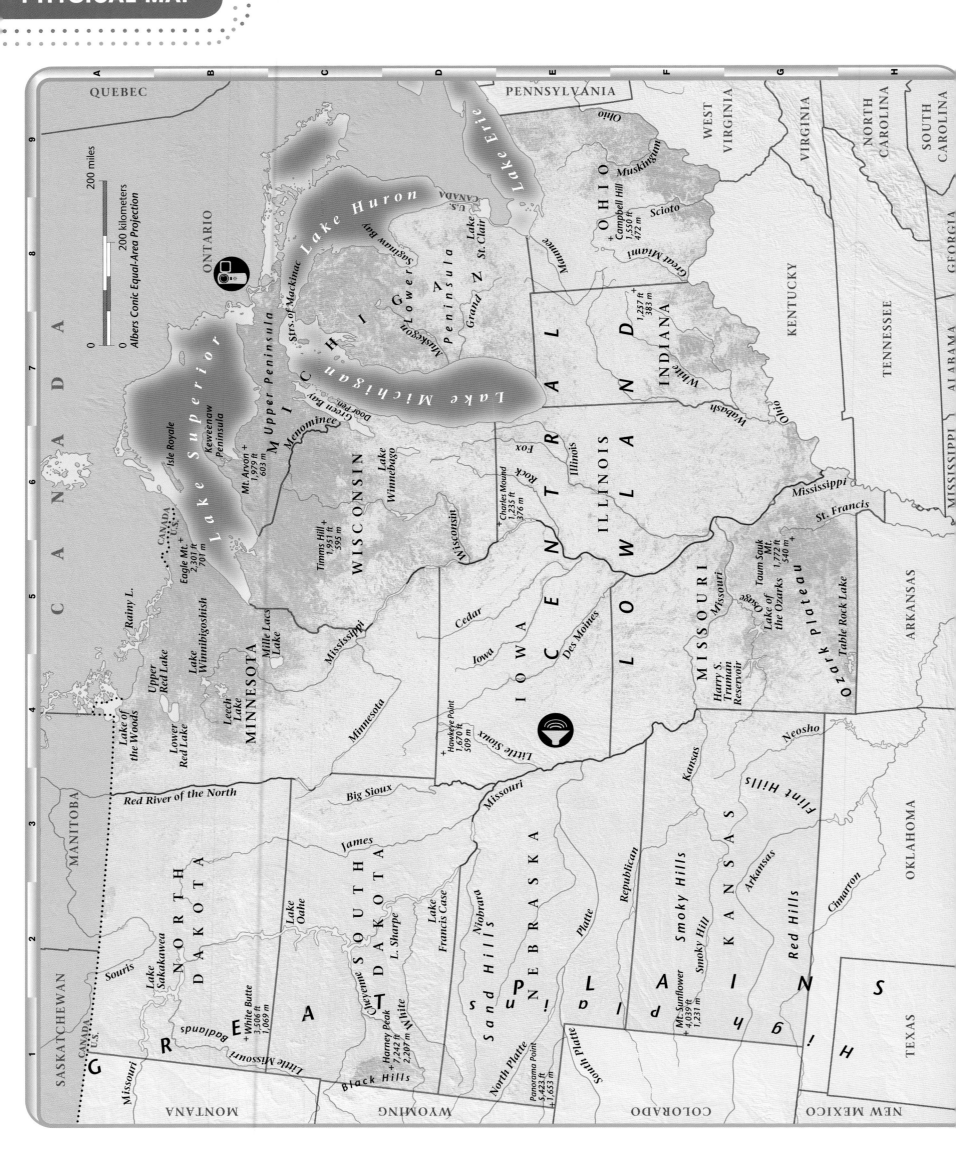

QUEBEC

PENNSYLVANIA

200 miles

200 kilometers
Albers Conic Equal-Area Projection

0

0

C A N A D A

ONTARIO

OHIO

WEST VIRGINIA

VIRGINIA

NORTH CAROLINA

SOUTH CAROLINA

GEORGIA

Lake Erie

Lake Huron

Lake Superior

Isle Royale

Keweenaw Peninsula

Upper Peninsula

Strs. of Mackinac

Saginaw Bay

M I C H I G A N

Lower Peninsula

Lake St. Clair

Grand

U.S.
CANADA

Muskegon

Muskingum

Campbell Hill
1,550 ft
472 m

Scioto

Great Miami

Ohio

Green Bay

Door Pen.

Lake Michigan

Maumee

Mt. Arvon +
1,979 ft
603 m

Menominee

Lake Winnebago

Fox

White

INDIANA
1,257 ft
383 m

Wabash

Ohio

KENTUCKY

TENNESSEE

CANADA
U.S.

Eagle Mt. +
2,301 ft
701 m

Rainy L.

WISCONSIN

Wisconsin

Rock

Illinois

C E N T R A L

L O W L A N D

ILLINOIS

Mississippi

St. Francis

Timms Hill +
1,951 ft
595 m

+ Charles Mound
1,235 ft
376 m

Upper Red Lake

Lake Winnibigoshish

Lower Red Lake

Leech Lake

Mille Lacs Lake

MINNESOTA

Mississippi

Cedar

Iowa

I O W A

Des Moines

MISSOURI

Missouri

Osage

Lake of the Ozarks

Taum Sauk Mt.
1,772 ft +
540 m

Ozark Plateau

Table Rock Lake

ARKANSAS

Harry S.
Truman
Reservoir

Lake of the Woods

MANITOBA

Red River of the North

Minnesota

+ Hawkeye Point
1,670 ft
509 m

Little Sioux

Big Sioux

Missouri

Neosho

Kansas

Flint Hills

SASKATCHEWAN

CANADA
U.S.

Souris

Lake Sakakawea

N O R T H D A K O T A

James

Lake Oahe

S O U T H D A K O T A

L. Sharpe

Lake Francis Case

Niobrara

N E B R A S K A

Sand Hills

Platte

Republican

Smoky Hills

Smoky Hill

K A N S A S

Arkansas

Red Hills

Cimarron

OKLAHOMA

Missouri

Little Missouri

G R E A T

Badlands

+ White Butte
3,506 ft
1,069 m

Cheyenne

White

+ Harney Peak
7,242 ft
2,207 m

Black Hills

North Platte

Panorama Point
5,423 ft +
1,653 m

South Platte

P l a i n s

Mt. Sunflower
4,039 ft +
1,231 m

P L A I N S

G

MONTANA

WYOMING

COLORADO

NEW MEXICO

TEXAS

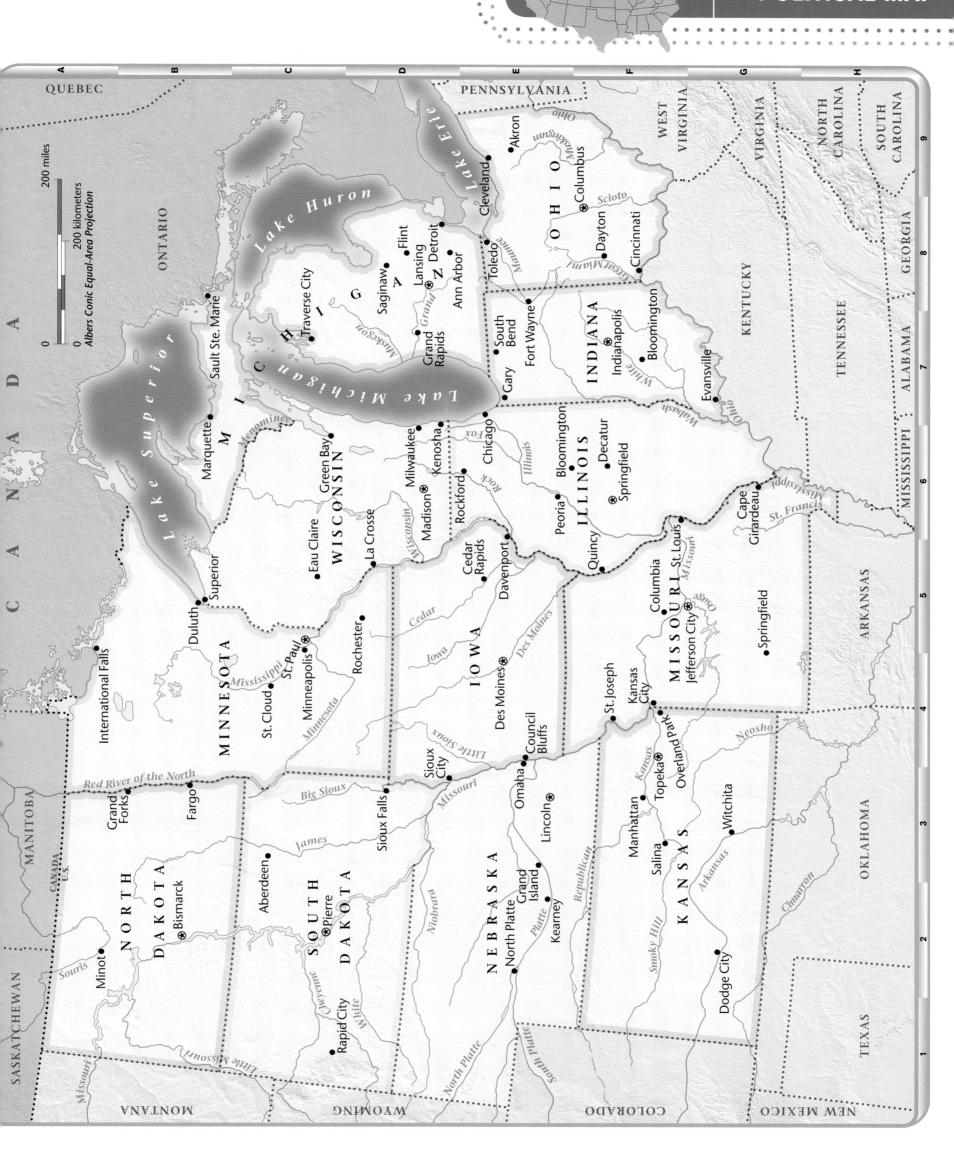

200 miles

200 kilometers

Albers Conic Equal-Area Projection

QUEBEC

PENNSYLVANIA

CANADA

ONTARIO

Lake Superior

Lake Huron

Lake Erie

OHIO

Akron

Cleveland

Columbus

Scioto

Dayton

Cincinnati

WEST VIRGINIA

VIRGINIA

NORTH CAROLINA

SOUTH CAROLINA

GEORGIA

KENTUCKY

TENNESSEE

ALABAMA

MISSISSIPPI

ARKANSAS

Flint

Lansing

Detroit

Ann Arbor

M I C H I G A N

Saginaw

Grand Rapids

Traverse City

Sault Ste. Marie

Marquette

Toledo

Maumee

Muskegon

South Bend

Fort Wayne

Gary

I N D I A N A

Indianapolis

Bloomington

White

Wabash

Evansville

Ohio

Green Bay

Milwaukee

Kenosha

Chicago

Rockford

Fox

I L L I N O I S

Bloomington

Decatur

Springfield

Peoria

Quincy

Illinois

Rock

Cape Girardeau

St. Francis

Mississippi

W I S C O N S I N

Madison

La Crosse

Eau Claire

Wisconsin

Superior

Duluth

Cedar Rapids

Davenport

Cedar

I O W A

Des Moines

Iowa

Des Moines

St. Louis

Columbia

M I S S O U R I

Jefferson City

Missouri

Osage

Springfield

International Falls

M I N N E S O T A

St. Cloud

St. Paul

Minneapolis

Rochester

Mississippi

Minnesota

CANADA

U.S.

Grand Forks

Fargo

Aberdeen

Red River of the North

Big Sioux

James

Sioux City

Sioux Falls

Little Sioux

Council Bluffs

Omaha

Lincoln

St. Joseph

Kansas City

Kansas City

Overland Park

Topeka

Manhattan

Salina

Kansas

K A N S A S

Wichita

Dodge City

N E B R A S K A

Grand Island

Kearney

North Platte

Niobrara

Platte

Republican

North Platte

South Platte

Smoky Hill

Arkansas

Neosho

Cimarron

N O R T H D A K O T A

Bismarck

Minot

Souris

S O U T H D A K O T A

Pierre

Rapid City

White

Cheyenne

Missouri

Little Missouri

MANITOBA

SASKATCHEWAN

MONTANA

WYOMING

COLORADO

NEW MEXICO

TEXAS

OKLAHOMA

MONTANA

⇨ FIERCE GIANT. Students in Chicago's Field Museum eye the skeleton of *Tyrannosaurus rex*, a dinosaur that roamed North America's plains 65 million years ago.

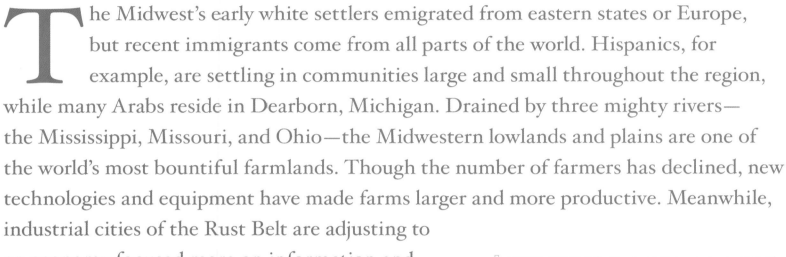

The Midwest
GREAT LAKES, GREAT RIVERS

The Midwest's early white settlers emigrated from eastern states or Europe, but recent immigrants come from all parts of the world. Hispanics, for example, are settling in communities large and small throughout the region, while many Arabs reside in Dearborn, Michigan. Drained by three mighty rivers—the Mississippi, Missouri, and Ohio—the Midwestern lowlands and plains are one of the world's most bountiful farmlands. Though the number of farmers has declined, new technologies and equipment have made farms larger and more productive. Meanwhile, industrial cities of the Rust Belt are adjusting to an economy focused more on information and services than on manufacturing.

⇩ CROP CIRCLES. Much of the western part of the region receives less than 20 inches (50 cm) of rain yearly—not enough to support agriculture. Large circular center-pivot irrigation systems draw water from underground reserves called aquifers to provide life-giving water to crops.

⇩ DAIRY HEARTLAND. Dairy cows, such as these in Wisconsin, are sometimes treated with growth hormones to increase milk production. These animals play an important role in the economy of the Midwest, which supplies much of the country's milk, butter, and cheese.

— MIDWEST URBAN HUB. Chicago, the third largest urban area in the U.S., with almost 10 million people, is the economic and cultural core of the Midwest and a major transportation hub.

⇒ PRESERVING THE PAST. A young Cherokee man, dressed in beaded costume and feathered headband, dances at a powwow in Milwaukee. Such gatherings provide Indians from across the country with a chance to share their traditions.

⇧ NATURE'S MOST VIOLENT STORMS. Parts of the midwestern U.S. have earned the nickname Tornado Alley because these destructive, swirling storms, which develop in association with thunderstorms along eastward-moving cold fronts, occur here more than any other place on Earth.

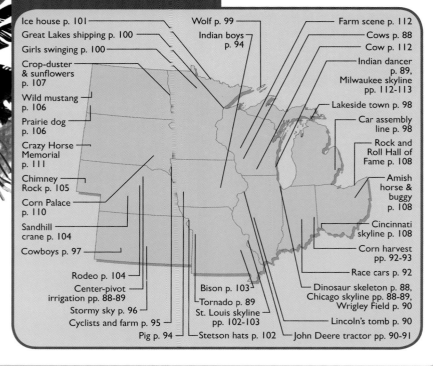

WHERE THE PICTURES ARE

Ice house p. 101
Great Lakes shipping p. 100
Girls swinging p. 100
Crop-duster & sunflowers p. 107
Wild mustang p. 106
Prairie dog p. 106
Crazy Horse Memorial p. 111
Chimney Rock p. 105
Corn Palace p. 110
Sandhill crane p. 104
Cowboys p. 97
Rodeo p. 104
Center-pivot irrigation pp. 88-89
Stormy sky p. 96
Cyclists and farm p. 95
Pig p. 94

Wolf p. 99
Indian boys p. 94

Bison p. 103
Tornado p. 89
St. Louis skyline pp. 102-103
Stetson hats p. 102

Farm scene p. 112
Cows p. 88
Cow p. 112
Indian dancer p. 89, Milwaukee skyline pp. 112-113
Lakeside town p. 98
Car assembly line p. 98
Rock and Roll Hall of Fame p. 108
Amish horse & buggy p. 108
Cincinnati skyline p. 108
Corn harvest pp. 92-93
Race cars p. 92
Dinosaur skeleton p. 88, Chicago skyline pp. 88-89, Wrigley Field p. 90
Lincoln's tomb p. 90
John Deere tractor pp. 90-91

THE LAND OF LINCOLN STATE:
ILLINOIS

ILLINOIS

ILLINOIS

Two rivers that now form the borders of Illinois aided the state's early white settlement. Frenchmen first explored the area in 1673 by traveling down the Mississippi, and the Ohio brought many 19th-century settlers to southern Illinois. Most Indians were forced out by the 1830s, more than a decade after Illinois became the 21st state. Ethnically diverse Chicago, the most populous city in the Midwest, is an economic giant and one of the country's busiest rail, highway, and air transit hubs. Barges from its port reach the Gulf of Mexico via rivers and canals, while ships reach the Atlantic Ocean via the Great Lakes and St. Lawrence Seaway. Flat terrain and fertile prairie soils in the northern and central regions help make the state a top producer of corn and soybeans. The more rugged, forested south has deposits of bituminous coal. Springfield, capital of the Land of Lincoln, welcomes tourists visiting the home and tomb of the country's 16th president.

⇧ REMEMBERING A PRESIDENT. Dedicated in 1874, the National Lincoln Monument in Springfield honors Abraham Lincoln, who was assassinated in 1865. A special vault holds the remains of the slain president, who led the country during the Civil War.

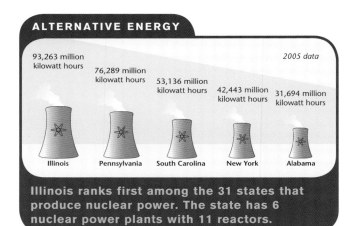

ALTERNATIVE ENERGY

2005 data

93,263 million kilowatt hours	76,289 million kilowatt hours	53,136 million kilowatt hours	42,443 million kilowatt hours	31,694 million kilowatt hours
Illinois	Pennsylvania	South Carolina	New York	Alabama

Illinois ranks first among the 31 states that produce nuclear power. The state has 6 nuclear power plants with 11 reactors.

⇧ PLAY BALL! Wrigley Field, home to the Chicago Cubs baseball team, is affected by wind conditions more than any other major league park due to its location near Lake Michigan.

⇧ FIELDS OF GRAIN. Illinois has long been a major grain producer, but farming today is highly mechanized. Above, a tractor moves bales of rolled hay.

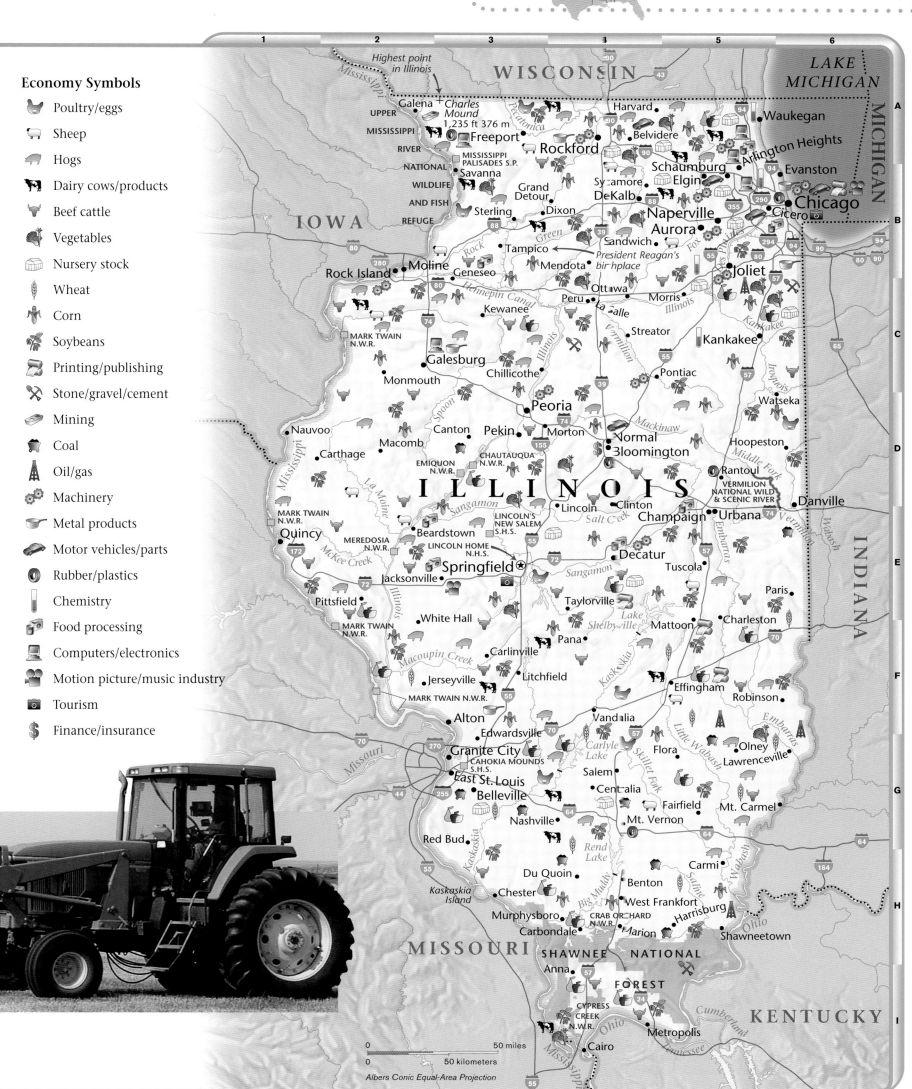

Economy Symbols

- Poultry/eggs
- Sheep
- Hogs
- Dairy cows/products
- Beef cattle
- Vegetables
- Nursery stock
- Wheat
- Corn
- Soybeans
- Printing/publishing
- Stone/gravel/cement
- Mining
- Coal
- Oil/gas
- Machinery
- Metal products
- Motor vehicles/parts
- Rubber/plastics
- Chemistry
- Food processing
- Computers/electronics
- Motion picture/music industry
- Tourism
- Finance/insurance

WISCONSIN

LAKE MICHIGAN

IOWA

MICHIGAN

INDIANA

MISSOURI

KENTUCKY

Highest point in Illinois

Charles Mound 1,235 ft 376 m

UPPER MISSISSIPPI RIVER NATIONAL WILDLIFE AND FISH REFUGE

Galena
Freeport
Rockford
Savanna
MISSISSIPPI PALISADES S.P.
Grand Detour
Sycamore
DeKalb
Sterling
Dixon
Harvard
Belvidere
Schaumburg
Elgin
Arlington Heights
Evanston
Waukegan
Chicago
Cicero

Moline
Rock Island
Geneseo
Tampico
Mendota
President Reagan's birthplace
Sandwich
Aurora
Naperville
Joliet

Hennepin Canal
Kewanee
Ottawa
Peru
La Salle
Morris
Streator
Kankakee

MARK TWAIN N.W.R.
Galesburg
Chillicothe
Pontiac
Watseka

Monmouth

Nauvoo
Canton
Pekin
Morton
Normal
Bloomington
Hoopeston
Rantoul
VERMILION NATIONAL WILD & SCENIC RIVER
Danville

Carthage
Macomb
Peoria
EMIQUON N.W.R.
CHAUTAUQUA N.W.R.

MARK TWAIN N.W.R.
Lincoln
Clinton
Champaign
Urbana

Quincy
MEREDOSIA N.W.R.
Beardstown
LINCOLN'S NEW SALEM S.H.S.
LINCOLN HOME N.H.S.
Springfield
Decatur
Tuscola

Pittsfield
Jacksonville
White Hall
Taylorville
Paris
Charleston
Mattoon

MARK TWAIN N.W.R.
Carlinville
Pana
Lake Shelbyville

Jerseyville
Litchfield
Effingham
Robinson

MARK TWAIN N.W.R.
Alton
Edwardsville
Vandalia
Olney
Lawrenceville

Granite City
CAHOKIA MOUNDS S.H.S.
East St. Louis
Belleville
Carlyle Lake
Flora
Salem

Red Bud
Nashville
Centralia
Fairfield
Mt. Carmel

Du Quoin
Mt. Vernon
Carmi

Kaskaskia Island
Chester
Benton
West Frankfort
Harrisburg

Murphysboro
Carbondale
CRAB ORCHARD N.W.R.
Marion
Shawneetown

SHAWNEE NATIONAL FOREST
Anna

CYPRESS CREEK N.W.R.
Metropolis
Cairo

0   50 miles
0   50 kilometers
Albers Conic Equal-Area Projection

THE BASICS

STATS

Area
36,418 sq mi (94,322 sq km)

Population
6,345,289

Capital
Indianapolis
Population 795,484

Largest city
Indianapolis
Population 795,484

Ethnic/racial groups
88.3% white; 8.9% African American; 1.3% Asian; .3% Native American. Hispanic (any race) 4.8%.

Industry
Transportation equipment, steel, pharmaceutical and chemical products, machinery, petroleum, coal

Agriculture
Corn, soybeans, hogs, poultry and eggs, cattle, dairy products

Statehood
December 11, 1816; 19th state

GEO WHIZ

Every July during Circus Festival, in Peru, a couple hundred local kids and a couple thousand volunteers put on a three-ring circus complete with clowns, snow cones, and standing ovations from sellout crowds. The city is home to the International Circus Hall of Fame.

Every year Fort Wayne hosts the Johnny Appleseed Festival to honor John Chapman, the man who planted apple orchards from Pennsylvania to Illinois.

The Indianapolis Children's Museum, in partnership with National Geographic and the Environmental Research Systems Institute, has created an international traveling exhibit to teach children and parents that maps are tools of adventure.

CARDINAL
PEONY

INDIANA

Indiana's name, meaning "Land of the Indians," honors the tribes who lived in the region before the arrival of Europeans. The first permanent white settlement was Vincennes, established by the French in the early 1700s. Following statehood in 1816, most Indians were forced out to make way for white settlement. Lake Michigan, in the state's northwest corner, brings economic and recreational opportunities. The lakefront city of Gary anchors a major industrial region. Nearby, the natural beauty and shifting sands of the Indiana Dunes National Lakeshore attract many visitors. Corn, soybeans, and hogs are the most important products from Indiana's many farms. True to the state motto, "The Crossroads of America," highways from all directions converge at Indianapolis. Traveling at a much higher speed are cars on that city's famed Motor Speedway, home to the Indy 500 auto race since 1911. Cheering for a favorite high school or college team is a favorite pastime for many Hoosiers who catch basketball fever.

⇧ START YOUR ENGINES. The Indianapolis Motor Speedway seats 250,000 sports fans. Nicknamed the Brickyard, its track was once paved with 3.2 million bricks.

⇨ FUEL FARMING. Indiana farming is undergoing dramatic changes as corn is used in the production of ethanol, a non-fossil fue energy source that is increasingly popular.

HEAVY INDUSTRY

Indiana		27.34 million tons
Ohio		15.75 million tons
Pennsylvania		6.9 million tons
Michigan		6.44 million tons

2004 data

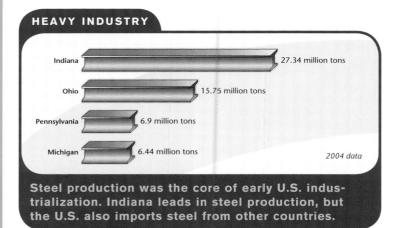

Steel production was the core of early U.S. industrialization. Indiana leads in steel production, but the U.S. also imports steel from other countries.

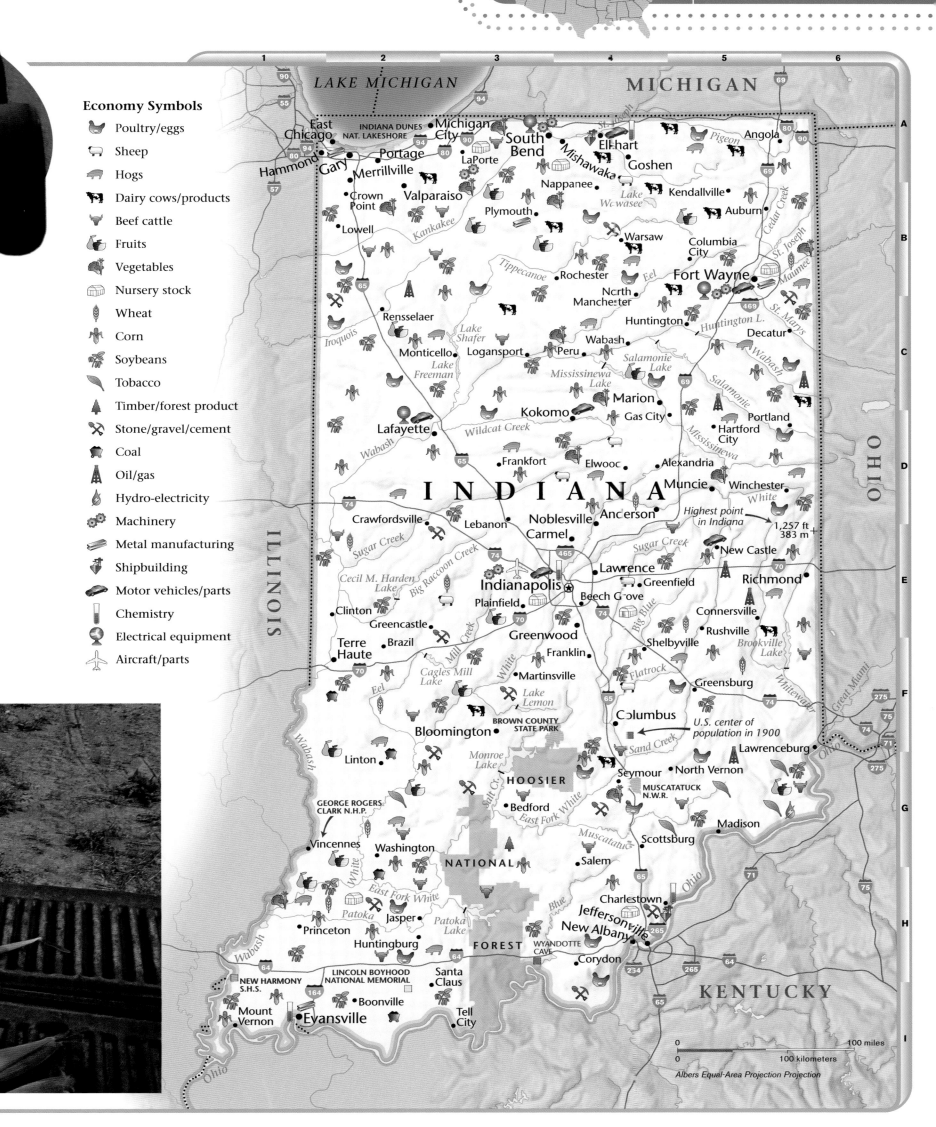

Economy Symbols

- Poultry/eggs
- Sheep
- Hogs
- Dairy cows/products
- Beef cattle
- Fruits
- Vegetables
- Nursery stock
- Wheat
- Corn
- Soybeans
- Tobacco
- Timber/forest product
- Stone/gravel/cement
- Coal
- Oil/gas
- Hydro-electricity
- Machinery
- Metal manufacturing
- Shipbuilding
- Motor vehicles/parts
- Chemistry
- Electrical equipment
- Aircraft/parts

LAKE MICHIGAN

MICHIGAN

ILLINOIS

OHIO

KENTUCKY

I N D I A N A

East Chicago
Hammond
Gary
Merrillville
Crown Point
Lowell
Valparaiso
Portage
Michigan City
INDIANA DUNES NAT. LAKESHORE
LaPorte
South Bend
Mishawaka
Elkhart
Goshen
Nappanee
Plymouth
Warsaw
Kendallville
Auburn
Columbia City
Angola
Rochester
Fort Wayne
North Manchester
Huntington
Decatur
Rensselaer
Monticello
Logansport
Peru
Wabash
Marion
Kokomo
Gas City
Hartford City
Portland
Lafayette
Frankfort
Elwood
Alexandria
Muncie
Winchester
Crawfordsville
Lebanon
Noblesville
Carmel
Anderson
New Castle
Richmond
Indianapolis
Lawrence
Greenfield
Connersville
Clinton
Greencastle
Plainfield
Beech Grove
Rushville
Shelbyville
Terre Haute
Brazil
Greenwood
Franklin
Greensburg
Martinsville
Columbus
Bloomington
BROWN COUNTY STATE PARK
Linton
Seymour
North Vernon
Lawrenceburg
GEORGE ROGERS CLARK N.H.P.
Bedford
MUSCATATUCK N.W.R.
Madison
Vincennes
Washington
Salem
Scottsburg
NATIONAL
Charlestown
Jeffersonville
New Albany
Jasper
Princeton
Huntingburg
FOREST
WYANDOTTE CAVE
Corydon
NEW HARMONY S.H.S.
LINCOLN BOYHOOD NATIONAL MEMORIAL
Santa Claus
Boonville
Mount Vernon
Evansville
Tell City
HOOSIER

Highest point in Indiana → 1,257 ft 383 m

U.S. center of population in 1900

Lake Wawasee
Lake Shafer
Lake Freeman
Lake Lemon
Monroe Lake
Patoka Lake
Brookville Lake
Salamonie Lake
Mississinewa Lake
Cecil M. Harden Lake
Cagles Mill Lake
Huntington L.
St. Joseph
Pigeon
Cedar Creek
Maumee
St. Marys
Salamonie
Mississinewa
Wabash
Tippecanoe
Eel
Kankakee
Iroquois
Wildcat Creek
Sugar Creek
Sugar Creek
Big Raccoon Creek
Mill Creek
White
Big Blue
Flatrock
Sand Creek
Whitewater
Great Miami
Ohio
Blue
Muscatatuck
East Fork White
Salt Cr.
Patoka
East Fork White
Eel
White

100 miles
100 kilometers
Albers Equal-Area Projection Projection

THE HAWKEYE STATE:
IOWA

IOWA

THE BASICS

STATS

Area
56,272 sq mi (145,743 sq km)

Population
2,988,046

Capital
Des Moines
Population 193,886

Largest city
Des Moines
Population 193,886

Ethnic/racial groups
94.6% white; 2.5% African
American; 1.6% Asian;
.4% Native American. Hispanic
(any race) 3.8%.

Industry
Real estate, health services,
industrial machinery, food processing,
construction

Agriculture
Hogs, corn, soybeans, oats, cattle,
dairy products

Statehood
December 28, 1846; 29th state

GEO WHIZ

The most famous house in Iowa and
one of the most famous houses in
America is in Eldon. It was immor-
talized in Grant Wood's famous
painting "American Gothic." The
stern-faced, pitchfork-holding farmer
and his wife shown in the art were not
farmers at all. Wood's sister and his
dentist posed for the painting.

Effigy Mounds National Monument,
in the northeast corner of Iowa, is the
only place in the country with such
a large collection of mounds in the
shapes of mammals, birds, and reptiles.
Of the 191 mounds, 29 are shaped
like animals. Eastern Woodland
Indians built these mounds from
about B.C. 500 to 1300 A.D.

Iowa, along with California
and Texas, is one
of the country's
leading producers
of wind energy.

AMERICAN
GOLDFINCH
WILD ROSE

IOWA

Iowa's prehistoric inhabitants built earthen mounds—
some shaped like birds and bears—that are visible in
the state's northeast. Nineteenth-century white
settlers found rolling prairies covered
by a sea of tall grasses that soon yielded
to the plow. A decade after statehood in
1846, a group of religious German immigrants
established the Amana Colonies, a communal
society that still draws visitors. Blessed with
ample precipitation and rich soils, Iowa
is the heart of one of the world's most
productive farming regions. The state is the
country's top producer of corn, soybeans,
hogs, and eggs. Food processing
and manufacturing machinery are two of the
biggest industries. Much of the grain crop
feeds livestock destined to reach
dinner plates in the U.S. and around
the world. An increasing amount of
corn is used to make ethanol, which
is mixed with gasoline to fuel cars
and trucks. Des Moines,
the capital and largest
city, is a center of
insurance and publishing.

⇧ PIG BUSINESS.
Hogs outnumber
people five to one in
Iowa. The state raises
25 percent of the
nation's hogs, making
it the leading producer.

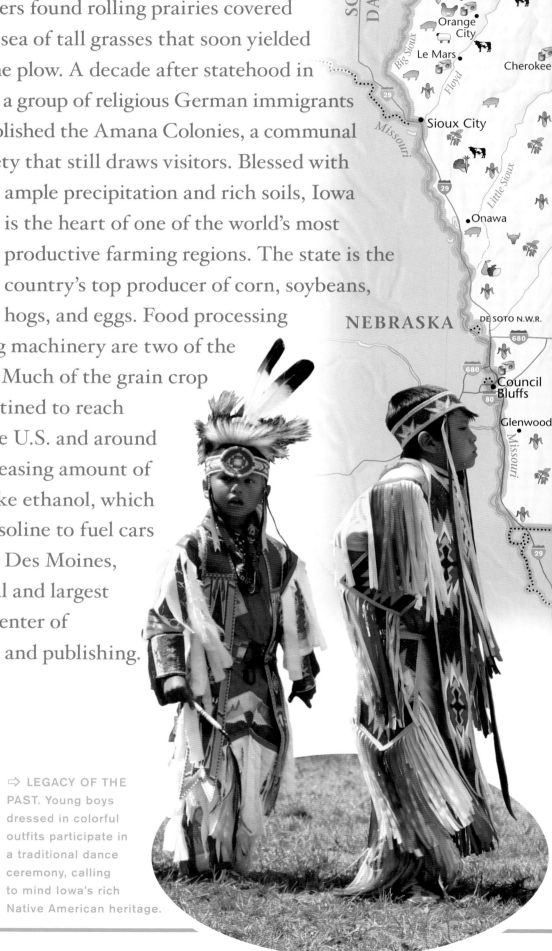

⇨ LEGACY OF THE
PAST. Young boys
dressed in colorful
outfits participate in
a traditional dance
ceremony, calling
to mind Iowa's rich
Native American heritage.

GREEN ENERGY

*2007 production capacity in
millions of gallons (liters)

Iowa	Nebraska	Illinois	Minnesota	South Dakota
3,357 (12,709)*	1,745 (6,607)	1,172 (4,436)	1,102 (4,172)	985 (3,729)

Iowa is the leading producer of ethanol fuel,
a clean-burning, renewable, non-fossil fuel
energy source made mainly from corn.

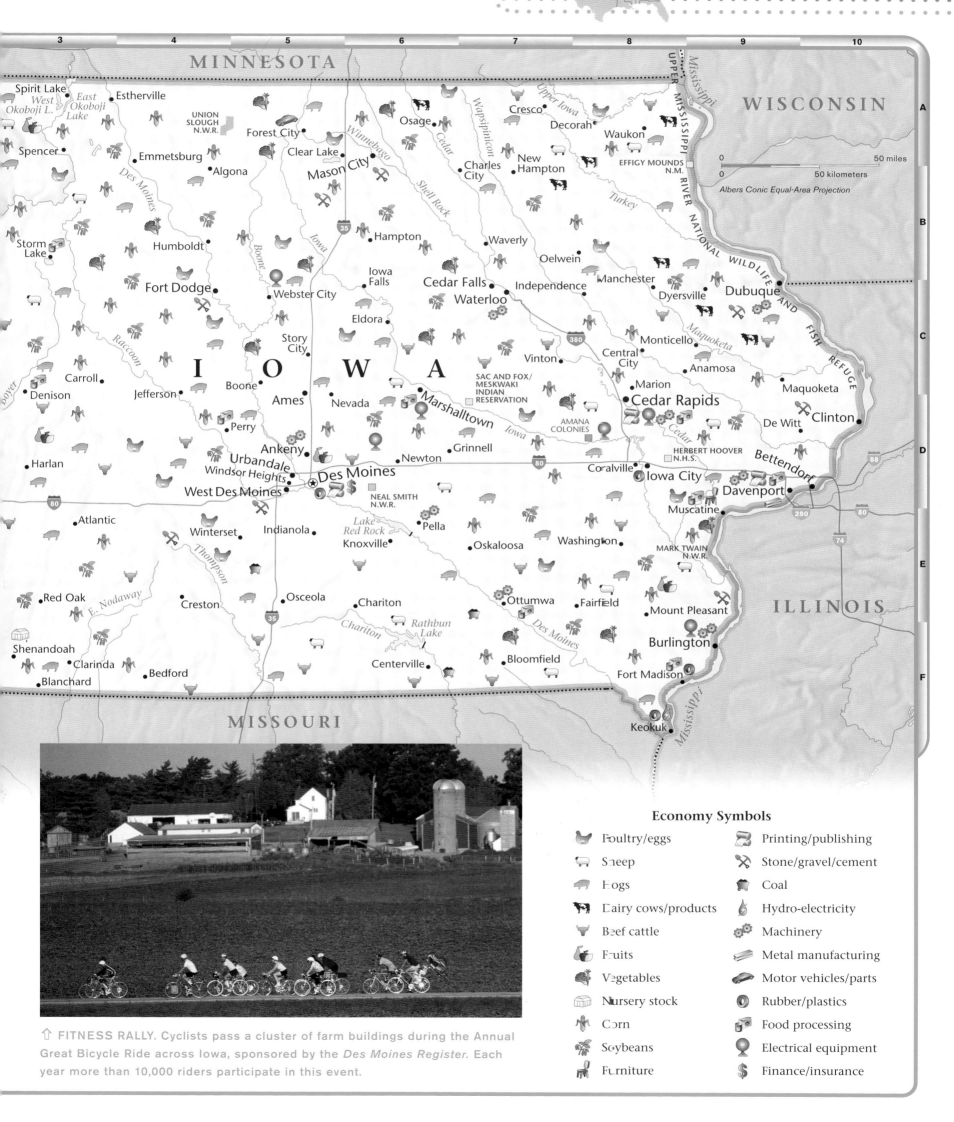

MINNESOTA

WISCONSIN

3   4   5   6   7   8   9   10

Spirit Lake
West Okoboji L.
East Okoboji Lake
Estherville
UNION SLOUGH N.W.R.
Forest City
Osage
Cresco
Decorah
Waukon
EFFIGY MOUNDS N.M.

0 50 miles
0 50 kilometers
Albers Conic Equal-Area Projection

Spencer
Emmetsburg
Algona
Clear Lake
Mason City
Charles City
New Hampton

Storm Lake
Humboldt
Hampton
Iowa Falls
Waverly
Oelwein
Manchester
Dyersville
Dubuque

Fort Dodge
Webster City
Cedar Falls
Waterloo
Independence

Eldora

Story City
Vinton
Central City
Monticello
Anamosa

IOWA

Carroll
Boone
Ames
Nevada
Marshalltown
SAC AND FOX/ MESKWAKI INDIAN RESERVATION
Marion
Cedar Rapids
Maquoketa

Denison
Jefferson
Perry
Grinnell
AMANA COLONIES
De Witt
Clinton

Harlan
Urbandale
Ankeny
Newton
HERBERT HOOVER N.H.S.
Coralville
Bettendorf

Windsor Heights
Des Moines
West Des Moines
NEAL SMITH N.W.R.
Iowa City
Davenport

Atlantic
Winterset
Indianola
Pella
Muscatine

Red Oak
Creston
Osceola
Chariton
Knoxville
Oskaloosa
Washington
MARK TWAIN N.W.R.

Shenandoah
Clarinda
Blanchard
Bedford
Lake Red Rock
Rathbun Lake
Centerville
Chariton
Bloomfield
Ottumwa
Fairfield
Mount Pleasant
Burlington
Fort Madison

ILLINOIS

MISSOURI

Keokuk

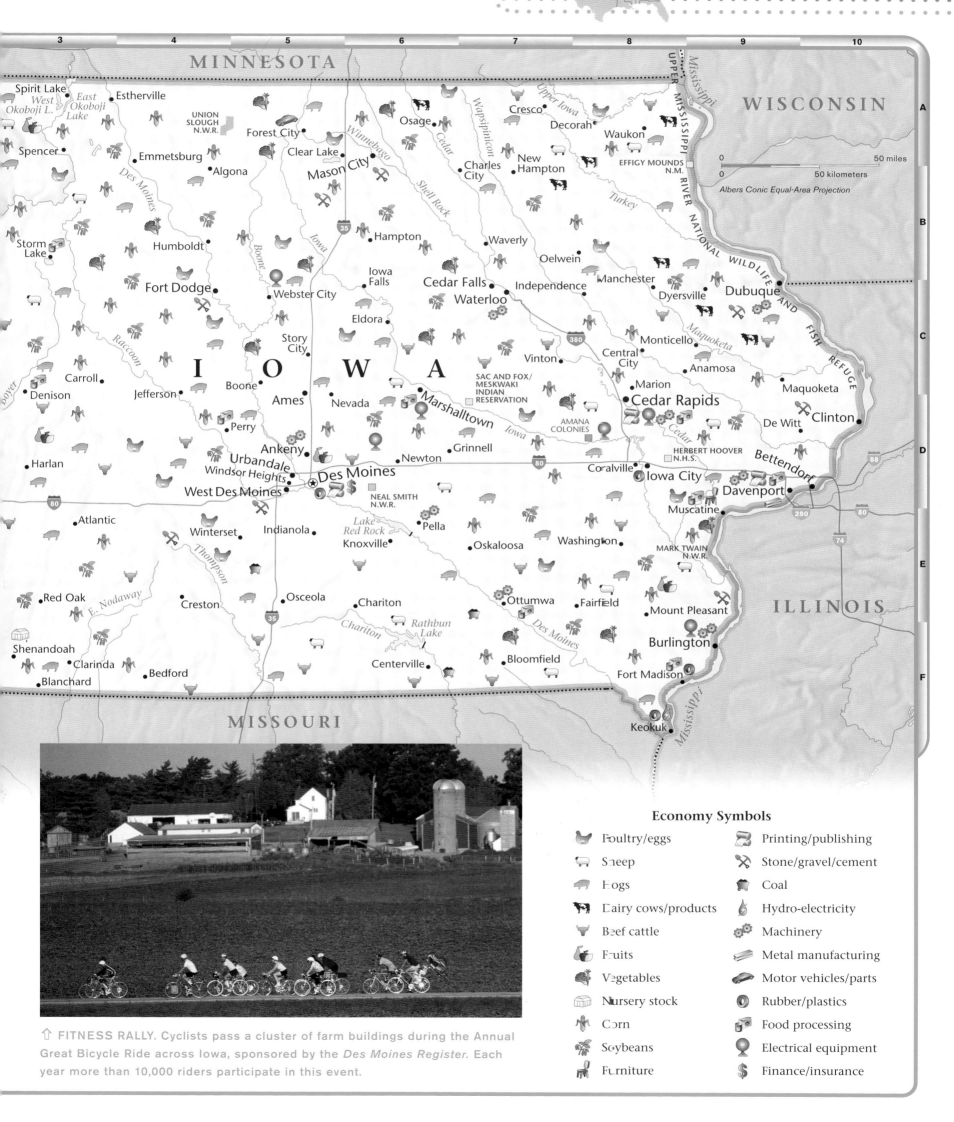

⇧ FITNESS RALLY. Cyclists pass a cluster of farm buildings during the Annual Great Bicycle Ride across Iowa, sponsored by the *Des Moines Register*. Each year more than 10,000 riders participate in this event.

Economy Symbols

Poultry/eggs		Printing/publishing	
Sheep		Stone/gravel/cement	
Hogs		Coal	
Dairy cows/products		Hydro-electricity	
Beef cattle		Machinery	
Fruits		Metal manufacturing	
Vegetables		Motor vehicles/parts	
Nursery stock		Rubber/plastics	
Corn		Food processing	
Soybeans		Electrical equipment	
Furniture		Finance/insurance	

KANSAS

STATS

Area
82,277 sq mi (213,097 sq km)

Population
2,775,997

Capital
Topeka
Population 122,113

Largest city
Wichita
Population 357,698

Ethnic/racial groups
89.1% white; 6.0% African American; 2.2% Asian; 1.0% Native American. Hispanic (any race) 8.6%.

Industry
Aircraft manufacturing, transportation equipment, construction, food processing, printing and publishing, health care

Agriculture
Cattle, wheat, sorghum, soybeans, hogs, corn

Statehood
January 29, 1861; 34th state

GEO WHIZ

Plesiosaur skeletons and many other marine reptile fossils have been unearthed in Kansas. In 2007 National Geographic released the IMAX film *Sea Monsters,* which explores the kinds of animals that lived in the prehistoric sea that covered Kansas and much of North America 82 million years ago.

The Tallgrass Prairie National Preserve, the nation's last great expanse of tallgrass prairie, anchors a world renewed by fire. It is in the Flint Hills of Kansas.

Lindsborg is proud of its Swedish heritage and the fact that it is home to the Anatoly Karpov International School of Chess. The school is named for the Russian player who succeeded American Bobby Fischer as world champion in 1975.

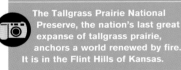

WESTERN MEADOWLARK
SUNFLOWER

KANSAS

Considered by whites to be unsuitable for settlement, Kansas was made part of Indian Territory—a vast tract of land between Missouri and the Rockies—in the 1830s. By the 1850s whites were fighting Indians for more land and among themselves over the issue of slavery. In 1861 Kansas entered the Union as a free state. After the Civil War, cowboys drove Texas cattle to railheads in the Wild West towns of Abilene and Dodge City, where waiting trains hauled cattle to slaughterhouses in the East. Today, the state remains a major beef producer and the country's top wheat grower. Oil and natural gas wells dot the landscape, while factories in Wichita, the largest city, make aircraft equipment. A preserve in the Flint Hills boasts one of the few tallgrass prairies to escape farmers' plows. Heading west toward the Rockies, elevations climb slowly, and the climate gets drier. Threats of fierce thunderstorms accompanied by tornados have many Kansans keeping an eye on the sky.

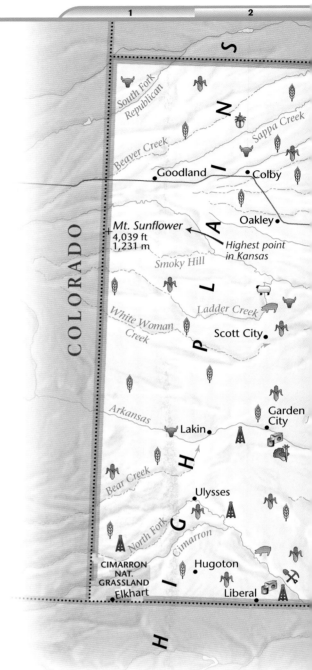

⬆ OMINOUS SKY. Lightning splits the sky as black clouds of a thunderstorm roll across a field of wheat. Such storms bring heavy rain and often spawn dangerous tornados.

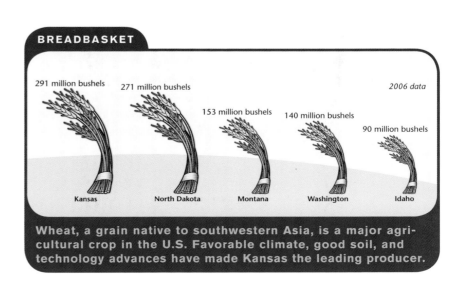

BREADBASKET

291 million bushels — Kansas
271 million bushels — North Dakota
153 million bushels — Montana
140 million bushels — Washington
90 million bushels — Idaho

2006 data

Wheat, a grain native to southwestern Asia, is a major agricultural crop in the U.S. Favorable climate, good soil, and technology advances have made Kansas the leading producer.

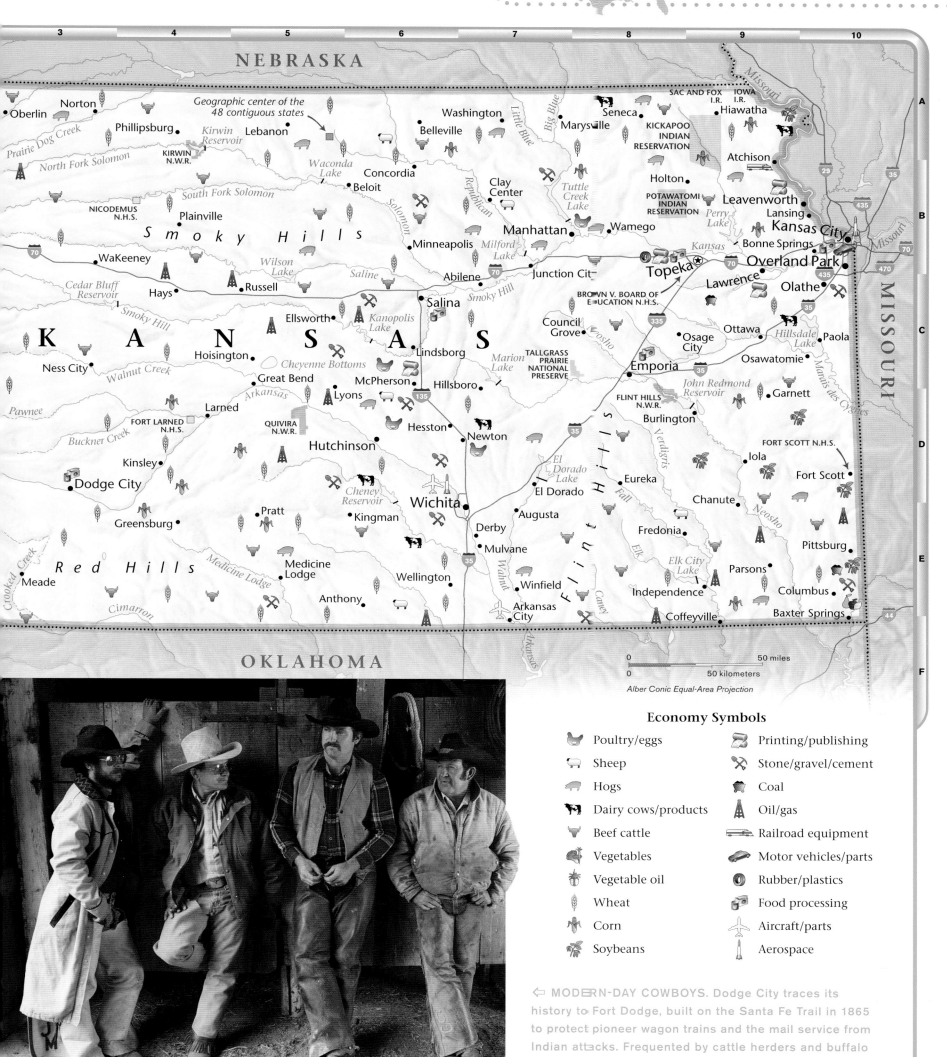

NEBRASKA

3   4   5   6   7   8   9   10

Oberlin
Norton
Phillipsburg
Prairie Dog Creek
North Fork Solomon
KIRWIN N.W.R.
Kirwin Reservoir
Lebanon
Geographic center of the 48 contiguous states
Washington
Belleville
Little Blue
Big Blue
Marysville
Seneca
SAC AND FOX I.R.
IOWA I.R.
Hiawatha
KICKAPOO INDIAN RESERVATION
Atchison
Concordia
Beloit
Clay Center
Holton
Leavenworth
Lansing
Missouri
NICODEMUS N.H.S.
Plainville
South Fork Solomon
Waconda Lake
Tuttle Creek Lake
POTAWATOMI INDIAN RESERVATION
Perry Lake
Kansas City
Minneapolis
Manhattan
Wamego
Bonner Springs
Overland Park
WaKeeney
Smoky Hills
Milford Lake
Solomon
Republican
Bonne Springs
Missouri
Wilson Lake
Saline
Abilene
Junction City
Topeka
Lawrence
Olathe
Cedar Bluff Reservoir
Hays
Russell
Smoky Hill
BROWN V. BOARD OF EDUCATION N.H.S.
K A N S A S
Ellsworth
Kanopolis Lake
Salina
Council Grove
Osage City
Ottawa
Hillsdale Lake
Paola
Ness City
Hoisington
Cheyenne Bottoms
Lindsborg
Marion Lake
TALLGRASS PRAIRIE NATIONAL PRESERVE
Emporia
Osawatomie
Walnut Creek
Great Bend
McPherson
Hillsboro
Neosho
John Redmond Reservoir
Garnett
Pawnee
Lyons
Arkansas
Larned
FORT LARNED N.H.S.
FLINT HILLS N.W.R.
Burlington
Buckner Creek
QUIVIRA N.W.R.
Hesston
Newton
FORT SCOTT N.H.S.
Kinsley
Hutchinson
Verdigris
Iola
Fort Scott
Dodge City
Cheney Reservoir
El Dorado Lake
Eureka
Chanute
Greensburg
Pratt
Wichita
El Dorado
Fall
Pittsburg
Kingman
Augusta
Fredonia
Parsons
Medicine Lodge
Derby
Mulvane
Elk City Lake
Columbus
Red Hills
Medicine Lodge
Wellington
Winfield
Independence
Baxter Springs
Meade
Cimarron
Anthony
Arkansas City
Coffeyville
Crooked Creek
Flint Hills
Wahut
Caney
Elk
Neosho

OKLAHOMA

MISSOURI

0   50 miles
0   50 kilometers
Alber Conic Equal-Area Projection

Economy Symbols

Poultry/eggs		Printing/publishing	
Sheep		Stone/gravel/cement	
Hogs		Coal	
Dairy cows/products		Oil/gas	
Beef cattle		Railroad equipment	
Vegetables		Motor vehicles/parts	
Vegetable oil		Rubber/plastics	
Wheat		Food processing	
Corn		Aircraft/parts	
Soybeans		Aerospace	

⬅ MODERN-DAY COWBOYS. Dodge City traces its history to Fort Dodge, built on the Santa Fe Trail in 1865 to protect pioneer wagon trains and the mail service from Indian attacks. Frequented by cattle herders and buffalo hunters, the town was known for its lawlessness.

THE GREAT LAKE STATE:
MICHIGAN

THE BASICS

STATS

Area
96,716 sq mi (250,495 sq km)

Population
10,071,822

Capital
Lansing
Population 114,276

Largest city
Detroit
Population 871,121

Ethnic/racial groups
81.2% white; 14.3% African American; 2.4% Asian; .6% Native American. Hispanic (any race) 3.9%.

Industry
Motor vehicles and parts, machinery, metal products, office furniture, tourism, chemicals

Agriculture
Dairy products, cattle, vegetables, hogs, corn, nursery stock, soybeans, hay, fruit

Statehood
January 26, 1837; 26th state

GEO WHIZ

Researchers at the Seney National Wildlife Refuge near Seney, Michigan, have discovered that male loons change the sound of their call when they move to a new territory. The reason is still a mystery, but it does explain why people say that loons sound different on different lakes.

The Keweenaw Peninsula is an adventurer's paradise. There's a 100-mile (161-km) water trail for canoers, scores of wrecks for divers, 14 miles (23 km) of forested bike paths, and more than 150 miles (240 km) of hiking trails on nearby Isle Royale National Park.

Climate change is causing Lake Michigan and the other Great Lakes to shrink, a fact that is very costly to shipping. For every inch (2.5 cm) of draft that a ship loses, a freighter must lighten its cargo by as much as 270 tons to keep from running aground. The collective annual cost can be in the billions of dollars.

ROBIN
APPLE BLOSSOM

WINTER SPORT

Registered snowmobiles 2006–2007 data

302,000* Michigan
277,290 Minnesota
232,320 Wisconsin
146,662 New York
53,400 Alaska

Snowmobiling has become a popular winter sport. Michigan and other states of the upper Midwest lead in number of registered snowmobiles.

MICHIGAN

Indians had friendly relations with early French fur traders who came to what is now Michigan, but they waged battles with the British who later assumed control. Completion of New York's Erie Canal in 1825 made it easier for settlers to reach the area, and statehood came in 1837. Michigan consists of two large peninsulas that border four of the five Great Lakes— Erie, Huron, Michigan, and Superior.

⇧ ROLLING OFF THE ASSEMBLY LINE. Motor vehicle production is the largest manufacturing sector in the U.S., and Michigan is the center of the industry. At Chrysler's Sterling Heights assembly plant, more than 700 robots speed production by making it possible to build different car models on the same assembly line.

Most of the population is on the state's Lower Peninsula, while the Upper Peninsula, once a productive mining area, now is popular among vacationing nature lovers. The five-mile- (8-km-) long Mackinac Bridge has linked the peninsulas since 1957. In the 20th century Michigan became the center of the American auto industry, and the state's fortunes have risen and fallen with those of the Big Three car companies. Though it remains a big producer of cars and trucks, the state is working to diversify its economy. Michigan's farms grow crops ranging from grains to fruits and vegetables.

⇧ REFLECTION OF THE PAST. Victorian-style summer homes, built on Mackinac Island in the late 19th century by wealthy railroad families, now welcome vacationers to the island. To protect the environment, cars are not allowed.

ONTARIO

CANADA
U.S.

MINNESOTA

0   50 miles
0   50 kilometers
Alber Conic Equal-Area Projection

LAKE SUPERIOR

CANADA
U.S.

⬅ SOLEMN PREDA-
TOR. Wolves on Isle
Royale, in upper
Lake Superior,
live in packs that
hunt moose in
this isolated
national park.

Soo Canals: among the busiest ship
canals in the Western Hemisphere

ISLE ROYALE
NATIONAL
PARK
Isle Royale

KEWEENAW
N.H.P.   Laurium   *Keweenaw
Peninsula*

ONTONAGON
INDIAN
RESERVATION   Houghton

HURON
N.W.R.

PORCUPINE MTS.
S.P.   ONTONAGON
N.W.&S.R.   Mt. Arvon
1,979 ft
+603 m   YELLOW DOG N.W.&S.R.

BLACK
N.W.&S.R.   OTTAWA   STURGEON
N.W.&
S.R.   L'Anse
L'ANSE
I.R.   *Highest point
in Michigan*   Marquette
GRAND ISLAND
N.R.A.

PICTURED
ROCKS
NATIONAL
LAKESHORE

TAHQUAMENON
FALLS S.P.   *Whitefish
Bay*   Sault Sainte Marie
SAULT SAINTE MARIE I.R.

PRESQUE
ISLE
N.W.&S.R.   NAT.   Ishpeming   OTTAWA
N.F.   Munising   SENEY
N.W.R.   TAHQUAMENON
(EAST BRANCH)
N.W.&S.R.   BAY
MILLS
I.R.   BAY MILLS I.R.

ONTARIO

Ironwood   FOREST   PAINT
N.W.&S.R.   *Ford*   UPPER   PENINSULA   INDIAN
N.W.
&S.R.   HIAWATHA   NATIONAL   FOREST   CARP N.W.&S.R.   *Drummond
Island*   HARBOR ISLAND N.W.R.

LAC VIEUX DESERT I.R.   *Brule*   WHITEFISH
N.W.
&S.R.   Manistique   FATHER MARQUETTE
NATIONAL MEMORIAL   St. Ignace   *Mackinac I.*

Economy Symbols

🐟 Fishing

🐓 Poultry/eggs

🐷 Hogs

🐄 Dairy cows/products

🐂 Beef cattle

🍒 Fruits

🥬 Vegetables

🪴 Nursery stock

🌾 Wheat

🌽 Corn

🫘 Soybeans

🌲 Timber/forest products

🪑 Furniture

⚒ Stone/gravel/cement

⛏ Mining

🛢 Oil/gas

💧 Hydro-electricity

⚙ Machinery

🔧 Metal products

🚗 Motor vehicles/parts

🧪 Chemistry

🍲 Food processing

📷 Tourism

HANNAHVILLE
I.R.   *Cedar*   STURGEON N.W.&S.R.   Gladstone   Escanaba   Garden
Peninsula   Manistique

Iron
Mountain   *Garden
Peninsula*   *Beaver
I.*   Cheboygan

Menominee   Garden
Peninsula   *Burt
Lake*   *Mullett
L.*

Menominee   *Green Bay*   *Manitou
Islands*   *Grand Traverse Bay*   Site of at least
50 shipwrecks   Petoskey   Boyne
City   *Pigeon*   Rogers City

WISCONSIN   *Menominee*   *Manitou Passage*   GRAND
TRAVERSE
I.R.   Gaylord   *Thunder Bay*   Alpena
Thunder Bay

SLEEPING
BEAR DUNES
NAT. LAKESHORE   Traverse City   Kalkaska   *Au Sable*   Mio   AU SABLE
N.W.&S.R.   *Hubbard L.*

BEAR CREEK
N.W.
&S.R.   LITTLE RIVER I.R.   *Manistee*   PINE
N.W.&S.R.   Cadillac   HURON
NAT.   *Houghton
Lake*   FOREST

Manistee   MANISTEE N.W.&S.R.   MANISTEE   *Houghton
Lake*   *Rifle*   Tawas
City

Ludington   PERE
MARQUETTE
N.W.&S.R.   NATIONAL   *Muskegon*   Big Rapids   ISABELLA I.R.   *Saginaw
Bay*   Bad Axe   Harbor
Beach

PERE MARQUETTE
N.W.&S.R.   FOREST   Mt. Pleasant   ISABELLA
I.R.   Midland   Bay City   *Cass*

Fremont   FLAT
N.W.&
S.R.   Alma   SHIAWASSEE
N.W.R.   Saginaw   Caro   Sandusky

Muskegon   Greenville   Belding   Ionia   St. Johns   Owosso   *Flint*   Flint   Port
Huron

Grand Haven   *Grand*   LOWER   PENINSULA   Burton   St. Clair

Grand Rapids   Kentwood   *Looking Glass*   East Lansing   Pontiac   Warren   St. Clair
Shores

Holland   Zeeland   Hastings   Lansing   Mason   Troy   Livonia   *Lake
St. Clair*

South Haven   Charlotte   *Kalamazoo*   Battle
Creek   Jackson   Ann Arbor   696   Detroit

Kalamazoo   Marshall   Albion   Ypsilanti   Dearborn

Benton Harbor   Portage   *Raisin*   Tecumseh   Monroe
St. Joseph   Dowagiac   *St. Joseph*   Coldwater   Hillsdale   Adrian   *Temperance*

Three Rivers   Sturgis   Lambertville   *LAKE
ERIE*
Niles

ILLINOIS   INDIANA   OHIO

Straits of Mackinac   Bois Blanc I.

LAKE   MICHIGAN

LAKE   HURON

ONTARIO

CANADA
U.S.

THE BASICS

STATS

Area
86,939 sq mi (225,172 sq km)

Population
5,197,621

Capital
St. Paul
Population 273,535

Largest city
Minneapolis
Population 372,833

Ethnic/racial groups
89.3% white; 4.5% African American;
3.5% Asian; 1.2% Native American.
Hispanic (any race) 3.8%.

Industry
Health services, tourism, real estate,
banking and insurance, industrial
machinery, printing and publishing,
food processing, scientific equipment

Agriculture
Corn, soybeans, dairy products, hogs,
cattle, turkeys, wheat

Statehood
May 11, 1858; 32nd state

GEO WHIZ

Nett Lake on the Bois Forte Chippewa
reservation, in northern Minnesota,
is the largest contiguous wild
rice lake in the world. Native
people have been gathering
what the Indians call *manoomin*
for thousands of years.

The Mayo Clinic, a world-famous medical research center founded in 1889 by
Dr. William W. Mayo, is in Rochester.

The Boundary Waters Canoe Area
Wilderness, along the Minnesota-
Ontario border, was the
first wilderness
area in the U.S. to
be set aside for canoeing.

COMMON LOON

SHOWY LADY'S
SLIPPER

MINNESOTA

French fur traders began arriving in present-day Minnesota in the mid-17th century. Statehood was established in 1858, and most remaining Indians were forced from the state after a decisive battle in 1862. During the late 1800s large numbers of Germans, Scandinavians, and other immigrants settled a land rich in wildlife, timber, minerals, and fertile soils. Today, farming is concentrated in the south and west. In the northeast, the Mesabi Range's open-pit mines make the state the country's source of iron ore. Most of the ore is shipped from Duluth. It, along with Superior, in nearby Wisconsin (see p. 113), is the leading Great Lakes port. Ships from the port reach the Atlantic Ocean via the St. Lawrence Seaway. Scattered across the state's landscape are thousands of lakes—ancient footprints of retreating glaciers—that draw anglers and canoeists. One of those lakes, Lake Itasca, is the source of the mighty Mississippi River, which flows through the Twin Cities of Minneapolis and St. Paul.

⇧ SUMMER FUN. Young girls play on a rope swing near Leech Lake in northern Minnesota. The state's many lakes are remnants of the last ice age, when glaciers gouged depressions that filled with water as the ice sheets retreated.

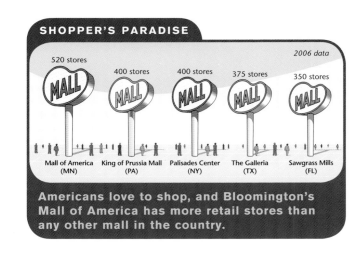

SHOPPER'S PARADISE

2006 data

520 stores	400 stores	400 stores	375 stores	350 stores
MALL	MALL	MALL	MALL	MALL
Mall of America (MN)	King of Prussia Mall (PA)	Palisades Center (NY)	The Galleria (TX)	Sawgrass Mills (FL)

Americans love to shop, and Bloomington's
Mall of America has more retail stores than
any other mall in the country.

⇐ INLAND PORT. Duluth, on the northern shore of Lake Superior, is the westernmost deep-water port on the St. Lawrence Seaway. Barges and container ships move products such as iron ore and grain along the Great Lakes to the Atlantic Ocean and to markets around the world.

The "Northwest Angle" is the northernmost point in the 48 contiguous states

0 ___ 100 miles
0 ___ 100 kilometers
Albers Conic Equal-Area Projection

MANITOBA

CANADA
U.S.

RED LAKE
INDIAN RES.

• Hallock
• Roseau
Baudette
Lake of the Woods
Rainy Lake
International Falls
VOYAGEURS NATIONAL PARK
Namakan Lake
ONTARIO

Roseau
AGASSIZ N.W.R.
Mud Lake
• Warren
Thief River Falls
East Grand Forks
• Crookston
Red Lake
RED LAKE INDIAN RESERVATION
Upper Red Lake
Lower Red Lake
Big Fork
BOIS FORTE I.R.
Vermilion Lake
BOIS FORTE (VERMILION LAKE) I.R.
• Ely
BOUNDARY WATERS CANOE AREA WILDERNESS
Highest point in Minnesota
Eagle Mt. 2,301 ft 701 m
Pigeon
GRAND PORTAGE I.R.
GRAND PORTAGE NAT. MON.
CANADA U.S.

NORTH DAKOTA

Red River of the North

Source of the Mississippi River
• Bemidji
WHITE EARTH INDIAN RESERVATION
Wild Rice
Winnibigoshish
CHIPPEWA NATIONAL LEECH LAKE INDIAN RES. FOREST
Lake Itasca
• Walker
Leech Lake
BOIS FORTE (DEER CREEK) I.R.
• Grand Rapids
Mesabi Range
• Virginia
• Chisholm
• Hibbing
SUPERIOR
NATIONAL FOREST
Two Harbor
Grand Marais
LAKE SUPERIOR

HAMDEN SLOUGH N.W.R.
• Moorhead
Detroit Lakes
Menahga
TAMARAC N.W.R.
Park Rapids
SANDY LAKE I.R.
St. Louis
Duluth
FOND DU LAC I.R.
Cloquet
Proctor
MICHIGAN

Pelican Rapids
• Perham
• Wadena
Crow Wing
Mississippi
RICE LAKE N.W.R.
Mille-Lacs Lake
Fergus Falls
Otter Tail Lake
• Aitkin
• Brainerd

MINNESOTA

• Wheaton
Lake Traverse
• Morris
Big Stone Lake
Ortonville
Alexandria
Long Prairie
• Little Falls
MILLE LACS I.R.
• Mora
Pine City
Sandstone
St. Croix
MILLE LACS I.R.
ST. CROIX NATIONAL SCENIC RIVERWAY

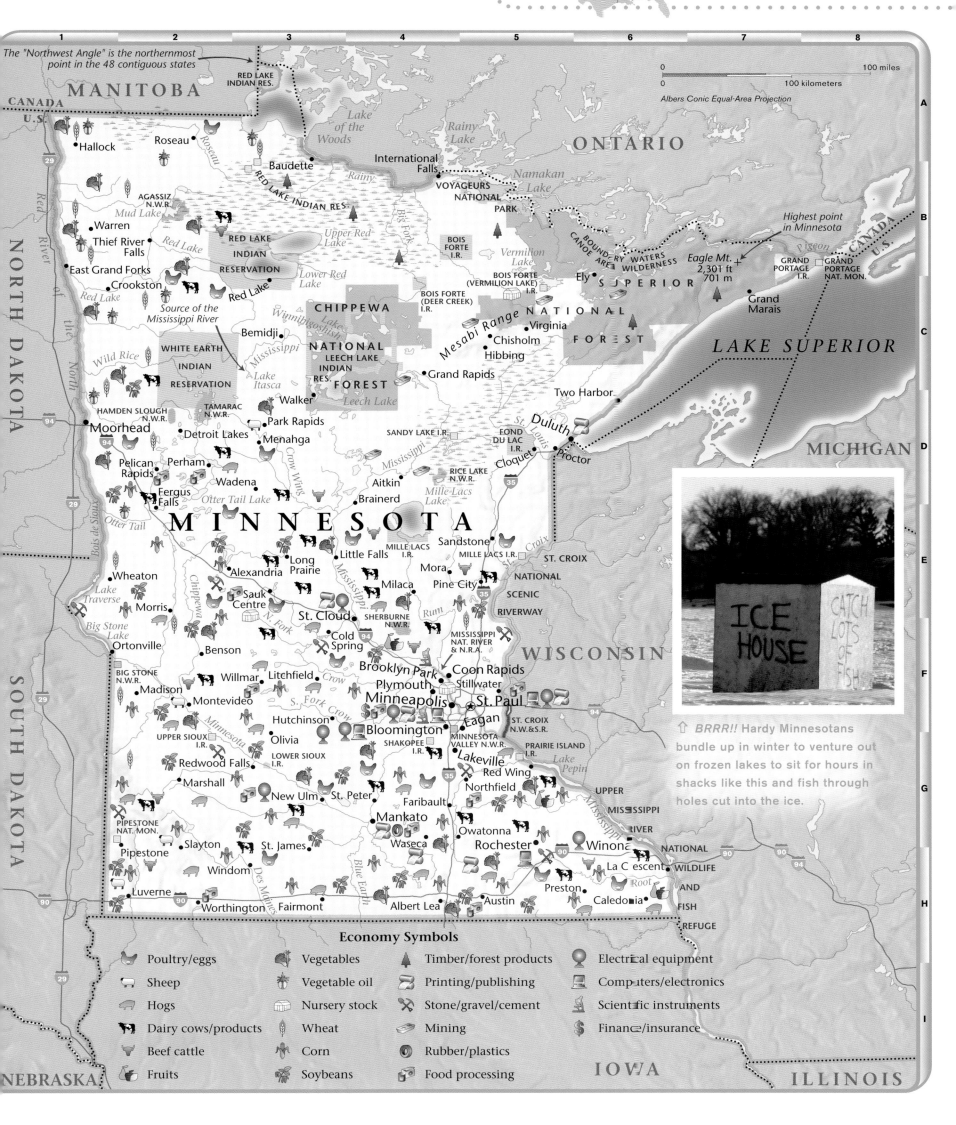

Chippewa
Sauk Centre
Cold Spring
St. Cloud
SHERBURNE N.W.R.
N. Fork
Rum
Milaca

BIG STONE N.W.R.
• Madison
• Benson
• Willmar
Litchfield
• Montevideo
Crow
Brooklyn Park
Plymouth
Minneapolis
Coon Rapids
Stillwater
St. Paul
MISSISSIPPI NAT. RIVER & N.R.A.
WISCONSIN

UPPER SIOUX I.R.
Minnesota
• Hutchinson
• Olivia
Bloomington
SHAKOPEE I.R.
Eagan
MINNESOTA VALLEY N.W.R.
ST. CROIX N.W.&S.R.
Lakeville
PRAIRIE ISLAND I.R.
Lake Pepin

SOUTH DAKOTA

Redwood Falls
LOWER SIOUX I.R.
• Marshall
New Ulm
S. Fork Crow
St. Peter
• Faribault
Red Wing
• Northfield
Mankato
Owatonna
UPPER MISSISSIPPI RIVER

PIPESTONE NAT. MON.
• Pipestone
• Slayton
St. James
• Waseca
Rochester
Winona
La Crescent
NATIONAL WILDLIFE

Des Moines
Blue Earth
• Windom
• Luverne
Worthington
• Fairmont
Albert Lea
• Austin
• Preston
Caledonia
Root
AND FISH REFUGE

NEBRASKA
IOWA
ILLINOIS

Economy Symbols

Poultry/eggs	Vegetables	Timber/forest products
Sheep	Vegetable oil	Printing/publishing
Hogs	Nursery stock	Stone/gravel/cement
Dairy cows/products	Wheat	Mining
Beef cattle	Corn	Rubber/plastics
Fruits	Soybeans	Food processing

Electrical equipment
Computers/electronics
Scientific instruments
Finance/insurance

⇧ *BRRR!!* Hardy Minnesotans bundle up in winter to venture out on frozen lakes to sit for hours in shacks like this and fish through holes cut into the ice.

THE SHOW-ME STATE:
MISSOURI

THE BASICS

STATS

Area
69,704 sq mi (180,534 sq mi)

Population
5,878,415

Capital
Jefferson City
Population 37,550

Largest city
Kansas City
Population 447,306

Ethnic/racial groups
85.1% white; 11.5% African American;
1.4% Asian; .5% Native American.
Hispanic (any race) 2.8%.

Industry
Transportation equipment, food
processing, chemicals, electrical
equipment, metal products

Agriculture
Cattle, soybeans, hogs, corn, poultry
and eggs, dairy products

Statehood
August 10, 1821; 24th state

GEO WHIZ

Camp Wood, near St. Louis, was
the starting point for Lewis and
Clark's Corps of Discovery,
commissioned by President
Thomas Jefferson to seek a water route
to the Pacific. Along the way
their encounters included hundreds
of new species of plants and animals,
nearly 50 Indian tribes, and the
Rocky Mountains.

In Ash Grove, near Springfield,
Father Moses Berry has turned his
family history into a museum for
slavery education. His family was
one of the few who didn't flee the
area after three falsely accused
black men were lynched in 1906.
The museum is the only one of
its kind in the Ozark region.

EASTERN BLUEBIRD
HAWTHORN

MISSOURI

The Osage people were among the largest tribes in present-day Missouri when the French began establishing permanent settlements in the 1700s. The U.S. obtained the territory in the 1803 Louisiana Purchase, and Lewis and Clark began exploring the vast wilderness by paddling up the Missouri River from the St. Louis area. Missouri entered the Union as a slave state in 1821. Though it remained in the Union during the Civil War, sympathies were split between the North and South. For much of the 1800s the state was the staging ground for pioneers traveling to western frontiers on the Santa Fe and Oregon Trails. Today, Missouri leads the country in lead mining. Farmers raise cattle, hogs, poultry, corn, and soybeans. Cotton and rice are grown in the southeastern Bootheel region. Cross-state river-port rivals St. Louis and Kansas City are centers of transportation, manufacturing, and finance. Lakes, caves, scenic views, and Branson's country music shows bring many tourists to the Ozarks.

⇧ TALL HATS. Since its founding in 1865 in St. Joseph, the Stetson Company has been associated with western hats worn by men and women around the world.

HISTORICAL MARKERS

630 feet (192 m) — Gateway Arch (MO)
570 feet (174 m) — San Jacinto Monument (TX)
555 feet (169 m) — Washington Monument (DC)
352 feet (107 m) — Perry's Victory and International Peace Memorial (OH)
351 feet (107 m) — Jefferson Davis Monument (KY)

The tallest of all monuments in the U.S. is Gateway Arch in St. Louis, which marks the departure point for westward-bound pioneers during the 19th century.

⇨ HEADING WEST. The 630-foot (192-m) Gateway Arch honors the role St. Louis played in U.S. westward expansion. Trams carry one million tourists to the top of the arch each year.

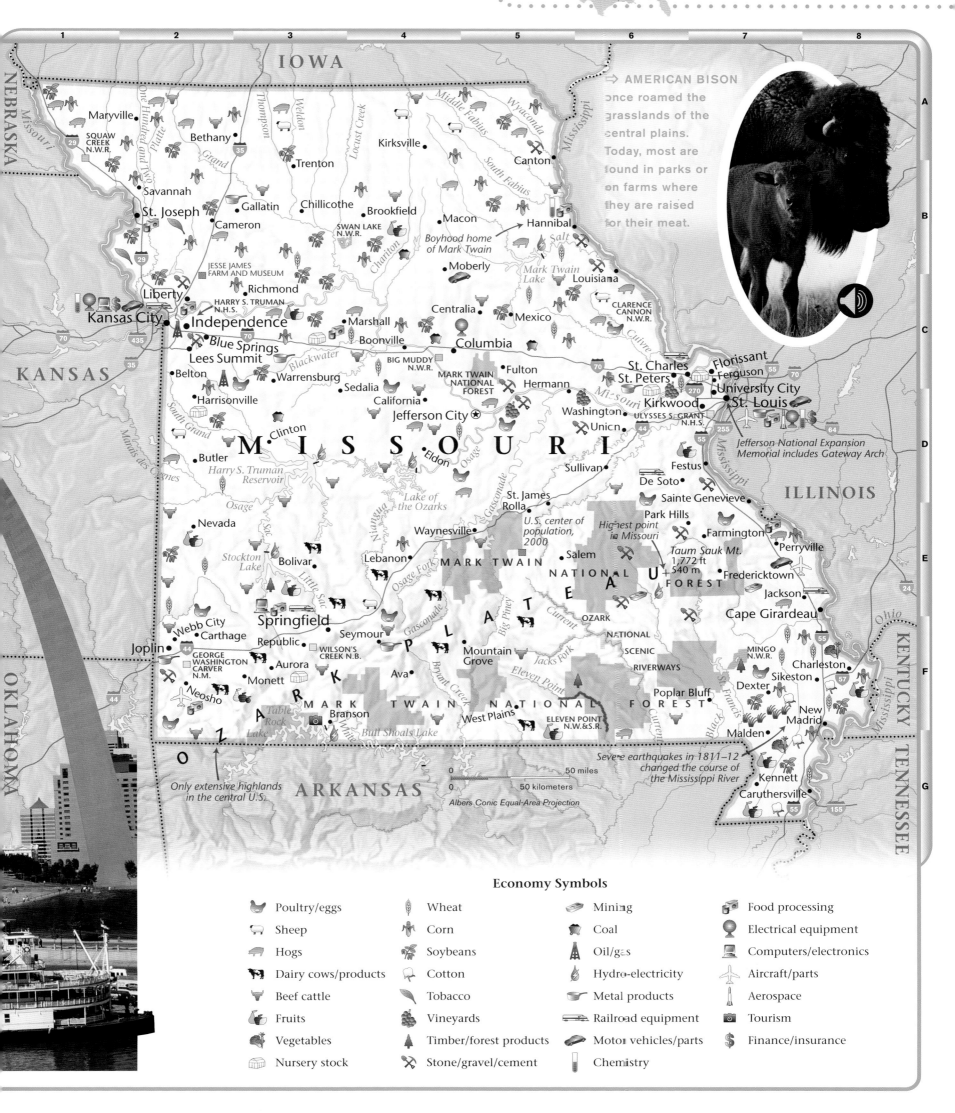

→ AMERICAN BISON once roamed the grasslands of the central plains. Today, most are found in parks or on farms where they are raised for their meat.

IOWA

NEBRASKA

Maryville
SQUAW CREEK N.W.R.
Bethany
Trenton
Kirksville
Canton
Savannah
Gallatin
Chillicothe
Brookfield
Macon
Hannibal
St. Joseph
Cameron
SWAN LAKE N.W.R.
Boyhood home of Mark Twain
Richmond
Moberly
Louisiana
Liberty
JESSE JAMES FARM AND MUSEUM
Mark Twain Lake
HARRY S. TRUMAN N.H.S.
Centralia
Mexico
CLARENCE CANNON N.W.R.
Kansas City
Independence
Marshall
Columbia
St. Charles
Florissant
Ferguson
Blue Springs
Boonville
St. Peters
Lees Summit
Blackwater
BIG MUDDY N.W.R.
Fulton
University City
Belton
Warrensburg
Sedalia
Hermann
Kirkwood
St. Louis
Harrisonville
California
MARK TWAIN NATIONAL FOREST
Washington
ULYSSES S. GRANT N.H.S.
Jefferson City ✪
Union
Jefferson National Expansion Memorial includes Gateway Arch

M·I·S·S·O·U·R·I

Clinton
Eldon
Osage
Sullivan
Festus
Butler
Harry S. Truman Reservoir
De Soto
Sainte Genevieve
Lake of the Ozarks
St. James
Rolla
Park Hills
ILLINOIS
Nevada
U.S. center of population, 2000
Farmington
Waynesville
Highest point in Missouri
Perryville
Lebanon
Salem
Taum Sauk Mt. 1,772 ft 540 m
Fredericktown
Stockton Lake
Bolivar
MARK TWAIN
Jackson
NATIONAL
Cape Girardeau
Springfield
Seymour
FOREST
OZARK
Webb City
Carthage
Mountain Grove
NATIONAL
Joplin
Republic
WILSON'S CREEK N.B.
Ava
SCENIC
MINGO N.W.R.
GEORGE WASHINGTON CARVER N.M.
Aurora
RIVERWAYS
Charleston
Monett
West Plains
Sikeston
Neosho
Table Rock Lake
Branson
Poplar Bluff
Dexter
M A R K   T W A I N   N A T I O N A L   F O R E S T
New Madrid
O Z A R K
Bull Shoals Lake
ELEVEN POINT N.W.&S.R.
Malden
KENTUCKY

Only extensive highlands in the central U.S.

ARKANSAS

Severe earthquakes in 1811–12 changed the course of the Mississippi River

Kennett
Caruthersville
TENNESSEE

OKLAHOMA

0   50 miles
0   50 kilometers
Albers Conic Equal-Area Projection

Economy Symbols

Poultry/eggs	Wheat	Mining	Food processing
Sheep	Corn	Coal	Electrical equipment
Hogs	Soybeans	Oil/gas	Computers/electronics
Dairy cows/products	Cotton	Hydro-electricity	Aircraft/parts
Beef cattle	Tobacco	Metal products	Aerospace
Fruits	Vineyards	Railroad equipment	Tourism
Vegetables	Timber/forest products	Motor vehicles/parts	Finance/insurance
Nursery stock	Stone/gravel/cement	Chemistry	

THE BASICS

STATS

Area
77,354 sq mi (200,346 sq km)

Population
1,774,571

Capital
Lincoln
Population 241,167

Largest city
Omaha
Population 419,545

Ethnic/racial groups
91.8% white; 4.4% African American; 1.7% Asian; 1.0% Native American. Hispanic (any race) 7.4%.

Industry
Food processing, machinery, electrical equipment, printing and publishing

Agriculture
Cattle, corn, hogs, soybeans, wheat, sorghum

Statehood
March 1, 1867; 37th state

GEO WHIZ

Many of Nebraska's early settlers were called sodbusters because they cut chunks of the grassy prairie (sod) to build their houses. These building blocks became known as "Nebraska marble."

Nebraska's state fossil is the mammoth. Fossils of these prehistoric elephants have been found in all 93 counties. The state estimates that as many as 10 mammoths are buried beneath an average square mile of territory.

Boys Town, founded in 1917 as a home for troubled boys, has provided a haven for girls since 1979. They now make up about half the population of 500 kids in this village-style community near Omaha.

WESTERN MEADOWLARK
GOLDENROD

NEBRASKA

For thousands of westbound pioneers on the Oregon and California Trails, Scotts Bluff and Chimney Rock were unforgettable landmarks, towering above the North Platte River. Once reserved for Indians by the government, Nebraska was opened for white settlement in 1854. Following statehood in 1867, ranchers clashed with farmers in an unsuccessful bid to preserve open rangelands. Before white settlers arrived, Indians hunted bison and grew corn, pumpkins, beans, and squash. Today, farms and ranches cover nearly all of the state. Ranchers graze beef cattle on the grass-covered Sand Hills, while farmers grow corn, soybeans, and wheat elsewhere. The vast underground Ogallala Aquifer feeds center-pivot irrigation systems needed to water crops in areas that do not receive enough rain. Processing the state's farm products, especially meatpacking, is a big part of the economy. Omaha, which sits along the Missouri River, is a center of finance, insurance, and agribusiness. Lincoln, the state capital, has the only unicameral, or one-house, legislature in the United States.

⇧ TAKING FLIGHT. Migratory Sandhill cranes pass through Nebraska in late winter, stopping in the Platte River Valley to feed and rest.

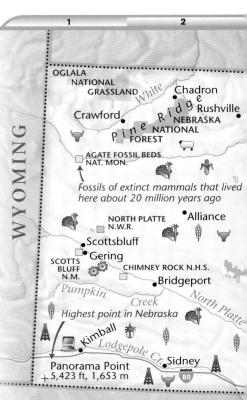

⇩ RIDER DOWN. The Big Rodeo is an annual event in tiny Burwell (population 1,130) in Nebraska's Sand Hills. The town, sometimes called "the place where the Wild West meets the 21st century," has hosted the rodeo for more than 80 years.

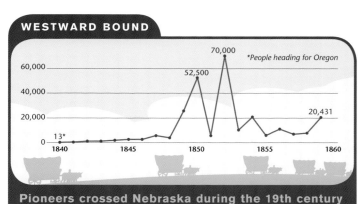

WESTWARD BOUND

*People heading for Oregon

Pioneers crossed Nebraska during the 19th century on their way to Oregon. Traffic fluctuated with the occurrence of cholera epidemics and Indian wars.

SOUTH DAKOTA

Gordon

Valentine

Niobrara

SAMUEL R. McKELVIE
NATIONAL FOREST

FORT
NIOBRARA
N.W.R.

NIOBRARA
NATIONAL SCENIC
RIVERWAY

Keya Paha

Niobrara

Ainsworth

Atkinson

O'Neill

Lewis and Clark Lake

MISSOURI NATIONAL RECREATIONAL RIVER

SANTEE
INDIAN
RES.

Hartington

Missouri

IOWA

Gordon Cr.

20,000 square miles of grass-covered dunes, the largest such area in North America

Mullen

Dismal

NEBRASKA
NAT. FOREST

North Loup

Middle Loup

Calamus
Reservoir

Holt Creek

Verdigre Cr.

Elkhorn

Neligh

Norfolk

Logan Creek

Wayne

Pender

South
Sioux City

WINNEBAGO
I.R.

OMAHA
I.R.

West Point

Tekamah

Blair

29

CRESCENT LAKE
N.W.R.

Sand Hills

PLAINS

Lake
C.W. McConaughy

Burwell

Cedar

Albion

Ord

Shell Cr.

Columbus

Schuyler

DE SOTO N.W.R.

Fremont

BOYER CHUTE
N.W.R.

680

80

NEBRASKA

Broken
Bow

South Loup

St. Paul

Fullerton

Loup

David City

Wahoo

Omaha

Papillion

Bellevue

President Ford's birthplace

Wild West Show
began in 1883

BUFFALO BILL
S.H.P.

North Platte

Ogallala

South Platte

76

Grant

Imperial

Platte

Gothenburg

Cozad

Lexington

Kearney

Ravenna

Gibbon

Grand
Island

Central
City

Aurora

York

Big Blue

Seward

Ashland

Waverly

NINE-MILE PRAIRIE

Milford

Lincoln

Plattsmouth

80

Platte

Nebraska
City

Largest mammoth fossil ever found, 1922

Red Willow Creek

Minden

Hastings

Geneva

Crete

Wilber

Big Nemaha

Auburn

29

Frenchman Cr.

Hugh Butler
Lake

Holdrege

Swanson
Res.

Cambridge

McCook

Republican

Alma

Little Blue

Harlan County
Lake

Red Cloud

Superior

Hebron

Fairbury

HOMESTEAD
NAT. MON.
OF AMERICA

Beatrice

MISSOURI

Falls
City

SAC AND FOX I.R.

IOWA
I.R.

KANSAS

HIGH

0 — 50 miles
0 — 50 kilometers
Albers Conic Equal-Area Projection

Economy Symbols

Poultry/eggs	Printing/publishing
Sheep	Stone/gravel/cement
Hogs	Oil/gas
Dairy cows/products	Hydro-electricity
Beef cattle	Machinery
Vegetables	Railroad equipment
Vegetable oil	Food processing
Nursery stock	Computers/electronics
Wheat	Scientific instruments
Corn	Finance/insurance
Soybeans	

⬅ THE WAY WEST. Longhorn cattle and a bison stand knee-deep in grass below Chimney Rock, which rises more than 300 feet (91 m) above western Nebraska's rolling landscape. An important landmark on the Oregon Trail for 19th-century westbound pioneers and now a national historic site, the formation is being worn away by forces of erosion.

NORTH DAKOTA

During the winter of 1804–05, Lewis and Clark camped at a Mandan village where they met Sacagawea, the Shoshone woman who helped guide them through the Rockies and onto the Pacific Ocean. White settlement of the vast grassy plains coincided with the growth of railroads, and statehood was gained in 1889. The geographic center of North America is southwest of Rugby. The state's interior location helps give it a huge annual temperature range. A record low temperature of -60°F (-51°C) and record high of 121°F (49°C) were recorded in 1936. Fargo, located on the northward flowing Red River of the North, is the state's largest city. Garrison Dam, on the Missouri River, generates electricity and provides water for irrigation. The state leads the country in the production of flax-seed, canola, sunflowers, and barley, but it is wheat, cattle, and soybeans that provide the greatest income. Oil and lignite coal are important in the western part of the state.

THE BASICS

STATS

Area
70,700 sq mi (183,113 sq km)

Population
639,715

Capital
Bismarck
Population 56,344

Largest city
Fargo
Population 91,484

Ethnic/racial groups
91.9% white; 5.4% Native American; .8% African American; .7% Asian. Hispanic (any race) 1.7%.

Industry
Services, government, finance, construction, transportation, oil and gas

Agriculture
Wheat, cattle, sunflowers, barley, soybeans

Statehood
November 2, 1889; 39th state

GEO WHIZ

Teenage Indian guide Sakakawea (also known as Sacagawea) joined the Lewis and Clark expedition in the spring of 1805 after the explorers spent the winter in the Mandan-Hidatsa villages near present-day Washburn. Today, the state's largest reservoir is named in her honor.

Devils Lake has earned the title Perch Capital of the World for the large number of walleye—a kind of perch—that anglers catch there.

North Dakota's landscape boasts some of the world's largest outdoor animal sculptures, including Salem Sue, the world's largest Holstein cow; a 60-ton buffalo; a 40-by-60-foot (12-by-18-m) grasshopper; a giant snowmobiling turtle; and Wally the Giant Walleye.

WESTERN MEADOWLARK

WILD PRAIRIE ROSE

⇧ VIGILANT LOOKOUT. A black-tailed prairie dog watches for signs of danger. This member of the squirrel family lives in burrows in the Great Plains.

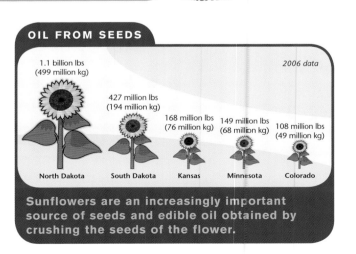

OIL FROM SEEDS

2006 data

1.1 billion lbs (499 million kg) — North Dakota

427 million lbs (194 million kg) — South Dakota

168 million lbs (76 million kg) — Kansas

149 million lbs (68 million kg) — Minnesota

108 million lbs (49 million kg) — Colorado

Sunflowers are an increasingly important source of seeds and edible oil obtained by crushing the seeds of the flower.

⇨ RUNNING FREE. A wild horse runs through a landscape dramatically eroded by the Little Missouri River in Theodore Roosevelt National Park in North Dakota's Badlands region.

SASKATCHE...

Crosby
WRITING ROCK S.H.S
LAKE ZAHL N.W.R.
Little Muddy
Tioga
Williston
Lake Sakakawea
Missouri
FORT UNION TRADING POST N.H.S.
LITTLE
Watford City
Yellowstone
THEODORE ROOSEVELT N.P. (NORTH UNIT)
MISSOURI
THEODORE ROOSEVELT N.P. (ELKHORN RANCH SITE)
Little Missouri
MONTANA
NATIONAL
94
Beach
Medora
THEODORE ROOSEVELT N.P. (SOUTH UNIT)
Dickinson
GRASSLAND
White Butte 3,506 ft 1,069 m
Cedar
Bowman
Highest point in North Dakota

North Dakota
South Dakota
Kansas
Minnesota
Colorado

Little Missouri

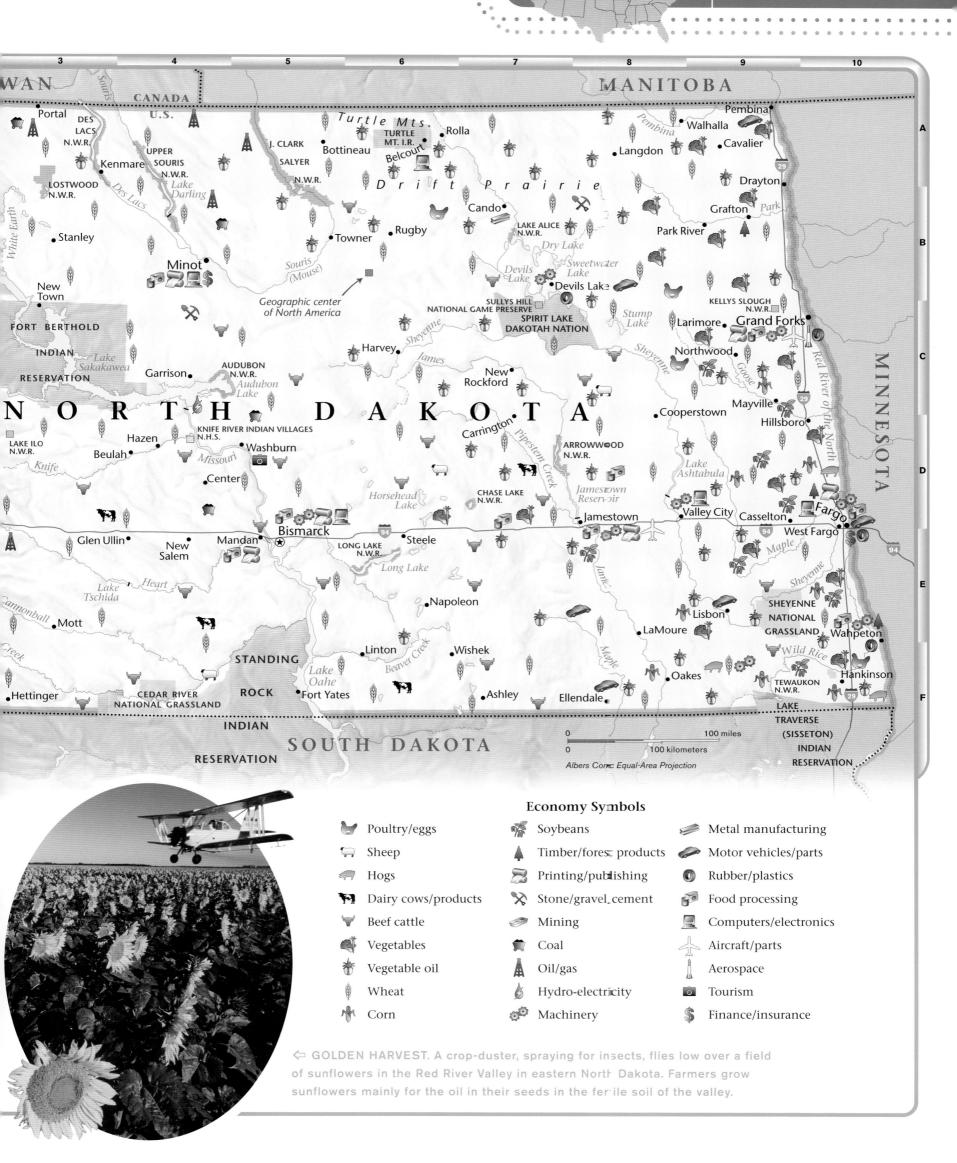

WAN

CANADA
U.S.

MANITOBA

3   4   5   6   7   8   9   10

Portal
DES LACS N.W.R.
Kenmare
UPPER SOURIS N.W.R.
LOSTWOOD N.W.R.
Stanley
Lake Darling
Des Lacs
White Earth

Turtle Mts.
TURTLE MT. I.R.
Rolla
Belcourt
J. CLARK SALYER N.W.R.
Bottineau
Drift Prairie
Langdon
Cando
LAKE ALICE N.W.R.
Pembina
Walhalla
Cavalier
Drayton
Grafton
Park River
Park

Minot
New Town
FORT BERTHOLD
INDIAN
RESERVATION
Lake Sakakawea

Towner
Rugby
Souris (Mouse)

Geographic center of North America

Devils Lake
Sweetwater Lake
Devils Lake
SULLYS HILL NATIONAL GAME PRESERVE
SPIRIT LAKE DAKOTAH NATION
Dry Lake
Stump Lake
KELLYS SLOUGH N.W.R.
Larimore
Grand Forks
Northwood
Sheyenne

Garrison
AUDUBON N.W.R.
Audubon Lake
Harvey
James
Sheyenne
New Rockford
Cooperstown
Mayville
Hillsboro
Goose

N O R T H   D A K O T A

LAKE ILO N.W.R.
Hazen
KNIFE RIVER INDIAN VILLAGES N.H.S.
Beulah
Washburn
Center
Knife
Missouri
Carrington
Pipestem Creek
ARROWWOOD N.W.R.
Lake Ashtabula

Horsehead Lake
CHASE LAKE N.W.R.
Jamestown Reservoir

Glen Ullin
Mandan
Bismarck
New Salem
LONG LAKE N.W.R.
Long Lake
Steele
Jamestown
Valley City
Casselton
West Fargo
Fargo
Maple

Lake Tschida
Heart
Napoleon
James
SHEYENNE NATIONAL GRASSLAND
Lisbon
Wahpeton
Sheyenne

Mott
Linton
Beaver Creek
Wishek
LaMoure
Wild Rice
Oakes
Hankinson
TEWAUKON N.W.R.

Cannonball Creek
Hettinger
STANDING ROCK
CEDAR RIVER NATIONAL GRASSLAND
Lake Oahe
Fort Yates
Ashley
Ellendale
Maple

INDIAN RESERVATION

SOUTH DAKOTA

LAKE TRAVERSE (SISSETON) INDIAN RESERVATION

MINNESOTA

29
94
94
29

0   100 miles
0   100 kilometers
Albers Conic Equal-Area Projection

Economy Symbols

- Poultry/eggs
- Sheep
- Hogs
- Dairy cows/products
- Beef cattle
- Vegetables
- Vegetable oil
- Wheat
- Corn

- Soybeans
- Timber/forest products
- Printing/publishing
- Stone/gravel/cement
- Mining
- Coal
- Oil/gas
- Hydro-electricity
- Machinery

- Metal manufacturing
- Motor vehicles/parts
- Rubber/plastics
- Food processing
- Computers/electronics
- Aircraft/parts
- Aerospace
- Tourism
- Finance/insurance

⇐ GOLDEN HARVEST. A crop-duster, spraying for insects, flies low over a field of sunflowers in the Red River Valley in eastern North Dakota. Farmers grow sunflowers mainly for the oil in their seeds in the fertile soil of the valley.

THE BASICS

STATS

Area
44,825 sq mi (116,097 sq km)

Population
11,466,917

Capital
Columbus
Population 733,203

Largest city
Columbus
Population 733,203

Ethnic/racial groups
84.9% white; 12.0% African American; 1.5% Asian; .2% Native American. Hispanic (any race) 2.3%.

Industry
Transportation equipment, metal products, machinery, food processing, electrical equipment

Agriculture
Soybeans, dairy products, corn, hogs, cattle, poultry and eggs

Statehood
March 1, 1803; 17th state

GEO WHIZ

Cedar Point Amusement Park, in Sandusky, is known as the Rollercoaster Capital of the World. Top Thrill Dragster, claimed to be the tallest and fastest rollercoaster on Earth, is 420 feet (128 m) high with a top speed of 120 miles per hour (193 kmph)!

Ohio's state tree is the buckeye, so-called because the nut it produces resembles the eye of a buck. A buck is a male deer.

Ohio's state insect is the ladybird beetle, more commonly known as the ladybug. Use of these beetles to control plant-eating pests greatly reduces the need for chemical pesticides.

CARDINAL
SCARLET CARNATION

OHIO

Ohio and the rest of the Northwest Territory became part of the United States after the Revolutionary War. The movement of white settlers into the region led to conflicts with the native inhabitants until 1794 when Indian resistance was defeated at Fallen Timbers. Ohio entered the Union nine years later. Lake Erie in the north and the Ohio River in the south, along with canals and railroads, provided transportation links that spurred early immigration and commerce. The state became an industrial giant, producing steel, machinery, rubber, and glass. From 1869 to 1923, 7 of 12 U.S. presidents were Ohioans. With 20 electoral votes, sixth highest in the country, Ohio is still a big player in presidential elections. Education, government, and finance employ many people in Columbus, the capital and largest city. Manufacturing in Cleveland, Toledo, Cincinnati, and other cities remains a vital segment of the state's economy. Farmers on Ohio's western, glaciated plains grow soybeans and corn, the two largest cash crops.

⇧ INLAND URBAN CENTER. Cincinnati's skyline sparkles in the red glow of twilight. Founded in 1788, the modern city boasts education and medical centers as well as headquarters for companies such as Procter & Gamble.

⇩ TRADITIONAL TRAVEL. Horse and buggy are a familiar sight in central Ohio, location of the world's largest Amish population.

⇧ SOUND OF MUSIC. Colorful guitars mark the entrance to the Rock and Roll Hall of Fame in downtown Cleveland. The museum, through its Rockin' the School's program, attracts more than 50,000 students annually to experience the sounds of rock and roll music and learn about its history.

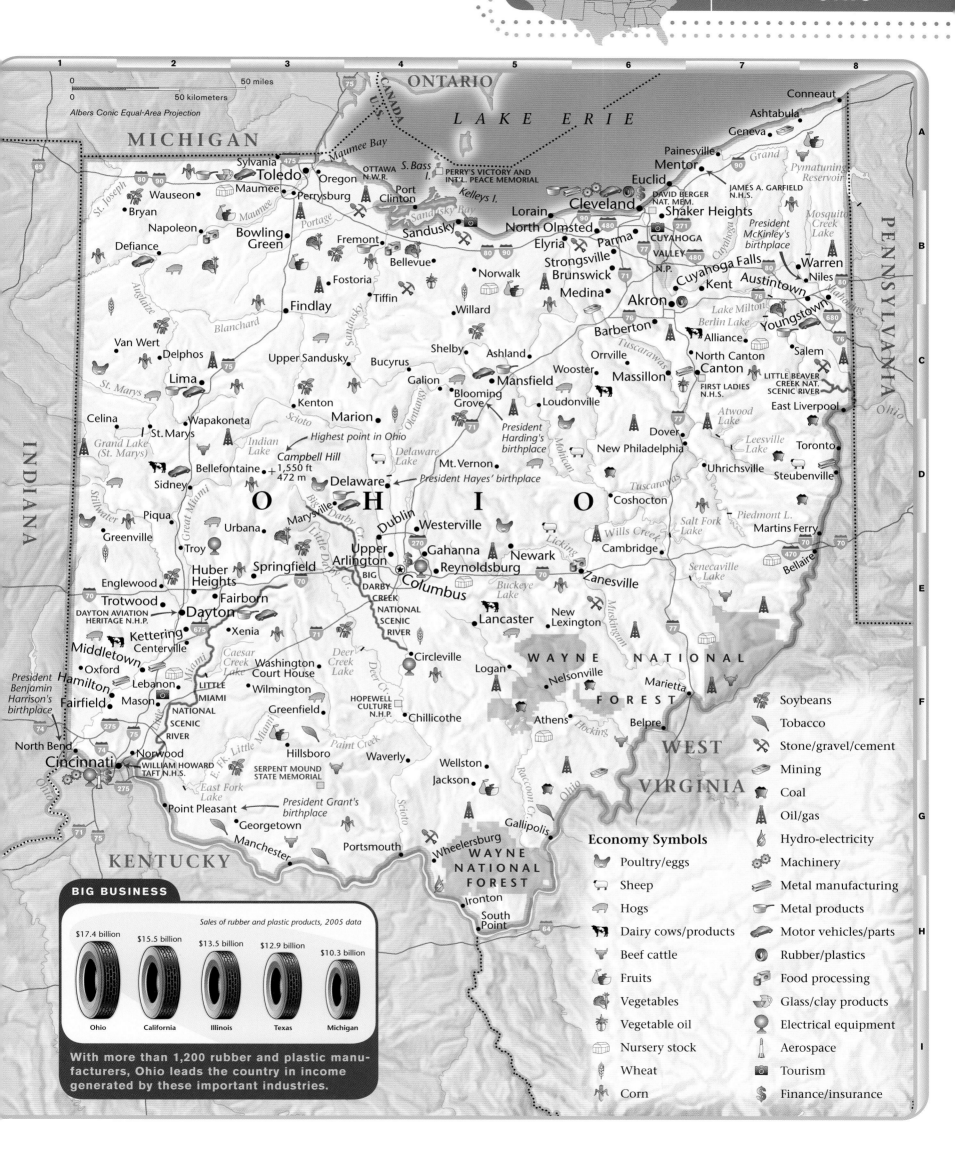

LAKE ERIE

ONTARIO
CANADA
U.S.

MICHIGAN

INDIANA

PENNSYLVANIA

WEST VIRGINIA

KENTUCKY

O H I O

Conneaut
Ashtabula
Geneva
Painesville
Mentor
Euclid
Cleveland
Shaker Heights
DAVID BERGER NAT. MEM.
JAMES A. GARFIELD N.H.S.
President McKinley's birthplace
Pymatuning Reservoir
Mosquito Creek Lake
CUYAHOGA VALLEY N.P.
Cuyahoga Falls
Warren
Niles
Austintown
Youngstown
Salem
LITTLE BEAVER CREEK NAT. SCENIC RIVER
East Liverpool
Toronto
Steubenville
Martins Ferry
Bellaire
Piedmont L.

Sylvania
Toledo
Oregon
Maumee Bay
OTTAWA N.W.R.
S. Bass I.
PERRY'S VICTORY AND INT'L. PEACE MEMORIAL
Kelleys I.
Maumee
Perrysburg
Port Clinton
Wauseon
Bryan
Napoleon
Defiance
Bowling Green
Fremont
Sandusky
Sandusky Bay
Bellevue
Lorain
North Olmsted
Elyria
Parma
Strongsville
Brunswick
Medina
Norwalk
Fostoria
Findlay
Tiffin
Willard
Akron
Barberton
Kent
Lake Milton
Berlin Lake
Van Wert
Delphos
Shelby
Ashland
Orrville
Wooster
North Canton
Canton
Massillon
FIRST LADIES N.H.S.
Atwood Lake
Leesville Lake
Lima
Upper Sandusky
Bucyrus
Galion
Mansfield
Loudonville
Dover
New Philadelphia
Uhrichsville
Kenton
Blooming Grove
President Harding's birthplace
Celina
Wapakoneta
Marion
St. Marys
Indian Lake
Highest point in Ohio
Campbell Hill 1,550 ft 472 m
Delaware Lake
Mt. Vernon
President Hayes' birthplace
Coshocton
Salt Fork Lake
Bellefontaine
Delaware
Sidney
Piqua
Greenville
Urbana
Marysville
Dublin
Westerville
Cambridge
Senecaville Lake
Troy
Huber Heights
Springfield
Upper Arlington
Gahanna
Reynoldsburg
Newark
Zanesville
Englewood
Trotwood
Fairborn
Dayton
Columbus
Buckeye Lake
BIG DARBY CREEK NATIONAL SCENIC RIVER
DAYTON AVIATION HERITAGE N.H.P.
Kettering
Xenia
Lancaster
New Lexington
Middletown
Centerville
Oxford
Lebanon
Mason
Washington Court House
Circleville
Logan
Nelsonville
Marietta
Caesar Creek Lake
LITTLE MIAMI NATIONAL SCENIC RIVER
Wilmington
Deer Creek Lake
WAYNE NATIONAL FOREST
President Benjamin Harrison's birthplace
Hamilton
Fairfield
Greenfield
HOPEWELL CULTURE N.H.P.
Chillicothe
Athens
Belpre
North Bend
Cincinnati
Norwood
WILLIAM HOWARD TAFT N.H.S.
Hillsboro
Waverly
Wellston
Jackson
SERPENT MOUND STATE MEMORIAL
East Fork Lake
President Grant's birthplace
Point Pleasant
Georgetown
Manchester
Portsmouth
Gallipolis
Wheelersburg
WAYNE NATIONAL FOREST
Ironton
South Point

St. Joseph
Maumee
Portage
Auglaize
Blanchard
Sandusky
St. Marys
Scioto
Great Miami
Stillwater
Grand Lake (St. Marys)
Little Miami
Miami
Olentangy
Darby Cr.
Big Darby Cr.
Little Darby Cr.
Deer Cr.
Paint Creek
E. Fk. Little Miami
Scioto
Licking
Wills Creek
Mohican
Tuscarawas
Muskingum
Hocking
Raccoon Cr.
Ohio
Cuyahoga
Mahoning
Grand

Economy Symbols

- Soybeans
- Tobacco
- Stone/gravel/cement
- Mining
- Coal
- Oil/gas
- Hydro-electricity
- Machinery
- Metal manufacturing
- Metal products
- Motor vehicles/parts
- Rubber/plastics
- Food processing
- Glass/clay products
- Electrical equipment
- Aerospace
- Tourism
- Finance/insurance

- Poultry/eggs
- Sheep
- Hogs
- Dairy cows/products
- Beef cattle
- Fruits
- Vegetables
- Vegetable oil
- Nursery stock
- Wheat
- Corn

BIG BUSINESS

Sales of rubber and plastic products, 2005 data

$17.4 billion — Ohio
$15.5 billion — California
$13.5 billion — Illinois
$12.9 billion — Texas
$10.3 billion — Michigan

With more than 1,200 rubber and plastic manufacturers, Ohio leads the country in income generated by these important industries.

0 — 50 miles
0 — 50 kilometers
Albers Conic Equal-Area Projection

THE MOUNT RUSHMORE STATE:
SOUTH DAKOTA

THE BASICS

STATS

Area
77,117 sq mi (199,732 sq km)

Population
796,214

Capital
Pierre
Population 14,095

Largest city
Sioux Falls
Population 142,396

Ethnic/racial groups
88.4% white; 8.5% Native American;
.9% African American; .7% Asian.
Hispanic (any race) 2.1%.

Industry
Finance, services, manufacturing,
government, retail trade, transportation and utilities, wholesale trade,
construction, mining

Agriculture
Cattle, corn, soybeans, wheat, hogs,
hay, dairy products

Statehood
November 2, 1889; 40th state

GEO WHIZ

Thirty years ago, black-footed ferrets
were on the brink of extinction.
Now, thanks to captive breeding
programs, the world's largest wild
black-footed ferret population is
thriving in a black-tailed prairie dog
colony in south-central South Dakota.

Called Shrine of Democracy by its
creator Gutzon Borglum, Mount
Rushmore National Monument
features the faces of George
Washington, Thomas Jefferson,
Abraham Lincoln, and Theodore
Roosevelt. Each is 60 feet (18 m) tall.

The Black Hills Institute of Geological
Research in Hill City has been
involved in digging up eight
Tyrannosaurus rex
skeletons, including Sue,
Stan, Bucky, and WREX.
In addition to research work,
the institute prepares museum-
quality reproductions.

RING-NECKED
PHEASANT

PASQUEFLOWER

SOUTH DAKOTA

After the discovery of Black Hills gold in 1874,
prospectors poured in and established lawless mining towns such as Deadwood. Indians fought this
invasion but were defeated, and statehood came
in 1889. Today, South Dakota has several reservations, and nearly nine percent of the state's people
are Native Americans. The Missouri River flows
through the center of the state, creating two
distinct regions. To the east, farmers grow corn
and soybeans on the fertile, rolling prairie. To the
west, where it is too dry for most crops, farmers
grow wheat and graze cattle and sheep on the
vast plains. In the southwest, the Black Hills,
named for the dark coniferous trees blanketing
their slopes, are still a rich source of gold.
Millions of tourists visit the area to see Mount
Rushmore and a giant sculpture of Crazy Horse
that has been in the works since 1948. Nearby,
the fossil-rich Badlands, a region of eroded
buttes and pinnacles, dominate the landscape.

⇨ HONORING AGRICULTURE.
The face of the Corn Palace
in Mitchell is renewed each
year using thousands of
bushels of grain to create
pictures depicting the
role of agriculture in
the state's history.

ALTERNATIVE BEEF

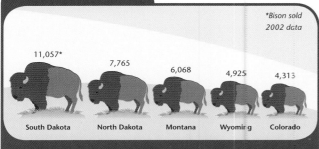

*Bison sold
2002 data

South Dakota	North Dakota	Montana	Wyoming	Colorado
11,057*	7,765	6,068	4,925	4,313

Bison meat is popular among health-conscious
consumers because it is lower in calories, fat,
and cholesterol than other meats.

Map labels:

MONTANA

WYOMING

CUSTER
NATIONAL
Buffalo
FOREST

Little Missouri
S. Fork Grand

Geographic center
of the 50 states

Belle Fourche
Spearfish
Deadwood · Sturgis
Lead
BLACK
Highest mountains
east of the Rockies
Black Hawk
Black Hills
Rapid City
HILLS
MOUNT
RUSHMORE
N.M.
CRAZY HORSE
MEMORIAL
Harney Peak
Custer
7,242 ft 2,207 m
CUSTER
S.P.
JEWEL
NAT.
CAVE
N.M.
WIND CAVE
N.P.
BADLANDS
Hot
Springs
GAP
Cheyenne
FOREST
INDIAN
NAT.
Edgemont
White
GRASSLAND

0   50 miles
0   50 kilometers
Albers Equal-Area Conic Projection

Map of South Dakota

NORTH DAKOTA

STANDING ROCK

GRAND RIVER NATIONAL GRASSLAND

Lemmon
McIntosh
INDIAN
POCASSE N.W.R.
Eureka
Leola
SAND LAKE N.W.R.
Britton
LAKE TRAVERSE (SISSETON)
Lake Traverse
Sisseton INDIAN RES.

RESERVATION

Bison
Mobridge
Selby
Ipswich
Aberdeen
Groton
Webster
Waubay L.
WAUBAY N.W.R.
Big Stone Lake
Milbank

Timber Lake
Lake Oahe
Watertown
Clear Lake

CHEYENNE RIVER

Dupree
SIOUX
Gettysburg
Faulkton
Redfield
Clark
Lake Poinsett

INDIAN RESERVATION

Onida
Highmore
Miller
Huron
De Smet
Brookings
Volga

S O U T H   D A K O T A

Fort Pierre
Pierre
CROW CREEK INDIAN RESERVATION
Wessington Springs
Woonsocket
Madison
FLANDREAU I.R.

MINUTEMAN MISSILE N.H.S.
FORT PIERRE NATIONAL GRASSLAND
Lake Sharpe
LOWER BRULE INDIAN RESERVATION
Fort Thompson
Howard
Flandreau

Wall
Philip
Murdo
Kennebec
Chamberlain
Plankinton
Mitchell
Salem
Sioux Falls

NATIONAL
Kadoka
Crow Creek
Alexandria

GRASSLAND

Huge rock barrier sculptured into pinnacles and gullies by running water

White River
Winner
Lake Francis Case
Platte
Parkston
Armour
Freeman
Parker
Lennox
Canton
Beresford

Last major conflict of the Indian Wars, December 1890

RIDGE RESERVATION

WOUNDED KNEE MASSACRE SITE
Martin
Rosebud
ROSEBUD INDIAN RESERVATION
Gregory
Burke
YANKTON
Lake Andes
LAKE ANDES N.W.R.
INDIAN RES.
Wagner
Tyndall
Yankton
Vermillion

Pine Ridge
LACREEK N.W.R.
NEBRASKA
Lewis and Clark Lake
Elk Point
N. Sioux City

MISSOURI NATIONAL RECREATIONAL RIVER

⬇ BRAVE WARRIOR. Begun in 1948, the Crazy Horse Memorial in South Dakota's Black Hills honors the culture, tradition, and living heritage of North American Indians. In the background sculptors are recreating the statue of the Lakota chief and his horse in the mountainside.

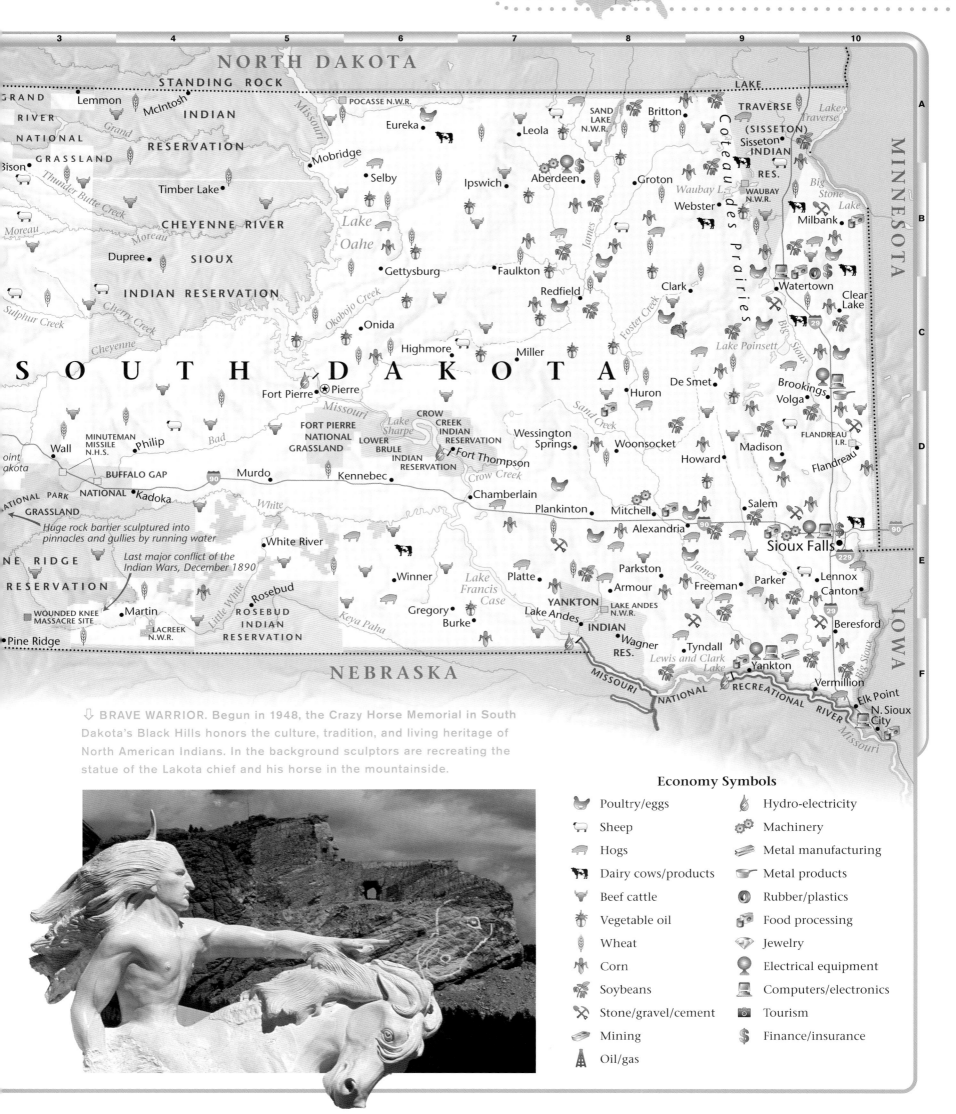

Economy Symbols

Poultry/eggs	Hydro-electricity
Sheep	Machinery
Hogs	Metal manufacturing
Dairy cows/products	Metal products
Beef cattle	Rubber/plastics
Vegetable oil	Food processing
Wheat	Jewelry
Corn	Electrical equipment
Soybeans	Computers/electronics
Stone/gravel/cement	Tourism
Mining	Finance/insurance
Oil/gas	

WISCONSIN

1848

THE BASICS

STATS

Area
65,498 sq mi (169,639 sq km)

Population
5,601,640

Capital
Madison
Population 223,389

Largest city
Milwaukee
Population 573,358

Ethnic/racial groups
90.0% white; 6.0% African American; 2.0% Asian; .9% Native American. Hispanic (any race) 4.7%.

Industry
Industrial machinery, paper products, food processing, metal products, electronic equipment, transportation

Agriculture
Dairy products, cattle, corn, poultry and eggs, soybeans

Statehood
May 29, 1848; 30th state

GEO WHIZ

The Indian Community School in Milwaukee offers courses in native languages, history, and rituals. In all of its programs—from math to tribal creation stories—seven core values are stressed: bravery, love, truth, wisdom, humility, loyalty, and respect.

Bogs left by retreating ice-age glaciers provide excellent conditions for raising cranberries. Wisconsin leads the nation in cranberry farming, producing more than half of the estimated 575 million pounds (261 million kg) consumed by Americans annually.

Wisconsin is nicknamed the Badger State, not for the animal but for the men who mined lead in the state during the 1820s. They dug living spaces by burrowing like badgers into the hillside.

ROBIN
WOOD VIOLET

WISCONSIN

Frenchman Jean Nicolet was the first European to reach present-day Wisconsin when he stepped ashore from Green Bay in 1634. After decades of getting along, relations with the region's Indians soured as the number of settlers increased. The Black Hawk War in 1832 ended the last major Indian resistance, and statehood came in 1848. Many Milwaukee residents are descendants of German immigrants who labored in the city's breweries and meatpacking plants. Even as the economic importance of health care and other services has increased, food processing and the manufacture of machinery and metal products remains significant for the state. More than one million dairy cows graze in America's Dairyland, as the state is often called. It leads the country in cheese production, and is the second-largest producer of milk and butter. Other farmers grow crops ranging from corn and soybeans to potatoes and cranberries. Northern Wisconsin is sparsely populated but heavily forested, and is the source of paper and paper products produced by the state.

⇧ CITY BY THE LAKE. Milwaukee, on the shore of Lake Michigan, derives its name from the Algonquian word for "beautiful land." The city, known for brewing and manufacturing, also has a growing service sector.

⇧ TASTY GRAZING. The largest concentration of Brown Swiss cows in the U.S. is in Wisconsin, where the milk of this breed is prized by cheese manufacturers.

⇦ RURAL ECONOMY. The dairy industry is an important part of Wisconsin's rural economy, and dairy farmers control most of the state's farmland.

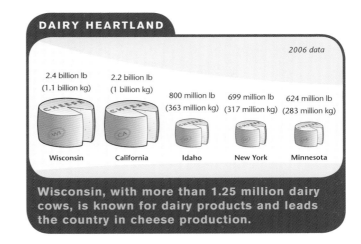

DAIRY HEARTLAND

2006 data

Wisconsin	California	Idaho	New York	Minnesota
2.4 billion lb (1.1 billion kg)	2.2 billion lb (1 billion kg)	800 million lb (363 million kg)	699 million lb (317 million kg)	624 million lb (283 million kg)

Wisconsin, with more than 1.25 million dairy cows, is known for dairy products and leads the country in cheese production.

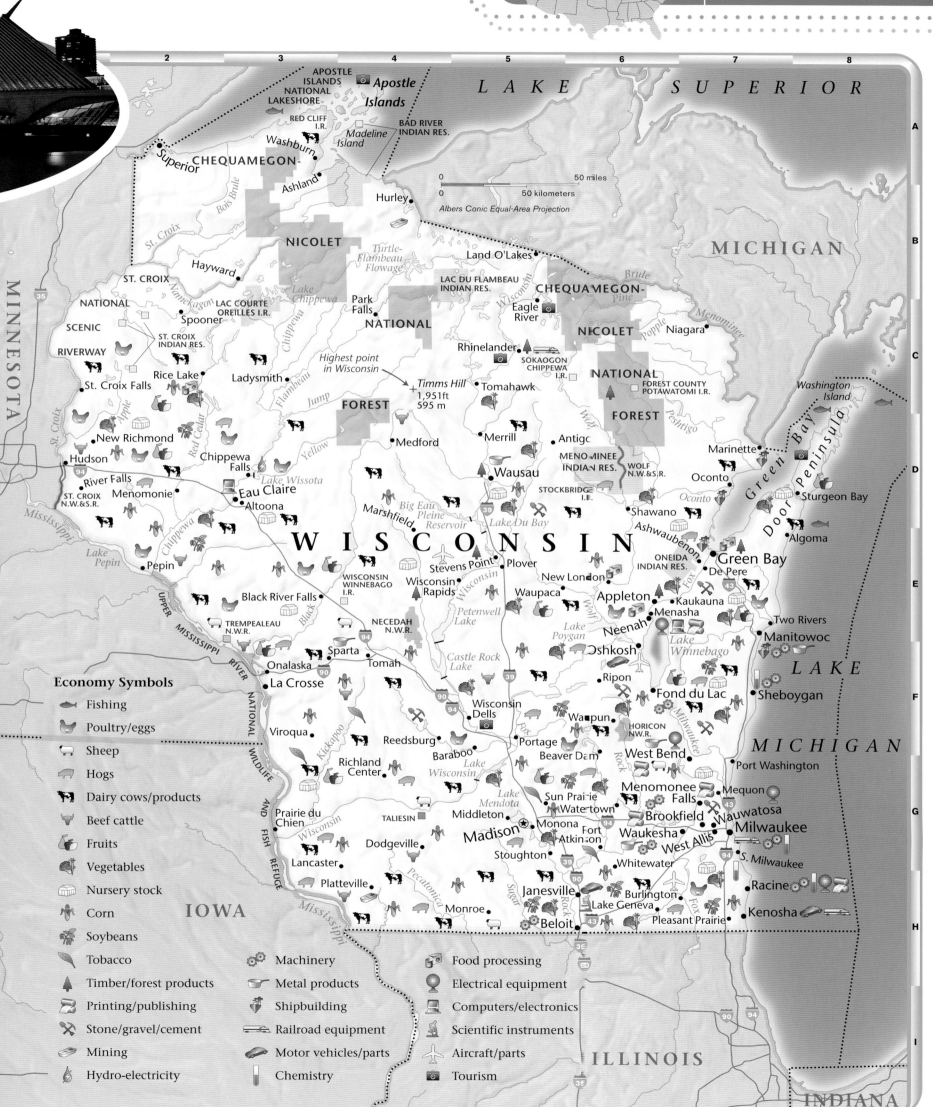

Economy Symbols

- 🐟 Fishing
- 🐔 Poultry/eggs
- 🐑 Sheep
- 🐗 Hogs
- 🐄 Dairy cows/products
- 🐂 Beef cattle
- 🍎 Fruits
- 🌿 Vegetables
- 🏠 Nursery stock
- 🌽 Corn
- 🌱 Soybeans
- 🍃 Tobacco
- 🌲 Timber/forest products
- 🖨 Printing/publishing
- ⚒ Stone/gravel/cement
- ⛏ Mining
- 💧 Hydro-electricity

- ⚙ Machinery
- 🍳 Metal products
- ⚓ Shipbuilding
- 🚃 Railroad equipment
- 🚗 Motor vehicles/parts
- 🧪 Chemistry

- 📷 Food processing
- 🔌 Electrical equipment
- 💻 Computers/electronics
- 🔬 Scientific instruments
- ✈ Aircraft/parts
- 📷 Tourism

Map labels

LAKE SUPERIOR
MICHIGAN
MINNESOTA
IOWA
ILLINOIS
INDIANA

WISCONSIN

APOSTLE ISLANDS NATIONAL LAKESHORE
Apostle Islands
RED CLIFF I.R.
Madeline Island
BAD RIVER INDIAN RES.
CHEQUAMEGON-
Superior
Washburn
Ashland
Hurley
NICOLET
Hayward
Bois Brule
St. Croix
Lake Chippewa
Turtle-Flambeau Flowage
Land O'Lakes
LAC DU FLAMBEAU INDIAN RES.
CHEQUAMEGON-
Eagle River
Niagara
Menominee
NICOLET
Park Falls
Rhinelander
SOKAOGON CHIPPEWA I.R.
NATIONAL
ST. CROIX
NATIONAL
SCENIC
RIVERWAY
Spooner
LAC COURTE OREILLES I.R.
ST. CROIX INDIAN RES.
Rice Lake
Ladysmith
Highest point in Wisconsin
Timms Hill 1,951ft 595 m
Tomahawk
Merrill
Antigo
FOREST
FOREST COUNTY POTAWATOMI I.R.
NATIONAL
FOREST
Washington Island
St. Croix Falls
New Richmond
Chippewa Falls
Medford
Wausau
Marinette
Green Bay
Door Peninsula
Hudson
River Falls
Menomonie
Altoona
Eau Claire
Lake Wissota
Big Eau Pleine Reservoir
Marshfield
MENOMINEE INDIAN RES.
WOLF N.W.&S.R.
Oconto
Sturgeon Bay
ST. CROIX N.W.&S.R.
Lake Pepin
Pepin
Lake Du Bay
STOCKBRIDGE I.R.
Shawano
Ashwaubenon
ONEIDA INDIAN RES.
Green Bay
De Pere
Algoma
WISCONSIN
Black River Falls
WISCONSIN WINNEBAGO I.R.
Stevens Point
Plover
Wisconsin Rapids
New London
Waupaca
Appleton
Kaukauna
Menasha
Two Rivers
Manitowoc
TREMPEALEAU N.W.R.
NECEDAH N.W.R.
Petenwell Lake
Lake Poygan
Neenah
Oshkosh
LAKE MICHIGAN
UPPER MISSISSIPPI RIVER NATIONAL WILDLIFE AND FISH REFUGE
Sparta
Onalaska
Tomah
Castle Rock Lake
Lake Winnebago
Ripon
Fond du Lac
Sheboygan
La Crosse
Wisconsin Dells
Reedsburg
Baraboo
Portage
Beaver Dam
Waupun
HORICON N.W.R.
West Bend
Port Washington
Viroqua
Richland Center
Lake Wisconsin
Sun Prairie
Watertown
Menomonee Falls
Mequon
Prairie du Chien
TALIESIN
Middleton
Lake Mendota
Madison
Monona
Fort Atkinson
Brookfield
Wauwatosa
Milwaukee
Dodgeville
Stoughton
Waukesha
West Allis
S. Milwaukee
Lancaster
Platteville
Whitewater
Racine
Monroe
Janesville
Burlington
Lake Geneva
Pleasant Prairie
Kenosha
Beloit

Mississippi
St. Croix
Namekagon
Chippewa
Flambeau
Jump
Yellow
Red Cedar
Black
Kickapoo
Wisconsin
Pecatonica
Sugar
Rock
Fox
Wolf
Peshtigo
Oconto
Brule
Pine
Popple
Menominee
Milwaukee

0 — 50 miles
0 — 50 kilometers
Albers Conic Equal-Area Projection

THE REGION

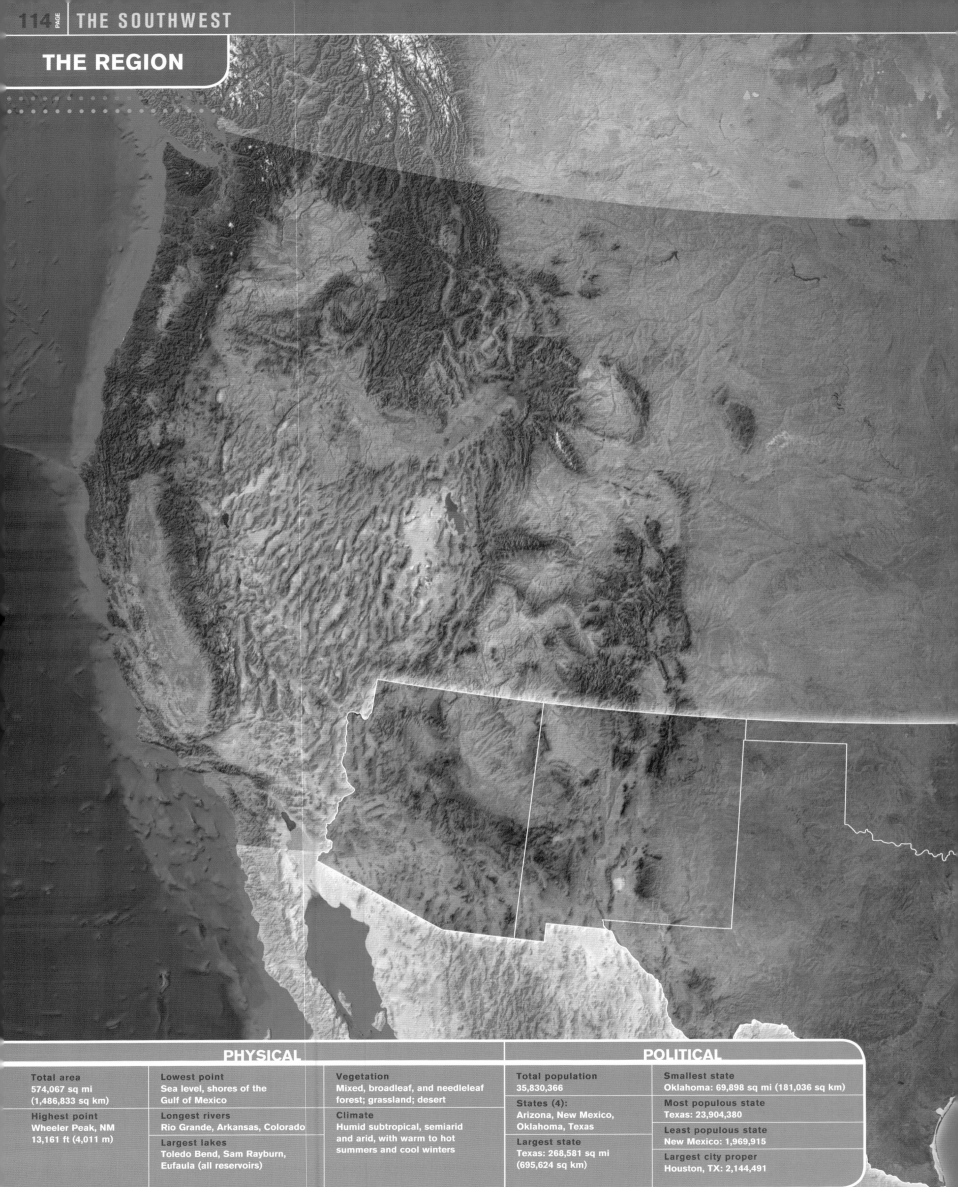

PHYSICAL			POLITICAL	
Total area 574,067 sq mi (1,486,833 sq km)	**Lowest point** Sea level, shores of the Gulf of Mexico	**Vegetation** Mixed, broadleaf, and needleleaf forest; grassland; desert	**Total population** 35,830,366	**Smallest state** Oklahoma: 69,898 sq mi (181,036 sq km)
Highest point Wheeler Peak, NM 13,161 ft (4,011 m)	**Longest rivers** Rio Grande, Arkansas, Colorado	**Climate** Humid subtropical, semiarid and arid, with warm to hot summers and cool winters	**States (4):** Arizona, New Mexico, Oklahoma, Texas	**Most populous state** Texas: 23,904,380
	Largest lakes Toledo Bend, Sam Rayburn, Eufaula (all reservoirs)		**Largest state** **Texas: 268,581 sq mi** **(695,624 sq km)**	**Least populous state** New Mexico: 1,969,915
				Largest city proper Houston, TX: 2,144,491

The Southwest

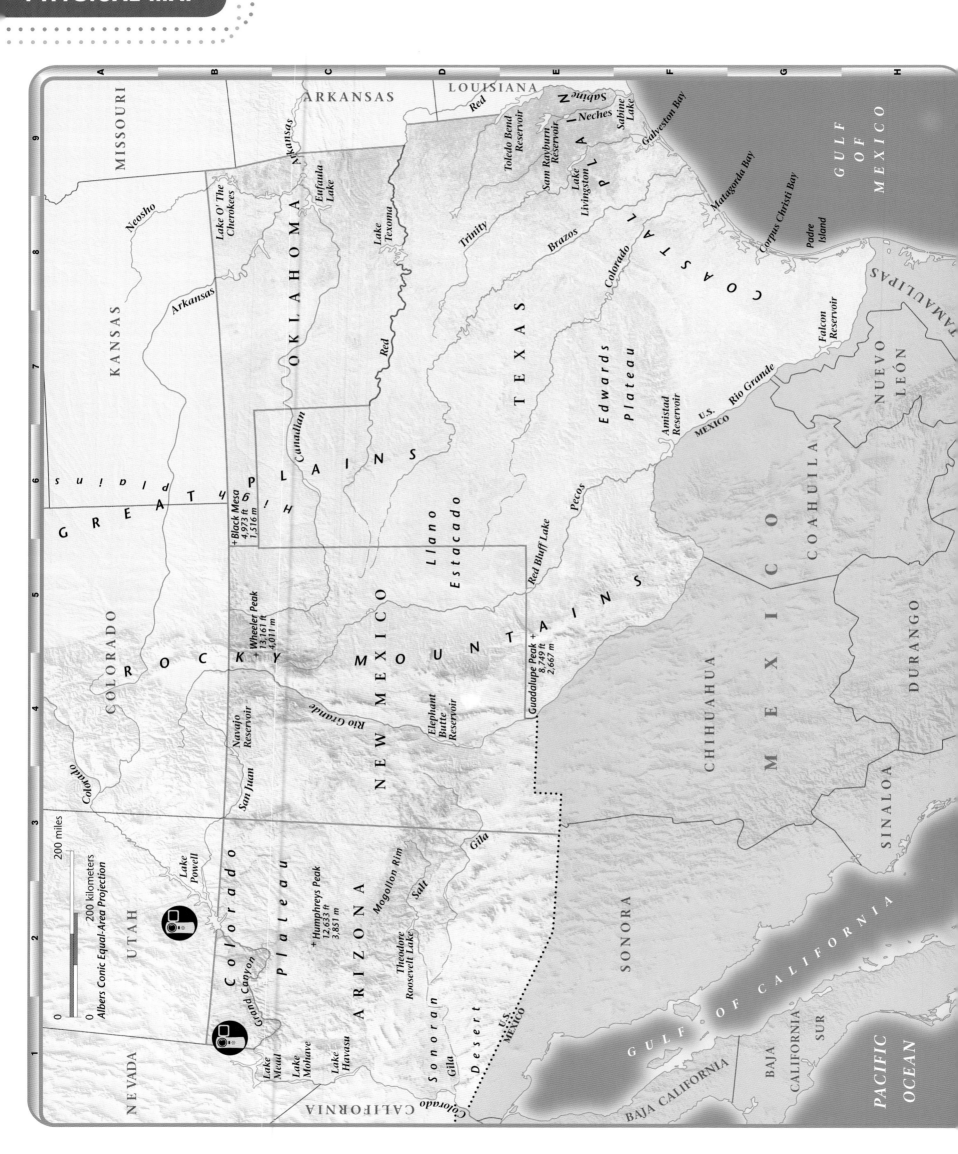

MISSOURI

ARKANSAS

LOUISIANA

KANSAS

OKLAHOMA

Neosho

Lake O' The Cherokees

Arkansas

Eufaula Lake

Lake Texoma

Red

Arkansas

Red

Trinity

Brazos

Colorado

Canadian

T E X A S

COASTAL

P L A I N

Neches

Sabine

Sabine Lake

Toledo Bend Reservoir

Sam Rayburn Reservoir

Lake Livingston

Galveston Bay

Matagorda Bay

Corpus Christi Bay

Padre Island

GULF OF MEXICO

TAMAULIPAS

NUEVO LEÓN

Falcon Reservoir

COAHUILA

Edwards Plateau

Amistad Reservoir

U.S. Rio Grande MEXICO

Pecos

Red Bluff Lake

Llano Estacado

+ Black Mesa 4,973 ft 1,516 m

G R E A T

P L A I N S

Great Plains

COLORADO

R O C K Y

+ Wheeler Peak 13,161 ft 4,011 m

N E W   M E X I C O

M O U N T A I N S

Guadalupe Peak + 8,749 ft 2,667 m

M E X I C O

CHIHUAHUA

DURANGO

SINALOA

Colorado

San Juan

Navajo Reservoir

Rio Grande

Elephant Butte Reservoir

UTAH

200 miles

200 kilometers

Albers Conic Equal-Area Projection

Lake Powell

Colorado Plateau

+ Humphreys Peak 12,633 ft 3,851 m

A R I Z O N A

Mogollon Rim

Salt

Gila

Theodore Roosevelt Lake

Grand Canyon

Gila

Sonoran Desert

U.S. MEXICO

SONORA

BAJA CALIFORNIA

BAJA CALIFORNIA SUR

G U L F   O F   C A L I F O R N I A

PACIFIC OCEAN

NEVADA

CALIFORNIA

Lake Mead

Lake Mohave

Lake Havasu

Colorado

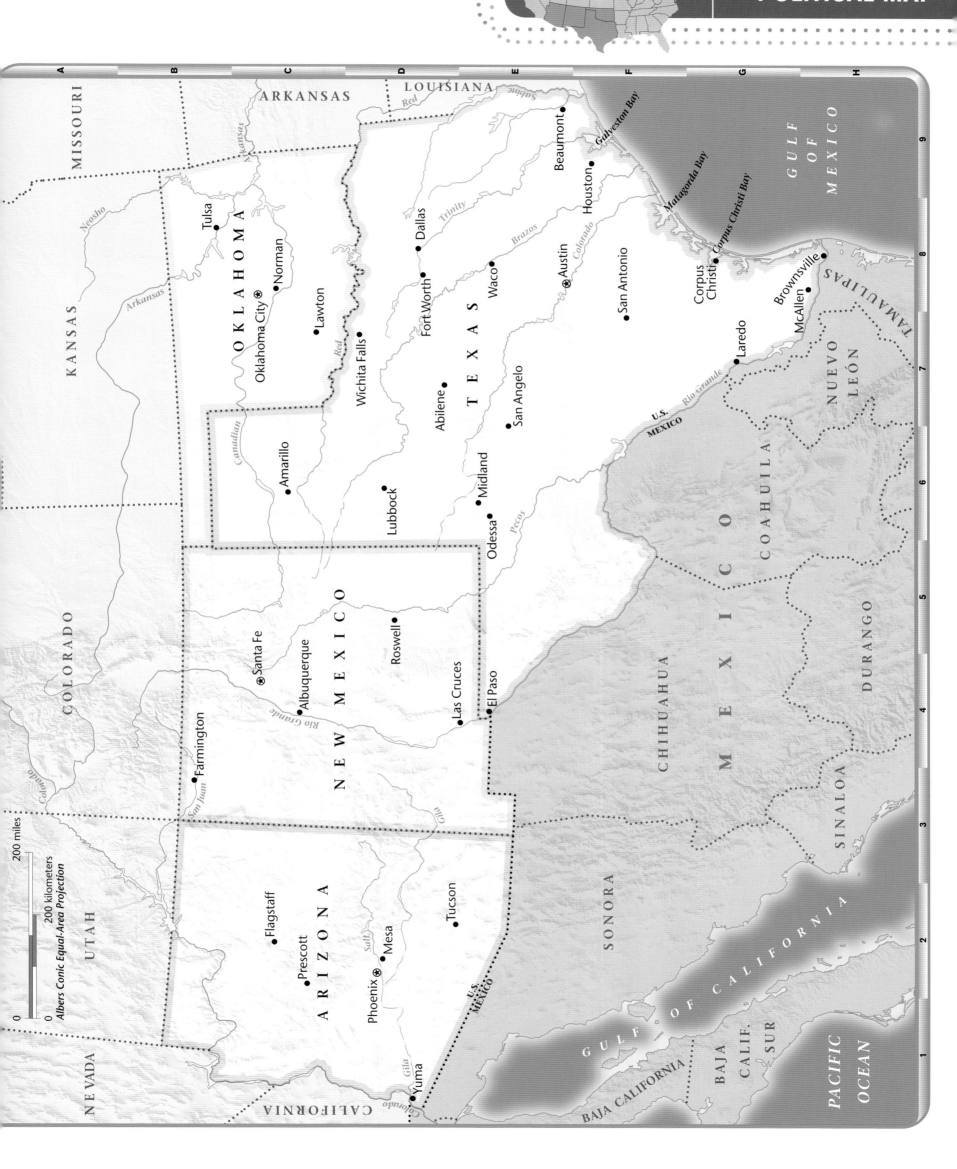

A   B   C   D   E   F   G   H

MISSOURI

ARKANSAS

LOUISIANA

Red

Sabine

Trinity

GULF OF MEXICO

Beaumont

Galveston Bay

Houston

Colorado

Brazos

Matagorda Bay

Corpus Christi Bay

KANSAS

Neosho

Arkansas

OKLAHOMA

Tulsa

Norman

Oklahoma City ⊛

Lawton

Dallas

Fort Worth

Waco

Austin ⊛

San Antonio

Corpus Christi

Brownsville

McAllen

Laredo

TAMAULIPAS

Wichita Falls

Red

TEXAS

Canadian

Amarillo

Abilene

San Angelo

U.S.

MEXICO

Rio Grande

NUEVO LEÓN

Lubbock

Midland

Odessa

Pecos

COAHUILA

COLORADO

Santa Fe ⊛

Albuquerque

Roswell

Las Cruces

El Paso

NEW MEXICO

Rio Grande

CHIHUAHUA

MEXICO

DURANGO

Farmington

San Juan

Colorado

NEVADA

UTAH

200 miles

200 kilometers

Albers Conic Equal-Area Projection

Flagstaff

Prescott

Mesa

Phoenix ⊛

ARIZONA

Salt

Gila

Tucson

SONORA

SINALOA

U.S.

MEXICO

CALIFORNIA

Yuma

Gila

Colorado

BAJA CALIFORNIA

GULF OF CALIFORNIA

BAJA CALIF. SUR

PACIFIC OCEAN

9   8   7   6   5   4   3   2   1

⇨ SKY STONE. According to Indian legend, turquoise stole its color from the sky. This Zuni woman is wearing turquoise jewelry for a festival in Phoenix. Zuni Indians, whose reservation is in western New Mexico, have made jewelry for more than one thousand years.

The Southwest
FROM CANYONS TO GRASSLANDS

Legendary cities of gold lured Spanish conquistadors to the Southwest in the 1500s. Today, the promise of economic opportunities brings people from other states as well as immigrants, both legal and illegal, from countries south of the border. This part of the Sunbelt region boasts future-oriented cities while preserving Wild West tales and Native American traditions. Stretching from the humid Gulf Coast to Arizona's deserts, the landscape is as diverse as its climate, ranging from sprawling plains in the east to plateaus cut by dramatic canyons in the west. Water is a major concern in the Southwest, one of the country's fastest-growing regions.

⇩ HIGH SOCIETY. Dressed in an elegant ball gown, a young woman participates in the Society of Martha Washington Pageant in Laredo, Texas. This event presents daughters of wealthy and long-established Hispanic families to the local community.

⇑ MODERN METROPOLIS. Lights sparkle in the skyline of Dallas, Texas. Although incorporated as a town in 1856, it was not until 1930 that it experienced explosive growth and prosperity due to the discovery of oil. Today, Dallas is a center of the U.S. oil industry and a leader in technology-based industries.

⇑ DEADLY VIPER. Shaking the rattles on the tip of its tail, this diamondback rattlesnake—coiled for attack—warns intruders to stay away. Common throughout the arid Southwest, the snake eats mainly small rodents.

⇐ STANDING TALL. The saguaro cactus, which often rises more than 30 feet (9 m) above the shrubs of the Sonoran Desert, frequently has several branches and produces creamy-white flowers that bloom at night. The Sonoran, hottest desert in North America, is located in the borderlands of southern Arizona and California and extends into northern Mexico.

WHERE THE PICTURES ARE

Copper worker p. 120

Grand Canyon p. 120

Rattlesnake p. 119

Bison grazing p. 124

Historic plane p. 125

Saguaro cactus pp. 118-119

Turquoise jewelry p. 118

Gila monster p. 122

Hot-air balloons p. 122

Los Alamos scientists p. 122

Dallas skyline pp. 118-119

Oil drillers p. 126

Rio Grande ferry pp. 126-127

Texas debutante p. 118

ARIZONA

⇧ HOT WORK. A man in protective clothing works near a furnace that melts and refines copper ore at Magma Copper Company near Tucson. Arizona is one of the largest copper-producing regions in the world.

The Europeans to first visit what is now Arizona were the Spanish in the 1500s. The territory passed from Spain to Mexico and then to the United States over the next three centuries. In the 1800s settlers clashed with the Apache warriors Cochise and Geronimo—and with one another in lawless towns like Tombstone. Youngest of the 48 contiguous states, statehood arrived in 1912. Arizona's economy was long based on the Five C's—copper, cattle, cotton, citrus, and climate—but manufacturing and service industries have gained prominence. A fast-growing population, sprawling cities, and agricultural irrigation strain limited water supplies in this dry state, which depends on water from the Colorado River and underground aquifers. Tourists flock to the Colorado Plateau in the north to see stunning vistas of the Grand Canyon, Painted Desert, and Monument Valley. To the south, the Sonoran Desert's unique ecosystem includes the giant saguaro cactus. Indian reservations scattered around the state offer outsiders the chance to learn about tribal history and culture.

THE BASICS

STATS

Area
113,998 sq mi (295,256 sq km)

Population
6,338,755

Capital
Phoenix
Population 1,512,986

Largest city
Phoenix
Population 1,512,986

Ethnic/racial groups
87.3% white; 4.8% Native American; 3.8% African American; 2.4% Asian. Hispanic (any race) 29.2%.

Industry
Real estate, manufactured goods, retail, state and local government, transportation and public utilities, wholesale trade, health services, tourism, electronics

Agriculture
Vegetables, cattle, dairy products, cotton, fruit, nursery stock, nuts

Statehood
February 14, 1912; 48th state

GEO WHIZ

The California condor, once common throughout the Southwest, nearly became extinct in 1987. Through captive breeding and other conservation measures, the species has been reintroduced to the wild in areas such as the Grand Canyon.

People have been carving pictures called petroglyphs into rock cliffs in Verde Valley near Flagstaff for thousands of years. The meanings of most are a mystery, but others reveal the plants and animals of bygone eras.

Introduced as wild game for sportsmen, bullfrogs have made Arizona their new home on the range. With no natural predators and plenty to eat, bullfrogs are taking over.

CACTUS WREN
SAGUARO

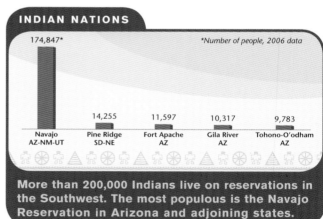

INDIAN NATIONS

174,847*   *Number of people, 2006 data

| | 14,255 | 11,597 | 10,317 | 9,783 |
| Navajo AZ-NM-UT | Pine Ridge SD-NE | Fort Apache AZ | Gila River AZ | Tohono-O'odham AZ |

More than 200,000 Indians live on reservations in the Southwest. The most populous is the Navajo Reservation in Arizona and adjoining states.

⇩ NATURAL WONDER. Carved by the rushing waters of the Colorado River, the Grand Canyon's geologic features and fossil record reveal almost two billion years of Earth's history. Archaeological evidence indicates human habitation dating back 12,000 years.

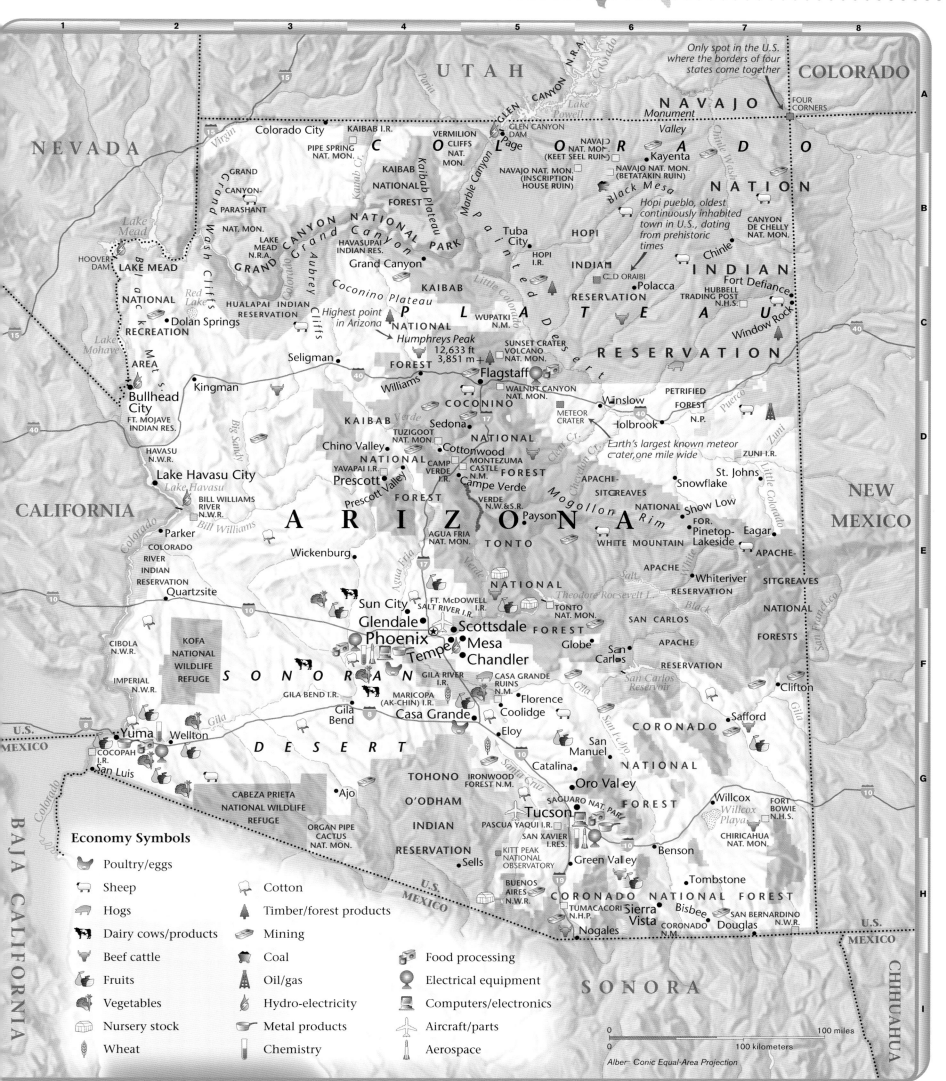

Only spot in the U.S. where the borders of four states come together

UTAH

COLORADO

NEVADA

N.R.A.

GLEN CANYON

Colorado City

KAIBAB I.R.

Page

NAVAJO NAT. MON.
(KEET SEEL RUIN)

Kayenta

NAVAJO
Monument
Valley

NAVAJO NAT. MON.
(BETATAKIN RUIN)

CANYON
DE CHELLY
NAT. MON.

N A T I O N

PIPE SPRING
NAT. MON.

VERMILION
CLIFFS
NAT.
MON.

GRAND
CANYON-
PARASHANT
NAT. MON.

KAIBAB

KAIBAB
NATIONAL

FOREST

GLEN CANYON
DAM

Lake
Powell

Black Mesa

Hopi pueblo, oldest
continuously inhabited
town in U.S., dating
from prehistoric
times

Chinle

Tuba
City

HOPI

HOPI
I.R.

ORAIBI

INDIAN

Polacca

Fort Defiance

HUBBELL
TRADING POST
N.H.S.

Window Rock

LAKE
MEAD
N.R.A.

HOOVER
DAM

Lake
Mead

LAKE MEAD

Red
Lake

GRAND

CANYON

NATIONAL

PARK

Grand Canyon

HAVASUPAI
INDIAN RES.

Coconino Plateau

KAIBAB
NATIONAL

RESERVATION

INDIAN

RESERVATION

NATIONAL

HUALAPAI INDIAN
RESERVATION

Dolan Springs

RECREATION

Lake
Mohave

AREA

Seligman

FOREST

Highest point
in Arizona

P L A T E A U

Humphreys Peak
12,633 ft
3,851 m

WUPATKI
N.M.

SUNSET CRATER
VOLCANO
NAT. MON.

PETRIFIED

Kingman

Williams

Flagstaff

WALNUT CANYON
NAT. MON.

Winslow

FOREST

Bullhead
City

FT. MOJAVE
INDIAN RES.

COCONINO

Holbrook

N.P.

RESERVATION

Puerco

Zuni

HAVASU
N.W.R.

KAIBAB

Verde

Sedona

NATIONAL

METEOR
CRATER

Earth's largest known meteor
crater, one mile wide

ZUNI I.R.

Lake Havasu City

Chino Valley

TUZIGOOT
NAT. MON.

Cottonwood

MONTEZUMA
CASTLE
N.M.

St. Johns

NEW

BILL WILLIAMS
RIVER
N.W.R.

NATIONAL

CAMP
VERDE
I.R.

Snowflake

Little Colorado

MEXICO

Lake Havasu

Parker

Bill Williams

YAVAPAI I.R.

Prescott

Prescott Valley

CAMP
VERDE

Campe Verde

FOREST

VERDE
N.W.&S.R.

APACHE-
SITGREAVES

NATIONAL

Show Low

CALIFORNIA

COLORADO
RIVER
INDIAN
RESERVATION

A R I Z O N A

FOREST

AGUA FRIA
NAT. MON.

Payson

Mogollon Rim

WHITE MOUNTAIN

FOR.
Pinetop-
Lakeside

Eagar

APACHE-
SITGREAVES

Wickenburg

TONTO

APACHE

NATIONAL

Quartzsite

Whiteriver

FORESTS

San Francisco

CIBOLA
N.W.R.

KOFA
NATIONAL
WILDLIFE
REFUGE

Sun City

FT. McDOWELL
I.R.

SALT RIVER I.R.

NATIONAL

TONTO
NAT. MON.

Theodore Roosevelt L.

Salt

SAN CARLOS

Black

RESERVATION

Glendale

Scottsdale

FOREST

Globe

San
Carlos

APACHE

IMPERIAL
N.W.R.

Phoenix

Tempe

Mesa

Chandler

GILA RIVER
I.R.

CASA GRANDE
RUINS
N.M.

Florence

San Carlos
Reservoir

RESERVATION

Clifton

S O N O R A N

GILA BEND I.R.

MARICOPA
(AK-CHIN) I.R.

Gila
Bend

Casa Grande

Coolidge

Eloy

Gila

CORONADO

Safford

U.S.

Gila

Yuma

Wellton

San
Manuel

San Pedro

NATIONAL

MEXICO

COCOPAH
I.R.

D E S E R T

Catalina

Santa Cruz

San Luis

Ajo

TOHONO

IRONWOOD
FOREST N.M.

Oro Valley

FOREST

Willcox

FORT
BOWIE
N.H.S.

Willcox
Playa

CABEZA PRIETA
NATIONAL WILDLIFE
REFUGE

O'ODHAM

SAGUARO NAT. PARK

Tucson

PASCUA YAQUI I.R.

CHIRICAHUA
NAT. MON.

ORGAN PIPE
CACTUS
NAT. MON.

INDIAN

SAN XAVIER
I.RES.

Benson

BAJA

CALIFORNIA

Colorado

RESERVATION

KITT PEAK
NATIONAL
OBSERVATORY

Sells

Green Valley

Tombstone

U.S.

MEXICO

BUENOS
AIRES
N.W.R.

C O R O N A D O   N A T I O N A L   F O R E S T

Bisbee

SAN BERNARDINO
N.W.R.

U.S.

MEXICO

TUMACACORI
N.H.P.

Sierra
Vista

San Bernardino

CORONADO
N.M.

Nogales

Douglas

S O N O R A

CHIHUAHUA

Economy Symbols

- Poultry/eggs
- Sheep
- Hogs
- Dairy cows/products
- Beef cattle
- Fruits
- Vegetables
- Nursery stock
- Wheat
- Cotton
- Timber/forest products
- Mining
- Coal
- Oil/gas
- Hydro-electricity
- Metal products
- Chemistry
- Food processing
- Electrical equipment
- Computers/electronics
- Aircraft/parts
- Aerospace

0   100 miles

0   100 kilometers

Alber Conic Equal-Area Projection

NEW MEXICO

New Mexico is among the youngest states—statehood was established in 1912—but its capital city is the country's oldest. The Spanish founded Santa Fe in 1610, a decade before the *Mayflower* reached America. Beginning in the 1820s, the Santa Fe Trail brought trade and settlers, and the United States acquired all the territory from Mexico by 1853. Most large cities are in the center of the state, along the Rio Grande. The Rocky Mountains divide the plains in the east from eroded mesas and canyons in the west. Cattle and sheep ranching on the plains is the chief agricultural activity, but hay, onions, and chili peppers are also important. Copper, potash, and natural gas produce mineral wealth. Cultural richness created by the historic interaction of Indian, Hispanic, and Anglo peoples abounds. Visitors experience this unique culture in the state's spicy cuisine, the famous art galleries of Taos, and the crafts made by Indians on the state's many reservations.

THE BASICS

STATS

Area
121,590 sq mi (314,917 sq km)

Population
1,969,915

Capital
Santa Fe
Population 66,476

Largest city
Albuquerque
Population 504,949

Ethnic/racial groups
84.6% white; 9.8% Native American; 2.5% African American; 1.3% Asian. Hispanic (any race) 44.0%.

Industry
Electronic equipment, state and local government, real estate, business services, federal government, oil and gas extraction, health services

Agriculture
Cattle, dairy products, hay, chili peppers, onions

Statehood
January 6, 1912; 47th state

GEO WHIZ

Carlsbad Caverns National Park has more than a hundred caves, including the deepest limestone cavern in the U.S. From May through October, visitors can watch hundreds of thousands of Mexican free-tailed bats emerge from the cavern on their nightly search for food.

Taos Pueblo, in north-central New Mexico, has been continuously inhabited by Pueblo people for more than 1,000 years. When Spanish explorers reached it in 1540, they thought they had found one of the fabled golden cities of Cibola.

In 2007 voters in a county in south-central New Mexico approved a tax to help fund construction of a spaceport where rockets will launch tourists into space.

ROADRUNNER

YUCCA

⇧ PAINFUL BITE. The strikingly patterned gila monster, the most poisonous lizard native to the United States, lives in desert areas of the Southwest.

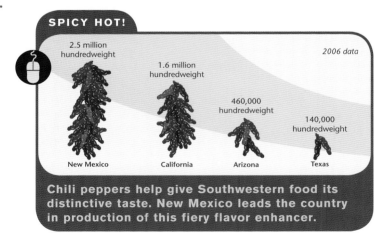

⇧ FLYING HIGH. Brightly colored balloons rise into a brilliant blue October sky during Albuquerque's annual International Balloon Fiesta, the largest such event in the world. During the 9-day festival more than 700 hot-air balloons drift on variable air currents created by surrounding mountains.

SPICY HOT!

2006 data

2.5 million hundredweight — New Mexico

1.6 million hundredweight — California

460,000 hundredweight — Arizona

140,000 hundredweight — Texas

Chili peppers help give Southwestern food its distinctive taste. New Mexico leads the country in production of this fiery flavor enhancer.

⇦ NUCLEAR MYSTERIES. Scientists at Los Alamos National Laboratory, a leading scientific and engineering research institution responsible for national security, use 3-D simulations to study nuclear explosions.

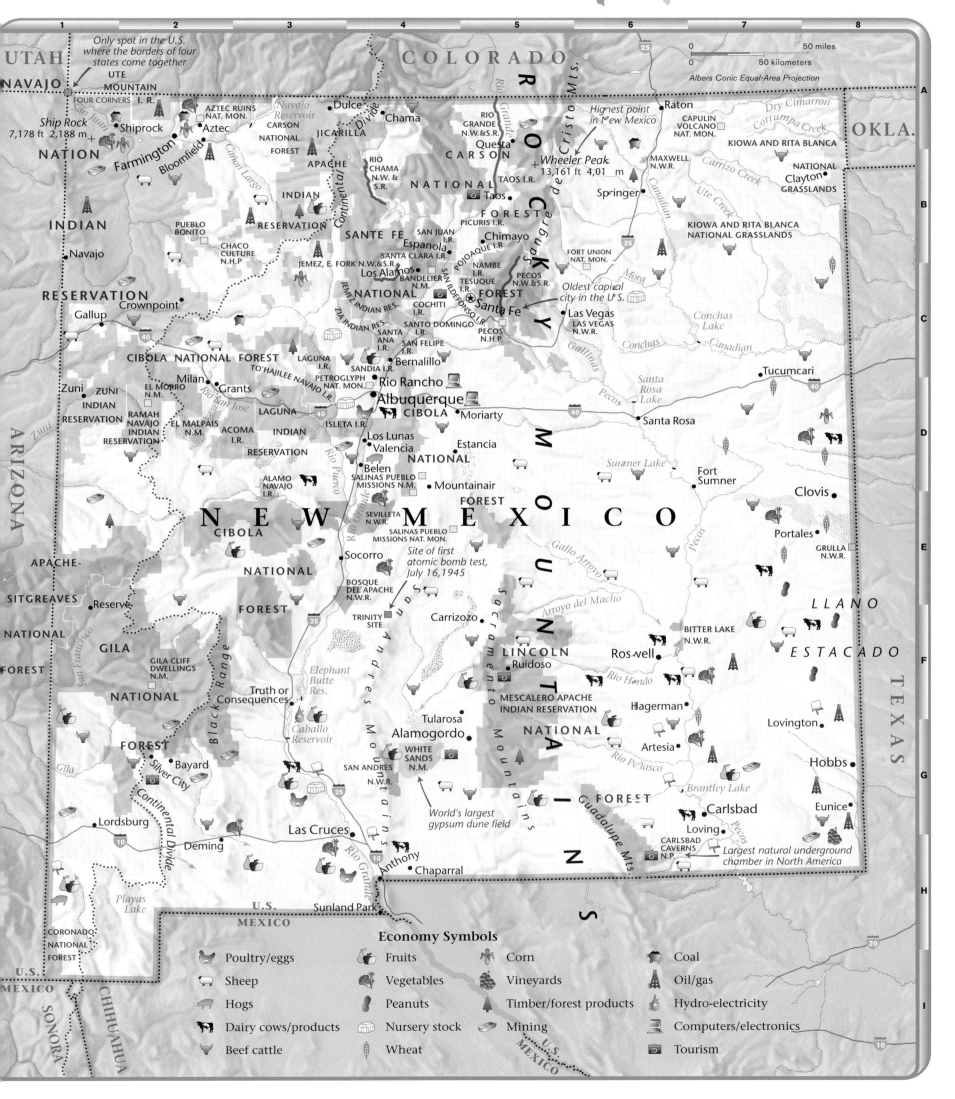

UTAH

NAVAJO

Only spot in the U.S. where the borders of four states come together UTE MOUNTAIN

FOUR CORNERS I.R.

Ship Rock 7,178 ft 2,188 m

Shiprock

NATION

Farmington

Bloomfield

Aztec

AZTEC RUINS NAT. MON.

Dulce

Navajo Reservoir

CARSON NATIONAL FOREST

JICARILLA

APACHE

INDIAN

Chama

Continental Divide

RIO CHAMA N.W. & S.R.

RIO GRANDE N.W.&S.R.

COLORADO

Questa

CARSON

NATIONAL

Raton

CAPULIN VOLCANO NAT. MON.

KIOWA AND RITA BLANCA

Dry Cimarron

Corrumpa Creek

OKLA.

Highest point in New Mexico

Carrizo Creek

INDIAN

RESERVATION

PUEBLO BONITO

CHACO CULTURE N.H.P.

JEMEZ, E. FORK N.W.&S.R.

SANTE FE

San Juan I.R.

Espanola

SANTA CLARA I.R.

Los Alamos

BANDELIER N.M.

FOREST

TAOS I.R.

Taos

PICURIS I.R.

Chimayo

POJOAQUE I.R.

NAMBE I.R.

TESUQUE I.R.

PECOS N.W.&S.R.

Wheeler Peak 13,161 ft 4,01 m

Sangre de Cristo Mts.

MAXWELL N.W.R.

Springer

FORT UNION NAT. MON.

Mora

Canadian

KIOWA AND RITA BLANCA NATIONAL GRASSLANDS

NATIONAL Clayton GRASSLANDS

Ute Creek

INDIAN

Navajo

RESERVATION

Crownpoint

Gallup

JEMEZ INDIAN RES.

ZIA INDIAN RES.

Los Alamos

COCHITI I.R.

SANTO DOMINGO I.R.

SANTA ANA I.R.

SAN FELIPE I.R.

Bernalillo

SAN ILDEFONSO I.R.

FOREST

Santa Fe

PECOS N.H.P.

Oldest capital city in the U.S.

Las Vegas

LAS VEGAS N.W.R.

Conchas Lake

Conchas

Canadian

Santa Rosa Lake

Gallinas

Pecos

Tucumcari

CIBOLA NATIONAL FOREST

Milan

Grants

EL MORRO N.M.

TO'HAJIILEE NAVAJO I.R.

PETROGLYPH NAT. MON.

Rio Rancho

Albuquerque

CIBOLA

Moriarty

Santa Rosa

Zuni

ZUNI INDIAN RESERVATION

RAMAH NAVAJO INDIAN RESERVATION

EL MALPAIS N.M.

LAGUNA I.R.

ACOMA I.R.

LAGUNA INDIAN

RESERVATION

ISLETA I.R.

Los Lunas

Valencia

Rio Puerco

Rio San Jose

Estancia

Suñer Lake

Fort Sumner

Clovis

ARIZONA

APACHE-

SITGREAVES

NATIONAL

Reserve

FOREST

GILA

NATIONAL

FOREST

Belen

ALAMO NAVAJO I.R.

SALINAS PUEBLO MISSIONS N.M.

Mountainair

SALINAS PUEBLO MISSIONS NAT. MON.

N E W   **M E X I C O**

SEVILLETA N.W.R.

Socorro

Rio Grande

FOREST

Site of first atomic bomb test, July 16, 1945

BOSQUE DEL APACHE N.W.R.

TRINITY SITE

Portales

GRULLA N.W.R.

M O U N

Gallo Arroyo

Carrizozo

Arroyo del Macho

BITTER LAKE N.W.R.

Zuni

CIBOLA

NATIONAL

FOREST

GILA

Gila

Reserve

GILA CLIFF DWELLINGS N.M.

Black Range

Elephant Butte Res.

Truth or Consequences

Caballo Reservoir

San Francisco

Andres

Mountains

LINCOLN

Ruidoso

T

A

Roswell

Rio Hondo

L L A N O

E S T A C A D O

T E X A S

FOREST

Bayard

Silver City

Continental Divide

San Andres

SAN ANDRES N.W.R.

Tularosa

Alamogordo

WHITE SANDS N.M.

World's largest gypsum dune field

MESCALERO APACHE INDIAN RESERVATION

Sacramento

Hagerman

NATIONAL

Artesia

Rio Peñasco

Lovington

Hobbs

Lordsburg

Deming

Las Cruces

Rio Grande

Anthony

Chaparral

I

N

S

Mountains

Guadalupe Mts.

FOREST

Brantley Lake

Carlsbad

Loving

Pecos

Eunice

CARLSBAD CAVERNS N.P.

Largest natural underground chamber in North America

Playas Lake

U.S.

MEXICO

Sunland Park

CORONADO NATIONAL FOREST

U.S. MEXICO

CHIHUAHUA

SONORA

U.S. MEXICO

Economy Symbols

Poultry/eggs	Fruits	Corn	Coal
Sheep	Vegetables	Vineyards	Oil/gas
Hogs	Peanuts	Timber/forest products	Hydro-electricity
Dairy cows/products	Nursery stock	Mining	Computers/electronics
Beef cattle	Wheat		Tourism

0   50 miles

0   50 kilometers

Albers Conic Equal-Area Projection

OKLAHOMA

THE BASICS

STATS

Area
69,898 sq mi (181,036 sq km)

Population
3,617,316

Capital
Oklahoma City
Population 537,734

Largest city
Oklahoma City
Population 537,734

Ethnic/racial groups
78.3% white; 8.0% Native American;
7.8% African American; 1.7% Asian.
Hispanic (any race) 6.9%.

Industry
Manufacturing, services, government,
finance, insurance, real estate

Agriculture
Cattle, wheat, hogs, poultry, nursery
stock

Statehood
November 16, 1907; 46th state

GEO WHIZ

An area of Oklahoma City has earned
the nickname Little Saigon. In the
1960s the city opened its doors
to tens of thousands of refugees
from Vietnam. Today, the area is a
thriving business district that includes
people of other Asian nationalities.

"Hillbilly Speed Bump" is one of several
nicknames for the armadillo.
Native to South America, large
populations of this armor-plated
mammal are found as far north
as Oklahoma.

Before it became a state in 1907,
Oklahoma was known as Indian
Territory. Today 39 tribes, including
Cherokees, Osages, Creeks,
and Choctaws, have their
headquarters in the state.

SCISSOR-TAILED
FLYCATCHER

MISTLETOE

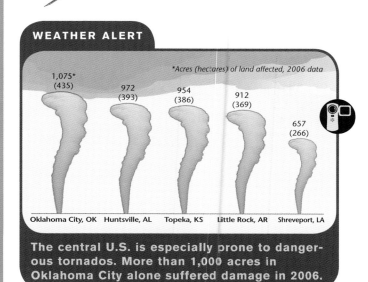

OKLAHOMA

The U.S. government declared most of present-day Oklahoma Indian Territory in 1834. To reach this new homeland, southeastern Indians were forced to travel the Trail of Tears, named for its brutal conditions. By 1889 areas were opened for white homesteaders who staked claims in frenzied land runs. White and Indian lands were combined to form the state of Oklahoma in 1907. During the 1930s, many Okies fled drought and dust storms that smothered everything in sight. Some traveled as far as California in search of work. Better farming methods and the return of rain helped agriculture recover, and today cattle and wheat are the chief products. Oil and natural gas wells are found throughout the state. The Red River, colored by the region's iron-rich soils, marks the state's southern boundary. Along the eastern border, the Ozark Plateau and Ouachita Mountains form rugged bluffs and valleys. To the west, rolling plains rise toward the High Plains in the state's panhandle.

COLORADO

NEW MEXICO

Black Mesa 4,973 ft 1,516 m
• Boise City
Highest point in Oklahoma
Cimarron
Guymon •
OPTIMA N.W.R.
Optima Lake

KIOWA AND RITA BLANCA NATIONAL GRASSLAND

H I G H   P L A I N S

Beaver
Beaver •

WEATHER ALERT

*Acres (hectares) of land affected, 2006 data

1,075* (435) — Oklahoma City, OK
972 (393) — Huntsville, AL
954 (386) — Topeka, KS
912 (369) — Little Rock, AR
657 (266) — Shreveport, LA

The central U.S. is especially prone to dangerous tornados. More than 1,000 acres in
Oklahoma City alone suffered damage in 2006.

⇧ NATURAL LANDSCAPE. A bison herd grazes in the Tallgrass Prairie
Preserve, near Pawhuska. In years when rain is abundant, the grasses can
grow as tall as 8 feet (2.5 m). Tallgrass prairie once covered 140 million
acres (57 million ha), extending from Minnesota to Texas, but today less
than 10 percent remains because of urban sprawl and cropland expansion.

KANSAS

5 6 7 8 9 10 11 12

A

MISSOURI

•Buffalo

•Alva
SALT PLAINS N.W.R.

Blackwell
Ponca City

Kaw Lake

OSAGE

NATION

•Bartlesville

Vinita

Lake O' The Cherokees

•Grove

Great Salt Plains Lake

RESERVATION

Pawhuska

Oologah Lake

44 TURNPIKE

Woodward

Fairview

•Enid

•Perry

Sooner Lake

CIMARRON TURNPIKE

Sziatook Lake

Owasso

WILL ROGERS

Pryor

Lake Hudson

B

Claremore

Keystone Lake

Tulsa

Broken Arrow

Wagoner

•Tahlequah

Stillwater

Sand Springs

Sapulpa

Jenks

Bixby

Ft. Gibson L.

Stilwell

•Watonga

•Kingfisher

Guthrie

Cushing

Bristow

TURNER TURNPIKE

Muskogee

OKLAHOMA

BLACK KETTLE NATIONAL GRASSLAND

WASHITA N.W.R.

Edmond

Deep Fork

DEEP FORK N.W.R.

Okmulgee

Tenkiller Lake

C

WASHITA BATTLEFIELD N.H.S.

•Weatherford

El Reno

Yukon

Oklahoma City

Checotah

SEQUOYAH N.W.R.

Sallisaw

40

Clinton

Bethany

Henryetta

•Sayre

Elk City

Oklahoma City Nat. Mem.

•Moore

Shawnee

Robert S. Kerr Lake

•Hollis

•Mangum

Anadarko

•Norman

Tecumseh

Seminole

Eufaula Lake

Poteau

D

•Hobart

Lake Altus

Chickasha

Wewoka

Holdenville

Wilburton

OUACHITA

McAlester

Heavener

WICHITA MTS. WILDLIFE REFUGE

Purcell

Pauls Valley

Ada

Sardis Lake

•Altus

Marlow

Lawton

Sulphur

Atoka

McGee Cr. Lake

NATIONAL

•Frederick

Walters

Duncan

CHICKASAW N.R.A.

Antlers

Broken Bow Lake

E

Arbuckle Mts.

Tishomingo

Coleman

LITTLE RIVER N.W.R.

Broken Bow

Waurika Lake

Lone Grove

Ardmore

TISHOMINGO N.W.R.

Hugo Lake

Hugo

Idabel

FOREST

Madill

Durant

Lake Texoma

0 50 miles
0 50 kilometers
Albers Equal-Area Projection

TEXAS

F

Economy Symbols

- Poultry/eggs
- Sheep
- Hogs
- Dairy cows/products
- Beef cattle
- Fruits
- Vegetables
- Peanuts
- Nursery stock
- Wheat
- Corn
- Soybeans
- Cotton
- Stone/gravel/cement
- Mining

- Coal
- Oil/gas
- Hydro-electricity
- Machinery
- Metal products
- Motor vehicles/parts
- Rubber/plastics
- Chemistry
- Food processing
- Clothing/textiles
- Electrical equipment
- Computers/electronics
- Aircraft/parts
- Finance/insurance

⇩ HISTORY IN THE AIR. Tulsa's mayor pilots one of the Spirit of Tulsa Squadron's vintage PT-17 airplanes above the city. In 1990 the squadron became part of the Commemorative Air Force, a national organization committed to preserving aviation history by restoring and flying World War II aircraft.

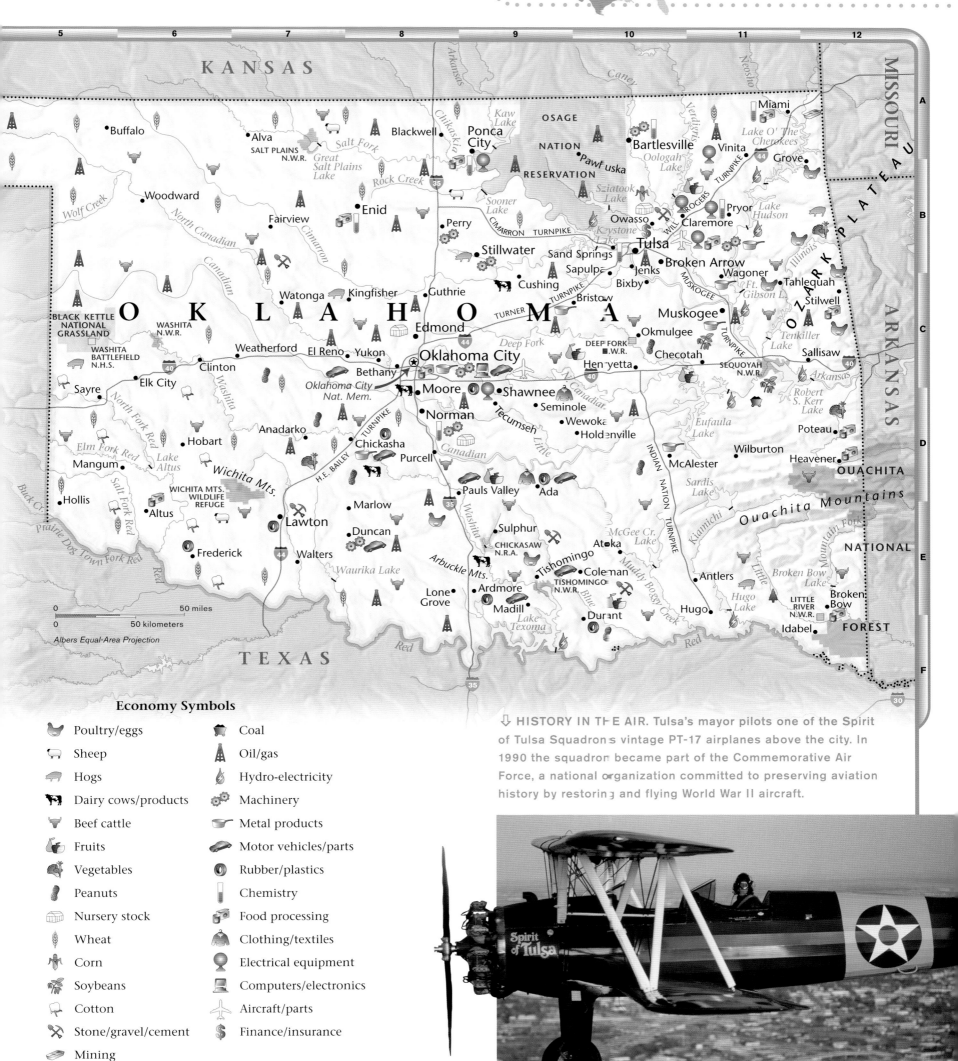

TEXAS

Huge size, geographic diversity, and rich natural resources make Texas seem like its own country. In fact, it was an independent republic after throwing off Mexican rule in 1836. A famous battle in the fight for independence produced the Texan battle cry "Remember the Alamo!" In 1845 Texas was annexed by the United States. Texas is the second largest state (behind Alaska) and the second most populous (behind California). It is a top producer of many agricultural products, including cattle, sheep, cotton, citrus fruits, vegetables, rice, and pecans. It also has huge oil and natural gas fields and is a manufacturing powerhouse. Pine forests cover East Texas, the wettest region. The Gulf Coast has swamps and extensive barrier islands. Grassy plains stretch across the northern panhandle, while the rolling Hill Country is famous for beautiful wildflowers. Mountains, valleys, and sandy plains sprawl across dry West Texas. The Rio Grande, sometimes barely a trickle, separates Texas and Mexico.

THE BASICS

STATS

Area
268,581 sq mi (695,624 sq km)

Population
23,904,380

Capital
Austin
Population 709,893

Largest city
Houston
Population 2,144,491

Ethnic/racial groups
82.7% white; 11.9% African American; 3.4% Asian; .7% Native American. Hispanic (any race) 35.7%.

Industry
Chemicals, machinery, electronics and computers, food products, petroleum and natural gas, transportation equipment

Agriculture
Cattle, sheep, poultry, cotton, sorghum, wheat, rice, hay, peanuts, pecans

Statehood
December 29, 1845; 28th state

GEO WHIZ

The Fossil Rim Wildlife Research Center in the Texas Hill Country is breeding black rhinos and other endangered African animals. The goal is to reintroduce offspring into the wild in their native environment. Meanwhile, visitors get a chance to see a bit of Africa in Texas.

Six national flags have flown over Texas during the course of its history—the Spanish, French, Mexican, Texan, Confederate, and American.

Texas has a long history of Bigfoot sightings. The ape-man creature was part of local Indian lore, and white settlers told stories about a wild woman along the Navidad River. The Texas Bigfoot Research Center has collected hundreds of eyewitness reports, footprint casts, and hair samples of what locals call Wooly Booger.

MOCKINGBIRD
BLUEBONNET

⇧ BLACK GOLD. Workers plug an oil well. Discovery of oil early in the 20th century transformed life in Texas. Today, the state leads the U.S. in oil and natural gas production.

Chamizal National Memorial
NEW MEXICO
U.S.
MEXICO El Paso
GUADALUPE MTS. N.P. Guadalupe Peak
8,749 ft
2,667 m
YSLETA DEL SUR I.R.
Fabens
Pecos
Highest point in Texas
CHIHUAHUA
Rio Grande
Davis Mts.
FORT DAVIS N.H.S.
Alpine
Marfa
Presidio
BIG
NATI
PA

2007 data

14 million cattle
6.6 million cattle
6.4 million cattle
5.5 million cattle
5.2 million cattle

Texas Nebraska Kansas California Oklahoma

Texas has more cattle than most states have people. Only California, Texas, New York, and Florida have larger human populations.

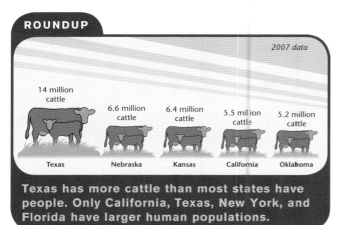

⇨ BORDERLAND RELIC. Los Ebanos Ferry, which takes its name from a grove of ebony trees growing nearby, is the last remaining government-licensed, hand-pulled ferry on any U.S. border. The privately owned ferry, near Mission, Texas, can carry three cars at a time across the Rio Grande.

Economy Symbols

- 🐟 Fishing
- 🐚 Shellfish
- 🐔 Poultry/eggs
- 🐑 Sheep
- 🐖 Hogs
- 🐄 Dairy cows/products
- 🐂 Beef cattle
- 🍒 Fruits
- 🥬 Vegetables

- Peanuts
- Nursery stock
- Wheat
- Corn
- Rice
- Soybeans
- Cotton
- Timber/forest products
- Stone/gravel/cement
- Mining

- Oil/gas
- Hydro-electricity
- Machinery
- Metal manufacturing
- Metal products
- Motor vehicles/parts
- Rubber/plastics
- Chemistry
- Food processing
- Clothing/textiles
- Leather products
- Computers/electronics
- Aircraft/parts
- Tourism

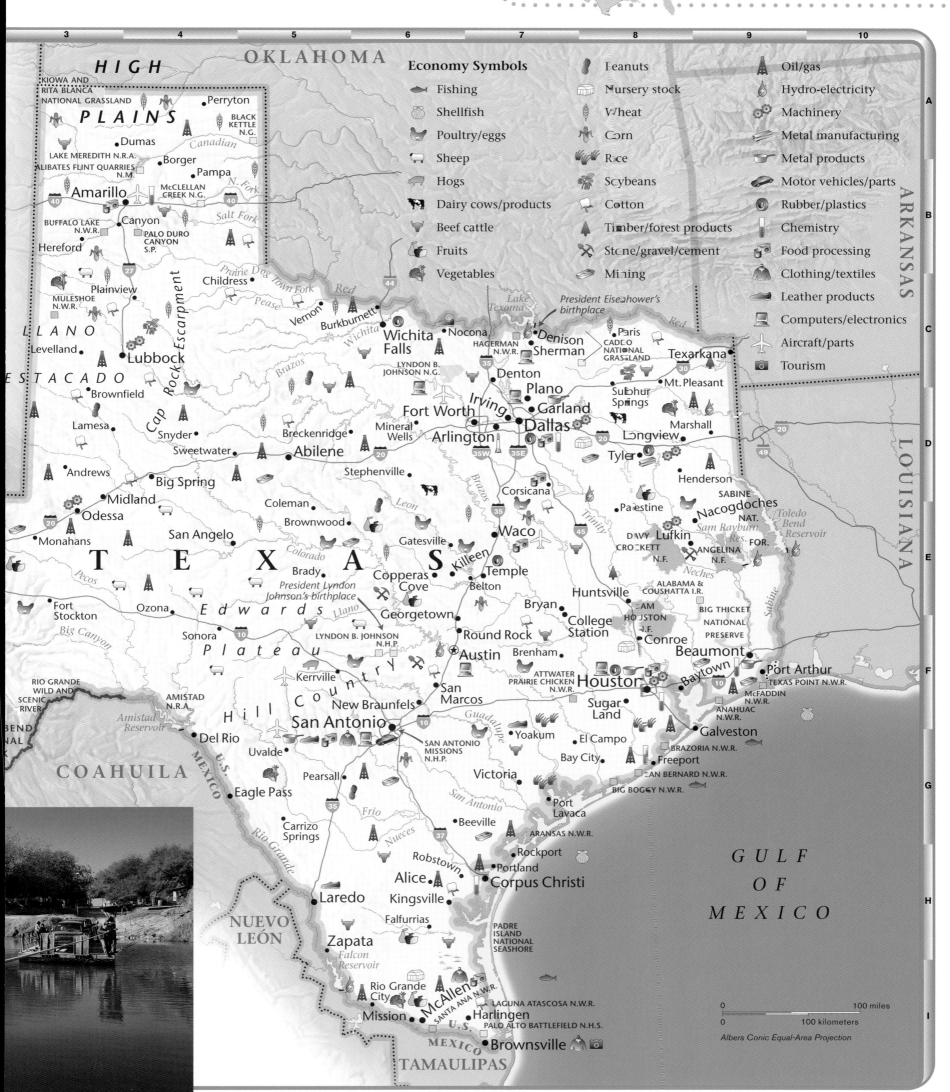

OKLAHOMA

HIGH PLAINS

KIOWA AND RITA BLANCA NATIONAL GRASSLAND
BLACK KETTLE N.G.
Perryton
Dumas
Canadian
Borger
Pampa
LAKE MEREDITH N.R.A.
ALIBATES FLINT QUARRIES N.M.
McCLELLAN CREEK N.G.
N. Fork
Amarillo
Canyon
Salt Fork
BUFFALO LAKE N.W.R.
PALO DURO CANYON S.P.
Hereford
Prairie Dog Town Fork
LLANO
Plainview
Childress
Red
Pease
Lake Texoma
President Eisenhower's birthplace
MULESHOE N.W.R.
Levelland
Lubbock
Brazos
Vernon
Burkburnett
Wichita
Nocona
Denison
Paris
CADDO NATIONAL GRASSLAND
Texarkana
ESTACADO
Brownfield
LYNDON B. JOHNSON N.G.
Wichita Falls
HAGERMAN N.W.R.
Sherman
Cap Rock Escarpment
Lamesa
Snyder
Breckenridge
Mineral Wells
Denton
Plano
Sulphur Springs
Mt. Pleasant
ARKANSAS
LOUISIANA
Andrews
Sweetwater
Abilene
Irving
Fort Worth
Arlington
Garland
Dallas
Longview
Marshall
Big Spring
Stephenville
Brazos
Corsicana
Tyler
Henderson
SABINE
Midland
Coleman
Leon
Palestine
Nacogdoches NAT.
Toledo Bend Reservoir
Odessa
Brownwood
Sam Rayburn Res.
FOR.
Monahans
San Angelo
Waco
DAVY CROCKETT N.F.
Lufkin
ANGELINA N.F.
TEXAS
Gatesville
Trinity
Neches
Sabine
Pecos
Colorado
Brady
Killeen
Temple
ALABAMA & COUSHATTA I.R.
Fort Stockton
Copperas Cove
Belton
Huntsville
BIG THICKET NATIONAL PRESERVE
Ozona
Edwards
Llano
President Lyndon Johnson's birthplace
Georgetown
Bryan
SAM HOUSTON N.F.
Conroe
Beaumont
Sonora
Plateau
LYNDON B. JOHNSON N.H.P.
Round Rock
College Station
Big Canyon
Round Rock
Austin
Brenham
Baytown
Port Arthur
RIO GRANDE WILD AND SCENIC RIVER
Kerrville
Hill Country
San Marcos
ATTWATER PRAIRIE CHICKEN N.W.R.
Houston
TEXAS POINT N.W.R.
AMISTAD N.R.A.
New Braunfels
Sugar Land
McFADDIN N.W.R.
BEND
Amistad Reservoir
San Antonio
ANAHUAC N.W.R.
NAL
Del Rio
SAN ANTONIO MISSIONS N.H.P.
Yoakum
El Campo
Galveston
COAHUILA
Uvalde
Bay City
BRAZORIA N.W.R.
MEXICO
Pearsall
Victoria
Freeport
SAN BERNARD N.W.R.
U.S.
Eagle Pass
Frio
Port Lavaca
BIG BOGGY N.W.R.
Rio Grande
Carrizo Springs
Nueces
Beeville
ARANSAS N.W.R.
San Antonio
Rockport
GULF
Robstown
Portland
OF
Alice
Corpus Christi
MEXICO
Laredo
Kingsville
NUEVO LEÓN
Falfurrias
PADRE ISLAND NATIONAL SEASHORE
Zapata
Falcon Reservoir
Rio Grande City
McAllen
SANTA ANA N.W.R.
LAGUNA ATASCOSA N.W.R.
Mission
Harlingen
PALO ALTO BATTLEFIELD N.H.S.
U.S.
MEXICO
Brownsville
TAMAULIPAS

0   100 miles
0   100 kilometers
Albers Conic Equal-Area Projection

THE REGION

The West

PHYSICAL

Total area
1,635,555 sq mi
(4,236,083 sq km)

Highest point
Mount McKinley (Denali),
AK: 20,320 ft (6,194 m)

Lowest point
Death Valley, CA:
-282 ft (-86 m)

Longest rivers
Missouri, Yukon,
Rio Grande, Colorado

Largest lakes
Great Salt, Iliamna,
Becharof

Vegetation
Needleleaf, broadleaf, and mixed
forest; grassland; desert; tundra
(Alaska); tropical (Hawai'i)

Climate
Mild along the coast, with warm
summers and mild winters; semiarid
to arid inland; polar in parts of
Alaska; tropical in Hawai'i

POLITICAL

Total population
61,788,780

States (11):
Alaska, California, Colorado, Hawai'i,
Idaho, Montana, Nevada, Oregon,
Utah, Washington, Wyoming

Largest state
Alaska: 663,267 sq mi
(1,717,852 sq km)

Smallest state
Hawai'i: 10,931 sq mi (28,311 sq km)

Most populous state
California: 36,553,215

Least populous state
Wyoming: 522,830

Largest city proper
Los Angeles, CA: 3,849,378

PHYSICAL MAP

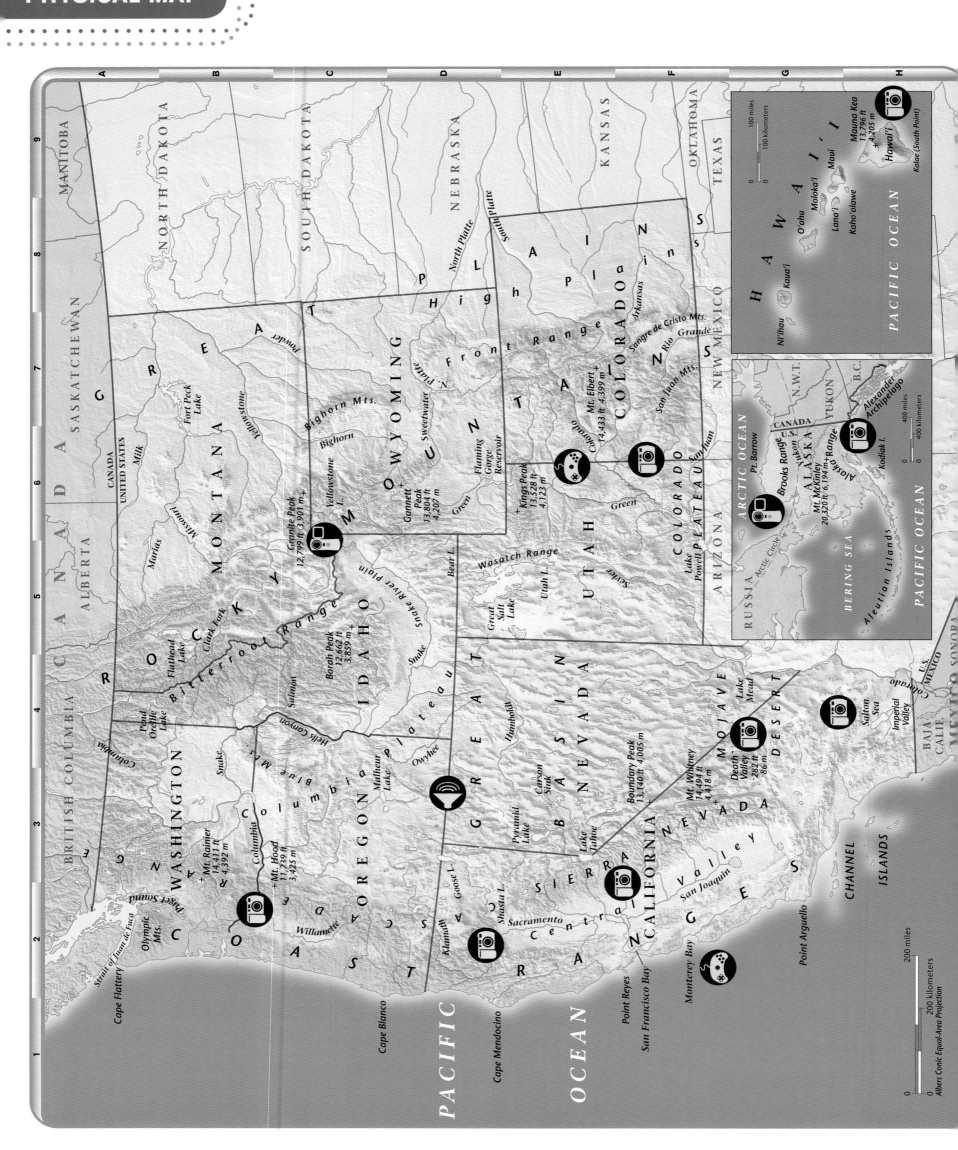

PACIFIC OCEAN

MANITOBA

SASKATCHEWAN

ALBERTA

BRITISH COLUMBIA

CANADA

UNITED STATES

NORTH DAKOTA

SOUTH DAKOTA

NEBRASKA

KANSAS

OKLAHOMA

TEXAS

NEW MEXICO

COLORADO

WYOMING

MONTANA

IDAHO

WASHINGTON

OREGON

NEVADA

UTAH

ARIZONA

CALIFORNIA

ROCKY MOUNTAINS

GREAT PLAINS

High Plains

Front Range

COLORADO PLATEAU

GREAT BASIN

SIERRA NEVADA

COAST RANGES

MOJAVE DESERT

Central Valley

CHANNEL ISLANDS

PACIFIC OCEAN

Powder

Milk

Marias

Missouri

Yellowstone

Bighorn Mts.

Bighorn

Sweetwater

N. Platte

North Platte

South Platte

Platte

Flaming Gorge Reservoir

Green

Colorado

Mt. Elbert +
14,433 ft 4,399 m

Sangre de Cristo Mts.

Rio Grande

Arkansas

San Juan Mts.

San Juan

Kings Peak
13,528 ft
4,123 m

Gannett
Peak
13,804 ft
4,207 m

Granite Peak
12,799 ft 3,901 m +

Yellowstone
L.

Fort Peck
Lake

Hoosink

Clark Fork

Flathead
Lake

Pend
Oreille
Lake

Bitterroot Range

Snake River Plain

Borah Peak
12,662 ft
3,859 m +

Bear L.

Wasatch Range

Great
Salt
Lake

Utah L.

Sevier

Green

Lake
Powell

Colorado

Columbia

Snake

Salmon

Blue Mts.

Malheur
Lake

Owyhee

Humboldt

Snake

Columbia
Plateau

Carson
Sink

Pyramid
Lake

Lake
Tahoe

Boundary Peak
13,140 ft 4,005 m +

Mt. Whitney
14,494 ft
4,418 m +

Death
Valley
-282 ft
-86 m

Lake
Mead

Salton
Sea

Imperial
Valley

Colorado

Mt. Rainier
14,411 ft
4,392 m +

Mt. Hood
11,739 ft
3,425 m +

Columbia

Olympic
Mts.

Strait of Juan de Fuca

Puget Sound

Cape Flattery

Goose L.

Klamath

Shasta L.

Sacramento

San Joaquin

Willamette

Cape Blanco

Cape Mendocino

Point Reyes

San Francisco Bay

Monterey Bay

Point Arguello

BAJA CALIF.

MEXICO

SONORA

U.S.
MEXICO

Albers Conic Equal-Area Projection

200 miles

200 kilometers

0

HAWAI'I

Ni'ihau

Kaua'i

O'ahu

Moloka'i

Lana'i

Maui

Kaho'olawe

Mauna Kea
13,796 ft
4,205 m

Hawai'i

Kalae (South Point)

PACIFIC OCEAN

100 miles

100 kilometers

ALASKA

ARCTIC OCEAN

Pt. Barrow

Brooks Range

Yukon

Mt. McKinley
20,320 ft 6,194 m +

Alaska Range

N.W.T.

YUKON

B.C.

CANADA

U.S.

RUSSIA

BERING SEA

Aleutian Islands

Kodiak I.

Alexander
Archipelago

Arctic Circle

PACIFIC OCEAN

400 miles

400 kilometers

⇨ OLD AND NEW. A cable car carries passengers on a steep hill in San Francisco. In the background modern buildings, including the Transamerica Pyramid, rise above older neighborhoods in this earthquake-prone city.

The West
THE HIGH FRONTIER

The western states, which make up almost half of the country's land area, have diverse landscapes and climates, ranging from the frozen heights of Denali, in Alaska, to the desolation of Death Valley, in California, and the lush, tropical islands of Hawai'i. More than half the region's population lives in California, and the Los Angeles metropolitan area is second only to New York City. Yet many parts of the region are sparsely populated, and much of the land is set aside as parkland and military bases. The region also faces many natural hazards— earthquakes, landslides, wild-fires, and even volcanic eruptions.

⇨ NORTHERN GIANT. Mount McKinley, called Denali—the "High One"— by native Athabascans, is North America's highest peak, rising more than 20,000 feet (6,100 m) in the Alaska Range. The same tectonic forces that trigger earthquakes in Alaska are slowly pushing this huge block of granite ever higher.

WHERE THE PICTURES ARE

Wheat farm p. 152
Seattle skyline p. 152
Astoria Column p. 148
Sea stacks p. 148
Log walker p. 133
Giant sequoia p. 136
Open-pit mine p. 147
Trolley car p. 132
Golden Gate Bridge p. 136
0   200 miles
Mount McKinley p. 132
0   400 mi
Fishing grizzly p. 134
Anchorage p. 134
0   100 mi
Honolulu skyline p. 140
Outrigger canoe p. 133

Logger p. 142
Sheepherders pp. 142-143
Mountain lake p. 145
Potatoes p. 143
Cowboys and cattle p. 144
Hot spring pp. 132-133
Old Faithful p. 155
Pronghorn p. 154
Barn with horse p. 154
Skier p. 138
Mountain lion p. 133
Ancient pueblo p. 138
Delicate Arch pp. 150-151
Mormon temple p. 150
Las Vegas hotel pp. 146-147
Desert scene p. 146
Erupting volcano p. 141

⇑ ELUSIVE PREDATOR. Known by many names, including cougar and mountain lion, these big cats are found mainly in remote mountainous areas of the West, where they hunt deer and smaller animals.

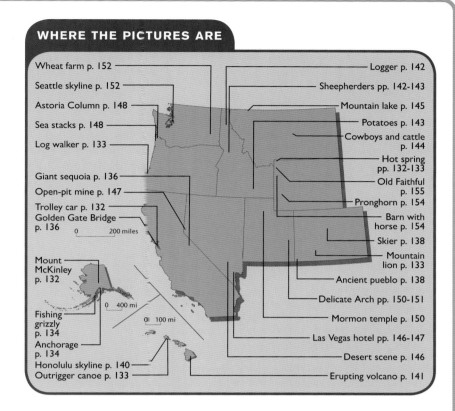

⇐ STEAMY BATH. Colorful, mineral-rich hot springs are just one geothermal feature of Yellowstone National Park. Runoff from rain and snowmelt seeps into cracks in the ground, sinking to a depth of 10,000 feet (3,050 m), where it is heated by molten rock before rising back to the surface.

⇓ BALANCING ACT. For many years, rivers have been used to move logs from forest to market, taking advantage of the buoyancy of logs and the power of moving water. A logger stands on a floating log raft in Coos Bay, Oregon.

⇑ TRADITIONAL SAILING CRAFT. A Hawaiian outrigger canoe on Waikiki Beach promises fun in the surf for visitors to the 50th state. An important part of Polynesian culture, the canoes were once used to travel from island to island.

THE LAST FRONTIER STATE:
ALASKA

ALASKA

Alaska—from *Alyeska*, an Aleut word meaning "great land"—was purchased by the U.S. from Russia in 1867 for just two cents an acre. Many people thought it was a bad investment, but it soon paid off when gold was discovered, and again when major petroleum deposits were discovered in 1968. Today, an 800-mile- (1,287-km-) long pipeline links North Slope oil fields to the ice-free port at Valdez, but opponents worry about long-term environmental impact.

Everything is big in Alaska. It is the largest state, with one-sixth of the country's land area; it has the highest peak in the U.S., Mt. McKinley (Denali); and the largest earthquake ever recorded in the U.S.—a 9.2 magnitude—occurred there in 1964. It is first in forestland, a leading source of seafood, and a major oil producer. Alaska's population includes a higher percentage of native people than that of any other state.

THE BASICS

STATS

Area
663,267 sq mi (1,717,862 sq km)

Population
683,478

Capital
Juneau
Population 31,187

Largest city
Anchorage
Population 278,700

Ethnic/racial groups
70.7% white; 15.4% Native American; 4.6% Asian; 3.7% African American. Hispanic (any race) 5.6%.

Industry
Petroleum products, government, services, trade

Agriculture
Shellfish, seafood, nursery stock, vegetables, dairy products, feed crops

Statehood
January 3, 1959; 49th state

GEO WHIZ

During the summer humpback whales migrate to Alaskan waters, where they work together to catch fish. While swimming in circles, the whales blow bubbles that form a net around schools of herring. Each whale can eat hundreds of fish in one gulp.

Global warming and population growth are changing the route of the Iditarod, the world's most famous sled-dog race. Since 2002 lack of snow in Wasilla has forced the starting point for the competition to move 30 miles (48 km) farther north to Willow.

The Tongass National Forest, where conservationists are battling to stop the harvesting of 1,000-year-old trees, is the largest national forest in the United States.

WILLOW PTARMIGAN
FORGET-ME-NOT

⇧ TIME FOR LUNCH.
A grizzly bear wades into the rushing waters of Brooks Falls, in Katmai National Park, to catch a leaping salmon.

CHUKCHI SEA

RUSSIA

Bering Strait
RUSSIA
U.S.
Little Diomede I.
Cape Prince of Wales
only 2.5 miles from Russia
Nome
P

St. Lawrence I.

Yukon Delta
Emmonak
Mountain Village
Hooper Bay • YUKON
St. Matthew I.
ALASKA MARITIME N.W.R.
NA
Nelson I.
WILD
Nunivak I.
R

B E R I N G
S E A

St. Paul
Pribilof Islands
ALASKA MARITIME N.W.R.

A L E U T I A N   I S L A N D S
IZEMBEK N.W.R.
Unimak I.
AI
ALAS
Unalaska I.
ALEUTIAN WORLD WAR II N.H.A.
Dutch Harbor •
Umnak I.
Unalaska
Sanak I.
Yunaska I.
Islands of Four Mountains
ALASKA MARITIME NATIONAL WILDLIF

⇦ NORTHERN METROPOLIS. Anchorage, established in 1915 as a construction port for the Alaska Railroad, sits in the shadow of the snow-covered Chugach Mountains.

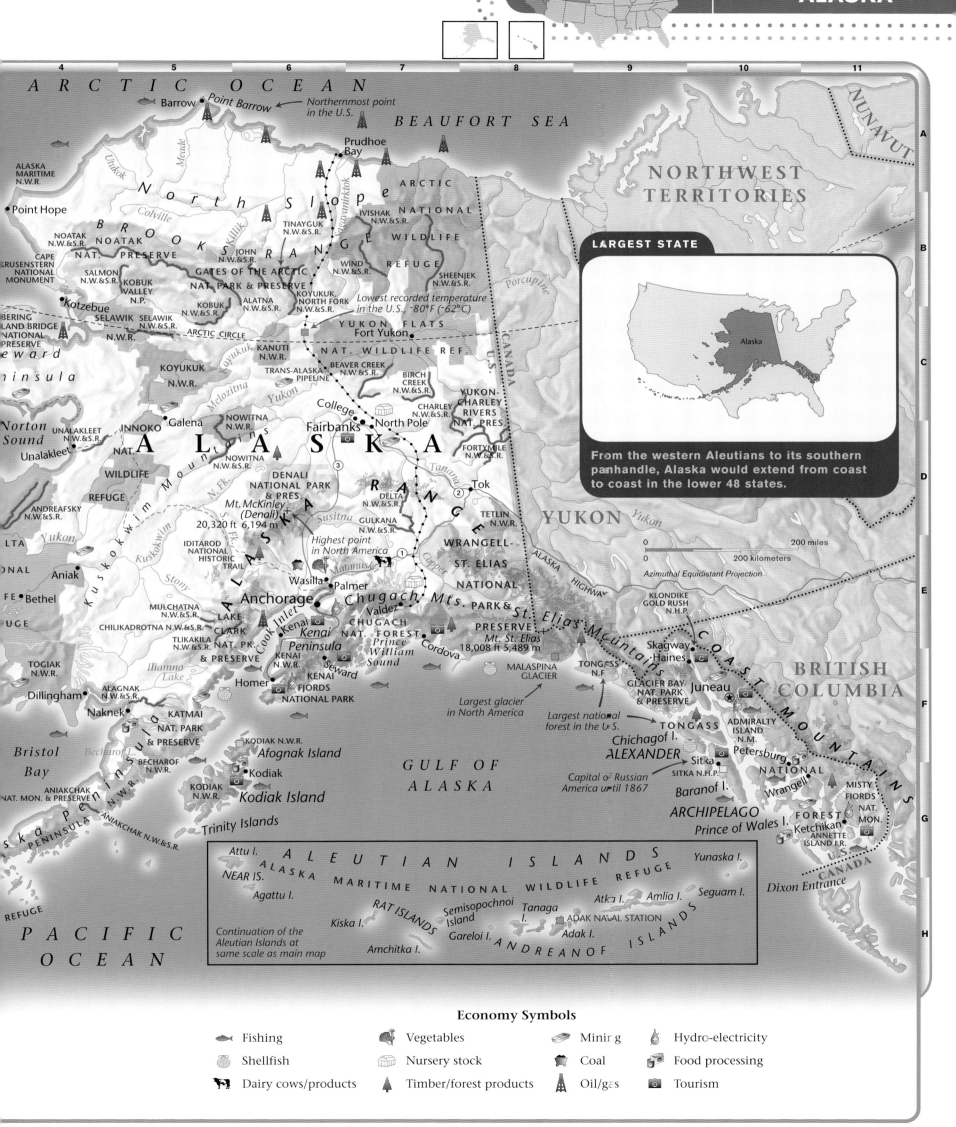

LARGEST STATE

Alaska

From the western Aleutians to its southern panhandle, Alaska would extend from coast to coast in the lower 48 states.

ARCTIC OCEAN

Barrow • Point Barrow ← Northernmost point in the U.S.

BEAUFORT SEA

NUNAVUT

Prudhoe Bay

ARCTIC

NORTHWEST TERRITORIES

• Point Hope

North Slope

ALASKA MARITIME N.W.R.

Ukivok

Meade

Colville

Killik

IVISHAK N.W.&S.R.

NATIONAL

B R O O K S

NOATAK N.W.&S.R.

NOATAK NAT. PRESERVE

RANGE

WILDLIFE

CAPE KRUSENSTERN NATIONAL MONUMENT

SALMON N.W.&S.R.

KOBUK VALLEY N.P.

GATES OF THE ARCTIC NAT. PARK & PRESERVE

S. JOHN N.W.&S.R.

WIND N.W.&S.R.

REFUGE

SHEENJEK N.W.&S.R.

Porcupine

• Kotzebue

BERING LAND BRIDGE NATIONAL PRESERVE

KOBUK N.W.&S.R.

SELAWIK SELAWIK N.W.R.

ALATNA N.W.&S.R.

KOYUKUK, NORTH FORK N.W.&S.R.

Lowest recorded temperature in the U.S. -80°F (-62°C)

YUKON FLATS

Fort Yukon

ARCTIC CIRCLE

eward

Koyukuk

KANUTI N.W.R.

NAT. WILDLIFE REF.

CANADA U.S.

eninsula

Norton Sound

KOYUKUK N.W.R.

Koyukuk

Melozitna

Yukon

College

BEAVER CREEK N.W.&S.R.

BIRCH CREEK N.W.&S.R.

CHARLEY N.W.&S.R.

YUKON-CHARLEY RIVERS NAT. PRES.

UNALAKLEET N.W.&S.R.

INNOKO NAT.

NOWITNA N.W.R.

A L A S K A

Fairbanks

North Pole

CANADA U.S.

Unalakleet

Galena

NOWITNA N.W.&S.R.

Mountains

FORTYMILE N.W.&S.R.

WILDLIFE

REFUGE

ANDREAFSKY N.W.&S.R.

DENALI NATIONAL PARK & PRES.

③

Tanana

Tok

②

YUKON

Yukon

LTA

Yukon

Aniak

IDITAROD NATIONAL HISTORIC TRAIL

Mt. McKinley (Denali) 20,320 ft 6,194 m

Highest point in North America

DELTA N.W.&S.R.

GULKANA N.W.&S.R.

TETLIN N.W.R.

Yukon

ONAL

Bethel

Kuskokwim

Kuskokwim Mountains

A L A S K A

Susitna

①

Copper

WRANGELL-ST. ELIAS NATIONAL PARK & PRESERVE

St. Elias Mountains

KLONDIKE GOLD RUSH N.H.P.

0   200 miles

0   200 kilometers

Azimuthal Equidistant Projection

FE

UGE

Stony

N. Fk.

S. Fk.

Wasilla

Matanuska

RANGE

Mt. St. Elias 18,008 ft 5,489 m

ALASKA HIGHWAY

Skagway

Haines

COAST MOUNTAINS

BRITISH COLUMBIA

MULCHATNA N.W.&S.R.

Anchorage

Palmer

Chugach Mts.

CHUGACH

ST. ELIAS

MALASPINA GLACIER

GLACIER BAY NAT. PARK & PRESERVE

Juneau

CHILIKADROTNA N.W.&S.R.

LAKE CLARK NAT. PK. & PRESERVE

Kenai

CHUGACH NAT. FOREST

Valdez

Prince William Sound

Cordova

PRESERVE

Largest glacier in North America

Largest national forest in the U.S.

TONGASS N.F.

TONGASS

ADMIRALTY ISLAND N.M.

TLIKAKILA N.W.&S.R.

KENAI N.W.R.

KENAI Peninsula

Seward

Chichagof I.

ALEXANDER

Sitka

Petersburg

TOGIAK N.W.R.

Iliamna Lake

Homer

KENAI FJORDS NATIONAL PARK

Capital of Russian America until 1867

SITKA N.H.P.

Baranof I.

NATIONAL

Wrangell

MISTY FIORDS NAT. MON.

Dillingham

ALAGNAK N.W.&S.R.

KATMAI NAT. PARK & PRESERVE

KODIAK N.W.R.

Afognak Island

GULF OF ALASKA

ARCHIPELAGO

Prince of Wales I.

FOREST

Ketchikan

ANNETTE ISLAND I.R.

Naknek

Bristol Bay

Becharof L.

BECHAROF N.W.R.

Kodiak

KODIAK N.W.R.

Kodiak Island

Trinity Islands

ALASKA

MARITIME

NATIONAL

WILDLIFE

REFUGE

CANADA U.S.

ANIAKCHAK NAT. MON. & PRESERVE

ska Peninsula

ANIAKCHAK N.W.&S.R.

Dixon Entrance

REFUGE

PACIFIC OCEAN

Attu I.

NEAR IS.

ALASKA

A L E U T I A N   I S L A N D S

MARITIME   NATIONAL   WILDLIFE   REFUGE

Yunaska I.

Agattu I.

RAT ISLANDS

Semisopochnoi Island

Tanaga I.

Atka I.

Amlia I.

Seguam I.

ADAK NAVAL STATION

Continuation of the Aleutian Islands at same scale as main map

Kiska I.

Garoloi I.

Adak I.

Amchitka I.

A N D R E A N O F   I S L A N D S

Economy Symbols

Fishing	Vegetables	Mining
Shellfish	Nursery stock	Coal
Dairy cows/products	Timber/forest products	Oil/gas

Hydro-electricity
Food processing
Tourism

CALIFORNIA REPUBLIC

THE BASICS

STATS

Area
163,696 sq mi (423,972 sq km)

Population
36,553,215

Capital
Sacramento
Population 453,781

Largest city
Los Angeles
Population 3,849,378

Ethnic/racial groups
76.9% white; 12.4% Asian; 6.7% African American; 1.2% Native American. Hispanic (any race) 35.9%.

Industry
Electronic components and equipment, computers and computer software, tourism, food processing, entertainment, clothing

Agriculture
Fruits and vegetables, dairy products, cattle, forest products, commercial fishing

Statehood
September 9, 1850; 31st state

GEO WHIZ

Every December one of the largest gatherings of northern elephant seals in the world converges on the beaches of Año Nuevo State Reserve, south of San Francisco, to rest, mate, and give birth.

The Monterey Bay Aquarium has been working to save endangered sea otters for 20 years. Rescued animals that cannot be rehabilitated for re-release into the wild find a permanent home at the aquarium.

Castroville, known as the Artichoke Capital of the World, crowned future movie legend Marilyn Monroe its first-ever artichoke queen in 1947.

CALIFORNIA QUAIL
GOLDEN POPPY

CALIFORNIA

The coast of what is now California was visited by Spanish and English explorers in the mid-1500s, but colonization did not begin until 1769 when the first of 21 Spanish missions was established at San Diego. The missions, built to bring Christianity to the many native people living in the area, eventually extended up the coast as far as Sonoma along a road known as El Camino Real. The U.S. gained control of California in 1847, following a war with Mexico. The next year gold was discovered near Sutter's Mill, triggering a gold rush and migration from the eastern U.S. and around the world. Today, California is the most populous state, and its economy ranks above that of most of the world's countries. It is a major source of fruits, nuts, and vegetables, accounting for more than half of the U.S. output. The state is an industrial leader, producing jet aircraft, ships, and high-tech equipment. It is also a center for the entertainment industry.

⇧ ENGINEERING WONDER. Stretching more than a mile (1.6 km) across the entrance to San Francisco Bay, the Golden Gate Bridge opened to traffic in 1937. The bridge is painted vermilion orange, a color chosen in part because it is visible in fog.

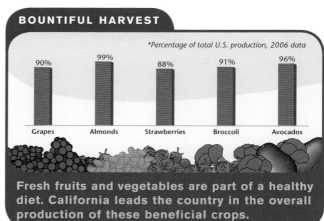

BOUNTIFUL HARVEST

*Percentage of total U.S. production, 2006 data

Grapes	Almonds	Strawberries	Broccoli	Avocados
90%	99%	88%	91%	96%

Fresh fruits and vegetables are part of a healthy diet. California leads the country in the overall production of these beneficial crops.

⇦ FOREST GIANT. Sequoias in Yosemite National Park's Mariposa Grove exceed 200 feet (61 m), making them the world's tallest trees. The trees, some of which are 3,000 years old, grow in isolated groves on the western slopes of the Sierra Nevada.

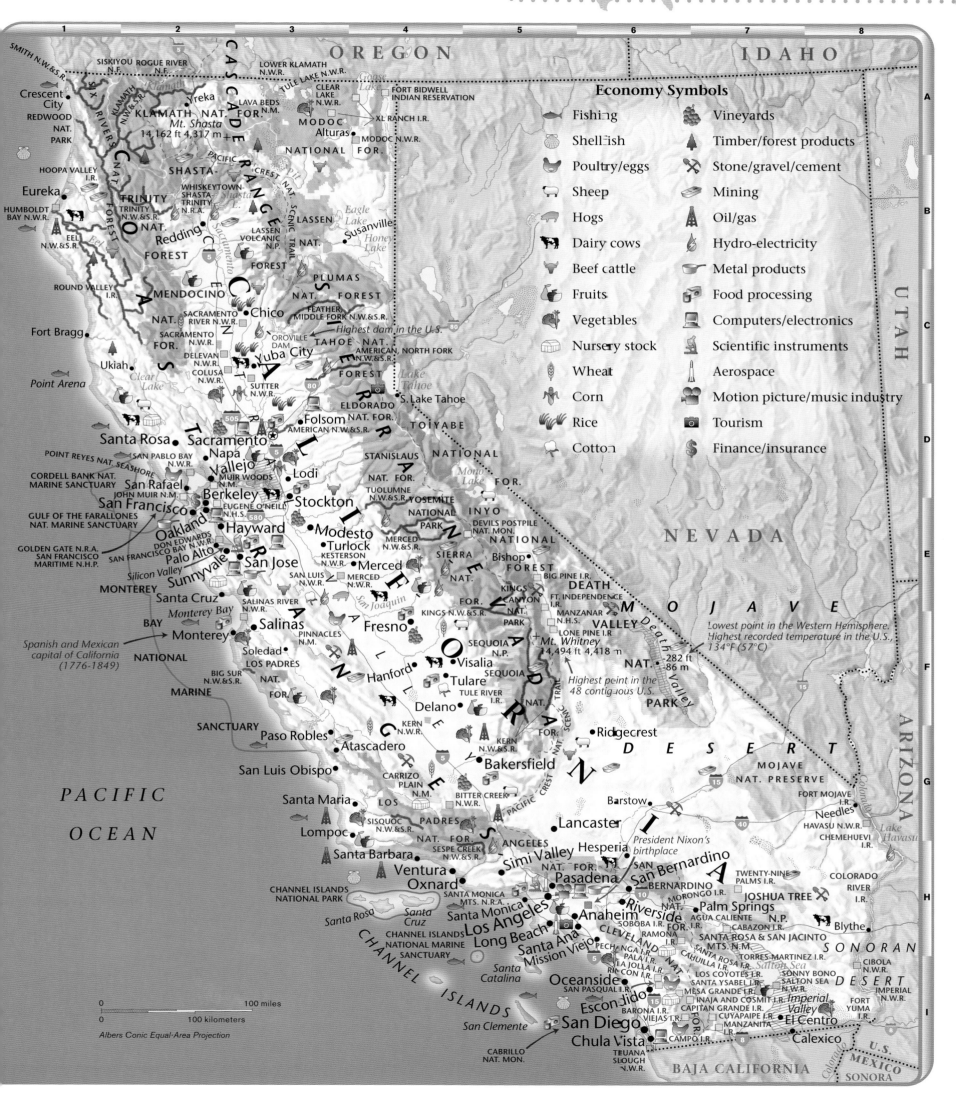

OREGON

IDAHO

SMITH N.W.&.S.R.

SISKIYOU ROGUE RIVER
N.F. N.F.

LOWER KLAMATH
N.W.R.

TULE LAKE N.W.R.

CLEAR LAKE N.W.R.

FORT BIDWELL
INDIAN RESERVATION

Crescent City

REDWOOD NAT. PARK

KLAMATH NAT. FOR.

Yreka

LAVA BEDS N.M.

MODOC

XL RANCH I.R.

Mt. Shasta
14,162 ft 4,317 m

Alturas

MODOC N.W.R.

NATIONAL FOR.

HOOPA VALLEY I.R.

SHASTA-

Eureka

TRINITY N.W.&.S.R.

WHISKEYTOWN-SHASTA-TRINITY N.R.A.

LASSEN

Eagle Lake

HUMBOLDT BAY N.W.R.

Redding

LASSEN VOLCANIC N.P.

Susanville

EEL N.W.&.S.R.

SACRAMENTO RIVER N.W.R.

Honey Lake

ROUND VALLEY I.R.

MENDOCINO NAT.

Chico

PLUMAS NAT. FOREST

Fort Bragg

SACRAMENTO N.W.R.

FEATHER, MIDDLE FORK N.W.&.S.R.

Highest dam in the U.S.

FOR.

DELEVAN N.W.R.

Yuba City

TAHOE NAT.

AMERICAN, NORTH FORK N.W.&.S.R.

Ukiah

COLUSA N.W.R.

OROVILLE DAM

Clear Lake

SUTTER N.W.R.

Point Arena

ELDORADO NAT. FOR.

S. Lake Tahoe

Lake Tahoe

Santa Rosa

Sacramento

Folsom

AMERICAN N.W.&.S.R.

TOIYABE

Napa

Lodi

STANISLAUS NAT. FOR.

NATIONAL

POINT REYES NAT. SEASHORE

Vallejo

MUIR WOODS N.M.

Mono Lake

CORDELL BANK NAT. MARINE SANCTUARY

San Rafael

JOHN MUIR N.M.

Berkeley

Stockton

TUOLUMNE N.W.&.S.R.

FOR.

San Francisco

EUGENE O'NEILL N.H.S.

YOSEMITE NATIONAL PARK

INYO

GULF OF THE FARALLONES NAT. MARINE SANCTUARY

Oakland

Hayward

Modesto

MERCED N.W.&.S.R.

GOLDEN GATE N.R.A., SAN FRANCISCO MARITIME N.H.P.

DON EDWARDS SAN FRANCISCO BAY N.W.R.

Palo Alto

Turlock

KESTERSON N.W.R.

DEVILS POSTPILE NAT. MON.

NATIONAL

NEVADA

Silicon Valley

Sunnyvale

San Jose

Merced

SIERRA

Bishop

MONTEREY

SAN LUIS N.W.R.

MERCED N.W.R.

NAT.

BIG PINE I.R.

Santa Cruz

San Joaquin

DEATH

Monterey Bay

SALINAS RIVER N.W.R.

Fresno

KINGS CANYON NAT.

KINGS N.W.&.S.R.

FT. INDEPENDENCE I.R.

VALLEY

BAY

Salinas

PINNACLES N.M.

PARK

MANZANAR N.H.S.

Lowest point in the Western Hemisphere. Highest recorded temperature in the U.S., 134°F (57°C)

Spanish and Mexican capital of California (1776-1849)

Monterey

Soledad

SEQUOIA N.P.

LONE PINE I.R.

NATIONAL

LOS PADRES

Hanford

SEQUOIA NAT.

Mt. Whitney 14,494 ft 4,418 m

-282 ft -86 m

Big Sur N.W.&.S.R.

NAT.

Tulare

Highest point in the 48 contiguous U.S.

MARINE

FOR.

TULE RIVER I.R.

SANCTUARY

Delano

Paso Robles

KERN N.W.R.

Ridgecrest

DESERT

Atascadero

KERN N.W.&.S.R.

MOJAVE NAT. PRESERVE

San Luis Obispo

CARRIZO PLAIN N.M.

Bakersfield

Barstow

FORT MOJAVE I.R.

PACIFIC

Santa Maria

BITTER CREEK N.W.R.

Needles

OCEAN

LOS

Lancaster

HAVASU N.W.R.

Lompoc

SISQUOC N.W.&.S.R.

PADRES

CHEMEHUEVI I.R.

Lake Havasu

NAT. FOR.

President Nixon's birthplace

Santa Barbara

SESPE CREEK N.W.R.

Simi Valley

Hesperia

San Bernardino

Ventura

NAT. FOR.

Pasadena

TWENTY-NINE PALMS I.R.

COLORADO RIVER

CHANNEL ISLANDS NATIONAL PARK

Oxnard

SANTA MONICA MTS. N.R.A.

San Bernardino

JOSHUA TREE

Palm Springs

Santa Rosa

Santa Cruz

Santa Monica

Riverside

MORONGO I.R.

N.P.

Blythe

CHANNEL ISLANDS NATIONAL MARINE SANCTUARY

Los Angeles

Anaheim

CLEVELAND NAT.

AGUA CALIENTE

CABAZON I.R.

SANTA ROSA & SAN JACINTO MTS. N.M.

SONORAN

Long Beach

Santa Ana

SOBOBA I.R.

FOR.

Mission Viejo

RAMONA I.R.

PECHANGA I.R.

CAHUILLA I.R.

TORRES-MARTINEZ I.R.

CIBOLA N.W.R.

Santa Catalina

PALA I.R.

LA JOLLA I.R.

LOS COYOTES I.R.

SANTA YSABEL I.R.

SONNY BONO SALTON SEA N.W.R.

DESERT

Oceanside

SAN PASQUAL I.R.

RINCON I.R.

Salton Sea

INAJA AND COSMIT I.R.

MESA GRANDE I.R.

FORT YUMA I.R.

San Clemente

Escondido

BARONA I.R.

CAPITAN GRANDE I.R.

Imperial Valley

San Diego

VIEJAS I.R.

CUYAPAIPE I.R.

MANZANITA I.R.

El Centro

CABRILLO NAT. MON.

Chula Vista

CAMPO I.R.

Calexico

TIJUANA SLOUGH N.W.R.

U.S. MEXICO

BAJA CALIFORNIA

SONORA

PACIFIC

OCEAN

CHANNEL ISLANDS

UTAH

ARIZONA

Economy Symbols

Fishing · Vineyards
Shellfish · Timber/forest products
Poultry/eggs · Stone/gravel/cement
Sheep · Mining
Hogs · Oil/gas
Dairy cows · Hydro-electricity
Beef cattle · Metal products
Fruits · Food processing
Vegetables · Computers/electronics
Nursery stock · Scientific instruments
Wheat · Aerospace
Corn · Motion picture/music industry
Rice · Tourism
Cotton · Finance/insurance

100 miles
100 kilometers
Albers Conic Equal-Area Projection

THE CENTENNIAL STATE:
COLORADO

THE BASICS

STATS

Area
104,094 sq mi (269,602 sq km)

Population
4,861,515

Capital
Denver
Population 566,974

Largest city
Denver
Population 566,974

Ethnic/racial groups
90.1% white; 4.1% African American; 2.6% Asian; 1.1% Native American. Hispanic (any race) 19.7%.

Industry
Real estate, government, durable goods, communications, health and other services, nondurable goods, transportation

Agriculture
Cattle, corn, wheat, dairy products, hay

Statehood
August 1, 1876; 38th state

GEO WHIZ

The Black Canyon of the Gunnison is one of the newest national parks in the Rockies. As it flows through the canyon, the Gunnison River drops an average of 95 feet (29 m) per mile—one of the steepest descents in North America. The craggy rock walls are a mecca for rock climbers.

Colorado's lynx population is making a comeback, thanks to a program that releases wild cats captured in Canada into Colorado's southern Rockies. The population in the wild has gone from 1 in 1973 to 170 in 2006.

LARK BUNTING
COLUMBINE

COLORADO

Indians were the earliest inhabitants of present-day Colorado. Some were cliff dwellers; others were plains dwellers. Spanish explorers arrived in Colorado in 1541. In 1803 eastern Colorado became U.S. territory as part of the Louisiana Purchase. Gold was discovered in 1858, and thousands were attracted by the prospect of quick wealth. The sudden jump in population led to conflict with native Cheyennes and Arapahos over control of the land, but the settlers prevailed. Completion of the transcontinental railroad in 1869 helped link Colorado to the eastern states and opened its doors for growth. Cattle ranching and farming developed on the High Plains of eastern Colorado, while the mountainous western part of the state focused on mining. Today, mining is still important in Colorado, but the focus has shifted to energy resources—oil, natural gas, and coal. Agriculture generates more than $15 billion each year, mostly cattle and dairy products. And Colorado's majestic mountains attract thousands of tourists each year.

⇧ THRILLING SPORT. Colorado's snow-covered mountains attract winter sports enthusiasts from near and far. In the past skis were used by gold prospectors. Today skiing and snowboarding are big moneymakers in the state's recreation and tourism industry.

⇐ ANCIENT CULTURE. Ancestral Puebloans lived from about A.D. 600 to A.D. 1300 in the canyons that today are a part of Mesa Verde National Park. More than 600 stone structures were built on protected cliffs of the canyon walls; others were located on mesas. These dwellings hold many clues to a past way of life.

BROWNS PARK N.W.R.
Green
Vermillion Cr.
DINOSAUR NATIONAL MONUMENT
White
Cathedral Bluffs
Rangely
Roan Plateau
UTAH
Grand Valley
70
COLORADO NAT. MON.
Grand Junction
GRAND MESA N.F.
Colorado
Dolores
Uncompahgre
MANTI-LA SAL N.F.
UNCO
San Miguel
NA
SAN
CANYONS OF THE ANCIENTS N.M.
Cortez
HOVENWEEP N.M.
MESA VERDE N.P.
YUCCA HOUSE N.M.
UTE MOUNTAIN I.R.
FOUR CORNERS
San Juan
Mancos
ARIZONA
Only spot in the U.S. where the borders of 4 states come together

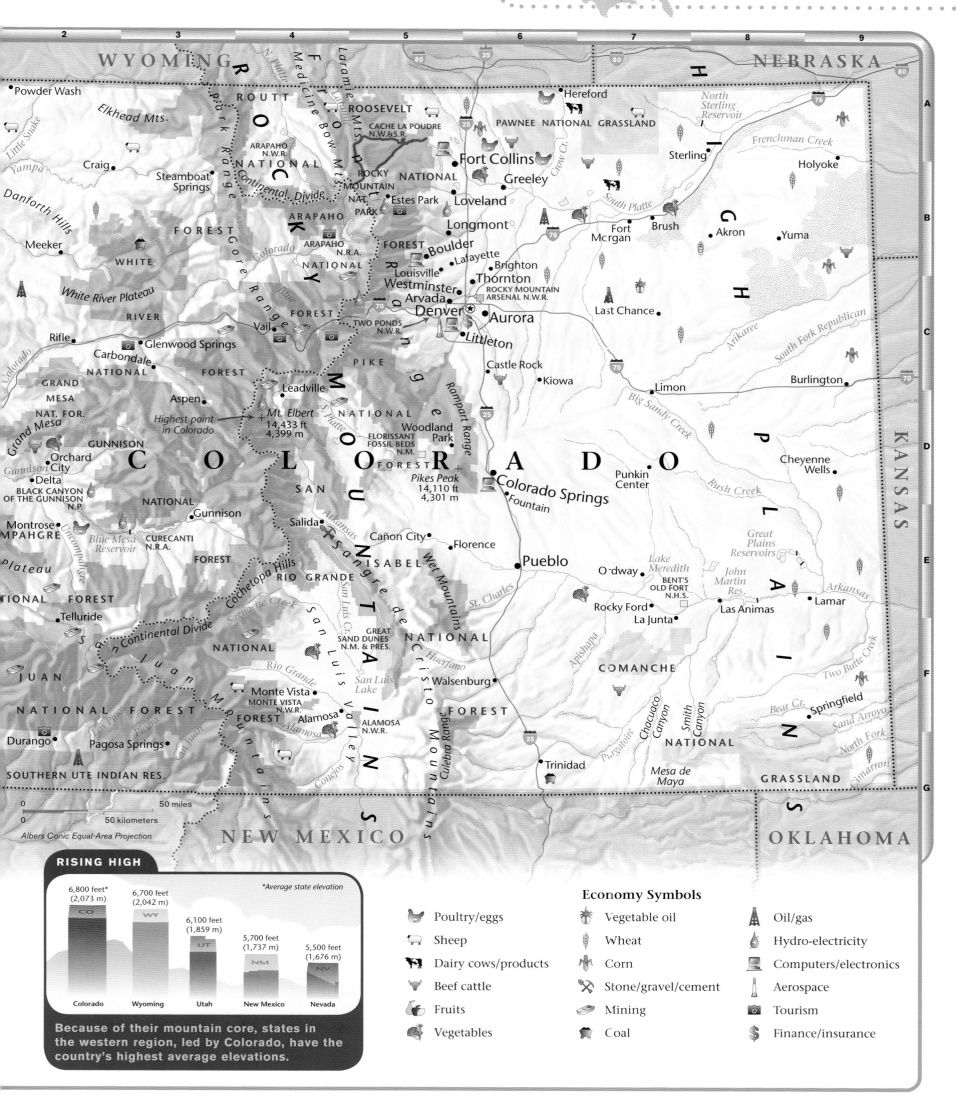

WYOMING

Powder Wash
Elkhead Mts.
Little Snake
Craig
Steamboat Springs
Yampa
Danforth Hills
Meeker
WHITE
White River Plateau
RIVER
Rifle
Carbondale
Glenwood Springs
Colorado
NATIONAL
FOREST
GRAND MESA
NAT. FOR.
Grand Mesa
GUNNISON
Orchard City
Delta
BLACK CANYON OF THE GUNNISON N.P.
Gunnison
Montrose
UMPAHGRE
NATIONAL
Blue Mesa Reservoir
CURECANTI N.R.A.
Plateau
Uncompahgre
NATIONAL FOREST
Telluride
Cochetopa Hills
Continental Divide
RIO GRANDE
SAN
Salida
Arkansas
NATIONAL
Cañon City
Florence
Sangre de Cristo
SAN JUAN
Saguache Creek
San Luis Cr.
NISABEL
Wet Mountains
St. Charles
NATIONAL FOREST
JUAN
NATIONAL FOREST
San Luis Valley
Rio Grande
San Luis Lake
GREAT SAND DUNES N.M. & PRES.
NATIONAL
Durango
Pagosa Springs
Los Pinos
Piedra
San Juan
Monte Vista
MONTE VISTA N.W.R.
Alamosa
ALAMOSA
Alamosa N.W.R.
Conejos
FOREST
Huerfano
Walsenburg
FOREST
SOUTHERN UTE INDIAN RES.
Culebra Range
Trinidad

ROUTT
ROCKY
Park Range
Medicine Bow Mts.
Laramie Mts.
N. Platte
FRONT
Laramie
ROOSEVELT
CACHE LA POUDRE N.W.&S.R.
ARAPAHO N.W.R.
NATIONAL
Continental Divide
ROCKY MOUNTAIN NAT. PARK
Estes Park
Fort Collins
Greeley
Loveland
NATIONAL
FOREST
Gore Range
Colorado
ARAPAHO N.R.A.
Longmont
ARAPAHO
FOREST
Boulder
Lafayette
Louisville
Brighton
Range
Westminster
Thornton
Blue R.
Vail
Arvada
ROCKY MOUNTAIN ARSENAL N.W.R.
TWO PONDS N.W.R.
Denver
Aurora
Littleton
PIKE
Leadville
Mt. Elbert 14,433 ft 4,399 m
Highest point in Colorado
NATIONAL
Front
Aspen
S. Platte
Woodland Park
FLORISSANT FOSSIL BEDS N.M.
Rampart Range
Castle Rock
Kiowa
FOREST
Pikes Peak 14,110 ft 4,301 m
Colorado Springs
Fountain
Pueblo
Rocky Ford
La Junta

NEBRASKA

HIGH
North Sterling Reservoir
Frenchman Creek
Sterling
Holyoke
Crow Cr.
PAWNEE NATIONAL GRASSLAND
Hereford
South Platte
Fort Morgan
Brush
Akron
Yuma
Last Chance
HIGH
Arikaree
South Fork Republican
Limon
Burlington
Big Sandy Creek
Rush Creek
PLAINS
Cheyenne Wells
Punkin Center
Great Plains Reservoirs
Lake Meredith
John Martin Res.
O'dway
BENT'S OLD FORT N.H.S.
Las Animas
Lamar
Arkansas
PLAIN
COMANCHE
Apishapa
Chacuaco Canyon
Smith Canyon
Two Butte Creek
Bear Cr.
Springfield
Sand Arroyo
NATIONAL
Purgatoire
Mesa de Maya
GRASSLAND
North Fork
Cimarron

KANSAS

COLORADO
MOUNTAINS

NEW MEXICO

OKLAHOMA

0 — 50 miles
0 — 50 kilometers
Albers Conic Equal-Area Projection

Economy Symbols

- Poultry/eggs
- Sheep
- Dairy cows/products
- Beef cattle
- Fruits
- Vegetables
- Vegetable oil
- Wheat
- Corn
- Stone/gravel/cement
- Mining
- Coal
- Oil/gas
- Hydro-electricity
- Computers/electronics
- Aerospace
- Tourism
- Finance/insurance

HAWAI'I

Some 1,500 years ago, Polynesians traveling in large canoes arrived from the south to settle the volcanic islands that make up Hawai'i. In 1778 Captain James Cook claimed the islands for Britain, and soon Hawai'i became a center of the whaling industry and a major producer of sugarcane. The spread of sugarcane plantations led to the importation of workers from Asia. Hawai'i became a U.S. territory in 1900. Naval installations, established as fueling depots and to protect U.S. interests in the Pacific, were attacked by the Japanese in 1941, an act that officially brought the U.S. into World War II. In 1959 Hawai'i became the 50th state. Tourism, agriculture, and the military, with bases centered on O'ahu's Pearl Harbor, are the cornerstone of Hawai'i's economy today. Jet airline service makes the distant islands accessible to tourists from both the mainland U.S. and Asia as well as from Australia and New Zealand. Hawai'i is still a major producer of sugarcane, along with nursery products and pineapples.

THE BASICS

STATS

Area
10,931 sq mi (28,311 sq km)

Population
1,283,388

Capital
Honolulu
Population 377,357

Largest city
Honolulu
Population 377,357

Ethnic/racial groups
40.0% Asian; 28.6% white; 9.1% Hawaiian/Pacific Islander; 2.5% African American. Hispanic (any race) 7.8%.

Industry
Tourism, trade, finance, food processing, petroleum refining, stone, clay, glass products

Agriculture
Sugarcane, pineapples, nursery stock, tropical fruit, livestock, macadamia nuts

Statehood
August 21, 1959; 50th state

GEO WHIZ

The shallow waters off the coast of Hawai'i are home to some of the world's most interesting sea creatures: marine worms. They were among the first sea animals more than 500 million years ago.

Hawai'i is the most isolated population center on Earth. It is more than 2,300 miles (3,700 km) from California, 3,850 miles (6,196 km) from Japan, and 4,900 miles (7,886 km) from China.

Everywhere else in the world caterpillars feed on plants. In Hawai'i there are 20 species that eat meat. Scientists have recorded the world's only known carnivorous caterpillars munching on ants.

You can ski two different ways on the same day in Hawai'i: on water at the beach and on snow on the slopes of Mauna Kea, a 13,796-foot- (4,205-m-) high volcano on the Big Island.

HAWAIIAN GOOSE (NENE)
HIBISCUS

One of the world's rainiest spots

KAUA'I
Princeville KILAUEA POINT N.W.R.
HANALEI N.W.R.
Wai'ale'ale
5,148 ft
1,569 m
Kapa'a
Hanama'ulu
Lehua I.
Kekaha
Lihu'e
Pu'uwai
Kalaheo
NI'IHAU
Kaulakahi Channel

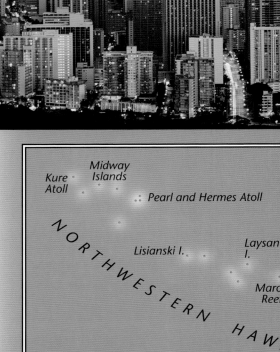

⇧ ISLAND PARADISE. High-rise hotels light up Waikiki, the center of Honolulu's tourist industry. Thousands of visitors flock to the islands each year to enjoy the warm climate, sandy beaches, and rich, multicultural heritage of Hawai'i.

Kure Atoll
Midway Islands
Pearl and Hermes Atoll
Lisianski I.
Laysan I.
Maro Reef
NORTHWESTERN HAWAI

0   400 miles
0   400 kilometers
Oblique Mercator Projection

DANGER FROM BELOW

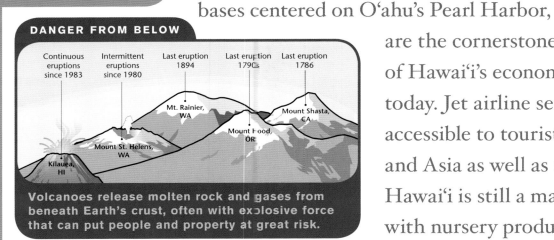

Continuous eruptions since 1983
Intermittent eruptions since 1980
Last eruption 1894
Last eruption 1790
Last eruption 1786
Mt. Rainier, WA
Mount St. Helens, WA
Mount Hood, OR
Mount Shasta, CA
Kilauea, HI

Volcanoes release molten rock and gases from beneath Earth's crust, often with explosive force that can put people and property at great risk.

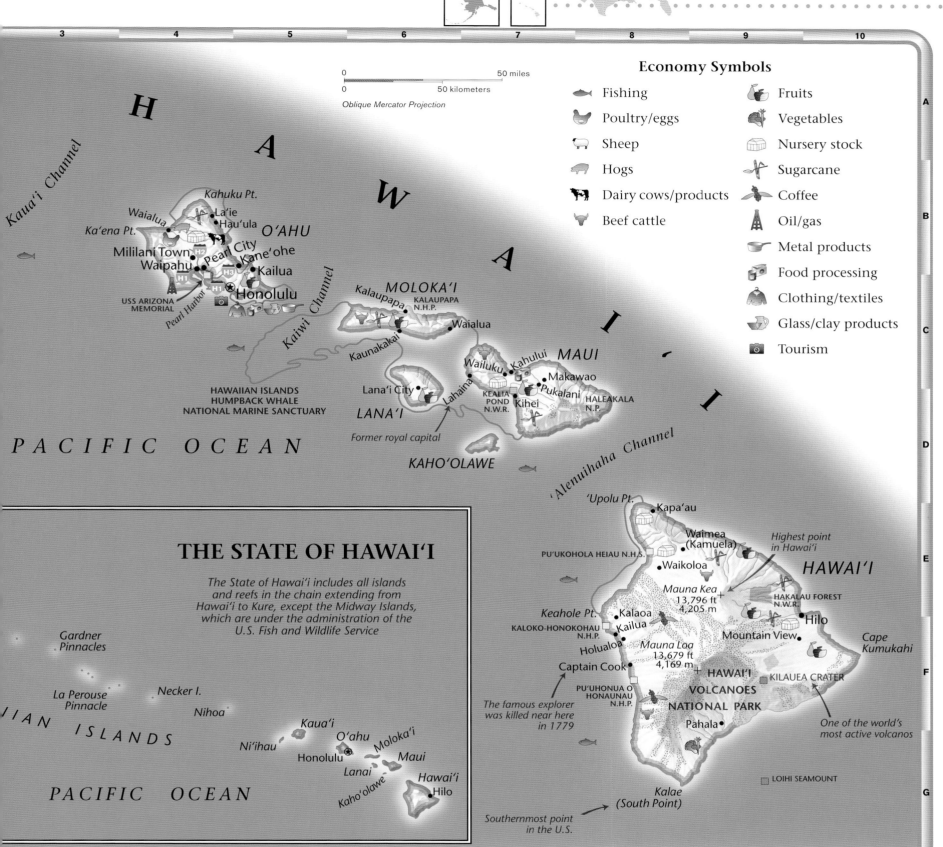

Economy Symbols

- Fishing
- Poultry/eggs
- Sheep
- Hogs
- Dairy cows/products
- Beef cattle
- Fruits
- Vegetables
- Nursery stock
- Sugarcane
- Coffee
- Oil/gas
- Metal products
- Food processing
- Clothing/textiles
- Glass/clay products
- Tourism

0 — 50 miles
0 — 50 kilometers
Oblique Mercator Projection

H A W A I ' I

Kaua'i Channel

Kahuku Pt.
Waialua · La'ie
Ka'ena Pt. · Hau'ula
Mililani Town · O'AHU
Waipahu · Pearl City · Kane'ohe
H2 · H1 · H3 · Kailua
USS ARIZONA · Honolulu
MEMORIAL · Pearl Harbor
Ka'iwi Channel

MOLOKA'I
Kalaupapa
KALAUPAPA N.H.P.
Waialua
Kaunakakai

HAWAIIAN ISLANDS
HUMPBACK WHALE
NATIONAL MARINE SANCTUARY

Lana'i City
LANA'I

Wailuku · Kahului · MAUI
Lahaina · Makawao
KEALIA · Pukalani
POND · Kihei · HALEAKALA
N.W.R. · N.P.

Former royal capital

KAHO'OLAWE

PACIFIC OCEAN

'Alenuihaha Channel

'Upolu Pt. · Kapa'au
Waimea (Kamuela) · Highest point in Hawai'i
PU'UKOHOLA HEIAU N.H.S.
· Waikoloa
Mauna Kea · HAKALAU FOREST N.W.R.
13,796 ft 4,205 m
Keahole Pt. · Kalaoa
KALOKO-HONOKOHAU · Kailua · HAWAI'I
N.H.P. · Mauna Loa · Mountain View · Hilo
Holualoa · 13,679 ft
Captain Cook · 4,169 m · Cape Kumukahi
PU'UHONUA O · HAWAI'I · KILAUEA CRATER
HONAUNAU · VOLCANOES
N.H.P. · NATIONAL PARK
The famous explorer · Pahala
was killed near here
in 1779 · One of the world's
most active volcanos

LOIHI SEAMOUNT

Kalae (South Point)
Southernmost point
in the U.S.

THE STATE OF HAWAI'I

The State of Hawai'i includes all islands
and reefs in the chain extending from
Hawai'i to Kure, except the Midway Islands,
which are under the administration of the
U.S. Fish and Wildlife Service

Gardner
Pinnacles

La Perouse
Pinnacle
Necker I.
Nihoa

Kaua'i
Ni'ihau · O'ahu
Honolulu · Moloka'i
Lanai · Maui
Kaho'olawe · Hawai'i
Hilo

'IAN ISLANDS

PACIFIC OCEAN

⇨ **FIERY CREATION.** Hawai'i is the fastest-
growing state in the U.S.—not in people,
but in land. Active volcanoes are constantly
creating new land as lava continues to flow.
The Pu'u 'O'o vent on Kīlauea has added
more than 568 acres (230 ha) of new land
since it began erupting in 1983.

THE GEM STATE:
IDAHO

IDAHO

Some of the earliest Native American sites in what is now Idaho date back 10,000 to 12,000 years. In the 18th and early 19th centuries, contact between native people and Europeans brought not only trade and cultural change but also diseases that wiped out many native groups. Present-day Idaho was part of the 1803 Louisiana Purchase, and in 1805 it was explored during the famous Lewis and Clark expedition. In 1843 wagons crossed into Idaho on the Oregon Trail. The arrival of white settlers brought conflict with the Indians, which continued until 1890 when Idaho became a state. Today, farming plays an important role in Idaho's economy. More than one-fifth of the land is planted with crops, especially wheat, sugar beets, barley, and potatoes. The state supports the use of alternative sources of energy, including geo-thermal, ethanol, wind, and biomass. The economy has diversified to include manufacturing and high-tech industries. The state's rugged natural beauty also attracts tourists year-round.

⬆ WOOLLY RUSH HOUR. Sheep fill a roadway in Idaho's Salmon River Valley. The herds move twice a year. In the spring they migrate north to mountain pastures. In the fall they return to the Snake River plains in the south.

ANCIENT STAPLE FOOD

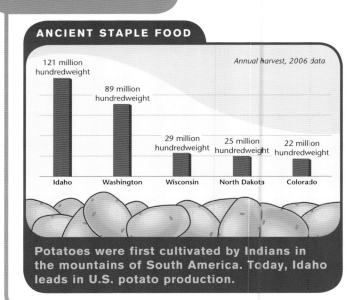

Annual harvest, 2006 data

Idaho	121 million hundredweight
Washington	89 million hundredweight
Wisconsin	29 million hundredweight
North Dakota	25 million hundredweight
Colorado	22 million hundredweight

Potatoes were first cultivated by Indians in the mountains of South America. Today, Idaho leads in U.S. potato production.

⬆ TIMBER! More than 40 percent of Idaho's land area is tree-covered, much of it in national forests. Lumber and paper products, most of which are sold to other states, are important to the state economy.

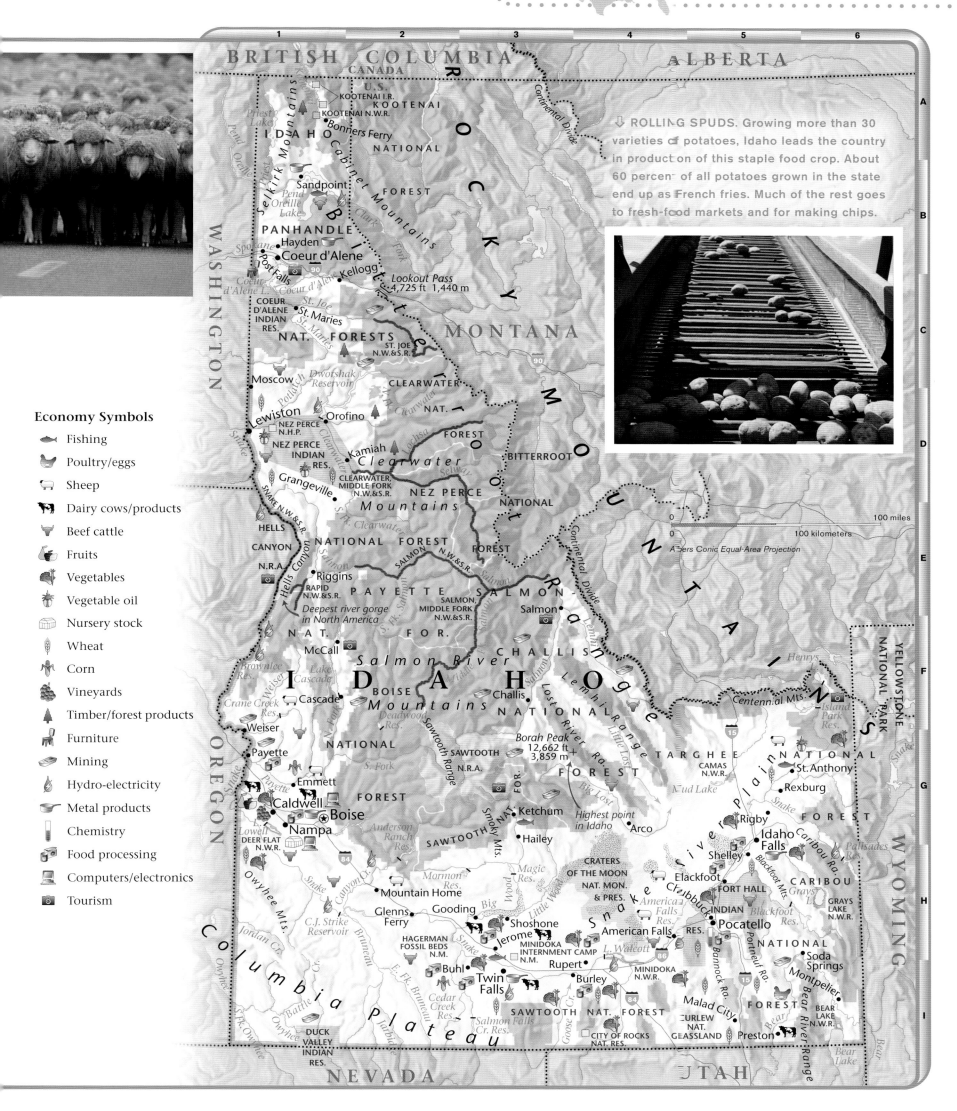

↓ ROLLING SPUDS. Growing more than 30 varieties of potatoes, Idaho leads the country in production of this staple food crop. About 60 percent of all potatoes grown in the state end up as French fries. Much of the rest goes to fresh-food markets and for making chips.

Economy Symbols

- 🐟 Fishing
- 🐔 Poultry/eggs
- 🐑 Sheep
- 🐄 Dairy cows/products
- 🐂 Beef cattle
- 🍒 Fruits
- 🥬 Vegetables
- 🌱 Vegetable oil
- 🏡 Nursery stock
- 🌾 Wheat
- 🌽 Corn
- 🍇 Vineyards
- 🌲 Timber/forest products
- 🪑 Furniture
- ▭ Mining
- 💧 Hydro-electricity
- 🍳 Metal products
- 🧪 Chemistry
- 📷 Food processing
- 💻 Computers/electronics
- 📷 Tourism

BRITISH COLUMBIA — ALBERTA
CANADA

Priest Lake
U.S.
KOOTENAI I.R.
KOOTENAI N.W.R.
Bonners Ferry
KOOTENAI
IDAHO
NATIONAL
Continental Divide

Sandpoint
FOREST
Pend Oreille Lake
PANHANDLE
Hayden
Coeur d'Alene
Kellogg
Post Falls
Coeur d'Alene L.
Lookout Pass 4,725 ft 1,440 m
MONTANA
COEUR D'ALENE INDIAN RES.
St. Joe
St. Maries
NAT. FORESTS
ST. JOE N.W.&S.R.
CLEARWATER
Moscow
Dworshak Reservoir
CLEARWATER
NAT.
Lewiston
Orofino
FOREST
NEZ PERCE N.H.P.
BITTERROOT
NEZ PERCE INDIAN RES.
Kamiah
Clearwater
NATIONAL
CLEARWATER, MIDDLE FORK N.W.&S.R.
NEZ PERCE
Grangeville
Mountains
FOREST
SNAKE N.W.&S.R.
HELLS
M. Fk. Clearwater
NATIONAL FOREST
SALMON N.W.&S.R.
CANYON
N.R.A.
Riggins
PAYETTE
SALMON, MIDDLE FORK N.W.&S.R.
Salmon
RAPID N.W.&S.R.
Deepest river gorge in North America
McCall
NAT. FOR.
CHALLIS
Salmon River
BOISE
Challis
IDAHO
Cascade
Mountains
CHALLIS NATIONAL FOREST
Brownlee Res.
Lake Cascade
Deadwood Res.
Centennial Mts.
Weiser
Crane Creek Res.
SAWTOOTH
Borah Peak 12,662 ft 3,859 m
Henrys
YELLOWSTONE NATIONAL PARK
Payette
NATIONAL
S. Fork
Range
N.R.A.
TARGHEE
Island Park Res.
Emmett
FOREST
CAMAS N.W.R.
St. Anthony
Caldwell
Anderson Ranch Res.
Smoky Mts.
Ketchum
Highest point in Idaho
Arco
Rexburg
Rigby
Boise
DEER FLAT N.W.R.
Nampa
Hailey
CRATERS OF THE MOON NAT. MON. & PRES.
Idaho Falls
Caribou Ra.
Palisades Res.
Mountain Home
SAWTOOTH NAT. FOR.
Magic Res.
Shelley
Mormon Res.
Blackfoot
FORT HALL
CARIBOU
Glenns Ferry
Gooding
Shoshone
American Falls Res.
Blackfoot Mts.
GRAYS LAKE N.W.R.
C.J. Strike Reservoir
HAGERMAN FOSSIL BEDS N.M.
Jerome
MINIDOKA INTERNMENT CAMP N.M.
American Falls
FORT HALL INDIAN RES.
Pocatello
NATIONAL
Buhl
Rupert
L. Walcott
Soda Springs
Twin Falls
Burley
MINIDOKA N.W.R.
FOREST
Montpelier
BEAR LAKE N.W.R.
SAWTOOTH NAT. FOREST
Malad City
CURLEW NAT. GRASSLAND
Salmon Falls Cr. Res.
CITY OF ROCKS NAT. RES.
Preston
Bear Lake

WASHINGTON
OREGON
Columbia Plateau
NEVADA
UTAH
WYOMING

0   100 miles
0   100 kilometers
Albers Conic Equal-Area Projection

MONTANA

MONTANA

Long before the arrival of Europeans, numerous native groups lived and hunted in the plains and mountains of present-day Montana. While contact between European explorers and Native Americans was often peaceful, Montana was the site of the historic 1876 Battle of the Little Bighorn, in which Lakota (Sioux) and Cheyenne warriors defeated George Armstrong Custer's troops. In the mid-19th century the discovery of gold and silver attracted many prospectors, and later cattle ranching became big business, adding to tensions with the Indians. Montana became the 41st state in 1889. Today, Indians still make up more than 6 percent of the state's population—only four other states have a larger percent. Agriculture is an important part of the economy, producing wheat, hay, and barley as well as beef cattle. Mining and timber industries have seen a decline, but service industries and tourism are growing. Montana's natural environment, including Glacier and Yellowstone National Parks, remains one of its greatest resources.

THE BASICS

STATS

Area
147,042 sq mi (380,840 sq km)

Population
957,861

Capital
Helena
Population 26,718

Largest city
Billings
Population 100,148

Ethnic/racial groups
90.8% white; 6.4% Native American .6% Asian; .4% African American. Hispanic (any race) 2.5%.

Industry
Forest products, food processing, mining, construction, tourism

Agriculture
Wheat, cattle, barley, hay, sugar beets, dairy products

Statehood
November 8, 1889; 41st state

GEO WHIZ

The fossil of a dinosaur about the size of a large turkey is being called the missing link between Asian and North American horned dinosaurs. Paleontologist Jack Horner, who served as the model for the character of Alan Grant in the *Jurassic Park* movies, discovered the fossil while sitting on it during a lunch break at a dig near Choteau.

Montana is the only state with river systems that empty into the Gulf of Mexico, Hudson Bay, and the Pacific Ocean.

Grasshopper Glacier is littered with the bodies of thousands of grasshoppers that became trapped in the ice sometime before the species became extinct 200 years ago.

WESTERN MEADOWLARK
BITTERROOT

⇧ STEP BACK IN TIME. Just like in the past, Montana ranchers move their cattle herds from low winter pastures to higher elevations for summer grazing. Some ranches allow adventurous tourists to participate in the drives.

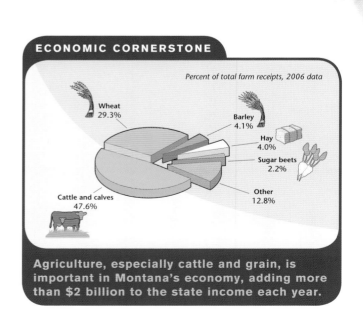

ECONOMIC CORNERSTONE

Percent of total farm receipts, 2006 data

Wheat 29.3%
Barley 4.1%
Hay 4.0%
Sugar beets 2.2%
Other 12.8%
Cattle and calves 47.6%

Agriculture, especially cattle and grain, is important in Montana's economy, adding more than $2 billion to the state income each year.

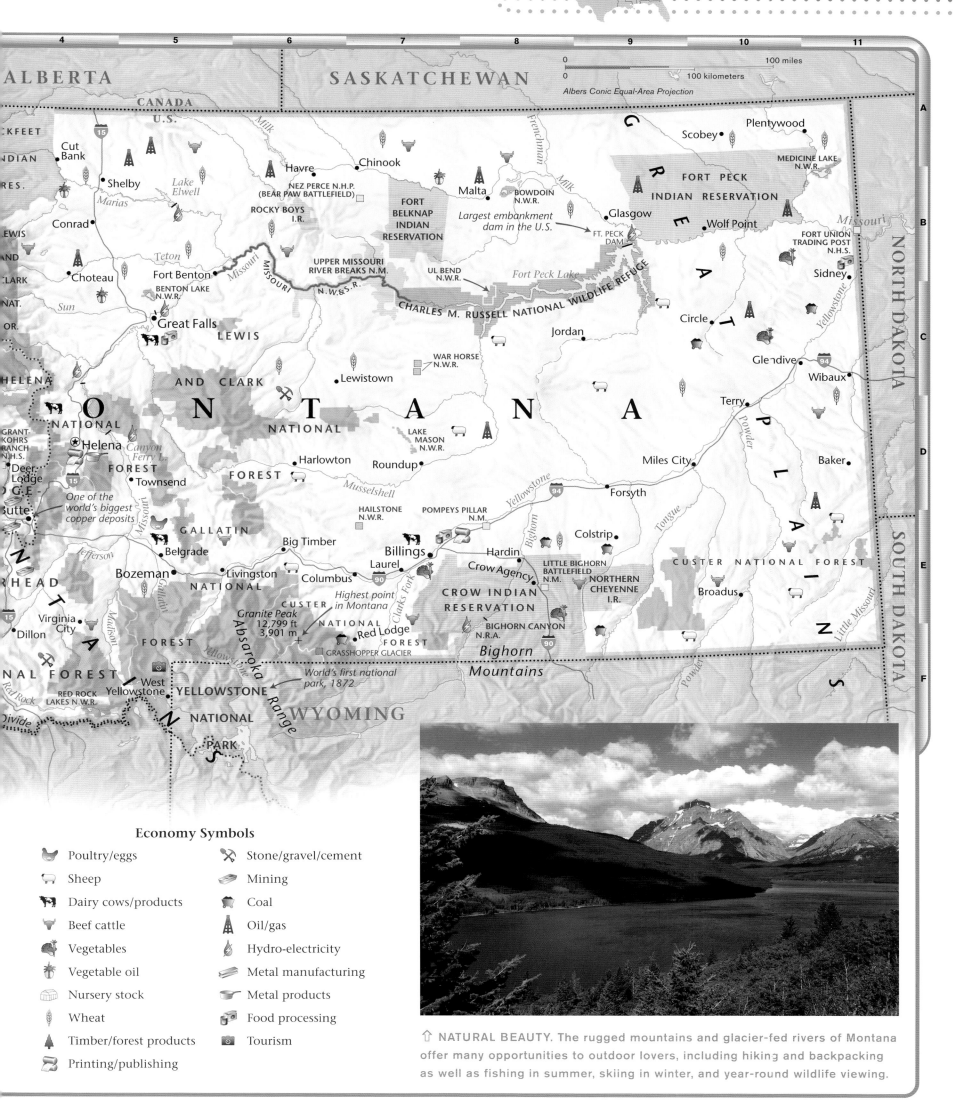

4 5 6 7 8 9 10 11

0   100 miles
0   100 kilometers
Albers Conic Equal-Area Projection

ALBERTA   SASKATCHEWAN

CANADA
U.S.

BLACKFEET INDIAN RES.

Cut Bank
Shelby
Conrad
Choteau

Lake Elwell
Marias
Teton
Sun

Havre
Chinook
NEZ PERCE N.H.P.
(BEAR PAW BATTLEFIELD)
ROCKY BOYS I.R.

Malta
BOWDOIN N.W.R.

FORT BELKNAP INDIAN RESERVATION

Milk

Frenchman

GREAT

Scobey
Plentywood

MEDICINE LAKE N.W.R.

FORT PECK INDIAN RESERVATION

Largest embankment dam in the U.S.

Glasgow
FT. PECK DAM

Wolf Point

Missouri

FORT UNION TRADING POST N.H.S.

Sidney

Fort Benton
BENTON LAKE N.W.R.

Missouri
Missouri

UPPER MISSOURI RIVER BREAKS N.M.
N.W.&S.R.

UL BEND N.W.R.

Fort Peck Lake

CHARLES M. RUSSELL NATIONAL WILDLIFE REFUGE

Circle

Yellowstone

Great Falls

LEWIS

WAR HORSE N.W.R.

Jordan

Glendive

94

Wibaux

LEWIS AND CLARK
NATIONAL

M O N T A N A
NATIONAL

Lewistown

LAKE MASON N.W.R.

Terry

Powder

Baker

HELENA

NATIONAL

Helena

Canyon Ferry L.

FOREST

Deer Lodge

GRANT-KOHRS RANCH N.H.S.

Townsend

FOREST

Harlowton
Roundup

Musselshell

Miles City

94

Forsyth

CUSTER NATIONAL FOREST

One of the world's biggest copper deposits

Butte

GALLATIN

Jefferson

Belgrade

HAILSTONE N.W.R.

POMPEYS PILLAR N.M.

Yellowstone

Bighorn

Colstrip

Tongue

Big Timber

Billings
Laurel

Hardin

Crow Agency

LITTLE BIGHORN BATTLEFIELD N.M.

NORTHERN CHEYENNE I.R.

Broadus

Little Missouri

Bozeman

Livingston

Columbus

90

CROW INDIAN RESERVATION

Virginia City

Dillon

Madison

Gallatin

NATIONAL

Highest point in Montana

CUSTER

NATIONAL

Granite Peak 12,799 ft 3,901 m

Red Lodge

FOREST

BIGHORN CANYON N.R.A.

90

BEAVERHEAD

Red Rock

RED ROCK LAKES N.W.R.

Yellowstone

Absaroka Range

GRASSHOPPER GLACIER

Clarks Fork

Bighorn Mountains

Divide

West Yellowstone

YELLOWSTONE

World's first national park, 1872

NATIONAL

WYOMING

PARK

NORTH DAKOTA

SOUTH DAKOTA

GREAT PLAINS

Economy Symbols

- Poultry/eggs
- Sheep
- Dairy cows/products
- Beef cattle
- Vegetables
- Vegetable oil
- Nursery stock
- Wheat
- Timber/forest products
- Printing/publishing

- Stone/gravel/cement
- Mining
- Coal
- Oil/gas
- Hydro-electricity
- Metal manufacturing
- Metal products
- Food processing
- Tourism

⬆ NATURAL BEAUTY. The rugged mountains and glacier-fed rivers of Montana offer many opportunities to outdoor lovers, including hiking and backpacking as well as fishing in summer, skiing in winter, and year-round wildlife viewing.

THE BASICS

STATS

Area
110,561 sq mi (286,352 sq km)

Population
2,565,382

Capital
Carson City
Population 55,311

Largest city
Las Vegas
Population 552,539

Ethnic/racial groups
81.7% white; 7.9% African American;
6.0% Asian; 1.4% Native American.
Hispanic (any race) 24.4%.

Industry
Tourism and gaming, mining, printing
and publishing, food processing,
electrical equipment

Agriculture
Cattle, hay, dairy products

Statehood
October 31, 1864; 36th state

GEO WHIZ

Lehman Caves, in Great Basin
National Park, contains the best
collection of shield, or angel wing,
formations in the country.

The Applegate Trail, named for two
brothers who first traveled it in 1846,
offered a shorter alternative to
the Oregon Trail. The trail
headed south from Idaho,
across Nevada's Black Rock
Desert into northern California
and then north into Oregon.

So many people claim to have seen
extraterrestrials along a 98-mile
(158-km) stretch of Nevada Highway
375 that the state transportation
board named it Extraterrestrial
Highway in 1996.

MOUNTAIN BLUEBIRD

SAGEBRUSH

NEVADA

Nevada's earliest settlers were native people about whom little is known. Around two thousand years ago, they began establishing permanent dwellings of clay and stone perched atop rocky ledges in what is today the state of Nevada. This was what Spanish explorers saw when they arrived in 1776. In years following, many expeditions passing through the area faced challenges of a difficult environment and native groups protecting their land. In the mid-1800s, gold and silver were discovered. In 1861, the Nevada Territory was created, and three years later statehood was granted. Today, the Nevada landscape is dotted with ghost towns—places once prosperous, but now abandoned except for curious tourists. Mining is now overshadowed by other economic activities. Casinos, modern hotels, and lavish entertainment attract thousands of visitors each year. Hoover Dam, on the Colorado River, supplies water and power to much of Nevada as well as two adjoining states. But water promises to be a challenge to Nevada's future growth.

⇧ TURNING BACK TIME. The Luxor, recreating a scene from ancient Egypt, is one of the many hotel-casinos that attract thousands of tourists to the four-mile (7-km) section of Las Vegas, known as the Strip.

THIRSTY LAND

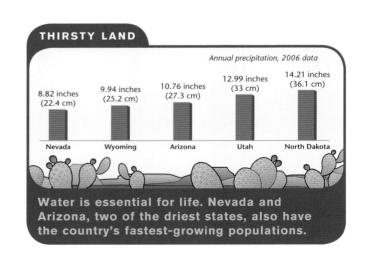

Annual precipitation, 2006 data

Nevada	Wyoming	Arizona	Utah	North Dakota
8.82 inches (22.4 cm)	9.94 inches (25.2 cm)	10.76 inches (27.3 cm)	12.99 inches (33 cm)	14.21 inches (36.1 cm)

Water is essential for life. Nevada and Arizona, two of the driest states, also have the country's fastest-growing populations.

⇦ PRICKLY GARDEN. Nevada's desert environment includes many varieties of cactuses. Saguaro and aloe plants as well as other xerophytes—plants that tolerate very dry conditions—thrive in this rocky garden.

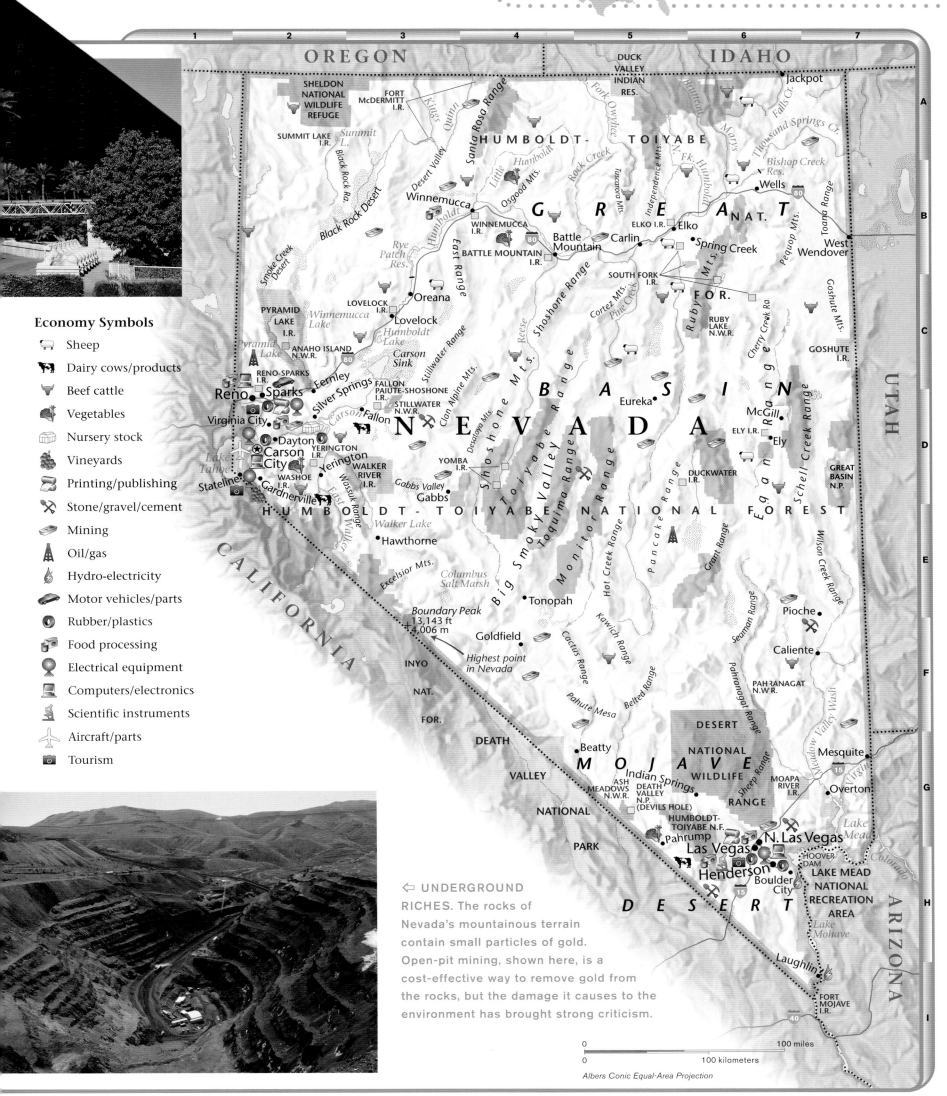

Economy Symbols

- 🐑 Sheep
- 🐄 Dairy cows/products
- 🐂 Beef cattle
- 🥬 Vegetables
- Nursery stock
- 🍇 Vineyards
- Printing/publishing
- ✖ Stone/gravel/cement
- Mining
- Oil/gas
- Hydro-electricity
- Motor vehicles/parts
- Rubber/plastics
- 📷 Food processing
- Electrical equipment
- 💻 Computers/electronics
- Scientific instruments
- ✈ Aircraft/parts
- 📷 Tourism

⬅ UNDERGROUND
RICHES. The rocks of
Nevada's mountainous terrain
contain small particles of gold.
Open-pit mining, shown here, is a
cost-effective way to remove gold from
the rocks, but the damage it causes to the
environment has brought strong criticism.

OREGON   IDAHO

Boundary Peak
13,143 ft
4,006 m
Highest point
in Nevada

0   100 miles
0   100 kilometers
Albers Conic Equal-Area Projection

STATE OF OREGON
1859

THE BASICS

STATS

Area
98,381 sq mi (254,806 sq km)

Population
3,747,455

Capital
Salem
Population 152,239

Largest city
Portland
Population 537,081

Ethnic/racial groups
90.5% white; 3.6% Asian; 1.9% African American; 1.4% Native American. Hispanic (any race) 10.2%.

Industry
Real estate, retail and wholesale trade, electronic equipment, health services, construction, forest products, business services

Agriculture
Nursery stock, hay, cattle, grass seed, wheat, dairy products, potatoes

Statehood
February 14, 1859; 33rd state

GEO WHIZ

To recover wetlands and save two endangered fish species, 100 tons of explosives were used to blast through levees so that water from the Williamson River could again flow into Upper Klamath Lake.

Crater Lake, at 1,943 feet (592 m), is the deepest in the United States. It fills a depression created when an eruption caused the top of a mountain to collapse. Wizard Island, at the center of the 6-mile- (10-km-) wide lake, is the top of a volcano.

Snow-covered Mount Hood dominates the Portland skyline. The peak is one of the most active volcanoes in the Cascade Range. Its last eruption occurred just a few years before Lewis and Clark reached the region.

WESTERN MEADOWLARK
OREGON GRAPE

OREGON

Long before the Oregon Trail brought settlers from the eastern U.S., Indians fished and hunted in Oregon's coastal waters and forested valleys. Spanish explorers sailed along Oregon's coast in 1543, and in the 18th century fur traders from Europe set up forts in the region. In the mid-1800s settlers began farming the rich soil of the Willamette Valley. Oregon achieved statehood in 1859, and by 1883 Oregon was linked to the East by railroad, and Portland had become an important shipping center. Today, forestry, fishing, and agriculture make up an important part of the state's economy, but Oregon is making an effort to diversify into manufacturing and high-tech industries, as well. Dams on the Columbia River generate inexpensive electricity to support energy-hungry industries, such as aluminum production. Computers, electronics, and research-based industries are expanding. The state's natural beauty—snow-capped volcanoes, old-growth forests, and rocky coastline—makes tourism an important growth industry.

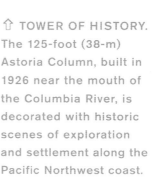

⇧ TOWER OF HISTORY. The 125-foot (38-m) Astoria Column, built in 1926 near the mouth of the Columbia River, is decorated with historic scenes of exploration and settlement along the Pacific Northwest coast.

⇦ CHANGING LANDSCAPE. Oregon's Pacific coast is a lesson on erosion and deposition. Rocky outcrops called sea stacks are leftovers of a former coastline that has been eroded by waves. The sandy beach is a result of eroded material being deposited along the shore.

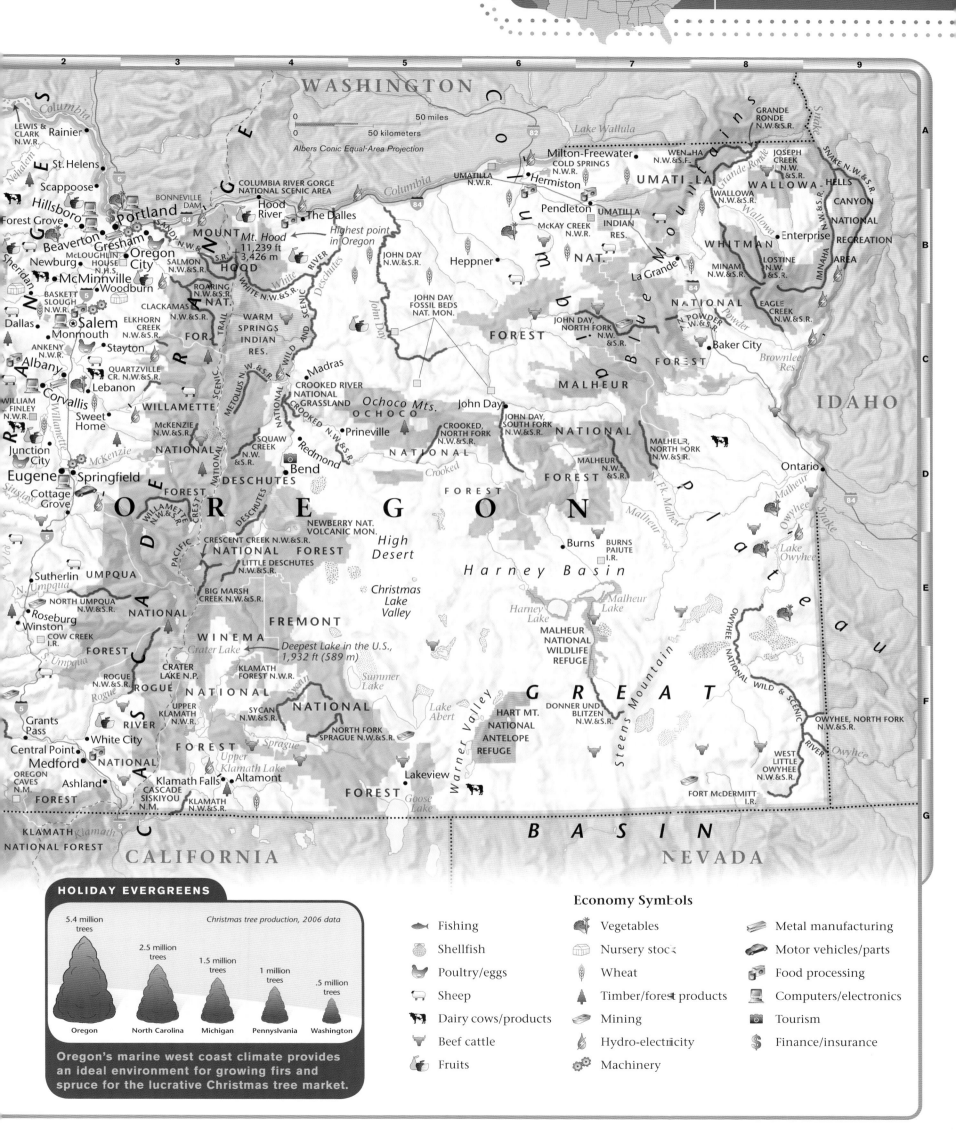

WASHINGTON

50 miles
50 kilometers
Albers Conic Equal-Area Projection

LEWIS & CLARK N.W.R.
Rainier
St. Helens
Scappoose
Hillsboro
Forest Grove
Portland
Beaverton
Gresham
McLOUGHLIN HOUSE N.H.S.
Newburg
Oregon City
Sheridan
McMinnville
Woodburn
BASKETT SLOUGH N.W.R.
Dallas
Salem
Monmouth
Stayton
ANKENY N.W.R.
Albany
Lebanon
WILLIAM L. FINLEY N.W.R.
Corvallis
Sweet Home
Junction City
Eugene
Springfield
Cottage Grove
Sutherlin
Roseburg
Winston
COW CREEK I.R.
Grants Pass
White City
Central Point
Medford
OREGON CAVES N.M.
Ashland
KLAMATH NATIONAL FOREST

Columbia
Nehalem

COLUMBIA RIVER GORGE NATIONAL SCENIC AREA
BONNEVILLE DAM
Hood River
The Dalles
Columbia
Mt. Hood +11,239 ft 3,426 m
Highest point in Oregon
MOUNT HOOD
SALMON N.W.&S.R.
ROARING N.W.&S.R.
ELKHORN CREEK N.W.&S.R.
CLACKAMAS N.W.&S.R.
QUARTZVILLE CR. N.W.&S.R.
McKENZIE N.W.&S.R.
WARM SPRINGS INDIAN RES.
METOLIUS N.W.&S.R.
CROOKED RIVER NATIONAL GRASSLAND
Madras
Prineville
Redmond
Bend
DESCHUTES
WILLAMETTE N.W.&S.R.
WILLAMETTE NATIONAL FOREST
McKenzie
CRESCENT CREEK N.W.&S.R.
NATIONAL FOREST
LITTLE DESCHUTES N.W.&S.R.
BIG MARSH CREEK N.W.&S.R.
UPPER KLAMATH N.W.R.
CRATER LAKE N.P.
Crater Lake
Deepest Lake in the U.S., 1,932 ft (589 m)
ROGUE N.W.&S.R.
Rogue
WINEMA NATIONAL FOREST
FREMONT
NATIONAL FOREST
KLAMATH FOREST N.W.R.
SYCAN N.W.&S.R.
NORTH FORK SPRAGUE N.W.&S.R.
Sprague
Upper Klamath Lake
Klamath Falls
Altamont
CASCADE SISKIYOU N.M.
KLAMATH N.W.&S.R.

UMATILLA N.W.R.
Milton-Freewater
COLD SPRINGS N.W.R.
Hermiston
Pendleton
McKAY CREEK N.W.R.
UMATILLA INDIAN RES.
Heppner
JOHN DAY N.W.&S.R.
JOHN DAY FOSSIL BEDS NAT. MON.
John Day
NAT. FOREST
MALHEUR
OCHOCO Mts.
OCHOCO
NATIONAL
CROOKED, NORTH FORK N.W.&S.R.
JOHN DAY, NORTH FORK N.W.&S.R.
JOHN DAY, SOUTH FORK N.W.&S.R.
Crooked
FOREST
NATIONAL
NEWBERRY NAT. VOLCANIC MON.
High Desert
Christmas Lake Valley
Summer Lake
Lake Abert
Warner Valley
HART MT. NATIONAL ANTELOPE REFUGE
Goose Lake
Lakeview

WEN-HA N.W.&S.R.
UMATILLA
GRANDE RONDE N.W.&S.R.
JOSEPH CREEK N.W. &S.R.
SNAKE N.W.&S.R.
WALLOWA
HELLS CANYON NATIONAL RECREATION AREA
Enterprise
WHITMAN
MINAM N.W.&S.R.
LOSTINE N.W.&S.R.
EAGLE CREEK N.W.&S.R.
IMNAHA N.W.&S.R.
La Grande
NATIONAL
POWDER N.W.&S.R.
Powder
Baker City
Brownlee Res.
FOREST
MALHEUR
MALHEUR N.W.&S.R.
MALHEUR, NORTH FORK N.W.&S.R.
NATIONAL
FOREST
Burns
BURNS PAIUTE I.R.
Harney Basin
Harney Lake
Malheur Lake
MALHEUR NATIONAL WILDLIFE REFUGE
GREAT
Steens Mountain
DONNER UND BLITZEN N.W.&S.R.
OWYHEE NATIONAL WILD & SCENIC RIVER
N. Fk. Malheur
Malheur
Ontario
Lake Owyhee
Owyhee
OWYHEE, NORTH FORK N.W.&S.R.
WEST LITTLE OWYHEE N.W.&S.R.
FORT McDERMITT I.R.
Snake
IDAHO

BASIN
CALIFORNIA
NEVADA

Economy Symbols

- Fishing
- Shellfish
- Poultry/eggs
- Sheep
- Dairy cows/products
- Beef cattle
- Fruits
- Vegetables
- Nursery stock
- Wheat
- Timber/forest products
- Mining
- Hydro-electricity
- Machinery
- Metal manufacturing
- Motor vehicles/parts
- Food processing
- Computers/electronics
- Tourism
- Finance/insurance

THE BASICS

STATS

Area
84,899 sq mi (219,888 sq km)

Population
2,645,330

Capital
Salt Lake City
Population 178,858

Largest city
Salt Lake City
Population 178,858

Ethnic/racial groups
93.5% white; 2.0% Asian; 1.3% Native American; 1.0% African American. Hispanic (any race) 11.2%.

Industry
Government, manufacturing, real estate, construction, health services, business services, banking

Agriculture
Cattle, dairy products, hay, poultry and eggs, wheat

Statehood
January 4, 1896; 45th state

GEO WHIZ

A giant, duck-billed dinosaur is among the many kinds of dinosaur fossils that have been found in the Grand Staircase-Escalante National Monument. Scientists think the plant eater was at least 30 feet (9 m) long and had a mouthful of 300 teeth.

Drought has caused the level of Lake Powell to drop by more than 100 feet (30 meters), revealing much of the spectacular scenery of Glen Canyon that was drowned in 1963 when a dam created the lake.

Great Salt Lake is the largest natural lake west of the Mississippi River. The lake, which has a high level of evaporation, is about eight times saltier than the ocean.

CALIFORNIA GULL
SEGO LILY

UTAH

For thousands of years, present-day Utah was populated by Native Americans living in small hunter-gatherer groups, including the Utes for whom the state is named. Spanish explorers passed through Utah in 1776, and in the early 19th century trappers came from the East searching for beavers. In 1847, the arrival of Mormons seeking freedom to practice their religion marked the beginning of widespread settlement of the territory. They established farms and introduced irrigation. Discovery of precious metals in the 1860s brought miners to the territory. Today, almost 70 percent of Utah's land is set aside by the federal government for use by the military and defense industries and as national parks, which attract large numbers of tourists annually. As a result, government is a leading employer in the state. Another important force in Utah is the Church of Latter-day Saints (Mormons), which has influenced culture and politics in the state for more than a century. More than half the state's population is Mormon.

⇧ NATURE'S HANDIWORK. Arches National Park includes more than 2,000 arches carved by forces of water and ice, extreme temperatures, and the shifting of underground salt beds over a period of 100 million years. Delicate Arch stands on the edge of a canyon, with the La Sal Mountains in the distance.

SPREADING THE FAITH

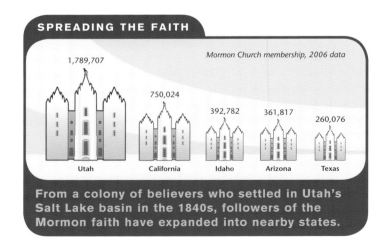

Mormon Church membership, 2006 data

Utah	California	Idaho	Arizona	Texas
1,789,707	750,024	392,782	361,817	260,076

From a colony of believers who settled in Utah's Salt Lake basin in the 1840s, followers of the Mormon faith have expanded into nearby states.

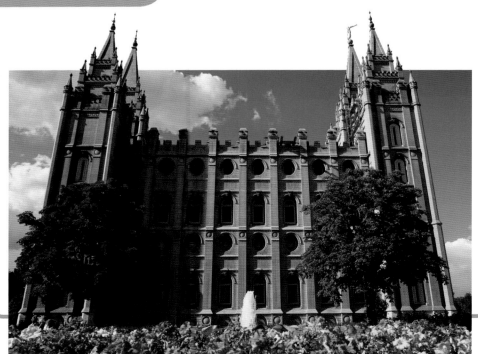

⇦ MONUMENT TO FAITH. Completed in 1893, the Salt Lake Temple is where Mormons gather to worship and participate in religious ceremonies. Church members regard temples as the most sacred places on Earth.

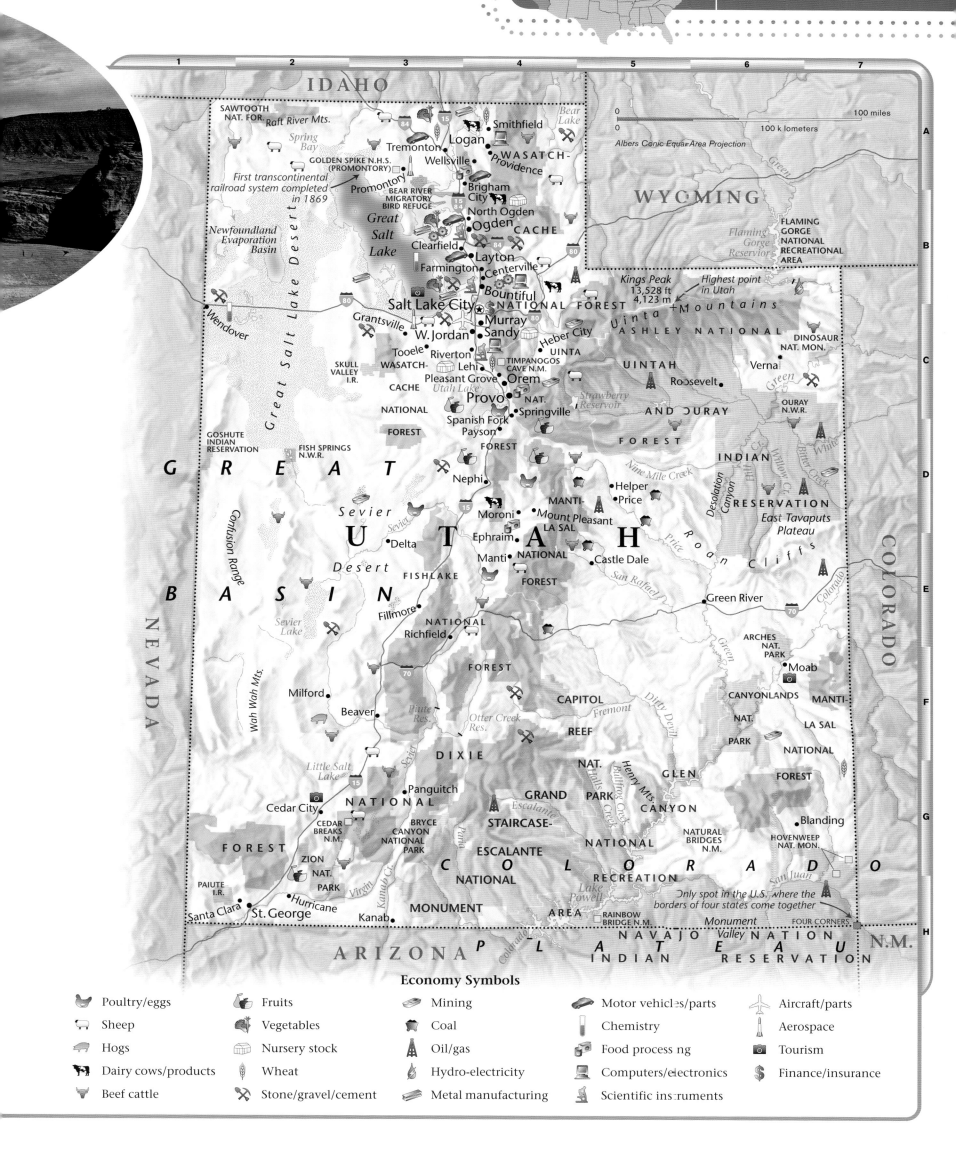

IDAHO

SAWTOOTH NAT. FOR.

Raft River Mts.

Spring Bay

Tremonton

Wellsville

Logan

Smithfield

Bear Lake

WASATCH-
Providence

GOLDEN SPIKE N.H.S. (PROMONTORY)

First transcontinental railroad system completed in 1869

Promontory

Brigham City

BEAR RIVER MIGRATORY BIRD REFUGE

North Ogden

Ogden

CACHE

WYOMING

Newfoundland Evaporation Basin

Great Salt Lake

Clearfield

Layton

Centerville

Flaming Gorge Reservoir

FLAMING GORGE NATIONAL RECREATIONAL AREA

Farmington

Bountiful

NATIONAL FOREST

Kings Peak 13,528 ft 4,123 m

Highest point in Utah

Uinta Mountains

Wendover

Salt Lake City

Murray

Uinta

ASHLEY NATIONAL

DINOSAUR NAT. MON.

Grantsville

W. Jordan

Sandy

Heber City

UINTAH

Verna

Great Salt Lake Desert

Tooele

Riverton

UINTA

UINTAH

Roosevelt

SKULL VALLEY I.R.

Lehi

WASATCH-

Pleasant Grove

TIMPANOGOS CAVE N.M.

Orem

AND OURAY

OURAY N.W.R.

CACHE

Utah Lake

Provo

NAT.

GOSHUTE INDIAN RESERVATION

NATIONAL

Spanish Fork

Springville

Strawberry Reservoir

FOREST

Payson

FOREST

INDIAN

G R E A T

FISH SPRINGS N.W.R.

Nephi

Nine Mile Creek

RESERVATION

East Tavaputs Plateau

Sevier

Helper

Price

Confusion Range

Moroni

MANTI-

Price

Desolation Canyon

Roan

Cliffs

U T A H

Mount Pleasant

LA SAL

Delta

Ephraim

NATIONAL

Castle Dale

Colorado

B A S I N

Desert

Manti

San Rafael

FISHLAKE

FOREST

Sevier Lake

Fillmore

NATIONAL

Green River

Sevier

Richfield

ARCHES NAT. PARK

NEVADA

FOREST

Moab

Wah Wah Mts.

Milford

Beaver

Piute Res.

Otter Creek Res.

Fremont

Ditty Devil

CAPITOL

CANYONLANDS

MANTI-

NAT.

LA SAL

REEF

PARK

NATIONAL

DIXIE

NAT.

Henry Mts.

GLEN

FOREST

Little Salt Lake

Panguitch

GRAND

Escalante

STAIRCASE-

CANYON

Cedar City

CEDAR BREAKS N.M.

BRYCE CANYON NATIONAL PARK

ESCALANTE

Blanding

NATURAL BRIDGES N.M.

HOVENWEEP NAT. MON.

FOREST

ZION NAT. PARK

C O L O R A D O

NATIONAL

RECREATION

PAIUTE I.R.

Virgin

Kanab Cr.

Paria

Lake Powell

San Juan

Santa Clara

Hurricane

St. George

Kanab

MONUMENT

AREA

RAINBOW BRIDGE N.M.

Only spot in the U.S. where the borders of four states come together

Monument Valley

FOUR CORNERS

NATION

N.M.

ARIZONA

P L A T E A U

NAVAJO

INDIAN

RESERVATION

Economy Symbols

- Poultry/eggs
- Sheep
- Hogs
- Dairy cows/products
- Beef cattle
- Fruits
- Vegetables
- Nursery stock
- Wheat
- Stone/gravel/cement
- Mining
- Coal
- Oil/gas
- Hydro-electricity
- Metal manufacturing
- Motor vehicles/parts
- Chemistry
- Food processing
- Computers/electronics
- Scientific instruments
- Aircraft/parts
- Aerospace
- Tourism
- Finance/insurance

THE EVERGREEN STATE:
WASHINGTON

WASHINGTON

Long before Europeans explored the coast of the Pacific Northwest, Native Americans inhabited the area, living mainly off abundant seafood found in coastal waters and rivers. In the late 18th century, first Spanish sailors and then British explorers, including Captain James Cook, visited the region. Under treaties with Spain (1819) and Britain (1846), the U.S. gained control of the land, and in 1853 the Washington Territory was formally separated from the Oregon Territory. Settlers soon based their livelihood on fishing, farming, and lumbering. Washington became the 42nd state in 1889. The 20th century was a time of growth and development in Washington. Seattle became a major Pacific seaport. The Grand Coulee Dam, completed in 1941, provided the region with inexpensive electricity. Today, manufacturing, led by Boeing and Microsoft, is a mainstay of the economy. Washington leads the country in production of apples and sweet cherries, and the state is home to the headquarters of the popular Starbucks chain of coffee shops.

⇩ HARVEST TIME. Once a semiarid grassland, the Palouse region north of the Snake River in eastern Washington is now a major wheat-producing area.

⇧ PACIFIC GATEWAY. The city of Seattle, easily recognizable by its distinctive Space Needle tower, is a major West Coast port and home to the North Pacific fishing fleet.

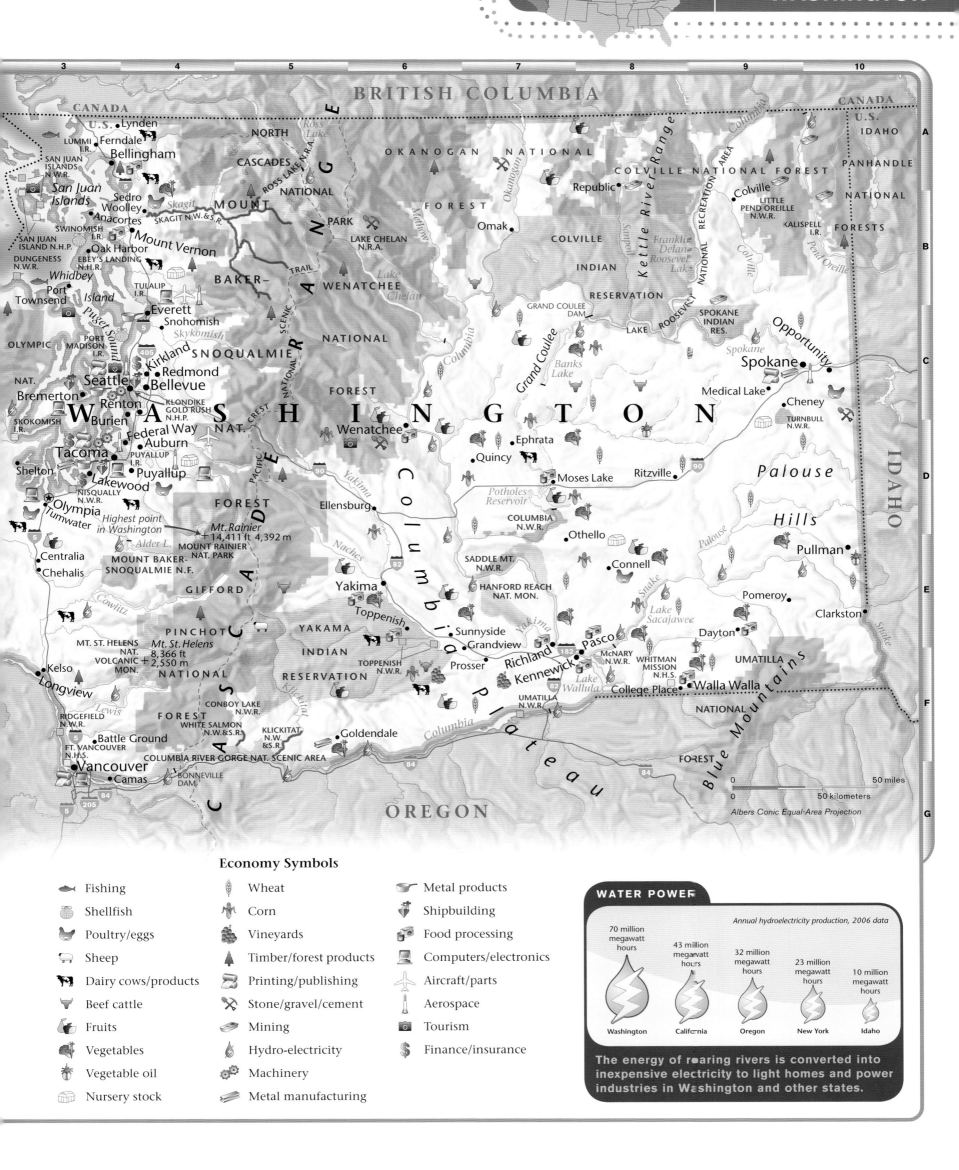

BRITISH COLUMBIA

CANADA
U.S.

CANADA
U.S.
IDAHO

PANHANDLE

Lynden
LUMMI I.R.
Ferndale
Bellingham

SAN JUAN
ISLANDS N.W.R.

NORTH

CASCADES

Ross
Lake

OKANOGAN   NATIONAL

COLVILLE NATIONAL FOREST

NATIONAL

Republic
Colville

LITTLE
PEND OREILLE
N.W.R.

KALISPEL
I.R.

NATIONAL

FORESTS

San Juan
Islands

Sedro
Woolley
Anacortes

Skagit
SKAGIT N.W.&S.R.

MOUNT

Omak

COLVILLE

FORESTS

SWINOMISH
I.R.

SAN JUAN
ISLAND N.H.P.

Oak Harbor
Mount Vernon

BAKER-

LAKE CHELAN
N.R.A.

INDIAN

DUNGENESS
N.W.R.

EBEY'S LANDING
N.H.R.

TULALIP
I.R.

WENATCHEE

Lake
Chelan

RESERVATION

Franklin
Delano
Roosevelt
Lake

Whidbey
Island

Port
Townsend

RANGE

GRAND COULEE
DAM

SPOKANE
INDIAN
RES.

OLYMPIC

Everett
Snohomish
Skykomish

NATIONAL

Columbia

Spokane

Opportunity

PORT
MADISON I.R.

SNOQUALMIE

Kirkland
Redmond

Grand Coulee

Banks
Lake

Spokane

NAT.

Seattle
Bellevue

FOREST

Wenatchee

Medical Lake

Cheney

Bremerton
Renton
Burien

WASHINGTON

KLONDIKE
GOLD RUSH
N.H.P.

NAT.

CREST

Quincy

Ephrata

Moses Lake

Ritzville

TURNBULL
N.W.R.

Palouse

SKOKOMISH
I.R.

Federal Way
Auburn

Tacoma

PUYALLUP
I.R.

Puyallup

Shelton

Lakewood

NISQUALLY
N.W.R.

FOREST

PACIFIC

90

Yakima

Ellensburg

Naches

COLUMBIA
N.W.R.

Othello

SADDLE MT.
N.W.R.

Connell

Hills

Pullman

Olympia
Tumwater

Highest point
in Washington

Mt. Rainier
+14,411 ft 4,392 m

MOUNT RAINIER
NAT. PARK

Potholes
Reservoir

Palouse

Alder L.

82

Centralia
Chehalis

MOUNT BAKER-
SNOQUALMIE N.F.

GIFFORD

HANFORD REACH
NAT. MON.

Pomeroy

Snake

Lake
Sacajawea

Clarkston

Cowlitz

MT. ST. HELENS
NAT.
VOLCANIC
MON.

Mt. St. Helens
8,366 ft
+2,550 m

PINCHOT

Toppenish

YAKAMA

Sunnyside
Grandview

Yakima

Pasco

McNARY
N.W.R.

WHITMAN
MISSION
N.H.S.

Dayton

UMATILLA

Kelso

INDIAN

TOPPENISH
N.W.R.

Prosser

Richland

182

Kennewick

College Place
Walla Walla

Longview

NATIONAL

RESERVATION

Lewis

82
Lake
Wallula

NATIONAL

Blue

RIDGEFIELD
N.W.R.

5

Battle Ground

FT. VANCOUVER
N.H.S.

FOREST

CONBOY LAKE
N.W.R.

WHITE SALMON
N.W.&S.R.

KLICKITAT
N.W.
&S.R

Klickitat

Goldendale

UMATILLA
N.W.R.

Columbia

Mountains

FOREST

Vancouver
Camas

BONNEVILLE
DAM

COLUMBIA RIVER GORGE NAT. SCENIC AREA

84

Columbia

Plateau

84

50 miles

0   50 kilometers

Albers Conic Equal-Area Projection

205

OREGON

CASCADE RANGE

Columbia Plateau

Puget Sound

Kettle River Range

Okanogan

Methow

Sampoil

Kettle

Colville

Pend Oreille

IDAHO

Economy Symbols

Fishing	Wheat	Metal products
Shellfish	Corn	Shipbuilding
Poultry/eggs	Vineyards	Food processing
Sheep	Timber/forest products	Computers/electronics
Dairy cows/products	Printing/publishing	Aircraft/parts
Beef cattle	Stone/gravel/cement	Aerospace
Fruits	Mining	Tourism
Vegetables	Hydro-electricity	Finance/insurance
Vegetable oil	Machinery	
Nursery stock	Metal manufacturing	

WATER POWER

Annual hydroelectricity production, 2006 data

70 million megawatt hours	43 million megawatt hours	32 million megawatt hours	23 million megawatt hours	10 million megawatt hours
Washington	California	Oregon	New York	Idaho

The energy of roaring rivers is converted into inexpensive electricity to light homes and power industries in Washington and other states.

THE EQUALITY STATE:
WYOMING

THE BASICS

STATS

Area
97,814 sq mi (253,337 sq km)

Population
522,830

Capital
Cheyenne
Population 54,374

Largest city
Cheyenne
Population 54,374

Ethnic/racial groups
94.5% white; 2.5% Native American; .9% African American; .7% Asian. Hispanic (any race) 6.9%.

Industry
Oil and natural gas, mining, generation of electricity, chemicals, tourism

Agriculture
Cattle, sugar beets, sheep, hay, wheat

Statehood
July 10, 1890; 44th state

GEO WHIZ

The successful reintroduction of wolves into Yellowstone National Park, a program that began in the mid-1990s, has become a model for saving endangered carnivores around the world. In 2001 there were 37 wolves in the Druid Peak pack, making it the largest known pack in history.

The National Elk Refuge, in Jackson Hole, provides a winter home for some 7,500 elk. The herd's migration from the refuge to their summer home in Yellowstone National Park is the longest elk herd migration in the lower 48 states.

Devils Tower, a huge formation of igneous rock near Sundance, was the country's first national monument. It was featured in the science-fiction classic *Close Encounters of the Third Kind*.

WESTERN MEADOWLARK
INDIAN PAINTBRUSH

WYOMING

When Europeans arrived in the 18th century in what would become Wyoming, various native groups were already there, living as nomads following herds of deer and bison across the plains. In the early 19th century fur traders moved into Wyoming, and settlers followed later along the Oregon Trail. Laramie and many of the state's other towns developed around old army forts built to protect wagon trains traveling through Wyoming. Today, fewer than 600,000 people live in all of Wyoming. The state's economy is based on agriculture—mainly grain and livestock production—and mining, especially energy resources. The state has some of the world's largest surface coal mines. In addition, it produces petroleum, natural gas, industrial metals, and precious gems. The natural environment is also a major resource. People come to Wyoming for fishing and hunting, for rodeos, and for the state's majestic mountains and parks. Yellowstone, established in 1872, was the world's first national park.

⇧ **WANT TO RACE?** Unique to the High Plains of the West, the pronghorn can sprint up to 60 miles per hour (97 kmph).

⇩ **DRAMATIC LANDSCAPE.** Rising more than 13,000 feet (3,900 m), the jagged peaks of the Tetons, one of the youngest mountain ranges of the West, tower over a barn on the valley floor.

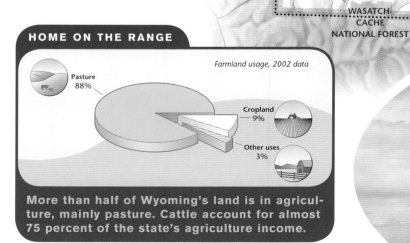

HOME ON THE RANGE

Farmland usage, 2002 data

Pasture
88%

Cropland
9%

Other uses
3%

More than half of Wyoming's land is in agriculture, mainly pasture. Cattle account for almost 75 percent of the state's agriculture income.

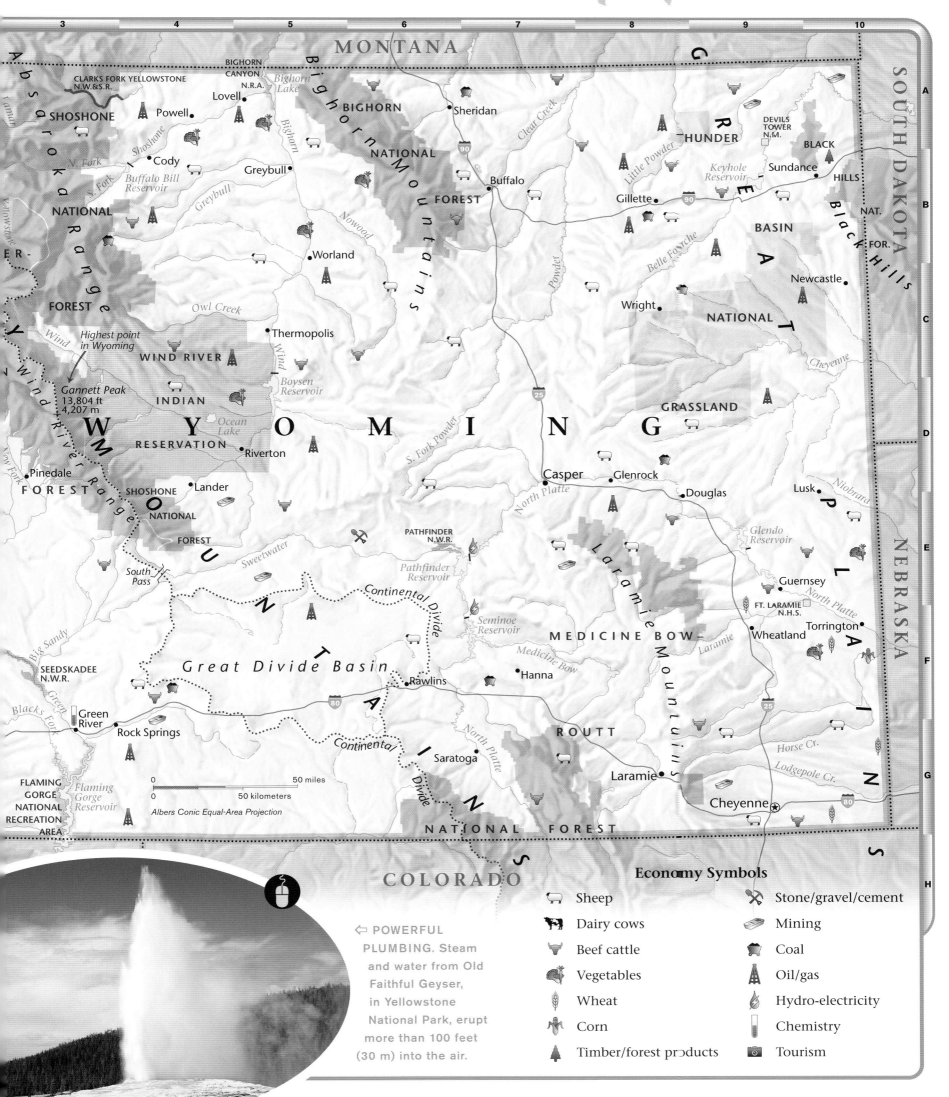

MONTANA

3   4   5   6   7   8   9   10

Absaroka Range

CLARKS FORK YELLOWSTONE N.W.&S.R.

SHOSHONE

Powell

Lovell

BIGHORN CANYON N.R.A.

Bighorn Lake

BIGHORN

Sheridan

G R E A T

DEVILS TOWER N.M.

BLACK

SOUTH DAKOTA

Cody

N. Fork

S. Fork

Shoshone

Buffalo Bill Reservoir

NATIONAL RANGE

Greybull

Greybull

Bighorn

NATIONAL

FOREST

THUNDER

Keyhole Reservoir

Sundance

Little Powder

Gillette

Black Hills

HILLS

NAT.

FOR.

FOREST

Worland

Nowood

Bighorn Mountains

Buffalo

90

BASIN

Newcastle

Cheyenne

Belle Fourche

Wright

NATIONAL

Powell

Owl Creek

Thermopolis

Wind

Boysen Reservoir

Highest point in Wyoming

Wind

WIND RIVER

Gannett Peak 13,804 ft 4,207 m

INDIAN

Ocean Lake

W Y O M I N G

GRASSLAND

RESERVATION

Riverton

Pinedale

New Fork

Wind River Range

SHOSHONE

Lander

FOREST

NATIONAL

FOREST

S. Fork Powder

Casper

Glenrock

Douglas

Lusk

Niobrara

Glendo Reservoir

Laramie Mountains

Sweetwater

PATHFINDER N.W.R.

Pathfinder Reservoir

North Platte

Guernsey

North Platte

South Pass

Continental Divide

Seminoe Reservoir

FT. LARAMIE N.H.S.

Torrington

Big Sandy

Great Divide Basin

Rawlins

Medicine Bow

MEDICINE BOW-

Laramie

Wheatland

SEEDSKADEE N.W.R.

Green Fork

Blacks Fork

Green River

Rock Springs

80

Continental Divide

Saratoga

North Platte

Hanna

R O U T T

Horse Cr.

Lodgepole Cr.

FLAMING GORGE NATIONAL RECREATION AREA

Flaming Gorge Reservoir

0   50 miles
0   50 kilometers

Albers Conic Equal-Area Projection

NATIONAL   FOREST

Laramie

Cheyenne

80

P L A I N S

NEBRASKA

COLORADO

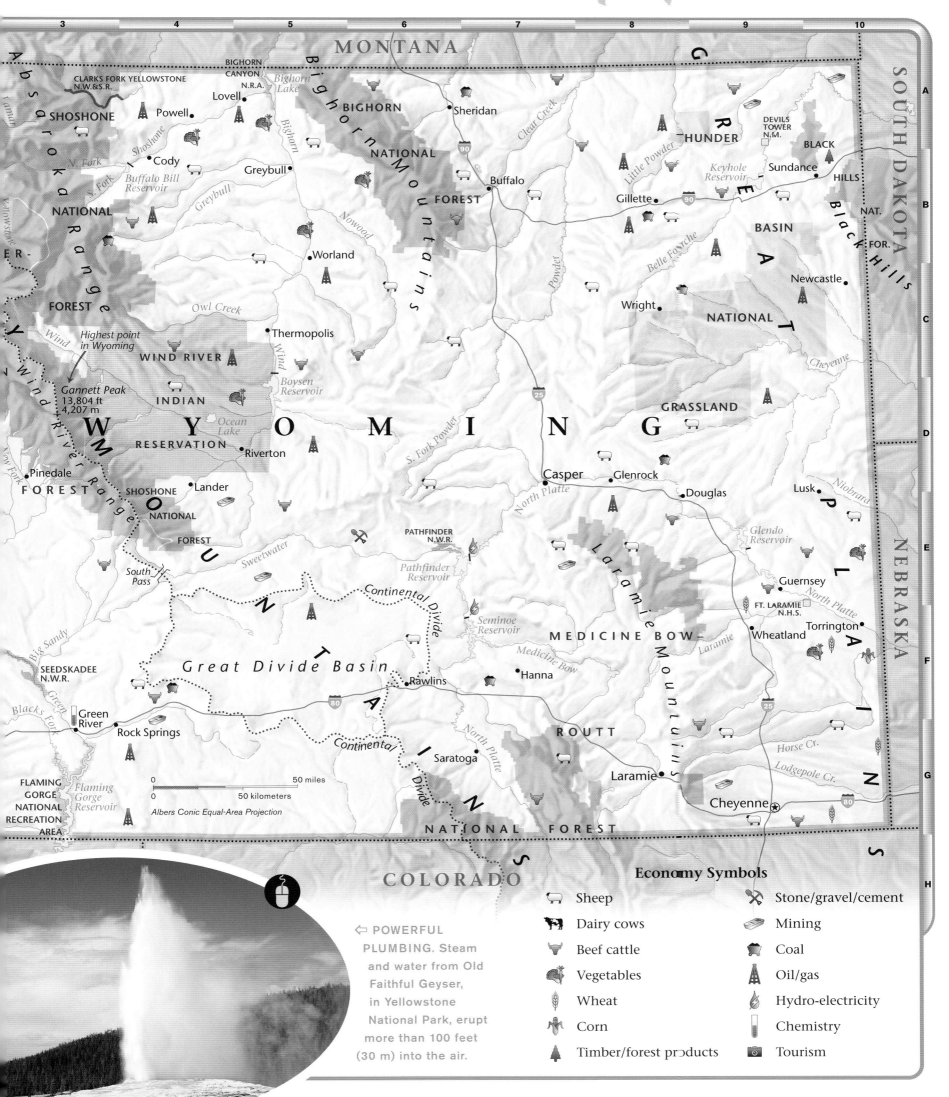

⇐ POWERFUL PLUMBING. Steam and water from Old Faithful Geyser, in Yellowstone National Park, erupt more than 100 feet (30 m) into the air.

Economy Symbols

Symbol		Symbol	
🐑	Sheep	⛏	Stone/gravel/cement
🐄	Dairy cows		Mining
	Beef cattle		Coal
	Vegetables		Oil/gas
🌾	Wheat		Hydro-electricity
🌽	Corn		Chemistry
🌲	Timber/forest products	📷	Tourism

The Territories
ACROSS TWO SEAS

Listed below are the 5 largest of the 14 U.S. territories, along with their flags and key information. Two of these are in the Caribbean Sea, and the other three are in the Pacific Ocean. Can you find the other 9 U.S. territories on the map?

U.S. CARIBBEAN TERRITORIES

PUERTO RICO

Area: 3,508 sq mi (9,086 sq km)

Population: 3,929,000

Capital: San Juan
Population 2,605,000

Languages: Spanish, English

U.S. VIRGIN ISLANDS

Area: 149 sq mi (386 sq km)

Population: 109,000

Capital: Charlotte Amalie
Population 52,000

Languages: English, Spanish or Spanish Creole, French or French Creole

U.S. PACIFIC TERRITORIES

AMERICAN SAMOA

Area: 77 sq mi (199 sq km)

Population: 67,000

Capital: Pago Pago
Population 55,000

Language: Samoan

GUAM

Area: 217 sq mi (561 sq km)

Population: 171,000

Capital: Hagåtña (Agana)
Population 144,000

Languages: English, Chamorro, Philippine languages

NORTHERN MARIANA ISLANDS

Area: 184 sq mi (477 sq km)

Population: 82,000

Capital: Saipan
Population 75,000

Languages: Philippine languages, Chinese, Chamorro, English

OTHER U.S. TERRITORIES

Baker Island, Howland Island, Jarvis Island, Johnston Atoll, Kingman Reef, Midway Islands, Navassa Island, Palmyra Atoll, Wake Island

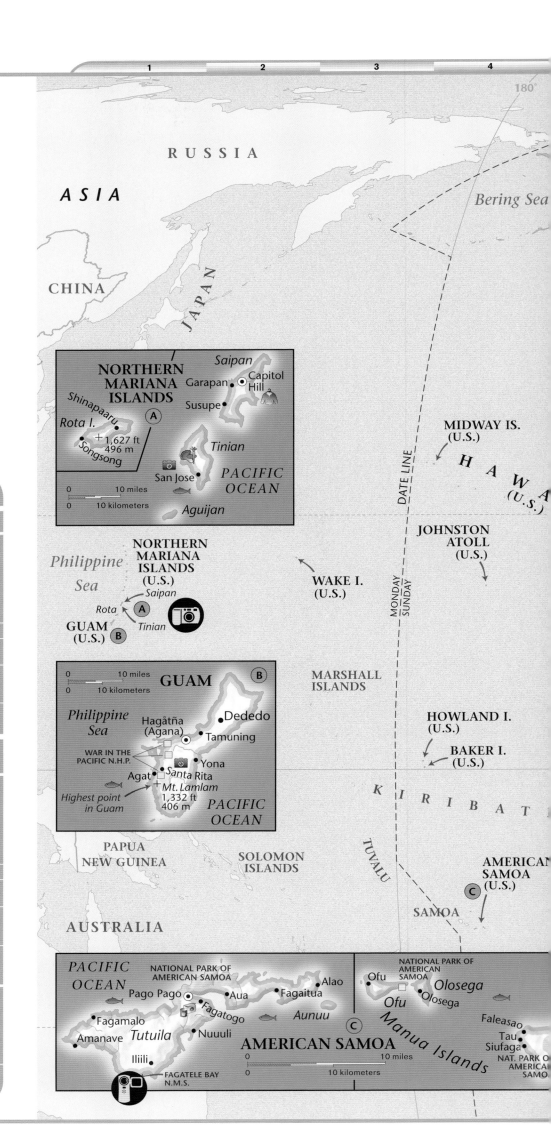

1 2 3 4

RUSSIA

ASIA

CHINA

JAPAN

Bering Sea

NORTHERN MARIANA ISLANDS

Saipan
Garapan • ⊙ Capitol Hill
Shinapaaru
Susupe •
Rota I.
(A)
+ 1,627 ft
496 m
Songsong
Tinian
San Jose
Aguijan
PACIFIC OCEAN

0   10 miles
0   10 kilometers

Philippine Sea

NORTHERN MARIANA ISLANDS (U.S.)
• Saipan
Rota (A)
GUAM (U.S.) Tinian
(B)

MIDWAY IS. (U.S.)

H A W A I I (U.S.)

DATE LINE

JOHNSTON ATOLL (U.S.)

WAKE I. (U.S.)

MONDAY SUNDAY

MARSHALL ISLANDS

GUAM (B)

0   10 miles
0   10 kilometers

Philippine Sea
Hagåtña (Agana) ⊙ • Dededo
• Tamuning
WAR IN THE PACIFIC N.H.P.
• Yona
Agat • Santa Rita
+ Mt. Lamlam 1,332 ft 406 m
Highest point in Guam
PACIFIC OCEAN

HOWLAND I. (U.S.)

BAKER I. (U.S.)

K I R I B A T I

PAPUA NEW GUINEA

SOLOMON ISLANDS

TUVALU

AMERICAN SAMOA (U.S.)
(C)

SAMOA

AUSTRALIA

PACIFIC OCEAN
NATIONAL PARK OF AMERICAN SAMOA
Pago Pago ⊙ • Aua • Fagaitua
• Fagatogo
• Fagamalo Tutuila • Nuuuli
Amanave
Aunuu
Iliili
FAGATELE BAY N.M.S.

NATIONAL PARK OF AMERICAN SAMOA
Ofu Olosega
Ofu • Olosega
Manua Islands
AMERICAN SAMOA
Faleasao
Tau
Siufaga
NAT. PARK O AMERICAN SAMOA

0   10 miles
0   10 kilometers

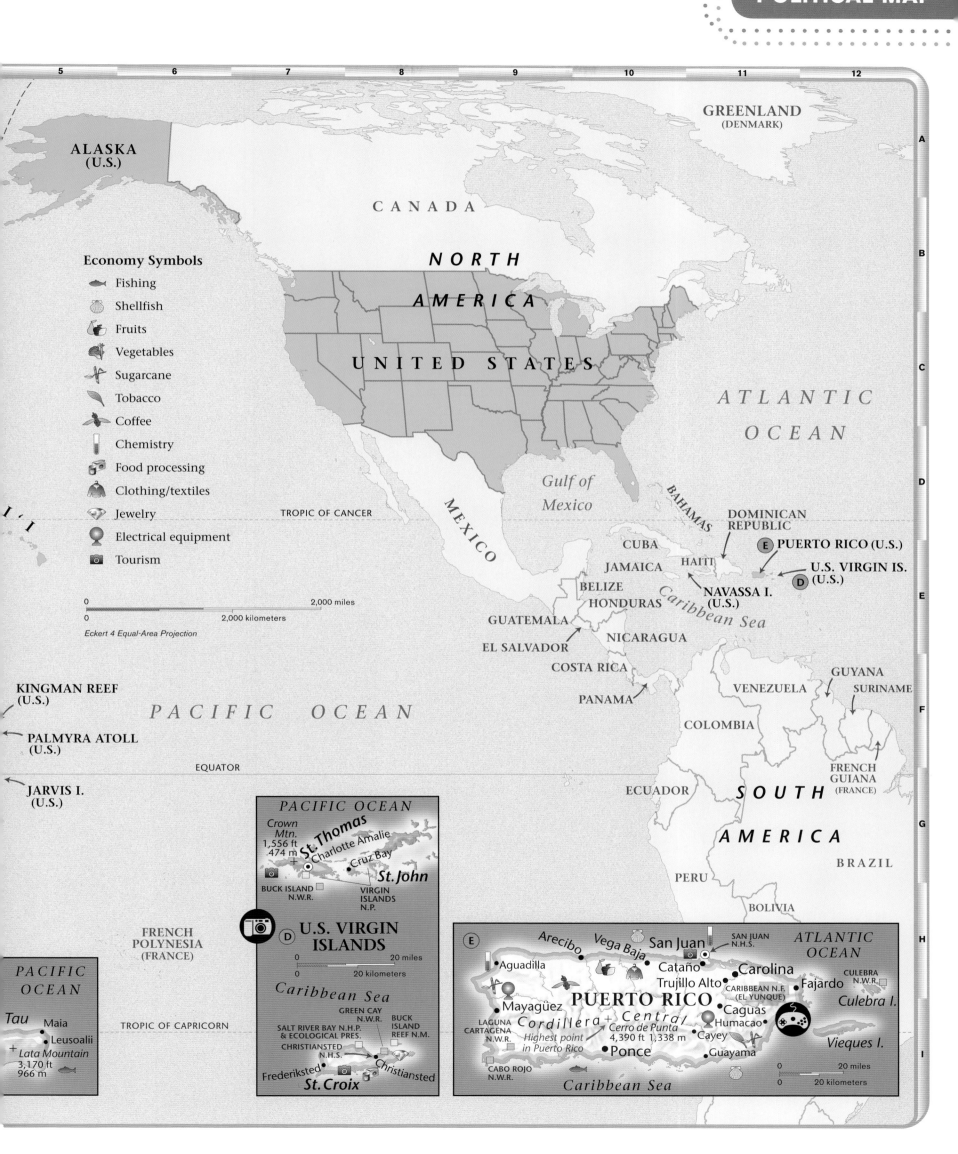

Economy Symbols

- Fishing
- Shellfish
- Fruits
- Vegetables
- Sugarcane
- Tobacco
- Coffee
- Chemistry
- Food processing
- Clothing/textiles
- Jewelry
- Electrical equipment
- Tourism

Eckert 4 Equal-Area Projection

GREENLAND
(DENMARK)

ALASKA
(U.S.)

CANADA

NORTH

AMERICA

UNITED STATES

ATLANTIC

OCEAN

MEXICO

Gulf of
Mexico

TROPIC OF CANCER

BAHAMAS

DOMINICAN
REPUBLIC

CUBA

PUERTO RICO (U.S.)

JAMAICA   HAITI

U.S. VIRGIN IS.
(U.S.)

NAVASSA I.
(U.S.)

BELIZE

HONDURAS   Caribbean Sea

GUATEMALA

EL SALVADOR   NICARAGUA

COSTA RICA

KINGMAN REEF
(U.S.)

PACIFIC   OCEAN

PANAMA

VENEZUELA

GUYANA

SURINAME

COLOMBIA

PALMYRA ATOLL
(U.S.)

EQUATOR

JARVIS I.
(U.S.)

ECUADOR

FRENCH
GUIANA
(FRANCE)

SOUTH

AMERICA

FRENCH
POLYNESIA
(FRANCE)

PERU

BRAZIL

BOLIVIA

PACIFIC
OCEAN

Tau

Maia

Leusoalii

Lata Mountain
3,170 ft
966 m

TROPIC OF CAPRICORN

PACIFIC OCEAN

Crown
Mtn.
1,556 ft
474 m

St. Thomas

Charlotte Amalie

Cruz Bay

St. John

BUCK ISLAND
N.W.R.

VIRGIN
ISLANDS
N.P.

U.S. VIRGIN
ISLANDS

Caribbean Sea

GREEN CAY
N.W.R.

BUCK
ISLAND
REEF N.M.

SALT RIVER BAY N.H.P.
& ECOLOGICAL PRES.

CHRISTIANSTED
N.H.S.

Christiansted

Frederiksted

St. Croix

Arecibo

Vega Baja

San Juan

SAN JUAN
N.H.S.

ATLANTIC
OCEAN

Aguadilla

Cataño

Carolina

CULEBRA
N.W.R.

Trujillo Alto

CARIBBEAN N.F.

Fajardo

Mayagüez

PUERTO RICO

CARIBBEAN N.F.
(EL YUNQUE)

Culebra I.

LAGUNA
CARTAGENA
N.W.R.

Cordillera Central

Caguas

Humacao

Cerro de Punta
4,390 ft 1,338 m
Highest point
in Puerto Rico

Cayey

Ponce

Guayama

Vieques I.

CABO ROJO
N.W.R.

Caribbean Sea

⇨ PRESERVING TRADITION. Young dancers from American Samoa, dressed in costumes of feathers and pandanus leaves, prepare to perform in the Pacific Arts Festival, which is held once every four years to promote Pacific cultures.

The Territories
ISLANDS IN THE FAMILY

Fourteen territories and commonwealths scattered across the Pacific and Caribbean came under U.S. influence after wars or various international agreements. Because they are neither states nor independent countries, the U.S. government provides economic and military aid. Puerto Rico's nearly four million residents give it a population greater than that of 24 U.S. states. Many tourists seeking sunny beaches visit the Virgin Islands, purchased from Denmark for $25 million in 1917. American Samoa, Guam, and the Northern Mariana Islands in the Pacific have sizable populations, but several tiny atolls have no civilian residents and are administered by the U.S. military or government departments. In most cases, citizens of these territories are also eligible for American citizenship.

⇧ RELIC OF THE PAST. Sugar mill ruins on St. John, in the U.S. Virgin Islands, recall a way of life that dominated the Caribbean in the 18th and 19th centuries. Plantations used slave labor to grow cane and make it into sugar and molasses.

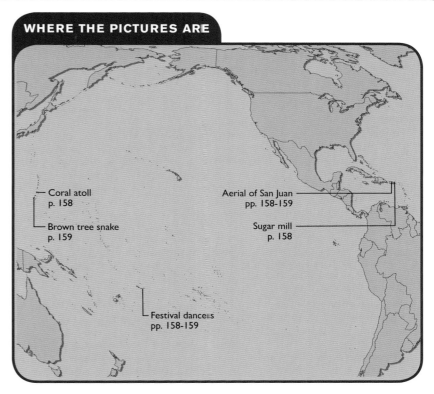

WHERE THE PICTURES ARE

Coral atoll
p. 158

Brown tree snake
p. 159

Aerial of San Juan
pp. 158-159

Sugar mill
p. 158

Festival dancers
pp. 158-159

⇐ PACIFIC JEWEL. Managaha Island sits in the blue-green waters of a lagoon formed by a long reef along Saipan's western coast. Marine biologists fear that portions of the reef are dying due to pollution. The lagoon holds wrecks from battles fought in Northern Mariana waters during World War II.

⇐ ATLANTIC PLAYGROUND. Modern hotels, catering to 2.5 million tourists annually, rise above sandy beaches in San Juan, Puerto Rico. Founded in 1521, the city has one of the best natural harbors in the Caribbean.

⇓ UNWELCOME STOWAWAY. The brown tree snake probably arrived in Guam on cargo ships in the 1950s. The snake has greatly reduced the island's bird and small mammal populations and causes power outages when it climbs electric poles.

U.S. FACTS & FIGURES

THE COUNTRY

STATS

Founding
1776

Area
3,794,083 sq mi (9,826,675 sq km)

Population (January 2008)
303,269,000

Capital
Washington, D.C.

Population
581,530

Largest city
New York

Population
8,214,426

Ethnic/racial groups
**80.1% white; 12.8% African American;
4.4% Asian; 1.0% Native American.
Hispanic (any race) 14.8%.**

**Languages
(most widely spoken)**
English, Spanish

Economy
**Services: 78.2% of GDP
Industry: 20.9% of GDP
Agriculture: .9% of GDP**

**BALD EAGLE,
NATIONAL SYMBOL**

Top States

Listed below are major farm products, fish, and minerals and the states that currently lead in their production. Following each list is a ranking of the top states in each category.

Farm Products

Cattle and calves: Texas, Nebraska, Kansas, California
Dairy products: California, Wisconsin, New York, Pennsylvania
Soybeans: Iowa, Illinois, Minnesota, Indiana
Corn for grain: Iowa, Illinois, Nebraska, Minnesota
Hogs and pigs: Iowa, North Carolina, Minnesota, Illinois
Broiler chickens: Georgia, Arkansas, Alabama, North Carolina
Wheat: Kansas, North Dakota, Montana, Washington
Cotton: Texas, California, Georgia, Mississippi
Eggs: Iowa, Ohio, Pennsylvania, Indiana
Hay: Texas, California, Pennsylvania, Idaho
Tobacco: North Carolina, Kentucky, Tennessee, South Carolina
Turkeys: Minnesota, North Carolina, Arkansas, Virginia
Oranges: Florida, California, Texas, Arizona
Potatoes: Idaho, Washington, Wisconsin, Colorado
Grapes: California, Washington, New York, Pennsylvania
Tomatoes: Florida, California, Ohio, Georgia
Rice: Arkansas, California, Louisiana, Missouri

Top Ten in Farm Products
(by net farm income)

1. California
2. Texas
3. North Carolina
4. Iowa
5. Minnesota
6. Georgia
7. Florida
8. Nebraska
9. Arkansas
10. Kentucky

Fish

Shrimp: Louisiana, Texas, Florida, Alabama
Crabs: Alaska, Louisiana, Oregon, Maryland, California
Lobsters: Maine, Massachusetts, Florida, Rhode Island
Salmon: Alaska, Washington, Oregon, California
Pollock: Alaska, Massachusetts, Maine, New Hampshire

Top Five in Fisheries
(by value of catch)

1. Alaska
2. Massachusetts
3. Maine
4. Louisiana
5. Texas

Minerals

Crude oil: Texas, Alaska, California, Louisiana, Oklahoma
Natural gas: Texas, Wyoming, Oklahoma, New Mexico, Louisiana
Coal: Wyoming, West Virginia, Kentucky, Pennsylvania
Crushed stone: Texas, Florida, Pennsylvania, Missouri
Copper: Arizona, Utah, New Mexico, Nevada
Cement: California, Texas, Pennsylvania, Florida
Construction sand and gravel: California, Arizona, Texas, Michigan
Gold: Nevada, Utah, Alaska, Colorado, Montana
Iron ore: Minnesota, Michigan, California
Clay: Georgia, South Carolina, Alabama, Arkansas
Phosphate rock: Florida, North Carolina, Idaho, Utah
Lime: Missouri, Kentucky, Alabama, Ohio, Texas
Salt: Louisiana, Texas, New York, Ohio
Sulfur: Louisiana, Texas

Top Ten in Minerals

1. Arizona
2. California
3. Nevada
4. Florida
5. Utah
6. Texas
7. Minnesota
8. Missouri
9. Georgia
10. Colorado

Extremes

World's Strongest Surface Wind
231 mph (372 kph), Mount Washington, New Hampshire, April 12, 1934

World's Tallest Living Tree
"Hyperion," a coast redwood in Redwood National Park, California, 379.1 ft (115.55 m) high

World's Oldest Living Tree
Methuselah bristlecone pine, California; 4,789 years old

World's Largest Gorge
Grand Canyon, Arizona; 290 mi (466 km) long, 600 ft to 18 mi (183 m to 29 km) wide, 1 mile (1.6 km) deep

Highest Temperature in U.S.
134°F (56.6°C), Death Valley, California, July 10, 1913

Lowest Temperature in U.S.
Minus 80°F (-62.2°C) at Prospect Creek, Alaska, January 23, 1971

Highest Point in U.S.
Mount McKinley (Denali), Alaska; 20,320 ft (6,194 m)

Lowest Point in U.S.
Death Valley, California; 282 feet (86 m) below sea level

Longest River System in U.S.
Mississippi-Missouri; 3,710 mi (5,971 km) long

Rainiest Spot in U.S.
Waiʻaleʻale (mountain), Hawaiʻi: average annual rainfall 460 in (1,168 cm)

**Metropolitan Areas with
More Than Five Million People**
A metropolitan area is a city and its surrounding suburban areas. (2006 data)

1. New York, pop. 21,976,224
2. Los Angeles, pop. 17,775,984
3. Chicago, pop. 9,725,317
4. Washington, D.C., pop. 8,211,213
5. Boston, pop. 7,465,634
6. San Francisco, pop. 7,228,948
7. Philadelphia, pop. 6,382,714
8. Dallas-Fort Worth, pop. 6,359,758
9. Houston, pop. 5,641,077
10. Atlanta, pop. 5,478,667
11. Detroit, pop. 5,410,014

GLOSSARY

aquaculture raising fish or shellfish in controlled ponds or waterways for commercial use

atoll a circular coral reef enclosing a tropical lagoon

arid climate type of dry climate in which annual precipitation is often less than 10 inches (25 cm)

biomass total weight of all organisms found in a given area

bituminous coal a soft form of coal used in industries and power plants

bog a poorly drained area with wet, spongy ground

broadleaf forest trees with wide leaves that are shed during the winter season

butte a high, steep-sided rock formation created by the erosion of a mesa

canal an artificial waterway that is used by ships or to carry water for irrigation

center-pivot irrigation an irrigation system that rotates around a piped water source at its middle, often resulting in circular field patterns

continental climate temperature extremes with long cold winters and heavy snowfall

continental divide an elevated area that separates rivers flowing toward opposite sides of a continent; in the U.S. this divide follows the crest of the Rocky Mountains

copra dried coconut meat from which oil is extracted to make a variety of products, including soap, candles, and cosmetics

Creole a simplified or modified form of a language, such as French or Spanish, used for communication between two groups; spoken in some Caribbean islands

delta lowland formed by silt, sand, and gravel deposited by a river at its mouth

desert vegetation plants such as cactus and dry shrubs that have adapted to conditions of low, often irregular precipitation

fork in a river, the place where two streams join

Fortune 500 company ranking of the top 500 U.S. companies based on total revenue

fossil remains of or an impression left by the remains of plants or animals preserved in rock

geothermal energy a clean, renewable form of energy derived from heat that flows continuously from Earth's interior

grassland areas with medium to short grasses; found where precipitation is not sufficient to support tree growth

gross domestic product (GDP) the total value of goods and services produced in a country in a year

highland climate found in association with high mountains where elevation affects temperature and precipitation

hundredweight in the U.S., a commercial unit of measure equal to 100 pounds

ice age a very long period of cold climate when glaciers often cover large areas of land

intermittent river/lake a stream or lake that contains water only part of the time, usually after heavy rain or snowmelt

lava molten rock from Earth's interior that flows out on the surface during volcanic activity

levee an embankment, usually earth or concrete, built to prevent a river from overflowing

lignite low-grade coal used mainly to produce heat in thermal-electric generators

marine west coast climate type of mild climate found on the mid-latitude West Coast of the U.S.

Mediterranean climate type of mild climate found on the West Coast of the U.S., south of the marine west coast climate

mesa an eroded plateau, broader than it is high, that is found in arid or semiarid regions

metropolitan area a city and its surrounding suburbs or communities

mild climate moderate temperatures with distinct seasons and ample precipitation

nursery stock young plants, including fruits, vegetables, shrubs, and trees, raised in a greenhouse or nursery

pinnacle a tall pillar of rock standing alone or on a summit

plain a large area of relatively flat land that is often covered with grasses

plateau a relatively flat area, larger than a mesa, that rises above the surrounding landscape

population density the average number of people living on each square mile or square kilometer of a specific land area

precipitate process of depositing dissolved minerals as water evaporates, as in limestone caves

rangeland areas of grass prairie that are used for grazing livestock

reactor a device that uses controlled nuclear fission to divide an atomic nucleus to generate power

Richter scale ranking of the power of an earthquake; the higher the number, the stronger the quake

Rust Belt a region made up of northeastern and midwestern states that have experienced a decline in heavy industry and an out-migration of population

scale on a map, a means of explaining the relationship between distances on the map and actual distances on Earth's surface

stalactite column of limestone hanging from the ceiling of a cave that forms as underground water drips down and evaporates, leaving dissolved minerals behind

stalagmite column of limestone that forms on the floor of a cave when underground water drips down and evaporates, leaving dissolved minerals behind

staple main item in an economy; also, main food for domestic consumption

Sunbelt a region made up of southern and western states that are experiencing major in-migration of population and rapid economic growth

territory land that is under the jurisdiction of a country but that is not a state or a province

tropical zone the area bounded by the Tropic of Cancer and the Tropic of Capricorn, where it is usually warm year-round

tundra vegetation plants, often stunted in size, that have adapted to periods of extreme cold and a short growing season; found in polar regions and high elevations

urban areas in which natural vegetation has been replaced by towns or cities, where the main economic activity is nonagricultural

volcanic pipe a vertical opening beneath a volcano through which molten rock has passed

wetland land that is either covered with or saturated by water; includes swamps, marshes, and bogs

OUTSIDE WEB SITES

The following Web sites will provide you with additional valuable information about various topics discussed in this atlas. You can find direct links to each by going to the atlas URL (www.nationalgeographic .com/kids-usa-atlas) and clicking on "Resources."

General information:
    States: www.state.al.us (This is for Alabama; for each state insert the two-letter state abbreviation where "al" is now.)

D.C. and the Territories:
    Washington, D.C.: http://kids.dc.gov/kids_main_content.html
    American Samoa: www.samoanet.com
    Guam: http://ns.gov.gu/
    Northern Marianas: www.saipan.com/gov
    Puerto Rico: www.prstar.net
    U.S. Virgin Islands: www.gov.vi

Natural Environment:
    Biomes: http://www.blueplanetbiomes.org
    Climate: http://www.eoearth.org/
    Global Warming: http://www.nrdc.org/globalWarming/

Climate:
    http://www.noaa.gov/climate.html
    http://www.worldclimate.com (for cities)
    http://www.cpc.noaa.gov/

Natural Hazards:
    General: http://www.usgs.gov/hazards/
    Droughts: http://www.drought.unl.edu/DM/monitor.html
    Earthquakes: http://earthquake.usgs.gov/
    Hurricanes: http://hurricanes.noaa.gov/
    Tornados: http://www.tornadoproject.com/
    Tsunamis: http://www.noaa.gov/tsunamis.html
    Volcanoes: http://www.geo.mtu.edu/volcanoes
    Wildfires: http://www.nifc.gov. and http://www.fs.fed.us/fire/

Population:
    States: http://quickfacts.census.gov/qfd/
    Cities: http://www.city-data.com/
    Population migration: http://www.census.gov/prod/2001pubs/p23-204.pdf
    Hispanic population: http://www.census.gov/prod/2003pubs/p20-545.pdf

Getting Green:
    http://www.epa.gov/
    http://www.earthday.net/Footprint/index.asp
    http://www.footprintnetwork.org/index.php

Bird sounds:
    http://www.animalbehaviorarchive.org/loginPublic.do

Mapping site:
    http://earth.google.com/

PLACE-NAME INDEX

Map references are in boldface (**50**) type. Letters and numbers following in lightface (D12) locate the place-names using the map grid. (Refer to page 7 for more details.)

A

Abbeville, AL **61** G6
Abbeville, LA **71** G4
Abbeville, SC **76** C2
Aberdeen, MD **39** A8
Aberdeen, MS **73** C5
Aberdeen, SD **111** B8
Aberdeen, WA **152** D2
Abert, Lake, OR **149** F5
Abilene, KS **97** C7
Abilene, TX **127** D5
Abingdon, VA **80** E3
Abraham Lincoln Birthplace National Historic Site, KY **69** D6
Absaroka Range, MT, WY **155** A3
Absecon, NJ **45** H3
Acadia N.P., ME **37** G6
Ada, OK **125** D9
Adak Island, AK **135** H8
Adams, MA **40** A1
Adamsville, RI **51** E7
Adel, GA **67** H4
Adirondack Mountains, NY **47** B7
Adirondack Park, NY **47** C7
Admiralty Island Nat. Mon., AK **135** F10
Adrian, MI **99** I7
Afognak Island, AK **135** F6
Afton, WY **154** E1
Agana *see* Hagåtña, GU **156** F1
Agat, GU **156** G1
Agate Fossil Beds Nat. Mon., NE **104** B1
Agattu Island, AK **135** H6
Agawam, MA **41** D3
Agua Fria (river), AZ **121** E4
Agua Fria Nat. Mon., AZ **121** E4
Aguadilla, PR **157** H9
Aguijan (island), MP **156** D1
Ahoskie, NC **75** B9
Aiken, SC **77** E4
Ainsworth, NE **105** B5
Aitkin, MN **101** D4
Ajo, AZ **121** G3
Akron, CO **139** B8
Akron, OH **109** B6
Alabama (river), AL **61** F3
Alabaster, AL **61** D3
Alagnak N.W.&S.R., AK **135** F5
Alamogordo, NM **123** G5
Alamosa, CO **139** F4
Alamosa (river), CO **139** F4
Alao, AS **156** H2
Alapaha (river), GA **67** H4
Alaska Highway, AK **135** E8
Alaska Peninsula, AK **134** G3
Alaska Range, AK **135** E6
Alaska, Gulf of, AK **135** G7
Alatna N.W.&S.R., AK **135** B6
Albany, GA **67** G3
Albany, KY **69** E7
Albany, NY **47** E8
Albany, OR **149** C2
Albemarle, NC **75** C5
Albemarle Sound, NC **75** B10
Albert Lea, MN **101** H4
Albertville, AL **61** B4
Albion, MI **99** H6
Albion, NE **105** C7
Albuquerque, NM **123** D4
Alburg, VT **53** A1
Alcoa, TN **79** C8
Alder Lake, WA **153** E4
'Alenuihaha Channel, HI **141** D7
Aleutian Islands, AK **135** G6
Aleutian World War II National Historic Area, AK **134** H2
Alexander Archipelago, AK **135** F9
Alexander City, AL **61** D5
Alexandria, IN **93** D4
Alexandria, LA **71** D4
Alexandria, MN **101** E2
Alexandria, SD **111** E9
Alexandria, VA **81** B10
Algoma, WI **113** E7
Algona, IA **95** B4
Alibates Flint Quarries Nat. Mon., TX **127** B4
Alice, TX **127** H6
Aliceville, AL **61** D1
Aliquippa, PA **48** D1
Allagash (river), ME **37** B4
Allagash, ME **37** A4
Allagash Lake, ME **37** C4
Allagash Wilderness Waterway, ME **37** C4
Allatoona Lake, GA **67** C2
Allegheny (river), PA **48** D2
Allegheny Mountains, **28** G2
Allegheny N.W.&S.R., PA **49** B3
Allegheny Portage Railroad National Historic Site, PA **49** D4
Allegheny Reservoir, PA **49** A3
Allendale, SC **77** F4
Allenton, RI **51** E4
Allentown, PA **49** D9
Alliance, NE **104** B2
Alliance, OH **109** C7
Alligator (river), NC **75** B10
Alma, MI **99** G6
Alma, NE **105** E6
Alpena, MI **99** E7
Alpine, TX **126** F2
Altamaha (river), GA **67** G6
Altamont, OR **149** G3
Altavista, VA **81** E7
Alton, IL **91** F3
Alton Bay, NH **43** G4
Altoona, PA **49** D4
Altoona, WI **113** D3
Alturas, CA **137** A4
Altus, OK **125** E6
Altus, Lake, OK **125** D6
Alva, OK **125** A7
Amana Colonies (site), IA **95** D8
Amanave, AS **156** I1
Amarillo, TX **127** B3
Amchitka Island, AK **135** H7
American Falls, ID **143** H4
American Falls Reservoir, ID **143** H4
American N.W.&S.R., CA **137** D3
American Samoa (territory), US **156** G4
American, North Fork N.W.&S.R., CA **137** C4
Americus, GA **67** F3
Ames, IA **95** D5
Amesbury, MA **41** A7
Amherst, MA **41** C3
Amherst, NY **46** D2
Amistad N.R.A., TX **127** F4
Amistad Reservoir, TX **127** F4
Amite, LA **71** F7
Amlia Island, AK **135** H9
Ammonoosuc (river), NH **43** D3
Amory, MS **73** C5
Amsterdam, NY **47** D8
Anaconda, MT **144** D3
Anacortes, WA **153** B3
Anadarko, OK **125** D7
Anamosa, IA **95** C9
Anchorage, AK **135** E6
Andalusia, AL **61** G4
Anderson, IN **93** D4
Anderson, SC **76** C2
Anderson Ranch Reservoir, ID **143** G2
Andersonville National Historic Site, GA **67** F3
Andreafsky N.W.&S.R., AK **135** D4
Andreanof Islands, AK **135** H8
Andrew Johnson National Historic Site, TN **79** B10
Andrews, TX **127** D3
Androscoggin (river), ME, NH **43** C4
Angola, IN **93** A5
Aniak, AK **135** E4
Aniakchak N.W.&S.R., AK **135** G4
Aniakchak Nat. Mon. and Preserve, AK **135** G4
Ankeny, IA **95** D5
Ann Arbor, MI **99** H7
Ann, Cape, MA **41** A8
Anna, IL **91** I4
Anna, Lake, VA **81** C9
Annapolis, MD **39** C8
Anniston, AL **61** C5
Ansonia, CT **33** D3
Anthony, KS **97** E6
Anthony, NM **123** H4
Anthony, RI **51** D4
Antietam N.B., MD **39** B5
Antigo, WI **113** D5
Antlers, OK **125** E11
Antrim, NH **43** H2
Apache-Sitgreaves National Forests, AZ, NM **121** E7
Apalachicola (river), FL **65** B3
Apishapa (river), CO **139** F7
Apostle Islands, WI **113** A4
Apostle Islands National Lakeshore, WI **113** A3
Appalachian Mountains, **56** C5
Appalachian National Scenic Trail, **47** G7
Appalachian Plateau, **28** F2
Apple (river), WI **113** D2
Appleton, WI **113** E6
Appomattox, VA **81** D7
Appomattox (river), VA **81** D8
Appomattox Court House N.H.P., VA **81** D7
Arapaho N.R.A., CO **139** B5
Arbuckle Mountains, OK **125** E8
Arcadia, FL **65** F7
Archbald, PA **49** B9
Arches N.P., UT **151** E6
Arco, ID **143** G4
Ardmore, OK **125** E9
Arecibo, PR **157** H10
Arena, Point, CA **137** D1
Arikaree (river), CO **139** C8
Arkabutla Lake, MS **73** A3
Arkadelphia, AR **63** E3
Arkansas (river), **56** C1
Arkansas City, KS **97** F7
Arkansas Post National Memorial, AR **63** E6
Arlington, TX **127** D7
Arlington, VA **81** B10
Arlington, VT **53** H2
Arlington Heights, IL **91** B5
Armour, SD **111** E8
Aroostook (river), ME **37** C5
Arroyo del Macho (river), NM **123** F5
Artesia, NM **123** G6
Arvada, CO **139** C5
Arvon, Mount, MI **99** C3
Asbury Park, NJ **45** E5
Ash Lawn-Highland (site), VA **81** C8
Ashaway, RI **51** F2
Ashdown, AR **63** F1
Asheboro, NC **75** B6
Asheville, NC **74** C2
Ashland, KY **69** B10
Ashland, ME **37** B5
Ashland, NE **105** D9
Ashland, NH **43** F3
Ashland, OH **109** C5
Ashland, OR **149** G2
Ashland, VA **81** D9
Ashland, WI **113** A3
Ashley, ND **107** F7
Ashtabula, OH **109** A7
Ashtabula, Lake, ND **107** D9
Ashton, RI **51** A4
Ashuelot (river), NH **43** I1
Ashwaubenon, WI **113** E7
Aspen, CO **139** D3
Assateague Island, MD **39** F11
Assateague Island National Seashore, MD, VA **39** F11
Assawoman Canal, DE **35** I7
Assawompset Pond, MA **41** D8
Astoria, OR **148** A1
Atascadero, CA **137** G3
Atchafalaya (river), LA **71** F5
Atchafalaya Bay, LA **71** H5
Atchison, KS **97** B9
Athens, AL **61** A3
Athens, GA **67** C4
Athens, OH **109** F5
Athens, TN **79** C8
Athol, MA **41** B4
Atka Island, AK **135** H9
Atkinson, NE **105** B6
Atkinson, NH **43** I4
Atlanta, GA **67** C2
Atlantic, IA **95** E3
Atlantic City, NJ **45** H4
Atlantic City Expressway, NJ **45** G2
Atmore, AL **61** H2
Atoka, OK **125** E10
Attleboro, MA **41** D6
Attu Island, AK **135** G6
Atwood Lake, OH **109** C7
Au Sable (river), MI **99** E6
Au Sable N.W.&S.R., MI **99** E7
Aua, AS **156** I2
Aubrey Cliffs, AZ **121** B3
Auburn, AL **61** E5
Auburn, IN **93** B5
Auburn, MA **41** C5
Auburn, ME **37** G3
Auburn, NE **105** D9
Auburn, NY **47** D5
Auburn, WA **153** D4
Audubon Lake, ND **107** C5
Auglaize (river), OH **109** B2
Augusta, GA **67** D6
Augusta, KS **97** E7
Augusta, ME **37** G3
Aunuu (island), AS **156** I2
Aurora, CO **139** C6
Aurora, IL **91** B5
Aurora, MO **103** F3
Aurora, NE **105** D7
Austin, MN **101** H5
Austin, RI **51** E3
Austin, TX **127** F6
Austintown, OH **109** B8
Ava, MO **103** F4
Avery Island, LA **71** G4
Aziscohos Lake, ME **37** E2
Aztec, NM **123** A2
Aztec Ruins Nat. Mon., NM **123** A2

B

B. Everett Jordan Lake, NC **75** B6
Backbone Mountain, MD **38** B1
Bad (river), SD **111** D4
Bad Axe, MI **99** F8
Badlands (region), ND **106** E2
Badlands N.P., SD **110** E2
Bainbridge, GA **67** H2
Baker, MT **145** D11
Baker (river), NH **43** F2
Baker City, OR **149** C8
Baker Island (territory), US **156** F4
Bakersfield, CA **137** G5
Bald Knob, AR **63** C5
Baldwyn, MS **73** B5
Baltic, CT **33** C7
Baltimore, MD **39** B7
Bamberg, SC **77** E5
Bandelier Nat. Mon., NM **123** C4
Bangor, ME **37** F5
Bangor, PA **49** E9
Banks Lake, WA **153** C7
Bannock Range, ID **143** H5
Bantam Lake, CT **33** B3
Bar Harbor, ME **37** G6
Baraboo, WI **113** F5
Baranof Island, AK **135** G10
Barataria Bay, LA **71** H8
Barberton, OH **109** C6
Bardstown, KY **69** C6
Barkhamsted Reservoir, CT **33** A4
Barkley, Lake, KY, TN **68** E3
Barnegat Bay, NJ **45** F5
Barnstable, MA **41** E9
Barnwell, SC **77** E4
Barre, VT **53** D3
Barren (river), KY **69** D5
Barren River Lake, KY **69** E5
Barrington, RI **51** C5
Barrow, AK **135** A5
Barrow, Point, AK **135** A5
Barstow, CA **137** G6
Bartholomew, Bayou (river), LA **71** B4
Bartlesville, OK **125** A10
Bartlett, TN **78** C1
Barton, VT **53** B4
Bastrop, LA **71** A5
Batavia, NY **46** D3
Batesburg-Leesville, SC **77** D4
Batesville, AR **63** B5
Batesville, MS **73** B3
Bath, ME **37** H3
Bath, NY **47** E4
Baton Rouge, LA **71** F6
Batten Kill (river), VT **53** H1
Battle Creek, ID **143** I1
Battle Creek, MI **99** H5
Battle Ground, WA **153** F3
Battle Mountain, NV **147** B4
Baudette, MN **101** A3
Baxter Springs, KS **97** E10
Bay City, MI **99** G7
Bay City, TX **127** G8
Bay Minette, AL **61** H2
Bay St. Louis, MS **73** I4
Bayard, NM **123** G2
Bayonet Point, FL **65** D6
Bayonne, NJ **45** C5
Bayou Bartholomew (river), AR **63** E5
Bayou La Batre, AL **61** I1
Baytown, TX **127** F8
Beach, ND **106** D1
Beach Haven, NJ **45** G4
Beacon, NY **47** G8
Bear, DE **35** B4
Bear (river), ID, WY **143** I5
Bear Creek, AL **61** B2
Bear Creek, CO, KS **139** F8
Bear Creek N.W.&S.R., MI **99** F5
Bear Lake, ID, UT **151** A5
Bear River Migratory Bird Refuge, UT **151** B3
Bear River Range, ID **143** I6
Bearcamp (river), NH **43** F4
Beardstown, IL **91** E2
Beatrice, NE **105** E9
Beatty, NV **147** G5
Beaufort, SC **77** G6
Beaufort Sea, AK **135** A7
Beaumont, TX **127** F9
Beaver, OK **124** A4
Beaver, UT **151** F3
Beaver (river), OK **124** A4
Beaver (river), PA **48** C1
Beaver Creek, KS **96** B1
Beaver Creek, ND **107** F6
Beaver Creek N.W.&S.R., AK **135** C7
Beaver Dam, WI **113** G6
Beaver Falls, PA **48** D1
Beaver Island, MI **99** D5
Beaver Lake (lake), AR **63** A2
Beaverton, OR **149** B2
Becharof Lake, AK **135** F5
Beckley, WV **83** G4
Bedford, IA **95** F4
Bedford, IN **93** G3
Bedford, PA **49** E4
Bedford, VA **81** D6
Beebe, AR **63** C5
Beech Grove, IN **93** E4
Beeville, TX **127** G6
Bel Air, MD **39** A8
Belcourt, ND **107** A6
Belding, MI **99** G5
Belen, NM **123** D4
Belfast, ME **37** G4
Belgrade, MT **145** E5
Bella Vista, AR **63** A1
Bellaire, OH **109** E8
Belle Fourche, SD **110** C1
Belle Fourche (river), SD, WY **110** C2
Belle Glade, FL **65** F9
Bellefontaine, OH **109** D3
Bellefonte, DE **35** A5
Belleville, IL **91** G3
Belleville, KS **97** A6
Bellevue, NE **105** C9
Bellevue, OH **109** B4
Bellevue, WA **153** C4
Bellingham, MA **41** D6
Bellingham, WA **153** A3
Bellows Falls, VT **53** H4
Belmar, NJ **45** E5
Beloit, KS **97** B6
Beloit, WI **113** H6
Belpre, OH **109** F6
Belted Range, NV **147** F5
Belton, MO **103** C2
Belton, SC **76** C2
Belton, TX **127** E7
Belvidere, IL **91** A4
Bemidji, MN **101** C3
Bend, OR **149** D4
Bennettsville, SC **77** B8
Bennington, VT **53** I1
Benson, AZ **121** H6
Benson, MN **101** F2
Benton, AR **63** D4
Benton, IL **91** H4
Benton Harbor, MI **99** H4
Bentonville, AR **63** A1
Bent's Old Fort National Historic Site, CO **139** E7
Berea, KY **69** D8
Beresford, SD **111** F10
Bering Sea, AK **134** F2
Bering Strait, AK **134** C2
Berkeley, CA **137** E2
Berkeley (site), VA **81** D10
Berkeley Heights, NJ **45** C4
Berlin, MD **39** E11
Berlin, NH **43** C4
Berlin Lake, OH **109** C7
Bernalillo, NM **123** C4
Bernardsville, NJ **45** C3
Berryville, AR **63** A2
Bessemer, AL **61** D3
Bethany, MO **103** A3
Bethany, OK **125** C8
Bethany Beach, DE **35** I7
Bethel, AK **135** E4
Bethel, CT **33** D2
Bethel, ME **37** G2
Bethesda, MD **39** C6
Bethlehem, CT **33** C3
Bethlehem, PA **49** D9
Bettendorf, IA **95** D10

Beulah — Cascade

Beulah, ND **107** D4
Beverly, MA **41** B8
Biddeford, ME **37** H2
Big Bend N.P., TX **127** F3
Big Black (river), MS **73** E2
Big Blue (river), KS, NE **97** A7
Big Blue (river), IN **93** E4
Big Canyon (river), TX **127** F3
Big Coal (river), WV **83** G3
Big Cypress National Preserve, FL **65** G8
Big Cypress Swamp, FL **65** G8
Big Darby Creek, OH **109** D3
Big Darby Creek National Scenic River, OH **109** E4
Big Eau Pleine Reservoir, WI **113** D4
Big Fork (river), MN **101** B4
Big Hole N.B., MT **144** E3
Big Lake, ME **37** E6
Big Lost (river), ID **143** G4
Big Marsh Creek N.W.&S.R., OR **149** E3
Big Muddy (river), IL **91** H4
Big Nemaha (river), NE **105** E9
Big Piney (river), MO **103** F5
Big Piney Creek, AR **63** C3
Big Piney Creek N.W.&S.R., AR **63** B3
Big Raccoon Creek, IN **93** E2
Big Rapids, MI **99** G5
Big Sandy (river), AZ **121** D3
Big Sandy (river), KY, WV **82** F1
Big Sandy (river), WY **155** F3
Big Sandy Creek, CO **139** D7
Big Sioux (river), IA, SD **94** B1
Big Smoky Valley, NV **147** E4
Big South Fork National River and Recreation Area, KY, TN **79** A7
Big Spring, TX **127** D4
Big Stone Gap, VA **80** E2
Big Stone Lake, MN, SD **101** F1
Big Sunflower (river), MS **73** C2
Big Sur N.W.&S.R., CA **137** F3
Big Thicket National Preserve, TX **127** E9
Big Timber, MT **145** F6
Big Wood (river), ID **143** H3
Bighorn (river), MT, WY **130** C6
Bighorn Canyon N.R.A., MT, WY **145** F8
Bighorn Lake, WY **155** A5
Bighorn Mountains, MT, WY **155** A5
Bill Williams (river), AZ **121** E2
Billings, MT **145** E7
Biloxi, MS **73** I5
Biltmore House (site), NC **74** C2
Bingham, ME **37** E3
Binghamton, NY **47** F6
Birch Creek N.W.&S.R., AK **135** C7
Birmingham, AL **61** C3
Bisbee, AZ **121** H7
Biscayne Bay, FL **65** H9
Biscayne N.P., FL **65** H9
Bishop, CA **137** E5
Bishop Creek Reservoir, NV **147** B6
Bismarck, ND **107** E5
Bison, SD **111** B3
Bistineau, Lake, LA **70** B2
Bitter Creek, UT **151** D7
Bitterroot Range, ID, MT **143** B1
Bixby, OK **125** C10
Black (river), VT **53** G3
Black (river), AR, MO **63** B6
Black (river), AZ **121** F7
Black (river), MI **99** G8
Black (river), NY **47** C6
Black (river), SC **77** E8
Black (river), WI **113** E3
Black Belt (region), AL **61** E2
Black Canyon of the Gunnison N.P., CO **139** D2
Black Creek, MS **73** H5
Black Creek N.W.&S.R., MS **73** H4
Black Hawk, SD **110** D2
Black Hills, SD **110** D1
Black Hills, WY **155** B10
Black Mesa (peak), OK **124** A1
Black Mesa, AZ **121** B6
Black Mountain, KY **69** E10
Black Mountain, NC **74** C3
Black Mountains, AZ **121** C2
Black N.W.&S.R., MI **99** C1
Black Range, NM **123** G2
Black River Falls, WI **113** E3
Black Rock Desert, NV **147** B2
Black Rock Range, NV **147** A2
Black Warrior (river), AL **61** E2
Blackfoot, ID **143** H5
Blackfoot Mountains, ID **143** H5
Blackfoot Reservoir, ID **143** H5
Blacks Fork (river), WY **154** G2
Blacksburg, VA **81** E5
Blackstone, VA **81** E9
Blackstone (river), MA, RI **51** A4
Blackwater (river), MO **103** C3
Blackwell, OK **125** A8
Blades, DE **35** H5
Blair, NE **105** C9
Blakely, GA **67** G1
Blanchard, IA **95** F3
Blanchard (river), OH **109** C2
Blanco, Cape, OR **148** F1
Blanding, UT **151** G6
Block Island, RI **51** I3
Block Island, RI **51** H3
Block Island Sound, NY **47** G11
Bloodsworth Island, MD **39** F9
Bloomfield, CT **33** B5
Bloomfield, IA **95** F7
Bloomfield, NM **123** A2
Blooming Grove, OH **109** C4
Bloomington, IL **91** D4
Bloomington, IN **93** F3
Bloomington, MN **101** F4
Bloomsburg, PA **49** C7
Blue (river), CO **139** C4
Blue (river), IN **93** H3
Blue (river), OK **125** E10
Blue Earth (river), MN **101** H4
Blue Grass Parkway, KY **69** C6
Blue Hill Bay, ME **37** G5
Blue Mesa Reservoir, CO **139** E3
Blue Mountain, NH **43** B3
Blue Mountain, PA **49** D7
Blue Mountains, OR **149** C7
Blue Ridge, GA, NC, VA **56** C5
Blue Ridge Parkway, VA **81** F5
Blue Springs, MO **103** C2
Bluefield, VA **80** E4
Bluefield, WV **83** H3
Bluegrass Region, KY **69** B7
Bluestone (river), WV **83** H3
Bluestone Lake, WV **83** H4
Bluestone National Scenic River, WV **83** H4
Blythe, CA **137** H8
Blytheville, AR **63** B8
Boaz, AL **61** B4
Boca Raton, FL **65** G9
Bogalusa, LA **71** E8
Bogue Chitto (river), LA, MS **71** E8
Bois Blanc Island, MI **99** D6
Bois Brule (river), WI **113** B3
Bois de Sioux (river), MN **101** E1
Boise, ID **143** G1
Boise City, OK **124** A2
Bolivar, MO **103** E3
Bolivar, TN **78** C2
Bombay Hook Island, DE **35** D5
Bomoseen, Lake, VT **53** F1
Bonne Springs, KS **97** B10
Bonners Ferry, ID **143** A1
Bonneville Dam, OR, WA **149** B3
Booker T. Washington Nat. Mon., VA **81** E6
Boone, IA **95** C5
Boone, NC **74** B3
Boone (river), IA **95** B5
Booneville, AR **63** C2
Booneville, MS **73** A5
Boonsboro, MD **39** A5
Boonville, IN **93** I2
Boonville, MO **103** C4
Boothbay Harbor, ME **37** H4
Borah Peak, ID **143** G3
Borger, TX **127** B4
Borgne, Lake, LA **71** G8
Bossier City, LA **70** B1
Boston, MA **41** C7
Boston Harbor Islands N.R.A., MA **41** C7
Boston Mountains, AR **63** B2
Boston N.H.P., MA **41** B7
Bottineau, ND **107** A5
Boulder, CO **139** B5
Boulder City, NV **147** H6
Boundary Peak, NV **147** E3
Boundary Waters Canoe Area Wilderness, MN **101** B5
Bountiful, UT **151** B4
Bow Lake (lake), NH **43** H4
Bowers Beach, DE **35** F6
Bowie, MD **39** C7
Bowling Green, KY **69** E5
Bowling Green, OH **109** B3
Bowman, ND **106** F2
Boyer (river), IA **95** D3
Boyne City, MI **99** E6
Boysen Reservoir, WY **155** D5
Bozeman, MT **145** E5
Bradenton, FL **65** E6
Bradford, PA **49** A4
Bradford, RI **51** F2
Bradford, VT **53** E4
Brady, TX **127** E5
Brainerd, MN **101** D4
Brandenburg, KY **69** C5
Brandon, MS **73** F3
Brandon, VT **53** E2
Brandywine, DE **35** A5
Brandywine Creek, DE **35** A5
Branford, CT **33** E4
Branson, MO **103** F3
Brantley Lake, NM **123** G7
Brasstown Bald (peak), GA **67** A3
Brattleboro, VT **53** I3
Brazil, IN **93** F2
Brazos (river), TX **127** C5
Breaks Interstate Park, KY **69** D11
Breaux Bridge, LA **71** F4
Breckenridge, TX **127** D5
Bremerton, WA **153** C3
Brenham, TX **127** F7
Brentwood, NY **47** H9
Brentwood, TN **79** B5
Breton Islands, LA **71** H10
Breton Sound, LA **71** H9
Brevard, NC **74** C2
Brewer, ME **37** F5
Brewton, AL **61** H3
Brices Cross Roads National Battlefield Site, MS **73** B5
Bridgeport, CT **33** E3
Bridgeport, NE **104** C2
Bridgeport, WV **83** D5
Bridgeton, NJ **45** H1
Bridgeville, DE **35** H5
Bridgewater, MA **41** D7
Bridgewater, VA **81** C7
Bridgton, ME **37** G2
Brigantine, NJ **45** H4
Brigham City, UT **151** A4
Brighton, CO **139** B6
Brinkley, AR **63** D6
Bristol, NH **43** F3
Bristol, RI **51** D6
Bristol, TN **79** A11
Bristol, VA **80** F3
Bristol, VT **53** D2
Bristol Bay, AK **135** F4
Bristow, OK **125** C10
Britton, SD **111** A8
Britton Hill (peak), FL **64** A2
Broad (river), GA **67** C5
Broad (river), NC, SC **77** A4
Broad Brook, CT **33** A5
Broadkill Beach, DE **35** G7
Broadus, MT **145** E10
Brockton, MA **41** D7
Broken Arrow, OK **125** B10
Broken Bow, NE **105** C5
Broken Bow, OK **125** E12
Broken Bow Lake, OK **125** E12
Bromley Mountain, VT **53** G2
Brookfield, MO **103** B4
Brookfield, WI **113** G7
Brookhaven, MS **73** G2
Brookings, OR **148** G1
Brookings, SD **111** D10
Brookline, MA **41** C7
Brooklyn, CT **33** B8
Brooklyn Park, MN **101** F4
Brooks Range, AK **135** B4
Brookside, DE **35** B4
Brookville Lake, IN **93** F5
Brown v. Board of Education N.H.S., KS **97** C8
Brownfield, TX **127** D3
Browning, MT **144** B3
Brownlee Reservoir, ID, OR **143** F1
Browns Mills, NJ **45** F3
Brownsville, TN **78** C2
Brownsville, TX **127** I7
Brownville Junction, ME **37** E4
Brownwood, TX **127** E5
Brule (river), MI, WI **113** B6
Bruneau (river), ID, NV **143** H2
Bruneau, East Fork (river), ID **143** I2
Brunswick, GA **67** H7
Brunswick, MD **39** B5
Brunswick, ME **37** H3
Brunswick, OH **109** B6
Brush, CO **139** B7
Bryan, OH **109** B2
Bryan, TX **127** E7
Bryant, AR **63** D4
Bryant Creek, MO **103** F4
Bryce Canyon N.P., UT **151** G3
Buck Creek, OK **125** D5
Buck Island Reef Nat. Mon., VI **157** I8
Buckeye Lake, OH **109** E5
Buckhannon, WV **83** D5
Buckner Creek, KS **97** D3
Bucksport, ME **37** F5
Bucktown, MD **39** E9
Bucyrus, OH **109** C4
Budd Lake, NJ **45** B3
Buena Vista, VA **81** D7
Buffalo, NY **46** D2
Buffalo, OK **125** A5
Buffalo, SD **110** A2
Buffalo (river), TN **79** C4
Buffalo, WY **155** B7
Buffalo (river), AR **63** B2
Buffalo Bill Reservoir, WY **155** B4
Buffalo N.W.&S.R., AR **63** B2
Buffalo National River, AR **63** B3
Buhl, ID **143** I3
Bull Shoals Lake, AR, MO **63** A3
Bullfrog Creek, UT **151** G5
Bullhead City, AZ **121** D2
Bunkie, LA **71** E4
Burien, WA **153** C4
Burkburnett, TX **127** C6
Burke, SD **111** F7
Burley, ID **143** I5
Burlington, CO **139** C9
Burlington, IA **95** F9
Burlington, KS **97** D9
Burlington, NC **75** B6
Burlington, NJ **45** E2
Burlington, VT **53** C1
Burlington, WI **113** H6
Burns, OR **149** E6
Burt Lake, MI **99** D6
Burton, MI **99** G7
Burton, SC **77** G6
Burwell, NE **105** C6
Butler, MO **103** D2
Butler, PA **48** C2
Butte, MT **145** E4
Buzzards Bay, MA **41** E8

C

C.J. Strike Reservoir, ID **143** H1
C.W. McConaughy, Lake, NE **105** C3
Caballo Reservoir, NM **123** G3
Cabinet Mountains, ID, MT **144** A1
Cabot, AR **63** D5
Cabot, Mount, NH **43** C4
Cabrillo Nat. Mon., CA **137** I5
Cacapon (river), WV **83** D8
Cache (river), AR **63** C6
Cache La Poudre N.W.&S.R., CO **139** A5
Cactus Range, NV **147** F4
Caddo Lake, LA **70** A1
Cadillac, MI **99** F5
Cadillac Mountain, ME **37** G6
Caesar Creek Lake, OH **109** F2
Cagles Mill Lake, IN **93** F2
Caguas, PR **157** I11
Cahaba (river), AL **61** E3
Cairo, GA **67** H3
Cairo, IL **91** I4
Calais, ME **37** E7
Calamus (river), NE **105** B5
Calamus Reservoir, NE **105** B6
Calcasieu (river), LA **71** F3
Calcasieu Lake, LA **70** G2
Caldwell, ID **143** G1
Caldwell, NJ **45** C4
Caledonia, MN **101** H6
Calexico, CA **137** I7
Calhoun, GA **67** B2
Caliente, NV **147** F7
California, MO **103** D4
California, Gulf of, **116** F1
Caloosahatchee (river), FL **65** F8
Calvert City, KY **68** E2
Camas, WA **153** G3
Cambridge, MA **41** B7
Cambridge, MD **39** D9
Cambridge, NE **105** E5
Cambridge, OH **109** E6
Camden, AR **63** F3
Camden, DE **35** E5
Camden, ME **37** G4
Camden, NJ **45** F2
Camden, SC **77** C6
Camels Hump (peak), VT **53** C2
Cameron, MO **103** B2
Camilla, GA **67** H3
Campbell Hill (peak), OH **109** D3
Campbellsville, KY **69** D6
Campe Verde, AZ **121** D5
Canaan, CT **33** A2
Canaan, NH **43** F2
Canaan, VT **53** A6
Canadian (river), NM, OK, TX **116** C6
Canadian, North (river), OK **125** B6
Canandaigua, NY **47** D4
Canaveral National Seashore, FL **65** C8
Canaveral, Cape, FL **65** D9
Candlewood, Lake, CT **33** D2
Cando, ND **107** B7
Cane River Creole N.H.P. and Heritage Area, LA **70** D2
Caney (river), KS, OK **125** A10
Caney Fork (river), TN **79** C6
Cannonball (river), ND **107** E3
Cañon City, CO **139** E5
Cañon Largo (river), NM **123** B3
Canoochee (river), GA **67** F6
Canterbury, NH **43** G3
Canton, IL **91** D3
Canton, MO **103** A5
Canton, MS **73** E3
Canton, OH **109** C7
Canton, SD **111** E10
Canyon, TX **127** B3
Canyon Creek, ID **143** H1
Canyon de Chelly Nat. Mon., AZ **121** B7
Canyon Ferry Lake, MT **145** D5
Canyonlands N.P., UT **151** F6
Canyons of the Ancients Nat. Mon., CO **138** F1
Cap Rock Escarpment, TX **127** D4
Cape Charles, VA **81** D11
Cape Cod Bay, MA **41** D9
Cape Cod Canal, MA **41** D8
Cape Cod National Seashore, MA **41** D10
Cape Coral, FL **65** G7
Cape Elizabeth, ME **37** H3
Cape Fear (river), NC **75** D7
Cape Girardeau, MO **103** E8
Cape Hatteras National Seashore, NC **75** C11
Cape Island, SC **77** F8
Cape Krusenstern Nat. Mon., AK **135** B4
Cape Lookout National Seashore, NC **75** D10
Cape May, NJ **45** I2
Cape May Canal, NJ **45** I2
Cape May Court House, NJ **45** I3
Capitol Hill, MP **156** C2
Capitol Reef N.P., UT **151** F5
Captain Cook, HI **141** F8
Capulin Volcano Nat. Mon., NM **123** A7
Carbondale, CO **139** C3
Carbondale, IL **91** H4
Carbondale, PA **49** B9
Caribou, ME **37** B6
Caribou Range, ID **143** G6
Carl Sandburg Home National Historic Site, NC **74** C3
Carlin, NV **147** B5
Carlinville, IL **91** F3
Carlisle, PA **49** E6
Carlsbad, NM **123** G7
Carlsbad Caverns N.P., NM **123** H6
Carlyle Lake, IL **91** G4
Carmel, IN **93** E4
Carmi, IL **91** H5
Caro, MI **99** G7
Carolina, PR **157** H11
Carolina, RI **51** F3
Carp N.W.&S.R., MI **99** D5
Carrington, ND **107** D7
Carrizo Creek, NM **123** B7
Carrizo Plain Nat. Mon., CA **137** G4
Carrizo Springs, TX **127** G5
Carrizozo, NM **123** F5
Carroll, IA **95** C3
Carrollton, GA **67** D1
Carson (river), NV **147** D2
Carson City, NV **147** D2
Carson Sink (river), NV **147** C3
Carthage, IL **91** D2
Carthage, MO **103** F2
Carthage, MS **73** E4
Caruthersville, MO **103** G8
Cary, NC **75** B7
Casa Grande, AZ **121** F5
Casa Grande Ruins Nat. Mon., AZ **121** F5
Cascade, ID **143** F1

Cascade Range — Crossville

Cascade Range, **130** C2
Cascade Siskiyou Nat. Mon., OR **149** G3
Cascade, Lake, ID **143** F1
Casco Bay, ME **37** H3
Casper, WY **155** D7
Cass (river), MI **99** G7
Casselman (river), PA **49** F3
Casselton, ND **107** D9
Castillo de San Marcos Nat. Mon., FL **65** B8
Castine, ME **37** G5
Castle Dale, UT **151** E5
Castle Rock, CO **139** C6
Castle Rock Lake, WI **113** F5
Castleton, VT **53** F2
Catahoula Lake, LA **71** D4
Catalina, AZ **121** G6
Cataño, PR **157** H11
Catawba (river), NC, SC **77** B5
Cathedral Bluffs, CO **138** B1
Catoctin Mountain Park, MD **39** A5
Catonsville, MD **39** B7
Catskill, NY **47** E8
Catskill Mountains, NY **47** F8
Catskill Park, NY **47** F7
Cattaraugus Creek, NY **46** E2
Cavalier, ND **107** A9
Cave City, KY **69** D6
Cave Run Lake, KY **69** C9
Cayce, SC **77** D5
Cayey, PR **157** I11
Cayuga Lake, NY **47** E5
Cecil M. Harden Lake, IN **93** E2
Cedar (river), NE **105** C6
Cedar (river), IA **95** A6
Cedar (river), MI **99** D3
Cedar Bluff Reservoir, KS **97** C3
Cedar Breaks Nat. Mon., UT **151** G2
Cedar City, UT **151** G2
Cedar Creek, ND **106** E2
Cedar Creek, IN **93** B5
Cedar Creek Reservoir, ID **143** I2
Cedar Falls, IA **95** C7
Cedar Rapids, IA **95** D8
Celina, OH **109** D2
Centennial Mountains, ID **143** F5
Center, ND **107** D4
Center Hill Lake, TN **79** B6
Center Ossipee, NH **43** F4
Center Point, AL **61** C3
Center Sandwich, NH **43** F4
Centereach, NY **47** H9
Centerville, IA **95** F6
Centerville, OH **109** E2
Centerville, UT **151** B4
Central City, IA **95** C8
Central City, NE **105** C7
Central Falls, RI **51** B5
Central Lowland (plain), **86** E5
Central Point, OR **149** F2
Central Valley, CA **137** B2
Centralia, IL **91** G4
Centralia, MO **103** C5
Centralia, WA **153** E3
Centreville, MS **73** H1
Cerro de Punta (mountains), PR **157** I10
Chaco Culture N.H.P., NM **123** B2
Chacuaco Canyon, CO **139** F7
Chadron, NE **104** A2
Challis, ID **143** F3
Chalmette, LA **71** G8
Chama, NM **123** A4
Chamberlain, SD **111** D7
Chamberlain Lake, ME **37** C4
Chambersburg, PA **49** E5
Champaign, IL **91** E5
Champlain, Lake, NY, VT **47** B9
Chandeleur Islands, LA **71** G10
Chandeleur Sound, LA **71** G10
Chandler, AZ **121** F5
Channel Islands, CA **137** H3
Channel Islands N.P., CA **137** H3
Channel Islands National Marine Sanctuary, CA **137** H4
Chanute, KS **97** E9
Chaparral, NM **123** H4
Chapel Hill, NC **75** B6
Chappaquiddick Island, MA **41** F9
Chariton, IA **95** E6
Chariton (river), IA, MO **103** B4
Charles (river), MA **41** C6
Charles City, IA **95** B7
Charles Mound, IL **91** A3
Charles Pinckney National Historic Site, SC **77** F8
Charles Town, WV **83** D10
Charleston, IL **91** F5
Charleston, MO **103** F8
Charleston, SC **77** G7
Charleston, WV **83** F3
Charlestown, IN **93** H4
Charlestown, NH **43** G1
Charlestown, RI **51** G3
Charley N.W.&S.R., AK **135** C7
Charlotte, MI **99** H6
Charlotte, NC **75** C4
Charlotte Amalie, VI **157** G7
Charlotte Harbor, FL **65** F7
Charlottesville, VA **81** C8
Chatham, MA **41** E10
Chattahoochee (river), AL, GA **56** D5
Chattahoochee River N.R.A., GA **67** C2
Chattanooga, TN **79** D6
Chattooga (river), SC **76** B1
Chattooga N.W.&S.R., GA, NC, SC **67** A4
Chautauqua Lake, NY **46** E1
Cheaha Mountain, AL **61** C5
Cheat (river), WV **83** C6
Cheat Mountain, WV **83** F6
Cheboygan, MI **99** D6
Checotah, OK **125** C11
Cheektowaga, NY **46** D2
Cheesequake, NJ **45** D4
Chehalis, WA **153** E3
Chehalis (river), WA **152** D2
Chelan, Lake, WA **153** B6
Chelmsford, MA **41** B6
Chemung (river), NY **47** E4
Cheney, WA **153** C9
Cheney Reservoir, KS **97** D6
Chepachet, RI **51** B3
Cheraw, SC **77** B7
Cherokee, IA **94** B2
Cherokee Lake, TN **79** A9
Cherokee Village, AR **63** A5
Cherokees, Lake O' The, OK **125** A11
Cherry Creek, SD **111** C3
Cherry Creek Range, NV **147** C6
Cherry Hill, NJ **45** F2
Chesapeake, VA **81** E11
Chesapeake and Delaware Canal, DE, MD **35** C4
Chesapeake and Ohio Canal, MD **38** A2
Chesapeake and Ohio Canal N.H.P., MD **39** B5
Chesapeake Bay, MD, VA **28** H4
Chesapeake Bay Bridge *see* William Preston Lane Jr. Memorial Bridge, MD **39** C8
Chesapeake Bay Bridge-Tunnel, VA **81** E11
Chesapeake Beach, MD **39** D8
Cheshire, CT **33** D4
Cheshire Reservoir, MA **40** B1
Chester, IL **91** H3
Chester, PA **49** F9
Chester, SC **77** B5
Chester, VA **81** D9
Chester, VT **53** G3
Chester, WV **83** A5
Chester (bay), MD **39** C8
Chesterfield, CT **33** D7
Chestertown, MD **39** B9
Chesuncook Lake, ME **37** D4
Cheswold, DE **35** E5
Chetco (river), OR **148** G1
Chetco N.W.&S.R., OR **148** G1
Chevelon Creek, AZ **121** D6
Cheyenne, WY **155** G9
Cheyenne (river), SD, WY **111** C3
Cheyenne Bottoms (lake), KS **97** C5
Cheyenne Wells, CO **139** D9
Chicago, IL **91** B6
Chichagof Island, AK **135** F9
Chickamauga and Chattanooga N.M.P., GA, TN **67** A1
Chickamauga Lake, TN **79** C7
Chickasaw N.R.A., OK **125** E9
Chickasawhay (river), MS **73** G5
Chickasha, OK **125** D8
Chico, CA **137** C3
Chicopee (river), MA **41** C3
Chicopee, MA **41** C3
Chikaskia (river), OK **125** A8
Childress, TX **127** C5
Chilikadrotna N.W.&S.R., AK **135** E5
Chillicothe, IL **91** C3
Chillicothe, MO **103** B3
Chillicothe, OH **109** F4
Chimayo, NM **123** B5
Chimney Rock National Historic Site, NE **104** C1
Chincoteague, VA **81** C12
Chincoteague Bay, MD **39** F11
Chinle, AZ **121** B7
Chinle Wash (river), AZ **121** A7
Chino Valley, AZ **121** D4
Chinook, MT **145** B7
Chippewa (river), MN **101** E2
Chippewa (river), WI **113** C3
Chippewa Falls, WI **113** D3
Chippewa, Lake, WI **113** B3
Chiputneticook Lakes, ME **37** D6
Chiricahua Nat. Mon., AZ **121** H7
Chisholm, MN **101** C5
Chittenden Reservoir, VT **53** E2
Choctawhatchee (river), AL, FL **64** B2
Choptank (bay), MD **39** D8
Choptank (river), MD **39** D9
Choteau, MT **145** B4
Chowan (river), NC **75** A9
Christiansburg, VA **81** E5
Christiansted, VI **157** I8
Christiansted National Historic Site, VI **157** I7
Christina (river), DE **35** B4
Christmas Lake Valley, OR **149** E5
Chubbuck, ID **143** H5
Chugach Mountains, AK **135** E7
Chukchi Sea, AK **134** A3
Chula Vista, CA **137** I6
Church Hill, TN **79** A10
Churchill Lake, ME **37** C4
Cicero, IL **91** B5
Cimarron (river), CO, KS, OK **125** B7
Cimarron Turnpike, OK **125** B9
Cimarron, North Fork (river), CO, KS **96** E1
Cincinnati, OH **109** G1
Cinnaminson, NJ **45** F2
Circle, MT **145** C10
Circleville, OH **109** F4
Citronelle, AL **61** H1
City of Rocks National Reserve, ID **143** I4
Clackamas N.W.&S.R., OR **149** C3
Clan Alpine Mountains, NV **147** D3
Clanton, AL **61** E3
Clara Barton National Historic Site, MD **39** C6
Claremont, NH **43** G1
Claremore, OK **125** B10
Clarinda, IA **95** F3
Clarion, PA **49** C3
Clarion (river), PA **49** C3
Clarion N.W.&S.R., PA **49** C3
Clark, SD **111** C9
Clark Fork (river), MT **144** B1
Clarks Fork (river), MT **145** E7
Clarks Fork Yellowstone N.W.&S.R., WY **155** A3
Clarksburg, WV **83** D5
Clarksdale, MS **73** B2
Clarkston, WA **153** E10
Clarksville, AR **63** C2
Clarksville, TN **79** A4
Clay Center, KS **97** B7
Claymont, DE **35** A6
Clayton, DE **35** D4
Clayton, NM **123** B8
Clear Creek, AZ **121** D5
Clear Creek, WY **155** A7
Clear Lake, CA **137** C2
Clear Lake, IA **95** A5
Clear Lake, SD **111** C10
Clearfield, PA **49** C4
Clearfield, UT **151** B3
Clearwater, FL **65** E6
Clearwater, SC **77** E3
Clearwater (river), ID **143** D1
Clearwater Mountains, ID **143** D2
Clearwater, Middle Fork N.W.&S.R., ID **143** D2
Clearwater, North Fork (river), ID **143** D2
Clearwater, South Fork (river), ID **143** E2
Clemson, SC **76** B2
Cleveland, MS **73** C2
Cleveland, OH **109** B6
Cleveland, TN **79** D7
Clifton, AZ **121** F7
Clifton, NJ **45** B4
Clifton Forge, VA **81** D6
Clinch (river), TN, VA **79** A9
Clinch Mountain, VA **80** E3
Clingmans Dome (peak), TN **79** C9
Clinton, AR **63** B4
Clinton, CT **33** E5
Clinton, IA **95** D10
Clinton, IL **91** E4
Clinton, IN **93** E2
Clinton, MO **103** D3
Clinton, MS **73** E2
Clinton, NC **75** C7
Clinton, OK **125** C6
Clinton, SC **77** C3
Clinton, TN **79** B8
Cloquet, MN **101** D5
Clovis, NM **123** E8
Clyde (river), VT **53** A5
Coast Mountains, AK **135** E10
Coast Ranges, CA **137** B2
Coast Ranges, **130** B2
Coastal Plain, **56** E2
Coatesville, PA **49** E8
Cobble Mountain Reservoir, MA **40** C2
Cobleskill, NY **47** E7
Cocheco (river), NH **43** G5
Cochetopa Hills, CO **139** E4
Cockeysville, MD **39** A7
Coconino Plateau, AZ **121** C4
Cod, Cape, MA **41** E9
Cody, WY **155** B4
Coeur d'Alene, ID **143** B1
Coeur d'Alene (river), ID **143** C1
Coeur d'Alene Lake, ID **143** C1
Coffeyville, KS **97** F9
Cohansey (river), NJ **45** H1
Colby, KS **96** B2
Colchester, CT **33** C6
Cold Spring, MN **101** F3
Coldwater, MI **99** I6
Coldwater (river), MS **73** B2
Colebrook, NH **43** B3
Coleman, OK **125** E10
Coleman, TX **127** E5
College, AK **135** C7
College Place, WA **153** F8
College Station, TX **127** E7
Collierville, TN **78** D1
Collins, MS **73** G4
Collinsville, CT **33** B4
Collinsville, VA **81** E6
Colonial Beach, VA **81** C10
Colonial N.H.P., VA **81** D10
Colorado (river), **130** H4
Colorado City, AZ **121** A3
Colorado Nat. Mon., CO **138** D1
Colorado Plateau, AZ **116** B2
Colorado Springs, CO **139** D6
Colstrip, MT **145** E9
Columbia, MD **39** B7
Columbia, MO **103** C4
Columbia, MS **73** G3
Columbia, PA **49** E7
Columbia, SC **77** D5
Columbia, TN **79** C4
Columbia (river), OR, WA **149** A2
Columbia City, IN **93** B5
Columbia Falls, MT **144** B2
Columbia Plateau, OR **130** B3
Columbia River Gorge National Scenic Area, OR, WA **153** F4
Columbus, GA **67** F1
Columbus, IN **93** F4
Columbus, KS **97** E10
Columbus, MS **73** C5
Columbus, MT **145** E7
Columbus, NE **105** C8
Columbus, OH **109** E4
Columbus Salt Marsh (river), NV **147** E3
Colville, WA **153** B9
Colville (river), AK **135** B5
Colville (river), WA **153** B9
Combahee (river), SC **77** G6
Combs Mountain Parkway, KY **69** C9
Compensating Reservoir, CT **33** B4
Conanicut Island, RI **51** E5
Conchas (river), NM **123** C6
Conchas Lake, NM **123** C7
Concord, MA **41** B6
Concord, NC **75** C5
Concord, NH **43** H3
Concord (river), MA **41** B6
Concordia, KS **97** B6
Conecuh (river), AL **61** G4
Conejos (river), CO **139** G4
Conemaugh (river), PA **49** D3
Confusion Range, UT **151** D1
Congamond Lakes, CT **33** A4
Congaree (river), SC **77** D5
Congaree N.P., SC **77** D5
Conneaut, OH **109** A8
Connecticut (river), CT, MA, NH, VT **28** D6
Connell, WA **153** E8
Connellsville, PA **48** E2
Connersville, IN **93** E5
Conrad, MT **145** B4
Conroe, TX **127** F8
Continental Divide, CO, ID, MT, NM, WY **143** E4
Contoocook, NH **43** H3
Contoocook (river), NH **43** H3
Conway, AR **63** C4
Conway, NH **43** E4
Conway, SC **77** D9
Conway Lake, NH **43** E4
Cook Inlet, AK **135** E6
Cookeville, TN **79** B6
Coolidge, AZ **121** F5
Coon Rapids, MN **101** F4
Cooper (river), SC **77** F7
Cooperstown, ND **107** D8
Cooperstown, NY **47** E7
Coos (river), OR **148** E1
Coos Bay, OR **148** E1
Coosa (river), AL, GA **61** D4
Coosawattee (river), GA **67** B2
Coosawhatchie (river), SC **77** F5
Copper (river), AK **135** E7
Copperas Cove, TX **127** E6
Coquille, OR **148** E1
Coral Springs, FL **65** G9
Coralville, IA **95** D8
Coram, NY **47** H9
Corbin, KY **69** E8
Cordele, GA **67** F3
Cordell Bank National Marine Sanctuary, CA **137** D1
Cordillera Central (mountains), PR **157** I9
Cordova, AK **135** E7
Core Sound, NC **75** D10
Corinth, MS **73** A5
Corning, AR **63** A7
Corning, NY **47** F4
Coronado Nat. Mon., AZ **121** H6
Corpus Christi, TX **127** H7
Corpus Christi Bay, TX **116** G8
Corrumpa Creek, NM **123** A7
Corry, PA **48** A2
Corsicana, TX **127** D7
Cortez, CO **138** F1
Cortez Mountains, NV **147** C5
Cortland, NY **47** E5
Corvallis, OR **149** C2
Corydon, IN **93** H4
Coshocton, OH **109** D6
Cossatot (river), AR **63** E1
Cossatot N.W.&S.R., AR **63** E1
Coteau des Prairies, SD **111** A9
Cottage Grove, OR **149** D2
Cottonwood, AZ **121** D4
Coudersport, PA **49** B5
Council Bluffs, IA **94** E2
Council Grove, KS **97** C8
Coventry, CT **33** B6
Coventry Center, RI **51** D3
Covington, GA **67** D3
Covington, KY **69** A8
Covington, LA **71** F8
Covington, VA **81** D6
Cowlitz (river), WA **153** E3
Cowpasture (river), VA **81** C6
Cowpens N.B., SC **77** A4
Cozad, NE **105** D5
Craig, CO **139** B2
Crane Creek Reservoir, ID **143** F1
Cranston, RI **51** C4
Crater Lake, OR **149** F3
Crater Lake N.P., OR **149** F3
Craters of the Moon Nat. Mon. and Preserve, ID **143** H4
Crawford, NE **104** A1
Crawfordsville, IN **93** D2
Crazy Horse Memorial, SD **110** D1
Crescent City, CA **137** A1
Crescent Creek N.W.&S.R., OR **149** E3
Cresco, IA **95** A7
Creston, IA **95** E4
Crestview, FL **64** A2
Crestwood Village, NJ **45** F4
Crete, NE **105** D8
Crisfield, MD **39** F9
Crooked (river), OR **149** D5
Crooked N.W.&S.R., OR **149** C4
Crooked, North Fork N.W.&S.R., OR **149** D5
Crookston, MN **101** C1
Crosby, ND **106** A2
Crossett, AR **63** G5
Crossville, TN **79** B7

Crow Agency, MT **145** E8
Crow Creek, CO **139** B6
Crow Creek, SD **111** D7
Crow Wing (river), MN **101** D3
Crow, North Fork (river), MN **101** E3
Crow, South Fork (river), MN **101** F3
Crowley, LA **71** G4
Crowleys Ridge, AR **63** C7
Crown Mountain, VI **157** G7
Crown Point, IN **93** B2
Crownpoint, NM **123** C2
Cruz Bay, VI **157** G8
Crystal Lake, NH **43** G4
Crystal Springs, MS **73** F2
Cuivre (river), MO **103** C6
Culebra Island, PR **157** I12
Culebra Range, CO **139** G5
Cullman, AL **61** B3
Culpeper, VA **81** B8
Cumberland, KY **69** E10
Cumberland, MD **38** A2
Cumberland (river), KY, TN **56** C4
Cumberland Gap, KY, VA **69** E9
Cumberland Gap N.H.P., KY, TN, VA **69** E9
Cumberland Hill, RI **51** A4
Cumberland Island, GA **67** H7
Cumberland Island National Seashore, GA **67** H7
Cumberland Mountains, KY **69** E9
Cumberland Plateau, **56** C5
Cumberland, Lake, KY **69** E7
Curecanti N.R.A., CO **139** E3
Current (river), MO **103** E5
Currituck Sound, NC **75** A10
Cushing, OK **125** C9
Custer, SD **110** D1
Cut Bank, MT **145** A4
Cuyahoga (river), OH **109** B7
Cuyahoga Falls, OH **109** B6
Cuyahoga Valley N.P., OH **109** B6
Cynthiana, KY **69** B8
Cypress Swamp, DE **35** I6

D
Dagsboro, DE **35** I6
Dahlonega, GA **67** B3
Dale City, VA **81** B9
Dale Hollow Lake, KY,TN **79** A7
Daleville, AL **61** G5
Dallas, OR **149** C2
Dallas, TX **127** D7
Dalton, GA **67** B2
Dalton, MA **40** B1
Dan (river), NC, VA **75** A6
Danbury, CT **33** D2
Danforth, ME **37** D6
Danielson, CT **33** B8
Dannemora, NY **47** A8
Dansville, NY **46** E3
Danvers, MA **41** B7
Danville, IL **91** E6
Danville, KY **69** D7
Danville, VA **81** F7
Daphne, AL **61** I1
D'Arbonne, Bayou (river), LA **71** B3
Dardanelle, AR **63** C3
Dardanelle, Lake, AR **63** C2
Darien, CT **33** F2
Darling, Lake, ND **107** B4
Darlington, SC **77** C7
Daufuskie Island, SC **77** H5
Dauphin Island, AL **61** I1
Davenport, IA **95** D9
David Berger National Memorial, OH **109** B6
David City, NE **105** C8
Davis Mountains, TX **126** F2
Davis, Mount, PA **49** F3
Dawson, GA **67** G2
Dayton, NV **147** D2
Dayton, OH **109** E2
Dayton, TN **79** C7
Dayton, WA **153** E9
Dayton Aviation Heritage N.H.P., OH **109** E2
Daytona Beach, FL **65** C8
Dayville, CT **33** B8
De Gray Lake, AR **63** E3
De Land, FL **65** C8
De Pere, WI **113** E7
De Queen, AR **63** E1
De Quincy, LA **70** F2
De Ridder, LA **70** E2
De Smet, SD **111** C9
De Soto, MO **103** D6
De Soto National Memorial, FL **65** E6
De Witt, AR **63** E6
De Witt, IA **95** D9
Dead (river), ME **37** E3
Deadwood, SD **110** C1
Deadwood Reservoir, ID **143** F2
Deale, MD **39** D8
Dearborn, MI **99** H7
Death Valley, CA **137** F6
Death Valley N.P., CA, NV **137** E6
Decatur, AL **61** B3
Decatur, IL **91** E4
Decatur, IN **93** C6
Decorah, IA **95** A8
Dededo, GU **156** F2
Deep (river), NC **75** C6
Deep Creek Lake, MD **38** A1
Deep Fork (river), OK **125** C9
Deep River, CT **33** D6
Deepwater Point, DE **35** E6
Deer Creek, OH **109** F4
Deer Creek, MS **73** E2
Deer Creek Lake, OH **109** F4
Deer Isle, ME **37** G5
Deer Lodge, MT **145** D4
Deerfield, MA **41** B3
Deerfield (river), MA **40** B2
Defiance, OH **109** B2
DeKalb, IL **91** B4
Del Rio, TX **127** G4
Delano, CA **137** F4
Delaware, OH **109** D4
Delaware (river), DE, NJ, PA **28** F4
Delaware and Raritan Canal, NJ **45** E3
Delaware Bay, DE, NJ **28** G4
Delaware City, DE **35** B5
Delaware Lake, OH **109** D4
Delaware Memorial Bridge, DE **35** B5
Delaware Water Gap N.R.A., NJ, PA **45** B2
Delaware, East Branch (river), NY **47** F7
Delaware, West Branch (river), NY **47** F7
Delmar, DE **35** I5
Delmarva Peninsula, DE, MD, VA **28** H4
Delphos, OH **109** C2
Delray Beach, FL **65** G9
Delta, CO **139** D2
Delta, UT **151** E3
Delta N.W.&S.R., AK **135** D7
Deltona, FL **65** D8
Deming, NM **123** H2
Demopolis, AL **61** E2
Denali (peak) *see* McKinley, Mount, AK **135** D6
Denali N.P. and Preserve, AK **135** D6
Denham Springs, LA **71** F6
Denison, IA **95** C3
Denison, TX **127** C7
Dennis, MA **41** E10
Denton, MD **39** C9
Denton, TX **127** C7
Denver, CO **139** C6
Derby, KS **97** E7
Derby Center, VT **53** A4
Derby Line, VT **53** A4
Dermott, AR **63** F6
Derry, NH **43** I4
Des Lacs (river), ND **107** B4
Des Moines, IA **95** D5
Des Moines (river), IA, MN **95** B4
Des Plaines (river), IL **91** B5
Desatoya Mountains, NV **147** D4
Deschutes (river), OR **149** B4
Deschutes N.W.&S.R., OR **149** D4
Desert National Wildlife Range, NV **147** F6
Desert Valley, NV **147** B3
Desolation Canyon, UT **151** D6
Detroit, MI **99** H8
Detroit (river), MI **99** H8
Detroit Lakes, MN **101** D2
Devils Lake (lake), ND **107** B7
Devils Lake, ND **107** B7
Devils Postpile Nat. Mon., CA **137** E5
Devils Tower Nat. Mon., WY **155** A9
Dewey Beach, DE **35** H7
Dexter, ME **37** E4
Dexter, MO **103** F7
Dickinson, ND **106** D2
Dickson, TN **79** B4
Dillingham, AK **135** F4
Dillon, MT **145** F4
Dillon, SC **77** C8
Dinosaur Nat. Mon., CO, UT **138** A1
Dirty Devil (river), UT **151** F5
Disappointment, Cape, WA **152** E1
Dismal (river), NE **105** C4
Dixon, IL **91** B3
Dixon Entrance (strait), AK **135** H10
Dodge City, KS **97** D3
Dodgeville, WI **113** G4
Dolan Springs, AZ **121** C2
Dolores, CO **138** E1
Donaldsonville, LA **71** G6
Donner Und Blitzen N.W.&S.R., OR **149** F7
Door Peninsula, WI **113** E7
Dothan, AL **61** G5
Double Trouble, NJ **45** F4
Douglas, AZ **121** H7
Douglas, GA **67** G5
Douglas, WY **155** E8
Douglas Lake, TN **79** B9
Dover, DE **35** E5
Dover, NH **43** H5
Dover, NJ **45** B3
Dover, OH **109** D6
Dover-Foxcroft, ME **37** E4
Dowagiac, MI **99** I5
Doylestown, PA **49** E10
Dracut, MA **41** A6
Drayton, ND **107** A9
Drift Prairie, ND **107** B7
Driskill Mountain, LA **71** B3
Drummond Island, MI **99** D7
Dry Cimarron (river), NM **123** A7
Dry Lake, ND **107** B7
Dry Tortugas N.P., FL **65** I6
Du Bay, Lake, WI **113** D5
Du Bois, PA **49** C4
Du Quoin, IL **91** H4
Dublin, GA **67** E5
Dublin, OH **109** E4
Dubuque, IA **95** C9
Duck (river), TN **79** C4
Dulce, NM **123** A3
Duluth, MN **101** D5
Dumas, AR **63** F6
Dumas, TX **127** A3
Dunbar, WV **83** F3
Duncan, OK **125** E8
Dundalk, MD **39** B8
Dunkirk, NY **46** E1
Dunmore, PA **49** B9
Dunmore, Lake, VT **53** E2
Dunn, NC **75** C7
Dupree, SD **111** B4
Durango, CO **139** G2
Durant, OK **125** F10
Durham, CT **33** D5
Durham, NC **75** B7
Durham, NH **43** H5
Dutch Harbor, AK **134** H2
Dworshak Reservoir, ID **143** C2
Dyersburg, TN **78** B1
Dyersville, IA **95** C9

E
Eagan, MN **101** F5
Eagar, AZ **121** E7
Eagle Creek, KY **69** B7
Eagle Creek N.W.&S.R., OR **149** C8
Eagle Lake, CA **137** B4
Eagle Lake, ME **37** B5
Eagle Lake, ME **37** C4
Eagle Lake, ME **37** A5
Eagle Mountain, MN **101** B7
Eagle Pass, TX **127** G4
Eagle River, WI **113** C5
Earle, AR **63** C7
Easley, SC **76** B2
East Brunswick, NJ **45** D4
East Chicago, IN **93** A2
East Derry, NH **43** I4
East Falmouth, MA **41** E9
East Fork Lake, OH **109** G2
East Grand Forks, MN **101** B1
East Greenwich, RI **51** D4
East Hampton, CT **33** C6
East Hartford, CT **33** B5
East Hartland, CT **33** A4
East Haven, CT **33** E4
East Lansing, MI **99** H6
East Liverpool, OH **109** C8
East Millinocket, ME **37** D5
East Mountain, VT **53** B5
East Okoboji Lake, IA **95** A3
East Point, GA **67** C2
East Providence, RI **51** B5
East Range, NV **147** B3
East Ridge, TN **79** D7
East River, CT **33** E5
East St. Louis, IL **91** G3
East Tavaputs Plateau, UT **151** D6
Eastern Bay, MD **39** C8
Easthampton, MA **40** C2
Eastman, GA **67** F4
Easton, MD **39** D9
Easton, PA **49** D9
Eastport, ME **37** F7
Eatonton, GA **67** D4
Eatontown, NJ **45** D5
Eau Claire, WI **113** D3
Ebey's Landing National Historical Reserve, WA **153** B3
Eden, NC **75** A6
Edenton, NC **75** B9
Edgartown, MA **41** F9
Edgefield, SC **77** D3
Edgemont, SD **110** E1
Edgewood, MD **39** B8
Edison, NJ **45** D4
Edison National Historic Site, NJ **45** C4
Edisto (river), SC **77** F6
Edisto Island, SC **77** G6
Edisto, North Fork (river), SC **77** E5
Edisto, South Fork (river), SC **77** E4
Edmond, OK **125** C8
Edward T. Breathitt Parkway, KY **68** D3
Edwards Plateau, TX **127** E5
Edwardsville, IL **91** G3
Eel (river), CA **137** B1
Eel (river), IN **93** B4
Eel (river), IN **93** F2
Eel N.W.&S.R., CA **137** B1
Effigy Mounds Nat. Mon., IA **95** A8
Effingham, IL **91** F5
Egan Range, NV **147** E6
Egg Harbor City, NJ **45** G3
Eisenhower National Historic Site, PA **49** F6
El Campo, TX **127** G7
El Centro, CA **137** I7
El Dorado, AR **63** G4
El Dorado, KS **97** D7
El Dorado Lake, KS **97** D7
El Malpais Nat. Mon., NM **123** D2
El Morro Nat. Mon., NM **123** D2
El Paso, TX **126** D1
El Reno, OK **125** C7
Elbert, Mount, CO **139** D4
Elberton, GA **67** C5
Eldon, MO **103** D4
Eldora, IA **95** C6
Eleanor Roosevelt National Historic Site, NY **47** F8
Elephant Butte Reservoir, NM **123** F3
Eleven Point (river), MO **103** F5
Eleven Point N.W.&S.R., MO **103** F6
Elgin, IL **91** B5
Elizabeth, NJ **45** C4
Elizabeth City, NC **75** A10
Elizabeth Islands, MA **41** F7
Elizabethton, TN **79** B11
Elizabethtown, KY **69** C5
Elizabethtown, PA **49** E7
Elk (river), KS **97** E8
Elk (river), WV **83** F5
Elk City, OK **125** C6
Elk City Lake, KS **97** E9
Elk N.W.&S.R., OR **148** F1
Elk Point, SD **111** F10
Elkhart, IN **93** A4
Elkhart, KS **96** F1
Elkhead Mountains, CO **139** A2
Elkhorn (river), NE **105** F7
Elkhorn Creek N.W.&S.R., OR **149** C3
Elkins, WV **83** E6
Elko, NV **147** B5
Elkton, MD **39** A9
Ellendale, DE **35** G6
Ellendale, ND **107** F8
Ellensburg, WA **153** D6
Ellicott City, MD **39** B7
Ellington, CT **33** A6
Ellis (river), NH **43** D4
Ellis Island, NY, NJ **47** E8
Ellisville, MS **73** G4
Ellsworth, KS **97** C5
Ellsworth, ME **37** F5
Elmira, NY **47** F4
Eloy, AZ **121** G5
Elsmere, DE **35** A5
Elwell, Lake, MT **145** B5
Elwood, IN **93** D4
Ely, MN **101** C6
Ely, NV **147** D6
Elyria, OH **109** B5
Embarras (river), IL **91** F5
Emmetsburg, IA **95** A4
Emmett, ID **143** G1
Emmonak, AK **134** D3
Emporia, KS **97** C8
Emporia, VA **81** E9
Emporium, PA **49** B5
Endicott, NY **47** F5
Endwell, NY **47** F6
Enfield, CT **33** A5
Enfield, NH **43** F2
England, AR **63** D5
Englewood, OH **109** E2
Enid, OK **125** B8
Enid Lake, MS **73** B3
Enosburg Falls, VT **53** A3
Enterprise, AL **61** G5
Enterprise, OR **149** B8
Ephraim, UT **151** E4
Ephrata, PA **49** E8
Ephrata, WA **153** D7
Equinox, Mount, VT **53** H2
Erie, PA **48** A2
Erie Canal, NY **46** D2
Erie, Lake, **86** E9
Erling, Lake, AR **63** G2
Erwin, TN **79** B10
Escalante (river), UT **151** G4
Escanaba, MI **99** D4
Escondido, CA **137** I6
Esmond, RI **51** B4
Espanola, NM **123** B4
Essex, CT **33** D6
Essex, MD **39** B8
Essex Junction, VT **53** C2
Estancia, NM **123** D4
Estes Park, CO **139** B5
Estherville, IA **95** A3
Etowah (river), GA **67** B1
Euclid, OH **109** A6
Eudora, AR **63** G6
Eufaula, AL **61** F6
Eufaula Lake, OK **125** D11
Eugene, OR **149** D2
Eugene O'Neill National Historic Site, CA **137** E2
Eunice, LA **71** F4
Eunice, NM **123** G8
Eureka, CA **137** B1
Eureka, KS **97** D8
Eureka, MT **144** A2
Eureka, NV **147** D5
Eureka, SD **111** A6
Eureka Springs, AR **63** A2
Evangeline, LA **71** F3
Evans, GA **67** D6
Evanston, IL **91** B6
Evanston, WY **154** G1
Evansville, IN **93** I1
Everett, WA **153** C4
Everglades N.P., FL **65** H9
Evergreen, AL **61** G3
Ewing, NJ **45** E3
Excelsior Mountains, NV **147** E3
Exeter, NH **43** H5
Exeter, RI **51** E4

F
Fabens, TX **126** E1
Fabius, Middle (river), MO **103** A4
Fabius, South (river), MO **103** B5
Fagaitua, AS **156** H2
Fagamalo, AS **156** I1
Fagatele Bay National Marine Sanctuary, AS **156** I1
Fagatogo, AS **156** I1
Fair Haven, VT **53** F1
Fairbanks, AK **135** D7
Fairborn, OH **109** E2
Fairbury, NE **105** E8
Fairfield, CT **33** E2
Fairfield, IA **95** E8
Fairfield, IL **91** G5
Fairfield, OH **109** F1
Fairfield, VT **53** B3
Fairfield Bay, AR **63** B4
Fairhaven, MA **41** E8
Fairhope, AL **61** I1
Fairmont, MN **101** H3
Fairmont, WV **83** C5
Fairmount, NY **47** D5
Fairview, KY **69** E4
Fairview, OK **125** B7
Fajardo, PR **157** H12
Falcon Reservoir, TX **127** H5
Faleasao, AS **156** I4
Falfurrias, TX **127** H6
Fall (river), KS **97** D8

Fall Line — Green River

Fall Line (escarpment), NJ, PA **28** G4
Fall River, MA **41** E7
Fallon, NV **147** D3
Falls City, NE **105** E10
Falls Creek, NV **147** A6
Falls Lake, NC **75** B7
Falmouth, MA **41** F8
Falmouth, ME **37** H3
Fargo, ND **107** D10
Faribault, MN **101** G4
Farmington, ME **37** F3
Farmington, MO **103** E7
Farmington, NH **43** G5
Farmington, NM **123** A2
Farmington, UT **151** B4
Farmington (river), CT **33** B4
Farmington N.W.&S.R., CT **33** A3
Farmington, East Branch (river), CT **33** A4
Farmington, West Branch (river), CT, MA **33** A3
Farmville, VA **81** D8
Farragut, TN **79** B8
Father Marquette National Memorial, MI **99** D6
Faulkton, SD **111** B7
Fayette, AL **61** C2
Fayetteville, AR **63** B1
Fayetteville, NC **75** C7
Fayetteville, TN **79** D5
Fayetteville, WV **83** G4
Fear, Cape, NC **75** E8
Feather, Middle Fork N.W.&S.R., CA **137** C3
Federal Way, WA **153** D4
Federalsburg, MD **39** D9
Felton, DE **35** F5
Fenwick Island, DE **35** I7
Fergus Falls, MN **101** D2
Ferguson, MO **103** C7
Fernandina Beach, FL **65** A8
Ferndale, WA **153** A3
Fernley, NV **147** C2
Ferriday, LA **71** D5
Festus, MO **103** D7
Fillmore, UT **151** E3
Findlay, OH **109** C3
Finger Lakes, NY **47** E4
Fire Island National Seashore, NY **47** H9
First Connecticut Lake, NH **43** A4
First Ladies National Historic Site, OH **109** C7
Fish (river), ME **37** B5
Fish Creek, WV **83** C4
Fishing Bay, MD **39** E9
Fitchburg, MA **41** B5
Fitzgerald, GA **67** G4
Flagstaff, AZ **121** C5
Flagstaff Lake, ME **37** E2
Flambeau (river), WI **113** C3
Flaming Gorge N.R.A., WY **155** G3
Flaming Gorge Reservoir, UT, WY **155** G3
Flandreau, SD **111** D10
Flat N.W.&S.R., MI **99** G5
Flat River Reservoir, RI **51** D3
Flathead (river), MT **144** C2
Flathead Lake, MT **144** B3
Flathead N.W.&S.R., MT **144** B3
Flathead, South Fork (river), MT **144** B3
Flatrock (river), IN **93** F4
Flattery, Cape, WA **152** B1
Flatwoods, KY **69** B10
Flemington, NJ **45** D2
Flint, MI **99** G7
Flint (river), GA **67** E2
Flint (river), MI **99** G7
Flint Hills, KS **97** E7
Flora, IL **91** G5
Florence, AL **61** A2
Florence, AZ **121** F5
Florence, CO **139** E5
Florence, KY **69** A7
Florence, OR **148** D1
Florence, SC **77** C8
Florida Bay, FL **65** H9
Florida Keys (islands), FL **65** I8
Florida Keys National Marine Sanctuary, FL **65** I7
Florida, Straits of, FL **65** I9
Florida's Turnpike, FL **65** E8
Florissant, MO **103** C7
Florissant Fossil Beds Nat. Mon., CO **139** D5
Floyd (river), IA **94** B2
Foley, AL **61** I2
Follansbee, WV **83** A5
Folsom, CA **137** D3
Fond du Lac, WI **113** F6
Fontana Lake, NC **74** C1
Fontenelle Reservoir, WY **154** F2
Ford (river), MI **99** C3
Fordyce, AR **63** F4
Forest, MS **73** E4
Forest Acres, SC **77** D5
Forest City, IA **95** A5
Forest City, NC **74** C3
Forest Grove, OR **149** B2
Forrest City, AR **63** D7
Forsyth, MT **145** D9
Fort Atkinson, WI **113** G6
Fort Benton, MT **145** B5
Fort Bowie National Historic Site, AZ **121** G7
Fort Bragg, CA **137** C1
Fort Caroline National Memorial, FL **65** B8
Fort Clatsop National Memorial, OR **148** A1
Fort Collins, CO **139** B5
Fort Davis National Historic Site, TX **126** E2
Fort Defiance, AZ **121** C7
Fort Dodge, IA **95** C4
Fort Donelson N.B., TN **78** A3
Fort Fairfield, ME **37** B6
Fort Foote Park, MD **39** D6
Fort Frederica Nat. Mon., GA **67** H7
Fort Gibson Lake, OK **125** C11
Fort Kent, ME **37** A5
Fort Knox (site), KY **69** C6
Fort Laramie National Historic Site, WY **155** F9
Fort Larned National Historic Site, KS **97** D4
Fort Lauderdale, FL **65** G9
Fort Lee, NJ **45** C5
Fort Loudoun Lake, TN **79** B8
Fort Madison, IA **95** F8
Fort Matanzas Nat. Mon., FL **65** B8
Fort McHenry Nat. Mon. and Historic Shrine, MD **39** B8
Fort Mill, SC **77** A5
Fort Morgan, CO **139** B7
Fort Myers, FL **65** F7
Fort Necessity N.B., PA **48** F2
Fort Payne, AL **61** B5
Fort Peck Dam, MT **145** B9
Fort Peck Lake, MT **145** B8
Fort Pickens, FL **64** B1
Fort Pierce, FL **65** E9
Fort Pierre, SD **111** D5
Fort Pulaski Nat. Mon., GA **67** F8
Fort Raleigh National Historic Site, NC **75** B10
Fort Scott, KS **97** D10
Fort Scott National Historic Site, KS **97** D10
Fort Smith, AR **63** C1
Fort Smith National Historic Site, AR **63** B1
Fort Stanwix Nat. Mon., NY **47** C6
Fort Stockton, TX **127** E3
Fort Sumner, NM **123** D7
Fort Sumter Nat. Mon., SC **77** G7
Fort Thompson, SD **111** D6
Fort Ticonderoga, NY **47** C9
Fort Union Nat. Mon., NM **123** B6
Fort Union Trading Post National Historic Site, MT, ND **145** B11
Fort Vancouver National Historic Site, WA **153** F3
Fort Walton Beach, FL **64** B2
Fort Washington Park, MD **39** D6
Fort Wayne, IN **93** B5
Fort Worth, TX **127** D7
Fort Yates, ND **107** F5
Fort Yukon, AK **135** C7
Fortymile N.W.&S.R., AK **135** D8
Fossil Butte Nat. Mon., WY **154** F2
Foster Center, RI **51** C2
Foster Creek, SD **111** C8
Fostoria, OH **109** B3
Fountain, CO **139** D6
Four Corners (site), AZ, CO, NM, UT **121** A7
Four Mountains, Islands of, AK **134** H1
Fox, IL, WI **91** B5
Framingham, MA **41** C6
Francis Case, Lake, SD **111** E7
Francis, Lake, NH **43** B4
Franconia, NH **43** D3
Frankford, DE **35** I7
Frankfort, IN **93** D3
Frankfort, KY **69** B7
Franklin, IN **93** F4
Franklin, KY **69** E5
Franklin, LA **71** G5
Franklin, MA **41** D6
Franklin, NC **74** C1
Franklin, NH **43** G3
Franklin, NJ **45** B3
Franklin, TN **79** B5
Franklin, VA **81** E10
Franklin Delano Roosevelt Lake, WA **153** B9
Frederica, DE **35** F5
Frederick, MD **39** B5
Frederick, OK **125** E6
Fredericksburg, VA **81** C9
Fredericksburg and Spotsylvania County Battlefields Memorial N.M.P., VA **81** C9
Fredericktown, MO **103** E7
Frederiksted, VI **157** I7
Fredonia, KS **97** E8
Fredonia, NY **46** E1
Freehold, NJ **45** E4
Freeman, SD **111** E9
Freeman, Lake, IN **93** C3
Freeport, IL **91** A3
Freeport, TX **127** G8
Freeport, NY **47** H9
Fremont, MI **99** G5
Fremont, NE **105** C9
Fremont, OH **109** B4
Fremont (river), UT **151** F5
French Broad (river), TN **79** B10
Frenchman (river), MT **145** A8
Frenchman Creek, CO, NE **105** E4
Frenchville, ME **37** A5
Fresno, CA **137** F4
Friendship Hill National Historic Site, PA **48** F2
Frio (river), TX **127** G6
Frissell, Mount, CT **33** A2
Front Range, CO,WY **130** D7
Front Royal, VA **81** B8
Frostburg, MD **38** A2
Fruitland, MD **39** E10
Fryeburg, ME **37** G2
Fullerton, NE **105** C7
Fulton, KY **68** E1
Fulton, MO **103** C5
Fulton, MS **73** B5
Fulton, NY **47** D5
Fundy, Bay of, **28** C9

G

Gabbs, NV **147** D3
Gabbs Valley, NV **147** D3
Gadsden, AL **61** C4
Gaffney, SC **77** A4
Gahanna, OH **109** E4
Gaillard, Lake, CT **33** D4
Gainesville, FL **65** C7
Gainesville, GA **67** B3
Gaithersburg, MD **39** C6
Galax, VA **81** F5
Galena, AK **135** C5
Galena, IL **91** A2
Galesburg, IL **91** C2
Galilee, RI **51** G4
Galion, OH **109** C4
Gallatin, MO **103** B3
Gallatin, TN **79** B5
Gallatin (river), MT **145** E5
Gallinas (river), NM **123** C6
Gallipolis, OH **109** G5
Gallo Arroyo (river), NM **123** E5
Gallup, NM **123** C1
Galveston, TX **127** F9
Galveston Bay, TX **116** F9
Gannett Peak, WY **155** D3
Gantt, SC **76** B2
Garapan, MP **156** C2
Garden City, KS **96** D2
Garden City, SC **77** E9
Garden Peninsula, MI **99** D4
Garden State Parkway, NJ **45** G4
Gardiner, ME **37** G3
Gardner, MA **41** B4
Gardner Lake, CT **33** C6
Gardner Pinnacles, HI **141** F3
Gardnerville, NV **147** D2
Gareloi Island, AK **135** H8
Garland, TX **127** D7
Garner, NC **75** B7
Garnett, KS **97** D9
Garrison, ND **107** C4
Gary, IN **93** A2
Gas City, IN **93** D4
Gasconade (river), MO **103** F4
Gaston, Lake, NC, VA **75** A8
Gastonia, NC **75** C4
Gates, NY **46** D3
Gates of the Arctic N.P. and Preserve, AK **135** B6
Gatesville, TX **127** E6
Gateway N.R.A., NJ, NY **45** D5
Gatlinburg, TN **79** C9
Gauley (river), WV **83** F4
Gauley River N.R.A., WV **83** F4
Gay Head (point), MA **41** F8
Gaylord, MI **99** E6
Genesee (river), NY **46** E3
Geneseo, IL **91** C3
Geneseo, NY **46** E3
Geneva, AL **61** H5
Geneva, NE **105** D8
Geneva, NY **47** D4
Geneva, OH **109** A7
George Rogers Clark N.H.P., IN **93** G1
George Washington Birthplace Nat. Mon., VA **81** C10
George Washington Carver Nat. Mon., MO **103** F2
George, Lake, FL **65** C7
George, Lake, NY **47** C8
Georgetown, DE **35** H6
Georgetown, KY **69** C8
Georgetown, OH **109** G3
Georgetown, SC **77** E9
Georgetown, TX **127** F6
Georgia, Strait of, WA **152** A2
Gering, NE **104** B1
Germantown, MD **39** C6
Germantown, TN **78** D1
Gettysburg, PA **49** F6
Gettysburg, SD **111** B6
Gettysburg N.M.P., PA **49** F6
Gibbon, NE **105** D6
Gila (river), AZ **121** F7
Gila Bend, AZ **121** F4
Gila Cliff Dwellings Nat. Mon., NM **123** F2
Gilford Park, NJ **45** F5
Gillette, WY **155** B8
Glacier Bay N.P. and Preserve, AK **135** F9
Glacier N.P., MT **144** A3
Gladstone, MI **99** D4
Glasgow, DE **35** B4
Glasgow, KY **69** E6
Glasgow, MT **145** B9
Glassboro, NJ **45** G2
Glastonbury, CT **33** B5
Glen Burnie, MD **39** C7
Glen Canyon Dam, AZ **121** A5
Glen Canyon N.R.A., AZ, UT **151** G5
Glen Ullin, ND **107** E4
Glendale, AZ **121** F4
Glendale, RI **51** A3
Glendive, MT **145** C10
Glendo Reservoir, WY **155** E9
Glenns Ferry, ID **143** H2
Glenrock, WY **155** D8
Glens Falls, NY **47** D8
Glenwood, IA **94** E2
Glenwood Springs, CO **139** C3
Globe, AZ **121** F6
Gloucester, MA **41** B8
Gloversville, NY **47** D8
Gold Beach, OR **148** F1
Golden Beach, MD **39** E7
Golden Gate N.R.A., CA **137** E1
Golden Spike National Historic Site, UT **151** A3
Goldendale, WA **153** F5
Goldfield, NV **147** F4
Goldsboro, NC **75** C8
Gonzales, LA **71** G6
Gooding, ID **143** H3
Goodland, KS **96** B1
Goodlettsville, TN **79** B5
Goose (river), ND **107** C9
Goose Creek, ID **143** I3
Goose Creek, SC **77** F7
Goose Lake, CA, OR **137** A4
Goose Point, DE **35** D6
Gordon, NE **105** A3
Gordon Creek, NE **105** B4
Gore Range, CO **139** B4
Gorham, NH **43** D4
Goshen, IN **93** A4
Goshute Mountains, NV **147** C7
Gothenburg, NE **105** D5
Gouverneur, NY **47** B6
Grafton, ND **107** B9
Grafton, WV **83** D6
Graham Lake, ME **37** F5
Grambling, LA **71** B3
Granby, CT **33** A4
Grand (river), MI **99** G6
Grand (river), MO **103** A2
Grand (river), OH **109** A7
Grand (river), SD **111** A3
Grand Canyon, AZ **121** B4
Grand Canyon (canyon), AZ **121** B3
Grand Canyon N.P., AZ **121** B3
Grand Canyon-Parashant Nat. Mon., AZ **121** B3
Grand Coulee (valley), WA **153** C7
Grand Coulee Dam, WA **153** C8
Grand Detour, IL **91** B4
Grand Forks, ND **107** C10
Grand Haven, MI **99** G4
Grand Island, NE **105** D7
Grand Island N.R.A., MI **99** C4
Grand Isle, LA **71** I8
Grand Isle, VT **53** B1
Grand Junction, CO **138** D1
Grand Lake, LA **71** G3
Grand Lake, ME **37** D6
Grand Lake (St. Marys Lake), OH **109** D2
Grand Manan Channel, ME **37** F7
Grand Marais, MN **101** C7
Grand Mesa, CO **139** D2
Grand Portage Nat. Mon., MN **101** B8
Grand Rapids, MI **99** G5
Grand Rapids, MN **101** C4
Grand Staircase-Escalante Nat. Mon., UT **151** G4
Grand Teton N.P., WY **154** C2
Grand Traverse Bay, MI **99** D5
Grand Valley, CO **138** D1
Grand Wash Cliffs, AZ **121** B2
Grand, South (river), MO **103** D2
Grand, South Fork (river), SD **110** A2
Grande Ronde (river), OR **149** A8
Grande Ronde N.W.&S.R., OR **149** A8
Grandfather Mountain, NC **74** B3
Grandview, WA **153** E7
Grangeville, ID **143** D1
Granite City, IL **91** G3
Granite Peak, MT **145** E6
Graniteville, VT **53** D4
Grant, NE **105** D3
Grant Range, NV **147** E6
Grant-Kohrs Ranch National Historic Site, MT **145** D4
Grants, NM **123** D2
Grants Pass, OR **149** F2
Grantsville, UT **151** C3
Grasonville, MD **39** C8
Grasshopper Glacier (site), MT **145** F6
Grays Harbor, WA **152** D1
Grays Lake, ID **143** H6
Gray's Reef National Marine Sanctuary, GA **67** G8
Great Barrington, MA **40** C1
Great Basin, NV **147** B5
Great Basin N.P., NV **147** D7
Great Bay, NH **43** H5
Great Bay, NJ **45** G4
Great Bend, KS **97** C5
Great Dismal Swamp, NC, VA **56** B8
Great Divide Basin, WY **155** F5
Great Egg Harbor (river), NJ **45** G3
Great Egg Harbor N.W.&S.R., NJ **45** G3
Great Falls, MT **145** C5
Great Miami (river), OH **109** D2
Great Pee Dee (river), NC, SC **56** C6
Great Plains, **86** A1
Great Plains Reservoirs, CO **139** E8
Great Pond, ME **37** F3
Great Quittacus Pond, MA **41** E8
Great Sacandaga Lake, NY **47** D8
Great Salt Lake, UT **151** B3
Great Salt Lake Desert, UT **151** D2
Great Salt Plains Lake, OK **125** B7
Great Sand Dunes Nat. Mon. and Preserve, CO **139** F5
Great Smoky Mountains, NC, TN **74** C1
Great Smoky Mountains N.P., NC, TN **74** B1
Great Swamp, RI **51** F3
Greece, NY **46** D3
Greeley, CO **139** B6
Green (river), CO, UT, WY **130** F6
Green Bay, WI **113** E7
Green Bay (bay), WI **113** D7
Green Mountains, VT **53** H2
Green River, UT **151** E6

Green River — Jamestown

Green River, WY **155** G3
Green River Lake, KY **69** D7
Green Swamp, NC **75** E7
Green Valley, AZ **121** H6
Greenbelt Park, MD **39** C7
Greenbrier, AR **63** C4
Greenbrier (river), WV **83** G5
Greencastle, IN **93** E2
Greeneville, TN **79** B10
Greenfield, IN **93** E4
Greenfield, MA **41** B3
Greenfield, OH **109** F3
Greensboro, NC **75** B6
Greensburg, IN **93** F5
Greensburg, KS **97** E4
Greensburg, PA **49** E3
Greenville, AL **61** F3
Greenville, DE **35** A5
Greenville, ME **37** E4
Greenville, MS **73** D1
Greenville, NC **75** C8
Greenville, NH **43** I3
Greenville, OH **109** D1
Greenville, PA **48** B1
Greenville, RI **51** B3
Greenville, SC **76** B2
Greenville, MI **99** G5
Greenway (site), VA **81** D10
Greenwich, CT **33** F1
Greenwood, AR **63** C1
Greenwood, DE **35** G5
Greenwood, IN **93** E4
Greenwood, MS **73** C3
Greenwood, SC **77** C3
Greer, SC **77** B3
Greers Ferry Lake, AR **63** C4
Greeson, Lake, AR **63** E2
Gregory, SD **111** E6
Grenada, MS **73** C3
Grenada Lake, MS **73** C3
Gresham, OR **149** B3
Greybull, WY **155** B5
Greybull (river), WY **155** B4
Greylock, Mount, MA **40** A1
Greys (river), WY **154** D2
Griffin, GA **67** D3
Grinnell, IA **95** D6
Gros Ventre (river), WY **154** C2
Groton, SD **111** B8
Groton, CT **33** D7
Grove, OK **125** B12
Grove City, PA **48** C2
Groveton, NH **43** C3
Guadalupe (river), TX **127** F7
Guadalupe Mountains, NM **123** G6
Guadalupe Mountains N.P., TX **126** E1
Guadalupe Peak, TX **126** E2
Guam (territory), US **156** E1
Guayama, PR **157** I11
Guernsey, WY **155** E9
Guilford, CT **33** E5
Guilford, ME **37** E4
Guilford Courthouse N.M.P., NC **75** B6
Gulf Islands National Seashore, FL, MS **64** B1
Gulf of the Farallones National Marine Sanctuary, CA **137** E2
Gulf Shores, AL **61** I2
Gulfport, MS **73** I4
Gulkana N.W.&S.R., AK **135** D7
Gunnison, CO **139** E3
Guntersville, AL **61** B4
Guntersville Lake, AL **61** B4
Gurdon, AR **63** F3
Guthrie, OK **125** C8
Guyandotte (river), WV **82** G2
Guymon, OK **124** A3

H

H.E. Bailey Turnpike, OK **125** D7
Hackensack, NJ **45** B5
Hackettstown, NJ **45** C3
Haddam, CT **33** D5
Haddonfield, NJ **45** F2
Hagåtña (Agana), GU **156** F1
Hagerman, NM **123** F6
Hagerman Fossil Beds Nat. Mon., ID **143** H2
Hagerstown, MD **39** A5
Hailey, ID **143** G3
Haines, AK **135** F9
Haines City, FL **65** E7
Hal Rogers Parkway, KY **69** D8
Haleakala N.P., HI **141** D8
Hallock, MN **101** A1
Halls Creek, UT **151** G5
Hamburg, AR **63** G5
Hamburg, NY **46** E2
Hamden, CT **33** D4
Hamilton, AL **61** B1
Hamilton, MT **144** D2
Hamilton, OH **109** F1
Hamilton, RI **51** E4
Hammonasset (river), CT **33** D5
Hammond, IN **93** A1
Hammond, LA **71** F7
Hammonton, NJ **45** G3
Hampton, IA **95** B6
Hampton, NH **43** H5
Hampton, SC **77** F5
Hampton, VA **81** E11
Hampton National Historic Site, MD **39** B7
Hams Fork (river), WY **154** F2
Hanahan, SC **77** F7
Hanama'ulu, HI **140** A2
Hancock, MD **39** A4
Hanford, CA **137** F4
Hanford Reach Nat. Mon., WA **153** E7
Hankinson, ND **107** F10
Hanna, WY **155** F7
Hannibal, MO **103** B5
Hanover, NH **43** F2
Hanover, PA **49** F7
Harbeson, DE **35** H6
Harbor Beach, MI **99** F8
Hardin, MT **145** E8
Harding, Lake, GA **67** E1
Hardinsburg, KY **69** C5
Hardwick, VT **53** C4
Harlan, IA **95** D3
Harlan County Lake, NE **105** E6
Harlingen, TX **127** I7
Harlowton, MT **145** D6
Harmony, RI **51** B3
Harney Basin, OR **149** E6
Harney Lake, OR **149** E6
Harney Peak, SD **110** D2
Harpers Ferry N.H.P., WV **83** D10
Harriman, TN **79** B8
Harriman Reservoir, VT **53** I2
Harrington, DE **35** F5
Harris, RI **51** C4
Harrisburg, IL **91** H5
Harrisburg, PA **49** E7
Harrison, AR **63** A3
Harrison, TN **79** D7
Harrisonburg, VA **81** C7
Harrisonville, MO **103** D2
Harrisville, RI **51** A3
Harrodsburg, KY **69** C7
Harry S. Truman National Historic Site, MO **103** C2
Harry S. Truman Reservoir, MO **103** D3
Hart Mountain National Antelope Refuge, OR **149** F6
Hartford, CT **33** B5
Hartford City, IN **93** D5
Hartington, NE **105** A8
Hartland, ME **37** F4
Hartland, VT **53** F4
Hartselle, AL **61** B3
Hartsville, SC **77** C7
Hartwell, GA **67** B4
Hartwell Lake, GA, SC **76** C1
Harvard, IL **91** A4
Harvey, ND **107** C6
Harwinton, CT **33** B3
Hastings, MI **99** H5
Hastings, NE **105** D7
Hatchie (river), TN **78** C2
Hatteras Island, NC **75** B11
Hatteras, Cape, NC **75** C11
Hattiesburg, MS **73** G4
Hau'ula, HI **141** B4
Havasu, Lake, AZ, CA **121** D2
Havelock, NC **75** D9
Haverhill, MA **41** A7
Haverhill, NH **43** E2
Haverhill-Bath Bridge, NH **43** D2
Havre, MT **145** B6
Havre de Grace, MD **39** A9
Haw (river), NC **75** B6
Hawai'i (island), HI **141** E9
Hawai'i Volcanoes N.P., HI **141** F9
Hawaiian Islands Humpback Whale National Marine Sanctuary, HI **141** D5
Hawkeye Point (peak), IA **94** A2
Hawthorne, NV **147** E3
Hayden, ID **143** B1
Hays, KS **97** C4
Hayward, CA **137** E2
Hayward, WI **113** B3
Hazard, KY **69** D10
Hazardville, CT **33** A5
Hazen, ND **107** D4
Hazlehurst, GA **67** G5
Hazlehurst, MS **73** F2
Hazleton, PA **49** C8
Heart (river), ND **107** E4
Heavener, OK **125** D12
Heber City, UT **151** C4
Heber Springs, AR **63** C5
Hebron, NE **105** E8
Helena, AR **63** D7
Helena, MT **145** D4
Hells Canyon, ID **143** E1
Hells Canyon N.R.A., ID, OR **149** A9
Helper, UT **151** D5
Henderson, KY **68** C3
Henderson, NC **75** B7
Henderson, NV **147** H6
Henderson, TN **78** C2
Henderson, TX **127** D8
Hendersonville, NC **74** C2
Hendersonville, TN **79** B5
Henlopen, Cape, DE **35** G7
Hennepin Canal, IL **91** C3
Henniker, NH **43** H3
Henry Mountains, UT **151** G5
Henryetta, OK **125** C10
Henrys Lake, ID **143** F6
Heppner, OR **149** B6
Herbert Hoover National Historic Site, IA **95** D8
Hereford, CO **139** A6
Hereford, TX **127** B3
Hermann, MO **103** C5
Hermiston, OR **149** A6
Hershey, PA **49** E7
Hesperia, CA **137** H6
Hesston, KS **97** D6
Hettinger, ND **107** F3
Hialeah, FL **65** G9
Hiawatha, KS **97** A9
Hibbing, MN **101** C5
Hickory, NC **75** B4
High Bridge, NJ **45** C2
High Desert, OR **149** E5
High Plains, **130** D7
High Point, NC **75** B5
High Point (peak), NJ **45** A3
Highland Lake, NH **43** H2
Highland Lakes, NJ **45** A4
Highmore, SD **111** C6
Hightstown, NJ **45** E3
Hill Country (region), TX **127** H5
Hill Creek, UT **151** D6
Hillsboro, KS **97** D7
Hillsboro, ND **107** D10
Hillsboro, NH **43** H2
Hillsboro, OH **109** F3
Hillsboro, OR **149** B2
Hillsdale, MI **99** I6
Hillsdale Lake, KS **97** C10
Hilo, HI **141** F9
Hilton Head Island (island), SC **77** H6
Hilton Head Island, SC **77** H6
Hinesville, GA **67** G7
Hinsdale, NH **43** I1
Hinton, WV **83** G4
Hiwassee (river), TN **79** D8
Hiwassee Lake, NC **74** C1
Hobart, OK **125** D6
Hobbs, NM **123** G8
Hockanum (river), CT **33** B5
Hockessin, DE **35** A4
Hocking (river), OH **109** F6
Hoisington, KS **97** C5
Holbrook, AZ **121** D6
Holdenville, OK **125** D10
Holdrege, NE **105** D6
Holland, MI **99** H5
Hollandale, MS **73** D2
Hollidaysburg, PA **49** D4
Hollis, OK **125** E5
Holly Springs, MS **73** A4
Hollywood, FL **65** G9
Holston (river), TN, VA **79** A10
Holston, North Fork (river), VA **80** F3
Holston, South Fork (river), VA **80** F3
Holt Creek, NE **105** B6
Holton, KS **97** B9
Holualoa, HI **141** F8
Holyoke, CO **139** A9
Holyoke, MA **41** C3
Home of Franklin D. Roosevelt National Historic Site, NY **47** F8
Homer, AK **135** F6
Homer, LA **71** A3
Homestead, FL **65** H9
Homestead Nat. Mon. of America, NE **105** E8
Homewood, AL **61** D3
Homochitto (river), MS **73** G1
Homosassa Springs, FL **65** D6
Hondo, Rio (river), NM **123** F6
Honey Lake, CA **137** B4
Honolulu, HI **141** C4
Hood River, OR **149** B4
Hood, Mount, OR **149** B4
Hooper Bay, AK **134** E3
Hoopeston, IL **91** D6
Hoosic (river), MA **40** A1
Hoover, AL **61** D3
Hoover Dam, AZ, NV **121** B1
Hopatcong, NJ **45** B3
Hopatcong, Lake, NJ **45** B3
Hope, AR **63** F2
Hope, RI **51** C3
Hope Mills, NC **75** C7
Hope Valley, RI **51** E2
Hopewell, VA **81** D10
Hopewell Culture N.H.P., OH **109** F4
Hopewell Furnace National Historic Site, PA **49** E8
Hopkinsville, KY **68** E3
Hoquiam, WA **152** D2
Horn Lake, MS **73** A3
Hornell, NY **46** E3
Horse Creek, WY **155** G9
Horsehead Lake, ND **107** D6
Horseheads, NY **47** F4
Horsepasture N.W.&S.R., NC **74** C2
Horseshoe Bend, AR **63** A5
Horseshoe Bend N.M.P., AL **61** D5
Hot Creek Range, NV **147** E5
Hot Springs, AR **63** E3
Hot Springs, SD **110** E2
Hot Springs N.P., AR **63** D3
Houghton, MI **99** B2
Houghton Lake (lake), MI **99** F6
Houghton Lake, MI **99** F6
Houlton, ME **37** C6
Houma, LA **71** H7
Housatonic (river), CT, MA **33** D3
Houston, DE **35** F5
Houston, MS **73** C4
Houston, TX **127** F8
Hovenweep Nat. Mon., CO **138** F1
Howard, SD **111** D9
Howland, ME **37** E5
Howland Island (territory), US **156** F3
Hubbard Lake, MI **99** E7
Hubbell Trading Post National Historic Site, AZ **121** C7
Huber Heights, OH **109** E2
Hudson (river), NJ, NY **47** C8
Hudson, NY **47** E8
Hudson, WI **113** D1
Hudson, Lake, OK **125** B11
Huerfano (river), CO **139** F5
Hueytown, AL **61** D3
Hugh Butler Lake, NE **105** D4
Hugo, OK **125** E11
Hugo Lake, OK **125** E11
Hugoton, KS **96** E2
Humacao, PR **157** I11
Humboldt, IA **95** B4
Humboldt, TN **78** B2
Humboldt (river), NV **147** B3
Humboldt Lake, NV **147** C3
Humboldt, North Fork (river), NV **147** A5
Humphreys Peak, AZ **121** C5
Huntingburg, IN **93** H2
Huntingdon, PA **49** D5
Huntington, IN **93** C5
Huntington, WV **82** F[illegible]
Huntington, NY **47** H[illegible]
Huntington Lake, IN **93** C5
Huntsville, AL **61** A4
Huntsville, TX **127** E8
Hurley, WI **113** B4
Hurlock, MD **39** D9
Huron, SD **111** D8
Huron, Lake, **86** C8
Hurricane, UT **151** H2
Hurricane, WV **82** F2
Hurricane Creek N.W.&S.R., AR **63** B3
Hutchinson, KS **97** D6
Hutchinson, MN **101** F3
Hyannis, MA **41** E9
Hyattsville, MD **39** C7

I

Idabel, OK **125** F12
Idaho Falls, ID **143** G5
Iditarod National Historic Trail, AK **135** E5
Iliamna Lake, AK **135** F5
Iliili, AS **156** I1
Ilion, NY **47** D7
Illinois (river), IL **91** E2
Illinois (river), OK **125** B12
Illinois (river), OR **148** G1
Illinois N.W.&S.R., OR **148** F1
Immokalee, FL **65** G8
Imnaha N.W.&S.R., OR **149** B9
Imperial, NE **105** D3
Imperial Valley, CA **137** I7
Independence, IA **95** C8
Independence, KS **97** E9
Independence, MO **103** C2
Independence Mountains, NV **147** B5
Indian (river), FL **65** E9
Indian Head, MD **39** D6
Indian Lake, OH **109** D3
Indian N.W.&S.R., MI **99** C4
Indian Nation Turnpike, OK **125** D10
Indian River Bay, DE **35** I7
Indian River Inlet, DE **35** H8
Indian Springs, NV **147** G6
Indiana, PA **49** D3
Indiana Dunes National Lakeshore, IN **93** A2
Indianapolis, IN **93** E4
Indianola, IA **95** E5
Indianola, MS **73** D2
International Falls, MN **101** B4
Intracoastal Waterway, AL, FL, LA, NC, SC **61** I2
Iola, KS **97** D9
Ionia, MI **99** G6
Iowa (river), IA **95** B5
Iowa City, IA **95** D8
Iowa Falls, IA **95** C6
Ipswich, MA **41** A8
Ipswich, SD **111** B7
Irmo, SC **77** D5
Iron Mountain, MI **99** D3
Irondequoit, NY **46** D4
Ironton, OH **109** H5
Ironwood, MI **99** C1
Ironwood Forest Nat. Mon., AZ **121** G5
Iroquois (river), IL, IN **91** C5
Irving, TX **127** D7
Irvington, NJ **45** C4
Ishpeming, MI **99** C3
Island Falls, ME **37** C5
Island Park, RI **51** D6
Island Park Reservoir, ID **143** F6
Island Pond, VT **53** B5
Isle au Haut, ME **37** G5
Isle Royale, MI **99** A2
Isle Royale N.P., MI **99** A2
Isles of Shoals, ME, NH **37** I2
Itasca, Lake, MN **101** C3
Ithaca, NY **47** E5
Iuka, MS **73** A6
Ivishak N.W.&S.R., AK **135** B7

J

J. Percy Priest Lake, TN **79** B5
J. Strom Thurmond Reservoir, GA, SC **67** C5
Jack Lee, Lake, AR **63** G4
Jackman, ME **37** D3
Jackpot, NV **147** A6
Jacks Fork (river), MO **103** F5
Jackson, AL **61** G2
Jackson, KY **69** D9
Jackson, MI **99** H6
Jackson, MO **103** E7
Jackson, MS **73** F3
Jackson, OH **109** G5
Jackson, TN **78** C2
Jackson, WY **154** C2
Jackson Lake, WY **154** C2
Jacksonville, AL **61** C5
Jacksonville, AR **63** D5
Jacksonville, FL **65** B7
Jacksonville, IL **91** E3
Jacksonville, NC **75** D8
Jacksonville Beach, FL **65** B8
Jaffrey, NH **43** I2
James (river), ND, SD **86** C3
James (river), VA **81** D8
James A. Garfield National Historic Site, OH **109** A7
Jamestown, ND **107** D8

Jamestown — Little Deschutes N.W.&S.R.

Jamestown, NY **46** F2
Jamestown, RI **51** E5
Jamestown, VA **81** D10
Jamestown Reservoir, ND **107** D8
Janesville, WI **113** H6
Jarbidge (river), ID **143** I2
Jarvis Island (territory), US **157** G5
Jasper, AL **61** C2
Jasper, IN **93** H2
Jay Peak, VT **53** A3
Jeanerette, LA **71** G5
Jeannette, PA **48** E2
Jefferson, IA **95** D4
Jefferson (river), MT **145** E4
Jefferson City, MO **103** D5
Jefferson City, TN **79** B9
Jeffersontown, KY **69** B6
Jeffersonville, IN **93** H4
Jekyll Island, GA **67** H7
Jemez, E. Fork N.W.&S.R., NM **123** C4
Jenks, OK **125** B10
Jennings, LA **71** G3
Jericho, VT **53** C2
Jerimoth Hill (peak), RI **51** B2
Jerome, ID **143** H3
Jersey City, NJ **45** C5
Jersey Shore, PA **49** C6
Jerseyville, IL **91** F2
Jerusalem, RI **51** G4
Jesse James Farm and Museum, MO **103** B2
Jesup, GA **67** G6
Jewel Cave Nat. Mon., SD **110** E1
Jewett City, CT **33** C8
Jimmy Carter National Historic Site, GA **67** F2
John D. Rockefeller, Jr. Memorial Parkway, WY **154** B2
John Day, OR **149** C6
John Day (river), OR **149** C5
John Day Fossil Beds Nat. Mon., OR **149** C5
John Day N.W.&S.R., OR **149** B5
John Day, North Fork N.W.&S.R., OR **149** C7
John Day, South Fork N.W.&S.R., OR **149** D6
John F. Kennedy Space Center (site), FL **65** D9
John H. Kerr Reservoir, NC, VA **81** E8
John Martin Reservoir, CO **139** E8
John Muir Nat. Mon., CA **137** D2
John N.W.&S.R., AK **135** B6
John Redmond Reservoir, KS **97** D9
Johnson, VT **53** B3
Johnson City, TN **79** B10
Johnston, RI **51** B4
Johnston Atoll (territory), US **156** E4
Johnstown, PA **49** E3
Johnstown Flood National Memorial, PA **49** D4
Joliet, IL **91** C5
Jonesboro, AR **63** B7
Jonesboro, LA **71** C3
Jonesport, ME **37** F6
Joplin, MO **103** F2
Jordan, MT **145** C9
Jordan Creek, ID **143** H1
Joseph Creek N.W.&S.R., OR **149** A8
Joshua Tree N.P., CA **137** H7
Juan de Fuca, Strait of, WA **152** B1
Julia Butler Hansen Refuge, WA **152** E2
Julian M. Carroll Parkway, KY **68** E1
Jump (river), WI **113** C3
Junction City, KS **97** B7
Junction City, OR **149** D2
Juneau, AK **135** F10
Juniata (river), PA **49** D6
Jupiter, FL **65** F9

K
Ka'ena Point, HI **141** B4
Kadoka, SD **111** D4
Kaho'olawe (island), HI **141** D7
Kahuku Point, HI **141** B4
Kahului, HI **141** C7
Kaibab Plateau, AZ **121** B4
Kailua, HI **141** B5
Kailua, HI **141** F8
Kaiwi Channel, HI **141** C5
Kalae (South Point), HI **141** G8
Kalaheo, HI **140** A2
Kalamazoo, MI **99** H5
Kalamazoo (river), MI **99** H5
Kalaoa, HI **141** F8
Kalaupapa, HI **141** C6
Kalaupapa N.H.P., HI **141** C6
Kalispell, MT **144** B2
Kalkaska, MI **99** E5
Kaloko-Honokohau N.H.P., HI **141** F8
Kamiah, ID **143** D2
Kamuela *see* Waimea, HI **141** E8
Kanab, UT **151** H3
Kanab Creek, AZ, UT **121** B4
Kanawha (river), WV **83** F3
Kane'ohe, HI **141** B5
Kankakee, IL **91** C5
Kankakee (river), IL, IN **91** C5
Kannapolis, NC **75** C5
Kanopolis Lake, KS **97** C6
Kansas (river), KS **97** B9
Kansas City, KS **97** B10
Kansas City, MO **103** C2
Kapa'a, HI **140** A2
Kapa'au, HI **141** E8
Kaskaskia (river), IL **91** F4
Kaskaskia Island, IL **91** H3
Katahdin, Mount, ME **37** D5
Katmai N.P. and Preserve, AK **135** F5
Kaua'i (island), HI **140** A2
Kaukauna, WI **113** E6
Kaulakahi Channel, HI **140** A1
Kaunakakai, HI **141** C6
Kaw Lake, OK **125** A9
Kawich Range, NV **147** E5
Kayenta, AZ **121** B6
Keahole Point, HI **141** F8
Keansburg, NJ **45** D4
Kearney, NE **105** D6
Keene, NH **43** H2
Kekaha, HI **140** A1
Kelleys Island, OH **109** B5
Kellogg, ID **143** C1
Kelso, WA **153** F3
Kemmerer, WY **154** F2
Kenai, AK **135** E6
Kenai Fjords N.P., AK **135** F6
Kenai Peninsula, AK **135** E6
Kendall, FL **65** H9
Kendall Park, NJ **45** D3
Kendallville, IN **93** B5
Kenmare, ND **107** A3
Kennebec, SD **111** D6
Kennebec (river), ME **37** G3
Kennebunk, ME **37** I2
Kenner, LA **71** G7
Kennesaw Mountain National Battlefield Park, GA **67** C2
Kennett, MO **103** G7
Kennett Square, PA **49** F9
Kennewick, WA **153** F7
Kenosha, WI **113** H7
Kenova, WV **82** F1
Kent, CT **33** B2
Kent, OH **109** B7
Kent Island, MD **39** C8
Kenton, OH **109** C3
Kentucky (river), KY **69** B7
Kentucky Lake, KY **68** E2
Kentucky, Middle Fork (river), KY **69** D9
Kentucky, North Fork (river), KY **69** C9
Kentucky, South Fork (river), KY **69** D9
Kentwood, MI **99** G5
Keokuk, IA **95** F8
Keowee, Lake, SC **76** B2
Kern N.W.&S.R., CA **137** G5
Kernersville, NC **75** B5
Kerrville, TX **127** F5
Ketchikan, AK **135** G11
Ketchum, ID **143** G3
Kettering, OH **109** E2
Kettle River Range, WA **153** B8
Keuka Lake, NY **47** E4
Kewanee, IL **91** C3
Keweenaw N.H.P., MI **99** B2
Keweenaw Peninsula, MI **99** B3
Key Largo, FL **65** H9
Key West, FL **65** I7
Keya Paha (river), NE, SD **105** A5
Keyhole Reservoir, WY **155** B9
Keyser, WV **83** C8
Keystone Lake, OK **125** B10
Kiamichi (river), OK **125** E11
Kickapoo (river), WI **113** G3
Kihei, HI **141** D7
Kilauea Crater (site), HI **141** F9
Killeen, TX **127** E6
Killik (river), AK **135** B6
Killington Peak, VT **53** F3
Kimball, NE **104** C1
Kinderhook, NY **47** E8
Kingfield, ME **37** F3
Kingfisher, OK **125** C8
Kingman, AZ **121** D2
Kingman, KS **97** E6
Kingman Reef (territory), US **157** F5
Kings (river), NV **147** A3
Kings Canyon N.P., CA **137** E5
Kings Mountain, NC **75** C4
Kings Mountain N.M.P., SC **77** A4
Kings N.W.&S.R., CA **137** F5
Kings Peak, UT **151** B5
Kingsland, GA **67** H7
Kingsport, TN **79** A10
Kingston, NH **43** H5
Kingston, NY **47** F8
Kingston, PA **49** C8
Kingston, RI **51** F4
Kingstree, SC **77** E7
Kingsville, TX **127** H6
Kingwood, WV **83** C6
Kinsley, KS **97** D4
Kinston, NC **75** C8
Kiowa, CO **139** C6
Kirkland, WA **153** C4
Kirksville, MO **103** A4
Kirkwood, MO **103** D7
Kirwin Reservoir, KS **97** A4
Kiska Island, AK **135** H7
Kissimmee, FL **65** D8
Kissimmee (river), FL **65** E8
Kitt Peak National Observatory, AZ **121** H5
Kittanning, PA **49** D3
Kittatinny Mountains, NJ **45** B2
Kittery, ME **37** I2
Kitts Hummock, DE **35** E6
Kitty Hawk, NC **75** B10
Klamath (river), CA, OR **130** D2
Klamath Falls, OR **149** G3
Klamath N.W.&S.R., CA, OR **137** A1
Klickitat (river), WA **153** F5
Klickitat N.W.&S.R., WA **153** F5
Klondike Gold Rush N.H.P., AK **135** E9
Knife (river), ND **107** D3
Knife River Indian Villages National Historic Site, ND **107** D4
Knoxville, IA **95** E6
Knoxville, TN **79** B8
Kobuk N.W.&S.R., AK **135** C5
Kobuk Valley N.P., AK **135** B5
Kodiak, AK **135** G6
Kodiak Island, AK **135** G6
Kokomo, IN **93** D4
Koocanusa, Lake, MT **144** A2
Kootenai (river), ID, MT **143** A1
Kosciusko, MS **73** D4
Kotzebue, AK **135** B4
Koyukuk (river), AK **135** C5
Koyukuk, North Fork N.W.&S.R., AK **135** B6
Kumukahi, Cape, HI **141** F10
Kure Atoll, HI **140** E1
Kuskokwim (river), AK **135** C6
Kuskokwim Mountains, AK **135** E4
Kuskokwim, North Fork (river), AK **135** D5

L
L'Anse, MI **99** C2
La Crescent, MN **101** H6
La Crosse, WI **113** F3
La Follette, TN **79** B8
La Grande, OR **149** B7
La Grange, GA **67** E1
La Grange, KY **69** B6
La Junta, CO **139** F7
La Moine (river), IL **91** D2
La Perouse Pinnacle (island), HI **141** F3
La Plata, MD **39** E7
La Salle, IL **91** C4
La'ie, HI **141** B4
Laconia, NH **43** G4
Ladder Creek, KS **96** C2
Ladson, SC **77** F7
Ladysmith, WI **113** C3
LaFayette, GA **67** B1
Lafayette, IN **93** D2
Lafayette, LA **71** G4
Lafayette, CO **139** B5
Lafayette, Mount, NH **43** D3
Lafourche, Bayou (river), LA **71** H7
Lahaina, HI **141** C7
Lake Andes, SD **111** F8
Lake Charles, LA **70** G2
Lake City, FL **65** B6
Lake City, SC **77** D8
Lake Clark N.P. and Preserve, AK **135** E5
Lake Erie Beach, NY **46** E2
Lake Geneva, WI **113** H6
Lake Havasu City, AZ **121** D2
Lake Mead N.R.A., AZ, NV **121** C2
Lake Meredith N.R.A., TX **127** A4
Lake Placid, NY **47** B8
Lake Providence, LA **71** A6
Lake Roosevelt N.R.A., WA **153** C8
Lake Village, AR **63** G6
Lakehurst, NJ **45** F4
Lakeland, FL **65** E7
Lakeview, OR **149** G5
Lakeville, CT **33** A2
Lakeville, MN **101** G4
Lakewood, NJ **45** E4
Lakewood, WA **153** D3
Lakin, KS **96** D2
Lamar, CO **139** E9
Lambertville, MI **99** I7
Lambertville, NJ **45** D2
Lamesa, TX **127** D3
Lamlam, Mount, GU **156** G1
Lamoille (river), VT **53** B2
LaMoure, ND **107** E8
Lamprey (river), NH **43** H4
Lamprey N.W.&S.R., NH **43** H5
Lana'i (island), HI **141** D6
Lana'i City, HI **141** D6
Lancaster, CA **137** G5
Lancaster, NH **43** C3
Lancaster, OH **109** E5
Lancaster, PA **49** E8
Lancaster, SC **77** B6
Lancaster, WI **113** G4
Land Between the Lakes N.R.A., KY, TN **68** E3
Land O'Lakes, WI **113** B5
Lander, WY **155** D4
Lanett, AL **61** E6
Langdon, ND **107** A8
L'Anguille (river), AR **63** C6
Lansing, KS **97** B10
Lansing, MI **99** H6
LaPorte, IN **93** A3
Laramie, WY **155** G8
Laramie (river), CO, WY **155** F9
Laramie Mountains, CO, WY **155** E8
Laredo, TX **127** H5
Larimore, ND **107** C9
Larned, KS **97** D4
Larose, LA **71** H7
Las Animas, CO **139** E8
Las Cruces, NM **123** G4
Las Vegas, NM **123** C5
Las Vegas, NV **147** G6
Lassen Volcanic N.P., CA **137** B3
Last Chance, CO **139** C7
Lata Mountain, AS **157** I5
Laughlin, NV **147** I6
Laurel, DE **35** I5
Laurel, MS **73** G4
Laurel, MT **145** E7
Laurens, SC **77** C3
Laurinburg, NC **75** D6
Laurium, MI **99** B2
Lava Beds Nat. Mon., CA **137** A3
Lawrence, IN **93** E4
Lawrence, KS **97** B9
Lawrence, MA **41** A7
Lawrenceburg, IN **93** F6
Lawrenceburg, KY **69** C7
Lawrenceburg, TN **79** C4
Lawrenceville, IL **91** G6
Lawton, OK **125** E7
Laysan Island, HI **140** E2
Layton, UT **151** B4
Le Mars, IA **94** B2
Lead, SD **110** C1
Leadville, CO **139** D4
Leaf (river), MS **73** G5
Leavenworth, KS **97** B10
Lebanon, IN **93** D3
Lebanon, KS **97** A5
Lebanon, KY **69** D7
Lebanon, MO **103** E4
Lebanon, NH **43** F2
Lebanon, OH **109** F2
Lebanon, OR **149** C2
Lebanon, PA **49** E7
Lebanon, TN **79** B5
Lebanon, VA **80** E3
Lee, MA **40** C1
Leech Lake, MN **101** D3
Lees Summit, MO **103** C2
Leesburg, FL **65** D7
Leesburg, VA **81** A9
Leesville, LA **70** E2
Leesville Lake, OH **109** D7
Lehi, UT **151** C4
Lehigh (river), PA **49** C8
Lehua Island, HI **140** A1
Leitchfield, KY **69** D5
Leland, MS **73** D2
Lemhi (river), ID **143** F4
Lemhi Pass, MT **144** F3
Lemhi Range, ID **143** F3
Lemmon, SD **111** A3
Lemon, Lake, IN **93** F3
Lennox, SD **111** E10
Lenoir, NC **75** B4
Lenoir City, TN **79** B8
Lenox, MA **40** B1
Leola, SD **111** A7
Leominster, MA **41** B5
Leon (river), TX **127** E6
Leusoalii, AS **157** I5
Levelland, TX **127** C3
Levisa Fork (river), KY **69** C10
Levittown, NY **47** H9
Levittown, PA **49** E10
Lewes, DE **35** G7
Lewes and Rehoboth Canal, DE **35** G7
Lewis (river), WA **153** F3
Lewis and Clark Lake, NE, SD **111** F9
Lewis and Clark Memorial, MT **144** F3
Lewis Smith Lake, AL **61** B3
Lewisburg, PA **49** C7
Lewisburg, TN **79** C5
Lewisburg, WV **83** G5
Lewiston, ID **143** D1
Lewiston, ME **37** G3
Lewistown, MT **145** C6
Lewistown, PA **49** D6
Lexington, KY **69** C8
Lexington, MA **41** B7
Lexington, NC **75** B5
Lexington, NE **105** D5
Lexington, TN **78** C3
Lexington, VA **81** D7
Lexington Park, MD **39** E8
Libby, MT **144** B1
Liberal, KS **96** F2
Liberty, MO **103** C2
Licking (river), KY **69** A8
Licking (river), OH **109** E5
Licking, North Fork (river), KY **69** B8
Licking, South Fork (river), KY **69** B8
Lihu'e, HI **140** A2
Lillinonah, Lake, CT **33** D2
Lima, OH **109** C2
Limestone, ME **37** B6
Limon, CO **139** D7
Lincoln, DE **35** G6
Lincoln, IL **91** E4
Lincoln, ME **37** E5
Lincoln, NE **105** D9
Lincoln, NH **43** E3
Lincoln Boyhood National Memorial, IN **93** H2
Lincoln City, OR **148** C1
Lincoln Home National Historic Site, IL **91** E3
Lincolnton, NC **75** C4
Lindenwold, NJ **45** F2
Lindsborg, KS **97** C6
Linton, IN **93** G2
Linton, ND **107** F6
Lisbon, ND **107** E9
Lisbon, NH **43** D2
Lisbon Falls, ME **37** G3
Lisianski Island, HI **140** E2
Liston Point, DE **35** C5
Litchfield, CT **33** B3
Litchfield, IL **91** F3
Litchfield, MN **101** F3
Little (river), AR, OK **63** F1
Little (river), KY **68** E3
Little (river), LA **71** D4
Little (river), OK **125** D9
Little Beaver Creek National Scenic River, OH **109** C8
Little Bighorn Battlefield Nat. Mon., MT **145** E8
Little Blue (river), KS, NE **97** A7
Little Colorado (river), AZ **121** D7
Little Compton, RI **51** E6
Little Darby Creek, OH **109** E3
Little Deschutes N.W.&S.R., OR **149** E4

Little Diomede Island, AK **134** C3
Little Egg Harbor, NJ **45** G4
Little Falls, MN **101** E3
Little Falls, NY **47** D7
Little Humboldt (river), NV **147** B4
Little Kanawha (river), WV **83** D3
Little Lost (river), ID **143** F4
Little Miami (river), OH **109** F2
Little Miami National Scenic River, OH **109** F2
Little Miami, East Fork (river), OH **109** G2
Little Missouri (river), AR, ND, SD **86** C1
Little Missouri, MT **145** F11
Little Missouri N.W.&S.R., AR **63** E2
Little Muddy (river), ND **106** B2
Little Pee Dee (river), NC, SC **77** D9
Little Powder (river), WY **155** B8
Little Red (river), AR **63** C5
Little River Canyon National Preserve, AL **61** B5
Little Rock, AR **63** D4
Little Rock Central High School National Historic Site, AR **63** D5
Little Sac (river), MO **103** E3
Little Salt Lake (dry lake), UT **151** G2
Little Sandy (river), KY **69** B10
Little Sioux (river), IA **94** C2
Little Snake (river), CO **139** A2
Little Tallahatchie (river), MS **73** B4
Little Wabash (river), IL **91** G5
Little White (river), SD **111** F4
Little Wood (river), ID **143** H3
Littleton, CO **139** C6
Littleton, ME **37** C6
Littleton, NH **43** D3
Live Oak, FL **65** B6
Livingston, AL **61** E1
Livingston, MT **145** E5
Livingston, Lake, TX **116** E9
Livonia, MI **99** H7
Llano (river), TX **127** E5
Llano Estacado (plain), NM, TX **116** D5
Lochsa (river), ID **143** D2
Lock Haven, PA **49** C6
Lockport, NY **46** D2
Locust Creek, MO **103** A4
Locust Fork (river), AL **61** C3
Lodgepole Creek, NE, WY **104** C1
Lodi, CA **137** D3
Logan, OH **109** F5
Logan, UT **151** A4
Logan, WV **82** G2
Logan Creek, NE **105** B8
Logansport, IN **93** C3
Lolo Pass, MT **144** D2
Lompoc, CA **137** G4
London, KY **69** D8
Londonderry, NH **43** I4
Lone Grove, OK **125** E8
Long Bay, NC, SC **75** E7
Long Beach, CA **137** H5
Long Beach, MS **73** I4
Long Beach, NY **47** H9
Long Beach Island, NJ **45** G5
Long Branch, NJ **45** D5
Long Island, NY **47** H9
Long Island Sound, NY **47** G9
Long Lake (lake), ME **37** A5
Long Lake (lake), ME **37** B4
Long Lake, ND **107** E6
Long Pond, MA **41** E7
Long Prairie, MN **101** E3
Long Trail, VT **53** D2
Longfellow Mountains, ME **37** F2
Longmont, CO **139** B5
Longview, TX **127** D8
Longview, WA **153** F3
Lonsdale, RI **51** B5
Looking Glass (river), MI **99** G6
Lookout Pass, ID **143** C2
Lookout, Cape, NC **75** D10
Lookout, Point, MD **39** F8
Lorain, OH **109** B5
Lordsburg, NM **123** G1
Loris, SC **77** D9
Los Alamos, NM **123** C4
Los Angeles, CA **137** H5
Los Lunas, NM **123** D4
Los Pinos (river), CO **139** F2
Lost River Range, ID **143** F3
Lostine N.W.&S.R., OR **149** B8
Loudonville, OH **109** C5
Louie B. Nunn Parkway, KY **69** E6
Louisiana, MO **103** B6
Louisville, CO **139** B5
Louisville, KY **69** B6
Louisville, MS **73** D4
Loup (river), NE **105** C7
Loup, Middle (river), NE **105** C5
Loup, North (river), NE **105** B5
Loup, South (river), NE **105** C5
Loveland, CO **139** B5
Lovell, WY **155** A5
Lovelock, NV **147** C3
Loving, NM **123** G7
Lovington, NM **123** G8
Lowell, IN **93** B2
Lowell, MA **41** A6
Lowell N.H.P., MA **41** A6
Lowell, Lake, ID **143** G1
Lower Bay, NJ **45** D5
Lower Peninsula, MI **99** F5
Lower Red Lake, MN **101** B3
Lowville, NY **47** C6
Loxahatchee N.W.&S.R., FL **65** F10
Lubbock, TX **127** C4
Lucedale, MS **73** H5
Ludington, MI **99** F4
Ludlow, MA **41** C3
Ludlow, VT **53** G3
Lufkin, TX **127** E8
Lumber (river), NC **75** D6
Lumber N.W.&S.R., NC **75** D6
Lumberton, NC **75** D7
Luray, VA **81** B8
Lusk, WY **155** D10
Luverne, MN **101** H2
Lyman, WY **154** G2
Lynchburg, TN **79** C5
Lynchburg, VA **81** D7
Lynches (river), SC **77** D8
Lynden, WA **153** A3
Lyndon B. Johnson N.H.P., TX **127** F6
Lyndonville, VT **53** C5
Lynn, MA **41** B7
Lyons, KS **97** D5

M

Machias, ME **37** F7
Machias (river), ME **37** F6
Machiasport, ME **37** F7
Mackinac Island, MI **99** D6
Mackinac, Straits of, MI **99** D5
Mackinaw (river), IL **91** D4
Macomb, IL **91** D2
Macon, GA **67** E3
Macon, MO **103** B4
Macon, Bayou (river), LA **71** B5
Macoupin Creek, IL **91** F2
Mad (river), VT **53** D3
Madawaska, ME **37** A5
Madeline Island, WI **113** A4
Madill, OK **125** E9
Madison, AL **61** A3
Madison, CT **33** E5
Madison, IN **93** G5
Madison, ME **37** F3
Madison, MN **101** F2
Madison, NE **105** C8
Madison, SD **111** D9
Madison, WI **113** G5
Madison, WV **82** G2
Madison (river), WY **154** A1
Madison (river), MT **145** E4
Madison Heights, VA **81** D7
Madisonville, KY **68** D3
Madras, OR **149** C4
Magazine Mountain (peak), AR **63** C2
Magee, MS **73** F3
Maggie L. Walker National Historic Site, VA **81** D9
Magic Reservoir, ID **143** H3
Magnolia, AR **63** G3
Mahoning (river), OH **109** B8
Maia, AS **157** I5
Maine, Gulf of, ME **37** H5
Makawao, HI **141** C7
Malad City, ID **143** I4
Malden, MA **41** B7
Malden, MO **103** G7
Malheur (river), OR **149** D8
Malheur Lake, OR **149** E7
Malheur N.W.&S.R., OR **149** D7
Malheur, North Fork (river), OR **149** D7
Malheur, North Fork N.W.&S.R., OR **149** D7
Malone, NY **47** A8
Malta, MT **145** B8
Malvern, AR **63** E3
Mammoth Cave N.P., KY **69** D5
Manalapan (river), NJ **45** D4
Manasquan, NJ **45** E5
Manassas, VA **81** B9
Manassas National Battlefield Park, VA **81** B9
Manchester, CT **33** B5
Manchester, IA **95** C8
Manchester, MD **39** A7
Manchester, NH **43** H4
Manchester, OH **109** G3
Manchester, TN **79** C6
Manchester Center, VT **53** H2
Mancos (river), CO **138** G1
Mandan, ND **107** E5
Mandeville, LA **71** F8
Mangum, OK **125** D6
Manhattan, KS **97** B7
Manila, AR **63** B8
Manistee, MI **99** F4
Manistee (river), MI **99** F5
Manistee N.W.&S.R., MI **99** F5
Manistique, MI **99** D4
Manitou Islands, MI **99** E4
Manitou Passage, MI **99** E5
Manitowoc, WI **113** E7
Mankato, MN **101** G4
Manning, SC **77** D7
Mannington, WV **83** C5
Mansfield, LA **70** C1
Mansfield, OH **109** C5
Mansfield, PA **49** B6
Mansfield Hollow Lake, CT **33** B7
Mansfield, Mount, VT **53** C2
Manti, UT **151** E4
Manua Islands (islands), AS **156** I3
Manville, RI **51** A4
Many, LA **70** D2
Manzanar National Historic Site, CA **137** F5
Maple (river), ND **107** E9
Maple (river), ND **107** F8
Maquoketa, IA **95** C9
Maquoketa (river), IA **95** C9
Marais des Cygnes (river), KS, MO **97** C10
Marathon, FL **65** I8
Marble Canyon, AZ **121** B5
Marblehead, MA **41** B8
Marcy, Mount, NY **47** B8
Marfa, TX **126** F2
Marianna, AR **63** D7
Marianna, FL **65** A3
Marias (river), MT **145** B4
Marietta, GA **67** C2
Marietta, OH **109** F7
Marinette, WI **113** D7
Marion, AL **61** E2
Marion, IA **95** C8
Marion, IL **91** H4
Marion, IN **93** C4
Marion, KY **68** D3
Marion, OH **109** D4
Marion, SC **77** C8
Marion, VA **80** E4
Marion Lake, KS **97** C7
Marion, Lake, SC **77** E6
Mark Twain Lake, MO **103** B5
Marked Tree, AR **63** C7
Marksville, LA **71** E4
Marlborough, CT **33** C6
Marlborough, MA **41** C6
Marlow, OK **125** E8
Maro Reef, HI **140** F2
Marquette, MI **99** C3
Mars Hill, ME **37** B6
Marsh Island, LA **71** H4
Marshall, MI **99** H6
Marshall, MN **101** G2
Marshall, MO **103** C4
Marshall, TX **127** D9
Marshallton, DE **35** B4
Marshalltown, IA **95** C6
Marsh-Billings-Rockefeller N.H.P., VT **53** F3
Marshfield, WI **113** D4
Marshyhope Creek, DE, MD **35** G4
Martha's Vineyard (island), MA **41** F8
Martin, SD **111** E4
Martin, TN **78** B2
Martin Luther King, Jr. National Historic Site, GA **67** C2
Martin Van Buren National Historic Site, NY **47** E8
Martin, Lake, AL **61** E5
Martins Ferry, OH **109** D8
Martinsburg, WV **83** C9
Martinsville, IN **93** F3
Martinsville, VA **81** E6
Marydel, DE **35** E4
Marys (river), NV **147** A6
Marysville, KS **97** A7
Marysville, OH **109** D3
Maryville, MO **103** A2
Maryville, TN **79** C8
Mascoma Lake, NH **43** F2
Mason, MI **99** H6
Mason, OH **109** F2
Mason City, IA **95** A6
Massabesic Lake, NH **43** H4
Massachusetts Bay, MA **41** B8
Massena, NY **47** A7
Massillon, OH **109** C6
Matagorda Bay, TX **116** F8
Matanuska (river), AK **135** E6
Mattawamkeag (river), ME **37** D6
Matthews, NC **75** C4
Mattoon, IL **91** F5
Maui (island), HI **141** C7
Mauldin, SC **77** B3
Maumee, OH **109** B3
Maumee (river), IN, OH **93** B6
Maumee Bay, OH **109** A3
Maumelle, AR **63** D4
Mauna Kea (peak), HI **141** E9
Mauna Loa (peak), HI **141** F9
Maurepas, Lake, LA **71** F7
Maurice (river), NJ **45** G2
Maurice N.W.&S.R., NJ **45** H2
May, Cape, NJ **45** I2
Mayagüez, PR **157** I9
Mayfield, KY **68** E2
Mayfield Creek, KY **68** E1
Mays Landing, NJ **45** H3
Maysville, KY **69** B9
Mayville, ND **107** C9
McAlester, OK **125** D10
McAllen, TX **127** I6
McCall, ID **143** F1
McCandless, PA **48** D2
McComb, MS **73** G2
McCook, NE **105** E4
McGee Creek Lake, OK **125** E10
McGehee, AR **63** F6
McGill, NV **147** D6
McIntosh, SD **111** A4
McKee Creek, IL **91** E2
McKeesport, PA **48** E2
McKenzie, TN **78** B3
McKenzie (river), OR **149** D2
McKenzie N.W.&S.R., OR **149** D3
McKinley, Mount (Denali), AK **135** D6
McLean, VA **81** A9
McLoughlin House National Historic Site, OR **149** B2
McMinnville, OR **149** B2
McMinnville, TN **79** C6
McPherson, KS **97** C5
Mead, Lake, AZ, NV **121** B2
Meade, KS **97** E3
Meade (river), AK **135** A5
Meadow Valley Wash (river), NV **147** G7
Meadville, PA **48** B2
Mechanicsburg, PA **49** E6
Mechanicsville, VA **81** D9
Medford, MA **41** B7
Medford, OR **149** G2
Medford, WI **113** D4
Medical Lake, WA **153** C9
Medicine Bow (river), WY **155** F7
Medicine Bow Mountains, CO **139** A4
Medicine Lodge (river), KS **97** E4
Medicine Lodge, KS **97** E5
Medina, NY **46** D3
Medina, OH **109** B6
Medora, ND **106** D2
Meeker, CO **139** B2
Meherrin (river), VA **81** E8
Melbourne, FL **65** D9
Melozitna (river), AK **135** C5
Memphis, TN **78** C1
Memphremagog, Lake, VT **53** A4
Mena, AR **63** D1
Menahga, MN **101** D3
Menasha, WI **113** E6
Mendota, IL **91** B4
Mendota, Lake, WI **113** G5
Menlo Park, NJ **45** D4
Menominee, MI **99** E3
Menominee (river), MI, WI **99** D3
Menomonee Falls, WI **113** G7
Menomonie, WI **113** D2
Mentor, OH **109** A7
Mequon, WI **113** G7
Merced, CA **137** E4
Merced N.W.&S.R., CA **137** E4
Mercersburg, PA **49** F5
Mercerville, NJ **45** E3
Meredith, NH **43** F3
Meredith, Lake, CO **139** E7
Meriden, CT **33** C4
Meridian, MS **73** E5
Merrill, WI **113** D5
Merrillville, IN **93** A2
Merrimack, NH **43** I3
Merrimack (river), MA, NH **41** A7
Merritt Island, FL **65** D9
Merrymeeting Lake, NH **43** G4
Mesa, AZ **121** F5
Mesa de Maya, CO **139** G7
Mesa Verde N.P., CO **138** G1
Mesabi Range, MN **101** C4
Mesquite, NV **147** G7
Metairie, LA **71** G8
Meteor Crater, AZ **121** D5
Methow (river), WA **153** B6
Methuen, MA **41** A7
Metolius N.W.&S.R., OR **149** D3
Metropolis, IL **91** I4
Mettawee (river), VT **53** G1
Mexico, ME **37** F2
Mexico, MO **103** C5
Mexico, Gulf of, **56** G3
Miami, FL **65** G9
Miami, OK **125** A11
Miami Beach, FL **65** G9
Miami Canal, FL **65** F9
Michigan City, IN **93** A2
Michigan, Lake, **86** D7
Middleboro, MA **41** D8
Middlebury, VT **53** E2
Middlesboro, KY **69** E9
Middleton, WI **113** G5
Middletown, CT **33** C5
Middletown, DE **35** C4
Middletown, NY **47** G8
Middletown, OH **109** F2
Middletown, RI **51** E5
Midland, MI **99** G6
Midland, TX **127** D3
Midway, DE **35** H7
Midway Islands (territory), US **156** D4
Milaca, MN **101** E4
Milan, NM **123** D2
Milan, TN **78** B2
Milbank, SD **111** B10
Miles City, MT **145** D10
Milford, CT **33** E3
Milford, DE **35** G6
Milford, MA **41** C6
Milford, NE **105** D8
Milford, NH **43** I3
Milford, UT **151** F2
Milford Lake, KS **97** B7
Mililani Town, HI **141** B4
Milk (river), MT **145** B8
Mill Creek, IN **93** F3
Millbrook, AL **61** E4
Millcreek, PA **48** A2
Mille Lacs Lake, MN **101** D4
Milledgeville, GA **67** D4
Millen, GA **67** E6
Miller, SD **111** C7
Millers (river), MA **41** A4
Millington, TN **78** C1
Millinocket, ME **37** D5
Millsboro, DE **35** I6
Millville, NJ **45** H2
Millwood Lake, AR **63** F2
Milo, ME **37** E4
Milton, DE **35** G6
Milton, MA **41** C7
Milton, NH **43** G5
Milton, VT **53** B2
Milton, Lake, OH **109** C7
Milton-Freewater, OR **149** A7
Milwaukee, WI **113** G7
Milwaukee (river), WI **113** F6
Minam N.W.&S.R., OR **149** B8
Minden, LA **70** B2
Minden, NE **105** D6
Mineral Wells, TX **127** D6
Minidoka Internment Camp Nat. Mon., ID **143** H3
Minneapolis, KS **97** B6
Minneapolis, MN **101** F4
Minnesota (river), MN **101** F2
Minot, ND **107** B4
Minute Man N.H.P., MA **41** B6
Minuteman Missile National Historic Site, SD **111** D3
Mio, MI **99** E6

Mishawaka — Odessa

Mishawaka, IN **93** A4
Mission, TX **127** I6
Mission Viejo, CA **137** H6
Missisquoi (river), VT **53** A2
Mississinewa (river), IN **93** D5
Mississinewa Lake, IN **93** C4
Mississippi (river), **56** B2
Mississippi National River and N.R.A., MN **101** F4
Mississippi Petrified Forest, MS **73** E2
Mississippi River Delta, LA **71** I10
Mississippi Sound, AL, MS **73** I5
Missoula, MT **144** C3
Missouri (river), **86** F5
Missouri N.W.&S.R., MT **145** B6
Missouri National Recreational River, NE, SD **105** A7
Misty Fiords Nat. Mon., AK **135** G11
Mitchell, SD **111** E8
Mitchell, Mount, NC **74** B3
Moab, UT **151** F6
Moberly, MO **103** B4
Mobile, AL **61** H1
Mobile (river), AL **61** H1
Mobile Bay, AL **61** I1
Mobridge, SD **111** B5
Modesto, CA **137** E3
Mogollon Rim, AZ **121** E6
Mohave, Lake, AZ, NV **121** C1
Mohawk (river), NY **47** D7
Mohican (river), OH **109** D5
Mojave Desert, CA, NV **130** F4
Mojave National Preserve, CA **137** G7
Moline, IL **91** C2
Moloka'i (island), HI **141** C6
Monadnock Mountain, NH **43** I2
Monahans, TX **127** E3
Moncks Corner, SC **77** F7
Monessen, PA **48** E2
Monett, MO **103** F3
Monhegan Island, ME **37** H4
Monitor Range, NV **147** E4
Monmouth, IL **91** C2
Monmouth, OR **149** C2
Mono Lake, CA **137** D5
Monocacy (river), MD **39** A6
Monocacy N.B., MD **39** B6
Monomoy Island, MA **41** E10
Monona, WI **113** G5
Monongahela (river), PA, WV **28** G1
Monroe, GA **67** C3
Monroe, LA **71** B4
Monroe, MI **99** I7
Monroe, NC **75** C5
Monroe, WI **113** H5
Monroe Lake, IN **93** G3
Monroeville, AL **61** G2
Montauk Point, NY **47** G11
Monte Vista, CO **139** F4
Monterey, CA **137** F2
Monterey Bay, CA **137** F2
Monterey Bay National Marine Sanctuary, CA **137** E2
Montevallo, AL **61** D3
Montevideo, MN **101** F2
Montezuma Castle Nat. Mon., AZ **121** D5
Montgomery, AL **61** E4
Montgomery, WV **83** F3
Montgomery Village, MD **39** B6
Monticello, AR **63** F5
Monticello, IA **95** C9
Monticello, IN **93** C3
Monticello, NY **47** F7
Monticello (site), VA **81** C8
Montpelier, ID **143** I6
Montpelier (site), VA **81** C8
Montpelier, VT **53** D3
Montrose, CO **139** E2
Monument Valley, AZ, UT **151** H6
Moodus, CT **33** D6
Moore, OK **125** D8
Moore Reservoir, NH, VT **53** C5
Moorefield, WV **83** D8
Moores Creek N.B., NC **75** D8
Moorhead, MN **101** D1
Moose (river), VT **53** C5
Moose (river), ME **37** D2
Moosehead Lake, ME **37** D4
Mooselookmeguntic Lake, ME **37** F2
Moosup, CT **33** B8
Moosup (river), RI **51** C2
Mora, MN **101** E4
Mora (river), NM **123** C6
Moreau (river), SD **111** B4
Morehead, KY **69** B9
Morehead City, NC **75** D9
Morgan City, LA **71** H6
Morgan Horse Farm (site), VT **53** D1
Morganfield, KY **68** C3
Morganton, NC **74** B3
Morgantown, WV **83** C6
Moriarty, NM **123** D4
Mormon Reservoir, ID **143** H3
Moroni, UT **151** D4
Morrilton, AR **63** C4
Morris, IL **91** C5
Morris, MN **101** E2
Morristown, NJ **45** C3
Morristown, TN **79** B9
Morristown N.H.P., NJ **45** C3
Morrisville, VT **53** B3
Morton, IL **91** D4
Moscow, ID **143** C1
Moses Lake, WA **153** D7
Mosquito Creek Lake, OH **109** B8
Moss Point, MS **73** I5
Mott, ND **107** E3
Moultrie, GA **67** H3
Moultrie, Lake, SC **77** E7
Moundsville, WV **83** B4
Mount Airy, NC **75** A5
Mount Desert Island, ME **37** G6
Mount Holly, NJ **45** F3
Mount Hope Bay, RI **51** D6
Mount Pleasant, IA **95** E8
Mount Pleasant, UT **151** D4
Mount Rainier N.P., WA **153** E4
Mount Rushmore Nat. Mon., SD **110** D2
Mount St. Helens National Volcanic Monument, WA **153** E4
Mount Vernon, IN **93** I1
Mount Vernon, KY **69** D8
Mount Vernon (site), VA **81** B10
Mount Vernon, WA **153** B4
Mountain Fork (river), OK **125** E12
Mountain Grove, MO **103** F5
Mountain Home, AR **63** A4
Mountain Home, ID **143** H2
Mountain View, AR **63** B5
Mountain View, HI **141** F9
Mountain Village, AK **134** D3
Mountainair, NM **123** D4
Mouse (river) *see* Souris, ND **107** B5
Mt. Carmel, IL **91** G5
Mt. Carmel, PA **49** D7
Mt. Pleasant, MI **99** G6
Mt. Pleasant, SC **77** G7
Mt. Pleasant, TX **127** C8
Mt. Sterling, KY **69** C8
Mt. Vernon, IL **91** G4
Mt. Vernon, OH **109** D5
Mud Lake, ID **143** G5
Mud Lake, MN **101** B2
Muddy Boggy Creek, OK **125** E10
Muir Woods Nat. Mon., CA **137** D2
Mulberry (river), AR **63** B2
Mulberry Fork (river), AL **61** B3
Mulberry N.W.&S.R., AR **63** B2
Mulchatna N.W.&S.R., AK **135** E5
Mullen, NE **105** B4
Mullens, WV **83** H3
Mullett Lake, MI **99** D6
Mullica (river), NJ **45** G3
Mullins, SC **77** C9
Mulvane, KS **97** E7
Muncie, IN **93** D5
Munising, MI **99** C4
Murdo, SD **111** D5
Murfreesboro, AR **63** E2
Murfreesboro, TN **79** B5
Murphysboro, IL **91** H4
Murray, KY **68** E2
Murray, UT **151** C4
Murray, Lake, SC **77** C4
Muscatatuck (river), IN **93** G4
Muscatine, IA **95** E9
Muscle Shoals, AL **61** A2
Musconetcong (river), NJ **45** C2
Muscongus Bay, ME **37** H4
Muskegon, MI **99** G4
Muskegon (river), MI **99** G5
Muskingum (river), OH **109** E6
Muskogee, OK **125** C11
Muskogee Turnpike, OK **125** C11
Musselshell (river), MT **145** D7
Myrtle Beach, SC **77** D9
Mystic, CT **33** D8
Mystic Island, NJ **45** G4
Mystic Seaport (site), CT **33** D8

N

Naches (river), WA **153** E5
Nacogdoches, TX **127** E9
Naknek, AK **135** F5
Namakan Lake, MN **101** B5
Namekagon (river), WI **113** B2
Nampa, ID **143** G1
Nanticoke (river), DE, MD **39** E9
Nantucket, MA **41** F10
Nantucket Island, MA **41** F10
Nantucket Sound, MA **41** F9
Napa, CA **137** D2
Napatree Point, RI **51** G1
Naperville, IL **91** B5
Naples, FL **65** G7
Napoleon, ND **107** E6
Napoleon, OH **109** B2
Nappanee, IN **93** B4
Narragansett Bay, RI **51** E5
Narragansett Pier, RI **51** F4
Nashua, NH **43** I4
Nashua (river), MA **41** B5
Nashville, AR **63** F2
Nashville, IL **91** G4
Nashville, TN **79** B5
Natchaug (river), CT **33** B7
Natchez, MS **73** G1
Natchez N.H.P., MS **73** F1
Natchez Trace Parkway, AL, MS **73** D4
Natchitoches, LA **70** C2
National Park of American Samoa, AS **156** I4
Natural Bridges Nat. Mon., UT **151** G6
Naugatuck, CT **33** D3
Naugatuck (river), CT **33** D3
Nauvoo, IL **91** D1
Navajo, NM **123** B1
Navajo Nat. Mon., AZ **121** B6
Navajo Reservoir, NM **123** A3
Navassa Island (territory), US **157** E11
Nazareth, PA **49** D9
Near Islands, AK **135** G5
Nebraska City, NE **105** D9
Neches (river), TX **127** E8
Necker Island, HI **141** F4
Needles, CA **137** G8
Neenah, WI **113** E6
Nehalem (river), OR **149** A2
Neligh, NE **105** B7
Nelson Island, AK **134** E3
Nelsonville, OH **109** F5
Neosho, MO **103** F2
Neosho (river), KS, OK **86** G4
Nepaug Reservoir, CT **33** B4
Nephi, UT **151** D4
Neptune, NJ **45** E5
Ness City, KS **97** C3
Neuse (river), NC **75** C8
Nevada, IA **95** D5
Nevada, MO **103** E2
New (river), VA **80** F4
New Albany, IN **93** H4
New Albany, MS **73** B4
New Bedford, MA **41** E7
New Bedford Whaling N.H.P., MA **41** E7
New Bern, NC **75** C9
New Braunfels, TX **127** F6
New Brunswick, NJ **45** D4
New Canaan, CT **33** E1
New Castle, DE **35** B5
New Castle, IN **93** E5
New Castle, PA **48** C1
New City, NY **47** G8
New Echota State Historic Site, GA **67** B2
New Fairfield, CT **33** D2
New Hampton, IA **95** B7
New Harmony State Historic Site, IN **93** H1
New Hartford, CT **33** B4
New Haven, CT **33** D4
New Iberia, LA **71** G5
New Ipswich, NH **43** I3
New Jersey Turnpike, NJ **45** E3
New Lexington, OH **109** E5
New London, CT **33** D7
New London, NH **43** G2
New London, WI **113** E6
New Madrid, MO **103** F8
New Martinsville, WV **83** C4
New Milford, CT **33** C2
New N.W.&S.R., NC **75** A4
New Orleans, LA **71** G8
New Paltz, NY **47** F8
New Philadelphia, OH **109** D6
New Richmond, WI **113** D1
New River Gorge Bridge, WV **83** F4
New River Gorge National River, WV **83** G4
New Rochelle, NY **47** H8
New Rockford, ND **107** C7
New Salem, ND **107** E4
New Smyrna Beach, FL **65** C8
New Town, ND **107** C3
New Ulm, MN **101** G3
New York, NY **47** H8
New York State Thruway, NY **47** D4
New, South Fork (river), NC **75** A4
Newark, DE **35** B4
Newark, NJ **45** C4
Newark, OH **109** E5
Newberry, SC **77** C4
Newberry National Volcanic Monument, OR **149** D4
Newburg, OR **149** B2
Newburgh, NY **47** G8
Newbury, VT **53** D5
Newburyport, MA **41** A8
Newcastle, WY **155** C10
Newfound Lake, NH **43** F3
Newfoundland Evaporation Basin (dry lake), UT **151** B2
Newington, CT **33** C5
Newmarket, NH **43** H5
Newnan, GA **67** D2
Newport, AR **63** B6
Newport, DE **35** B5
Newport, KY **69** A8
Newport, ME **37** F4
Newport, NH **43** G2
Newport, OR **148** C1
Newport, RI **51** F5
Newport, TN **79** B9
Newport, VT **53** A4
Newport News, VA **81** E11
Newton, IA **95** D6
Newton, KS **97** D7
Newton, MS **73** F4
Newton, NC **75** B4
Newton, NJ **45** B3
Newtown, CT **33** D2
Nez Perce N.H.P., ID **143** D1
Nez Perce Pass, MT **144** E2
Ni'ihau (island), HI **140** B1
Niagara, WI **113** C7
Niagara Falls, NY **46** D2
Niagara Falls (waterfall), NY **28** D2
Niagara River (river), NY **46** D2
Niangua (river), MO **103** E4
Niantic, CT **33** D7
Niceville, FL **64** A2
Nicodemus National Historic Site, KS **97** B4
Nihoa (island), HI **141** F4
Niles, MI **99** I4
Niles, OH **109** B8
Nine Mile Creek, UT **151** D5
Nine-Mile Prairie, NE **105** D8
Ninety Six National Historic Site, SC **77** C3
Ninigret Pond, RI **51** G3
Niobrara (river), NE, WY **105** A4
Niobrara National Scenic Riverway, NE **105** A5
Niskayuna, NY **47** E8
Nitro, WV **82** F2
Noatak N.W.&S.R., AK **135** B4
Noatak National Preserve, AK **135** B5
Noblesville, IN **93** D4
Nocona, TX **127** C6
Nodaway, East (river), IA **95** E3
Nogales, AZ **121** H6
Nolichucky (river), TN **79** B10
Nolin River Lake, KY **69** D5
Nomans Land (island), MA **41** F8
Nome, AK **134** C3
Nonquit Pond, RI **51** E6
Norfolk, CT **33** A3
Norfolk, NE **105** B8
Norfolk, VA **81** E11
Norfork Lake, AR **63** A5
Normal, IL **91** D4
Norman, OK **125** D8
Norman, Lake, NC **75** B4
Norris Lake, TN **79** B8
Norristown, PA **49** E9
North Adams, MA **40** A1
North Attleboro, MA **41** D6
North Augusta, SC **77** E3
North Bend, OH **109** F1
North Bend, OR **148** E1
North Bennington, VT **53** I1
North Branford, CT **33** D4
North Canton, OH **109** C7
North Cascades N.P., WA **153** A5
North Charleston, SC **77** F7
North Conway, NH **43** E4
North Fork Sprague N.W.&S.R., OR **149** F4
North Grosvenor Dale, CT **33** A8
North Haven, CT **33** D4
North Hero, VT **53** B1
North Hero Island, VT **53** A1
North Island, SC **77** E9
North Las Vegas, NV **147** G6
North Little Rock, AR **63** D4
North Manchester, IN **93** B4
North Myrtle Beach, SC **77** D10
North Ogden, UT **151** B4
North Olmsted, OH **109** B6
North Platte, NE **105** D4
North Pole, AK **135** D7
North Powder N.W.&S.R., OR **149** C7
North Providence, RI **51** B4
North Scituate, RI **51** B3
North Sioux City, SD **111** F10
North Slope, AK **135** B5
North Springfield, VT **53** G3
North Sterling Reservoir, CO **139** A8
North Stratford, NH **43** C3
North Sylamore Creek N.W.&S.R., AR **63** B4
North Troy, VT **53** A4
North Umpqua N.W.&S.R., OR **149** E2
North Vernon, IN **93** G5
North Walpole, NH **43** H1
North Wildwood, NJ **45** I3
Northampton, MA **41** C3
Northern Mariana Islands (territory), US **156** E1
Northfield, MN **101** G5
Northfield, NH **43** G3
Northfield, VT **53** D3
Northwestern Hawaiian Islands, HI **140** E1
Northwood, ND **107** C9
Norton, KS **97** A3
Norton, VA **80** E2
Norton Sound, AK **135** D4
Norwalk, CT **33** F2
Norwalk, OH **109** B5
Norway, ME **37** G2
Norwich, CT **33** C7
Norwich, NY **47** E6
Norwich, VT **53** F4
Norwood, MA **41** C7
Norwood, OH **109** F2
Nottoway (river), VA **81** E10
Nowitna N.W.&S.R., AK **135** D6
Nowood (river), WY **155** B5
Noxontown Pond, DE **35** C4
Noxubee (river), MS **73** D5
Nubanusit Lake, NH **43** H2
Nueces (river), TX **127** G6
Nunivak Island, AK **134** E3
Nuuuli, AS **156** I1

O

O'ahu (island), HI **141** B5
Oahe, Lake, ND, SD **111** B6
Oak Bluffs, MA **41** F9
Oak Harbor, WA **153** B3
Oak Hill, WV **83** G4
Oak Orchard, DE **35** H7
Oak Ridge, TN **79** B8
Oakdale, LA **71** E3
Oakes, ND **107** F8
Oakland, CA **137** E2
Oakland, MD **38** B1
Oakland, ME **37** F3
Oakley, KS **96** B2
Oakville, CT **33** C3
Obed (river), TN **79** B7
Obed N.W.&S.R., TN **79** B7
Oberlin, KS **97** A3
Obion (river), TN **78** B1
Ocala, FL **65** C7
Ocean City, MD **39** E11
Ocean City, NJ **45** H3
Ocean Lake, WY **155** D4
Ocean Pines, MD **39** E11
Ocean Shores, WA **152** D1
Ocean Springs, MS **73** I5
Ocean View, DE **35** I7
Oceanside, CA **137** I6
Ochlockonee (river), FL, GA **65** B4
Ochoco Mountains, OR **149** C5
Ocmulgee (river), GA **67** G4
Ocmulgee Nat. Mon., GA **67** E4
Oconee (river), GA **67** F5
Oconee, Lake, GA **67** D4
Oconto, WI **113** D7
Oconto (river), WI **113** D7
Ocracoke Island, NC **75** C10
Odessa, DE **35** C4

Odessa — Potomac

Odessa, TX **127** E3
Oelwein, IA **95** B8
Ofu (island), AS **156** I3
Ofu, AS **156** H3
Ogallala, NE **105** D3
Ogden, UT **151** B4
Ogdensburg, NY **47** A6
Ogeechee (river), GA **67** E6
Ogunquit, ME **37** I2
Ohio (river), **86** G7
Ohoopee (river), GA **67** F6
Oil City, PA **48** B2
Okanogan (river), WA **153** B7
Okatibbee Lake, MS **73** E5
Okeechobee, Lake, FL **65** F8
Okefenokee Swamp, GA **67** H5
Oklahoma City, OK **125** C8
Okmulgee, OK **125** C10
Okobojo Creek, SD **111** C5
Okolona, MS **73** C5
Olathe, KS **97** C10
Old Faithful (site), WY **154** B2
Old Hickory Lake, TN **79** B5
Old Oraibi (site), AZ **121** C6
Old Orchard Beach, ME **37** H2
Old Saybrook, CT **33** E6
Old Town, ME **37** F5
Olean, NY **46** F3
Olentangy (river), OH **109** D4
Oliver, Lake, GA **67** E1
Olivia, MN **101** G3
Olney, IL **91** G5
Olosega (island), AS **156** H3
Olosega, AS **156** H3
Olympia, WA **153** D3
Olympic Coast National Marine Sanctuary, WA **152** B1
Olympic Mountains, WA **152** C2
Olympic N.P., WA **152** C2
Olympus, Mount, WA **152** C2
Omaha, NE **105** C9
Omak, WA **153** B7
Onalaska, WI **113** F3
Onancock, VA **81** D12
Onawa, IA **94** C2
One Hundred and Two (river), MO **103** A2
Oneida, NY **47** D6
Oneida Lake, NY **47** D6
O'Neill, NE **105** B6
Oneonta, NY **47** E7
Onida, SD **111** C6
Onslow Bay, NC **75** D9
Ontario, OR **149** D9
Ontario, Lake, **28** D2
Ontonagon N.W.&S.R., MI **99** B2
Oologah Lake, OK **125** B10
Oostanaula (river), GA **67** B1
Opelika, AL **61** E5
Opelousas, LA **71** F4
Opp, AL **61** G4
Opportunity, WA **153** C10
Optima Lake, OK **124** B4
Orange, CT **33** E3
Orange, MA **41** B3
Orange, VA **81** C8
Orange City, IA **94** B2
Orangeburg, SC **77** E5
Orchard City, CO **139** D2
Ord, NE **105** C6
Ordway, CO **139** E7
Oreana, NV **147** C3
Oregon, OH **109** A3
Oregon Caves Nat. Mon., OR **149** G2
Oregon City, OR **149** B3
Oregon Dunes N.R.A., OR **148** D1
Orem, UT **151** C4
Orford, NH **43** E2
Organ Pipe Cactus Nat. Mon., AZ **121** G3
Orlando, FL **65** D8
Orleans, MA **41** E10
Orleans, VT **53** B4
Oro Valley, AZ **121** G6
Orofino, ID **143** D1
Orono, ME **37** F5
Oroville Dam, CA **137** C3
Orrville, OH **109** C6
Ortonville, MN **101** F1
Osage, IA **95** A6
Osage (river), MO **103** E3
Osage City, KS **97** C8
Osage Fork (river), MO **103** E4
Osawatomie, KS **97** C10
Osceola, AR **63** B8
Osceola, IA **95** E5
Osgood Mountains, NV **147** B4
Oshkosh, WI **113** F6
Oskaloosa, IA **95** E7
Ossabaw Island, GA **67** G7
Ossabaw Sound, GA **67** G7
Ossipee Lake, NH **43** F4
Oswego, NY **47** C5
Oswego (river), NY **47** D5
Othello, WA **153** E7
Otis Reservoir, MA **40** C1
Ottawa, IL **91** C4
Ottawa, KS **97** C9
Otter Creek (river), VT **53** E1
Otter Creek Reservior, UT **151** F4
Otter Tail (river), MN **101** E1
Otter Tail Lake, MN **101** D2
Ottumwa, IA **95** E7
Ouachita (river), AR, LA **56** D2
Ouachita Mountains, AR, OK **63** D1
Ouachita, Lake, AR **63** D3
Outer Banks (islands), NC **75** C10
Overland Park, KS **97** B10
Overton, NV **147** G7
Owasso, OK **125** B10
Owatonna, MN **101** G4
Owensboro, KY **69** C4
Owl Creek, WY **155** C4
Owosso, MI **99** G6
Owyhee (river), OR **149** D8
Owyhee Mountains, ID **143** H1
Owyhee N.W.&S.R., OR **149** E8
Owyhee, Lake, OR **149** E8
Owyhee, North Fork N.W.&S.R., OR **149** F9
Owyhee, South Fork (river), ID, NV **143** I1
Oxford, MA **41** C5
Oxford, MS **73** B4
Oxford, NC **75** B7
Oxford, OH **109** F1
Oxnard, CA **137** H4
Oxon Cove Park and Oxon Hill Farm, MD **39** D6
Ozark, AL **61** G5
Ozark, AR **63** C2
Ozark National Scenic Riverways, MO **103** F6
Ozark Plateau, **86** G5
Ozarks, Lake of the, MO **103** D4
Ozona, TX **127** E4

P

Pachaug Pond, CT **33** C8
Pacific Crest National Scenic Trail, CA **137** G5
Paden City, WV **83** C4
Padre Island, TX **116** G8
Padre Island National Seashore, TX **127** H7
Paducah, KY **68** D2
Page, AZ **121** A5
Pago Pago, AS **156** I1
Pagosa Springs, CO **139** G3
Pahala, HI **141** F9
Pahranagat Range, NV **147** F6
Pahrump, NV **147** G5
Pahute Mesa, NV **147** F4
Painesville, OH **109** A7
Paint Creek, OH **109** F3
Paint N.W.&S.R., MI **99** C2
Painted Desert, AZ **121** B5
Palatka, FL **65** C7
Palestine, TX **127** E8
Palisades Reservoir, ID **143** H6
Palm Bay, FL **65** E9
Palm Coast, FL **65** C8
Palm Springs, CA **137** H7
Palmer, AK **135** E6
Palmer (river), RI **51** C5
Palmyra Atoll (territory), US **157** F5
Palo Alto, CA **137** E2
Palo Alto Battlefield National Historical Site, TX **127** I7
Palouse (river), WA **153** E9
Palouse Hills, WA **153** D9
Pamlico (river), NC **75** C9
Pamlico Sound, NC **75** C10
Pampa, TX **127** B4
Pana, IL **91** F4
Panama City, FL **65** B3
Pancake Range, NV **147** E5
Panguitch, UT **151** G3
Panorama Point (peak), NE **104** C1
Paola, KS **97** C10
Papillion, NE **105** C9
Paragould, AR **63** B7
Paramus, NJ **45** B5
Paria (river), AZ **121** A4
Paris, AR **63** C2
Paris, IL **91** E6
Paris, KY **69** B8
Paris, TN **78** B3
Paris, TX **127** C8
Park (river), ND **107** B9
Park Falls, WI **113** C4
Park Hills, MO **103** E6
Park Range, CO **139** A3
Park Rapids, MN **101** D3
Park River, ND **107** B9
Parker, AZ **121** E2
Parker, SD **111** E9
Parkersburg, WV **83** D3
Parkston, SD **111** E8
Parkville, MD **39** B8
Parma, OH **109** B6
Parris Island, SC **77** H6
Parsippany, NJ **45** C4
Parsons, KS **97** E9
Pasadena, CA **137** H5
Pascagoula, MS **73** I5
Pascagoula (river), MS **73** H5
Pasco, WA **153** F8
Pascoag, RI **51** A2
Pascoag Lake, RI **51** A2
Paso Robles, CA **137** G3
Passaic, NJ **45** C5
Passaic (river), NJ **45** C4
Passamaquoddy Bay, ME **37** E7
Passumpsic (river), VT **53** C5
Paterson, NJ **45** B4
Pathfinder Reservoir, WY **155** E6
Patoka (river), IN **93** H2
Patoka Lake, IN **93** H3
Patten, ME **37** C5
Patuxent (bay), MD **39** E7
Patuxent (river), MD **39** B6
Pauls Valley, OK **125** D9
Paulsboro, NJ **45** F1
Pawcatuck, CT **33** D8
Pawcatuck (river), CT, RI **33** D8
Pawhuska, OK **125** A10
Pawnee (river), KS **97** D3
Pawtucket, RI **51** B5
Pawtucket Reservoir, RI **51** A5
Pawtuxet (river), RI **51** C4
Payette, ID **143** G1
Payette (river), ID **143** G1
Payette, North Fork (river), ID **143** G1
Payette, South Fork (river), ID **143** G2
Payson, AZ **121** E5
Payson, UT **151** D4
Pea (river), AL **61** G4
Pea Patch Island, DE **35** B5
Pea Ridge N.M.P., AR **63** A1
Peabody, MA **41** B7
Peace (river), FL **65** F7
Peachtree City, GA **67** D2
Peaked Mountain, ME **37** B5
Pearl, MS **73** E3
Pearl (river), LA, MS **71** F9
Pearl and Hermes Atoll, HI **140** E1
Pearl City, HI **141** B4
Pearl Harbor, HI **141** C4
Pearsall, TX **127** G5
Pease (river), TX **127** C5
Pecatonica (river), WI **113** H4
Pecos, TX **126** E2
Pecos (river), NM, TX **116** E6
Pecos N.H.P., NM **123** C5
Pecos N.W.&S.R., NM **123** C5
Peekskill, NY **47** G8
Pekin, IL **91** D3
Pelican Rapids, MN **101** D2
Pell City, AL **61** C4
Pella, IA **95** E6
Pembina, ND **107** A9
Pembina (river), ND **107** A8
Pemigewasset (river), NH **43** E3
Peñasco, Rio (river), NM **123** G6
Pend Oreille (river), WA **153** B10
Pend Oreille Lake, ID **143** B1
Pender, NE **105** B8
Pendleton, OR **149** B7
Penn Hills, PA **48** D2
Penn Yan, NY **47** E4
Penns Grove, NJ **45** G1
Pennsauken, NJ **45** F2
Pennsville, NJ **45** G1
Pennsylvania Turnpike, PA **49** E3
Penobscot (river), ME **37** E5
Penobscot Bay, ME **37** G5
Penobscot, East Branch (river), ME **37** C5
Penobscot, West Branch (river), ME **37** D3
Pensacola, FL **64** B1
Peoria, IL **91** D3
Pepin, WI **113** E2
Pepin, Lake, MN **101** G5
Pequop Mountains, NV **147** B6
Perdido (river), AL, FL **61** H2
Pere Marquette N.W.&S.R., MI **99** F4
Perham, MN **101** D2
Perry, FL **65** B5
Perry, GA **67** F3
Perry, IA **95** D4
Perry, OK **125** B8
Perry Hall, MD **39** B8
Perry Lake, KS **97** B9
Perry's Victory and International Peace Memorial, OH **109** A4
Perrysburg, OH **109** B3
Perryton, TX **127** A4
Perryville, MO **103** E7
Perth Amboy, NJ **45** D4
Peru, IL **91** C4
Peru, IN **93** C4
Peshtigo (river), WI **113** C6
Petal, MS **73** G4
Petenwell Lake, WI **113** E5
Peterborough, NH **43** I2
Petersburg, AK **135** F10
Petersburg, VA **81** D9
Petersburg, WV **83** D7
Petersburg N.B., VA **81** E9
Petoskey, MI **99** D6
Petrified Forest N.P., AZ **121** D7
Petroglyph Nat. Mon., NM **123** D4
Phenix City, AL **61** E6
Philadelphia, MS **73** E4
Philadelphia, PA **49** E10
Philip, SD **111** D4
Philippi, WV **83** D6
Phillipsburg, KS **97** A4
Phillipsburg, NJ **45** C2
Phoenix, AZ **121** F4
Picayune, MS **73** I3
Pickwick Lake, AL, MS, TN **61** A1
Pictured Rocks National Lakeshore, MI **99** C4
Piedmont, AL **61** C5
Piedmont (region), **56** D5
Piedmont Lake, OH **109** D7
Piedra (river), CO **139** F3
Pierre, SD **111** D5
Pigeon (river), IN **93** A5
Pigeon (river), MI **99** D6
Pigeon (river), MN **101** B8
Pikes Peak, CO **139** D5
Pikeville, KY **69** D11
Pine (river), WI **113** C6
Pine Barrens (region), NJ **45** G3
Pine Bluff, AR **63** E5
Pine City, MN **101** E5
Pine Creek, NV **147** C5
Pine Creek, PA **49** B6
Pine Creek Gorge, PA **49** B6
Pine Hill, NJ **45** F2
Pine Mountain, KY **69** E9
Pine N.W.&S.R., MI **99** F5
Pine Ridge, NE **104** A2
Pine Ridge, SD **111** F3
Pinedale, WY **155** D3
Pinehurst, NC **75** C6
Pinelands National Reserve, NJ **45** F4
Pinetop-Lakeside, AZ **121** E7
Pineville, LA **71** D4
Pinnacles Nat. Mon., CA **137** F3
Pioche, NV **147** E7
Pioneer Valley, MA **41** B3
Pipe Spring Nat. Mon., AZ **121** A4
Pipestem Creek, ND **107** D7
Pipestone, MN **101** G2
Pipestone Nat. Mon., MN **101** G1
Piqua, OH **109** D2
Piscataqua (river), NH **43** H5
Piscataquis (river), ME **37** E4
Piscataway, NJ **45** D4
Piscataway Park, MD **39** D6
Pit (river), CA **137** B3
Pittsburg, KS **97** E10
Pittsburgh, PA **48** D2
Pittsfield, IL **91** E2
Pittsfield, MA **40** B1
Pittsfield, ME **37** F4
Pittsfield, NH **43** G4
Pittsford, VT **53** F2
Piute Reservior, UT **151** F3
Plainfield, CT **33** C8
Plainfield, IN **93** E3
Plainfield, NJ **45** C4
Plainfield, VT **53** D4
Plains, GA **67** F2
Plainview, TX **127** C4
Plainville, CT **33** C4
Plainville, KS **97** B4
Plaistow, NH **43** I5
Plankinton, SD **111** E8
Plano, TX **127** D7
Plaquemine, LA **71** F6
Platte (river), NE **105** D9
Platte, SD **111** E7
Platte, North (river), CO, NE, WY **130** D8
Platte, South (river), CO, NE **130** E8
Platteville, WI **113** H4
Plattsburgh, NY **47** A8
Plattsmouth, NE **105** D9
Playas Lake, NM **123** H2
Pleasant Grove, UT **151** C4
Pleasant Prairie, WI **113** H7
Pleasantville, NJ **45** H3
Pleasure Ridge Park, KY **69** C6
Plentywood, MT **145** A11
Plover, WI **113** E5
Plum, PA **48** D2
Plymouth, IN **93** B3
Plymouth, MA **41** D8
Plymouth, MN **101** F4
Plymouth, VT **53** F3
Pocahontas, AR **63** A6
Pocatello, ID **143** H5
Pocomoke (river), MD **39** F10
Pocomoke City, MD **39** F10
Pocono Mountains, PA **49** C9
Pocotopaug Lake, CT **33** C5
Poinsett, Lake, SD **111** C9
Point Hope, AK **135** B4
Point Judith, RI **51** G4
Point Judith Pond, RI **51** F4
Point Pleasant, NJ **45** E5
Point Pleasant, OH **109** G2
Point Pleasant, WV **82** E2
Point Reyes National Seashore, CA **137** D2
Polacca, AZ **121** C6
Polson, MT **144** C3
Pomeroy, WA **153** E9
Pompeys Pillar Nat. Mon., MT **145** E8
Ponaganset (river), RI **51** B2
Ponaganset Reservoir, RI **51** B2
Ponca City, OK **125** A9
Ponce, PR **157** I10
Pond (river), KY **69** D4
Pontchartrain, Lake, LA **71** G8
Pontiac, IL **91** C4
Pontiac, MI **99** H7
Pontoosuc Lake, MA **40** B1
Pontotoc, MS **73** B4
Poplar Bluff, MO **103** F7
Poplarville, MS **73** H4
Popple (river), WI **113** C6
Poquonock Bridge, CT **33** D7
Poquoson, VA **81** E11
Porcupine (river), AK **135** B8
Port Allen, LA **71** F6
Port Angeles, WA **152** B2
Port Arthur, TX **127** F9
Port Charlotte, FL **65** F7
Port Clinton, OH **109** B4
Port Huron, MI **99** G8
Port Jervis, NY **47** G7
Port Lavaca, TX **127** G7
Port Penn, DE **35** C5
Port Royal, SC **77** H6
Port Royal Sound (river), SC **77** H6
Port St. Lucie, FL **65** F9
Port Sulphur, LA **71** H8
Port Townsend, WA **153** B3
Port Washington, WI **113** G7
Portage, IN **93** A2
Portage, MI **99** H5
Portage, WI **113** F5
Portage (river), OH **109** B3
Portal, ND **107** A3
Portales, NM **123** E8
Portland, CT **33** C5
Portland, IN **93** D6
Portland, ME **37** H3
Portland, TN **79** A5
Portland, TX **127** H7
Portland, OR **149** B2
Portneuf Range, ID **143** H5
Portsmouth, NH **43** H5
Portsmouth, OH **109** G4
Portsmouth, RI **51** E6
Portsmouth, VA **81** E11
Post Falls, ID **143** B1
Poteau, OK **125** D12
Potholes Reservoir, WA **153** D7
Potlatch (river), ID **143** D1
Potomac, MD **39** C6
Potomac (river), MD, VA, WV **39** E7

Potomac — Sandstone

Potomac, North Branch (river), MD, WV **38** B2
Potomac, South Branch (river), WV **38** B2
Potsdam, NY **47** A7
Pottstown, PA **49** E9
Pottsville, PA **49** D8
Poughkeepsie, NY **47** F8
Poultney, VT **53** F1
Poultney (river), VT **53** F1
Poverty Point Nat. Mon., LA **71** B5
Powder (river), MT, WY **130** C7
Powder (river), OR **149** C8
Powder Wash, CO **139** A2
Powder, South Fork (river), WY **155** D6
Powell, WY **155** A4
Powell (river), TN, VA **79** A9
Powell, Lake, UT **151** H5
Pownal Center, VT **53** I1
Poygan, Lake, WI **113** E6
Prairie Dog Creek, KS **97** A3
Prairie du Chien, WI **113** G3
Pratt, KS **97** E5
Prattville, AL **61** E4
Prescott, AR **63** F3
Prescott, AZ **121** D4
Prescott Valley, AZ **121** D4
Presidential Range, NH **43** D4
Presidio, TX **126** F2
Presque Isle, ME **37** B6
Presque Isle N.W.&S.R., MI **99** C1
Preston, ID **143** I5
Preston, MN **101** H6
Prestonsburg, KY **69** C10
Pribilof Islands, AK **134** F2
Price (river), UT **151** E5
Price, UT **151** D5
Prichard, AL **61** H1
Priest (river), ID **143** B1
Priest Lake, ID **143** A1
Prince Frederick, MD **39** E7
Prince of Wales Island, AK **135** G10
Prince of Wales, Cape, AK **134** C2
Prince William Forest Park, VA **81** B9
Prince William Sound, AK **135** E7
Princeton, IN **93** H1
Princeton, KY **68** D3
Princeton, ME **37** E6
Princeton, NJ **45** D3
Princeton, WV **83** H4
Princeville, HI **140** A2
Prineville, OR **149** D4
Proctor, MN **101** D5
Proctor, VT **53** F2
Promontory, UT **151** A3
Prospect, CT **33** C4
Prosser, WA **153** F7
Providence, RI **51** B5
Providence, UT **151** A4
Providence (river), RI **51** C5
Provincetown, MA **41** D10
Provo, UT **151** C4
Prudence Island, RI **51** D5
Prudhoe Bay, AK **135** A6
Pryor, OK **125** B11
Pu'uhonua O Honaunau N.H.P., HI **141** F8
Pu'ukohola Heiau National Historic Site, HI **141** E8
Pu'uwai, HI **140** A1
Pueblo, CO **139** E6
Pueblo Bonito (site), NM **123** B2
Puerco (river), AZ **121** D7
Puerco, Rio (river), NM **123** D3
Puerto Rico (territory), US **157** E11
Puget Sound, WA **153** C3
Pukalani, HI **141** C7
Pulaski, TN **79** C4
Pulaski, VA **81** E5
Pullman, WA **153** E10
Pumpkin Creek, NE **104** C1
Punkin Center, CO **139** D7
Punta Gorda, FL **65** F7
Punxsutawney, PA **49** C3
Purcell, OK **125** D8
Purgatoire (river), CO **139** G7
Putnam, CT **33** A8
Putney, VT **53** H3
Puyallup, WA **153** D4
Pymatuning Reservoir, PA, OH **48** B1
Pyramid Lake (river), NV **147** C2

Q

Quabbin Reservoir, MA **41** B4
Quaddick Reservoir, CT **33** A8
Quaker Hill, CT **33** D7
Quakertown, PA **49** D9
Quartzsite, AZ **121** E2
Quartzville Creek N.W.&S.R., OR **149** C3
Queen (river), RI **51** E3
Queets (river), WA **152** C1
Questa, NM **123** A5
Quincy, IL **91** E1
Quincy, MA **41** C7
Quincy, WA **153** D7
Quinebaug (river), CT **33** C7
Quinn (river), NV **147** A3
Quinnipiac (river), CT **33** D4
Quinsigamond, Lake, MA **41** C5
Quitman, GA **67** H4
Quitman, MS **73** F5
Quonochontaug, RI **51** G2
Quonochontaug Pond, RI **51** G2

R

Rabun Gap, GA **67** A4
Raccoon (river), IA **95** C4
Raccoon Creek, OH **109** G5
Racine, WI **113** H7
Radcliff, KY **69** C6
Radford, VA **81** E5
Raft River Mountains, UT **151** A2
Rahway, NJ **45** C4
Rainbow Bridge Nat. Mon., UT **151** H5
Rainier, OR **149** A2
Rainier, Mount, WA **153** D4
Rainy (river), MN **101** B4
Rainy Lake, MN **101** A4
Raisin (river), MI **99** H6
Raleigh, NC **75** B7
Raleigh Bay, NC **75** D10
Rampart Range, CO **139** D5
Ramsey, NJ **45** B4
Randolph, MA **41** C7
Randolph, VT **53** E3
Randolph Center, VT **53** E3
Rangeley, ME **37** E2
Rangeley Lake, ME **37** F2
Rangely, CO **138** B1
Rantoul, IL **91** D5
Rapid City, SD **110** D2
Rapid N.W.&S.R., ID **143** E1
Rappahannock (river), VA **81** C10
Raquette (river), NY **47** B7
Raritan (river), NJ **45** D4
Rat Islands, AK **135** H7
Rathbun Lake, IA **95** F6
Raton, NM **123** A6
Ravenna, NE **105** D6
Ravenswood, WV **83** E3
Rawlins, WY **155** F6
Raymond, NH **43** H4
Raymond, WA **152** E2
Rayne, LA **71** G4
Raystown Lake, PA **49** E5
Rayville, LA **71** B5
Reading, PA **49** E8
Red (river), **116** C7
Red Bank, NJ **45** D5
Red Bank, TN **79** D7
Red Bay, AL **61** B1
Red Bluff Lake, TX **116** E5
Red Bud, IL **91** G3
Red Cedar (river), WI **113** D2
Red Cloud, NE **105** E7
Red Hills, KS **97** E3
Red Lake, AZ **121** C2
Red Lake, MN **101** C3
Red Lake (river), MN **101** B2
Red Lion, PA **49** E7
Red Lodge, MT **145** F7
Red N.W.&S.R., KY **69** C9
Red Oak, IA **95** E3
Red River of the North (river), MN, ND **86** A3
Red Rock, Lake, IA **95** E6
Red Willow Creek, NE **105** D4
Red Wing, MN **101** G5
Red, Elm Fork (river), OK **125** D5
Red, North Fork (river), OK **125** D5
Red, North Fork (river), TX **127** B4
Red, Prairie Dog Town Fork (river), OK, TX **125** E5
Red, Salt Fork (river), OK, TX **125** D5
Redding, CA **137** B2
Redfield, SD **111** C8
Redmond, OR **149** D4
Redmond, WA **153** C4
Redwood Falls, MN **101** G3
Redwood N.P., CA **137** A1
Reedsburg, WI **113** F4
Reedsport, OR **148** D1
Reedy Island, DE **35** C5
Reelfoot Lake, TN **78** B2
Reese (river), NV **147** C4
Rehoboth Bay, DE **35** H7
Rehoboth Beach, DE **35** H7
Reidsville, NC **75** A6
Reisterstown, MD **39** B7
Rend Lake, IL **91** H4
Reno, NV **147** D2
Rensselaer, IN **93** C2
Renton, WA **153** C4
Republic, MO **103** F3
Republic, WA **153** A8
Republican (river), KS, NE **86** F2
Republican, South Fork (river), KS, CO **96** A1
Reserve, NM **123** F1
Reston, VA **81** B9
Rexburg, ID **143** G5
Reynoldsburg, OH **109** E4
Rhinelander, WI **113** C5
Rhode Island (island), RI **51** E6
Rhode Island Sound, RI **51** G4
Rice City, RI **51** D2
Rice Lake, WI **113** C2
Richard B. Russell Lake, GA, SC **67** C5
Richardson lakes, ME **37** F2
Richfield, UT **151** E3
Richford, VT **53** A3
Richland, WA **153** E7
Richland Center, WI **113** G4
Richland Creek N.W.&S.R., AR **63** B3
Richlands, VA **80** E3
Richmond, IN **93** E6
Richmond, MO **103** C3
Richmond, VA **81** D9
Richmond, VT **53** C2
Richmond N.B. Park, VA **81** D9
Richwood, WV **83** F5
Ridgecrest, CA **137** G6
Ridgefield, CT **33** E2
Ridgeland, MS **73** E3
Ridgewood, NJ **45** B5
Ridgway, PA **49** B4
Rifle, CO **139** C2
Rifle (river), MI **99** F7
Rigby, ID **143** G5
Riggins, ID **143** E1
Ringwood, NJ **45** B4
Rio Chama N.W.&S.R., NM **123** B4
Rio Grande (river), CO, NM, TX **116** G7
Rio Grande City, TX **127** I6
Rio Grande N.W.&S.R., NM **123** A5
Rio Grande Wild and Scenic River, TX **127** F3
Rio Rancho, NM **123** D4
Ripley, MS **73** A4
Ripley, TN **78** C1
Ripley, WV **83** E3
Ripon, WI **113** F6
Ritzville, WA **153** D8
River Falls, WI **113** D1
Riverside, CA **137** H6
Riverton, UT **151** C4
Riverton, WY **155** D5
Roan Cliffs, UT **151** E6
Roan Mountain, TN **79** B11
Roan Plateau, CO **138** C1
Roanoke, AL **61** D5
Roanoke, VA **81** D6
Roanoke (river), NC, VA **56** C7
Roanoke (Staunton) (river), VA **81** E7
Roanoke Island, NC **75** B10
Roanoke Rapids, NC **75** A8
Roaring N.W.&S.R., OR **149** B3
Robert South Kerr Lake, OK **125** D12
Robinson, IL **91** F6
Robstown, TX **127** H6
Rochester, IN **93** B4
Rochester, MN **101** G5
Rochester, NH **43** G5
Rochester, NY **47** D4
Rock (river), IL, WI **91** B3
Rock Creek, NV **147** B5
Rock Creek, OK **125** B8
Rock Hill, SC **77** B5
Rock Island, IL **91** C2
Rock Springs, WY **155** G3
Rockcastle (river), KY **69** D8
Rockford, IL **91** A4
Rockingham, NC **75** D6
Rockland, MA **41** C8
Rockland, ME **37** G4
Rockport, ME **37** G4
Rockport, TX **127** H7
Rockville, MD **39** C6
Rocky Ford, CO **139** E7
Rocky Mount, NC **75** B8
Rocky Mount, VA **81** E6
Rocky Mountain N.P., CO **139** B5
Rocky Mountains, **130** A4
Rogers, AR **63** A1
Rogers City, MI **99** D7
Rogers, Mount, VA **80** F4
Rogue (river), OR **149** F2
Rogue N.W.&S.R., OR **148** F1
Rolla, MO **103** E5
Rolla, ND **107** A6
Rolling Fork (river), KY **69** D6
Rome, GA **67** B1
Rome, NY **47** D6
Romney, WV **83** D8
Roosevelt, UT **151** C6
Root (river), MN **101** H6
Roseau, MN **101** A2
Roseau (river), MN **101** A2
Rosebud, SD **111** E5
Roseburg, OR **149** E2
Rosepine, LA **70** E2
Ross Barnett Reservoir, MS **73** E3
Ross Lake, WA **153** A5
Ross Lake N.R.A., WA **153** A5
Roswell, GA **67** C2
Roswell, NM **123** F6
Rota Island, MP **156** D1
Rough (river), KY **69** D4
Rough River Lake, KY **69** C5
Round Rock, TX **127** F6
Round Valley Reservoir, NJ **45** C3
Roundup, MT **145** D7
Roxboro, NC **75** A7
Ruby Mountains, NV **147** C6
Rugby, ND **107** B6
Ruidoso, NM **123** F5
Ruleville, MS **73** C2
Rum (river), MN **101** E4
Rumford, ME **37** F2
Rupert, ID **143** I4
Rush Creek, CO **139** D8
Rushville, IN **93** E5
Rushville, NE **104** A2
Russell, KS **97** C5
Russell Cave Nat. Mon., AL **61** A5
Russellville, AL **61** B2
Russellville, AR **63** C3
Ruston, LA **71** B3
Rutland, VT **53** F2
Rye, NH **43** H5
Rye Patch Reservoir, NV **147** B3

S

Sabine (river), LA, TX **56** E2
Sabine Lake, LA **70** G1
Sable, Cape, FL **65** H8
Sac (river), MO **103** E3
Sacajawea, Lake, WA **153** E8
Saco, ME **37** H2
Saco (river), ME, NH **37** H2
Sacramento, CA **137** D3
Sacramento (river), CA **137** B2
Sacramento Mountains, NM **123** F5
Safford, AZ **121** F7
Sag Harbor, NY **47** G10
Sagamore Hill National Historic Site, NY **47** H9
Sagavanirktok (river), AK **135** B6
Saginaw, MI **99** G7
Saginaw Bay, MI **99** F7
Saguache Creek, CO **139** E3
Saguaro N.P., AZ **121** G5
Saint Albans, VT **53** B2
Saint John (river), ME **37** B4
Saint John, Baker Branch (river), ME **37** C3
Saint John, Northwest Branch (river), ME **37** B3
Saint John, Southwest Branch (river), ME **37** C3
Sainte Genevieve, MO **103** D7
Saint-Gaudens National Historic Site, NH **43** G1
Saipan (island), MP **156** C2
Sakakawea, Lake, ND **107** C3
Sakonnet Point, RI **51** F6
Sakonnet River, RI **51** E6
Salamanca, NY **46** F2
Salamonie (river), IN **93** C5
Salamonie Lake, IN **93** C4
Salem, IL **91** G4
Salem, IN **93** G4
Salem, MA **41** B8
Salem, MO **103** E5
Salem, NH **43** I4
Salem, NJ **45** G1
Salem, OH **109** C7
Salem, OR **149** C2
Salem, SD **111** E9
Salem, VA **81** D6
Salem, WV **83** D5
Salem (river), NJ **45** G1
Salem Maritime National Historic Site, MA **41** B8
Salida, CO **139** E4
Salina, KS **97** C6
Salinas, CA **137** F3
Salinas Pueblo Missions Nat. Mon., NM **123** E4
Saline (river), KS **97** C6
Saline (river), AR **63** E4
Saline (river), IL **91** H5
Saline Bayou (river), LA **71** B3
Saline Bayou N.W.&S.R., LA **71** C3
Salisbury, MD **39** E10
Salisbury, NC **75** B5
Salish Mountains, MT **144** A2
Sallisaw, OK **125** C12
Salmon, ID **143** E3
Salmon (river), CT **33** C6
Salmon (river), ID **143** F3
Salmon Falls (river), ME, NH **37** I2
Salmon Falls Creek Reservoir, ID **143** I3
Salmon N.W.&S.R., AK **135** B4
Salmon N.W.&S.R., ID **143** E2
Salmon N.W.&S.R., OR **149** B3
Salmon River Mountains, ID **143** F2
Salmon, Middle Fork (river), ID **143** F3
Salmon, Middle Fork N.W.&S.R., ID **143** E3
Salmon, South Fork (river), ID **143** F2
Salt (river), AZ **121** E6
Salt (river), KY **69** C6
Salt (river), MO **103** B5
Salt Creek (river), IN **93** G3
Salt Creek, IL **91** E4
Salt Fork Lake, OH **109** D7
Salt Lake City, UT **151** C4
Salt River Bay N.H.P. and Ecological Preserve, VI **157** I8
Salton Sea (lake), CA **137** I7
Saluda (river), SC **77** C4
Salvador, Lake, LA **71** H7
Sam Rayburn Reservoir, TX **127** E9
San Andres Mountains, NM **123** F5
San Angelo, TX **127** E4
San Antonio, TX **127** F6
San Antonio (river), TX **127** G6
San Antonio Missions N.H.P., TX **127** G6
San Bernardino, CA **137** H6
San Blas, Cape, FL **56** F5
San Carlos, AZ **121** F6
San Carlos Reservoir, AZ **121** F6
San Clemente (island), CA **137** I5
San Diego, CA **137** I6
San Francisco, CA **137** E2
San Francisco (river), NM **123** F1
San Francisco Maritime N.H.P., CA **137** E1
San Joaquin (river), CA **137** E4
San Jose, CA **137** E3
San Jose, MP **156** D1
San Jose, Rio (river), NM **123** D2
San Juan, PR **157** H11
San Juan (river), CO, NM, UT **116** B3
San Juan Island N.H.P., WA **153** B3
San Juan Islands, WA **153** B3
San Juan Mountains, CO **139** F2
San Juan National Historic Site, PR **157** H11
San Luis, AZ **121** G1
San Luis Creek, CO **139** E4
San Luis Lake, CO **139** F5
San Luis Obispo, CA **137** G3
San Luis Valley, CO **139** F4
San Manuel, AZ **121** G6
San Marcos, TX **127** F6
San Miguel (river), CO **138** E1
San Pedro (river), AZ **121** G6
San Rafael, CA **137** D2
San Rafael (river), UT **151** E5
Sanak Island, AK **134** H3
Sanbornville, NH **43** F5
Sand Arroyo (river), CO **139** F9
Sand Creek, IN **93** F4
Sand Creek, SD **111** D8
Sand Hills, NE **105** B3
Sand Springs, OK **125** B10
Sandersville, GA **67** E5
Sandpoint, ID **143** B1
Sandstone, MN **101** E5

Sandusky — Stilwell

Sandusky, MI **99** G8
Sandusky, OH **109** B4
Sandusky (river), OH **109** C4
Sandusky Bay, OH **109** B4
Sandwich, IL **91** B4
Sandwich, MA **41** E9
Sandy, UT **151** C4
Sandy Hook (point), NJ **45** D5
Sandy Hook Bay, NJ **45** D5
Sandy N.W.&S.R., OR **149** B3
Sandy Point, RI **51** H3
Sandy Springs, GA **67** C2
Sanford, FL **65** D8
Sanford, ME **37** I2
Sanford, NC **75** C6
Sangamon (river), IL **91** E4
Sangre de Cristo Mountains, CO,
    NM **130** F7
Sanibel Island, FL **65** G7
Sanpoil (river), WA **153** B8
Santa Ana, CA **137** H5
Santa Barbara, CA **137** H4
Santa Catalina (island), CA **137** I5
Santa Clara, UT **151** H2
Santa Claus, IN **93** H2
Santa Cruz (island), CA **137** H4
Santa Cruz, CA **137** E2
Santa Cruz (river), AZ **121** G5
Santa Fe, NM **123** C5
Santa Maria, CA **137** G4
Santa Monica, CA **137** H5
Santa Monica Mountains N.R.A.,
    CA **137** H5
Santa Rita, GU **156** G1
Santa Rosa (island), CA **137** H3
Santa Rosa, CA **137** D2
Santa Rosa, NM **123** D6
Santa Rosa and San Jacinto
    Mountains Nat. Mon., CA
    137 H7
Santa Rosa Lake, NM **123** D6
Santa Rosa Range, NV **147** A4
Santee (river), SC **77** E8
Santee Dam, SC **77** E7
Sapelo Island, GA **67** G7
Sapelo Sound, GA **67** G7
Sappa Creek, KS **96** A2
Sapulpa, OK **125** B10
Saraland, AL **61** H1
Saranac Lake, NY **47** B8
Sarasota, FL **65** F6
Saratoga, WY **155** G7
Saratoga N.H.P., NY **47** D8
Saratoga Springs, NY **47** D8
Sardis Lake, MS **73** B3
Sardis Lake, OK **125** D11
Sassafras (bay), MD **39** B4
Sassafras Mountain, SC **76** A2
Satilla (river), GA **67** H5
Saugatuck Reservoir, CT **33** E2
Saugus Iron Works National
    Historic Site, MA **41** B7
Sauk Centre, MN **101** E3
Sault Sainte Marie, MI **99** C6
Saunderstown, RI **51** E4
Savanna, IL **91** B3
Savannah, GA **67** F7
Savannah, MO **103** B2
Savannah, TN **78** C3
Savannah (river), GA, SC **56** D6
Sawtooth N.R.A., ID **143** G3
Sawtooth Range, ID **143** F2
Saylesville, RI **51** B5
Sayre, OK **125** D5
Sayre, PA **49** A7
Sayreville, NJ **45** D4
Scantic (river), CT **33** B5
Scappoose, OR **149** B2
Scarborough, ME **37** H2
Schaumburg, IL **91** B5
Schell Creek Range, NV **147** D6
Schenectady, NY **47** D8
Schuyler, NE **105** C8
Schuylkill (river), PA **49** D8
Scioto (river), OH **109** C3
Scituate Reservoir, RI **51** C3
Scobey, MT **145** A10
Scott City, KS **96** C2
Scotts Bluff Nat. Mon., NE **104** C1
Scottsbluff, NE **104** B1
Scottsboro, AL **61** A4
Scottsburg, IN **93** G4
Scottsdale, AZ **121** F4
Scranton, PA **49** B9
Sea Islands, GA, SC **56** E6
Sea Isle City, NJ **45** I3
Seaford, DE **35** H5
Seaman Range, NV **147** F6
Searcy, AR **63** C5

Searsport, ME **37** F5
Seaside, OR **148** A1
Seaside Heights, NJ **45** F5
Seattle, WA **153** C4
Sebago Lake, ME **37** H2
Sebec Lake, ME **37** E4
Sebring, FL **65** E8
Second Lake, NH **43** A4
Sedalia, MO **103** D3
Sedona, AZ **121** D5
Sedro Woolley, WA **153** B4
Seekonk, MA **41** E6
Seekonk (river), RI **51** B5
Seguam Island, AK **135** H10
Selawik N.W.&S.R., AK **135** C5
Selby, SD **111** B6
Selbyville, DE **35** I7
Seligman, AZ **121** C3
Selinsgrove, PA **49** D7
Selkirk Mountains, ID **143** B1
Sells, AZ **121** H5
Selma, AL **61** E3
Selway (river), ID **143** D2
Seminoe Reservoir, WY **155** F7
Seminole, OK **125** D9
Seminole, Lake, FL, GA **67** I2
Semisopochnoi Island, AK **135** H7
Senatobia, MS **73** B3
Seneca, KS **97** A3
Seneca, SC **76** B1
Seneca Falls, NY **47** D4
Seneca Lake, NY **47** E4
Senecaville Lake, OH **109** E7
Sequatchie (river), TN **79** C7
Sequoia N.P., CA **137** F5
Sespe Creek N.W.&S.R., CA **137** H5
Severn (river), MD **39** C7
Severna Park, MD **39** C8
Sevier (river), UT **151** G3
Sevier Desert, UT **151** D3
Sevier Lake (dry lake), UT **151** E2
Sevierville, TN **79** B9
Seward, NE **105** D8
Seward, AK **135** F6
Seward Peninsula, AK **135** C4
Seymour, CT **33** D3
Seymour, IN **93** G4
Seymour, MO **103** F4
Seymour Lake, VT **53** A5
Shafer, Lake, IN **93** C3
Shaker Heights, OH **109** B6
Shamokin, PA **49** D7
Shannock, RI **51** F3
Sharon, CT **33** B2
Sharon, PA **48** C1
Sharpe, Lake, SD **111** D6
Sharpsburg, MD **39** B4
Shasta Lake, CA **137** B3
Shasta, Mount, CA **137** A2
Shawano, WI **113** D6
Shawnee, OK **125** D9
Shawneetown, IL **91** H5
Sheboygan, WI **113** F7
Sheenjek N.W.&S.R., AK **135** B7
Sheep Range, NV **147** G6
Shelburne, VT **53** C1
Shelburne Falls, MA **40** B2
Shelby, MS **73** C2
Shelby, MT **145** B4
Shelby, OH **109** C5
Shelbyville, IN **93** F4
Shelbyville, KY **69** B7
Shelbyville, TN **79** C5
Shelbyville, Lake, IL **91** F4
Sheldon, IA **94** A2
Shell Creek, NE **105** C7
Shell Rock (river), IA **95** B6
Shelley, ID **143** H5
Shelton, CT **33** E3
Shelton, WA **153** D3
Shenandoah, IA **95** F3
Shenandoah (river), VA **81** A8
Shenandoah Mountain, VA **81** C7
Shenandoah N.P., VA **81** B8
Shenipsit Lake, CT **33** B6
Shepaug (river), CT **33** C2
Sheridan, AR **63** E4
Sheridan, OR **149** B2
Sheridan, WY **155** A6
Sherman, TX **127** C7
Sherman Mills, ME **37** D5
Sheyenne (river), ND **107** C6
Shiloh N.M.P., TN **78** C3
Shinapaaru, MP **156** D1
Shinnston, WV **83** D5
Ship Bottom, NJ **45** G4
Ship Rock (peak), NM **123** A1
Shippensburg, PA **49** E6

Shiprock, NM **123** A2
Shoshone, ID **143** H3
Shoshone (river), WY **155** B4
Shoshone Mountains, NV **147** D4
Shoshone Range, NV **147** C4
Shoshone, North Fork (river), WY
    155 B3
Shoshone, South Fork (river), WY
    155 B3
Show Low, AZ **121** E6
Shreveport, LA **70** B1
Shrewsbury, MA **41** C5
Sidney, MT **145** B11
Sidney, NE **104** C2
Sidney, NY **47** E6
Sidney, OH **109** D2
Sidney Lanier, Lake, GA **67** B3
Sierra Nevada, CA **137** C3
Sierra Vista, AZ **121** H6
Sikeston, MO **103** F8
Silicon Valley, CA **137** E2
Siloam Springs, AR **63** A1
Silver City, NM **123** G2
Silver Lake, MA **41** D8
Silver Spring, MD **39** C6
Silver Springs, NV **147** D2
Simi Valley, CA **137** H5
Simpsonville, SC **77** B3
Simsbury, CT **33** B4
Sinclair, Lake, GA **67** D4
Sioux Center, IA **94** A2
Sioux City, IA **94** C1
Sioux Falls, SD **111** E10
Sipsey (river), AL **61** D1
Sipsey Fork N.W.&S.R., AL **61** B2
Sisquoc N.W.&S.R., CA **137** G4
Sisseton, SD **111** A9
Sissonville, WV **83** E3
Sitka, AK **135** F10
Sitka N.H.P., AK **135** G10
Siufaga, AS **156** I4
Siuslaw (river), OR **149** D2
Skagit (river), WA **153** B4
Skagway, AK **135** E10
Skiatook Lake, OK **125** B10
Skillet Fork (river), IL **91** G4
Skowhegan, ME **37** F3
Skykomish (river), WA **153** C4
Skyline Drive, VA **81** C8
Slatersville, RI **51** A3
Slaughter Beach, DE **35** G6
Slayton, MN **101** H2
Sleeping Bear Dunes National
    Lakeshore, MI **99** E5
Slide Mountain, NY **47** F8
Slidell, LA **71** F8
Smackover, AR **63** G4
Smith Canyon, CO **139** F8
Smith Island, MD **39** F9
Smith Mountain Lake, VA **81** E6
Smith N.W.&S.R., CA **137** A1
Smith, North Fork N.W.&S.R., OR
    148 G1
Smithfield, NC **75** C7
Smithfield, UT **151** A4
Smithfield, VA **81** E10
Smoke Creek Desert, NV **147** C2
Smoky Hill (river), KS **96** C1
Smoky Hills, KS **97** B4
Smoky Mountains, ID **143** G3
Smyrna, DE **35** D5
Smyrna, GA **67** C2
Smyrna, TN **79** B5
Smyrna (river), DE **35** D5
Snake (river), ID, OR, WA, WY
    130 B3
Snake N.W.&S.R., ID, OR **143** D1
Snake River Plain, ID **143** H4
Snohomish, WA **153** C4
Snow Hill, MD **39** F10
Snow, Mount, VT **53** H2
Snowflake, AZ **121** D6
Snyder, TX **127** D4
Socastee, SC **77** D9
Socorro, NM **123** E3
Soda Springs, ID **143** H6
Soddy-Daisy, TN **79** C7
Sol Duc (river), WA **152** C1
Soledad, CA **137** F3
Solomon (river), KS **97** B6
Solomon, North Fork (river), KS
    97 B3
Solomon, South Fork (river), KS
    97 B4
Solomons, MD **39** E8
Somers Point, NJ **45** H3
Somerset, KY **69** D8
Somerset, MA **41** E7
Somerset, PA **49** E3

Somerset Reservoir, VT **53** H2
Somersworth, NH **43** G5
Somerville, NJ **45** D3
Songsong, MP **156** D1
Sonora, TX **127** F4
Sonoran Desert, AZ, CA **121** F3
Sooner Lake, OK **125** B9
Souhegan (river), NH **43** I3
Souris (Mouse) (river), ND **107** B5
South (river), NC **75** D7
South Bass Island, OH **109** A4
South Bend, IN **93** A3
South Berwick, ME **37** I2
South Boston, VA **81** E7
South Burlington, VT **53** C1
South Charleston, WV **83** F3
South Hadley, MA **41** C3
South Haven, MI **99** H4
South Hero Island, VT **53** B1
South Hill, VA **81** E8
South Lake Tahoe, CA **137** D4
South Milwaukee, WI **113** G7
South Paris, ME **37** G2
South Pass, WY **155** E4
South Point see Kalae, HI **141** G8
South Point, OH **109** H5
South Portland, ME **37** H3
South Sioux City, NE **105** B9
South Yarmouth, MA **41** E10
Southampton, NY **47** G10
Southaven, MS **73** A3
Southbridge, MA **41** D4
Southbury, CT **33** D3
Southern Pines, NC **75** C6
Southington, CT **33** C4
Southport, NC **75** E8
Southwest Harbor, ME **37** G5
Spanish Fork, UT **151** C4
Sparks, NV **147** D2
Sparta, NJ **45** B3
Sparta, TN **79** B6
Sparta, WI **113** F3
Spartanburg, SC **77** B3
Spearfish, SD **110** C1
Spencer, IA **95** A3
Spencer, MA **41** C4
Spencer, WV **83** E3
Spirit Lake, IA **95** A3
Spokane, WA **153** C9
Spokane (river), ID, WA **153** C9
Spoon (river), IL **91** D3
Spooner, WI **113** C2
Sprague (river), OR **149** F4
Spring (river), AR **63** A6
Spring Bay (dry lake), UT **151** A2
Spring Creek, NV **147** B6
Spring Hill, FL **65** D6
Spring Hill, TN **79** C5
Spring Lake, NC **75** C7
Spring Valley, NY **47** G8
Springdale, AR **63** A1
Springer, NM **123** B6
Springer Mountain, GA **67** B3
Springfield, CO **139** F9
Springfield, IL **91** E3
Springfield, MA **41** C3
Springfield, MO **103** F3
Springfield, OH **109** E3
Springfield, OR **149** D2
Springfield, TN **79** A5
Springfield, VT **53** G3
Springfield Armory National
    Historic Site, MA **41** C3
Springhill, LA **70** A2
Springvale, ME **37** H2
Springville, UT **151** C4
Spruce Knob (peak), WV **83** E7
Spruce Knob-Seneca Rocks N.R.A.,
    WV **83** E7
Squam Lake, NH **43** F3
Squapan Lake, ME **37** C5
Square Lake, ME **37** A5
Squaw Creek N.W.&S.R., OR
    149 D4
St. Albans, WV **82** F2
St. Andrew Sound, GA **67** H7
St. Anthony, ID **143** G5
St. Augustine, FL **65** B8
St. Catherine, Lake, VT **53** G1
St. Catherines Island, GA **67** G7
St. Catherines Sound, GA **67** G7
St. Charles, MD **39** D7
St. Charles, MO **103** C6
St. Charles (river), CO **139** E6
St. Clair, MI **99** H8
St. Clair Shores, MI **99** H8
St. Clair, Lake, MI **99** H8
St. Cloud, MN **101** E4
St. Croix (island), VI **157** I7

St. Croix (river), ME **37** D7
St. Croix (river), MN, WI **101** E5
St. Croix Falls, WI **113** C1
St. Croix Island International
    Historic Site, ME **37** E7
St. Croix N.W.&S.R., MN, WI
    113 D1
St. Croix National Scenic Riverway,
    MN, WI **113** B2
St. Elias Mountains, AK **135** E8
St. Elias, Mount, AK **135** E8
St. Francis (river), ME **37** A4
St. Francis, ME **37** A4
St. Francis (river), AR, MO **63** A7
St. George, UT **151** H2
St. Georges, DE **35** C4
St. Helena Island, SC **77** H6
St. Helena Sound, SC **77** G6
St. Helens, OR **149** A2
St. Helens, Mount, WA **153** F4
St. Ignace, MI **99** D6
St. James, MN **101** G3
St. James, MO **103** D5
St. Joe (river), ID **143** C1
St. Joe N.W.&S.R., ID **143** C2
St. John (island), VI **157** G8
St. Johns, AZ **121** D7
St. Johns, MI **99** G6
St. Johns (river), FL **65** D8
St. Johnsbury, VT **53** C5
St. Jones (river), DE **35** E5
St. Joseph, MI **99** I4
St. Joseph, MO **103** B2
St. Joseph (river), IN, MI **93** A4
St. Joseph (river), IN, OH **93** B5
St. Lawrence (river), NY **47** A6
St. Lawrence Island, AK **134** D2
St. Louis, MO **103** D7
St. Louis (river), MN **101** D5
St. Lucie Canal, FL **65** F9
St. Maries, ID **143** C1
St. Maries (river), ID **143** C1
St. Marys, GA **67** I7
St. Marys, OH **109** D2
St. Marys, PA **49** B4
St. Marys, WV **83** D4
St. Marys (river), FL **65** B7
St. Marys (river), IN, OH **93** C5
St. Marys (river), MI **99** C6
St. Marys City, MD **39** F8
St. Marys Lake see Grand Lake, OH
    109 D2
St. Matthew Island, AK **134** E1
St. Michaels, MD **39** D8
St. Paul, AK **134** F1
St. Paul, MN **101** F5
St. Paul, NE **105** C7
St. Paul's Church National Historic
    Site, NY **47** H8
St. Peter, MN **101** G4
St. Peters, MO **103** C6
St. Petersburg, FL **65** E6
St. Simons Island, GA **67** H7
St. Thomas (island), VI **157** G7
Stafford, CT **33** A6
Stafford Pond, RI **51** D6
Staffordville Reservoir, CT **33** A6
Stamford, CT **33** F1
Stamps, AR **63** G2
Stanley, ND **107** B3
Starkville, MS **73** C5
State College, PA **49** D5
Stateline, NV **147** D1
Staten Island, NY **47** H8
Statesboro, GA **67** F6
Statesville, NC **75** B4
Statue of Liberty Nat. Mon., NY
    47 H8
Staunton (river) see Roanoke, VA
    81 E7
Staunton, VA **81** C7
Stayton, OR **149** C2
Steamboat Springs, CO **139** B3
Steamtown National Historic Site,
    PA **49** B9
Steele, ND **107** E6
Steens Mountain, OR **149** F7
Stellwagen Bank National Marine
    Sanctuary, MA **41** B9
Stephenville, TX **127** D6
Sterling, CO **139** A8
Sterling, IL **91** B3
Steubenville, OH **109** D8
Stevens Point, WI **113** E5
Stillwater, MN **101** F5
Stillwater, OK **125** B9
Stillwater (river), OH **109** D1
Stillwater Range, NV **147** C3
Stilwell, OK **125** C12

Stockbridge — Waikoloa

Stockbridge, MA **40** C1
Stockton, CA **137** D3
Stockton Lake, MO **103** E3
Stone Mountain (site), GA **67** C3
Stones River N.B., TN **79** B5
Stonewall Jackson Lake, WV **83** D5
Stonington, ME **37** G5
Stony (river), AK **135** E5
Storm Lake, IA **95** B3
Storrs, CT **33** B6
Story City, IA **95** C5
Stoughton, MA **41** C7
Stoughton, WI **113** G5
Stowe, VT **53** C3
Stratford, CT **33** E3
Stratford Point, CT **33** E3
Stratton Mountain, VT **53** H2
Strawberry Reservoir, UT **151** C5
Streator, IL **91** C4
Strong (river), MS **73** F3
Strongsville, OH **109** B6
Stroudsburg, PA **49** C9
Stuarts Draft, VA **81** C7
Stump Lake, ND **107** C8
Sturbridge, MA **41** C4
Sturgeon Bay, WI **113** D8
Sturgeon N.W.&S.R., MI **99** D4
Sturgis, MI **99** I5
Sturgis, SD **110** C2
Stuttgart, AR **63** E5
Sudbury Reservoir, MA **41** C6
Sudbury, Assabet and Concord N.W.&S.R., MA **41** B6
Suffolk, VA **81** E11
Sugar (river), NH **43** G1
Sugar (river), WI **113** H5
Sugar Creek (creek), IN **93** E2
Sugar Creek (creek), IN **93** E4
Sugar Land, TX **127** F8
Sugarloaf Mountain, ME **37** E2
Suitland, MD **39** D7
Sullivan, MO **103** D6
Sullys Hill National Game Preserve, ND **107** C7
Sulphur, LA **70** G2
Sulphur, OK **125** E9
Sulphur Creek, SD **111** C3
Sulphur Springs, TX **127** C8
Summer Lake, OR **149** F5
Summersville, WV **83** F4
Summersville Lake, WV **83** F4
Summerville, SC **77** F7
Summit Lake, NV **147** A2
Sumner Lake, NM **123** D6
Sumter, SC **77** D6
Sun (river), MT **145** C4
Sun City, AZ **121** F4
Sun Prairie, WI **113** G5
Sunapee Lake, NH **43** G2
Sunapee, Mount, NH **43** G2
Sunbury, PA **49** C7
Suncook, NH **43** H4
Suncook (river), NH **43** H4
Suncook Lakes, NH **43** G4
Sundance, WY **155** B10
Sunflower, Mount, KS **96** B1
Sunland Park, NM **123** H4
Sunnyside, WA **153** E6
Sunnyvale, CA **137** E2
Sunset Crater Volcano Nat. Mon., AZ **121** C5
Superior, NE **105** E7
Superior, WI **113** A2
Superior, Lake, **86** B6
Surf City, NJ **45** G4
Surfside Beach, SC **77** E9
Surry Mountain Lake, NH **43** H1
Susanville, CA **137** B3
Susitna (river), AK **135** D6
Susquehanna (river), MD, NY, PA **39** A8
Susquehanna, West Branch (river), PA **49** C5
Susupe, MP **156** C2
Sutherlin, OR **149** E2
Sutton Lake, WV **83** E5
Suwannee (river), FL **65** C6
Swainsboro, GA **67** E5
Swanson Reservoir, NE **105** E4
Swanton, VT **53** A2
Sweet Home, OR **149** D2
Sweetwater, TN **79** C8
Sweetwater, TX **127** D4
Sweetwater (river), WY **155** E5
Sweetwater Lake, ND **107** B8
Swift (river), MA **41** C3
Sycamore, IL **91** B4
Sycan (river), OR **149** F4
Sycan N.W.&S.R., OR **149** F4
Sylacauga, AL **61** D4
Sylvania, OH **109** A3
Syracuse, NY **47** D5
Sysladobsis Lake, ME **37** E6

T

Table Rock Lake, MO **103** F3
Tacoma, WA **153** D3
Taconic Range, MA, NY, VT **47** F9
Tahlequah, OK **125** C11
Tahoe, Lake, CA, NV **137** C4
Tahquamenon (East Branch) N.W.&S.R., MI **99** C5
Taliesin (site), WI **113** G4
Talladega, AL **61** D4
Tallahala Creek, MS **73** G4
Tallahassee, FL **65** B4
Tallahatchie (river), MS **73** C3
Tallapoosa (river), AL **61** E4
Tallassee, AL **61** E5
Talleyville, DE **35** A5
Tallgrass Prairie National Preserve, KS **97** C7
Tallulah, LA **71** B6
Tamaqua, PA **49** D8
Tampa, FL **65** E6
Tampa Bay, FL **65** E6
Tampico, IL **91** B3
Tamuning, GU **156** F1
Tanaga Island, AK **135** H8
Tanana (river), AK **135** D7
Taneytown, MD **39** A6
Tangier Island, VA **81** C11
Tangier Sound, MD **39** F9
Tangipahoa (river), LA **71** E7
Taos, NM **123** B5
Tar (river), NC **75** B8
Tarboro, NC **75** B8
Tarpon Springs, FL **65** E6
Tarrytown, NY **47** G8
Tau (island), AS **157** I5
Tau, AS **156** I4
Taum Sauk Mountain, MO **103** E6
Taunton, MA **41** D7
Taunton (river), MA **41** E7
Tawas City, MI **99** F7
Taylors, SC **77** B3
Taylorville, IL **91** E4
Tazewell, VA **80** E4
Teche, Bayou (river), LA **71** G5
Tecumseh, MI **99** I7
Tecumseh, OK **125** D9
Tekamah, NE **105** C9
Tell City, IN **93** I3
Tellico Lake, TN **79** C8
Telluride, CO **139** F2
Telos Lake, ME **37** C4
Tempe, AZ **121** F4
Temperance, MI **99** I7
Temple, TX **127** E7
Ten Thousand Islands, FL **65** H8
Tenkiller Lake, OK **125** C11
Tennessee (river), AL, KY, MS, TN **56** C4
Tennessee-Tombigbee Waterway, AL, MS **73** B5
Tensas (river), LA **71** C5
Terre Haute, IN **93** F2
Terrebonne Bay, LA **71** I7
Terry, MT **145** D10
Terryville, CT **33** C3
Teton (river), MT **145** B5
Texarkana, AR **63** F1
Texarkana, TX **127** C9
Texoma, Lake, OK **125** F9
Thames (river), CT **33** D7
The Berkshires (hills), MA **40** C1
The Dalles, OR **149** B4
The Everglades, FL **65** H8
The Hermitage (site), TN **79** B5
Theodore Roosevelt Inaugural National Historic Site, NY **46** D1
Theodore Roosevelt Lake, AZ **121** E5
Theodore Roosevelt N.P. (Elkhorn Ranch Site), ND **106** D1
Theodore Roosevelt N.P. (South Unit), ND **106** D2
Thermopolis, WY **155** C5
Thibodaux, LA **71** G6
Thief River Falls, MN **101** B2
Third Lake, NH **43** A4
Thomas Stone National Historic Site, MD **39** D6
Thomaston, GA **67** E2
Thomaston, ME **37** G4
Thomasville, AL **61** F2
Thomasville, GA **67** H3
Thomasville, NC **75** B5
Thompson, CT **33** A8
Thompson (river), IA, MO **103** A3
Thompson Falls, MT **144** C1
Thomson, GA **67** D5
Thornton, CO **139** C6
Thousand Islands, NY **47** B5
Thousand Springs Creek, NV **147** A6
Three Mile Island, PA **49** E7
Three Rivers, MI **99** I5
Thunder Bay, MI **99** E7
Thunder Bay (river), MI **99** E6
Thunder Butte Creek (river), SD **111** B3
Thurmont, MD **39** A5
Ticonderoga, NY **47** C9
Tiffin, OH **109** B4
Tifton, GA **67** G4
Tillamook, OR **148** B1
Tillery, Lake, NC **75** C5
Tilton, NH **43** G3
Timbalier Bay, LA **71** I7
Timber Lake, SD **111** B4
Timberlake, VA **81** D7
Timms Hill (peak), WI **113** C4
Timpanogos Cave Nat. Mon., UT **151** C4
Tims Ford Lake, TN **79** C5
Timucuan Ecological and Historic Preserve, FL **65** A8
Tinayguk N.W.&S.R., AK **135** B6
Tinian (island), MP **156** D2
Tinton Falls, NJ **45** E5
Tioga, ND **106** B2
Tioga (river), PA **49** A6
Tiogue Lake, RI **51** D4
Tippecanoe (river), IN **93** B3
Tishomingo, OK **125** E9
Titusville, FL **65** D8
Titusville, PA **48** B2
Tiverton, RI **51** D6
Tlikakila N.W.&S.R., AK **135** E5
Toana Range, NV **147** B7
Toccoa, GA **67** B4
Toiyabe Range, NV **147** D4
Tok, AK **135** D8
Toledo, OH **109** A3
Toledo Bend Reservoir, LA, TX **70** D2
Tomah, WI **113** F4
Tomahawk, WI **113** C5
Tombigbee (river), MS **73** G6
Tombigee (river), AL **61** G1
Tombstone, AZ **121** H7
Toms (river), NJ **45** E4
Toms River, NJ **45** F4
Tonawanda, NY **46** D2
Tongue (river), MT **145** E9
Tonopah, NV **147** E4
Tonto Nat. Mon., AZ **121** F5
Tooele, UT **151** C3
Topeka, KS **97** B9
Toppenish, WA **153** E6
Toquima Range, NV **147** E4
Toronto, OH **109** D8
Torrington, CT **33** B3
Torrington, WY **155** F10
Touro Synagogue National Historic Site, RI **51** F5
Towanda, PA **49** B7
Towner, ND **107** B5
Townsend, DE **35** D4
Townsend, MT **145** D5
Towson, MD **39** B7
Tradewater (river), KY **68** D3
Trans-Alaska Pipeline, AK **135** C6
Trask (river), OR **148** B1
Traverse City, MI **99** E5
Traverse, Lake, MN, SD **101** E1
Tremonton, UT **151** A3
Trenton, MO **103** B3
Trenton, NJ **45** E3
Trenton, TN **78** B2
Trinidad, CO **139** G6
Trinity (river), TX **127** E8
Trinity Islands, AK **135** G5
Trinity N.W.&S.R., CA **137** B2
Trinity Site, NM **123** F4
Trotwood, OH **109** E2
Troy, AL **61** F5
Troy, MI **99** H7
Troy, NH **43** I2
Troy, NY **47** E8
Troy, OH **109** E2
Trujillo Alto, PR **157** H11
Trumann, AR **63** B7
Trumbull, CT **33** E3
Truro, MA **41** D10
Truth or Consequences, NM **123** F3
Tschida, Lake, ND **107** E3
Tuba City, AZ **121** B5
Tuckahoe (river), NJ **45** H3
Tuckerman, AR **63** B6
Tucson, AZ **121** G6
Tucumcari, NM **123** C7
Tug Fork (river), KY, WV **69** C11
Tugaloo (river), GA, SC **67** B4
Tulare, CA **137** F4
Tularosa, NM **123** F5
Tullahoma, TN **79** C5
Tulsa, OK **125** B10
Tumacacori N.H.P., AZ **121** H5
Tumwater, WA **153** D3
Tuolumne N.W.&S.R., CA **137** D4
Tupelo, MS **73** B5
Tupelo N.B., MS **73** B5
Turkey (river), IA **95** B8
Turlock, CA **137** E3
Turner Turnpike, OK **125** C9
Turners Falls, MA **41** B3
Turtle Mountains, ND **107** A6
Turtle-Flambeau Flowage, WI **113** B4
Tuscaloosa, AL **61** D2
Tuscarawas (river), OH **109** C6
Tuscarora Mountain, PA **49** E5
Tuscarora Mountains, NV **147** B5
Tuscola, IL **91** E5
Tuskegee, AL **61** E5
Tuskegee Institute National Historic Site, AL **61** F5
Tuttle Creek Lake, KS **97** B7
Tutuila (island), AS **156** I1
Tuxedo Park, NY **47** G8
Tuzigoot Nat. Mon., AZ **121** D4
Twin Falls, ID **143** I3
Twin Lakes, CT **33** A2
Two Butte Creek, CO **139** F9
Two Harbors, MN **101** D6
Two Rivers, WI **113** E7
Tybee Island, GA **67** F8
Tygart Lake, WV **83** D6
Tygart Valley (river), WV **83** E6
Tyler, TX **127** D8
Tyndall, SD **111** F9
Tyrone, PA **49** D4

U

U.S. Military Academy, NY **47** G8
U.S. Virgin Islands (territory), US **157** E12
Uhrichsville, OH **109** D7
Uinta Mountains, UT **151** C5
Ukiah, CA **137** C2
Ulysses, KS **96** E2
Ulysses S. Grant National Historic Site, MO **103** D7
Umbagog Lake, NH **43** B4
Umnak Island, AK **134** H1
Umpqua (river), OR **148** E1
Umpqua, North (river), OR **149** E2
Umpqua, South (river), OR **149** F2
Umsaskis Lake, ME **37** B4
Unalakleet, AK **135** D4
Unalakleet N.W.&S.R., AK **135** D4
Unalaska, AK **134** H2
Unalaska Island, AK **134** H2
Uncompahgre (river), CO **139** E2
Uncompahgre Plateau, CO **138** E1
Unimak Island, AK **134** G2
Union, MO **103** D6
Union, SC **77** B4
Union City, NJ **45** C5
Union City, TN **78** A2
Union Springs, AL **61** F5
Union Village, RI **51** A4
Uniontown, PA **48** E2
Unionville, CT **33** B4
University City, MO **103** D7
'Upolu Point, HI **141** D8
Upper Ammonoosuc (river), NH **43** C3
Upper Arlington, OH **109** E4
Upper Darby, PA **49** E9
Upper Delaware Scenic and Recreational River, PA, NY **49** B10
Upper Iowa (river), IA **95** A7
Upper Klamath Lake, OR **149** G3
Upper Mississippi River National Wildlife and Fish Refuge, IA, IL, MN, WI **101** G6
Upper Missouri River Breaks Nat. Mon., MT **145** B7
Upper Peninsula, MI **99** C3
Upper Red Lake, MN **101** B3
Upper Sandusky, OH **109** C4
Urbana, IL **91** E5
Urbana, OH **109** D3
Urbandale, IA **95** D5
USS Arizona Memorial, HI **141** C4
Utah Lake, UT **151** C4
Ute Creek, NM **123** B7
Utica, NY **47** D6
Utukok (river), AK **135** A4
Uvalde, TX **127** G5

V

Vail, CO **139** C4
Valdez, AK **135** E7
Valdosta, GA **67** H4
Valencia, NM **123** D4
Valentine, NE **105** A4
Vallejo, CA **137** D2
Valley, AL **61** E6
Valley City, ND **107** D8
Valley Falls, RI **51** B5
Valley Forge N.H.P., PA **49** E9
Valparaiso, IN **93** B2
Van Buren, AR **63** C1
Van Buren, ME **37** A6
Van Wert, OH **109** C2
Vanceburg, KY **69** B9
Vancouver, WA **153** G3
Vandalia, IL **91** F4
Vanderbilt Mansion National Historic Site, NY **47** F8
Vaughan, MS **73** E3
Vega Baja, PR **157** H10
Venice, FL **65** F6
Ventnor City, NJ **45** H4
Ventura, CA **137** H4
Verde (river), AZ **121** D4
Verde N.W.&S.R., AZ **121** E5
Verdigre Creek, NE **105** B7
Verdigris (river), KS, OK **125** A11
Vergennes, VT **53** D1
Vermilion (river), IL **91** C4
Vermilion (river), IL, IN **91** E6
Vermilion Cliffs Nat. Mon., AZ **121** A5
Vermilion Lake, MN **101** B5
Vermilion N.W.&S.R., IL **91** D5
Vermillion, SD **111** F10
Vermillion Creek, CO **138** A1
Vermillion, Middle Fork (river), IL **91** D5
Vernal, UT **151** C6
Vernon, CT **33** B6
Vernon, TX **127** C5
Vero Beach, FL **65** E9
Versailles, KY **69** C7
Vicksburg, MS **73** E2
Vicksburg N.M.P., MS **73** E2
Victoria, TX **127** G7
Vidalia, GA **67** F5
Vidalia, LA **71** D5
Vienna, WV **83** D3
Vieques Island, PR **157** I12
Villas, NJ **45** I2
Ville Platte, LA **71** F4
Vinalhaven, ME **37** G5
Vincennes, IN **93** G1
Vineland, NJ **45** G2
Vineyard Haven, MA **41** F8
Vineyard Sound, MA **41** F8
Vinita, OK **125** A11
Vinton, IA **95** C7
Virgin (river), AZ, NV, UT **147** G7
Virgin Islands N.P., VI **157** H8
Virginia, MN **101** C5
Virginia Beach, VA **81** E11
Virginia City, MT **145** E4
Virginia City, NV **147** D2
Viroqua, WI **113** F3
Visalia, CA **137** F4
Vivian, LA **70** A1
Volga, SD **111** D10
Voyageurs N.P., MN **101** B5

W

Wabash, IN **93** C4
Wabash (river), IL, IN **86** G7
Waccamaw (river), SC **77** E9
Waccamaw, Lake, NC **75** D7
Wachusett Reservoir, MA **41** B5
Waco, TX **127** E7
Waconda Lake, KS **97** B5
Wadena, MN **101** D3
Wagner, SD **111** F8
Wagoner, OK **125** C11
Wah Wah Mountains, UT **151** F2
Wahoo, NE **105** C9
Wahpeton, ND **107** E10
Wai'ale'ale (peak), HI **140** A2
Waialua, HI **141** B4
Waialua, HI **141** C6
Waikoloa, HI **141** E8

Wailuku — Zuni

Wailuku, HI **141** C7
Waimea (Kamuela), HI **141** E8
Waipahu, HI **141** B4
Wake Island (territory), US **156** E2
WaKeeney, KS **97** B3
Wakefield, RI **51** F4
Walcott, Lake, ID **143** H4
Waldoboro, ME **37** G4
Waldorf, MD **39** D7
Waldron, AR **63** D1
Walhalla, ND **107** A9
Walker, MN **101** D3
Walker Lake, NV **147** E3
Walker, East (river), NV **147** D2
Walkersville, MD **39** B6
Wall, SD **111** D3
Walla Walla, WA **153** F9
Wallenpaupack, Lake, PA **49** B9
Wallingford, CT **33** D4
Wallingford, VT **53** G2
Wallkill (river), NJ **45** B3
Wallops Island, VA **81** C12
Wallowa (river), OR **149** B8
Wallowa N.W.&S.R., OR **149** B8
Wallula, Lake, WA **153** F8
Wallum Lake, RI **51** A2
Walnut (river), KS **97** E7
Walnut Canyon Nat. Mon., AZ **121** D5
Walnut Creek, KS **97** C4
Walnut Ridge, AR **63** B6
Walpole, NH **43** H1
Walsenburg, CO **139** F6
Walt Disney World and EPCOT Center, FL **65** D7
Walter F. George Reservoir, AL, GA **61** F6
Walterboro, SC **77** F6
Walters, OK **125** E7
Wamego, KS **97** B8
Wanaque, NJ **45** B4
Wanaque Reservoir, NJ **45** B4
Wapakoneta, OH **109** D2
Wapsipinicon (river), IA **95** A7
War in the Pacific N.H.P., GU **156** F1
Ware, MA **41** C4
Ware (river), MA **41** C4
Warner Robins, GA **67** E4
Warner Valley, OR **149** G5
Warren, AR **63** F5
Warren, MI **99** H8
Warren, MN **101** B1
Warren, NH **43** E2
Warren, OH **109** B8
Warren, PA **49** A3
Warren, RI **51** C5
Warrensburg, MO **103** C3
Warrensburg, NY **47** C8
Warrenton, VA **81** B9
Warrior, AL **61** C3
Warsaw, IN **93** B4
Warwick, RI **51** D5
Wasatch Range, UT **130** D5
Waseca, MN **101** G4
Washburn, ME **37** B6
Washburn, ND **107** D5
Washburn, WI **113** A3
Washington, GA **67** C5
Washington, IA **95** E8
Washington, IN **93** G2
Washington, KS **97** A7
Washington, MO **103** D6
Washington, NC **75** C9
Washington, NJ **45** C2
Washington, PA **48** E1
Washington Court House, OH **109** F3
Washington Island, WI **113** C8
Washington, Mount, NH **43** D4
Washita (river), OK **125** C6
Washita Battlefield National Historic Site, OK **125** C5
Wasilla, AK **135** E6
Wassuk Range, NV **147** D2
Watch Hill, RI **51** G1
Watchaug Pond, RI **51** F3
Water Valley, MS **73** B3
Waterbury, CT **33** C3
Waterbury, VT **53** C3
Wateree (river), SC **77** D6
Wateree Lake, SC **77** C6
Waterloo, IA **95** C7
Watertown, CT **33** C3
Watertown, NY **47** C6
Watertown, SD **111** C9
Watertown, WI **113** G6
Waterville, ME **37** F4
Watford City, ND **106** C2
Watkins Glen, NY **47** E4
Watonga, OK **125** C7
Watseka, IL **91** D6
Watts Bar Lake, TN **79** C7
Waubay Lake, SD **111** B9
Waukegan, IL **91** A5
Waukesha, WI **113** G6
Waukon, IA **95** A8
Waupaca, WI **113** E5
Waupun, WI **113** F6
Waurika Lake, OK **125** E7
Wausau, WI **113** D5
Wauseon, OH **109** B2
Wauwatosa, WI **113** G7
Waverly, IA **95** B7
Waverly, NE **105** D9
Waverly, OH **109** F4
Wawasee, Lake, IN **93** B4
Waycross, GA **67** H5
Wayne, NE **105** B8
Wayne, NJ **45** B4
Waynesboro, GA **67** D6
Waynesboro, MS **73** G5
Waynesboro, PA **49** F6
Waynesboro, VA **81** C7
Waynesburg, PA **48** E1
Waynesville, MO **103** E5
Waynesville, NC **74** C2
Weatherford, OK **125** C7
Webb City, MO **103** F2
Webster, MA **41** D5
Webster, SD **111** B9
Webster City, IA **95** C5
Weir Farm National Historic Site, CT **33** E2
Weirton, WV **83** A5
Weiser, ID **143** F1
Weiser (river), ID **143** F1
Weiss Lake, AL **61** B5
Welch, WV **83** H3
Weldon (river), MO **103** A3
Wellesley, MA **41** C6
Wellfleet, MA **41** D10
Wellington, KS **97** E6
Wells, ME **37** I2
Wells, NV **147** B6
Wells River, VT **53** D5
Wellsboro, PA **49** B6
Wellsburg, WV **83** B5
Wellston, OH **109** G5
Wellsville, NY **46** F3
Wellsville, UT **151** A4
Wellton, AZ **121** G2
Wenaha N.W.&S.R., OR **149** A8
Wenatchee, WA **153** D6
Wendell H. Ford Parkway, KY **69** D4
Wendover, UT **151** C1
Wentworth, Lake, NH **43** F4
Wessington Springs, SD **111** D8
West (river), VT **53** H3
West Allis, WI **113** G7
West Bend, WI **113** G7
West Chester, PA **49** E9
West Columbia, SC **77** D5
West Des Moines, IA **95** D5
West Fargo, ND **107** D10
West Frankfort, IL **91** H4
West Grand Lake, ME **37** E6
West Hartford, CT **33** B4
West Haven, CT **33** E4
West Helena, AR **63** D7
West Jordan, UT **151** C4
West Kingston, RI **51** F3
West Little Owyhee N.W.&S.R., OR **149** G8
West Memphis, AR **63** C8
West Milford, NJ **45** B4
West Monroe, LA **71** B4
West Okoboji Lake, IA **95** A3
West Palm Beach, FL **65** F9
West Plains, MO **103** F5
West Point, MS **73** C5
West Point, NE **105** B9
West Point, NY **47** G8
West Point, VA **81** D10
West Point Lake, AL, GA **67** D1
West Quoddy Head, ME **37** F8
West Rutland, VT **53** F2
West Seneca, NY **46** D2
West Warwick, RI **51** D4
West Wendover, NV **147** B7
West Yellowstone, MT **145** F5
Westbrook, CT **33** E6
Westbrook, ME **37** H2
Westerly, RI **51** G1
Westerville, OH **109** D4
Westfield, MA **40** C2
Westfield, NY **46** E1
Westfield (river), MA **40** C2
Westfield N.W.&S.R., MA **40** C2
Westfield, Middle Branch (river), MA **40** B2
Westfield, West Branch (river), MA **40** C1
Westminster, CO **139** C5
Westminster, MD **39** A6
Weston, WV **83** D5
Westport, CT **33** E2
Wet Mountains, CO **139** E5
Wethersfield, CT **33** B5
Wewoka, OK **125** D9
Weymouth, MA **41** C7
Wheatland, WY **155** F9
Wheaton, MN **101** E1
Wheeler Lake, AL **61** A3
Wheeler Peak, NM **123** B5
Wheelersburg, OH **109** G4
Wheeling, WV **83** B4
Whidbey Island, WA **153** B3
Whiskeytown-Shasta-Trinity N.R.A., CA **137** B2
White (river), CO, UT **151** D7
White (river), AR, MO **63** A2
White (river), AZ **121** E7
White (river), IN **93** D5
White (river), MI **99** G4
White (river), NE, SD **111** D5
White (river), OR **149** B4
White (river), VT **53** E3
White Butte (peak), ND **106** E2
White City, OR **149** F2
White Earth (river), ND **107** B3
White Hall, IL **91** F2
White Horse, NJ **45** E3
White Lake, LA **71** H3
White Mountains, NH **43** E2
White N.W.&S.R., OR **149** B4
White Oak Lake, AR **63** F3
White Plains, NY **47** G8
White River, SD **111** E5
White River Junction, VT **53** F4
White River Plateau, CO **139** C2
White Rocks N.R.A., VT **53** G2
White Salmon N.W.&S.R., WA **153** F5
White Sands Nat. Mon., NM **123** G4
White Sulphur Springs, WV **83** G5
White Woman Creek, KS **96** C1
White, East Fork (river), IN **93** G3
Whitefield, NH **43** D3
Whitefish, MT **144** B2
Whitefish Bay, MI **99** C6
Whitefish N.W.&S.R., MI **99** C4
Whiteriver, AZ **121** E7
Whiteville, NC **75** D7
Whitewater, WI **113** G6
Whitewater (river), IN **93** F6
Whitman, MA **41** D8
Whitman Mission National Historic Site, WA **153** F8
Whitney, Mount, CA **137** F5
Wibaux, MT **145** C11
Wichita, KS **97** E7
Wichita (river), TX **127** C6
Wichita Falls, TX **127** C6
Wichita Mountains, OK **125** D6
Wichita Mountains Wildlife Refuge, OK **125** D6
Wickenburg, AZ **121** E4
Wickford, RI **51** E4
Wiggins, MS **73** H4
Wilber, NE **105** D8
Wilburton, OK **125** D11
Wild Rice (river), MN **101** C1
Wild Rice (river), ND **107** F9
Wildcat Brook N.W.&S.R., NH **43** D4
Wildcat Creek, IN **93** D3
Wilder, VT **53** F4
Wildwood, NJ **45** I3
Wilkes-Barre, PA **49** C8
Will Rogers Turnpike, OK **125** B10
Willamette (river), OR **149** C2
Willamette N.W.&S.R., OR **149** D3
Willapa Bay, WA **152** E2
Willard, OH **109** C4
Willcox, AZ **121** G7
Willcox Playa (river), AZ **121** G7
William "Bill" Dannelly Reservoir, AL **61** F3
William H. Natcher Parkway, KY **69** D4
William Howard Taft National Historic Site, OH **109** G2
William Preston Lane Jr. Memorial Bridge (Chesapeake Bay Bridge), MD **39** C8
Williams, AZ **121** C4
Williamsburg, KY **69** E8
Williamsburg, VA **81** D10
Williamson, WV **82** G2
Williamsport, MD **39** A4
Williamsport, PA **49** C7
Williamston, NC **75** B9
Williamstown, KY **69** B8
Williamstown, NJ **45** G2
Williamstown, WV **83** C3
Willimantic, CT **33** B7
Willimantic (river), CT **33** E7
Willimantic Reservoir, CT **33** B7
Willingboro, NJ **45** E2
Williston, ND **106** B2
Williston, SC **77** E4
Willmar, MN **101** F3
Willoughby, Lake, VT **53** B[illegible]
Willow Creek, UT **151** D6
Wills Creek, OH **109** E6
Wilmington, DE **35** A5
Wilmington, NC **75** D8
Wilmington, OH **109** F3
Wilmington, MA **41** B7
Wilson, NC **75** B8
Wilson Creek Range, NV **147** E7
Wilson Lake, AL **61** A2
Wilson Lake, KS **97** B5
Wilson's Creek N.B., MO **103** F3
Wilton, CT **33** E2
Wilton, ME **37** F3
Wilton, NH **43** I3
Winchendon, MA **41** A4
Winchester, IN **93** D6
Winchester, KY **69** C8
Winchester, NH **43** I1
Winchester, TN **79** D6
Winchester, VA **81** A8
Wind (river), WY **155** C5
Wind Cave N.P., SD **110** E2
Wind N.W.&S.R., AK **135** E7
Wind River Range, WY **155** C3
Windber, PA **49** E4
Windom, MN **101** H3
Window Rock, AZ **121** C7
Windsor, CT **33** B5
Windsor, VT **53** F4
Windsor Heights, IA **95** D4
Windsor Locks, CT **33** A5
Winfield, AL **61** C2
Winfield, KS **97** E7
Winnebag, Lake, WI **113** F[illegible]
Winnebago (river), IA **95** A[illegible]
Winnemucca, NV **147** B4
Winnemucca Lake, NV **147** C2
Winner, SD **111** E6
Winnfield, LA **71** C3
Winnibigoshish, Lake, MN **101** C3
Winnipesaukee, Lake, NH **43** F4
Winnisquam Lake, NH **43** G3
Winnsboro, SC **77** C5
Winnsboro, LA **71** C5
Winona, MN **101** G6
Winona, MS **73** C3
Winooski (river), VT **53** C2
Winooski, VT **53** C2
Winslow, AZ **121** D6
Winslow, ME **37** F4
Winsted, CT **33** A3
Winston, OR **149** E2
Winston-Salem, NC **75** B5
Winter Haven, FL **65** E7
Winterset, IA **95** E5
Winterthur Museum and Gardens, DE **35** A5
Winthrop, ME **37** G3
Wiscasset, ME **37** G3
Wisconsin (river), WI **113** E5
Wisconsin Dells, WI **113** F5
Wisconsin Rapids, WI **113** [illegible]5
Wisconsin, Lake, WI **113** G5
Wishek, ND **107** F6
Wissota, Lake, WI **113** D3
Withlacoochee (river), GA **67** H4
Woburn, MA **41** B7
Wolf (river), WI **113** D6
Wolf Creek, OK **125** B5
Wolf N.W.&S.R., WI **113** [illegible]6
Wolf Point, MT **145** B10
Wolf Trap N.P. for the Performing Arts, VA **81** B9
Wolfeboro, NH **43** F4
Women's Rights N.H.P., NY **47** D5
Wood (river), RI **51** F2
Woodall Mountain, MS **73** [illegible]6
Woodbine, NJ **45** H3
Woodbridge, VA **81** B9
Woodburn, OR **149** B2
Woodbury, NJ **45** F2
Woodland, ME **37** E7
Woodland Park, CO **139** D5
Woods Hole, MA **41** F8
Woods, Lake of the, MN **101** A3
Woodstock, VT **53** F3
Woodstown, NJ **45** G1
Woodsville, NH **43** E2
Woodward, OK **125** B6
Woonasquatucket (river), RI **51** B4
Woonasquatucket Reservoir, RI **51** B3
Woonsocket, RI **51** A4
Woonsocket, SD **111** D8
Wooster, OH **109** C6
Worcester, MA **41** C5
Worden Pond, RI **51** F3
Worland, WY **155** B5
Worthington, MN **101** H2
Wounded Knee Massacre Site, SD **111** E3
Wrangell, AK **135** G11
Wrangell-St. Elias N.P. and Preserve, AK **135** E8
Wright, WY **155** C8
Wright Brothers National Memorial, NC **75** B10
Wrightsville Beach, NC **75** E8
Wupatki Nat. Mon., AZ **121** C5
Wyaconda (river), MO **103** A5
Wyandotte Cave, IN **93** H3
Wylie Lake, SC **77** A5
Wynne, AR **63** C7
Wyoming, RI **51** E2
Wyoming Range, WY **154** D2
Wytheville, VA **80** E4

X

Xenia, OH **109** E3

Y

Yadkin (river), NC **75** B4
Yakima, WA **153** E6
Yakima (river), WA **153** D6
Yalobusha (river), MS **73** C4
Yampa (river), CO **139** B2
Yankton, SD **111** F9
Yantic (river), CT **33** C7
Yarmouth, ME **37** H3
Yazoo (river), MS **73** E2
Yazoo City, MS **73** E2
Yellow (river), WI **113** D3
Yellow Dog N.W.&S.R., MI **99** C3
Yellowstone (river), MT, WY **145** C11
Yellowstone Lake, WY **154** A2
Yellowstone N.P., ID, MT, WY **154** A2
Yerington, NV **147** D2
Yoakum, TX **127** G7
Yocona (river), MS **73** B3
Yona, GU **156** F1
Yonkers, NY **47** G8
York, AL **61** E1
York, NE **105** D8
York, PA **49** E7
York, SC **77** A5
York (river), VA **81** D10
York Village, ME **37** I2
Yorktown, VA **81** D11
Yosemite N.P., CA **137** E4
Youghiogheny (river), PA **49** F3
Youngstown, OH **109** B8
Ypsilanti, MI **99** H7
Yreka, CA **137** A2
Yuba City, CA **137** C3
Yucca House Nat. Mon., CO **138** G1
Yukon, OK **125** C8
Yukon (river), AK **135** E4
Yukon Delta, AK **134** D3
Yukon-Charley Rivers National Preserve, AK **135** C8
Yuma, AZ **121** G2
Yuma, CO **139** B8
Yunaska Island, AK **135** G10

Z

Zachary, LA **71** F6
Zanesville, OH **109** E6
Zapata, TX **127** H5
Zeeland, MI **99** H5
Zion N.P., UT **151** G2
Zoar, Lake, CT **33** D3
Zuni, NM **123** D1
Zuni (river), AZ **121** D7

Published by the National Geographic Society

John M. Fahey, Jr.
President and Chief Executive Officer

Gilbert M. Grosvenor
Chairman of the Board

Tim T. Kelly
President, Global Media Group

Nina D. Hoffman
Executive Vice President; President, Book Publishing Group

Prepared by the Book Division

Nancy Laties Feresten,
Vice President, Editor in Chief, Children's Books

Bea Jackson, Director of Design and Illustrations, Children's Books

Jennifer Emmett, Executive Editor, Reference, Children's Books

Amy Shields, Executive Editor, Series, Children's Books

Carl Mehler, Director of Maps

Staff for this book

Suzanne Patrick Fonda, Project Editor

Bea Jackson, Art Director and Book Design

Ruthie Thompson, Thunder Hill Graphics, Designer

Sven M. Dolling, Laura Exner, Thomas L. Gray,
Nicholas P. Rosenbach, Map Editors

Matt Chwastyk, Sven M. Dolling, Steven D. Gardner,
Michael McNey, Gregory Ugiansky, Mapping Specialists, and
XNR Productions, Map Research and Production

Tibor G. Tóth, Map Relief

Priyanka Lamichhane, Editor

Lori Epstein, Illustrations Editor

Martha B. Sharma, Consultant

Martha B. Sharma, Timothy J. Hill, Writers

Stuart Armstrong, Graphics Illustrator

Chelsea M. Zillmer, Researcher

Dan Sherman, Web Page Design

Jennifer Kirkpatrick, Web Page Editor

Mark H. Bockenhauer, Clean Reader

Sandi Owatverot, Production Design Assistant

Stacy Gold, Nadia Hughes, Illustrations Research Editors

Rebecca Baines, Editorial Assistant

Debbie Guthrie Haer, Copy Editor

Lewis R. Bassford, Production Project Manager

Jennifer A. Thornton, Managing Editor

Grace Hill, Associate Managing Editor

R. Gary Colbert, Production Director

Susan Borke, Legal and Business Affairs

Manufacturing and Quality Management

Christopher A. Liedel, Chief Financial Officer

Phillip L. Schlosser, Vice President

Chris Brown, Technical Director

Nicole Elliott, Manager

Founded in 1888, the National Geographic Society is one of the largest nonprofit scientific and educational organizations in the world. It reaches more than 285 million people worldwide each month through its official journal, NATIONAL GEOGRAPHIC, and its four other magazines; the National Geographic Channel; television documentaries; radio programs; films; books; videos and DVDs; maps; and interactive media. National Geographic has funded more than 8,000 scientific research projects and supports an education program combating geographic illiteracy.

For more information, please call 1-800-NGS LINE (647-5463) or write to the following address:

NATIONAL GEOGRAPHIC SOCIETY
1145 17th Street N.W., Washington, D.C. 20036-4688 U.S.A.

Visit us online at www.nationalgeographic.com/books

For information about special discounts for bulk purchases, please contact National Geographic Books Special Sales: ngspecsales@ngs.org

For rights or permissions inquiries, please contact National Geographic Books Subsidiary Rights: ngbookrights@ngs.org

Teachers and librarians go to ngchildrensbooks.com

Printed in China

Illustrations Credits

Abbreviations for terms appearing below: (t)-top; (b)-bottom; (l)-left; (r)-right; NGS = National Geographic Image Collection; iS = iStockphoto.com; SH = Shutterstock.com

Art for state flowers and state birds by Robert E. Hynes

Locator globe page 16 created by Theophilus Britt Griswold

Front cover, Tibor G. Tóth

Back cover (t–b), FloridaStock/SH, Peder Digre/SH, Lou Ann M. Aepelbacher/SH, Olga Lyubkina/SH

Front of the Book
2 (l–r), Freerk Brouwer/SH; PhotoDisc; Brandon Laufenberg/iS; Richard Nowitz/NGS; 3 (l–r), Joel Sartore/NGS; Jeremy Edwards/iS; Eileen Hart/iS; PhotoDisc; 4 (l), PhotoDisc; 4 (r), Brian J. Skerry/NGS; 4–5, Lenice Harms/SH; 5 (l), italianestro/SH; 5 (r), James Davis Photography/Alamy; 5 (b), Digital Stock; 11 (t–b), Lane V. Erickson/SH; Elena Elisseeva/SH; SNEHIT/SH; Nic Watson/SH; FloridaStock/SH; Sai Yeung Chan/SH; TTphoto/SH; 12 (l) Lowell Georgia/NGS; 12 (r), NASA; 14 (l–r), George F. Mobley/NGS; Skip Brown/NGS; Jan Brons/SH; Michelle Pacitto/SH; Tammy Bryngelson/iS; 15 (l–r), Carsten Peter/NGS; Mark Thiessen/NGS; Michael Nichols/NGS; Steven Collins/SH; Robert Madden/NGS; 18, Ira Block/NGS; 20 (t), Penny de los Santos; 20 (bl), Steven Clevenger/Corbis; 20–21, Sarah Leen/NGS; 22 (l), Marcelo Piotti/iS; 22–23, Jim Richardson/NGS; 23 (r), Sorin Alb/iS; 24, PhotoDisc; 24–25, PhotoDisc; 25 (t), L. Kragt Bakker/SH; 25 (b), EyeWire.

The Northeast
30 (bl), Rudi Von Briel/Photo Edit; 30 (br), Les Byerley/SH; 30–31 (t), Michael Melford/NGS; 30–31 (b), Tim Laman/NGS; 31 (t), Donald Swartz/iS; 32 (both), David L. Arnold/NGS; 33, Catherine Karnow/NGS; 34 (bl), Kevin Fleming/NGS; 34 (br), Stephen R. Brown/NGS; 34–35, Stephen St. John/NGS; 36 (b), iS; 36–37, PhotoDisc; 37 (b), Roy Toft/NGS; 38 (t), Jeremy Edwards/iS; 38 (b), Justine Gecewicz/iS; 39, James L. Stanfield/NGS; 40 (t), Sarah Leen/NGS; 40 (b), Tim Laman/NGS; 41, Darlyne A. Murawski/NGS; 42 (t), Medford Taylor/NGS; 42–43, Steven Phraner/iS; 43 (t), Richard Nowitz/NGS; 44 (t), Richard Nowitz/NGS; 44 (bl), Iconica/Getty Images; 44 (br), Matt Rainey/Star Ledger/Corbis; 44–45, Mike Derer/Associated Press; 46 (t), Glenn Taylor/iS; 46 (b), James P. Blair/NGS; 47, Kenneth Garrett/NGS; 48 (t), Kenneth Garrett/NGS; 48 (b), Jeremy Edwards/iS; 49, William Albert Allard/NGS; 50 (t), Todd Gipstein/NGS; 50 (b), Onne van der Wal/Corbis; 50–51, Ira Block/NGS; 52, Michael S. Yamashita/NGS; 52–53, David McLain/Aurora/Getty Images; 53, Daniel W. Slocum/SH.

The Southeast
58 (t), Klaus Nigge/NGS; 58 (bl), Tyrone Turner/NGS; 58 (br), Richard Nowitz/Corbis; 58–59, Skip Brown/NGS; 59 (t), Raymond Gehman/NGS; 59 (b), Robert Clark/NGS; 60 (t), Raymond Gehman/NGS; 60 (b), Richard Nowitz/NGS; 62 (t), Harrison Shull/Aurora/Getty Images; 62 (b), Joel Sartore/NGS; 63, Cary Wolinsky/NGS; 64 (t), David Burnett/NGS; 64 (b), Brian J. Skerry/NGS; 64–65, Otis Imboden/NGS; 66 (tl), NGS; 66 (tr), PhotoDisc; 66 (b), Michael Melford/NGS; 68, Melissa Farlow/NGS; 69, Randy Olson/NGS; 70 (t), Tyrone Turner/NGS; 70 (b), Jason Major/iS; 72 (t), William Albert Allard/NGS; 72 (b), Ira Block/NGS; 73, Elena Vdovina/iS; 74 (l), Jack Fletcher/NGS; 74 (r), Pete Souza/NGS; 75, Raymond Gehman/NGS; 76, Terry Healy/iS; 76–77, Annie Griffiths Belt/NGS; 77, Raymond Gehman/NGS; 78, Melissa Farlow/NGS; 79 (t), Dennis R. Dimick/NGS; 79 (b), Jodi Cobb/NGS; 80 (t), Robert Clark/NGS; 80 (b), Richard Nowitz/NGS; 80–81, Medford Taylor/NGS; 82 (t), James L. Stanfield/NGS; 82 (b), Joel Sartore/NGS; 83, Robert Pernell/SH.

The Midwest
88 (t), James L. Stanfield/NGS; 88 (b), Jim Richardson/NGS; 88–89, NGS; 89 (tl), Nadia M. B. Hughes/NGS; 89 (tr), Sean Martin/iS; 89 (b), Aga/SH; 90 (t), Chas/SH; 90 (b), Jenny Solomon/SH; 90–91 (t), Lenice Harms/SH; 92–93 (t), iS; 92–93 (b), Joel Sartore/NGS; 94 (t), Joel Sartore/NGS; 94 (b), Madeleine Openshaw/SH; 95, Tom Bean/NGS; 96, Cotton Coulson/NGS; 97, Phil Schermeister/NGS; 98 (t), Kevin Fleming/Corbis; 98 (b), Vince Ruffa/SH; 99, Geoffrey Kuchera/SH; 100 (t), Joel Sartore/NGS; 100 (b), Medford Taylor/NGS; 101, Lawrence Sawyer/iS; 102, Phil Schermeister/NGS; 102–103 (b), PhotoDisc; 103, Sarah Leen/NGS; 104 (both), Joel Sartore/NGS; 105, Sarah Leen/NGS; 106 (t), Farrell Grehan/NGS; 106 (b), Beverley Vycital/iS; 107, Annie Griffiths Belt/NGS; 108 (t), PhotoDisc; 108 (bl), Weldon Schloneger/SH; 108 (br), Robert J. Daveant/SH; 110, Peter Digre/SH; 111, Dan Westergren/NGS; 112 (t), Paul Damien/NGS; 112 (b), PhotoDisc; 112–113 Medford Taylor/NGS.

The Southwest
118 (t), Joseph H. Bailey/NGS; 118 (b), Penny de los Santos; 118–119, Anton Folton/iS; 119 (t), Chih Hsueh Tseng/SH; 119 (b), Joel Sartore/NGS; 120 (t), Joel Sartore/NGS; 120 (b), George Burba/NGS; 122 (tl), James P. Blair/NGS; 122 (tr), italianestro/iS; 122 (b), Lynn Johnson/NGS; 124, Joel Sartore/NGS; 125, Annie Griffiths Belt/NGS; 126 (t), Sarah Leen/NGS; 126–127, Diane Cook & Len Jenshel/NGS.

The West
132 (both), PhotoDisc; 132–133, Digital Stock; 133 (t), Phillip Holland/SH; 133 (bl), Joel Sartore/NGS; 133 (br), Digital Stock; 134 (t), Joel Sartore/NGS; 134 (b), PhotoDisc; 136 (t), PhotoDisc; 136 (b), Randy Olson/NGS; 138 (both), PhotoDisc; 140, PhotoDisc; 141, Frans Lanting/NGS; 142 (b), Joel Sartore/NGS; 142–143, Michael Melford/NGS; 143 (r), J. Cameron Gull/SH; 144 (b), William Albert Allard/NGS; 145, SH; 146 (b), Sam Abell/NGS; 146–147, Andy Z./SH; 147 (b), Raymond Gehman/NGS; 148 (t), Jennifer Lynn Arnold/NGS; 148 (b), Peter Kunasz/SH; 150 (b), Digital Stock; 150–151, PhotoDisc; 152 (l), PhotoDisc; 152 (r), Digital Stock; 154 (t), Michael Rubin/SH; 154 (b), Digital Stock; 155, PhotoDisc.

The Territories and Back of the Book
158 (l), Kendra Nielsam/SH; 158–159 (t), James Davis Photography/Alamy; 158–159 (b), Ira Block/NGS; 159 (t), VisionsofParadise.com/Alamy; 159 (b), Gerry Ellis/Minden/Getty Images; 160, SH.

Map Acknowledgments

2–3, 26–27, 54–55, 84–85, 114–115, 128–129, Blue Marble: Next Generation NASA Earth Observatory; 12–13, climate data adapted from Peel, M. C., Finlayson, B. L., and McMahon, T. A.: Updated world map of the Köppen-Geiger climate classification, Hydrol. Earth Syst. Sci., 11, 1633–1644, 2007; 14–15, data from Billion Dollar Weather Disasters 1980–2007 (map), NOAA's National Climatic Data Center (NCDC); 18–19, data from Center for International Earth Science Information Network (CIESIN), Columbia University, and Centro Internacional de Agricultura Tropical (CIAT), 2005. Gridded Population of the World Version 3 (GPWv3): Population Density Grids—World Population Density, 2005 (map). Palisades, New York: Socioeconomic Data and Applications Center (SEDAC), Columbia University. Accessed October 2007. Available at http://sedac.ciesin.columbia.edu/gpw; 20–21, United States Atlas of Renewable Resources, National Renewable Energy Laboratory; 22–23, U.S. Census Bureau, Census 2000 Redistricting Data (PL 94-171) Summary File, Population Division.

Library of Congress Cataloging-in-Publication Data available upon request.

ISBN: 978-1-4263-0255-8 (hardcover);
ISBN: 978-1-4263-0271-8 Direct Mail Expanded Edition; ISBN: 978-1-4263-0272-5 Deluxe Direct Mail Expanded Edition

AMERICAN
HEROES

⇧ A statue in Arlington, Virginia, overlooking the Washington, D.C., skyline, commemorates the 1945 World War II Marine victory at Iwo Jima.

AMERICAN HEROES

MARFÉ FERGUSON DELANO

NATIONAL GEOGRAPHIC

WASHINGTON, D.C.

Contents

"What Is an American Hero?"
An Introduction by Robert D. Johnston ★ 181

Pocahontas ★ 182

Benjamin Franklin ★ 183

George Washington ★ 184

Lewis and Clark ★ 186

John Chapman ★ 187

Harriet Tubman ★ 188

Abraham Lincoln ★ 189

Elizabeth Cady Stanton and Susan B. Anthony ★ 190

Sitting Bull ★ 192

Queen Lili'uokalani ★ 193

Alexander Graham Bell ★ 194

Wright Brothers ★ 196

Theodore Roosevelt ★ 197

Matthew Henson ★ 198

Amelia Earhart ★ 199

Franklin Delano Roosevelt ★ 200

Rachel Carson ★ 202

Jackie Robinson ★ 203

Martin Luther King, Jr. ★ 204

César Chávez ★ 206

Resources, Quote Sources, Photo Credits ★ 207

What Is an American Hero?

⇧ The painting above portrays the legendary landing of the Pilgrims at Plymouth, Massachusetts, in 1620.

The best histories are about humanity. And with humanity comes heroism. Americans have always, rightly, been attracted to the heroes of the past whether they be high-and-mighty generals who have directed our wars or the powerless who have thirsted for justice. For we can learn much by looking at the lives of heroes. We can see how people we admire made courageous ethical choices. We can see that it is possible to have the gumption to stand up in a crowd and make an unpopular decision. And we can see how individuals can make a real difference in human affairs.

Some scholars, though, say that looking for heroes in history is misguided—even dangerous. Focusing on extraordinary lives, they claim, makes us look up into the stratosphere, leading us to forget that it is ordinary people like us who make history. I disagree. Heroes can help us learn life lessons. This is a group of great Americans, tested by time. They are not people whose feats of heroism come down to a single moment of bravery. They are heroes of history who can still speak to us today.

It's a fascinating and complex group. If this combination is complex, so too are the heroes themselves. Those with stringent standards might ask for our heroes to be perfect, but this seems wrong. It is important to understand not only that all people are imperfect, but that even our heroes are people—people who have reached beyond their flaws to make exceptional contributions to humanity. George Washington owned many slaves, for example. We may properly judge, and even condemn Washington and other heroes for their flawed actions—after all, people at the time they lived did so. Yet we can still recognize the heroism that inspired Washington to risk his life to lead his country to victory over the British. With humanity comes heroism, but with heroism also comes humanity.

In the end, we not only care about the heroes in our history—we need them.

By Robert D. Johnston, Ph.D.

Pocahontas

⇧ Pocahontas is famous for her legendary role in saving the life of Captain John Smith.

About four hundred years ago, the young Indian princess Pocahontas became the first heroine in American history. As the story goes, she was about 12 years old when she saved the life of John Smith, one of the leaders of Virginia's Jamestown Colony. According to Smith, in December 1607 a group of Native Americans took him captive and brought him before their chief, Powhatan. Suddenly Smith's captors flung him down on a stone and stood "ready with their clubs to beat out his brains." In rushed Pocahontas, Powhatan's "dearest daughter," who took Smith's "head in her arms, and laid her own upon his to save him from death."

This story won Pocahontas a place in history for her kindheartedness and bravery, but it may be more legend than fact. The only record of the adventure is Smith's memoir, published 17 years after the alleged event. Details about Pocahontas's life are scarce, but historians believe that she was a frequent visitor to Jamestown. She and other members of Powhatan's tribe may have helped the English settlers survive during the long winters by bringing them food. In 1613 the English kidnapped Pocahontas and held her hostage, hoping to convince Powhatan to release some English prisoners. During her captivity, Pocahontas became engaged to an English colonist named John Rolfe. After she converted to Christianity, they were married. The union brought about temporary goodwill between their peoples. In 1616 Pocahontas, Rolfe, and their infant son traveled to England, where she became a celebrity. The next year Pocahontas became ill and died at about age 22. She was buried at the Church of St. George, Gravesend, Kent, England. Her grave has not been located, but memorial windows and a marker can be found there today.

THE BASICS

BIOGRAPHY	DID YOU KNOW
Born circa 1595, Virginia	The word "pocahontas" means "playful one." It was reported that as a young girl, Pocahontas was seen doing handsprings with young boys living at the Jamestown colony.
Died March 1617, Gravesend, England	
Age at death 22?	Pocahontas may have acted as her father's ambassador, carrying messages from him to the colonists.
Other names Matoaka, her Native American name; Rebecca, her baptized Christian name	The image of Pocahontas is on the flag and seal of Henrico County, Virginia.
	John Rolfe married again after Pocahontas died and lived in Virginia until his death in 1622. He crossed native tobacco with a milder variety—and created Virginia's first cash crop.
Milestones 1616: Met King James I, England	
	Pocahontas's son, Thomas Rolfe, became a wealthy tobacco farmer in Virginia.

Benjamin Franklin

Printer, author, postmaster, businessman, scientist, inventor, musician, patriot, and diplomat. All of these labels—and more—fit Benjamin Franklin, America's most versatile Founding Father and one of the most remarkable men the world has ever known.

Born in Boston, Benjamin was the child of Josiah Franklin, a poor candle and soap maker. As a boy, Ben loved books and reading and writing, so his father apprenticed him to his older brother James, a printer. When he was 17, Ben ran away to Philadelphia. He eventually acquired his own printing business and was appointed postmaster. Franklin founded the first lending library in the Colonies, as well as Philadelphia's first fire company, a public hospital, and a militia.

Franklin was a prolific writer. His best known publication, *Poor Richard's Almanack*, helped make him rich. In 1748, at the age of 42, he retired from the printing business to devote the rest of his life to his two main passions: scientific research and public service.

With his famous kite-flying experiment, Franklin proved that lightning and electricity were one and the same. He also invented the lightning rod, bifocal glasses, and a smokeless fireplace.

In the 1750s, Franklin became involved in politics. He eventually became a leader in the American Revolution. In 1776 he helped draft the Declaration of Independence. During the Revolutionary War Franklin served as a diplomat in France, helping to organize the war effort. In 1783 he helped negotiate a peace treaty with Great Britain that granted full independence to the American colonies.

In his final years, Benjamin Franklin penned his autobiography. He also joined an abolitionist group and freed the two slaves he owned. He spoke up for the need to educate freed slaves, which he believed would "promote the public good, and the happiness of these hitherto much neglected fellow-creatures."

⇧ One of America's most beloved Founding Fathers, Benjamin Franklin valued freedom above all else. "They that can give up essential liberty to obtain a little temporary safety," he wrote in 1759, "deserve neither liberty nor safety."

THE BASICS

BIOGRAPHY

Born
January 17, 1706,
Boston, Massachusetts

Died
April 17, 1790,
Philadelphia, Pennsylvania

Age at death
84

Other names
Silence Dogood, Richard Saunders,
Poor Richard

DID YOU KNOW

Ben Franklin was still teaching swimming in his seventies. He is the only Founding Father in the Swimming Hall of Fame.

The composer Mozart wrote two pieces for Franklin's musical invention, the glass armonica, which produced sound through vibrating glass spheres.

Franklin taught himself to read in five languages: German, French, Spanish, Italian, and Latin.

Franklin's son, William, became the colonial governor of New Jersey and remained loyal to Great Britain during the American Revolution, which led to an estrangement with his father. William was arrested in 1776 and lived out the rest of his life in England.

Benjamin Franklin was the only Founding Father to sign the Declaration of Independence, the Constitution, and the Treaty of Paris, which formally ended the Revolutionary War.

George Washington

⇧ The first President of the United States, George Washington is honored today in countless ways—from monuments across the country to the many schools and towns named for him to his image on both the one-dollar bill and the quarter. He is the only President to have a state named for him.

Called the "Father of His Country," George Washington is best known today for being the first President of the United States. But Washington deserves equal honor for his courage and skill as a military leader. As the commanding general of America's Continental Army, he led the 13 Colonies to victory during the Revolutionary War. Had the Americans failed to defeat the British, the United States as we know it would not exist.

Washington was the son of a Virginia landowner and planter. When he was 16 he found work as a surveyor and set off to chart the wilds of Virginia's Shenandoah Valley.

Washington joined the Virginia militia at the age of 22 and became a lieutenant colonel. He fought for the British in the French and Indian War. During one battle, two horses were shot from under him and bullets flew through his coat, but somehow he escaped without injury. Brave and calm in the face of danger, Washington gained the respect and loyalty of his men. His reputation as a gifted leader spread throughout the Colonies.

When he was 26, Washington retired from military service. For the next 17 years, he devoted himself to managing his Virginia plantation, Mount Vernon, which he ran with slave labor. He also served in Virginia's colonial legislature. In 1759, he married Martha Dandridge Custis, a wealthy widow with two young children.

Meanwhile, resistance to British rule began to grow in the Colonies. Washington was one of those who thought that British demands and taxes were unfair. In a July 1774 letter he wrote, "I think the Parliament of Great Britain hath no more Right to put their hands into my Pocket, without my consent, than I have to put my hands into your's, for money." When Washington attended the Second Continental

THE BASICS

BIOGRAPHY	DID YOU KNOW
Born February 22, 1732, Westmoreland County, Virginia	While the legend of Washington chopping down a cherry tree and then confessing to his father illustrates Washington's character, historians think it never happened.
Died December 14, 1799, Mount Vernon, Virginia	Washington only traveled outside the United States once—to Barbados.
Age at death 67	Washington did not have wooden teeth, but he did have several sets of false teeth.
Other names Father of His Country	On October 3, 1789, Washington declared that a date be set aside to celebrate the nation's first Thanksgiving.
Milestones 1789–1797: Served as first President of the United States	According to Washington's birth record, he had no middle name.
Honors National holiday, Presidents Day	

⬆ This famous painting of General George Washington crossing the icy Delaware River to lead an attack on the British captures his heroic role in American history. The fate of the new nation depended in large part on him—first as commander-in-chief of the Continental Army and then as the nation's first President. A legend in his own time, George Washington remains one of America's most enduring heroes.

Congress as a delegate from Virginia in May 1775, the first shots of the American war for independence had already been fired. The delegates chose George Washington to lead the new Continental Army against the British.

The troops of the Continental Army were poorly equipped and largely untrained, but Washington held them together for six years of fighting against the world's most powerful empire. He decided early on that the best strategy was to avoid major battles whenever possible and to harass the British instead. He used surprise attacks and organized a spy network to outfox the enemy. Washington's courage and commitment to the revolutionary cause inspired the ragtag American army. With help from the French, Washington forced the British to surrender in October 1781.

Washington again retired from military service in 1783 and returned to Mount Vernon. His stay there, however, lasted just a few years. The new nation he had helped create was in danger of falling apart. Washington realized that the federal government needed to be strengthened if the United States was to survive. In May 1787, he gathered

in Philadelphia with delegates from other states for a meeting that came to be known as the Constitutional Convention. By September the delegates had written the new Constitution of the United States. After the document was ratified by the states, the nation's first presidential election took place.

> "Observe good faith
> and justice toward all nations.
> Cultivate peace and
> harmony with all...."
>
> Farewell Address, September 17, 1796

George Washington, the war hero, was everyone's first choice for President. He was elected unanimously by a group of electors in the nation's first electoral college. He journeyed to New York, which was then the nation's capital, and he took the oath of office on April 30, 1789. An account from the time noted of Washington: "There was in his whole appearance an unusual dignity and gracefulness which at once secured him profound respect, and cor-

dial esteem. He seemed born to command his fellow men."

Washington did his best to live up to the trust his country had placed in him. He knew that everything he did in office would set a precedent, or model, for future presidents to follow. He used his powers as President to appoint Cabinet members and judges, to command the armed forces, and to negotiate treaties. He left it to Congress to make laws, as provided for in the Constitution. President Washington was so popular that he was reelected unanimously.

By the end of his second term, Washington had grown weary of politics. In his farewell address, he urged his fellow citizens to avoid splitting into political parties and to strive for unity: "With slight shades of difference you have the same religion, manner, habits, and political principles."

In 1797, George and Martha Washington returned to Mount Vernon. Less than three years later, Washington died of a throat infection at age 67. The entire nation mourned for months the man praised as "first in war, first in peace, and first in the hearts of his countrymen."

Lewis And Clark

⇧ As captains Meriwether Lewis and William Clark and their men pushed west to the Pacific Ocean, they ran into dangerous rapids—just one of the many perils they faced on their legendary journey into uncharted lands.

On June 19, 1803, President Thomas Jefferson's private secretary, Captain Meriwether Lewis, wrote a letter to his friend Captain William Clark. Lewis said that Jefferson wished him to lead a military expedition to explore "those western rivers which may run all the way across North America to the western ocean," with the aim of beginning trade with Indian tribes, discovering new plants and animals, and making maps.

A month earlier the United States had purchased the vast Louisiana Territory from France, and Jefferson was eager to learn just what America now owned. Lewis asked Clark to join him on the mission. Several years earlier he had served under Clark in the Army, and the two men had developed a strong mutual trust. A skilled waterman, surveyor, and mapmaker, Clark jumped at the chance to blaze new trails with his old friend.

Lewis and Clark recruited about 40 men, including Clark's slave York, for the Corps of Discovery. In May 1804 the expedition set out from St. Louis. Eighteen months later they reached the Pacific Ocean. Along the way they made maps and kept detailed journals of what they saw. The explorers returned to St. Louis in September 1806. Their maps and journals, their accounts of the Native Americans they encountered, and the thousands of plant and animal specimens they brought back from their travels excited curiosity throughout the nation. Their report that the new territory teemed with game and lands for farming sent thousands of Americans heading west.

Meriwether Lewis and William Clark were the very first U.S. citizens to cross the American continent. During their trip to the Pacific and back, they covered almost 8,000 miles (12,872 km) of wilderness. Today the brave adventurers still excite admiration for boldly going into uncharted lands and blazing a path for others to follow.

THE BASICS

BIOGRAPHY	DID YOU KNOW
MERIWETHER LEWIS	Thomas Jefferson taught Lewis how to navigate by sextant. He also saw to it that Lewis received lessons in surveying, mapmaking, astronomy, botany, zoology, and medicine to prepare him for the expedition.
Born August 18, 1774, near Charlottesville, Virginia	
Died October 11, 1809, near Nashville, Tennessee	To show their friendly intentions, the Corps of Discovery gave the Native Americans they met in their travels calico shirts, beads, and fishhooks.
Age at death 35	The expedition noted some 80 plants and 122 animals they had never seen before, including the gray wolf and grizzly bear.
WILLIAM CLARK	Lewis and Clark kept expedition journals and wrote more than a million words.
Born August 1, 1770, Caroline County, Virginia	Throughout the grueling journey, there is no hint that Lewis and Clark argued.
Died September 1, 1838, St. Louis, Missouri	An American Indian teenager called Sacagawea joined the expedition in North Dakota. She helped Lewis and Clark bargain with her tribe, the Shoshone, for horses to carry them across the Rocky Mountains.
Age at death 68	

John Chapman

Some frontiersmen, such as Daniel Boone and Davy Crockett, made names for themselves with their hunting and fighting skills. John Chapman earned his place in history by gentler means: He planted apple trees.

Better known as Johnny Appleseed, Chapman was born in 1774 in Leominster, Massachusetts. Little is known of his early years. At age 23 or so he made his way to the wilds of northwestern Pennsylvania, where he planted the seeds for his first apple tree nursery. He sold his seedlings to settlers moving into the region.

Around 1800 Chapman headed west into frontier territory, laden with burlap bags of apple seeds he had collected from cider presses. He had a knack for judging where pioneers would be likely to settle, and he planted his nurseries there. By the time the homesteaders arrived, Chapman had apple seedlings ready for them to start their own orchards. If people couldn't afford to buy the seedlings, he traded them for food or just gave them away.

For nearly half a century, Chapman roamed what would become Ohio and Indiana, tending his nurseries and planting new ones. He earned enough cash to buy more than a thousand acres, yet he dressed in ragged clothes and often went barefoot.

Chapman became a legend in his own time, known for his eccentric appearance, his generosity, his wilderness skills, his friendship with Native Americans, his knowledge of the Bible, and of course his apples, which were a mainstay of the pioneer diet. His mythic image grew when he risked his life to warn settlers of Indian attacks during the War of 1812. Chapman died of pneumonia in 1845. In 1996 he was designated the official folk hero of the Commonwealth of Massachusetts, and he lives on as one of America's favorite folk heroes: Johnny Appleseed.

⬆ John Chapman, better known as Johnny Appleseed, is celebrated in songs, folk tales, books, poems, postage stamps, and even a Disney film. His life has become so intertwined with legend that it's hard to tell what is fact about him and what is fiction. What we do know is that he won his fame by planting apple trees.

THE BASICS

BIOGRAPHY	DID YOU KNOW
Born September 26, 1774, Leominster, Massachusetts	Chapman's father was a minuteman at Concord.
	Planting an apple orchard served as a way of claiming a parcel of land.
Died circa March 18, 1845, near Fort Wayne, Indiana	Chapman collected his apple seeds from cider presses. He wore a sack or a shirt, and was fond of walking barefoot. Although he is usually pictured wearing an inverted mush pan for a hat, there's no evidence that he did—that's part of the myth that's grown up around him.
Age at death 71	As he traveled the frontier, he slept outdoors or sheltered overnight with pioneer families. He also would preach sermons on the spur of the moment.
Other names Johnny Appleseed	Chapman's faith was important to him, and one way he practiced his beliefs was by being kind to people and animals.
	At the time of his death he owned more than a thousand acres of land.

Harriet Tubman

⇧ The most famous conductor on the Underground Railroad, Harriet Tubman risked her life again and again to lead some 300 slaves out of bondage in the South to freedom in Canada.

In the years before the Civil War, thousands of slaves made their way to freedom along escape routes that became known as the Underground Railroad. One of the most daring conductors, or escorts, on the Railroad was an ex-slave named Harriet Tubman. She helped lead so many blacks to freedom that she became known as Moses, after the Biblical leader who led the Hebrews out of bondage in Egypt.

Harriet Tubman was born on a Maryland plantation around 1820. She began to work as a house slave at age five, and at 13 she was put to work in the fields. In 1849 Harriet decided to run away. After walking a hundred miles, she reached Pennsylvania—and sweet liberty. Once there, she recalled, "I looked at my hands to see if I was the same person now I was free."

Harriet settled in Philadelphia, where she found work as a domestic. She learned all about the Underground Railroad—a secret network of individuals who assisted runaway blacks and provided safe places for them to hide from slave catchers.

In 1851 Tubman slipped back into Maryland to rescue her sister and her sister's children and take them to the North. That was the beginning of her career as an Underground Railroad conductor. Over the next 10 years she made the dangerous journey back to the South another 18 times and guided more than 300 slaves, including her 70-year-old parents and several of her brothers and sisters, to freedom in Canada.

During the Civil War Tubman served the Union Army as a nurse, cook, and spy. Fearless as ever, she stole across Confederate lines and scouted out warehouses, ammunition depots, and other military sites.

After the war Harriet Tubman settled with her elderly parents on a small farm near Auburn, New York. She supported schooling for free blacks and campaigned for women's voting rights.

THE BASICS

BIOGRAPHY	DID YOU KNOW
Born circa 1820, Dorchester County, Maryland	While the Fugitive Slave Act of 1850 made it illegal to help runaway slaves, neither Tubman, nor any of the people she helped escape from slavery, were ever caught.
Died March 10, 1913, Auburn, New York	Harriet Tubman was buried with military honors in recognition of her contributions to her country.
Age at death 93?	Tubman made at least 19 trips herself on the Underground Railroad.
Other names Araminta Ross (birth name). She later adopted her mother's name, Harriet. She was called "The Moses of Her People."	Sometimes, if Tubman was being chased while leading slaves to freedom, she would head them back South to confuse her pursuers.
	Harriet tried for years to get the government to pay her a pension for her Civil War services. She received a small pension starting in 1890.
	The Harriet Tubman Family Living Center in New York City offers shelter to the homeless.

Abraham Lincoln

Abraham Lincoln led our nation through its greatest crisis—civil war. His determination to reunite the states and save the Union made him one of America's greatest national heroes.

Lincoln was elected to the Illinois Legislature at age 25. He went on to serve a term in the U.S. House of Representatives, where he spoke out against the spread of slavery. In 1860 he was elected President.

President Lincoln promised to end the spread of slavery into American territories. Rather than accept Lincoln's plan, seven southern states seceded, or withdrew, from the Union and combined to form the Confederate States of America. The Civil War began on April 12, 1861, when Confederate forces opened fire on Fort Sumter near Charleston, South Carolina.

Lincoln made it clear from the start of the war that he fought to save the Union, not to destroy slavery. As the war dragged on, however, he changed his position. This was partly in response to the growth of anti-slavery sentiment in the North, and partly because he concluded that freeing slaves would weaken the Confederacy. On January 1, 1863, Lincoln issued the Emancipation Proclamation. This famous decree called for an end to slavery in states fighting the Union. To make emancipation official, he encouraged Congress to pass the 13th Amendment, which outlawed slavery everywhere in the nation.

Lincoln won reelection in 1864. The war raged on until April 9, 1865, when the Confederates finally surrendered. But Lincoln had little time to savor the victory. On April 14, 1865, he was shot by a Confederate sympathizer named John Wilkes Booth. Abraham Lincoln died the following morning. Millions of Americans mourned the courageous leader who had reunited a divided nation and brought freedom for African Americans.

⇧ Before Abraham Lincoln entered politics at the age of 25, he worked as a rail splitter, flatboat navigator, storekeeper, postmaster, and soldier. This photograph of him was taken four days before his assassination.

THE BASICS

BIOGRAPHY	DID YOU KNOW
Born February 12, 1809, near Hodgenville, Kentucky	At six feet four inches tall, Lincoln was the tallest President.
	Lincoln established the Department of Agriculture and opened up federal land to settlers.
Died April 15, 1865, in Washington, D.C.; assassinated by John Wilkes Booth	Some of Lincoln's favorite books were *Aesop's Fables* and *Robinson Crusoe*. He also enjoyed history and works by Shakespeare.
Age at death 56	During his lifetime, Lincoln also worked as a blacksmith and as a lobbyist for Illinois Central Railroad.
Other names Honest Abe, the Great Emancipator	Neither of Lincoln's parents could read or write. As a boy, Lincoln educated himself by reading borrowed books and newspapers.

Elizabeth Cady Stanton and Susan B. Anthony

⬆ Friends for more than 50 years, Elizabeth Cady Stanton (seated) and Susan B. Anthony led the fight for a woman's right to vote. The mother of seven children, Stanton wrote the fiery speeches that Anthony delivered across the country. As Stanton remarked, "I forged the thunderbolts, and she [Anthony] fired them."

Elizabeth Cady Stanton and Susan B. Anthony's friendship lasted more than 50 years. So did their commitment to women's rights. Together they led the fight for a right that most American women today take for granted: the right to vote.

Elizabeth was born into a wealthy family in upstate New York in 1815. When she married Henry Stanton in 1840, she insisted that the part about the wife obeying the husband be dropped from the wedding vows. Soon after their marriage, the couple traveled to London, where Henry was a delegate to the World Anti-Slavery Convention. There Elizabeth met the famous American abolitionist Lucretia Mott. When the male delegates refused to let women participate at the meeting, Elizabeth and Lucretia faced facts: Slaves weren't the only ones denied justice. The new friends resolved to launch a women's rights movement back in the United States.

> "We demand in the Reconstruction suffrage for all the citizens of the Republic. I would not talk of Negroes or women, but of citizens."
>
> Elizabeth Cady Stanton, letter of January 13, 1868

American women at that time had little or no say in their own lives. According to the law, a married woman could not own property. Anything she inherited—a farm, a house, money— became the property of her husband. Women could not sign a contract or serve on a jury. Most important, women lacked the right to vote. And without the vote, they could not change the laws that oppressed them.

In July 1848 Elizabeth Stanton and Lucretia Mott organized the first women's rights convention. Held in

THE BASICS

BIOGRAPHY

SUSAN B. ANTHONY

Born
February 15, 1820, Adams, Massachusetts

Died
March 13, 1906, Rochester, New York

Age at death
86

ELIZABETH CADY STANTON

Born
November 12, 1815, Johnstown, New York

Died
October 26, 1902, New York, New York

Age at death
86

DID YOU KNOW

Stanton's suffrage demand was the most radical resolution at the 1848 Seneca Falls Convention and caused the most debate.

Stanton and Anthony published a paper called *The Revolution*, whose motto was "Men, their rights and nothing more; women their rights and nothing less!"

In 1872 Anthony dared to cast a ballot in the presidential election, and then was arrested. She was sentenced to pay a $100 fine. "I will never pay a dollar of your unjust penalty," she told the judge—and she didn't.

Susan B. Anthony was the first woman to be featured on U.S. currency—the dollar coin issued in 1979.

Seneca Falls, New York, it was attended by more than 200 women and 40 men. Stanton presented the Declaration of Sentiments she had drafted. Modeled on the Declaration of Independence, the document proclaimed, "We hold these truths to be self-evident: that all men and women are created equal." Stanton demanded social and political equality for all women—in particular the right to vote.

The press of the day ridiculed the Declaration of Sentiments, and many clergymen and politicians denounced it. Nonetheless, women across the country began holding their own meetings to air their complaints and call for action. The women's rights revolution really took off, however, when Stanton joined forces with Susan B. Anthony.

Born in 1820 in Adams, Massachusetts, Susan Brownell Anthony came from a family of reformers. Her parents were Quakers who supported abolition and women's rights. They encouraged their daughters to be self-reliant and to stand up for what they believed in. Susan taught school for ten years, then turned to reform work. She threw herself into the temperance movement, which sought to ban the drinking of alcohol. Temperance supporters believed that drunkenness contributed to many of society's problems, including poverty and the abuse of women and children.

In 1851 Anthony's temperance work took her to Seneca Falls, where she met Elizabeth Stanton. The two women liked each other at once, and they soon became allies in the fight for women's rights.

Stanton and Anthony made a great team. Stanton, who was tied to home life by motherhood, researched legal matters, drafted pamphlets, plotted strategy, and wrote speeches. Anthony, who never married, crisscrossed the state delivering Stanton's fiery speeches, holding meetings, and going door-to-

⬆ Carrying on the battle started by Elizabeth Cady Stanton and Susan B. Anthony, protesters in New York City in 1911 march to demand women's rights.

door to circulate petitions. Their efforts paid off: In 1860 the New York state legislature finally passed a law granting married women rights to property, income, and child custody.

Voting rights, however, were much harder to obtain. The struggle to win the ballot was put on hold during the Civil War. Stanton and Anthony focused instead on human rights—the abolition of slavery. When the war ended, they lobbied for an amendment to the Constitution that would give voting rights to African Americans and women. But politicians and many abolitionists told women that votes for freed slaves had priority over votes for women. Stanton and Anthony fumed when the 14th Amendment, promising voting rights to all "male citizens," was ratified.

Stanton and Anthony continued their crusade for women's suffrage for the rest of their lives. Seemingly tireless, Anthony traveled throughout the country seeking support for the cause. In 1878 Elizabeth Cady Stanton wrote a

women's suffrage amendment and had it submitted to the U.S. Senate. Sadly, she did not live to see it passed. She died in 1902.

Susan B. Anthony, who lived four years longer than her friend, knew that she would not see voting rights in her lifetime either. But she had "not a shadow of doubt" that the next generation of women's rights leaders would "carry our cause to victory." In one of her last speeches, she declared that "Failure is impossible." In 1920 Congress finally passed the 19th Amendment giving all women in America the right to vote.

"Marriage, to women as to men, must be a luxury, not a necessity; an incident of life, not all of it."

Susan B. Anthony, speech, March 1875

Sitting Bull

⇧ The great Lakota chief Sitting Bull and his warriors wiped out George Custer and his troops at the Battle of Little Bighorn. The bloody defeat shocked white Americans, but for American Indians it was a blow for freedom.

True to his name, the great Lakota Sioux chief Sitting Bull refused to budge when the United States ordered his people off South Dakota's Great Plains and onto reservations. Instead, he led the Lakota and their Cheyenne allies in the struggle against the white invaders. Along the way he gained two reputations. Many whites of the time saw him as a bloodthirsty savage standing in the way of civilization. To Native Americans, however, he was a heroic freedom fighter striving to save his people's land and way of life.

Sitting Bull belonged to the Hunkpapa tribe, one of seven branches of the Lakota Sioux. In the 1860s he and his warriors began to clash with the U.S. Army. Some of the Plains tribes signed treaties with the U.S. government and agreed to live on reservations. Other tribes, including Sitting Bull's Hunkpapas, refused to cooperate. Around 1868 these so-called nontreaty bands recognized Sitting Bull as their head chief.

In 1874 gold was discovered in South Dakota's Black Hills, an area considered sacred by many tribes. The U.S. told the Indians to leave the region and report to reservations. When Sitting Bull and his followers refused, the U.S. Army set out to drive them off the Plains. On June 25, 1876, Lieutenant Colonel George Custer and 210 troops attacked Sitting Bull's camp near the Little Bighorn River. Some 1,800 well-armed warriors were waiting for them. Led by Sitting Bull and Oglala Sioux chief Crazy Horse, they surrounded Custer and his men and killed them all.

The bloody defeat at Little Bighorn shocked the American public. The government sent many more troops to pursue the defiant tribes. Sitting Bull finally surrendered to the U.S. Army in July 1881. He died 9 years later after a clash with policemen at Standing Rock reservation in North Dakota.

THE BASICS

BIOGRAPHY

Born
circa 1831, near Grand River, Dakota Territory (now in South Dakota)

Died
December 15, 1890, on the Grand River in South Dakota

Age at death
59?

Other names
Tatanka Iyotanka, which means "sitting bull." When he was born, he was named Jumping Badger, but was renamed Slow to match his serious nature.

Milestones
June 25, 1876: Battle of Little Bighorn

DID YOU KNOW

Sitting Bull killed his first buffalo at age ten.

When he was 14 he fought in his first battle, proving his courage by charging ahead to land the first strike against the enemy tribe.

As a young man, Sitting Bull earned many more honors in battle, and he became a high-ranking member of the Strong Heart warrior society. He also mastered the ways of a holy man. Sometimes called medicine men, holy men were believed to have a special link with the spirit world.

In 1883, Sitting Bull was sent to the Standing Rock Reservation, where he hoed the land.

In Chicago at the 1893 Columbian Exposition, the cabin where Sitting Bull died was on view in an exhibit marking the 400th anniversary of Christopher Columbus's arrival to the New World.

Queen Lili'uokalani

When Queen Lili'uokalani assumed the Hawaiian throne in 1891, the island kingdom was on the brink of being taken over by the United States. She did her best to prevent it.

Born into a royal family, Lili'u's childhood years were spent playing and studying. She attended a special school run by white American missionaries, but she never lost her pride in Hawaiian traditions. When she was 24, she married an American named John Dominis.

Despite her husband's nationality, Lili'u criticized the increasing power Americans had in Hawai'i. They owned almost all the sugar plantations and were trying to control the kingdom's affairs.

In 1887 white business leaders forced King David Kalakaua, Lili'uokalani's brother, to sign a new constitution at gunpoint. It put great power in the hands of the American members of his cabinet and deprived most Hawaiians of the right to vote.

When King Kalakaua died in 1891, Lili'uokalani became Hawai'i's first queen. One of her first acts was to have a new constitution drafted that returned power to native Hawaiians. Meanwhile, the wealthy American community plotted to overthrow her. In 1893 they called in U.S. Marines, and Queen Lili'uokalani was forced to surrender. The Americans proclaimed a new government.

Hawai'i was annexed as an American territory in 1898. Lili'uokalani, like most Hawaiians, refused to watch the ceremony in which the Hawaiian flag was lowered and the Stars and Stripes raised in its place. She died 19 years after the takeover. Today Queen Lili'uokalani is still honored for her efforts to preserve Hawaiian independence. A statue of her stands on the grounds of the state capitol in Honolulu.

⬆ Lili'uokalani was Hawai'i's first queen and last monarch. She came from a long line of royal chiefs, who were honored by the Hawaiians as gods. Today Queen Lili'uokalani is praised for her efforts to prevent the overthrow of the Hawaiian kingdom by the United States and to preserve Hawaiian traditions, including ancient chants.

THE BASICS

BIOGRAPHY	DID YOU KNOW
Born September 2, 1838, Honolulu, Hawai'i	Lili'uokalani was a talented musician and composer. She composed 165 pieces, and wrote one of Hawai'i's most famous songs, "Aloha 'Oe." Lili'uokalani later wrote in her memoirs that "to compose was as natural to me as to breathe. This gift remains a source of the greatest consolation."
Died November 11, 1917, Honolulu, Hawai'i	Lili'uokalani attended Queen Victoria's Golden Jubilee in London in 1887 and was welcomed as royalty by the queen herself. On the way to London, Lili'uokalani visited Washington, D.C., where she was received by President Grover Cleveland.
Age at death 79	
Other names Lydia Kamakaeha, Lydia Lili'uokalani (lih-lee-ah-WOE-keh-LAHN-ee) Paki	She helped lead the movement against annexation. The movement's motto was "Hawai'i for the Hawaiians."
Milestones July 1898: The United States annexed the Hawaiian Islands.	In 1878 she visited California and was impressed by Mills Seminary College. She dreamed of starting a college for women in Hawai'i.
	The Queen Lili'uokalani Trust assists poor and orphaned children.

Alexander Graham Bell

⬆ Best known for inventing the telephone, Alexander Graham Bell was fascinated by "the world and all that is in it." A founding father of the National Geographic Society, he remarked, "The study of Nature is undoubtedly one of the most interesting of all pursuits. God has strewn our paths with wonders, and we certainly should not go through Life with our eyes shut."

Inventing the telephone made Alexander Graham Bell famous. But it was his boundless energy, passion for science and inventing, and commitment to improving the quality of life for people everywhere that made him truly extraordinary.

Born and raised in Edinburgh, Scotland, Alexander—called Alec— came from a family of communicators. His grandfather Bell was a well-known speech teacher in London. Alec's father, Melville Bell, also taught speech. In addition, Melville studied how the human voice produces sound. His research led him to create a universal phonetic alphabet—a system of symbols that represented any sound the human voice could make. He called this system Visible Speech.

> "The inventor is a man who looks around upon the world and... wants to improve whatever he sees"
>
> Speech to patent congress in Washington, D.C., 1891

Alec's mother kindled her son's interest in music. She was a talented pianist, despite being very nearly deaf. By putting one end of her ear tube on the piano's soundboard, she could hear, or feel, the vibrations of the music. Alec grew up fascinated by sounds and how they are made.

When Alec was 16, he visited London and saw a "speaking machine"— a device that mechanically produced vocal sounds. Alec and his older brother decided to make one of their own. After studying the larynx, or voice box, of a dead lamb, the brothers built a model of the vocal organs. It actually worked. When one blew into the contraption and manipulated its levers, it produced human-like cries.

THE BASICS

BIOGRAPHY	DID YOU KNOW
Born March 3, 1847, Edinburgh, Scotland	The "Graham" in Bell's name wasn't added until he was 11 years old.
Died August 2, 1922, Beinn Bhreagh, Cape Breton Island, Nova Scotia, Canada	The race to patent the telephone was intense; Bell submitted his plans a mere two hours before his chief rival.
Age at death 75	Bell showed his new invention, the telephone, at the Centennial Exhibition in Philadelphia, Pennsylvania, on June 25, 1876—the same day as the Battle of Little Bighorn, where Sitting Bull and his fighters defeated Lt. Col. George Custer.
Honors 1880: Volta Prize from France	Bell's hydrofoil set a speed record that lasted for ten years. In 1919 it traveled almost 71 miles per hour (114 km/h).
	It wasn't until January 1915 that a telephone call could be made from New York to California. This coast-to-coast call took place with the help of 130,000 telephone poles.

In 1870, Alec and his parents moved to Ontario, Canada. The following year Alec began teaching at a school for deaf children in Boston, Massachusetts. Using his father's Visible Speech system, he helped the students learn to speak. Bell found great joy in working with the deaf. One of his pupils in Boston, Mabel Hubbard, eventually became his wife.

In the evenings, after he had finished teaching, Bell thought about how to send speech over a wire. He theorized that the rising and falling pitches of the human voice could be converted into a rising and falling, or undulatory, electric current that could be transmitted over a wire. At the end of the wire a receiving device could convert the electrical energy back into sound.

To find out whether his ideas would work, Bell needed supplies and a technician to build things. In January 1875, he hired 20-year-old Thomas Watson, a skilled craftsman and electrician, as his assistant. Watson turned Bell's sketches into machines.

In their quest to send vocal sound over a wire, Bell and Watson tried dozens of combinations of electric current and materials to transmit it. The breakthrough came on March 10, 1876. On that day Bell spoke these now-famous words into his latest design: "Mr. Watson—Come here—I want to see you." To Bell's delight, Watson heard and understood his words through a duplicate device in another room. It was the first telephone call.

Three months later, Bell introduced the telephone to the public at the Centennial Exhibition in Philadelphia. The emperor of Brazil was so impressed by the demonstration that he ordered 100 telephones for his country.

In 1877, Alexander Graham Bell and Mabel Hubbard were married. Mabel's father helped lead the new Bell Telephone Company. For a while, Bell helped advise the company that bore his

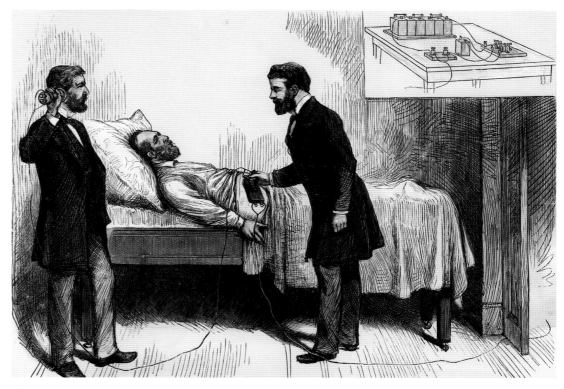

⇧ In this drawing, Bell and an assistant use a metal-detecting machine invented by Bell to find the assassin's bullet in President Garfield. Although his efforts failed to help Garfield, Bell later developed a telephonic probe that was used in military hospitals to save soldiers' lives. "Certainly no man can have a higher incentive," he said, "than the hope of relieving suffering and saving life."

name, but he refused to limit himself to that line of work. Fortunately, the money he earned from the company gave him the freedom "to follow the ideas that interest me most."

And that's just what he did for the rest of his life. He pursued his love of science and he kept on inventing. In 1881, the Bells' newborn son died from breathing problems. Alec's grief led him to develop an invention called a "vacuum jacket," which used a pump to force air into and out of the lungs. It was a forerunner of the iron lung, which was developed for polio victims five decades later. Bell experimented with flight by designing and flying huge kites, and he designed a hydrofoil—a boat that moves just above the water—that set a world water-speed record.

Throughout his life, Bell remained devoted to his work for and with the deaf. He became a leader in the education of deaf children and enjoyed visiting them at their schools. Bell studied the

scientific causes of deafness and investigated whether heredity might play a role. He also invented the audiometer, which measures a person's hearing.

Alexander Graham Bell once said that a true inventor "can no more help inventing than he can help thinking or breathing." This was certainly true of Bell himself. When he died in 1922, the phone company silenced all telephones for one minute in tribute to the man who, in the words of Thomas Edison, "brought the human family in closer touch."

"I believe that in the future... a man in one part of the Country may communicate by word of mouth with another in a distant place."

Prospectus to British financiers, March 5, 1878

Wright Brothers

⇧ Among the qualities that helped Orville (left) and Wilbur Wright solve the mystery of flight was bravery. Every time they flew the brothers took enormous risks. The 1903 *Flyer* was especially dangerous because its engine and propellers made it heavier than anything they had flown before.

In December 1903 Wilbur and Orville Wright did what no human being had done before: They flew. This stunning feat ushered in the age of flight and made the Wright brothers the first American heroes of the 20th century.

Both brothers loved to tinker. When they were in their 20s, they opened a bicycle shop in Dayton, Ohio. They designed and built their own models based on the latest technology. But eventually the brothers wanted more of a challenge. They decided to build a full-size flying machine.

In the workroom behind their bicycle shop, the brothers started building giant kites and gliders to test their design ideas. They focused on creating a mechanical system that would allow a pilot to control an aircraft up, down, and around. Along the way they invented the technology they needed to build their flying machines. To test wing curvatures, for example, they built their own wind tunnel using a six-foot-long wooden box, bicycle spokes, old hacksaw blades, and a belt-operated fan.

Between 1900 and 1903, the Wrights traveled to the village of Kitty Hawk, on North Carolina's Outer Banks, several times to test their designs. The location provided steady winds, tall sand dunes from which to launch their gliders, a soft landing place, and privacy. In Kitty Hawk, on December 17, 1903, they tested their first airplane powered by an engine. With Orville at the controls, *Flyer* lifted off from the ground on its own power and flew 120 feet. The 12-second flight proved that humans could fly.

The secrets of flight had baffled great minds for centuries. Wilbur and Orville Wright focused all their intellectual and engineering skills on finding the answers. When they did, it changed the world.

THE BASICS

BIOGRAPHY	DID YOU KNOW
WILBUR WRIGHT	When he was 17, Orville started a printing business using a press he made out of odds and ends.
Born April 16, 1867, near Millville, Indiana	
	The Wrights read through everything their local library and the Smithsonian Institution had to offer on aeronautics, the science of flight.
Died May 30, 1912, Dayton, Ohio	
Age at death 45	By 1905 the Wrights had made a plane that stayed in the air for 39 minutes and survived repeated takeoffs and landings. In 1908 they signed contracts to build airplanes for the U.S. military.
ORVILLE WRIGHT	
Born August 19, 1871, Dayton, Ohio	The first powered flight on December 17, 1903, was 120 feet (36 m) long, with an airspeed of 34 miles per hour. The brothers made three more powered flights that morning.
Died January 30, 1948, Dayton, Ohio	
Age at death 76	In September 1908, Orville was working with the U.S. Army when a propeller split and the airplane crashed. His passenger, Thomas Selfridge, died—the first casualty of powered flight.

Theodore Roosevelt

To Theodore Roosevelt, America's wilderness areas were a major part of the nation's "rich heritage." He believed such places should be "preserved for [Americans'] children and their children's children forever with their majestic beauty unmarred." He used his power as President to help make that happen.

Teddy Roosevelt was born into a wealthy New York family in 1858. After the death of his first wife in 1884, he moved west and took up cowboy life in the Dakota Territory. Two years later barrel-chested Teddy returned to the East Coast, remarried, and plunged into politics. When the Spanish-American War broke out, he recruited a cavalry company and headed for combat in Cuba. Colonel Roosevelt and his "Rough Riders" became famous for their daring charge near San Juan Hill.

After the war Roosevelt was elected governor of New York, then became William McKinley's Vice President. In September 1901 McKinley was assassinated, and Roosevelt was sworn in as the youngest President ever at age 42.

T.R charged into office with the same enthusiasm that made him a war hero, and he wowed the public with his boundless energy and keen intellect. In the 1904 election, he won by a landslide.

The Progressive-minded President injected government regulation into such areas as industry, labor, and consumer protection. He became known as a "trust-buster" for breaking up monopolies, or trusts, of companies that dominated certain businesses and prevented competition. T.R.'s most far-sighted achievements, however, may have been his preservation of more than 150 million acres of government land—a legacy for which he is admired to this day.

⇧ President Theodore Roosevelt, shown here in California's Yosemite Valley, created 150 national forests, 53 federal bird sanctuaries, and 5 national parks.

THE BASICS

BIOGRAPHY	DID YOU KNOW
Born October 27, 1858, New York, New York	Roosevelt dealt with other governments by thinking of the United States as a police force that would act if the nation felt threatened. This was known as "Big Stick Diplomacy."
Died January 6, 1919, Oyster Bay, New York	Many people criticized his role in expanding America's empire.
Age at death 60	After leaving office, T.R. went on safari in Africa and collected hundreds of animals for the Smithsonian Institution. He also spent seven months exploring the jungles of Brazil.
Other names Teddy, T.R.	Roosevelt was a respected ornithologist.
Honors 1905: Nobel Peace Prize for negotiating peace between Russia and Japan	Sagamore Hill, the Roosevelt's home, was known as the "summer White House."

Matthew Henson

⬆ Matthew Henson played a key role in Robert E. Peary's successful expedition to the North Pole in 1909. In 2000 the National Geographic Society posthumously awarded Henson its highest honor, the Hubbard Medal, "for distinction in exploration, discovery, and research." The Society noted, "Henson embodies what this award stands for."

In the early 20th century, explorers from several nations raced to see who would be first to stand on top of the world at the North Pole. On April 6, 1909, two Americans claimed victory: Commander Robert E. Peary and his right-hand man, African-American explorer Matthew Henson.

Born in Maryland in 1866, Henson signed on as a cabin boy on a sailing ship when he was 12 or 13. After six years at sea, Henson returned to land life. He eventually found work at a hat shop in Washington, D.C. That's where he met Peary. Peary, an engineer and explorer, was preparing for an expedition to Nicaragua, and he hired Henson to go along as his valet. When they returned, Peary asked Henson to join him on a quest for the Pole. Adventure-loving Henson agreed.

In 1891 Henson and Peary embarked on the first of seven Arctic expeditions they would make together. Henson quickly became a skilled dogsled driver and hunter, and he also learned the language and customs of the native Inuits. Henson was so fluent in the Inuit language and so adept in their ways that Peary remarked that he was "more of an Eskimo than some of them." He found Henson's abilities so valuable in the harsh, frozen land that he stated, "I can't get on without him." On their last trip, the two men, accompanied by four Inuit, left the rest of the crew behind and made a dash for the Pole. Henson got there first, which he later recalled made Peary "hopping mad." From that time on, the commander scarcely spoke to him.

The feat brought Peary worldwide acclaim. However, it took decades—and changing racial attitudes—for Henson to receive the recognition he deserved for his contributions to Arctic exploration.

THE BASICS

BIOGRAPHY	DID YOU KNOW
Born August 8, 1866, Charles County, Maryland	Henson and Peary had 24 men, 130 sled dogs, and 20 sleds with them on their 1909 attempt to reach the North Pole.
Died March 9, 1955, New York, New York	After his time exploring the northern latitudes, Henson was a customs house clerk in New York City, an appointment made by President William Howard Taft. He worked at the job until 1936.
Age at death 88	Henson's autobiography, *A Negro Explorer at the North Pole,* was published in 1912.
Family Henson married twice. He wed his second wife, Lucy Jane Ross, in 1907.	In the spring of 2005 a team of adventurers retraced Peary's route from base camp to the North Pole to prove that he could have made it in just 37 days—a claim long doubted by critics. The modern team made the 420-mile trip in 36 days, 22 hours, and 11 minutes.
Honors 1937: Made a member of the Explorers Club 1944: Congressional Medal	

Amelia Earhart

Amelia Earhart first saw an airplane fly in 1908, when her family went to the Iowa State Fair to celebrate her 11th birthday. About 12 years later she took her first plane ride. "As soon as we left the ground," she recalled, "I knew I myself had to fly." She worked odd jobs to pay for flying lessons, and in 1922 she set a women's altitude record of 14,000 feet (4,267 km).

In June 1928, Amelia caused a sensation when she became the first woman ever to fly across the Atlantic Ocean. She only rode as a passenger, but in the early days of aviation people were as amazed that a woman was brave enough to go along at all on such a dangerous adventure. Astounded by all the attention she received, Amelia hoped to someday pilot a transatlantic flight herself. She wanted "to prove that I deserved at least a small fraction of the nice things said about me."

From this point on, Amelia achieved one "first" after another. She became the first woman to make a round-trip solo flight across the United States, she competed in the first Women's Air Derby, and she set three women's world speed records. In 1932, Amelia crossed the Atlantic again—this time as the first woman to make the flight alone. Braving violent thunderstorms and heavy fog, she flew from Newfoundland to Ireland in record time.

On May 21, 1937, Amelia took off on her most ambitious voyage ever in a quest to become the first female pilot to circle the globe. About six weeks later, however, she and copilot Fred Noonan lost radio contact over the central Pacific Ocean and were never heard from again. A massive sea and air search failed to find any trace of them. Amelia Earhart's accomplishments live on, inspiring generations of girls and women to believe in themselves and work toward their dreams.

⇧ Amelia Earhart, shown here in the photograph from her pilot's license, made history in May 1932 when she became the first woman to fly solo across the Atlantic Ocean. The record-breaking flight made her world famous, and she received many awards for her courage and skill.

THE BASICS

BIOGRAPHY	DID YOU KNOW
Born July 24, 1897, Atchison, Kansas	When Amelia attended the 1908 Iowa State Fair, she thought that the airplane she saw was, "a thing of rusty wire and wood and not at all interesting."
Died (Disappeared) July 2, 1937, near Howland Island, central Pacific Ocean	Earhart was not the only person in her family to have a "first." Her mother was the first woman to climb Colorado's Pike's Peak.
Age at death 39	Earhart encouraged women pilots to fly in a race from Los Angeles to Cleveland in 1929. The race was nicknamed the "Powder-Puff Derby."
Other names Lady Lindy	When Earhart vanished without a trace, a search team including 65 airplanes and 10 ships covered an area the size of Texas looking for her and her copilot.
Milestones May 20–21, 1932: Solo flight across the Atlantic; this flight took 14 hours and 54 minutes.	It wasn't until 1964 that a woman—two American women flying independently—circumnavigated the globe. They were Geraldine Mock and Joan Merriam Smith.

Franklin Delano Roosevelt

⇑ During his first presidential campaign in 1932, Franklin Delano Roosevelt took great joy in meeting citizens across the country, including this young patient in Seattle. As President, he took an activist approach to ending the Great Depression that many people credited with saving the nation.

Franklin Delano Roosevelt served the longest presidency in United States history. During his 12 years in office he lifted the nation out of the Great Depression and then guided it safely through the worst days of World War II. Roosevelt knew how high the stakes were. "We are fighting," he said in 1936, "to save a great and precious form of government for ourselves and for the world." His heroic leadership helped America survive these two crises.

Born at his wealthy family's estate in Hyde Park, New York, Franklin was an only child. His parents, James Roosevelt and Sara Delano Roosevelt, had him tutored at home until he was 14. After graduating from Harvard in 1904, Franklin attended Columbia Law School. Then he went to work for a New York law firm.

> "The only thing
> we have to fear is
> fear itself."
>
> First Inaugural Address, March 4, 1933

In the meantime, Franklin fell in love with a distant cousin, Eleanor Roosevelt. They married in 1905. At their wedding, the bride was given away by her uncle, Theodore Roosevelt (T.R.), the President of the United States.

Franklin greatly admired T.R., and he followed in his footsteps by entering politics. In 1910 he was elected to the New York Senate. Unlike the Republican T.R., however, Franklin Roosevelt ran as a Democrat—perhaps because the ambitious young man saw more opportunities for himself in that party. A few years later Roosevelt was appointed assistant secretary of the Navy by President Woodrow Wilson. He held the post for about seven years, gaining experience that would help prepare him for his future role as a

THE BASICS

BIOGRAPHY	DID YOU KNOW
Born January 30, 1882, Hyde Park, New York	The country was suffering when FDR came to office, and one out of every four people was without a job.
Died April 12, 1945, Warm Springs, Georgia	After Roosevelt won four terms in office, many Americans felt that there needed to be a limit on how many times someone could be elected President. In 1951, the 22nd Amendment limited Presidents to two terms.
Age at death 63	
Other names FDR	While FDR was stricken with polio in 1921, it was not until 1952 that the epidemic reached its peak in the United States. In 1952, 58,000 Americans were infected.
Milestones 1933–1945: 32nd President of the United States	During his presidency, a majority of African Americans supported FDR—dropping their historic allegiance to the Republican Party.

wartime leader. In 1920 Roosevelt ran as the Democratic nominee for U.S. Vice President.

Although the Democrats lost that election, Roosevelt gained a lot of national attention, and his political prospects looked bright. In the summer of 1921, however, Roosevelt's life changed drastically when he was stricken suddenly with polio. The disease stole his physical strength and left his legs paralyzed. Eleanor encouraged him to fight for his recovery. Meanwhile she helped keep his career alive by attending political events on his behalf.

After three years of painful physical therapy, Roosevelt learned to stand on leg braces and to walk a few steps using crutches. He plunged back into politics, and in 1928 he was elected governor of New York. Four years later he ran for President of the United States.

By this time the nation was suffering from the worst economic crisis in its history, the Great Depression. One out of four workers was unemployed, banks across the country were failing, factories were closing, and farmers and families were losing their land and homes to foreclosures. In cities and towns across the country, the hungry and the homeless lined up at free soup kitchens for meals. Never before had life for so many in America seemed so hopeless.

So when the optimistic Roosevelt promised a "new deal for the American people," voters flocked to him. He overwhelmingly defeated the incumbent, Republican President Herbert Hoover, in the 1932 election. In his first Inaugural Address, Roosevelt declared, "The only thing we have to fear is fear itself." His words reassured his fellow citizens and brought them new hope.

As President, Roosevelt took bold action to end the Depression. In his first hundred days in office, he proposed and Congress passed a flurry of legislation. Among other things, these new laws

⇧ President Roosevelt (center) shares a lighthearted moment with British Prime Minister Winston Churchill (left) and Soviet leader Joseph Stalin (right). The three men met at Yalta, on the Black Sea, in February 1945 to discuss how to reshape Europe at war's end.

restored faith in the banking industry; put people back to work building bridges, roads, dams, and power plants; aided farmers; and improved working conditions. Later measures regulated the stock market and created the Social Security system. These programs became known as the New Deal.

Roosevelt's New Deal helped many people get on their feet again, but he had many critics. Some were concerned that the New Deal gave the federal government too much power, and many of the rich—who called Roosevelt a "traitor to his class"—resented him for reducing their power and income. But most ordinary citizens, many of whom saw their lives improve, trusted Roosevelt so much that they elected him to three more terms.

When World War II broke out in Europe in 1939, Roosevelt saw the evil threat the Nazis posed to democratic nations everywhere. He promised "all aid to the Allies short of war." After the Japanese bombed Pearl Harbor on December 7, 1941, America entered the war. As Commander in Chief of the

nation's armed forces, Roosevelt took an active role in plotting military strategy and appointing key generals and admirals.

The strain of the war took a toll on Roosevelt's health. About a month before the Allied victory in Europe, President Franklin Delano Roosevelt died of a brain hemorrhage at his retreat in Warm Springs, Georgia. Americans everywhere mourned the brave man who had helped them pull through some of the nation's toughest challenges.

"The test of our progress
is not whether
we add more to the abundance
of those who have much;
it is whether
we provide enough for
those who have too little."
Second Inaugural Address, January 20, 1937

Rachel Carson

⬆ In *Silent Spring*, Rachel Carson opened Americans' eyes to the dangers of pesticides, which came into widespread use after World War II. The book's title refers to the effect of the poisons on birds: "Over increasingly large areas of the United States...the early mornings are strangely silent where once they were filled with the beauty of bird song."

In her 1962 book, *Silent Spring*, biologist and writer Rachel Carson sounded an alarm: The reckless use of pesticides such as DDT and other toxic chemicals, she said, was poisoning the Earth and all its inhabitants. She accused the chemical industry and the U.S. government of encouraging the use of pesticides without knowing enough about their long-term effects. The book shook the nation.

Carson had been fascinated with "the beauty of the living world" since childhood. She majored in biology in college, then focused her graduate studies on marine life. From 1936 to 1952 she worked for the U.S. Fish and Wildlife Service. Meanwhile she combined her passion for science and nature with her desire to write. She wrote a trilogy of books about the sea, which sold so well that she was able to quit her job and write full-time.

In 1958 Carson received a letter from a woman who said that all the songbirds on her property died after a mosquito control plane sprayed pesticide over her town. The story inspired Carson to write a book about chemical pollution. For the next four years she collected data from scientists around the globe and documented the deadly effects of dangerous chemicals on living things. The result was *Silent Spring*.

The book quickly became a best-seller. The powerful chemical companies attacked it as the work of a "hysterical woman," but independent investigations—including one ordered by President John F. Kennedy—soon supported Carson's conclusions. The public called for government regulation of pesticide use.

Rachel Carson's pioneering work helped launch the environmental protection movement in America. Her story shows the difference one person's voice can make in speaking out for change.

THE BASICS

BIOGRAPHY	DID YOU KNOW
Born May 27, 1907, Springdale, Pennsylvania	Carson was ten years old when her first story was published in a children's literary magazine called *St. Nicholas*.
Died April 14, 1964, Silver Spring, Maryland	The summer after Carson graduated from college in 1929, she went to Woods Hole Marine Biological Laboratory as a "beginning investigator." There were few women working there, and Carson felt isolated.
Age at death 56	Carson and her mother were very close. They lived together until her mother died in 1958.
Honors 1951: National Book Award for *The Sea Around Us*	Carson combined her writing talent with her love of science to write articles about the Chesapeake Bay for the *Baltimore Sun* newspaper. She wrote under the name R.L. Carson, in the hopes that readers would think she was male and take her writing more seriously.
	The general use of the pesticide DDT in the U.S. was finally banned by the Environmental Protection Agency in 1972.

Jackie Robinson

On April 15, 1947, Jackie Robinson stepped out of the Brooklyn Dodgers dugout at Ebbett's Field in Brooklyn and took his position at first base. With those steps, the 28-year-old African American athlete broke the unwritten law that had kept blacks out of major league baseball for decades.

The grandson of a slave and the son of a sharecropper, Jackie was raised in Pasadena, California. During his college years at UCLA, he was an All-American running back on the football team. He also excelled at basketball, track, and baseball. In 1944 he signed on with the Kansas City Monarchs to play baseball in the Negro leagues.

While Jackie was with the Monarchs, he came to the attention of Branch Rickey, the head of the Brooklyn Dodgers. Rickey wanted to integrate major league baseball. He persuaded Jackie to join the Dodgers and take the lead in what came to be called the "Noble Experiment."

In Jackie's first season with the Dodgers, he earned new fans with every game. His bold style of baseball made him fun to watch. At the end of the season, he was named the league's first ever Rookie of the Year.

But Jackie's success did not come easy. Some of his own teammates protested against having to play with an African American. Bigoted spectators threw bottles and screamed racial insults at him. Some pitchers threw the ball at his head on purpose.

Somehow Jackie found the strength to hold his anger in check. He believed that he was not just playing for himself, he was playing for all people of his race. Gradually other black players joined him in the major leagues. Eventually Jackie's tremendous talent, grace, and courage on and off the baseball field made him a hero to countless Americans of all colors.

⇧ Jackie Robinson broke major league baseball's color barrier on April 15, 1947, when he played his first game with the Brooklyn Dodgers. He endured heckling and racial taunts—some from his own teammates—during his first years as a Dodger, but he soon became a favorite of many young fans, who eagerly collected Jackie Robinson baseball cards and comics.

THE BASICS

BIOGRAPHY	DID YOU KNOW
Born January 31, 1919, Cairo, Georgia	Robinson's lifetime batting average was .311. He led the National League in stolen bases in 1947 and 1949.
Died October 24, 1972, Stamford, Connecticut	After leading the Dodgers to six league championships and their first ever World Series victory, Jackie retired from baseball in 1956. He turned his attention to business and the civil rights movement.
Age at death 53	In 1970, he began the Jackie Robinson Construction Company to build housing for low-income families.
Other names Jack Roosevelt Robinson (full name)	Besides playing baseball, Robinson held a variety of jobs. He was a second lieutenant in the U.S. Army, a businessman, and a spokesperson for the NAACP.
Milestones 1962: First African American inducted into the National Baseball Hall of Fame	Throughout his life, Robinson was an advocate for civil rights. He remarked, "I won't 'have it made' until the most underprivileged Negro in Mississippi can live in equal dignity with anyone else in America."

Martin Luther King, Jr.

⬆ Martin Luther King, Jr., dreamed of an America without racial prejudice, in which his "four little children will one day live in a nation where they will not be judged by the color of their skin but by the content of their character." He devoted his life to making this dream of equality come true.

He was arrested and thrown in jail many times. He faced hundreds of death threats, and his family's home was bombed. But civil rights leader Martin Luther King, Jr., never backed down in his stand against racism. He dedicated his life to achieving equality and justice for Americans of all colors.

King was born in Atlanta, Georgia. Both his father and grandfather were preachers. When he was growing up, segregation was both the law and custom in the South and other parts of America. Blacks could not go to school with white children, vote, serve on juries, sit anywhere they chose on a bus, or buy or rent a home wherever they wanted. They couldn't be treated at white hospitals, use whites-only restrooms, or eat in the same restaurants

> "If a man hasn't discovered something that he will die for, he isn't fit to live."
>
> Speech given in Detroit, June 23, 1963

as whites. In some parts of the South, African Americans even had to step off the sidewalk if a white person walked by.

King entered Morehouse College in Atlanta at the age of 15. In his senior year he decided to become a minister, in part because he felt "an inner urge to serve humanity." He believed the best way to do that was through the church, which was the strongest black institution. He had learned from his family that religion and politics were a powerful combination.

King graduated from Crozer Theological Seminary in Pennsylvania with the highest grade average in his class and a reputation as a passionate and persuasive speaker. After

THE BASICS

BIOGRAPHY	DID YOU KNOW
Born January 15, 1929, Atlanta, Georgia	When King told his first-grade teacher he was only five years old, he was barred from school until he was older.
Died April 4, 1968, Memphis, Tennessee: assassinated by James Earl Ray	King was stabbed in 1958 during a book-signing in Harlem by a woman wielding a seven-inch letter opener. Doctors removed the letter opener, and he recovered.
Age at death 39	Then Democratic presidential candidate John F. Kennedy interceded to have King released from jail in October 1960, an action that is credited with helping Kennedy to be elected President.
Other names MLK	FBI director J. Edgar Hoover tried to blackmail King because he hated his politics.
Milestones 1963: March on Washington 1964: Civil Rights Act Nobel Peace Prize	The band U2 wrote a hit song in 1984 about King, "Pride (in the Name of Love)."

graduating from seminary school, King obtained a doctorate in philosophy from Boston University. While he was in Boston, he met Coretta Scott, a music student. They soon found they shared a commitment to changing the racist system they had both grown up under. They married in 1953.

The following year Martin and Coretta moved to Montgomery, Alabama. King became pastor of the Dexter Avenue Baptist Church. In December of 1955, Montgomery's black leadership recruited King to lead a boycott of the city's segregated public bus system. The boycott began when an African-American woman named Rosa Parks refused to give up her bus seat to a white passenger. As a result she was arrested for breaking the city's segregation law.

Over the next year, King spoke night after night at rallies in churches. His impassioned sermons inspired the bus boycotters to keep their spirits up, their means peaceful, and their eyes on their goal. During the boycott King was arrested several times on trumped-up charges, and he received several death threats. Nonetheless, King came to believe that nonviolent resistance was the best way to bring about social change.

On December 20, 1956, the Montgomery bus boycott ended 382 days after it began, when the United States Supreme Court upheld a ruling that the bus segregation policy was unconstitutional. Inspired by this victory, King and other black clergymen organized the Southern Christian Leadership Conference (SCLC). The SCLC planned to challenge segregation throughout the South.

After Montgomery, the attention of the news media transformed King into a symbol of the struggle for civil rights, and the young preacher became famous around the world. By 1960, King was devoting most of his time to the SCLC

⇧ In March 1965, King and his wife led a black voting rights march from Selma, Alabama, to the state capital in Montgomery.

and the civil rights movement. He traveled the country speaking out against segregation and spreading the message of nonviolent resistance to unjust laws.

In 1963 King joined other civil rights leaders in organizing the March on Washington for Jobs and Freedom. On August 28, 1963, some 250,000 Americans from across the country, including 60,000 white supporters, gathered in front of the Lincoln Memorial in Washington, D.C., to demand equal justice for all citizens. The highlight of the peaceful protest was King's famous "I Have a Dream" speech, in which he declared, "I have a dream... that one day this nation will rise up and live out the true meaning of its creed: We hold these truths to be self-evident— that all men are created equal."

King's emotional speech, broadcast on television and printed in papers around the nation, touched the hearts and consciences of people everywhere and boosted public support for civil rights. In 1964, Congress passed the Civil Rights Act, which outlawed racial segregation in publicly owned facilities. In December of that same year, King received the Nobel Peace Prize.

Over the next few years, King looked on in sorrow as younger activists rejected his philosophy of nonviolence,

and riots broke out in the ghettoes of several big cities. He began to focus on economic inequality in addition to racial discrimination. He wanted to form a coalition of poor people of all races to address issues of poverty.

In 1968 King went to Memphis, Tennessee, to help support a strike by the city's sanitation workers. On April 4, 1968, as he relaxed on the balcony of his room at the Lorraine Motel, King was assassinated by a white racist named James Earl Ray. In a speech given the night before he died, King spoke these prophetic words: "Like anybody, I would like to live a long life...But I'm not concerned about that now. I just want to do God's will. And He's allowed me to go up to the mountain. And I've looked over, and I've seen the promised land. I may not get there with you, but I want you to know tonight that we as a people will get to the promised land."

> "Injustice anywhere
> is a threat to
> justice everywhere."
> Letter from Birmingham Jail, April 16, 1963

César Chávez

⇧ Labor and civil rights leader César Chávez made it his mission to improve the lives of poor migrant farm workers. In this photo from 1986, Chávez kicks off a new grape boycott to protest the use of toxic pesticides by grape growers.

César Chávez knew exactly what life was like for poor Mexican-American farm workers. That's because he was one. He spent many years toiling for low wages in the fruit and vegetable fields of California. The rest of his time he dedicated to improving the lives of his fellow workers.

During the Great Depression, César's family moved to California, where they became migrant workers—people who move from region to region to harvest crops. Living conditions for migrants were terrible. People slept in their cars or in tents, or in crowded camps built by farm owners. These camps usually lacked electricity, running water, and indoor bathrooms. Migrant workers were very poorly paid. Workers who dared to complain were fired.

César left school after eighth grade to work full time in the fields. After serving in the U.S. Navy, he returned to California and farm work. He began thinking about what he could do to change the way in which farm workers were treated. He decided the best way to help them was to organize a union.

With the help of community activist Dolores Huerta, in 1962 Chávez founded the union that would become the United Farm Workers (UFW). Three years later, Chávez and the UFW asked Americans everywhere to boycott grapes from California until the growers agreed to bargain with the union.

To gain public support for the union's cause, known as "La Causa," Chávez relied on tactics of nonviolent resistance. He went on a month-long fast to dramatize the suffering of farm workers. Inspired by his sacrifice, millions of Americans stopped buying grapes. The growers bowed to the pressure, and by 1970 a majority of them had signed contracts with the UFW. Over the next two decades, Chávez continued to lead the struggle for farm workers' rights.

THE BASICS

BIOGRAPHY	DID YOU KNOW
Born March 31, 1927, Yuma, Arizona	Chávez's mother, Juana, originally inspired his devotion to nonviolence. From her, he learned hundreds of *dichos* (proverbs), which he used throughout his life.
Died April 23, 1993, San Luis, Arizona	As a young man he was influenced by books on labor leaders such as John L. Lewis and Eugene V. Debs. He also read political philosophy. He was most influenced by the writings of Mahatma Gandhi.
Age at death 66	
Other names César Estrada Chávez	For the most part, César Chávez lived as simply and poorly as the workers he represented. He never owned a house or a car, and he never earned more than $6,000 a year.
Honors 1974: Martin Luther King, Jr. Nonviolent Peace Award	In 1975, the law that Chávez and the UFW had fought so long for—the Agricultural Labor Relations Act, which provided greater rights for farmworkers and their representatives—was passed in California.

Resources

A variety of books, Web sites, and magazine and newspaper articles were consulted for this book. Below are some of the sources I found most helpful.

BOOKS

Ambrose, *Stephen E. Lewis & Clark: Voyage of Discovery.* Washington, D.C.: National Geographic Society, 1998.

Bartlett, John. *Bartlett's Familiar Quotations, 16th ed.* Boston: Little Brown & Company, 1992.

Bausum, Ann. *Our Country's Presidents.* Washington, D.C.: National Geographic Society, 2001.
_____. *With Courage and Cloth: Winning the Fight for a Woman's Right to Vote.* Washington, D.C.: National Geographic Society, 2004.

Brinkley, Douglas. *American Heritage History of the United States.* New York: Viking, 1998.

Colbert, David, editor. *Eyewitness to America: 500 Years of America in the Words of Those Who Saw It Happen.* New York: Pantheon Books, 1997.

Daniels, Patricia S., and Stephen G. Hyslop. *National Geographic Almanac of World History.* Washington, D.C.: National Geographic Society, 2003.

Davis, Kenneth C. *Don't Know Much About History.* New York: HarperCollins, 2003.

Deford, Frank. *The Heart of a Champion: Celebrating the Spirit and Character of Great American Sports Heroes.* San Diego: Tehabi Books, 2002.

Denenberg, Dennis, and Lorraine Roscoe. *50 American Heroes Every Kid Should Meet.* Brookfield, CT: The Millbrook Press, 2001.

Faber, Doris, and Harold Faber. *American Government Great Lives.* New York: Charles Scribner's Sons, 1988.

Freidel, Frank. *The Presidents of the United States of America.* Washington, D.C.: White House Historical Association, 1995.

Garraty, John A. and Mark C. Carnes, editors. *American National Biography.* New York: Oxford University Press, 1999.

Jacobs, William Jay. *Human Rights Great Lives.* New York: Charles Scribner's Sons, 1990.

Johnston, Robert D. *The Making of America: The History of the United States from 1492 to the Present.* Washington, D.C.: National Geographic Society, 2002.

Keenan, Sheila. *Scholastic Book of Outstanding Americans: Profiles of More Than 450 Famous and Infamous Figures in U.S. History.* New York: Scholastic Reference, 2003.

Leadership. African Americans: Voices of Triumph series. Time-Life Books. Alexandria, Va: Time-Life Books, 1993.

Perseverance. African Americans: Voices of Triumph series. Time-Life Books. Alexandria, Va: Time-Life Books, 1993.

Rubel, David. *Scholastic Encyclopedia of the Presidents and Their Times.* New York: Scholastic Inc., 1994.

Thomas, David Hurst, et. al. *The Native Americans: An Illustrated History.* Atlanta: Turner Publishing, Inc., 1993.

Virga, Vincent. *Eyes of the Nation: A Visual History of the United States.* New York: Alfred A. Knopf, 1997.

War for the Plains. The American Indians series. Time-Life Books. Alexandria, Va.: Time-Life Books, 1994.

Ware, Susan, editor. *Forgotten Heroes: Inspiring American Portraits from Our Leading Historians.* New York: The Free Press, 1998.

WEB SITES

American Experience. PBS Online. http://www.pbs.org/wgbh/amex/index.html
Includes biographies of several of the heroes profiled in this book.

American Memory Timeline. The Learning Page. The Library of Congress. http://memory.loc.gov/ammem/ndlpedu/features/timeline/index.html
A great source for key events in American history.

Encyclopedia Britannica Online. www.britannica.com

Smithsonian Education—Students Home Page. Smithsonian Institution. http://smithsonian education.org/students/index.html
Explores people and places, history and culture.

Spotlight: Biography. Smithsonian Institution. http://smithsonianeducation.org/spotlight/start.html
Profiles of famous and not-so-famous Americans.

Time 100: *The Most Important People of the Century.* http://www.time.com/time/time100/
Includes articles on several of the heroes profiled in this book.

Quote Sources

Page 182: *Eyewitness to America,* edited by David Colbert (ETA), p. 19; Page 183: "promote the…" www.pbs.org/benfranklin/; "They that …" *Bartlett's Familiar Quotations,* p. 310; "promote the public…" www.pbs.org/benfranklin/; Page 184: "I think…" http://gwpapers.virginia.edu/revolution/letters/ bfairfax2.html; Page 185: "There was in his…" and "First in war…" www.pbs.org/; "With slight…" *The Making of America,* by Robert Johnston (MOA), p. 59; "Observe good…" *Bartlett's,* p.336; Page 186: "those western…" *How We Crossed the West,* by Rosalyn Schanzer; Page 188: "I looked at…" http://www.africanamericans.com/FBIBlackHistoryMonth.htm; Page 190: *Bartlett's,* p. 475; Page 191: "We hold…" ANB, p. 548; "not a…" ANB, p. 550; "Failure…" www.pbs.org/stantonanthony/; Page 194: "the world…" and "The study…" *Always Inventing,* by Tom L. Matthews (AI), pp. 55 and 48; "The inventor…" http://www.biographi.ca/EN/ShowBio.asp?BioId=42027; Page 195: "Mr. Watson…" AI, p. 27; "to follow …" AI, p. 33; "can no…" AI, p. 5; "brought the…" ANB, p. 500; "I believe…" http://www.biographi.ca/EN/ShowBio.asp?BioId=42027; Page 196: AHH, p. 331; Page 198: all quotes from news.nationalgeographic.com/news/2003/01/0110_030113_henson.html; Page 199: "a thing of…" www.ameliaearhart.com/about/index/php; "As soon…" ANB, p. 222; "to prove…" *Sky Pioneer,* by Corinne Szabo, p. 27; Page 200: Time 100; "The only…" OCP, p. 130; Page 201: "new deal…" and "The only…" OCP, p. 130; "traitor …" Time 100; "all aid…" MOA, p. 154; "The test…" *Bartlett's,* p. 649; Page 202: "beauty of …" and "hysterical woman" Time 100; "Over increasingly…" *Silent Spring,* by Rachel Carson, chapter 8; Page 204: "If a man…" *Bartlett's,* p. 760; Page 205: "I have a dream…" MOA, p. 169; "Like anybody…" *Bartlett's,* p. 761; "Injustice anywhere…" http://www.nobelprizes.com/nobel/peace/.

Photo Credits

178-179, David Alan Harvey / National Geographic Image Collection; 181, after the painting by Peter F. Rothermel/ The Granger Collection, NY; 182, Library of Congress; 183, Stock Montage/ Stock Montage/ Getty Images; 184, painting by Gilbert Stuart/ Museum of the City of New York/ Corbis; 185, North Wind Picture Archives; 186, "The Rapids" by Harold Von Schmidt, Oil on Canvas, 1954, Courtesy of the Montana Historical Society; 187, The Granger Collection, NY; 188, Library of Congress; 189, Library of Congress; 190, Library of Congress; 191, North Wind Picture Archives; 192, Library of Congress; 193, Hulton Archive/ Getty Images; 194, Library of Congress; 195, North Wind Picture Archives; 196, Library of Congress/ Getty Images; 197, Library of Congress; 198, Library of Congress; 199, Library of Congress; 200, Franklin D. Roosevelt Library; 201, Keystone/ Getty Images; 202, Alfred Eisenstaedt/ Time Life Pictures/ Getty Images; 203, Bettmann/ Corbis; 204, Bettmann/ Corbis; 205, William Lovelace/ Express/ Getty Images; 206, Bettmann/ Corbis